The Global Student's Companion:

10,001 Timeless Themes & Topics *for* Dialogue, Discussion & Debate Practice

Everett Ofori, MBA (Heriot-Watt University, Scotland, UK)

© Everett Ofori, 2016

All rights reserved. No part of this publication may be reproduced, stored in a retrieval system, or transmitted, in any form or by any means, without the prior permission in writing of Everett Ofori, or as expressly permitted by law, or under terms agreed with the appropriate reprographics rights organization.

Enquiries concerning reproduction outside the scope of the above should be sent to:

Everett Ofori
c/o Takarazuka University of Art and Design
Tokyo Campus Building 1F-123MBE
7-11-1 Nishi-Shinjuku
Shinjuku-ku
Tokyo, Japan 160-0023

10-digit ISBN: 1-894221-02-8
13-digit ISBN: 978-1-894221-02-3

Book Cover Design: Raphaël Genty, Paris, France

...the word 'why' not only taught me to ask, but also to think... And thinking has never hurt anyone. On the contrary, it does us all a world of good.

- Anne Frank
(Anne Frank's *Tales from the Secret Annex*)

Mastery of language affords remarkable power.

- Frantz Fanon
(Psychiatrist, Philosopher, Writer)

Acknowledgments

Thanks to the dozens of individuals, both instructors and English learners, who generously agreed to allow me to use some of their comments as illustrative examples.

Many thanks to Dr. Tomoya Oe, Dr. Mayuko Okabe, Ms. Mutsumi Matsugu, Ms. Yuri Yamada, and countless others for generously agreeing to "test-drive" some of the topics in the book.

English instructors who contributed sample comments include Mr. David Akagi, Ms. Diana Camargo, Mr. Jim Pagliaro, Mr. Jack Cunningham, Dr. Simon Downes, and Mr. Bob Akber.

To all of you: 10,001 thanks!

Other Books by Everett Ofori

- *Succeeding From the Margins of Canadian Society: A Strategic Resource for New Immigrants, Refugees and International Students* (with Dr. Francis Adu-Febiri, Professor, Canada)

- *Guaranteed Formula for Writing Success*

- *Guaranteed Formula for Public Speaking Success*

- *Read Assure: Guaranteed Formula for Reading Success with Phonics*

- *Guaranteed Formula for Effective Business Writing*

- *The Changing Japanese Woman: From Yamatonadeshiko to YamatonadeGucci*

If I went back to college again, I'd concentrate on two areas: learning to write and to speak before an audience. Nothing in life is more important than the ability to communicate effectively.

- Gerald Ford, President of the United States

CONTENTS

Acknowledgments	4
Preface	8
How to Use this Book	9
Three "Bags" of Topics	10
SAMPLE RESPONSES FROM ENGLISH INSTRUCTORS AND ESL LEARNERS	11

ENGLISH INSTRUCTORS - SAMPLE RESPONSES . . . 11

Topic #1: Money problems
Topic #2: Every cloud has a silver lining
Topic #3: Colin Powell:
"I don't want to spend the rest of my life giving speeches."
Topic #4: John Wooden: "We are many, but are we much?"
Topic #5: Needle in a haystack
Topic #6: Pepper spray
Topic #7: My family
Topic #8: Qualities of a good secretary
Topic #9: Albert Einstein:
"The hardest thing in the world to understand is the income tax."
Topic #10: White weddings

ENGLISH LEARNERS - SAMPLE RESPONSES . . . 17

Topic #1: My mother
Topic #2: Accounting
Topic #3: Blogging
Topic #4: Tamagotchi
Topic #5: Reggae music
Topic #6: My idol
Topic #7: Mattress
Topic #8: Starbucks
Topic #9: Nasi Goreng
Topic #10: Grace Under Fire

Topic #11: Horoscope
Topic #12: Taxation
Topic #13: Businessmen
Topic #14: Chocolate
Topic #15: Playground
Topic #16: Witchcraft
Topic #17: Jeans
Topic #18: Bluetooth

Ten Expansion Frameworks 23

Evaluating Oral Presentations 24

POSITIVE ELEMENTS IN PUBLIC SPEAKING . . . 25

COMMON PROBLEMS IN PUBLIC SPEAKING . . . 25

Common Errors in Oral English 26

Becoming a Master Communicator (Tips) 26

Oral Presentation Evaluation Form 27

Topics: 1-10,001 28

Preface

The idea for this book crystallized when I was teaching English at one of the more progressive English conversation schools in Tokyo, Japan. The clients were eager to communicate. Their number one complaint, however, was that many of the English teachers charged with teaching them to speak the language talked too much. Ouch!!! The students wondered how they could ever learn to speak if English teachers routinely monopolized the conversation.

As a new student of the Japanese language, the English learners' complaint resonated with me as I also found Japanese teachers who would not give me an opportunity to try out my less-than-perfect Japanese. My own love for those Japanese instructors who gave me an opportunity to speak made it abundantly clear to me that allowing students to express themselves, and giving them gentle, supportive feedback, was a good way to help eager learners of English, or indeed learners of any language, make some headway.

I began by collecting simple topics and asking students to share their thoughts on them: *Myself, My best friend, My family*. Many students were able to share their thoughts on these topics. Once the topics began to stray from the familiar, however, some students were unsure how to proceed beyond a sentence or two. By providing students with a number of frameworks (see page 23) to guide their thoughts, all were practically able to make intelligible and coherent comments.

Initially, I had a very limited number of topics and occasionally asked a student to speak on a topic that I had assigned before; when students began to protest having to speak again on the same topic, it became clear that having an inexhaustible supply of topics could be useful both for teachers and students.

In using this style of offering a topic and having students speak on the topic, a teacher needs to be alert to correct the students but also give them the freedom to speak. Too many corrections might be discouraging. At the same time, some students become livid when they are not corrected! My approach is to allow students to talk, but to jot down any errors they make. Once they have finished what they are saying, I make suggestions for improvement (see template on page 27).

Whatever you do, please don't be like the teacher who asked a student to tell a story...for which the student gladly obliged. Shy at first, the student soon got into the spirit of the narrative. The more she talked the more animated she became. Oh, she must have spoken for five minutes, maybe a little more. Surprised that she had spoken for so long she finally looked to the teacher for approval...and found that he was sound asleep!

HOW TO USE THIS BOOK

For those using this book as a classroom resource, Everett recommends using it as a complement to other exercises or textbooks. Variety, after all, is the soul of pleasure.

For a person with very limited experience of life, some of the more advanced topics may pose a challenge. But those who have read extensively would find no difficulty challenging themselves to speak on topics that might at first appear too difficult or obscure. Students who read extensively, listen to podcasts, peruse newspaper articles, weigh arguments from print and broadcast media will find that they are developing the breadth of knowledge that will allow them to share their opinions on a wide variety of topics.

In one sense, the topics in *The Global Student's Companion* can serve to test not only the breadth of one's knowledge of issues, problems, challenges, opportunities, opinions, assertions from both historical and contemporary sources, but also awaken one to how much more one needs to learn.

As a student of the English language, you will find much in this volume that will expand the boundaries of your understanding of the language. You will also find thoughts and ideas that challenge you to express those of your own. In short, don't expect to agree with everything in this volume.

Initial difficulties in sharing thoughts about a topic should not discourage the learner but serve as a spur for greater effort, wider reading, and a more intense effort to apply some of the frameworks introduced in this volume. As American motivational speaker Les Brown likes to say, "Practice makes improvement."

The complete beginner may find inspiration in the model responses (see page 11) given by English instructors and English learners. Take this as an invitation to indulge in the fine art of clear thinking.

Happy speaking!

NOTE:

NUMBER CATEGORY/CREDIT	TOPIC
After the number, the name of the person associated with a quote is noted. Other clues are provided such as nationality, place of residence, profession, etc. to help the curious user follow up for more information.	The topic is stated in this box. Every effort has been made to ensure accuracy. Any errors or omissions are strictly the responsibility of Everett Ofori who will make an effort to make corrections as they come to his attention and as he reviews the topics over time.

THREE "BAGS" OF TOPICS

Of the 10,001 topics presented in this volume, you might find that you can break the whole lot into three categories:

Bag 1: **Familiar topics**

    My favorite movie, my hometown, my best friend, etc.

Bag 2: **Topics that are not so obscure but require you to think**

    Some topics might seem so difficult that you are tempted to give up on responding to them. If you take time to think, however, you may surprise yourself.

    Proverbs, figurative expressions, and popular sayings often fall into this category.

Bag 3: **Obscure topics that you are totally unfamiliar with**

    If you know absolutely nothing about a topic, and you cannot relate anything about the topic to your experience, then this is your chance to do some research.

    An online search is likely to give you some basic familiarity with the topic. This then turns an "I don't know" into an opportunity to expand the boundaries of your knowledge.

SAMPLE RESPONSES FROM ENGLISH INSTRUCTORS AND ESL LEARNERS

As you read these sample responses, consider some of the techniques the speakers use. Often, one way to expand upon what you are saying is to give an example or tell a story. You can also make comparisons or make analogies that your listeners can relate to. As with most things in life, the beginning may be difficult, but if you persist, you will find yourself becoming more and more adept. You will also note that because these are impromptu speeches, they are not necessarily all perfect. Even English instructors may fumble or falter for a moment before they regain their rhetorical balance. So, perfection is not the goal here, especially not at the beginning stages. As you keep practicing, however, who knows what elegant strings of words you might weave together? But we wouldn't know until we make the effort to try, right?

ENGLISH INSTRUCTORS -- SAMPLE RESPONSES

TOPIC #1: MONEY PROBLEMS

Money problems are very common with adults. I am very used to having money problems. I have had money problems since I was in high school. I had part-time jobs but I could never get ahead, and I had credit cards that I fell behind on....I paid them back with another credit card...fell behind on that...but I found that over time, in order to avoid having money problems I should avoid taking loans. And that's my biggest problem. So now I have no loans and everything seems to have been settled, so my advice to anyone with money problems is not to take loans. I suggest that they find a way to pay for things and not live beyond their means.

Money problems. Money problems are things that we'd like to avoid but it's something that comes to us without any warning. In order to avoid money problems in the future, first look at what you have and know the difference between what you want and what you need. It's a good thing to know about these things.

Once there was a man and he lived in England. He lived in a very old house. He thought that he wanted to have a nicer house so he took a loan and went to buy lots of beautiful things. His house became more beautiful and he was able to enjoy these new things for a short time, but one day he realized that whatever he had he was going to get used to, and so, all he could see, was the loan that he had and he could not see the beautiful things that he had brought into his house and so my message to you is: Be happy with what you have.

TOPIC #2: EVERY CLOUD HAS A SILVER LINING

Let's talk about clouds with silver linings. When you think about clouds you might imagine a dark, gray cloud that makes you feel sad, and feeling sad is not something desirable. However, in life we often come across sad things; sometimes if you look at that sad thing you might find a good thing that might come out of it and that is what we call the silver lining. This may be the inner side or the edge of the cloud that tells you that you need to pick yourself up, count your blessings, and see a way out of your problems. This is one of the ways you can look at your difficulties in life. And, you may have heard the expression, "If life gives you lemons, make lemonade." This is similar in that you have to make the best of your situation. So let's remember this phrase, "Every cloud has a silver lining." It will make you feel good when you're feeling down. And it is also good to tell other people because sometimes they are not aware of a way out of their difficulties. Tell them about your story, share it with them, and try to help them understand what their blessings are. I think that there are many things in life that can be said to make others feel good…just with a kind word, a kind thought. And this is one phrase that can be easily remembered. So, let's say it clearly: EVERY CLOUD HAS A SILVER LINING.

TOPIC #3:
COLIN POWELL: "I DON'T WANT TO SPEND THE REST OF MY LIFE GIVING SPEECHES."

Speeches are very important, but even more important than speeches is taking action and following up on speeches. Therefore, although I value speeches I also value that we follow up and that we actualize what we speak about and I appreciate if the people I know actualize what they speak about.

So, instead of making speeches, one after another, I highly recommend that people make one speech and spend the rest of the time following up on it so we don't need any more speeches. So, telling people what you plan to do is less impressive than actually doing what you say.

As a child, my father always told me: "There is no time like the present." So, I am a strong believer that if my bicycle goes flat the best time to fix my flat tire is now. And if I make a speech to someone to do something, the best way to teach them is by example and to prod them and encourage them to take action as soon as possible.

So our biggest enemy is actually ourselves and procrastination. Therefore, I will highly advise everyone: Instead of focusing on making lots of speeches, to take action and put action into your words.

TOPIC #4:
JOHN WOODEN (USA/BASKETBALL COACH): "WE ARE MANY, BUT ARE WE MUCH?"

The topic of my speech is, "We are many, but are we much?" It was said by John Wooden, who was a UCLA basketball coach. I think the point here is a question between quality and quantity. So, I would like to speak [about] how nowadays many people seem to focus on quantity and to forget about quality. Quality is one hundred times better than quantity and quantity does not equal quality. Therefore, I would like to talk today about the importance of quality and to emphasize that quality can never be replaced by quantity. So, quality is very, very important not only in the quality of your life, in the quality of your work, and the quality of your presentations.

Let me stat start by talking about presentations. I have seen many presentations and I am always, always shocked by the quantity of graphs, the quantity of statistics, and the quantity of PowerPoint presentation pages I see...and very often, the main idea for what the person is trying to say has not clearly been developed and I cannot understand even what they are trying to say. In this case, I will highly advise the person to focus on quality and to worry a little less about quantity.

Now, let me talk about personal life. Once again, in my personal life, when I look at things that are important, I think friends are one of the most important things in our life. And once again, I sometimes worry about our new lives, especially now that we have Facebook and we can have thousands and thousands of friends. I fail to understand how thousands of people could be your friends. It seems that people have not looked in the dictionary and seen the definition of friend. Once again, one or two friends of quality are by far more valuable than thousands of friends on Facebook. So, I would like to advise everyone: Please think back to broader life and I would like to emphasize to you to choose quality over quantity, or as John Wooden said, "We are many, but are we much?"

TOPIC #5: NEEDLE IN A HAYSTACK

Needle in a haystack! Hmm. Okay. Needle in a haystack is a very common idiom that we often use in America to describe how difficult it is to find that special thing. In my case, I would imagine that, with my experience as a baseball manager, a needle in a haystack for me is trying to find a pitcher who can pitch almost as well as my ace pitcher. What I mean is that my ace pitcher is very good with his control. He manages to walk very few batters in a game. The last game we had, it was a six-inning game, he only walked one batter through the game, which was very impressive. I am managing fifth grade kids who are ages from about 10 and 11. I have two other pitchers but they can't seem to throw strikes. We had a practice game after our other game. Between my two other pitchers, they walked twelve batters. So, finding that special pitcher who can have good control, and I think, it can be true in the major leagues as well, it's just like trying to find a needle in a haystack. There are literally hundreds of pitchers in professional sports and finding that one that can actually be a true winner is pretty tough. So, I think that's a needle in a haystack from a sports perspective.

TOPIC #6: PEPPER SPRAY

Pepper spray is a very important tool for women to carry with them, especially in areas like New York, because it fends off potential criminals. Pepper spray used to be used by police because it would help to subdue certain violent criminals and enable the police to put handcuffs on them pretty quickly. However, because of the spread of drugs and cocaine...cocaine is a nose drug. Criminals tended to... be...what's the word I am looking for?...resistant...to that kind of pepper spray. However, for women, most of the dangers for women involve rape or muggings or some type of violent behavior so for women to have that pepper spray, it can be effective as long as they can spray it into the face of the attacker. If that doesn't work, it is very important for women to have steel-toed boots. The reason for that is, if the pepper spray loses its effectiveness, the steel-toed boots...put in the right place, can enable the woman to escape from her assailant at a very rapid pace.

So, pepper spray is a very good weapon but steel-toed boots are a little bit better. That's my impression.

TOPIC #7: MY FAMILY

Hmmm....where to begin...family history? My family originated from...as far as back as I do remember... it goes back to Baluchistan, in Pakistan, western Pakistan...where possibly before that, possible migration from Iran into Pakistan. I am not quite sure about the history there.

But my parents moved out [of] there before I was born so I was the first person in my family to be born in the U.S. ...My sister is a scientist, Ph.D. in geophysics. My father is an engineer. Now he teaches. My mother, just a sweetheart now at home. She's lived in America for about 48 years but her English is terrible. But, sometimes, she speaks four or five Pakistani languages...including... a language, I think Jergawi, which means secret tongue. So, she can be a spy! Apart from that, I try to talk to them about once a month. I try to go more than that but lately we've all been busy with our little things. Maybe, I'll see them in November.

TOPIC #8: QUALITIES OF A GOOD SECRETARY

Well, I think, first and foremost, the quality of a good secretary should obviously be people skills depending on what business she is in. Now, obviously, people skills are important dealing not only with customers but also with, perhaps, dealing with people in the office as well.

And I'll give you an example...There was a lady up at [a major corporation] who had been there for ten years who just found last Thursday that she was being let go. And this was, you know, disturbing to her but more interestingly, everyone in the office she told started to cry because she had such a good rapport with them. She had such good people skills, she was able to meet their needs and connect with them not only on a professional but on a personal basis that it was [more sad] for them than it was actually for her.

So, coming back to the point, people skills are quite important. Now, having said that, the second most important skills are office skills. By office skills, I mean, perhaps, using a computer. By what I mean using a computer, I think Excel is quite important, and perhaps Word...so we come to the various software programs that a secretary uses on a regular basis. And if a secretary doesn't know these programs she is going to not only waste time but she is going to waste money. So, just knowing how to use a computer isn't enough. You have to be almost, I would say, an expert in software usage.

After computer skills, I think we will go to the third most important part, which is running the office. And running the office could mean anywhere from cleaning up and making coffee to arranging meetings and greeting guests, which fall back into people skills. And just making sure that the office is going smoothly and everything is in its place and where it should be.

So, having said that, the three most important skills for a secretary are people skills, computer software skills, especially Excel and Word, and finally office skills, as in running an office much like a housewife running a home.

TOPIC #9:
ALBERT EINSTEIN: "THE HARDEST THING IN THE WORLD TO UNDERSTAND IS THE INCOME TAX."

That's a very loaded question. What do you mean the income tax or the income...tax. I am not quite sure how to interpret that, however, let's take it at face value. When you say income tax I am going to assume that you are perhaps talking about government income tax. Quite obviously, this is one of the hardest subjects to understand and this is why they make accountants and CPAs. I look at the tax forms every year and I shake my head because the rules change, the forms change. I have absolutely no idea. From question 1, go to page 10 paragraph 2 line 3, back to question 2, go to...so I am lost even before I start. I just put my name in the right place.

Now, the government, I am not sure why they make the income tax forms and the process so difficult. This is money that is going to be used by the people, for the people, so obviously they should make sure that it's collected and that it's spent wisely. Now, I look at California. Because I heard just recently that Stockton, California, has declared bankruptcy. This was interesting to me because when Arnold Schwarzenegger was in office, he did a survey on how much marijuana people smoked in the state of California because it was going bankrupt...the state was. And I think it came out about 70 percent of the people they surveyed in California smoked marijuana on a regular basis – monthly, weekly, daily, hourly, I am not sure, right?

Now, the point is this, if they were able to collect the tax on all the marijuana these people smoked, much like they collect the tax on the cigarettes, they calculated that the deficit for the state of California would be paid off in five years. So, we're talking income tax, coming back to the point, that this is a very important part, not just of the government system, but our daily personal lives, so for them to make it so difficult to understand is beyond me. This is something that should be easy to understand and done very quickly. And I don't want to go any further. I can talk all night about income tax.

TOPIC #10: WHITE WEDDINGS

Well, I think from when little girls are born, they get it engrained on their brains that they have to be a princess and in order to be a princess, they have to have a white wedding with all their friends and that they have to wear the beautiful white wedding gown, flowing, and they have to have the Prince Charming up there dressed in his tuxedo. They have to make a whole elaborate tradition of this. I have been to a lot of these. I am Italian so…Italian weddings are really big and exciting…All the relatives come. It's a huge production. It's a fun time actually and I think white weddings are probably really good.

And the wedding industry has maintained their status even though for a time marriage was not thought of as that popular. I think, still, this idea that little girls have to be a princess and get married in a church with a huge elaborate ceremony is part of what being a little girl is, at least in the West.

And in Japan, now, it's really popular even for Japanese people to get married in a church though they don't believe in Jesus. But, it's an industry and I think it will be a tradition and it will go on and on because I think women want that fantasy of being special.

ENGLISH LEARNERS -- SAMPLE RESPONSES

TOPIC #1: MY MOTHER

My mother is not only my mother but also my boss.

Thirty-three years ago, she began her own business when I was in junior high school. She began a telephone answering company in Yokohama [Japan] close to my home. She worked very hard but she also cooked our meals, cleaned our house, cooked our lunch box when I was in junior high school and senior high school. After graduating from high school, suddenly my father left my home. Suddenly, our income went down. Owing to my mother, I went to college in the United States. My sister could enter university in Tokyo. After graduating from university I decided to support my mother's job but I needed to get enough experience before entering my mom's organization. So I joined a school promotion organization.

Later, I worked in my mother's company. It [has been] 15 years already.

I would like to help and support our company very much. [I always felt] I did not have enough ability to support my mom. So I always feel sorry for my mom. But she advised me to do my own thing in the company and if I [found] something interesting I [could] do...do so. I feel sorry for my mom because she supported us for a long time. She is already 72 years old. Recently, always she says it is my company; that's why she likes to do her own thing... she needs to have free time. So, recently I do not regret my ability about [the] company. I continue to support our company and her life because I am her daughter. Recently, I changed my mind. I hope she will be fine and do her best [in] her life.

TOPIC #2: ACCOUNTING

I don't like accounting but in my team, usually we work with accounting. It is very sensitive for me because if I make a mistake in a figure it will cause a big problem. So I get very nervous and I don't like accounting. On another floor, we have an accounting team and every day they focus only on accounting. Maybe, they are not familiar with communication. They don't like to communicate with other people so they can do accounting everyday, every year.

TOPIC #3: BLOGGING

Blogging is…to make some comments on a website, right? So, I am not interested in blogging, and I don't read blogs. So, I can't understand what is fun, what is enjoyable for bloggers and [their] followers. But by the spread of blogs, we can get some information we want easily and people can easily [share] their knowledge [with] others.

So, for some people, blogging is one of the tools to [form] relationships with each other and one another. So blogging affects a lot [of people] in society. It includes both good and bad effects. But totally, I think blogging is a good communication tool. But unfortunately, I am not interested in blogging.

TOPIC #4: TAMAGOTCHI

Tamagotchi was [a] very popular game all over the world. The reason why Tamagotchi was so popular was that [the] playing time is very short. Previously, TV game[s] took a very long time to play or enjoy, but using Tamagotchi, players need only a few minutes before they stop. But usual[ly] for TV game[s] it is impossible [to stop] until each stage finishes; [the] player cannot stop the game.

Recently, Smartphone and Tablet PCs have games. Using tablet PC is becoming very popular instead of Tamagotchi. The games in these devices are very easy to play, like Tamagotchi, so most games can be stopped when players want. Recently, my kid likes TV games or games in these devices so I downloaded some minigames. I played some games. The games [are] very exciting even for adults like me. You can stop the game whenever you like. It's a very useful tool to fill the available time. For example, when we are wait[ing] for someone before a meeting, we don't have to be bored. We can play the game, so instead of Tamagotchi, the minigames with smart phone or PC will be more popular.

TOPIC #5: REGGAE MUSIC

Bob Marley is a favorite singer of Reggae. At the time he sang, many people listened to his music. But still, there are a few people….But recently, reggae music is not as popular compared to when Bob Marley was singing. I think the popularity of some specific music reflects the atmosphere of the world culture. When reggae music was popular, the people in the world wanted to relax; the world economy was pretty good so they need[ed] a rest. They felt they [were] happy but they need[ed] a rest. That's why they wanted to listen to relaxing music such as reggae music. On the other hand, [the] current world situation is becoming worse. So, lots of people have very strong complaints against somebody who has big power, for example, big company CEOs, or government people That's why recently…hip hop music is becoming popular because hip hop message has a strong message [for] high society people. So, I believe that [the] popularity of each type of music reflects the trend or atmosphere of the world. So, someday when the economy of the world becomes good, reggae music will be popular again.

TOPIC #6: MY IDOL

My idol is Tatsuro Yamashita. He is [a] Japanese singer. He [has] continued to sing for 30 years. He is…this year he became 68 years old and he has [been performing] 60s-[themed] concerts for 7 months from Hokkaido to Okinawa. I went to his concert in Hamamatsu because I could not get a ticket in Tokyo because he [is] one of [the most] popular singers in Japan. His singing fascinates Japanese people. He is already around 60 years old but his voice and singing style have not changed since he was 22 years old. Without using a mic he [is able to] sing in a hall and…[for him] the term of one concert is four hours every time. But he [is able to] maintain his voice from first to last. He's like an artisan. He concentrates on [being a] professional singer.

Also, before [the big] earthquake happened [on March 11, 2011], he concentrated on melody because he can compose and sing by himself…but after the earthquake happened he concentrated on description of people in the song. That's why one of his songs was supported by many people after the earthquake. He is a singer but I respect his attitude and his policy for how singer[s] should be and how singers should influence society. Since I was 14 years old I [have] continued to listen to his songs -- for 30 years -- so I would like to keep on listening to his singing.

TOPIC #7: MATTRESS

For me the image of mattress is very sophisticated. Traditional Japanese people [use] futon instead of mattress. In my image, mattress is advanced and cutting edge -- advanced material for sleeping. When I was a university student, I bought a bed with a mattress, but unfortunately [the] mattress didn't fit me. Maybe, that was because I bought a cheap mattress, but for me, the main reason was … it was not good for me. Basically, mattress has feeling. When we lie down, [the] heavy part of the body sinks…so it's impossible to sleep in a flat position. On the other hand, with futon, [the] body position is flat. [This is] because [the] futon is not thick…[it is just] very thin material on the floor. So, actually, our body does not bend so until I bought the mattress I was used to sleeping on a futon. For me, sleeping in a flat position is very comfortable. That's why when I bought a new mattress, my satisfaction level was low… so I changed from mattress to futon.

TOPIC #8: STARBUCKS

Last year, I had a training course to obtain…to learn business skills, as you know. In the course, the teacher taught us we need to change to survive this current changing situation. And as an example, the teacher [shared with] us Starbucks' example. Starbucks is just a coffee shop but the president of Starbucks is different from other [owners of] coffee shops. At Starbucks, the[y] offer the customers not only good coffee but also the experience of relax[ing] with good coffee. That is a big difference for customers. That's why we customers pay big money [for] expensive Starbucks coffee. So, they started [a] business model which [focuses on] our needs. So to grow our business, we need to change like Starbucks and we need [to take care of] the potential customers' needs. So we must [take on that kind of] challenge all the time.

TOPIC #9: NASI GORENG

I really love traveling [to] Bali for surfing. So, generally, when I go to Bali for surfing I eat *nasi goreng*. There [are] two reasons. First, *nasi goreng* is tasty everywhere. I think making *nasi goreng* is easy for Indonesian people so in every restaurant the taste of *nasi goreng* is very similar. That's why the [chance] of having bad *nasi goreng* is low.

In this developing country, we must take care [to avoid being infected] by virus[es] or bacteria. For example, salad can cause diarrhea for Japanese tourists but *nasi goreng* is heated in every restaurant so it's a safe food. That's why I eat *nasi*. I like to travel to Bali.

TOPIC #10: GRACE UNDER FIRE

The degree of pressure is quite different [for] professional sports player[s] but we need grace under fire to to do our job smoothly, because in my job as [a] researcher, to proceed [with] our project we have to make a presentation in front of many top managers and they often raise lots of difficult questions but if I [get] upset in front of those managers, my team and I will lose the trust [of] the top managers. Once we lose trust it's very difficult to recover our trust again…and once we lose trust it becomes more difficult to proceed [with] our project. Because to proceed [with] our project we need the approval [of the] top managers. But to approve some projects, they judge the project as well as the team leader. So we need trust. Trust is very important for our job too. That's why we must think about grace under fire. We should make effort not to [be] upset while we are working.

TOPIC #11: HOROSCOPE

I don't believe in the horoscope. I think we cannot separate character into 12 types because there are more character types among humans than just 12. Every morning, on TV, they broadcast the horoscope and everyday they rank the signs. When I see cancer is the last one, my feeling is very bad. The ranking is from the luckiest to the most unlucky. But a few years ago, I [realized that] if Cancer [was] the last one, my feeling went down. If Cancer [was] the last one I would face something bad. So, that was not good for me. So, I don't watch it any more. I want to avoid the horoscope broadcast.

TOPIC #12: TAXATION

Many actors and actresses [try to avoid] paying tax. So, they often get arrested by [the] police. In Japan, taxation is very high and even if we [earn] a salary, a big part is taxation so we cannot receive the full salary. But taxation is high [and] I cannot understand the government's use of the tax money. It is not clear [to] me. In other countries such as Sweden, I [have] heard that taxation is very high but…their lives are very rich but in Japan I can't find [how the tax money is used.

TOPIC #13: BUSINESSMEN

The typical Japanese businessman is Horiemon. He started a small business while a university student. After making a lot of effort he grew the company into a very big one. He [is] so influential [in] the Japanese market and [among] Japanese people but [on] the way to [creating a] big company, he and his colleagues made some mistakes. That's why he and his colleagues were arrested. And the company was kicked out of the [stock] market.

At that point he lost everything, but [before] becoming CEO of Livedoor he had made a big effort, so he [had] acquired a lot of know-how and experience and also, he still has a lot of trust from Japanese people. So, even after his resignation from Livedoor, he still has a lot of supporters. When he tweets something, lots of Japanese people give him comments.

Recently, he started writing some essays in magazines. So, he is now coming back into Japanese society. So, what I want to say is that even [though] he once fell from a very high position, those things...[those bad experiences]...will help our future...so one failure does not mean total failure. This is just one step to final success.

TOPIC #14: CHOCOLATE

There was an interesting hypothesis in making chocolate. Actually, I don't believe in this hypothesis because it is scientifically mistaken. But still this hypothesis is very wonderful so I would like to describe it – it is a hypothesis relating [to] chocolate. A few decades ago a scientist presented the hypothesis, which is called The Chocolate of Love. In this hypothesis, a substance called PEA, is a pheromone substance, to fall in love. Actually, chocolate has [a lot] of PEA and people, especially girls, who are in love, produce lots of PEA in their brains. On the other hand, people who are not in a love situation [are] lack[ing] in PEA. When people produce PEA in their brains [they] feel happy because of PEA's existence. That's why lots of people, especially girls, want to fall in love.

On the other hand, girls tend to like chocolate. So, the scientists thought about the linkage, about love and chocolate. And one link is PEA. So according to the Chocolate of Love theory, girls like chocolate because chocolate has a lot of pheromones. Chocolate has a substance which satisfies girls to [create their] dreams of love. So, that's [the] chocolate of love theory ....recently I have been studying this substance, PEA. When you eat PEA, it is metabolized in the blood. That's why this theory is wrong, but this theory is still wonderful.

TOPIC #15: PLAYGROUND

Recently, playgrounds for kids are shrinking...dramatically in number. When I was a kid there were lots of playgrounds for kids, for example, just a park and actual playgrounds in the elementary school or some flat land near our house could be a playground for us. But recently, flat lands [are] covered by lots of trees or signs of ownership, so it's almost impossible for kids to play [on] those flat lands. In terms of parks, parks [these days] [have] a lot of play [equipment], for example, seesaws. Parks [these days don't] have big flat lands so it's very difficult to run or play soccer or baseball. So…playgrounds for kids [today] are shifting into the house, for example, [more and more children are playing] video games or playing indoors. But we know playing outside is very important especially for kids. So we need to make an effort to create outdoor playgrounds for our kids.

TOPIC #16: WITCHCRAFT

As a scientist, I don't believe in the power…witchcraft power. What they do is not reproducible by other people, and…it's impossible to clarify the mechanism of how they affect other people. As a scientist, every phenomenon has to be explained by substances and molecules but spiritual power is impossible to be proven by substances and molecules. But on the other hand, I can understand how people want to believe those magical powers. Based on our scientific finding, still now we cannot explain all phenomena. To understand magical power we need very special, weird power to explain the unknown magical power. So, to satisfy those power requirements witchcraft exists and…the existence of witchcraft has a positive meaning for…daily life because when [some] people live [under the influence of] such power they feel happy. I don't believe in the power of witchcraft but I accept the existence of witchcraft.

TOPIC #17: JEANS

I have never paid much attention to jeans. Originally, jeans were pants for blue-collar workers because they [do] lots of physical activity so they need very strong clothes. That's why jeans were invented for that demand. On the other hand, now, pants are not for workers. Jeans are one of the most fashionable items for people. Recently, some jeans, which have special modifications, are expensive. The turning point of the role of jeans emerg[ed] because of James Dean in the all-American movie. In the movie, James Dean wore jeans as a fashionable item, especially for women. That's why jeans were considered fashionable, not as work pants. So, the change of the role of jeans was based on [how he wore the] jeans. So, the current jeans-related industry must appreciate James Dean.

TOPIC #18: BLUETOOTH

Recently, I [have come to] know what Bluetooth is. ….use Bluetooth, when I [heard about] …the possibility of [using] Bluetooth I thought this [was an] amazing tool because from now on, we [won't] need to carry wires to connect PC devices like iPad. On the other hand, I realize the [number of] PC devices that have Bluetooth function is limited. All PC devices do not have Bluetooth so when I want to use a Bluetooth headphone or keyboard, [I] don't know if the blue tooth device can connect to the PC. So I realize that to use these cutting edge tools…the penetration rate is very important. If the penetration rate is low, the cutting edge technology is not so useful …So, at the moment, I don't think Bluetooth is very useful because every PC does not have Bluetooth function..

TEN EXPANSION FRAMEWORKS

1) PPF - PAST, PRESENT, FUTURE

2) PREP - POINT, REASON, EXAMPLE, POINT

3) ADVANTAGES AND DISADVANTAGES; PROS AND CONS

4) PS: PROBLEM AND SOLUTION

5) PCS: PROBLEM, CAUSE, SOLUTION

6) PCRS: PROBLEM, CAUSE, REACTION, SOLUTION

7) IFONI: INDIVIDUAL, FAMILY, ORGANIZATION, NATION, INTERNATIONAL

8) ALS: AIR, LAND, SEA

9) CHIILD'S PERSPECTIVE, ADULT'S PERSPECTIVE, OLDER ADULTS' PERSPECTIVE

10) OREO - OPENING, REASON, EXAMPLE, OUTCOME

IT TAKES PRACTICE TO BECOME A SKILLED COMMUNICATOR

Master communicators have their little tricks for bringing a subject alive. As such, master communicators do not feel a paralyzing sense of dread when they have to speak in public. The frameworks above are just a small sampling of techniques that great communicators use to guide their thinking.

When you are suddenly called upon to speak on a topic, you can easily become confused, self-conscious, and unsure where to begin. This may even be the case when you know a lot about the subject. The pressure of having all eyes on you and the suddenness of the invitation may all conspire to throw you off your guard.

In those situations, you can let any of the above frameworks guide and channel your communication.

Let's say you have suddenly been called on to say something about "World Leaders." You could choose to use PREP as your framework.

P: World leaders have a responsibility to lead the world towards peace.

R: This is because they have the power to both create chaos and suppress the chaos that others create.

E: For example, when there is a conflict involving world leaders, the effect is not only on the parties involved. When the disagreement escalates to the point of war, it is the innocent men and women under them who end up fighting one another while the leaders themselves sit safely at home. Many countries make sure that they have a stockpile of weapons to protect their countries. If they put just as much energy into building bridges of friendship, there might never be a reason for the wars and skirmishes that we hear about all the time.

P: World leaders need to make the pursuit of peace a priority and stop making the buying of arms and weapons one of their main priorities as leaders.

Evaluating Oral Presentations

As with making impromptu oral presentations, the use of frameworks for evaluation can help you to smoothly comment on a given oral presentation.

Approaching the task of evaluation without a plan is not a good idea. Having a plan will make the task easy for the evaluator and perhaps be of greater help to the person who is the beneficiary of the evaluation.

It is important for the would-be evaluator to be thoroughly familiar with both the elements that signal good public speaking performance and those that signal the need for improvement. In addition, familiarity with some of the more common errors in English can be very useful.

See the next page for a list of Positive Elements and Common Problems in public speaking.

POSITIVE ELEMENTS IN PUBLIC SPEAKING	COMMON PROBLEMS IN PUBLIC SPEAKING
1 Introduction gets the attention of the audience	1 Introduction not arresting
2 Voice is clear	2 Title and speech do not seem to match
3 Volume is sufficient for the room	3 Speaker appears distracted and confused
4 Speaker uses signposting/gives preview of what is to come	4 Speaker cannot be heard/voice volume too low
5 Diction/vocabulary fit for the particular topic	5 Speaker makes no eye contact
6 Organized: Introduction, Body, Conclusion	6 Speaker makes eye contact with only one section of the room
7 Speech is logical	7 Speech is not well organized/no signposting to guide listeners
8 Audiovisual materials are effectively used	8 Speaker appears frozen / no body language
9 Speaker appears confident and poised	9 Speaker stares at one person for too long, making the person uncomfortable
10 Speaker makes eye contact across the room	10 Speaker does not establish authority/reason why he or she is qualified to speak on the subject
11 Pacing of the speech is perfect	11 Speech is too short/substance of speech is not clear
12 Information is engaging/stimulating	12 Speaker has too many distracting movements
13 Speaker's approach is original	13 No facial expressions to indicate emotion
14 Speaker is energetic/dynamic	14 Speech content does not match emotions (e.g. smiling & talking about death)
15 Speaker establishes rapport with listeners	15 Props not used properly
16 Speaker tells story engagingly	16 Clear lack of preparation / forgetting lines
17 Speaker uses expressive voice/vocal variety	17 Nervousness too obvious
18 Speaker is creative	18 Poor grammar
19 Points are easy to follow	19 Pacing is too fast
20 Speaker uses colorful language (metaphors, etc.)	20 Pacing is too slow
21 Humor is tastefully used	21 Poor appearance / sloppy dressing / clothing style does not fit occasion
22 Topic fits interest of audience	22 Too tied to notes
23 Speaker is not tied to his/her notes	23 Style is too stilted
24 Speaker uses conversational style	24 Speaker does not pause
25 Speaker uses repetition to reinforce point	25 Speaker pauses for so long that listeners begin to feel uncomfortable
26 Speaker signposts the conclusion	26 No sense of connection with the audience
27 Speaker makes good use of transition phrases and signals	27 Conclusion has no spark
28 Speaker is balanced, not dogmatic	
29 Main points are supported with examples, anecdotes, quotes, statistics, etc.	
30 Main points are clear	

Common Errors in Oral English

1. Pronunciation (reprise, months, mores, etc.); make the dictionary your ally
2. Articles (*a engineer* or *an engineer*?; *a historical document* or *an historical document*?
3. Articles (Yesterday, *I saw the cat on the roof* or *I saw a cat on the roof*)
4. Transitional phrases (Consequently, In effect, In addition, etc.)
5. Multiple adjectives (*Japanese young people* or *Young Japanese people*)
6. Which/That/What (This is the lady what gave me the umbrella) Huh?
7. Present perfect versus Simple past:
   (I have gone to the mall last weekend or I went to the mall last weekend)
8. Who/Which (The engineer which gave me the present is from England or The engineer who gave me the present is from England).
9. Form of a word: *I am boring* or *I am bored*.
10. *Your welcome* or *You're welcome*
11. Subject-verb agreement: *They seems to be enjoying themselves* or *They seem to be enjoying themselves*.
12. Prepositional phrases: We went on foot or by foot. We did it out of respect for his grandparents or We did it out of respect to his grandparents.
13. Commonly confused words: Accept/Except; Lie/Lay; Their/There/They're; Affect/Effect, etc.
14. I versus Me (The papers had to be approved by both David and I) Is that correct? Are you sure?
15. Tautology: (Free gift, 6 a.m. in the morning, close proximity, necessary requirement)

Becoming a Master Communicator (Tips)

1. Make reading in English a habit. Some of the best speakers are known to be avid readers.
2. Seek opportunities to speak English everyday.
3. Do shadowing, which involves listening to a speaker, e.g., a broadcaster, and repeating his or her words as fast as you can. You say what you hear almost as soon as you hear it. It's not easy but it forces you to listen carefully.
4. Start a journal. Write everyday.
5. Make frequent use of the dictionary.
6. Make frequent use of the thesaurus.
7. Make frequent use of books on English usage (e.g., Fowler's)
8. Read top quality newspapers (New York Times, The Economist, etc.)
9. Make a daily habit of eliminating word whiskers (um, ah, ee, you know) from your speech.
10. Keep a vocabulary notebook in which you jot down words and expressions you encounter.

ORAL PRESENTATION EVALUATION FORM

Evaluator:		Speaker:
Element	Commendation + Reason	Recommendation + Reason
Introduction		
Signposting		
Transitions		
Vocal Variety		
Eye contact		
Gestures		
Pausing / Pacing		

ACTUAL LANGUAGE	SUGGESTED LANGUAGE
1)	
2)	
3)	
4)	
5)	
6)	

10,001 Topics

NUMBER CATEGORY/CREDIT	TOPIC
1 PERSONAL	Myself
2 PERSONAL	My family
3 PERSONAL	My best friend
4 PERSONAL	My hometown
5 PERSONAL	My hobbies
6 PERSONAL/FOOD	My favorite dish
7 PERSONAL/CHILDHOOD	My first day in school
8 PERSONAL/SPORTS	My favorite sport
9 ENTERTAINMENT	My favorite movie
10 PERSONAL/TRAVEL	My favorite travel destination
11 PERSONAL/TASTE	My favorite beverage
12 PERSONAL/FAMILY	My father
13 PERSONAL/FAMILY	My mother
14 PERSONAL	My idol
15 PERSONAL/OCCUPATION	My career preference
16 PERSONAL/EXPERIENCE	My most memorable experience
17 LIFE/EXPERIENCE	My happiest day
18 LIFE/SORROW	The saddest day of my life
19 PERSONAL/TV	My favorite television show
20 PERSONAL/EXPERENCE	A visit to the zoo
21 PERSONAL	My health
22 PERSONAL	My country
23 PERSONAL/ OPINION	My pet/pets
24 PERSONAL/BOOKS	My favorite writer
25 PERSONAL/MUSIC	My favorite singer
26 PERSONAL/MOVIEW	My favorite actor
27 PERSONAL/TRADITION	My favorite festival
28 PERSONAL/PLACE	My favorite hangout
29 PERSONAL/SHOPPING	My favorite street
30 PERSONAL	My first day at work
31 HENRY FORD/USA/ BUSINESS	Quality means doing it right when no one is looking.
32 RICHARD BRANSON/ BRITISH BUSINESSMAN	Business opportunities are like buses; there's always another one coming.
33 PERSONAL/FAMILY	My siblings
34 PERSONAL/ROUTINE	A typical day
35 AIR TRAVEL	Traveling by plane
36 SEA VOYAGE	Traveling by ship
37 ALBERT EINSTEIN/ NOBEL PRIZE WINNER	Everybody is a genius. But if you judge a fish by its ability to climb a tree it will live its whole life believing that it is stupid.

NUMBER CATEGORY/CREDIT	TOPIC
38 ENVIRONMENT	Pollution
39 BOOKS/DREAMS	Writing books: a book you wish you could write
40 PAIN/SUFFERING	War
41 PERSONAL	Dreams
42 PERSONAL/OPINION	Laziness
43 PERSONAL/OPINION	Cleanliness
44 PERSONAL/HEALTH	Swimming
45 PERSONAL/PLANNING	Saving money
46 ENTERTAINMENT	My favorite cartoons
47 FRÉDÉRIC CHOPIN/ POLISH COMPOSER	It is dreadful when something weighs on your mind, not to have a soul to unburden yourself to.
48 TECHNOLOGY	The Internet
49 RUSSIA/PYOTR ILYICH TCHAIKOVSKY/COMPOSER	To regret the past, to hope in the future, and never to be satisfied with the present: that is what I spend my whole life doing.
50 DEBT	Credit cards
51 PERSONAL/HOME	Favorite place in the home (kitchen, living room, etc.)
52 CONFLICT/SOCIETY/	Lawyers
53 OCCUPATION	Engineers
54 WRITER/ROBERT LOUIS STEVENSON/SCOTTISH	I kept always two books in my pocket, one to read, one to write in.
55 ANNE FRANK/JEWISH AUTHOR/ HOLOCAUST	Memories mean more to me than dresses.
56 MEGYN KELLY/USA/ BROADCASTER	Just because you're good at something doesn't mean it makes you happy.
57 ABRAHAM LINCOLN/ 16th PRESIDENT/USA	No man has a good enough memory to make a successful liar.
58 USA/RALPH WALDO EMERSON/ESSAYIST	This time, like all times, is a very good one, if we but know what to do with it.
59 MAXIM GORKY/RUSSIAN AUTHOR	Only mothers can think of the future, because they give birth to it in their children.
60 WRITER/FRANCOIS DE LA ROCHEFOUCAULD	A true friend is the greatest of all blessings, and that which we take the least care of all to acquire.
61 G.K. CHESTERTON/ ENGLISH WRITER	The traveler sees what he sees. The tourist sees what he has come to see.
62 DREAM/REALITY	World peace
63 ROBERT FULGHUM/ AMERICAN WRITER	Don't take things that aren't yours.
64 POLLY ADLER/US WRITER	A house is not a home.
65 ROBERT FULGHUM/USA/ WRITER	Clean up your own mess.
66 BURUNDI/SAYING	What you do for me, without me, you do to me.
67 FOOD/FAMINE	Farming

NUMBER CATEGORY/CREDIT	TOPIC
68 HEALTH/CAREER	Doctors
69 HEALTH/CAREER	Nurses
70 HELEN KELLER/ AMERICAN WRITER	What we have once enjoyed deeply we can never lose. All that we love deeply becomes a part of us.
71 OPINION	Teenagers
72 FOOD/ENTERTAINMENT	Favorite restaurant
73 OPINION/SOCIETY	United States of America
74 NATIONAL IMAGE	Canada
75 MUSIC	My favorite pop song
76 ENTERTAINMENT	Dance
77 EDUCATION/MEMORIES	My favorite teacher
78 COMPUTERS	Favorite computer game
79 JESSE JACKSON/USA/ CIVIL RIGHTS ACTIVIST	America is not a blanket woven from one thread, one color, one cloth.
80 T. D. JAKES/US/PREACHER RELATIONSHIPS/USA	We are often taught not to communicate when we understand that our words will be used against us.
81 OPINION/FEELINGS	The moon
82 BILL BRADLEY/USA/ POLITICIAN	Leaders should be collaborative, modest, and generous.
83 ENERGY/WORSHIP	The sun
84 STRENGTH/WORK	Elephants
85 POWER/SYMBOL	Tigers
86 SEA/ANIMALS	Whales
87 LEWIS MUMFORD/USA/ HISTORIAN	A man of courage never needs weapons, but he may need bail.
88 AUSTIN KLEON/AUTHOR/ STEAL LIKE AN ARTIST	Don't just steal the style, steal the thinking behind the style. You don't want to look like your heroes, you want to see like your heroes.
89 JOSEPH CAMPBELL/USA/ AUTHOR	Follow your bliss and the universe will open doors where there were only walls.
90 SOCIETY/ART	Art
91 PETER BART/USA/ JOURNALIST	Study the public behavior of top stars and you can detect a keen attentiveness to brand value.
92 ROBERT FROST/USA/POET	The world is full of willing people, some willing to work, the rest willing to let them.
93 HENRY THOREAU/USA/ WRITER	When I hear music, I fear no danger.
94 ANNE RICE/AUTHOR/USA	Don't be a pawn in somebody's game.
95 MICHAEL NORTON/ HAPPINESS/TED.COM	Spending on other people has a bigger return for you than spending on yourself.
96 PERSONAL	Best advice I ever received.
97 H.L. MENCKEN/USA/ EDITOR	A man may be a fool and not know it, but not if he is married.

NUMBER CATEGORY/CREDIT	TOPIC
98 RACE/DISCRIMINATION	Racial profiling
99 DANIEL GILBERT/USA/ BUSINESSMAN	If someone offered you a pill that would make you permanently happy, you would be well advised to run fast and run far. Emotion is a compass that tells us what to do, and a compass that is perpetually stuck on north is worthless.
100 BIBLE STORY	Adam and Eve
101 BEAUTY/GOSSIP	Hair salons and barber shops
102 RELIGION/CHRISTIANITY	The Bible
103 RELIGION/ISLAM	The Quran
104 FAMILY/RELATIONSHIPS	Uncles and aunts
105 INTERNET/BREAK	Internet sabbath
106 EDUCATION/AMY CHUA/ USA/BOOK TITLE	Tiger Mom (Stereotype of Asian mothers who push their children to study hard)
107 LYNN TOLER/USA/TV/ DIVORCE COURT JUDGE	Don't call the SWAT Team and complain if someone gets shot.
108 SOCIETY/VALUES	Benefits of beauty
109 SOCIETY/IMPORTANCE	Relationships
110 BENJAMIN FRANKLIN/ USA/STATESMAN	He that displays too often his wife and his wallet is in danger of having both of them borrowed.
111 DANIEL GILBERT/USA/ BUSINESSMAN	What's so curious about human beings is that we can look deeply in the future, foresee disaster, and still do nothing in the present to stop it.
112 TERRORISM	Suicide bombers
113 KOREAN PROVERB	Do not draw your sword to kill a fly.
114 SOCIETY/FAMILY	Children
115 SIR THOMAS BROWN/ ENGLISH AUTHOR	No one should approach the temple of science with the soul of a money changer.
116 ROBERT H. JACKSON/ U.S. SUPREME COURT/ JUDGE	If we can cultivate in the world the idea that aggressive war-making is the way to the prisoner's dock rather than the way to honors, we will have accomplished something toward making the peace more secure.
117 MAIMONIDES/THE GUIDE FOR THE PERPLEXED	No disease that can be treated by diet should be treated with any other means.
118 ALEXANDER DUMAS/ FRENCH WRITER	Nothing succeeds like success.
119 SEASONS	Favorite season
120 FUN/TRAVEL	Favorite car
121 FRANCIS BACON/UK/ PHILOSOPHER	Silence is the virtue of fools.
122 BUSINESS/GOVERNMENT	Giving and receiving kickbacks
123 SYDNEY J. HARRIS/ USA/JOURNALIST	The real danger is not that computers will begin to think like men, but that men will begin to think like computers.
124 PROVERB	Any port in a storm
125 UK/POLITICIAN/EDWARD G. BULWER-LYTTON	A fool flatters himself, a wise man flatters the fool.

NUMBER CATEGORY/CREDIT	TOPIC
126 RALPH WALDO EMERSON/ USA/ESSAYIST/LECTURER	Adopt the pace of nature: her secret is patience.
127 GEORGE SANTAYANA/USA SPAIN/USA/WRITER	Before you contradict an old man, my fair friend, you should endeavor to understand him.
128 FUN/ROMANCE	Cruise ships
129 MORTIMER ADLER/USA/ PHILOSOPHER/AUTHOR	A good book deserves an active reading. The activity of reading does not stop with the work of understanding what a book says. It must be completed by the work of criticism, the work of judging.
130 CHINA/HONESTY	Miss Artificial Beauty (beauty contest for those who have undergone plastic surgery)
131 SEA/ANIMALS	Sharks
132 SHAKESPEARE/LOVE/ SONNET 116	Love is not love. Which alters when it alteration finds.
133 ANNE FRANK/WRITER	In spite of everything, I still believe people are really good at heart.
134 FRIENDSHIP/BUSINESS	Loyalty
135 CHINA/FAMILY CONFUCIANISM	Filial piety: the kind of loyalty one feels for one's family or country; a sense of duty. Considered highly important in Chinese culture.
136 RICHARD BRANSON/ BRITISH BUSINESSMAN	What is a business? A business is people coming up with an idea to make a difference in other people's lives.
137 BRENDON BURCHARD/ MONTANA PROVERB/USA	The time you want the map…is the time before you go into the woods.
138 DR. WAYNE DYER/USA/ WRITER/MOTIVATION	See the light in others, and treat them as if that is all you see.
139 JAPAN/COST OF LIVING	Home ownership
140 ENTERTAINMENT	Hollywood movies
141 ENTERTAINMENT	Bollywood movies
142 ASIA/CONFLICT	China-Japan relationship
143 ELIZABETH GILBERT/USA/ AUTHOR	To lose balance sometimes for love is part of living a balanced life.
144 GRAHAM GREENE/USA/ WRITER	Champagne, if you are seeking the truth, is better than a lie detector.
145 EARL WARREN/JUDGE/ U.S. SUPREME COURT	Many people consider the things government does for them to be social progress but they regard the things government does for others as socialism.
146 CAREER/JOB	Job hunting
147 FAIRNESS/SOCIETY	Fat salaries of sportsmen/women
148 BILL COSBY/US/ COMEDIAN	A word to the wise ain't necessary. It's the stupid ones who need advice.
149 JESSE JACKSON/U.S. CIVIL RIGHTS ACTIVIST	Tears will get you sympathy; sweat will get you change.
150 SHARON GANNON/ YOGA/NY TIMES	Yoga is whatever you want it to be.
151 PAULO FREIRE/BRAZIL/ EDUCATOR	Washing one's hands of the conflict between the powerful and the powerless means to side with the powerful, not to be neutral.

NUMBER CATEGORY/CREDIT	TOPIC
152 EARL WARREN/JUDGE/ U.S. SUPREME COURT	...the police must obey the law while enforcing the law.
153 CHRISTOPHER KURTZ/US/ LAW PROFESSOR	...once principles have a price all that is left is the bargaining.
154 GAMBLING	Gambling in Las Vegas / Macau
155 PERFORMANCE/SPORTS	Cheating in sports - steroids and other drugs
156 EARL WARREN/JUDGE/ U.S. SUPREME COURT	The man of character, sensitive to the meaning of what he is doing, will know how to discover the ethical paths in the maze of possible behavior.
157 JESSE JACKSON/USA	In politics, an organized minority is a political majority.
158 ROBERT L. STEVENSON/ SCOTTISH WRITER	Keep your fears to yourself, but share your courage with others.
159 LEE KUAN YEW/LEADER/ SINGAPORE/BOOK TITLE	Singapore: From third world to first
160 USA/CANADA	Thanksgiving (national holiday in the U.S. and Canada) US: 4th Thursday of November/Canada: 2nd Monday of October
161 WORLD PEACE	United Nations
162 USA/HAROLD KUSHNER/ AUTHOR/TIME MAGAZINE	God's job is not to make sick people healthy. That's the doctor's job.
163 SONIA SANCHEZ/USA/ POET/PROFESSOR	So much of growing up is an unbearable waiting. A constant longing for another time, another season.
164 SKILLS DEVELOPMENT/ MERRIAMWEBSTER	Apprentice: one who is learning by practical experience under skilled workers a trade, art, or calling.
165 CRIME/PUNISHMENT	Death penalty
166 GRAHAM GREENE/USA/ WRITER	Hate is a lack of imagination.
167 BUSINESS	Teamwork
168 MARGARET MEAD/USA/ ANTHROPOLOGIST	I was brought up to believe that the only thing worth doing was to add to the sum of accurate information in the world.
169 INDIA/LEADER	Mohandas Gandhi
170 HERODOTUS/HISTORIAN	Death is a delightful hiding place for weary men.
171 WALT WHITMAN/US POET LEAVES OF GRASS	Happiness is not in another place, but this place...not for another hour... but this hour.
172 WILLIAM JAMES/USA/ PHILOSOPHER	Everybody should do at least two things each day that he hates to do, just for practice.
173 WILL ROGERS/ AMERICAN COMEDIAN	When I die, I want to die peacefully like my grandfather who died peacefully in his sleep. Not screaming like all the passengers in his car.
174 USA/RALPH WALDO EMERSON/ESSAYIST	A great part of courage is the courage of having done the thing before.
175 EARL WARREN/JUDGE/ U.S. SUPREME COURT	I hate banks. They do nothing positive for anybody except take care of themselves. They're first in with their fees and first out when there's trouble.
176 PETER DRUCKER/USA/ CONSULTANT/WRITER	The purpose of a business is to create a customer.

NUMBER CATEGORY/CREDIT	TOPIC
177 BEN SAUNDERS/ BRITISH POLAR EXPLORER/TED.COM	Inspiration and growth only come from adversity and from challenge -- from stepping away from what's comfortable and familiar and stepping into the unknown.
178 RONALD REAGAN/USA/ PRESIDENT	Trust, but verify.
179 JOSEPH ADDISON/UK/ ESSAYIST/POET	Reading is to the mind what exercising is to the body.
180 HEALTH/MIND	Mental health
181 H.L. MENCKEN/USA/ EDITOR/WRITER	A good politician is quite as unthinkable as an honest burglar.
182 LOUIS PASTEUR/FRENCH/ SCIENTIST	One does not ask of one who suffers: What is your country and what is your religion? One merely says: You suffer, that is enough for me.
183 USA/PAUL BLOOM/THE ORIGINS OF PLEASURE/ TEDTALK/PSYCHOLOGIST	If you like somebody, they look better to you. This is why spouses in happy marriages tend to think that their husband or wife looks much better than anyone else thinks that they do.
184 ARGUMENT/UNKNOWN	Nothing sucks more than that moment during an argument when you realize you're wrong.
185 DEPRESSION	Comfort food
186 STUDY/WORK	Concentration
187 FUN/RELAXATION	Public holidays
188 RICHARD BRANSON/ BRITISH BUSINESSMAN	You don't learn by following rules. You learn by doing, and by falling over.
189 EGYPT	The pyramids
190 REINHOLD NIEBUHR/ AMERICAN THEOLOGIAN	God grant me the serenity / To accept the things I cannot change; Courage to change the things I can; And wisdom to know the difference
191 ULRICH BECK/GERMAN SOCIOLOGIST/RISK	We are living in a world that is beyond controllability.
192 DIVINATION/FUTURE	Astrology/Palmistry
193 IRISH/BRIAN GERALD O'DRISCOLL/RUGBY	Knowledge is knowing a tomato is a fruit. Wisdom is not putting it in a fruit salad.
194 BILL McGLASHEN/USA/ BUSINESSMAN	Patience is something you admire in the driver behind you, but not in one ahead.
195 BUSINESS/SPIRITS	Angels
196 EYE PROTECTION	Sunglasses
197 MAHATMA GANDHI/ INDIAN LEADER	An error does not become truth by reason of multiplied propagation, nor does truth become error because nobody sees it. Truth stands, even if there be no support. It is self sustaining.
198 GRAHAM GREENE/USA/ WRITER	One can't love humanity. One can only love people.
199 BEN BERGOR/MAGICIAN/ USA/CHILDREN/WORK	It is amazing how quickly the kids learn to drive a car, yet are unable to understand the lawnmower, snowblower, or vacuum cleaner.
200 JAPAN/TRADITION	Kimono
201 FRIEDRICH NIETZSCHE/ GERMAN/PHILOSOPHER	The higher we soar the smaller we appear to those who cannot fly.

NUMBER CATEGORY/CREDIT	TOPIC
202 USA/RALPH WALDO EMERSON/ESSAYIST	A man in debt is so far a slave.
203 EXPERIENCE	Encounters with the police
204 RELIGION/PHILOSOPHY	Buddhism
205 JACK KEROUAC/ USA/ NOVELIST/POET	Great things are not accomplished by those who yield to trends and fads and popular opinion.
206 PICO IYER/WRITER/USA/ KNOWLEDGE@WHARTON	...my sense is that most of us humans when put in the way of temptation nearly always lose out to the temptation.
207 MAHATMA GANDHI/ INDIAN LEADER	The only tyrant I accept in this world is the 'still small voice' within me. And even though I have to face the prospect of being a minority of one, I humbly believe I have the courage to be in such a hopeless minority.
208 LEO BUSCAGLIA/ AMERICAN WRITER	Don't spend your precious time asking, "Why isn't the world a better place?" It will only be time wasted. The question to ask is "How can I make it better?" To that there is an answer.
209 WHAT WOMEN WANT/ JAPAN/HUMOR	3 H's: Height (Tall); High Salary; High Education
210 JOSHUA FOER/MEMORY/ TED.COM	Our lives are the sum of our memories. How much are we willing to lose from our already short lives by...not paying attention.
211 DWARF TOSSING/GAME/ ABUSE/WIKIPEDIA	Dwarf tossing: practice where patrons in a bar toss dwarfs wearing specially padded clothing onto mattresses or walls that are Velcro-coated. Participants compete on who can throw the dwarf the farthest.
212 NELSON MANDELA/ PRESIDENT/S. AFRICA	It is better to lead from behind and to put others in front, especially when you celebrate victory when nice things occur. You take the front line when there is danger. Then people will appreciate your leadership.
213 ENGLAND/FRANCE	Chunnel
214 OSCAR WILDE/WRITER/ IRISH	Some cause happiness wherever they go; others whenever they go.
215 E. B. WHITE/USA/WRITER	We grow tyrannical fighting tyranny.
216 JACK KEROUAC/POET/ USA	My fault, my failure, is not in the passions I have, but in my lack of control of them.
217 GEN. COLIN POWELL/USA/ STATESMAN	...loyalty means giving me your honest opinion, whether you think I'll like it or not.
218 STEPHEN COVEY/USA/ WRITER	I am not a product of my circumstances. I am a product of my decisions.
219 LEE IACOCCA/USA	Talk to people in their own language. If you do it well, they'll say, 'God, he said exactly what I was thinking.' And when they begin to respect you, they'll follow you to the death.
220 JANE AUSTEN/UK/ WRITER	If a book is well written, I always find it too short.
221 F. SCOTT FITZGERALD/ USA/WRITER	Genius is the ability to put into effect what is on your mind.
222 MICHELLE NORRIS/USA/ RADIO JOURNALIST	Food can lubricate a conversation.
223 BANKING/SECURITY	PIN: Personal Identification Number

NUMBER CATEGORY/CREDIT	TOPIC
224 THUCYDIDES/HISTORIAN	War is a matter not so much of arms as of money.
225 JACK KEROUAC/US POET	I saw that my life was a vast glowing empty page and I could do anything I wanted.
226 KINDNESS/HUMANITY	Generosity
227 PUBLILIUS SYRUS/ WRITER	Anyone can hold the helm when the sea is calm.
228 WILL ROGERS/USA/ COMEDIAN	The quickest way to double your money is to fold it over and put it back in your pocket.
229 INSINCERITY	Crocodile tears
230 PROTECTION/SHARK ATTACKS	Shark repellent
231 WAYNE OATES/USA/ PSYCHOLOGIST/PASTOR	Alcoholics are amazed when I admit to them my addiction to work...I have dubbed this addiction of myself and my fellow ministers as "workaholism."
232 FASHION	Jeans
233 ROBERT FROST/ AMERICAN POET	By working faithfully eight hours a day you may eventually get to be boss and work twelve hours a day.
234 RICHARD BRANSON/UK ENTREPRENEUR	Innovation happens when people are given the freedom to ask questions and the resources and power to find the answers.
235 CHILDREN	Safe playgrounds
236 PRESSURE	Grace under fire
237 SUCCESS/FAILURE	The higher you go the harder the fall.
238 CLARENCE BEICHER/ FRANK GILBREITH/USA	I will always choose a lazy person to do a difficult job ....Because , he will find an easy way to do it
239 FOOD/PLEASURE	Chocolate
240 COMFORT/CHOICE	Mattress
241 WAYNE LAPIERRE/USA/ CEO/NRA	The only thing that stops a bad guy with a gun is a good guy with a gun.
242 RORY SUTHERLAND/ PERSPECTIVE/TED.COM	Google understood that if you're just a search engine, people assume you're a very, very, good search engine.
243 REST & RECREATION	Spa
244 ANDRE GIDE/FRENCH/ AUTHOR	One doesn't consent to find new lands without consenting to lose sight, for a very long time, of the shore.
245 DETERMINATION	Mission Impossible
246 HOWARD SCHULTZ/USA/ FOUNDER/BUSINESS	Starbucks: a third place between work and home
247 ANNIE DILLARD/USA/ WRITER	There is no shortage of good days. It is good lives that are hard to come by.
248 ST. AUGUSTINE/BISHOP/ RELIGION/CATHOLIC	He that is jealous is not in love.
249 USA/DWIGHT D. EISENHOWER/ 39TH PRESIDENT	Every gun that is made, every warship launched, every rocket fired signifies, in the financial sense, a theft from those who hunger and are not fed, those who are cold and not clothed.
250 JAPAN/RELIGION	Shintoism

NUMBER CATEGORY/CREDIT	TOPIC
251 ED MUSKIE/US SENATOR	You have the God-given right to kick the government around.
252 GROVER NORQUIST/USA/ TAX REFORM	Thinking something out loud is not treason.
253 ANDRE GIDE/FRENCH/ AUTHOR	It is better to be hated for what you are than to be loved for what you are not.
254 KRAMER & PERLROTH/ WARNING/NY TIMES	EUGENE KASPERSKY : Cyberweapons are the most dangerous innovation of this century.
255 VINCE LOMBARDI/USA/ FOOTBALL/COACH	Fatigue makes cowards of us all.
256 SIMON SINEK/WRITER/ AUSTRALIA/PROFESSOR	For the best companies, hiring is like adopting a child.
257 BAD EXPERIENCE/ PRESSURE	Bad hair day : day on which one's hair seems unmanageable. Also extended to mean a day when everything seems to go wrong.
258 DANIEL HILL/USA/ WRITER	Feminine wants to be adored; masculine wants to be believed in.
259 STEPHEN COVEY/ AUTHOR/USA	You have to decide what your highest priorities are and have the courage – pleasantly, smilingly, nonapologetically, to say "no" to other things. And the way you do that is by having a bigger "yes" burning inside. The enemy of the "best" is often the "good."
260 PETER DRUCKER/USA/ CONSULTANT	The most important thing in communication is to hear what isn't being said.
261 PETER DRUCKER/USA/ CONSULTANT	The purpose of business is to create a customer.
262 CHINA/CONFUCIUS	Confucianism
263 PABLO PICASSO/ARTIST	Good artists copy; great artists steal.
264 CHINA/COAL	Black Death: China's Coal Mining Industry
265 LAURYN HILL/USA/ HIP HOP ARTIST	I consider myself a crayon. I might not be your favorite color but one day you're going to need me to complete your picture.
266 SUN TZU/CHINESE GENERAL/AUTHOR	Treat your men as you would your own beloved sons. And they will follow you into the deepest valley.
267 DOOMSDAY/NUCLEAR	Nuclear winter
268 ROBERT GATES/USA/ STATESMAN	Great leaders must have vision.
269 SOPHOCLES	Time eases all things.
270 AMY CUDDY/HARVARD PROFESSOR/TEDTALK	Don't fake it till you make it. Fake it till you become it.
271 ALCOHOL/SAFETY	Designated drivers
272 WATER SHORTAGE	Desalinization of sea water
273 FASHION	Vintage clothing
274 JAMES BALDWIN/USA/ WRITER	The law is meant to be my servant and not my master. Still less my torturer and my murderer.
275 POLLUTION	Smog
276 WALTER ISAACSON/ WRITER/USA	To dwell on the things that depress or anger us does not help in overcoming them. One must knock them down alone.

NUMBER CATEGORY/CREDIT	TOPIC
277 DALE CARNEGIE/USA/ AUTHOR	You can conquer almost any fear if you will only make up your mind to do so. For remember, fear doesn't exist anywhere except in the mind.
278 ENVIRONMENT	Logging
279 KOREAN PROVERB	A day-old pigeon cannot fly over a mountain pass.
280 HEALTH/MONEY	Pharmaceutical companies
281 ROBERT MCCRUM/UK/ THE GUARDIAN	Small publishers are small for a very good reason.
282 HANNAH ARENDT/USA/ POLITICAL THEORIST	No punishment has ever possessed enough power of deterrence to prevent the commission of crimes.
283 ARTHUR CONNELL/ THIS I BELIEVE/USA	Self-control, self-criticism and a remorseless urge for self-improvement are the indispensable virtues.
284 HANNAH ARENDT/ GERMAN/POLITICAL PHILOSOPHER	Loving life is easy when you are abroad. Where no one knows you and you hold your life in your hands all alone, you are more master of yourself than at any other time.
285 AUNG SAN SUU KYI/ MYANMAR/WOMEN/ LEADERSHIP	To view the opposition as dangerous is to misunderstand the basic concept of democracy. To oppress the opposition is to assault the very foundation of democracy.
286 JEFFREY EUGENIDES/ USA/NOVELIST	There comes a time when you get lost in the woods, when the woods begin to feel like home.
287 BILL BRADLEY/ AMERICAN POLITICIAN	Sports are a metaphor for overcoming obstacles and achieving against great odds. Athletes, in times of difficulty, can be important role models.
288 VICTOR HUGO/FRENCH/ AUTHOR	He who opens a school door, closes a prison.
289 AUNG SAN SUU KYI/ MYANMAR/LEADER	I don't believe in people just hoping. We work for what we want. I always say that one has no right to hope without endeavor.
290 FEDERICO FELLINI/ ITALY/MOVIE DIRECTOR	A different language is a different vision of life.
291 PERSONAL/BUSINESS	Transformation
292 USA/THIS I BELIEVE/ C. BOTTIGHEIMER	Work is the sweetening of life.
293 JOHN F. KENNEDY/ USA/35TH PRESIDENT	The stories of past courage can...teach...offer hope...provide inspiration. But they cannot supply courage itself. For this each man must look into his own soul.
294 MAHATMA GANDHI/ INDIAN LEADER	SEVEN SOCIAL SINS: 5) Commerce without morality
295 HEALTH	Health insurance
296 HELEN KELLER/USA/ AUTHOR	Alone we can do so little; together we can do so much.
297 USA/GLEN WARREN/ FOREVER FATHERS	There's a difference between a deadbeat dad and a dead broke dad.
298 ROALD DAHL/BRITISH NOVELIST	The writer has to force himself to work. He has to make his own hours and if he doesn't go to his desk at all there is nobody to scold him.
299 PETER NORVIG/100,000 STUDENTS/TED.COM	Peers can be the best teachers, because they're the ones that remember what it's like to not understand.

NUMBER CATEGORY/CREDIT	TOPIC
300 VICTOR HUGO/FRENCH/ AUTHOR	Not being heard is no reason for silence..
301 J. F. KENNEDY/USA/ PRESIDENT	The time to repair the roof is when the sun is shining.
302 HUMOR/COMEDY	Parody
303 USA/ELYN SAKS/MENTAL ILLNESS /TED.COM/ MacARTHUR FELLOW	Some people still hold the view that restraints help psychiatric patients feel safe. I've never met a psychiatric patient who agreed.
304 VISION/GAMBLE	Leap of faith
305 INDIA/PAKISTAN/FAMILY	Honor killings
306 USA/THEODORE SORENSEN/ SPEECHWRITER	Global warming is for real. Every scientist knows that now, and we are on our way to the destruction of every species on earth, if we don't pay attention and reverse our course.
307 GEORGE W. BUSH/USA/ PRESIDENT	Weapons of Mass Destruction
308 RELATIONSHIPS/DEBATE	Agreeing to disagree
309 POLITICS/SAYING	An hour is a lifetime in politics.
310 USA/RALPH WALDO EMERSON/ESSAYIST	A hero is no braver than an ordinary man, but he is brave five minutes longer.
311 WILLIAM M. CHASE/ A QUESTION OF HONOR/NY TIMES	Some students cheat because of pressures to succeed in a competitive world. Some cheat because they are lazy, tired, or indifferent.
312 ABIGAIL VAN BUREN/USA/ ADVICE COLUMNIST	The less you talk, the more you're listened to.
313 INDIAN PROVERB	Better to have a diamond with a few small flaws than a rock that is perfect.
314 COLD WAR	Mutual Assured Destruction (MAD)
315 MARCUS TULLIUS CICERO/PHILOSOPHER	A happy life consists in tranquility of mind.
316 SUCCESS/SAYING	No pain no gain
317 SINGAPORE	Killer litter (throwing objects from heights/apartments)
318 MARC ANDREESSEN/ USA/ENTREPRENEUR	The difference between a vision and a hallucination is that other people can see the vision.
319 DAVID R. DOW/LESSONS FROM DEATH ROW INMATES/TED.COM	People might disagree about whether [a murderer] should have been executed. But I think everybody would agree that the best possible version... would be a story where no murder ever occurs.
320 LUDWIG MIES VAN DER ROHE/ARICHITECTURE	Less is more.
321 DEBATE/BUSINESS	The bigger the better
322 SOCIETY	Money matters
323 DR. BEN CARSON/USA/ NEUROSURGEON	Success is determined not by whether or not you face obstacles, but by your reaction to them. And if you look at these obstacles as a containing fence, they become your excuse for failure. If you look at them as a hurdle, each one strengthens you for the next.
324 THEODORE ROOSEVELT/ USA/26TH PRESIDENT	I wish to preach, not the doctrine of ignoble ease, but the doctrine of the strenuous life.

NUMBER CATEGORY/CREDIT	TOPIC
325 THELONIUS MONK/USA/ JAZZ MUSICIAN	Sometimes it's to your advantage for people to think you're crazy.
326 WILLIAM JENNINGS BRYAN/USA/LAWYER	My place in history will depend on what I can do for the people and not on what the people can do for me.
327 JANE AUSTEN/UK/ AUTHOR	Those who do not complain are never pitied..
328 BLESSING	A gift that keeps on giving
329 FAMILY/FAVORITISM	Nepotism
330 SECRETS	Skeletons in the closet
331 USA/NANNIE HELEN BURROUGHS/EDUCATION	The book, the Bible, and the broom.
332 CICERO/PHILOSOPHER	Advice is judged by results, not by intentions.
333 GEOLOGY/DANGER	Volcanoes
334 JOSEPH CAMPBELL/ AMERICAN AUTHOR	Preachers err by trying to talk people into belief; better they reveal the radiance of their own discovery.
335 SHIRLEY CHISHOLM/ USA/CONGRESSWOMAN	You don't make change by standing on the sidelines, whimpering and complaining. You make progress by implementing ideas.
336 WILLIAM OSLER/USA/ CANADIAN DOCTOR	One of the first duties of the physician is to educate the masses not to take medicine.
337 EDWARD GIBBON/MP/ ENGLISH HISTORIAN	My early and invincible love of reading – I would not exchange for the treasures of India.
338 ABIGAIL VAN BUREN/ COLUMNIST/USA	People are judged by the company they keep.
339 DAVID R. DOW/LESSONS FROM DEATH ROW INMATES/TED.COM	If you tell me the name of a death row inmate -- doesn't matter what state he's in, doesn't matter if I've ever met him before -- I'll write his biography for you.
340 CHIEF JOSEPH/NATIVE AMERICAN/NEZ PERCE	Hear me, my chiefs! I am tired. My heart is sick and sad. From where the sun now stands, I will fight no more forever.
341 YOKO ONO/ARTIST/USA/ JAPAN	It's better to dance than to march through life.
342 FOODIES	Exotic cuisine
343 BUSINESS	Investor relations
344 DANGER/CONFLICT	Street fighting
345 SCOT/ROBERT LOUIS STEVENSON/WRITER	The cruelest lies are often told in silence.
346 ZIG ZIGLAR/USA/ MOTIVATION	Rich people have small TVs and big libraries, and poor people have small libraries and big TVs.
347 HERMAN MELVILLE/ USA/WRITER	To produce a mighty book, you must choose a mighty theme.
348 THEODORE ROOSEVELT/ 26TH PRESIDENT /USA	The wildlife of today is not ours to do with as we please.
349 GEORGE R. MARTIN/USA/ NOVELIST	It is one thing to be clever and another to be wise.

NUMBER CATEGORY/CREDIT	TOPIC
350 INDONESIA/PARADISE	Bali
351 JOSEPH CAMPBELL/ USA/AUTHOR	A bit of advice / Given to a young Native American At the time of his initiation: As you go the way of life, You will see great chasms. Jump. It is not as wide as you think.
352 DEATH	Wills
353 LAURA BUSH/FIRST LADY/ USA	Libraries allow children to ask questions about the world and find the answers. And the wonderful thing is that once a child learns to use a library, the doors to learning are always open.
354 AUNG SAN SUU KYI/ MYANMAR/LEADER	The only real prison is fear, and the only real freedom is freedom from fear.
355 DR. BEN CARSON/ USA/ NEUROSURGEON	Everyone in the world is worth being nice to. Because God never creates inferior human beings, each person deserves respect and dignity.
356 ENVIRONMENT	3R's: Reduce, reuse, recycle
357 YOKO ONO/ARTIST	Cosmetics are a boon to every woman, but a girl's best beauty aid is still a near-sighted man.
358 THEODORE SORENSEN/USA/ SPEECHWRITER	We will be safer from terrorist attacks only when we have earned the respect of all other nations instead of their fear, respect for our values and merely our weapons.
359 DON MARQUIS/ USA/HUMORIST	If you make people think they're thinking, they'll love you. But if you really make them think, they'll hate you.
360 THEODORE ROOSEVELT/ USA/26TH PRESIDENT	A man who has never gone to school may steal from a freight train; but if he has a university education, he may steal the whole railroad.
361 PETER SINGER/USA/ PHILOSOPHER	Faith cannot tell us who is right and who is wrong, because each will simply assert that his or her faith is the true one.
362 CONFLICT	Turf wars
363 PARTIES/BEVERAGES	Cocktails
364 VICTOR HUGO/FRENCH/ AUTHOR	Nothing makes a man so adventurous as an empty pocket.
365 HANNAH ARENDT/ GERMAN-AMERICAN POLITICAL THEORIST	The chief reason warfare is still with us is neither a secret death-wish of the human species, nor an irrepressible instinct of aggression...but the simple fact that no substitute for this final arbiter in international affairs has yet appeared on the political scene.
366 NATURAL PHENOMENA	Thunder & Lightning
367 PETER SINGER/USA/ PHILOSOPHER	Cheats prosper until there are enough who bear grudges against them to make sure they do not prosper.
368 OSCAR WILDE/WRITER/ IRISH/POET	One can always be kind to people about whom one cares nothing.
369 WOODY ALLEN/USA/ MOVIE DIRECTOR	Eighty percent of success is showing up.
370 WILLIAM JENNINGS BRYAN/LAWYER/USA	Never be afraid to stand with the minority when the minority is right, for the minority which is right will one day be the majority.
371 FYODOR DOSTOEVSKY/ RUSSIAN WRITER	It takes something more than intelligence to act intelligently.
372 ELIZABETH GURLEY BROWN/EDITOR/USA	Never fail to know that if you are doing all the talking, you are boring somebody.

NUMBER CATEGORY/CREDIT	TOPIC
373 WOODROW WILSON/ USA/PRESIDENT	I not only use all the brains that I have, but all I can borrow.
374 SUSAN SONTAG/USA/ WRITER/PROFESSOR	Pay attention. It's all about paying attention. Attention is vitality. It connects you with others. It makes you eager. Stay eager.
375 NELSON MANDELA/ SOUTH AFRICA/ PRESIDENT	A good head and good heart are always a formidable combination. But when you add to that a literate tongue or pen, then you have something special.
376 ROBERT ANTON WILSON/ USA/POLYMATH	Belief is the death of intelligence.
377 MARTHA GRAHAM/ USA/MODERN DANCER	'Age' is the acceptance of a term of years. But maturity is the glory of years.
378 RICHARD M. RORTY/USA/ PHILOSOPHER	Truth is what your contemporaries let you get away with.
379 USA/STEPHEN COVEY	The way we see the problem is the problem.
380 BALANCE	Nature's wisdom
381 VICTOR HUGO/FRENCH/ AUTHOR	Be like the bird that, passing on her flight awhile on boughs too slight, feels them give way beneath her, and yet sings, knowing that she has wings.
382 GLOBAL/NATIONAL	Economic progress
383 BUSINESS	Trade fairs
384 NATIONALISM	Flag waving
385 STEPHEN KING/WRITER	Get busy living, or get busy dying.
386 FRANKLIN ROOSEVELT USA/32ND PRESIDENT	We cannot always build the future for our youth, but we can build our youth for the future.
387 PETER SINGER/USA/ PHILOSOPHER	In the United States, 97 percent of those classified by the Census Bureau as poor own a color TV.
388 INDIAN PROVERB	In love beggars and kings are equal.
389 CHARLIE CHAPLIN/UK/US	The saddest thing I can imagine is to get used to luxury.
390 JOHN F. KENNEDY/ USA/35TH PRESIDENT	We must use time as a tool, not as a crutch.
391 AUNG SAN SUU KYI/ MYANMAR/LEADER	Government leaders are amazing. So often it seems they are the last to know what the people want.
392 TEENAGERS	Party drugs
393 ALBERT EINSTEIN/ SCIENTIST/NOBEL	A table, a chair, a bowl of fruit and a violin; what else does a man need to be happy?
394 COLIN POWELL/ USA/STATESMAN	A dream doesn't become reality through magic; it takes sweat, determination and hard work.
395 CHARLIE CHAPLIN/US/UK	I always like walking in the rain, so no one can see me crying.
396 ALBERT CAMUS/ FRENCH AUTHOR	It is the job of thinking people not to be on the side of the executioners.
397 DAVID ADAMS RICHARDS/ CANADIAN NOVELIST	There is no worse flaw in a man's character than that of wanting to belong.
398 ENVIRONMENT	Water pollution
399 DON MARQUIS/ USA/HUMORIST	When a man tells you that he got rich through hard work, ask him: "Whose?"

NUMBER CATEGORY/CREDIT	TOPIC
400 AUNG SAN SUU KYI/ MYANMAR	It is not power that corrupts but fear. Fear of losing power corrupts those who wield it and fear of the scourge of power corrupts those who are subject to it.
401 THOMAS PAINE/USA	Sunshine patriot
402 ANCIENT/MODERN	Egypt
403 WOLE SOYINKA/NIGERIA/ NOBEL LAUREATE	The greatest threat to freedom is the absence of criticism.
404 BERNARD M. BARUCH/ USA/BUSINESSMAN	The main purpose of the stock market is to make fools of as many men as possible.
405 MARTHA GRAHAM/USA	Dance is the hidden language of the soul.
406 ANTOINE SAINT-EXUPERY/FRENCH NOVELIST	If you want to build a ship, don't drum up people to collect wood and don't assign them tasks and work, but rather teach them to long for the endless immensity of the sea.
407 INDIAN PROVERB	It is better to be blind than to see things from only one point of view.
408 LEADER/USA/THEODORE ROOSEVELT	Aggressive fighting for the right is the greatest sport in the world.
409 MORAL DILEMMA	What you would do if you saw a colleague stealing at work or elsewhere.
410 RESEARCH	Fighting cancer
411 LEADERSHIP	Change agents
412 PERSONAL/JAPAN	"MY PACE" - Doing things at one's own pace
413 ELYN SAKS/MENTAL ILLNESS/TED.COM	Please hear this: There are no 'schizophrenics,' there are people with schizophrenia.
414 DREAMS	What you would do with a million dollars.
415 FOOD/PERSONAL	Vegetables you like
416 WILLIAM ROSS WALLACE/ USA/POET	The hand that rocks the cradle is the hand that rules the world.
417 BARBARA KINGSOLVER/ AMERICAN NOVELIST	If you never stepped on anybody's toes, you've never been for a walk.
418 SENECA/DRAMATIST	An unpopular rule is never long maintained.
419 IMAGE	Greenland
420 RECOMMENDATION	A good read
421 EDUCATION	Art galleries
422 HALLOWEEN	Trick or treat
423 DALE CARNEGIE/USA/ LECTURER/WRITER	Listen first. Give your opponents a chance to talk. Let them finish. Do not resist, defend, or debate. This only raises barriers. Try to build bridges of understanding.
424 EDWARD GIBBON/UK/ HISTORIAN	Conversation enriches the understanding, but solitude is the school of genius.
425 THEODORE SORENSEN/ USA/ SPEECHWRITER	I believe in an America in which the fruits of productivity and prosperity are shared by all, by workers as well as owners, by those at the bottom as well.
426 HERMAN MELVILLE/USA/ WRITER	Truth is in things, and not in words.

NUMBER CATEGORY/CREDIT	TOPIC
427 MARTHA GRAHAM/ USA/MODERN DANCER	Nobody cares if you can't dance well. Just get up and dance.
428 INA CORINNE BROWN/ WHAT ARE PEOPLE GOOD FOR?/USA/THIS I BELIEVE	The one thing that really matters is to be bigger than the things that can happen to you. Nothing that can happen to you is half so important than the way in which you end it.
429 MADELEINE L'ENGLE/ USA/WRITER	The great thing about getting older is that you don't lose all the other ages.
430 J. PAUL GETTY/ USA/BILLIONAIRE	Going to work for a large company is like getting on a train. Are you going sixty miles an hour or is the train going sixty miles an hour and you're just sitting still?
431 SOCIETY/PEOPLE	Character assassination
432 RELATIONSHIPS	Lying
433 RICHARD NIXON USA/PRESIDENT	Only if you have been in the deepest valley, can you ever know how magnificent it is to be on the highest mountain.
434 JAPAN	Yakuza : an organized crime group in Japan
435 JAPAN/RELATIONSHIP-BREAKING COMPANIES	Wakaresaseya: Companies that specialize in breaking up relationships for people who are too timid to end the relationship themselves.
436 AMY SCHULMAN/ LEADERSHIP/NY TIMES	People who are drawn to teaching really like to help people.
437 MIGNON MCLAUGHLIN/ USA/JOURNALIST	The time to begin most things is ten years ago.
438 RICHARD BRANSON/UK/ ENTREPRENEUR	The suit and tie is an anachronism.
439 CELEBRITY/ BENEFITS	Benefits of celebrity
440 DUSTIN HOFFMAN/ USA/ACTOR	A good review from the critics is just another stay of execution.
441 ASSERTIVENESS	No more Mr. Nice Guy
442 HEALTH/AGING	Memory loss
443 TECHNOLOGY	Robots
444 LUXURY	Swarovski crystals
445 NAOMI WOLF/USA/ WRITER	She wins who calls herself beautiful and challenges the world to change to truly see her.
446 GEORGIA O'KEEFE/ USA/ARTIST	When you take a flower in your hand and really look at it, it's your world for the moment.
447 MARTHA GRAHAM/ USA/DANCER	What people in the world think of you is really none of your business.
448 RICHARD GERE/ACTOR/ USA	The secret of my success is hairspray.
449 SOLUTIONS	Band aid : a temporary solution
450 ART/FRANCE	The Louvre
451 PERSONAL	Absentmindedness
452 NAOMI WOLF/USA/ WRITER	Ideal beauty is ideal because it does not exist.

NUMBER CATEGORY/CREDIT	TOPIC
453 DEMOCRACY/ELECTIONS	Mail-in ballots
454 HERMAN MELVILLE/USA	Whatever my fate, I'll go to it laughing.
455 DOLLY PARTON/SINGER	When someone shows you their true colors, believe them.
456 MARTHA GRAHAM/DANCE	The only sin is mediocrity.
457 AFRICAN PROVERB	If you want to go fast, go alone. If you want to go far, go together.
458 BUSINESS/IDIOM	Kicking an executive upstairs
459 LEISURE	Escapism
460 IDIOM	Hiding in plain sight
461 SAYING	Life is a circus.
462 MARC GOODMAN/USA/ STRATEGIST/TED.COM	We are at the dawn of a technological arms race, an arms race between people who are using technology for good and those who are using it for ill.
463 LEROY R. PAIGE/USA/ BASEBALL PLAYER	Age is a question of mind over matter. If you don't mind, it doesn't matter.
464 TRANSPORTATION	Segway
465 STEPHEN COVEY/USA/ AUTHOR	To change ourselves effectively, we first have to change our perceptions.
466 RICHARD NIXON/ USA/PRESIDENT	Don't get the impression that you arouse my anger. You see, one can only be angry with those he respects.
467 BUSINESS/SALES	Making cold calls
468 USA/RALPH WALDO EMERSON/ESSAYIST	I hate quotations. Tell me what you know.
469 IDIOM	On the make : seeking personal gain
470 RICHARD BRANSON/UK/ ENTREPRENEUR	My mother was determined to make us independent. When I was four years old, she stopped the car a few miles from our house and made me find my own way home across the fields. I got hopelessly lost.
471 MALALA YOUSAFZAI/ PAKISTAN/NOBELIST	I don't mind if I have to sit on the floor at school. All I want is an education. I am afraid of no one.
472 STEPHEN COVEY/AUTHOR	Live, love, laugh, leave a legacy.
473 IDIOM	Hot property : highly valued for its commercial potential/ highly attractive
474 CREATE A STORY	Sole survivor
475 IDIOM	High flyer (flier) : successful, powerful, rich person
476 VIRGINIA WOOLF/UK/ WRITER	A room of one's own
477 J. PAUL GETTY/USA/ MILLIONAIRE	If you owe the bank $100 that's your problem. If you owe the bank $100 million, that's the bank's problem.
478 PETER DRUCKER/USA/ BUSINESS CONSULTANT	Never mind your happiness; do your duty.
479 STEPHEN AMBROSE/US/ HISTORIAN	Reading your own material aloud forces you to listen.
480 DR. SAMUEL M. BEST/ USA/THIS I BELIEVE	Personal success, business success, built upon materialism alone, are empty shells concealing disappointment, saddened lives.

NUMBER CATEGORY/CREDIT	TOPIC
481 ROBERT BENCHLEY/USA/ PROCRASTINATION	Anyone can do any amount of work providing it isn't the work he is supposed to be doing at that moment.
482 USA/DR. CHARLOTTE H. BROWN/FOUNDER/ PALMER MEM. INSTITUTE	Educational philosophy: education, religion, and deeds
483 MARK TWAIN/ USA/ NOVELIST	Get a bicycle. You will not regret it. If you live.
484 WILLIAM SHAKESPEARE/ PLAYWRIGHT/UK	Every one can master a grief but he that has it.
485 ABIGAIL VAN BUREN/ COLUMNIST/USA	A church is a hospital for sinners, not a museum for saints.
486 PARENTING	Tough love
487 IDIOM	In your face
488 LOUIS D. BRANDEIS/ AMERICAN JUDGE/	Neutrality is at times a graver sin than belligerence.
489 TUPAC SHAKUR/USA/ HIP HOP ARTIST	I don't have no fear of death. My only fear is coming back reincarnated.
490 CONFUCIUS/CHINA/ PHILOSOPHER	Study the past if you would divine the future.
491 MARGARET ATWOOD/ CANADIAN NOVELIST	I read for pleasure and that is the moment I learn the most.
492 HENRY FORD/USA/ BUSINESS	Exercise is bunk. If you are healthy, you don't need it. If you are sick you should not take it.
493 DESMOND TUTU/CLERGY/ SOUTH AFRICA	Leadership and morality are indivisible. Good leaders are the custodians of morals.
494 MARC GOODMAN/USA/ TED.COM/SECURITY	More connections to more devices means more vulnerabilities.
495 PEARL S. BUCK/USA/ NOVELIST/RACISM	We send missionaries to China so the Chinese can get to heaven, but we won't let them into our country.
496 JANE McGONIGAL/10 EXTRA YEARS OF LIFE/ TED.COM/USA	A traumatic event doesn't doom us to suffer indefinitely. Instead, we can use it as a springboard to unleash our best qualities and lead happier lives.
497 CULTURE/SOCIETY	Superhero
498 BEAUTY/SOCIETY	Supermodel
499 DR. BEN CARSON/USA/ NEUROSURGEON	Tell the truth. If you tell the truth all the time you don't have to worry three months down the line about what you said three months earlier.
500 WILLIAM BLAKE/POET	A truth that's told with bad intent beats all the lies you can invent.
501 SIDONIE-GABRIELLE COLETTE/USA/WRITER	Hope costs nothing.
502 STATUE OF LIBERTY/ USA/INSCRIPTION/EMMA LAZARUS	Give me your tired, your poor, your huddled masses yearning to breathe free. The wretched refuse of your teeming shore. Send these, the homeless, tempest-tost to me; I lift my lamp beside the golden door!
503 DORIS LESSING/UK/ NOVELIST	The great secret that all old people share is that you really haven't changed in 70 or 80 years. Your body changes, but you don't change at all.

NUMBER CATEGORY/CREDIT	TOPIC
504 COMEDY/BUSINESS/ MERRIAMWEBSTER	Sidekick : a person closely associated with another as a subordinate partner
505 HOPI PROVERB/ NATIVE AMERICAN	Don't be afraid to cry. It will free your mind of sorrowful thoughts.
506 GERTRUDE STEIN/ USA/WRITER/POET	A very important thing is not to make up your mind that you are any one thing.
507 ERICA JONG/USA/ AUTHOR	Advice is what we ask for when we already know the answer but wish we didn't.
508 ISLAM/ MERRIAMWEBSTER	Jihad : a holy war waged on behalf of Islam as a religious duty; a crusade for a principle or belief
509 ABRAHAM LINCOLN/ 16th PRESIDENT/USA	No man is good enough to govern another without that other's consent.
510 AYN RAND/RUSSIAN-AMERICAN WRITER	Learn to value yourself, which means: to fight for your happiness.
511 SOJOURNER TRUTH/USA/ ABOLITIONIST	Religion without humanity is very poor human stuff.
512 BARBARA BUSH/FIRST LADY/USA	Bias has to be taught. If you hear your parents downgrading women or people of different backgrounds, why, you are going to do that.
513 GERTRUDE STEIN/ AMERICAN WRITER	When I go around and speak on campuses, I still don't get young men standing up and saying, How can I combine career and family?
514 STEPHEN JAY GOULD/ AMERICAN SCIENTIST	We pass through this world but once. Few tragedies can be more extensive than the stunting of life, few injustices deeper than the denial of an opportunity to strive or even to hope, by a limit imposed from without, but falsely identified as lying within.
515 PRINCIPLE/ADAGE	Finders keepers
516 ROBERT GATES/USA/ STATESMAN/DEFENCE	An additional quality for leadership is deep conviction.
517 STEPHEN COVEY/USA/ AUTHOR	When the trust account is high, communication is easy, instant, and effective.
518 ELEANOR ROOSEVELT/ USA/FIRST LADY	Do what you feel in your heart to be right – for you'll be criticized anyway.
519 STANLEY FISH/USA/ EVIDENCE IN SCIENCE AND RELIGION/NY TIMES	If you want to build a better mousetrap or computer, you will look to scientists and engineers. If you want to improve your marriage or learn how to win friends and influence people, you will look elsewhere, perhaps to couples counselors or to a religious tradition.
520 MICHELLE OBAMA/ USA/FIRST LADY	One of the lessons I grew up with was to always stay true to yourself and never let what somebody else says distract you from your goals.
521 BARBARA BUSH/ USA/FIRST LADY	Some people give time, some money, some their skills and connections, some literally give their life's blood. But everyone has something to give.
522 HENRY W. LONGFELLOW/ USA/POET	A torn jacket is soon mended, but hard words bruise the heart of a child.
523 EDWARD GIBBON/UK/ HISTORIAN	I have but one lamp by which my feet are guided, and that is the lamp of experience. I know no way of judging of the future but by the past.
524 SAYING/RELATIONSHIP	Love me, love my dog

NUMBER CATEGORY/CREDIT	TOPIC
525 EDWARD EVERETT HALE/USA/AUTHOR	I am only one...I cannot do everything, but still I can do something; and because I cannot do everything, I will not refuse to do something that I can do.
526 JACK KEROUAC/WRITER/USA	I don't know, I don't care, and it doesn't make a difference.
527 WATER/SAFETY	Water filters
528 BETTY FRIEDAN/USA/FEMINIST/ACTIVIST	We need to see men and women as equal partners....
529 MORTIMER ADLER/USA/PHILOSOPHER	Think how different human societies would be if they were based on love rather than justice. But no such societies have ever existed on earth.
530 PARENTS/COMICS	Why some parents dislike comic books
531 WONDER	Goosebumps
532 J. PAUL GETTY/USA/BILLIONAIRE	No one can possibly achieve any real and lasting success or 'get rich' in business by being a conformist.
533 RICHARD BRANSON/UK/BUSINESSMAN	Ridiculous yachts, private planes, and big limousines won't make people enjoy life more and it sends out terrible messages to the people who work for them.
534 DAVID ADAMS RICHARDS/CANADIAN NOVELIST	You do not understand – no accomplishment overcomes the stigma of being different.
535 ENTERTAINMENT	Street performers
536 HERMAN MELVILLE/USA/WRITER	It's better to fail in originality than to succeed in imitation.
537 JANE McGONIGAL/THE GAME.../TEDTALK GAME DESIGNER	Avatars are a way to express our true selves, our most heroic, idealized version of who we might become.
538 AUNG SAN SUU KYI/MYANMAR/LEADER	If you're feeling helpless, help someone.
539 TAOIST SAYING	There is so much to do. There is so little time. We must go slowly.
540 SAYING	A fish wouldn't get into trouble if it kept its mouth shut.
541 FUTURE/FUN	Horoscopes
542 FUN/LEARNING	Crossword puzzles
543 DR. BEN CARSON/USA/NEUROSURGEON	Good surgeons must understand the consequences of each action, to think in three dimensions.
544 EDWARD GIBBON/UK/HISTORIAN	I make it a point never to argue with people for whose opinion I have no respect.
545 BARBARA BUSH/USA/1ST LADY	Get involved in some of the big ideas of your time.
546 FOOD/FUN	Pizza
547 SAYING	Politics makes for strange bedfellows.
548 CHARLIE CHAPLIN/ACTOR	To truly laugh, you must be able to take your pain, and play with it.
549 LIFE	Frustration
550 IDIOM	Stealing someone's thunder

NUMBER CATEGORY/CREDIT	TOPIC
551 MARGARET MEAD/USA/ THIS I BELIEVE/ ANTHROPOLOGIST	I believe that to understand human beings it is necessary to think of them as part of the whole living world.
552 COLIN POWELL/ USA/STATESMAN	Avoid having your ego so close to your position that when your position falls, your ego goes with it.
553 SUN TZU/CHINESE GENERAL/AUTHOR	Secret operations are essential in war; upon them the army relies to make its every move.
554 LOUIS ARMSTRONG/USA/ MUSICIAN	If ya ain't got it in ya, ya can't blow it out.
555 AUNG SAN SUU KYI/ MYANMAR	In societies where men are truly confident of their own worth, women are not merely tolerated but valued.
556 J. PAUL GETTY/USA	In times of rapid change, experience could be your worst enemy.
557 STEPHEN COVEY/USA/ WRITER	...to learn and not to do is really not to learn. To know and not to do is really not to know.
558 REALIZATION	Wake-up call
559 ROXANE GAY/USA/ WRITER/NY TIMES	...no form of justice after the fact can erase trauma, or bring people back to life.
560 FRANKLIN ROOSEVELT 32ND PRESIDENT /USA	We must remember that any oppression, any injustice, any hatred, is a wedge designed to attack our civilization.
561 FRANKLIN ROOSEVELT 32ND PRESIDENT/USA	If you treat people right they will treat you right – ninety percent of the time.
562 ESPIONAGE	National security
563 CHRIS GERDES/TED.COM/ ENGINEER/USA	Life is too short for boring cars.
564 TED.COM/MINA BISSELL/ BIOLOGIST/USA/IRAN	Don't be arrogant, because arrogance kills curiosity and passion.
565 AGRICULTURE	Drought
566 IDIOM	Burning the midnight oil
567 CLASS MATTERS/ NY TIMES/USA	At a time when education matters more than ever, success in school remains linked tightly to class.
568 NEIL HARBISSON/COLOR/ TED.COM	Life will be much more exciting when we stop creating applications for mobile phones and we start creating applications for our own body.
569 MAHATMA GANDHI/INDIA	SEVEN SOCIAL SINS: 4) Knowledge without character
570 STEDMAN GRAHAM/USA/ DIVERSITY – LEADERS	The 21ST century is a performance-based culture. What matters is how people are able to interact and produce results.
571 FRANKLIN ROOSEVELT 32ND PRESIDENT /USA	Repetition does not transform a lie into a truth.
572 INDIAN PROVERB	Blaming your faults on your nature does not change the nature of your faults.
573 ARNOLD GLASOW/USA	A good father lives so he is a credit to his children.
574 USA/RALPH WALDO EMERSON/ESSAYIST	A man is what he thinks about all day.
575 IDIOM	Giving someone the cold shoulder
576 COLLEGE/WORK	Working part-time job to pay for college.

NUMBER CATEGORY/CREDIT	TOPIC
577 LEADER/USA/THEODORE ROOSEVELT	Whenever you are asked if you can do a job, tell 'em, 'Certainly I can!' Then get busy and find out how to do it.
578 JOHN QUINCY ADAMS/ USA/PRESIDENT	The influence of each human being on others in this life is a kind of immortality.
579 CONFUCIAN/CHINA/ PHILOSOPHER	The father who does not teach his son his duties is equally guilty with the son who neglects them.
580 RICHARD WRIGHT/ USA/AUTHOR	Men can starve from a lack of self-realization as much as they can from a lack of bread.
581 FRANKLIN ROOSEVELT 32ND PRESIDENT /USA	Happiness lies in the joy of achievement and the thrill of creative effort.
582 ELEANOR ROOSEVELT/ USA/ LEADERSHIP	A woman is like a tea bag – you never know how strong she is until she gets in hot water.
583 ANNA QUINDLEN/ USA/AUTHOR	I would be most content if my children grew up to be the kind of people who think decorating consists mostly of building enough bookshelves.
584 MIKE MYATT/FORBES/ USA/WRITER	Real leaders don't take credit; they give it.
585 STEPHEN KING/ USA/WRITER	I guess when you turn off the main road, you have to be prepared to see some funny houses.
586 MARK TWAIN/ USA/NOVELIST	A banker is a fellow who lends you his umbrella when the sun is shining, but wants it back the minute it begins to rain.
587 USA/ALEXANDER HAMILTON/LEADER	Man is a reasoning, rather than, a reasonable animal.
588 THEODORE ROOSEVELT/ 26TH PRESIDENT /USA	To educate a man in mind and not in morals is to educate a menace to society.
589 FRENCH/PAINTER/ PIERRE A. RENOIR	It is after you have lost your teeth that you can afford to buy steaks.
590 COLIN POWELL/USA/ STATESMAN	Bad news isn't wine. It doesn't improve with age.
591 INDIAN PROVERB	Call on God, but be sure to row away from the rocks.
592 KAHLIL GIBRAN/POET/ LEBANESE	When love beckons to you follow him.
593 KOREAN PROVERB	A great river does not refuse to accept smaller streams.
594 SENECA/ROMAN DRAMATIST	To be feared is to fear: no one has been able to strike terror into others and at the same time enjoy peace of mind.
595 HERODOTUS/HISTORIAN/ ANCIENT GREECE	Circumstances rule men; men do not rule circumstances.
596 TINA SEELIG/USA/ PROFESSOR/BUSINESS	Essentially, your reputation is your most valuable asset – so guard it well.
597 JIMI HENDRIX/USA/ MUSICIAN	I've been imitated so well I've heard people copy my mistakes.
598 FAMILY/FRIENDS	A surprise party
599 TONI MORRISON/ USA/NOBEL LAUREATE	If there is a book that you want to read, but it hasn't been written yet, you must be the one to write it.

NUMBER CATEGORY/CREDIT	TOPIC
600 MARK TWAIN/ US/ WRITER	Clothes make the man.
601 GERONIMO/NATIVE AMERICAN LEADER	While living, I want to live well.
602 PROVERB/CHEYENNE/ NATIVE AMERICAN	Our first teacher is our own heart.
603 PROVERB/NAVAJO	There is nothing as eloquent as a rattlesnake's tail.
604 ALLEN GINSBURG/USA/ POET	Follow your inner moonlight; don't hide the madness.
605 LAURA CARSTENSEN/ OLDER PEOPLE/TED.COM	Older people seem to engage with sadness more comfortably; they're more accepting of sadness than younger people are.
606 HUANGZI/CHINESE PHILOSOPHER	When you realize where you come from, you naturally become tolerant, disinterested, amused, kindhearted as a grandmother, dignified as a king.
607 ANNA QUINDLEN/USA	In books I have traveled, not only to other worlds, but into my own.
608 EDGAR BRONFMAN SR/ CANADA/BUSINESSMAN	To turn $100 into $110 is work. To turn 100 million into $110 million is inevitable.
609 SCOT/ROBERT LOUIS STEVENSON/WRITER	Quiet minds cannot be perplexed or frightened but go on in fortune or misfortune at their own private pace, like a clock during a thunderstorm.
610 VICTOR HUGO/FRENCH/ AUTHOR	A doctor's door should never be closed; a priest's door should always be open.
611 MARGARET ATWOOD/ CANADIAN NOVELIST	We still think of a powerful man as a born leader and a powerful woman as an anomaly.
612 ARABIANPROVERB	A tree that affords thee shade, do not order it to be cut down.
613 COLIN POWELL/USA	Don't be afraid to challenge the pros, even in their own backyard.
614 KOREAN PROVERB	A hunter's knife cannot carve its own handle.
615 SWAHILI PROVERB	Habit is a skin.
616 MELINDA GATES/USA/ PHILANTHROPIST	Our desire to bring every good thing to our children is a force for good throughout the world. It's what propels societies forward.
617 IRIS CHANG/US/HISTORY	The chronicle of humankind's cruelty is a long and sorry tale.
618 WALTER HAGEN/USA/ GOLF PROFESSIONAL	No one remembers who came in second.
619 GERRY SPENCE/USA/ LAWYER/AUTHOR	If I believe in one proposition, I have become locked behind the door of that belief, and all other doors to learning and freedom, although standing open and waiting for me to enter, are now closed to me.
620 STEDMAN GRAHAM/USA/ SUCCESS MAGAZINE	The 21st century demands that you have a vision of your future unclouded by your past.
621 NATIONAL SECURITY	Wiretapping
622 J. F. KENNEDY/USA/ 35th PRESIDENT	Those who make peaceful revolution impossible will make violent revolution inevitable.
623 G.K. CHESTERTON/UK	An adventure is only an inconvenience rightly considered.
624 DEBATE	The hunting of animals is barbaric.
625 SIDONIE-GABRIELLE COLETTE/USA/WRITER	The true traveler is he who goes on foot.

NUMBER CATEGORY/CREDIT	TOPIC
626 J. F. KENNEDY/USA/ 35TH PRESIDENT	And so, my fellow Americans: ask not what your country can do for you – ask what you can do for your country.
627 INDIAN PROVERB	It's easy to forget a kindness, but one remembers unkindness.
628 REBBE NACHMAN/RABBI/ UKRAINE	One may distort [the truth] to preserve peace.
629 USA/HEIDI GRANT HALVORSON/WRITER	...successful people reach their goals not simply because of who they are, but more often because of what they do.
630 KOREAN PROVERB	Don't try to cover the whole sky with the palm of your hand.
631 VICTOR HUGO/FRENCH/ AUTHOR	Every blade has two edges; he who wounds with one wounds himself with the other.
632 ROBERT McCRUM/UK/ THE GUARDIAN	Narrative (aka storytelling) is in our DNA. It's called gossip.
633 RUSSIAN PROVERB	Draw not your bow till your arrow is fixed.
634 KOREAN PROVERB	A new-born baby has no fear of tigers.
635 JUNG CHANG/AUTHOR/ UK	When a man gets power, even his chickens and dogs rise to heaven.
636 HONESTY/NEED	What you would do if you found a wallet with $10,000 in it
637 RUSSIAN PROVERB	Appetite comes with eating.
638 RUSSIAN PROVERB	When the rich make war, it's the poor who suffer.
639 INDIAN PROVERB	It is easier to cover our feet with sandals than to cover the earth with carpets.
640 RUSSIAN PROVERB	A great ship needs deep waters.
641 DEBATE	Wearing a fur coat is unethical.
642 WILL ROGERS/COMEDIAN	I never met a man that I didn't like.
643 AUDREY TAUTOU/ ACTOR/FRANCE	When I was a little girl, I loved monkeys. I wanted to be a primatologist. I went to the careers office to ask how. Because nobody could give me a good answer, I opted for acting.
644 MARK TWAIN/USA/ WRITER	Courage is resistance to fear, mastery of fear – not absence of fear.
645 KAHLIL GIBRAN/POET	For even as love crowns you so shall he crucify you.
646 ALEXANDER HAMILTON/ USA/FOUNDING FATHER	Men often oppose a thing merely because they have had no agency in planning it, or because it may have been planned by those whom they dislike.
647 J. F. KENNEDY/USA/ 35TH PRESIDENT	Too often we enjoy the comfort of opinion without the discomfort of thought.
648 RUSSIAN PROVERB	A beard does not make a philosopher.
649 ST. FRANCIS OF ASSISI/ ITALIAN CATHOLIC FRIAR	He who works with his hands is a laborer. He who works with his hand and his head is a craftsman. He who works with his hands and his head and his heart is an artist.
650 ADDICTION/IDIOM	Falling off the wagon
651 ABRAHAM LINCOLN/USA	Tact is the ability to describe others as they see themselves.
652 BILL GATES/USA/ ENTREPRENEUR	The Internet is becoming the town square for the global village of tomorrow.

NUMBER CATEGORY/CREDIT	TOPIC
653 UNIVERSITIES/ FUNCTION/DEBATE	Universities should train students to serve the economic need of the society.
654 FREEMAN HRABOWSKY/ UNIV. PRESIDENT/USA	Speak up. You have to project! If people can't hear you, it doesn't matter what you say.
655 DR. JOYCE BROTHERS/ USA/PSYCHOLOGIST	A strong, positive self-image is the best possible preparation for success.
656 KOREAN PROVERB	If you kick a stone in anger, you will hurt your own foot.
657 ALAN LAKEIN/USA/ AUTHOR/TIME	Time is life. It is irreversible and irreplaceable. To waste your time is to waste your life, but to master your time is to master your life and make the most of it.
658 MAX BEERBOHM/UK	Nobody ever died of laughter.
659 WILLIAM LI/CANCER?/ TED.COM/USA	We're treating cancer too late in the game, when it's already established, and, oftentimes, it's already spread or metastasized.
660 STEPHEN KING/WRITER	The devil's voice is sweet to hear.
661 MARIA MONTESSORI/ ITALIAN EDUCATOR	Free the child's potential, and you will transform him into the world.
662 KOREAN PROVERB	Even a monk can't shave his own head.
663 PYTHAGORAS/GREEK MATHEMATICIAN	As soon as laws are necessary for men, they are no longer fit for freedom.
664 ELEANOR ROOSEVELT/ USA/LEADERSHIP	No one can make you feel inferior without your consent.
665 ITAY TALGAM/TED.COM LEAD LIKE THE GREAT CONDUCTORS	A conductor's happiness does not come from only his own story and his joy of the music. The joy is about enabling other people's stories to be heard at the same time.
666 MARCO TEMPEST/USA/ SWISS/MAGIC/TED.COM	We willingly enter fictional worlds where we cheer our heroes and cry for friends we never had.
667 VICTOR HUGO/FRENCH/ AUTHOR	Nothing is more powerful than an idea whose time has come.
668 PETER DRUCKER/USA/ MANAGEMENT	Follow effective action with quiet reflection. From the quiet reflection will come even more effective action.
669 FRANKLIN ROOSEVELT 32ND PRESIDENT /USA	Men are not prisoners of fate, but only prisoners of their own minds.
670 PEGGY NOONAN/USA/ SPEECHWRITER FOR PRESIDENT REAGAN	I love eulogies. They are the most moving kind of speech because they attempt to pluck meaning from the fog, and on short order, when the emotions are still ragged and raw and susceptible to leaps.
671 YES, VIRGINIA, THERE IS A SANTA CLAUS/NY SUN/ FRANCIS PHARCELLUS CHURCH	Yes, Virginia, there is a Santa Claus, as certainly as love and generosity and devotion exist...
672 NOVELIST/MIGUEL DE CERVANTES/SPANISH	A man must eat a peck of salt with his friend before he knows him.
673 PYTHAGORAS/THINKER	Choose rather to be strong of soul than strong of body.
674 RAGHAVA KK/SHAKE UP YOUR STORY/TED.COM	I can't promise my child a life without bias – we're all biased – but I promise to bias my child with multiple perspectives.

NUMBER CATEGORY/CREDIT	TOPIC
675 THEODORE ROOSEVELT/ 26TH PRESIDENT /USA	No man is justified in doing evil on the ground of expediency.
676 INDIAN PROVERB	Dependence on another is perpetual disappointment.
677 JUNG CHANG/AUTHOR/ UK/CHINA	If you have love, even plain water is sweet.
678 PICO IYER/WRITER/USA/ KNOWLEDGE@WHARTON	There are surveys which show that multitasking loses billions of dollars a year, that 28% of an office worker's time is lost through multitasking.
679 BILL GATES/TED.COM/ ENTREPRENEUR/USA	I want to admit that I am an optimist. Any tough problem, I think it can be solved.
680 MAIMONIDES/GUIDE FOR THE PERPLEXED/RABBI	Do not consider it proof just because it is written in books, for a liar who will deceive with his tongue will not hesitate to do the same with his pen.
681 SUSAN CAIN/THE POWER OF INTROVERTS/ TED.COM	Eleanor Roosevelt, Rosa Parks, Gandhi – all these people describe themselves as quiet and soft-spoken and even shy. And they all took the spotlight, even though every bone in their bodies was telling them not to.
682 INDIAN PROVERB	It is hard for an ex-king to become a watchman.
683 MIKE ROWE/CELBRATING DIRTY JOBS/TED.COM	People with dirty jobs are *happier* than you think. As a group, they're the happiest people I know.
684 INDIAN PROVERB	It is love that makes the impossible possible.
685 THEODORE ROOSEVELT/ 26TH PRESIDENT /USA	The most practical kind of politics is the politics of decency.
686 KOREAN PROVERB	Even if you know the way, ask one more time.
687 END OF LIFE FINAL FOUR/DISEASE/DEATH	Heart disease, cancer, diabetes, and COPD (Chronic Obstructive Pulmonary Disease)
688 DR. ANDREW WEIL/ 'DATA SMOG'/TIME	The modern downpour of data is largely worthless distraction…
689 LEROY ROBERT PAIGE/ USA/BASEBALL	Don't pray when it rains if you don't pray when the sun shines.
690 LAO-TZU/THINKER/ CHINA	To have little is to possess. To have plenty is to be perplexed.
691 DOCTORS/LAWSUITS	Medical errors
692 HAROLD CACCIA/ UK/DIPLOMAT	If you are to stand up for your government you must be able to stand up to your government.
693 RELATIONSHIPS	Single by choice
694 VICKI BAUM/AUTHOR/ AUSTRIAN-AMERICAN	You don't get ulcers from what you eat, but from what's eating you.
695 MARK TWAIN/US WRITER	Work consists of whatever a body is obliged to do, and play consists of whatever a body is not obliged to do.
696 FRENCH/ANTOINE SAINT-EXUPERY/WRITER	A chief is a man who assumes responsibility. He says, "I was beaten," he does not say, "My men were beaten."
697 J. CARL COOK/USA	Minor surgery is surgery someone else is having.
698 EVELYN GLENNIE/HOW TO LISTEN/TED.COM	Music really is our daily medicine.
699 ST. AUGUSTINE/ RELIGIOUS LEADER	A thing is not necessarily true because badly uttered, nor false because spoken magnificently.

NUMBER CATEGORY/CREDIT	TOPIC
700 GRATITUDE	People and things you are grateful for.
701 HERMAN MELVILLE/ USA/WRITER/MOBY DICK	I am a man who, from his youth upwards, has been filled with a profound conviction that the easiest way of life is the best.
702 JOHN GRISHAM/WRITER/ USA	I don't want to force my politics on my readers.
703 FUTURE/SIGNS	An air of expectation
704 ATTITUDE	Holier than thou
705 ST. AUGUSTINE/ RELIGIOUS LEADER	He that is kind is free, though he is a slave; he that is evil is a slave, though he be a king.
706 T-SHIRT SLOGAN	Just a waitress until I'm discovered
707 COURTNEY E. MARTIN/ REINVENTION/WOMEN	Growing up is about aiming to succeed wildly and being fulfilled by failing really well.
708 CHLOE/HERO/THIS I BELIEVE/USA	Being a hero for the sake of others is most widely honored, but the first small thing you can conquer is to be a hero to yourself.
709 DALON CONEY/NY TIMES/ ROOM FOR DEBATE	...in the United States today: the number of marriages in which the woman is the breadwinner is on the rise...
710 INGRID BERGMAN/ SWEDISH ACTRESS	Happiness is good health and a bad memory.
711 INDIAN PROVERB	Deceive me about the price but not about the goods.
712 CHARLES DARWIN/ NATURALIST/UK	It is not the strongest of the species that survive, nor the most intelligent, but the one most responsive to change.
713 RIC ELIAS/3 THINGS I LEARNED/TED.COM	I no longer want to postpone anything in life. That urgency, that purpose, has really changed my life.
714 H.L. MENCKEN/USA/ EDITOR	A society made up of individuals who were all capable of original thought would probably be unendurable.
715 YES, VIRGINIA, THERE IS A SANTA CLAUS/NY SUN	All minds, Virginia, whether they be men's or children's, are little.
716 JIM ROHN/AMERICAN BUSINESSMAN	If you are not willing to risk the unusual, you will have to settle for the ordinary.
717 DR. BEN CARSON/USA/ NEUROSURGEON/ AUTHOR/THINK BIG	Knowledge is the key that unlocks all the doors. You can be green-skinned with yellow polka dots and come from Mars, but if you have knowledge that people need, instead of beating you, they'll beat a path to your door.
718 KOREAN PROVERB	A stranger nearby is better than a family member far away.
719 HERMAN MELVILLE/ AMERICAN WRITER	I will have no man in my boat...who is not afraid of a whale...an utterly fearless man is a far more dangerous comrade than a coward.
720 DALE CARNEGIE/USA/ WRITER/LECTURER	If you want to gather honey, don't kick over the beehive.
721 FRANKLIN ROOSEVELT/ 32ND PRESIDENT /USA	The only limit to our realization of tomorrow will be our doubts of today.
722 CHILI DAVIS/USA/COACH/ JAMAICA/BASEBALL	Growing old is mandatory; growing up is optional.
723 DALE CARNEGIE/USA/ LECTURER	Most of us have far more courage than we ever dreamed we possessed.
724 BEAUTY	Photoshopped images

NUMBER CATEGORY/CREDIT	TOPIC
725 JOHN ADAMS/USA/ PRESIDENT	Facts are stubborn things; and whatever may be our wishes, our inclinations, or the dictates of our passions, they cannot alter the state of facts and evidence.
726 WARREN G. BENNIS/ USA/PSYCHOLOGIST	There are two ways of being creative. One can sing and dance. Or one can create an environment in which singers and dancers flourish.
727 HANS ROSLING/ASIA'S RISE.../TED.COM	Avoid war, because that always pushes human beings backward.
728 KOREAN PROVERB	Even the best song becomes tiresome if heard too often.
729 TONY PORTER/A CALL TO MEN/TED.COM/USA	The Centers for Diseases Control says that men's violence against women is at epidemic proportions.
730 COLIN POWELL/USA/ STATESMAN	Don't bother people for help without first trying to solve the problem yourself.
731 ARABIAN PROVERB	What comes with ease goes with ease.
732 HEALTH	Alternative medicine
733 ANONYMOUS	If you can't run with the big dogs, stay up on the porch.
734 INDIAN PROVERB	A fight in your neighbor's house is refreshing.
735 LIFE/DEATH/ LIVING	What you would do if you had only 24 hours left to live.
736 DIANNA BOOHER/ AUTHOR/USA	People with presence look confident and comfortable, speak clearly and persuasively, think clearly even under pressure.
737 INDIAN PROVERB	It is easy to throw something into the river but hard to get it out again.
738 KOREAN PROVERB	Give an extra piece of cake to a stepchild.
739 MARK TWAIN/USA/ WRITER	Do something every day that you don't want to do.
740 HERMAN MELVILLE/ USA/WRITER	Evil is the chronic malady of the universe, and checked in one place, breaks forth in another.
741 MICHAEL GATES GILL/ USA/AUTHOR	The first rule of life is to have a good time. There is no second rule.
742 FRANKLIN ROOSEVELT 32ND PRESIDENT /USA	When you get to the end of your rope, tie a knot and hang on.
743 KOREAN PROVERB	It is darkest under the lamp stand.
744 DEBATE	Emotional intelligence is more important than IQ
745 INDIAN PROVERB	Do not blame God for having created the tiger, but thank him for not having given it wings.
746 IRIS CHANG/USA/ AUTHOR/HISTORIAN	I don't mind solitude. I love talking to other people, but I do need my space.
747 G.K. CHESTERTON/UK/ WRITER	The word "good" has many meanings. For example, if a man were to shoot his grandmother at a range of five hundred yards, I should call him a good shot, but not necessarily a good man.
748 POVERTY/CHILDREN	Free meals at schools
749 HUEY NEWTON/USA/ POLITICAL ACTIVIST	If you stop struggling, then you stop life.
750 KAHLIL GIBRAN/POET/ LEBANON	Let there be spaces in your togetherness.

NUMBER CATEGORY/CREDIT	TOPIC
751 WILLIAM JENNINGS BRYAN/USA/LAWYER	No one can earn a million dollars honestly.
752 DR GREG E. SIMON/USA/ RESEARCHER/HEALTH	The fundamentals of helping people with depression are pretty low-tech. The core resource is humans.
753 RICHARD STEELE/UK/ DRAMATIST	I cannot think of any character below the flatterer, except he who envies him.
754 SOPHOCLES/TRAGEDIAN	The greatest griefs are those we cause ourselves.
755 H.L. MENCKEN/USA/ EDITOR	A prohibitionist is the sort of man one couldn't care to drink with, even if he drank.
756 IBO PROVERB/NIGERIA	A debt may get moldy, but it never decays.
757 CARL CARMER/WISDOM USA/THIS I BELIEVE	Dying for one's convictions is never loss of the battle.
758 TALI SHAROT/THE OPTIMISM BIAS/TED.COM	Regardless of outcome, the pure act of anticipation makes us happy.
759 SOCIETY	Equality of opportunity
760 INDONESIA/RELIGION/ TOLERANCE	Transreligious identity (a country or society with many different strong religious groupings)
761 USA/THEODORE FORST-MANN/PHILANTHROPIST	It is better to invest in education than in prisons.
762 FATHER FORGETS/ LETTER TO A SON	Tomorrow I will be a real daddy! I will chum with you, suffer when you suffer and laugh when you laugh.
763 CLASS MATTERS/NY TIMES/USA/2005	At a time of extraordinary advances in medicine, class differences in health and life span are wide and appear to be widening.
764 WILL ROGERS/USA	Heroing is one of the shortest-lived professions there is.
765 MARGARET MEAD/USA/ ANTHROPOLOGIST	Never believe that a few caring people can't change the world. For, indeed, that's all who ever have.
766 INDIAN PROVERB	Keep five yards from a carriage, ten yards from a horse, and a hundred yards from an elephant, but the distance one should keep from a wicked man cannot be measured.
767 MAX BEERBOHM/UK/ ESSAYIST	Only mediocrity can be trusted to be always at its best.
768 USA/LEADER/THEODORE ROOSEVELT	Far and away the best prize that life offers is the chance to work hard at work worth doing.
769 CHARACTER/RELIGION	Moral compass
770 PICO IYER/WRITER/USA/ KNOWLEDGE@WHARTON	...silence...is the cradle of creativity.
771 ANNIE MURPHY PAUL/ PSYCHOLOGY TODAY	First-generation college students – undergraduates whose parents did not attend university – have reason to be proud.
772 PROVERB	Don't bite off more than you can chew.
773 MARGARET MEAD/USA/ ANTHROPOLOGIST	I was wise enough to never grow up while fooling most people into believing I had.
774 MERYL STREEP/ AMERICAN ACTRESS	Expensive clothes are a waste of money.

NUMBER CATEGORY/CREDIT760	TOPIC
775 USA/WILLIAM OSLER/ CANADIAN SCIENTIST	The best preparation for tomorrow is to do today's work well.
776 BRAM STOKER AUTHOR/DRACULA	There are mysteries which men can only guess at, which age by age, they may solve only in part.
777 JOSEPH CAMPBELL/USA/ AUTHOR	When you make the sacrifice in marriage, you're sacrificing not to each other but to unity in a relationship.
778 PUBLILIUS SYRUS	Depend not on fortune, but on conduct.
779 DR. JOYCE BROTHERS/ USA/PSYCHOLOGIST	Being taken for granted can be a compliment. It means that you've become a comfortable, trusted element in another person's life.
780 ABRAHAM LINCOLN/ 16th PRESIDENT/USA	That some should be rich, shows that others may become rich, and hence is just encouragement to industry and enterprise.
781 BUDGET/BUSINESS	A budget is a statement of your values.
782 MARK TWAIN/USA/ WRITER	Don't part with your illusions. When they are gone you may still exist, but you have ceased to live.
783 BARBARA JORDAN/ AMERICAN POLITICIAN	Education remains the key to both economic and political empowerment.
784 THOMAS PAINE/UK-BORN AMERICAN PHILOSOPHER	I scarcely ever quote: the reason is, I always think.
785 ELEANOR ROOSEVELT/ USA/ LEADERSHIP	You gain strength, courage and confidence by every experience in which you really stop to look fear in the face.
786 THEODORE ROOSEVELT/ 26TH PRESIDENT/USA	Let us speak courteously, deal fairly, and keep ourselves armed and ready.
787 KOREAN PROVERB	A turtle travels only when it sticks its neck out.
788 DAN RATHER/USA/ JOURNALIST	Courage is being afraid but going on anyhow.
789 WILL ROGERS/USA/ COMEDIAN	Everything is funny as long as it is happening to somebody else.
790 HERMAN MELVILLE/ AMERICAN WRITER	There is nothing namable but that some men will, or undertake to, do it for pay.
791 CHINESE PROVERB	Money hides in the tiger's ear.
792 WRITER/ANTOINE SAINT-EXUPERY/FRENCH	I have no right, by anything I do or say, to demean a human being in his own eyes.
793 BRANCH RICKEY/USA/ MAJOR/BASEBALL	Luck is the residue of design.
794 RITA RUDNER/USA/ COMEDIAN	I love being married. It's so great to find that one special person you want to annoy for the rest of your life.
795 JRR TOLKIEN/WRITER/ BRITISH	If more of us valued food and cheer and song above hoarded gold, it would be a merrier world.
796 ANNA QUINDLEN/ AMERICAN AUTHOR	Negotiators with the strongest personal presence, not necessarily the strongest argument, walk away with the best deals.
797 MARK TWAIN/USA/ AUTHOR	The thing that is really hard, and really amazing, is giving up on being perfect and beginning the work of becoming yourself.
798 DAN RATHER/USA/ JOURNALIST	A tough lesson in life that one has to learn is that not everybody wishes you well.

NUMBER CATEGORY/CREDIT	TOPIC
799 MARK TWAIN/USA/ WRITER	The best way to cheer yourself is to try to cheer somebody else up.
800 ANTOINE SAINT-EXUPERY/NOVELIST	I know but one freedom, and that is the freedom of the mind.
801 GERMAN/ARTHUR SCHOPENHAUER	Honor has not to be won; it must only not be lost.
802 KAHLIL GIBRAN/POET	Love one another but make not a bond of love.
803 DALE CARNEGIE/USA	People rarely succeed unless they have fun in what they are doing.
804 LIVING/LEARNING	Life-changing lessons
805 DALE CARNEGIE/USA/ WRITER	Remember happiness doesn't depend upon who you are or what you have; it depends solely on what you think.
806 ALEXANDER HAMILTON/ USA/FOUNDING FATHER	I never expect to see a perfect work from an imperfect man.
807 DALE CARNEGIE/USA/ WRITER/LECTURER	The expression a woman wears on her face is far more important than the clothes she wears on her back.
808 PERSONAL	Narcissism
809 HERMAN MELVILLE/ USA/WRITER	Strange as it may seem, there is nothing in which a young and beautiful female appears to more advantage than in the art of smoking.
810 INDIAN PROVERB	God laughs when you steal from a thief.
811 SUSAN GEORGE/WRITER	Only around 2% of the earth's surface is cultivatable land.
812 KEN ROBINSON/SCHOOLS/ CREATIVITY/TED.COM	All kids have tremendous talents – and we squander them pretty ruthlessly.
813 PROVERB	Better the devil you know than the angel you don't know.
814 ELEANOR ROOSEVELT/ USA/LEADERSHIP	Learn from the mistakes of others. You can't live long enough to make them all yourself.
815 JOHN F. KENNEDY 35TH PRESIDENT/USA	Liberty without learning is always in peril; learning without liberty is always in vain.
816 ANAIS NIN/USA/AUTHOR	We don't see things as they are, we see them as we are.
817 DR. JOYCE BROTHERS/USA	Listening, not imitation, may be the sincerest form of flattery.
818 PEGGY NOONAN/USA	Abortion is either OK or it's not.
819 KIDNEYS/HEALTH	Dialysis
820 INDIAN PROVERB	Never strike your wife, not even with a flower.
821 POTENTIAL POWER	The butterfly effect
822 FAMILY/HEREDITY	Cumulative advantage and cumulative disadvantage
823 INDIA/CHINA/PROVERB	Learning is a treasure no thief can touch.
824 DALE CARNEGIE/USA	Only the prepared speaker deserves to be confident.
825 AUTHOR/TIME/HAROLD KUSHNER/AUTHOR	We have confused God with Santa Claus.
826 MARK TWAIN/USA	Facts are stubborn things, but statistics are more pliable.
827 ALAN LAKEIN/AUTHOR/ TIME MANAGEMENT	Effectiveness means selecting the best task to do from all the possibilities available and then doing it the best way.
828 INDIAN PROVERB	Never use a dwarf to measure the depth of the water.

NUMBER CATEGORY/CREDIT	TOPIC
829 TONY ROBBINS/USA/ TED.COM/COACH	The defining factor [for success] is never resources; it's resourcefulness.
830 JESSI ARRINGTON/USA/ TEDTALK/DESIGNER	Color is powerful. It is almost physiologically impossible to be in a bad mood when you're wearing bright red pants.
831 STEDMAN GRAHAM/ DIVERSITY/SUCCESS	We are moving into an ownership society where we must become more accountable for how we are viewed and defined.
832 DAN RATHER/USA	Don't taunt the alligator until after you have crossed the creek.
833 INSURANCE/USA	Pre-existing condition
834 JIM ROHN/AMERICAN BUSINESSMAN	It is the set of the sails, not the direction of the wind that determines which way we will go.
835 INDIAN PROVERB	No strength within, no respect without.
836 BENJAMIN ZANDER/ TED.COM	The conductor of an orchestra doesn't make a sound. He depends, for his power, on his ability to make other people powerful.
837 MAHATMA GANDHI/INDIA	My life is my message.
838 RITA RUDNER/US COMEDIAN	When I meet a man I ask myself, "Is this the man I want my children to spend their weekends with?"
839 ROBERT MCCRUM/UK	Keep a diary. It might keep you.
840 DAN MEYER/MATH CLASS.../TED.COM	I teach high school math. I sell a product to a market that doesn't want it, but is forced by law to buy it.
841 VICTOR HUGO/FRENCH/ AUTHOR	Sorrow is a fruit. God does not make it grow on limbs too weak to bear it.
842 SOUTH AFRICA	Apartheid
843 NANCY PELOSI/USA/ POLITICIAN/SENATE	You can't go to a baseball game without a bat.
844 MARK TWAIN/USA/ NOVELIST	Don't go around saying the world owes you a living. The world owes you nothing. It was here first.
845 SUSAN GEORGE/USA/ POLITICAL SCIENTIST	If you cut down a forest, it doesn't matter how many sawmills you have if there are no more trees.
846 HENRY BROOKS ADAMS/ USA/HISTORIAN	A teacher affects eternity; he can never tell where his influence stops.
847 OSCAR WILDE/IRISH WRITER/POET	The only thing worse that being talked about is not being talked about.
848 ADVICE	Do what you love but remain open to new possibilities.
849 SPACE TRAVEL	You have been invited to go on a trip to the moon. Your response?
850 MARK BEZOS/A LIFE LESSON/TED.COM	Don't wait until you make your first million to make a difference in somebody's life. It you have something to give, give it now.
851 ROBERT KENNEDY/ SENATOR/USA	Tragedy is a tool for the living to gain wisdom, not a guide by which to live.
852 KOREAN PROVERB	After three years at a village schoolhouse, even a dog can recite a poem.
853 BERTRAND RUSSELL/ BRITISH AUTHOR	Do not fear to be eccentric in opinion, for every opinion now accepted was once eccentric.
854 USA/ALEXANDER HAMILTON/STATESMAN	I think the first duty of society is justice.

NUMBER CATEGORY/CREDIT	TOPIC
855 INDIAN PROVERB	Not all buds on a bush will blossom.
856 DR. JOYCE BROTHERS/ USA/PSYCHOLOGIST/TV	Marriage is not just spiritual communion; it is also remembering to take out the trash.
857 JACK NICKLAUS/GOLF/ PROFESSIONAL	A kid grows up a lot faster on the golf course. Golf teaches you how to behave.
858 ELEANOR ROOSEVELT/ USA/LEADERSHIP	It is not fair to ask of others what you are unwilling to do yourself.
859 WAEL GHONIM/TED.COM	The power of the people is much stronger than the people in power.
860 INDIAN PROVERB	One and one sometimes make eleven.
861 JOHNNY CARSON/USA/ COMEDIAN	People will pay more to be entertained than educated.
862 ADOPTION/RACE/DEBATE	People should not be allowed to adopt children from another race.
863 ROBERT B. CIALDINI/USA/ PSYCHOLOGIST	The rule of Reciprocity simply states that people feel obliged to give back to others who have given to them.
864 DAN RATHER/USA/ JOURNALIST	I'm proud to say I've never been anybody's lapdog.
865 WRITER/SCOT/ROBERT LOUIS STEVENSON	There are no foreign lands. It is the traveler only who is foreign.
866 BABE RUTH/USA/ BASEBALL PROFESSIONAL	If it wasn't for baseball, I'd be in either the penitentiary or the cemetery.
867 ALEXANDER HAMILTON/ FOUNDING FATHER	A promise must never be broken.
868 GEORGE F. WEST SR. / K. WEST SAVALI/HUFFPO	What you do for yourself dies with you; what you do for others lives on.
869 USA/PRESIDENT/ FRANKLIN ROOSEVELT	The only thing we have to fear is fear itself.
870 JOHN WOODEN/USA/ BASKETBALL COACH	You can lose when you outscore somebody in a game. And you can win when you're outscored.
871 DEBATE	It is more expensive to raise girls than to raise boys.
872 DALE CARNEGIE/ AMERICAN LECTURER/ WRITER	The ideas I stand for are not mine. I borrowed them from Socrates. I swiped them from Chesterfield. I stole them from Jesus. And I put them in a book. If you don't like their rules, whose would you use?
873 WILLIAM JAMES/USA/ PHILOSOPHER	The art of being wise is the art of knowing what to overlook.
874 PABLO PICASSO/ SPANISH ARTIST	The genius of Einstein leads to Hiroshima.
875 ELEANOR ROOSEVELT/ USA/LEADERSHIP	If someone betrays you once, it's their fault; if they betray you twice, it's your fault.
876 RICHARD BRANSON/UK/ BUSINESS	A teacher hasn't taught until a student has learned.
877 POLITICS/NATIONS	Sanctions
878 HARRY T. BRUNDRIDGE/ USA/THIS I BELIEVE	I have known some criminals very well indeed. I have known, too, that I was no better than they were. I was only more fortunate.

NUMBER CATEGORY/CREDIT	TOPIC
879 WILL ROGERS/USA/ COMEDIAN	We can't all be heroes because somebody has to sit on the curb and clap as they go by.
880 MICHAEL DIRDA/BOOK COLUMNIST/USA/ WASHINGTON POST	The patient accretion of knowledge, the focusing of all one's energies on some problem in history or science, the dogged pursuit of excellence of whatever kind – these are right and proper ideals for life.
881 A.A. MILNE/ENGLISH AUTHOR	You can't stay in your corner of the Forest waiting for others to come to you. You have to go to them sometimes.
882 RELATIONSHIPS	Backstabbers
883 RELATIONSHIPS/WAR	Fighting words
884 PABLO PICASSO/GOALS/ SPANISH ARTIST/SUCCESS	You have to have an idea of what you're going to do, but it should be a vague idea.
885 COMPETITION	Going head to head
886 BENJAMIN DISRAELI/UK/ PRIME MINISTER	Almost everything that is great has been done by youth.
887 CLASS MATTERS/NY TIMES/USA/2005	Merit has replaced the old system of inherited privilege, in which parents to the manner born handed down the manor to their children.
888 ALAN LAKEIN/AUTHOR/ USA	The over-organized person is always making lists, updating lists, losing lists.
889 MIKE MYATT/ FORBES	Realizing that you need help is a sign of leadership.
890 BRYAN STEVENSON/ INJUSTICE/USA/TED.COM	We have a system of justice in [the US] that treats you much better if you're rich and guilty than if you're poor and innocent. Wealth, not culpability, shapes outcomes.
891 ANNA QUINDLIN/USA/ WRITER	A finished person is a boring person.
892 JIM ROHN/AMERICAN BUSINESSMAN	If you don't design your own life plan, chances are you'll fall into someone else's plan. And guess what the other has planned for you. Nothing.
893 ECKHART TOLLE/ CANADA/AUTHOR	Power over others is weakness disguised as strength.
894 PABLO PICASSO/ARTIST	To make oneself hated is more difficult than to make oneself loved.
895 DR. BEN CARSON/USA/ NEUROSURGEON/ AUTHOR/THINK BIG	Anyone who can't learn from other people's mistakes simply can't learn, and that's all there is to it. There is value in the wrong way of doing things. The knowledge gained from error contributes to our knowledge base.
896 JILL LEPORE/USA/ PROFESSOR/HISTORY	History is the study of dead people.
897 VINCE LOMBARDI/ USA/FOOTBALL COACH	Football is like life – it requires perseverance, self-denial, hard work, sacrifice, dedication and respect for authority.
898 ZEN BUDDHISM	*Satori* (enlightenment)
899 YANN MARTEL/ CANADIAN WRITER	It's important in life to conclude things properly. Only then can you let go.
900 PSYCHIATRY/SOCIETY	Psychopaths
901 PETER DRUCKER/USA	The only thing we know about the future is that it will be different.
902 USA/JAMES B. CAREY/ THIS I BELIEVE	I believe in liberty; liberty for myself, liberty for my fellow men.

NUMBER CATEGORY/CREDIT	TOPIC
903 STEPHEN COVEY/USA / WRITER/SUCCESS COACH	Be a model, not a critic.
904 DIANNA BOOHER/USA AUTHOR	Personal presence may be difficult to define, but we all know it when we see it.
905 A.A. MILNE/ENGLISH AUTHOR	If you live to a hundred, I want to live to be a hundred minus one day so I never have to live without you.
906 VINCENT VAN GOGH/ DUTCH ARTIST	I see drawings and pictures in the poorest of huts and the dirtiest of corners.
907 ECKHART TOLLE/CANADA AUTHOR/GERMANY	Whatever the present moment contains, accept it as if you had chosen it.
908 ROBERT B. CIALDINI/ AUTHOR/USA	A well-known principle of human behavior says that when we ask someone to do us a favor we will be more successful if we provide a reason. People simply like to have reasons for what they do.
909 RICHARD DAWKINS/ BIOLOGIST/AUTHOR	Faith is the great cop-out, the great excuse to evade the need to think and evaluate evidence.
910 DREAM LIFE	If money were no object and you could live anywhere in the world, where would that be and why?
911 STEVE BLANK/USA/ ENTREPRENEUR	If you find a lawyer who talks about solutions, not problems, hold on to them.
912 THOMAS PAINE/ POLITICAL PHILOSOPHER	But where, say some, is the king of America?...in America the law is king.
913 J. PAUL GETTY/ AMERICAN BILLIONAIRE	I hate to be a failure. I hate and regret the failure of my marriages. I would gladly give all my millions for just one lasting marital success.
914 FUN	Living only for pleasure
915 OLIVER WENDELL HOLMES/USA	Many people die with their music still in them. Too often it is because they are always getting ready to live. Before they know it time runs out.
916 THE ANIMALS/SONG	Inside looking out
917 LEADERSHIP	Charisma
918 FRENCH/JACQUES-YVES COUSTEAU/SCIENTIST	Water and air, the two essential fluids on which all life depends, have become global garbage cans.
919 MICHAEL DIRDA/BOOK COLUMNIST/USA/ WASHINGTON POST	Books, by their very nature and variety, help us grow in empathy for others, in tolerance and awareness. But they should increase our skepticism as well as our humanity, for all good readers know how easy it is to misread.
920 LEO BUSCAGLIA/ AMERICAN WRITER	A single rose can be my garden...a single friend, my world.
921 ANNE MICHAELS/ CANADIAN WRITER	Hold a book in your hand and you're a pilgrim at the gates of a new city.
922 WALT DISNEY/USA/ ARTIST/ENTREPRENEUR	Once a man has tasted freedom he will never be content to be a slave.
923 CHARLES WYZANSKI/USA JUDGE/THIS I BELIEVE	Humility is the noblest fruit of introspection.
924 JOSEPH CAMPBELL/ AMERICAN AUTHOR	Follow your bliss and the universe will open doors for you where there were only walls.

NUMBER CATEGORY/CREDIT	TOPIC
925 PETER BREGMAN/USA/ ENTREPRENEUR	People are often successful not despite their dysfunctions but because of them. Obsessions are one of the greatest telltale signs of success.
926 DREAMS	Wishful thinking
927 THOMAS PAINE/USA/ PHILOSOPHER	What we obtain too cheap, we esteem too lightly.
928 JULES VERNE/AUTHOR/ FRENCH	What you do for money you do badly.
929 TALI SHAROT/THE OPTIMISM BIAS/TED.COM	People prefer Friday [to Sunday], because Friday brings with it the anticipation of the weekend ahead.
930 ROLE PLAY	You have been invited to a friend's home. You are served food that you absolutely dislike. Your response?
931 DEBATE/ADOPTION	Under-populated countries should consider adopting children from other countries.
932 DONALD G. McNEIL Jr./ SNAKEBITE/NY TIMES	W.H.O. estimates that snakebites kill between 20,000 and 94,000 people a year.
933 CHILDREN/ELDERLY	Why should children obey their elders?
934 CHIEF JOSEPH/NATIVE AMERICAN/NEZ PERCE	It makes my heart sick when I remember all the good words and the broken promises.
935 A.A. MILNE/ENGLISH AUTHOR	One of the advantages of being disorganized is that one is always having surprising discoveries.
936 MARK TWAIN/ AMERICAN NOVELIST	Grief can take care of itself; but to get the full value of a joy you must have someone to divide it with.
937 DISCUSSION/DEBATE	Your classmate asks you for the answer to a question in an examination room. No one is looking. What do you do? Why?
938 STEVEN COVEY/USA/ SUCCESS COACH	The key is not to prioritize what's on your schedule, but to schedule your priorities.
939 ECKHART TOLLE/ AUTHOR/GERMANY	Whatever you fight, you strengthen, and what you resist, persists.
940 HARRY EMERSON FOSDICK/USA/PASTOR	Don't simply retire from something; have something to retire to.
941 SENECA/ROMAN WRITER	Where the speech is corrupted, the mind is also.
942 HARRY BROWNE/USA/ AUTHOR	The important thing is to concentrate upon what you can do – by yourself upon your own initiative.
943 SIDONIE-GABRIELLE COLETTE/USA/WRITER	A happy childhood is poor preparation for human contacts.
944 VIRGINIA WOOLF/UK	Some people go to priests; others to poetry; I to my friends.
945 SAYING	Out of sight, out of mind.
946 JOAN BAEZ/USA/SINGER	Action is the antidote to despair.
947 FRENCH/JACQUES-YVES COUSTEAU/SCIENTIST	The sea, once it casts its spell, holds one in its net of wonder forever.
948 COMPASSION	Bleeding hearts
949 ECKHART TOLLE/CANADA AUTHOR/GERMAN	Don't let a mad world tell you that success is anything other than a successful present moment.

NUMBER CATEGORY/CREDIT	TOPIC
950 HELEN KELLER/ USA/ AUTHOR/ LECTURER	Keep your face to the sun and you will never see the shadows.
951 CAROLINE DUER/ WHITE IS MADE OF MANY COLORS/USA/ THIS I BELIEVE/RADIO	I forget which of our great Generals said, "Let the other man tell his story first." But it is a good principle, a part of that wisdom and understanding, which helps to keep the world going round, even in the rather wobbly way it is going.
952 JAMES WELCH/NATIVE AMERICAN WRITER	Before, Indian people had been so defeated, they were always looking for outsiders, for the government, to somehow come in and fix things. But now, they seem to realize that they're the only ones who can save themselves.
953 EPITAPH/HUMOR	if you want to be remembered after you die, borrow money from everyone you know.
954 BERNARD M. BARUCH/ USA/BUSINESSSMAN	Two things are bad for the heart - running up stairs and running down people.
955 DANISH/HANS CHRISTIAN ANDERSEN/WRITER	My life will be the best illustration of all my work.
956 CHIEF JOSEPH/NATIVE AMERICAN/NEZ PERCE	The earth is the mother of all people, and all people should have equal rights upon it.
957 BERNARD M. BARUCH/ USA/BUSINESSMAN	Every man has a right to his opinion, but no man has a right to be wrong in his facts.
958 POPE FRANCIS/CHURCH/ LEADER	Big cities bring together all the different ways which we human beings have discovered to express the meaning of life, wherever we may be. But big cities also conceal the faces of all those who don't appear to belong, or are second-class citizens
959 BARBARA BUSH/FIRST LADY/USA	Your success as a family, our success as a society, depends not on what happens in the White House, but on what happens inside your house.
960 BUDDHA	My actions are my only true belongings: I cannot escape their consequences. My actions are the ground on which I stand.
961 JOSEPH CAMPBELL/USA	If the path before you is clear, you're probably on someone else's.
962 MAURICE RAVEL/ FRENCH/COMPOSER	I am not one of the great composers. All the great have produced enormously. There is everything in their work -- the best and the worst, but there is always quantity. But I have written relatively little.
963 IGOR STRAVINSKY/ AUTHOR/MUSICIAN	To listen is an effort, and just to hear is no merit. A duck hears also.
964 G.K. CHESTERTON/UK/ WRITER	Drink because you are happy, but never because you are miserable.
965 JOHN RALSTON SAUL/ CANADIAN WRITER/ ESSAYIST	All the lessons of psychiatry, psychology, social work, indeed culture, have taught us over the last hundred years that it is the acceptance of differences, not the search for similarities which enables people to relate to each other in their personal or family lives.
966 HELEN KELLER/ USA/ AUTHOR/ POLITICAL ACTIVIST	Character cannot be developed in ease and quiet. Only through experience of trial and suffering can the soul be strengthened, vision cleared, ambition inspired, and success achieved.
967 CANADIAN/DIANE SCHOEMPERLEN/ WRITER	I remind myself that not everything is a sign, that some things simply are what they appear to be and should not be analyzed, deconstructed, or forced to bear the burden of metaphor, symbol, omen, or portent.

NUMBER CATEGORY/CREDIT	TOPIC
968 IGOR STRAVINSKY/ AUTHOR/MUSICIAN	To continue in one path is to go backward.
969 QURAN 2:41/MUTUAL RESPECT/ TOLERANCE	Behold, we have created you from a male and a female and have made you into nations and tribes so that you might come to know one another.
970 SOCIETY/FITTING IN	Unwritten rules
971 INDIAN PROVERB	Many families are built on laughter.
972 JONATHAN HAIDT/USA/ RELIGION/TED.COM	The most powerful force ever known on this planet is human cooperation – a force for construction and destruction.
973 FRENCH/ANTOINE SAINT-EXUPERY/NOVELIST	For true love is inexhaustible; the more you give, the more you have.
974 IGOR STRAVINSKY/ AUTHOR/MUSICIAN	Too many pieces of music finish too long after the end.
975 CLIFFORD STOLL/THE CALL TO LEARN/TED.COM	If you want to know what society is going to be like in 20 years, ask a kindergarten teacher.
976 DEREK SIVERS/TED.COM MOVEMENT	Repeated psychology tests have proven that telling someone your goal makes it less likely to happen.
977 ALBERTO CAIRO/TED.COM ITALY/PHYSIOTHERAPIST	Dignity cannot wait for better times.
978 WAX MUSEUM	Madame Tussauds
979 MAHATMA GANDHI/INDIA	SEVEN SOCIAL SINS: 2) Wealth without work
980 FRENCH/JACQUES-YVES COUSTEAU/SCIENTIST	When one man, for whatever reason, has the opportunity to lead an extraordinary life, he has no right to keep it to himself.
981 J. R. R. TOLKIEN/WRITER/ UK	It's a job that's never started that takes the longest to finish.
982 BERNARD M. BARUCH/ USA/BUSINESSMAN	The art of living lies not in eliminating but in growing with troubles.
983 HARRY BROWNE/USA/ AUTHOR	Everything you want in life has a price connected to it. There's a price to pay if you want to make things better, a price to pay just for leaving things as they are, a price for everything.
984 HEIDI GRANT HALVORSON/WRITER	When you set yourself a goal, try to be as specific as possible. "Lose 5 pounds is a better goal than "lose some weight."
985 CHERIE BLAIR/ BRITISH LAWYER	Let's...celebrate the role men are now playing in helping women's rise to the top.
986 KOREAN PROVERB	Aim high in your career but stay humble in heart.
987 COMMUNICATION	Tête-à-tête
988 DR. BEN CARSON/ USA/ NEUROSURGEON	People are simply not willing to look at their problems honestly and admit that they have problems.
989 NEIL DEGRASSE TYSON/ USA/ASTROPHYSICIST	For me, I am driven by two main philosophies, know more today about the world than I knew yesterday. And lessen the suffering of others. You'd be surprised how far that gets you.
990 DOUGLAS COUPLAND/ CANADIAN NOVELIST	TV and the Internet are good because they keep stupid people from spending too much time out in public.
991 ANNE MICHAELS/POET/ CANADIAN	Reading a poem in translation is like kissing a woman through a veil.

NUMBER CATEGORY/CREDIT	TOPIC
992 MAHATMA GANDHI/ INDIAN LEADER	SEVEN SOCIAL SINS: 3) Pleasure without conscience
993 LEO BUSCAGLIA/ AMERICAN WRITER	I have a very strong feeling that the opposite of love is not hate – it's apathy. It is not giving a DAMN.
994 HARRY BROWNE/USA/ AUTHOR/FREEDOM	You don't need an explanation for everything. Recognize that there are such things as miracles – events for which here are no ready explanations. Later knowledge may explain those events quite easily.
995 WILL ROGERS/USA/ COMEDIAN	We are all here for a spell; get all the good laughs you can.
996 DOUGLAS COUPLAND/ CANADIAN NOVELIST	Remember: the time you feel lonely is the time you most need to be by yourself.
997 ALICE CHILDRESS/USA/ WRITER	Life is just a short walk from the cradle to the grave, and it sure behooves us to be kind to one another along the way.
998 GOVERNMENT/INCOME ASSISTANCE/WIKIPEDIA DEFINITION	Rent control: Rent control refers to laws or ordinances that set price controls on the renting of residential housing. It functions as a price ceiling.
999 USA/ELBERT GREEN HUBBARD/USA/WRITER	Self-discipline is the ability to make yourself do what you should do, when you should do it, whether you feel like it or not.
1000 FRENCH/JACQUES-YVES COUSTEAU/NAVY	For most of history, man has had to fight nature to survive; in this century he is beginning to realize that, in order to survive, he must protect it.
1001 NEIL DEGRASSE TYSON/ USA/ASTROPHYSICIST	Curious that we spend more time congratulating people who have succeeded than encouraging people who have not.
1002 JEAN COCTEAU/FRENCH POET/WRITER	Statues to great men are made of the stones thrown at them in their lifetime.
1003 CHARLES S. JOHNSON/ THIS I BELIEVE/FISK	Religion is most real to those who feel the need for comfort and refuge beyond the gift of man.
1004 INDIAN PROVERB	Only the humpback himself knows how he can lie comfortably.
1005 RICHARD STEELE/UK/ DRAMATIST	Fire and swords are slow engines of destruction, compared to the tongue of a Gossip.
1006 RALPH BUNCHE/USA/ POLITICAL SCIENTIST	If you want to get across an idea, wrap it up in a person.
1007 HAROLD BLOOM/ AMERICAN WRITER	Everyone wants a prodigy to fail; it makes our mediocrity more bearable.
1008 LEO BUSCAGLIA/ AMERICAN WRITER	Worry never robs tomorrow of its sorrow, it only saps today of its joy.
1009 IGOR STRAVINSKY/ AUTHOR/MUSICIAN	Silence will save me from being wrong (and foolish), but it will also deprive me of the possibility of being right.
1010 NEIL DEGRASSE TYSON/ USA/ASTROPHYSICIST	I want to put on the table, not why 85% of the members of the National Academy of Sciences reject God, I want to know why 15% of the National Academy don't.
1011 NADIA BOULANGER/ COMPOSER/FRENCH	Loving a child doesn't mean giving in to all his whims; to love him is to bring out the best in him, to teach him to love what is difficult.
1012 DAN RATHER/USA/ JOURNALIST	If all difficulties were known at the outset of a long journey, most of us would never start out at all.

NUMBER CATEGORY/CREDIT	TOPIC
1013 DEBATE/ADOPTION	If you must adopt a child, it is better to adopt a baby than an older child.
1014 JOSEPH ADDISON/ ENGLISH WRITER	Friendships, in general, are suddenly contracted; and therefore it is no wonder they are easily dissolved.
1015 STEPHEN COVEY/USA/ AUTHOR	Words are like eggs dropped from great heights. You could no more call them back than ignore the mess they left when they fell.
1016 DONALD DAY/SUCCESS/ THIS I BELIEVE/RADIO	I believe the rule should not be "rising in the world," but "rising with the world."
1017 PEMA CHODRON/ BUDDHIST TEACHER	The truth you believe and cling to makes you unavailable to hear anything new.
1018 LEADER/ALEXANDER HAMILTON/USA	What we have to do is strike a balance between the idea that government should do everything and the idea, the belief, that government ought to do nothing.
1019 HELEN KELLER/ USA/ AUTHOR/ LECTURER	Although the world if is full of suffering, it is full also of the overcoming of it.
1020 CHIEF JOSEPH/NATIVE AMERICAN/NEZ PERCE	It does not require many words to speak the truth.
1021 FRENCH/JACQUES-YVES COUSTEAU/NAVAL OFFICER	Sometimes we are lucky enough to know that our lives have been changed, to discard the old, embrace the new, and run headlong down an immutable course.
1022 USA/CAROLINE DUER/ COLORS/THIS I BELIEVE	I'm convinced that any religion in which a man is good and unbigoted is a good religion for him and should be held in esteem.
1023 PET CARE	Declawing of cats
1024 LEO BUSCAGLIA/ AMERICAN WRITER	Love is always bestowed as a gift – freely, willingly and without expectation. We don't love to be loved; we love to love.
1025 CHILDREN/FRIENDSHIP	Sleepovers
1026 ELIE WIESEL/USA/ NOVELIST/PROFESSOR	There may be times when we are powerless to prevent injustice, but there must never be a time when we fail to protest.
1027 LARRY KING/USA/ BROADCASTER	I remind myself every morning. Nothing I say this day will teach me anything. So if I'm going to learn, I must do it by listening.
1028 ANNE FRANK/JEWISH AUTHOR/ HOLOCAUST	Women, who struggle and suffer pain to ensure the continuation of the human race, make much tougher and more courageous soldiers than all those big-mouthed freedom-fighting heroes put together.
1029 PROVERB	Beauty is only skin-deep.
1030 BERTRAND RUSSELL/ BRITISH AUTHOR	I think we ought always to entertain our opinions with some measure of doubt.
1031 SUPERSTITION	False beliefs
1032 NEIL DEGRASSE TYSON/ USA/ASTROPHYSICIST	The good thing about science is that it's true whether you believe in it.
1033 NADIA BOULANGER/ COMPOSER/FRENCH	Do not take up music unless you would rather die than not do so.
1034 ROBERT GATES/USA/ SEC. OF DEFENSE/WAPO/ LEADERSHIP	True leadership is a fire in the mind that transforms all who feel its warmth, that transfixes all who see its shining light in the eyes of a man or woman.

NUMBER CATEGORY/CREDIT	TOPIC
1035 MAHATMA GANDHI/ INDIAN LEADER	I'm a lover of my own liberty, and so I would do nothing to restrict yours.
1036 VIRGINIA WOOLF/ BRITISH AUTHOR	One cannot think well, love well, sleep well, if one has not dined well.
1037 MALALA YOUSAFZAI/ NOBELIST/EDUCATION	Why is it that giving guns is so easy but giving books is so hard? Why is it that making tanks is so easy, but building schools is so difficult?
1038 HAROLD BLOOM/ AMERICAN WRITER	I am naïve enough to read incessantly because I cannot, on my own, get to know enough people profoundly enough.
1039 NELSON MANDELA/ SOUTH AFRICA/LEADER	Do not judge me by my successes. Judge me by how many times I fell down and got back again.
1040 HERBERT HOOVER/ USA/31ST PRESIDENT	Always growing societies record their faith in God. Decaying societies lack faith and deny God.
1041 THOMAS PAINE/USA	My country is the world, and my religion is to do good.
1042 CHINESE SAYING	When the winds of change blow, some people build walls and others build windmills.
1043 USA/ELEANOR ROOSEVELT/1ST LADY	Friendship with oneself is all-important because without it one cannot be friends with anyone else in the world.
1044 DAN RATHER/USA/ JOURNALIST	Once the herd starts moving in one direction, it's very hard to turn it, even slightly.
1045 T. BOONE PICKENS/ AMERICAN BUSINESS MAGNATE	Be willing to make decisions. That's the most important quality in a good leader. Don't fall victim to what I call the Ready – Aim-Aim-Aim Syndrome. You must be willing to fire.
1046 LENIN/RUSSIA/LEADER	You can't make omelets without breaking eggs.
1047 SCHADENFREUDE/ LEARNER'S DICTIONARY	Schadenfreude : a feeling of enjoyment that comes from seeing or hearing about the troubles of other people.
1048 JOHN NASH/NOBELIST/ PROFESSOR/MATH	People are always selling the idea that people with mental illness are suffering. I think madness can be an escape. If things are not so good, you maybe want to imagine something better.
1049 VICTOR HUGO/FRENCH/ AUTHOR	Revolutions are not born of chance, but of necessity.
1050 ELIE WIESEL/ USA/ PROFESSOR/WRITER	We must always take sides. Neutrality helps the oppressor, never the victim. Silence encourages the tormentor, never the tormented.
1051 POST OFFICE	Postal deliveries
1052 ABIGAIL VAN BUREN/US	People who fight fire with fire usually end up with ashes.
1053 OPINION/PRACTICE	Giving books to friends and family members as presents
1054 T. BOONE PICKENS/ USA/BUSINESSMAN	I've always believed that it's important to show a new look periodically. Predictability can lead to failure.
1055 DR. NELSON GLUECK/ USA/THIS I BELIEVE	...danger is far from disaster...
1056 P. T. BARNUM/ USA	No one went broke underestimating public taste.
1057 DALE CARNEGIE/USA	Any fool can criticize, condemn, and complain – and most fools do.
1058 NORMAN KEMP SMITH/ SCOT/PHILOSOPHER	The history of human thought is the record not of a progressive discovery of truth, but of our gradual emancipation from error.
1059 WILLIAM BLAKE/POET	It is easier to forgive an enemy than to forgive a friend.

NUMBER CATEGORY/CREDIT	TOPIC
1060 JEAN COCTEAU/ FRENCH POET	Art produces ugly things which frequently become more beautiful with time. Fashion, on the other hand, produces beautiful things which always become ugly with time.
1061 LEO BUSCAGLIA/ AMERICAN WRITER	The fact that I can plant a seed and it becomes a flower, share a bit of knowledge and it becomes another's, smile at someone and receive a smile in return, are to me continual spiritual exercises.
1062 BILL NYE/USA/ SCIENTIST	There really is, for humankind, there's really no such thing as race. There's different tribes but not different races. We're all one species.
1063 ABIGAIL VAN BUREN/ ADVICE COLUMNIST	If you want a place in the sun, you've got to put up with a few blisters.
1064 J. PAUL GETTY/USA	If you can count your money, you don't have a billion dollars.
1065 SOCIETY/PERSONAL	Failing to connect the dots
1066 VIRGINIA WOOLF/ BRITISH AUTHOR	If you do not tell the truth about yourself you cannot tell it about other people.
1067 DOUGLAS COUPLAND/ CANADIAN NOVELIST	Adventure without risk is Disneyland.
1068 HELEN KELLER/USA	The highest result of education is tolerance.
1069 USA/BERNARD M. BARUCH/BUSINESSMAN	Age is only a number, a cipher for the records. A man can't retire his experience. He must use it. Experience achieves more with less energy and time.
1070 GOVERNMENT	Regime change
1071 BLAME	Burden shifting
1072 J. PAUL GETTY/BUSINESS	The meek shall inherit the Earth, but not its mineral rights.
1073 MICHAEL DIRDA/USA/ COLUMNIST/WAPO	We learn best by placing our 'confidence in men and women whose examples invite us to love what they love' (Robert Wilken).
1074 TONY DANZA/US/ACTOR	Hold back the tide. Keep your kids innocent as long as possible.
1075 USA/ELBERT GREEN HUBBARD/PUBLISHER	The final proof of greatness lies in being able to endure criticism without resentment.
1076 P. T. BARNUM/ AMERICAN SHOWMAN	Unless a man enters upon the vocation intended for him by nature, and best suited to his peculiar genius, he cannot succeed.
1077 W. AFRICAN PROVERB	Speak softly and carry a big stick.
1078 DR NELSON GLUECK/ USA/THIS I BELIEVE	I can magnify but never lessen my problems by ignoring, evading, or exorcising them.
1079 JAMES BALDWIN/ AMERICAN AUTHOR	A child cannot be taught by anyone who despises him, and a child cannot afford to be fooled.
1080 COMMUNICATION	Language barrier
1081 SHIRLEY ANN JACKSON/ USA/PHYSICIST	We need to go back to discovery, to posing a question, to having a hypothesis and having kids know that they can discover the answers and can peel away a layer.
1082 ELEANOR ROOSEVELT/ USA/ LEADERSHIP	Great minds discuss ideas; average minds discuss events; small minds discuss people.
1083 RALPH BUNCHE/ AMERICAN DIPLOMAT	The United Nations is our one great hope for a peaceful and free world.
1084 CRIME/BURGLARY	Break and enter

NUMBER CATEGORY/CREDIT	TOPIC
1085 CORRUPTION/GREED	Unjust enrichment
1086 WILLIAM CARLOS WILLIAMS/USA/POET	Beauty is in the eye of the beholder.
1087 MAYA ANGELOU/ AMERICAN POET	I may be changed by what happens to me but I refuse to be diminished by it.
1088 LOWELL THOMAS/ AMERICAN WRITER	The ability to speak is a short cut to distinction. It puts a man in the limelight, raises him head and shoulders above the crowd.
1089 VICTOR HUGO/FRENCH/ AUTHOR	I would rather be the head of a fly than the tail of a lion.
1090 RICHARD NIXON/ USA/PRESIDENT	Those who hate you don't win unless you hate them, and then you destroy yourself.
1091 TECHNOLOGY	Robots
1092 BERTRAND RUSSELL/ BRITISH AUTHOR	It has been said that man is a rational animal. All my life I have been searching for evidence which could support this.
1093 HARRY EMERSON FOSDICK/AMERICAN PASTOR	No horse gets anywhere until he is harnessed. No stream or gas drives anything until it is confined. No Niagara is ever turned into light and power until it is tunneled. No life ever grows great until it is focused, dedicated, disciplined.
1094 CAROLINE ADDERSON/ CANADIAN WRITER	The golden rule of business is supply and demand. I venture to say that this is also the rule of happiness. When a balance is achieved between our desires and another's willingness to satisfy them, the result is a sympathetic, mutually rewarding relationship.
1095 JAPAN/NORTH KOREA	Kidnapping of Japanese (IN JAPAN) by North Korean agents
1096 CONFLIECT/ VALUES	Culture clash
1097 STEPHEN AMBROSE/ USA/ HISTORIAN	The past is a source of knowledge, and the future is a source of hope. Love of the past implies faith in the future.
1098 ROBERT B. POWERS/ GUNS/THIS I BELIEVE	Love is stronger than the trace chains on a twenty-mule team wagon.
1099 DOUGLAS COUPLAND/ CANADIAN NOVELIST	Below a certain point, if you keep too quiet, people no longer see you as thoughtful or deep; they simply forget you.
1100 PITIM SOROKIN/USA/ THIS I BELIEVE	Altruistic persons live longer than egoistic individuals.
1101 ROBERT E.M. COWIE/ BUSINESS	Unless the man who works in an office is able to sell himself and his ideas, unless he has the power to convince others of the soundness of his convictions, he can never achieve his goal.
1102 JAMES BALDWIN/ USA/AUTHOR	Anyone who has ever struggled with poverty knows how extremely expensive it is to be poor.
1103 SOCIETY	Children with learning disabilities
1104 LEOPOLD STOKOWSKY/ BRITISH CONDUCTOR	A painter paints pictures on canvas. But musicians paint their pictures on silence.
1105 DAG HAMMARSJOLD/ SECRETARY GENERAL	It is when we all play safe that we create a world of utmost insecurity.
1106 LEONARD COHEN/ CANADA/POET/SINGER	There's a crack in everything. That's how the light gets in.
1107 MARKETING/ PREVIEW	Movie trailers

NUMBER CATEGORY/CREDIT	TOPIC
1108 WILLIAM HUBBEN/ USA/THIS I BELIEVE/ RADIO	Mankind is one and indivisible. And starvation, suffering, and suppression in one part of the world cannot and must not leave other nations untouched.
1109 J F KENNEDY/USA/ PRESIDENT	Let every nation know, whether it wishes us well or ill, that we shall pay any price, bear any burden, meet any hardship, support any friend, oppose any foe to assure the survival and the success of liberty.
1110 SOCIAL REGARD	V.I.P. (Very Important Person)
1111 DEATH	R.I.P. (Rest In Peace)
1112 USA/ELBERT GREEN HUBBARD/PUBLISHER	The line between failure and success is so fine…that we are often on the line and do not know it.
1113 FIRST NATIONS/ART	Totem poles
1114 ENEMIES/FRIENDSHIP	The kinship of old foes
1115 ELECTRONICS/FUN	Earphones
1116 POVERTY/LAW	Squatting by homeless people
1117 MANNERS/BEAUTY	Finishing school
1118 ALBERT J. NESBITT/USA/ THIS I BELIEVE	But it seems to me better to have a little religion and practice it than think piously and do nothing about it
1119 LEONARDO DA VINCI/ART	It is easier to resist at the beginning than at the end.
1120 KURT VONNEGUT/USA/ WRITER	The best jokes are dangerous and dangerous because they're in some way truthful.
1121 CHARLES SCHWAB/USA/ BUSINESS LEADER	Most of my troubles have been due to being good to people. If young folks want to avoid trouble, they should be hardboiled and say no to everybody. Then they will walk through life unmolested. But they will do without friends, and won't have much fun.
1122 NANCY ASTOR/UK/ MEMBER/PARLIAMENT	The only thing I like about rich people is their money.
1123 RICHARD DAWKINS/UK/ SCIENTIST	Do not indoctrinate your children. Teach them how to think for themselves, how to evaluate evidence, and how to disagree with you.
1124 TRAVEL/CHEAP	Youth hostels
1125 JEAN COCTEAU/FRANCE/ NOVELIST/POET	The prettiest dresses are worn to be taken off.
1126 INDIAN PROVERB	One of the two partners always bites the best part of the apple.
1127 DR. JIM SIMONS/USA/ MATH/BILLIONAIRE	Do something new and don't run with the pack.
1128 LEONARD COHEN/ CANADA/POET	Do not be a magician - be magic!
1129 ANNE FRANK/AUTHOR	A quiet conscience makes one strong!
1130 T. BOONE PICKENS/ USA	I may have been born at night, but I wasn't born last night.
1131 WALTER CRONKITE/ USA/JOURNALIST	America's health care system is neither healthy, caring, nor a system.
1132 ANNE GEDDES/N.Z. PHOTOGRAPHER	I have a deep love and respect for children and I cannot imagine photographic life without them playing a major part.
1133 WILLIAM BUTLER YEATS/ POET/NOBEL LAUREATE	Think like a wise man but communicate in the language of the people.

NUMBER CATEGORY/CREDIT	TOPIC
1134 JAPAN/R & R	*Onsen* – Japanese hot springs
1135 DAN BUETTNER/HOW TO LIVE TO BE 100+/ TED.COM	In Sardinia, the older you get the more equity you have, the more wisdom you're celebrated for. You go into the bars in Sardinia, instead of seeing the Sports Illustrated swimsuit calendar, you see the centenarian of the month calendar.
1136 DR. JOYCE BROTHERS/ USA/PSYCHOLOGIST	The person interested in success has to learn to view failure as a healthy, inevitable part of the process of getting to the top.
1137 JAMES Q. DUPONT/USA/ THIS I BELIEVE	…life is not all hearts and flowers; indeed it's hard and cruel for most of us much of the time.
1138 PARENTING/ BABIES	Prams
1139 PARANORMAL	Telepathy
1140 BEN LUCIEN BURMAN/ USA/WAR	My code of living is simple: It consists of three parts: 1) never be cruel; 2) always be artistic; 3) never lose your sense of humor.
1141 ITALY/TOURISM	Leaning Tower of Pisa
1142 SHMULEY BOTEACH/ USA/RABBI	I don't believe in being my kids' friend. I am their parent.
1143 SWITZERLAND/SKIING	The Alps
1144 CRIME/MONEY	Money laundering
1145 HISTORY/EUROPE/ MERRIAMWEBSTER	**Inquisition**: a former Roman Catholic tribunal for the discovery and punishment of heresy
1146 REV. PETER GOMES/PROF	…entertain the value of impossible things.
1147 MIKE MYATT/FORBES/US	The best leaders don't seek credit – they seek results.
1148 VIKTOR FRANKL/ AUSTRIAN/AUTHOR	Everything can be taken from a man but one thing: the last of the human freedoms – to choose one's attitude in any given set of circumstances, to choose one's own way.
1149 DAN RATHER/USA/ JOURNALIST	The dream begins with a teacher who believes in you, who tugs and pushes and leads you to the next plateau, sometimes poking you with a sharp stick called "truth."
1150 USA/BERNARD M. BARUCH/BUSINESS	The ability to express an idea is well nigh as important as the idea itself.
1151 JEAN COCTEAU/POET/ FRENCH/WRITER	One should always talk well about oneself! The word spreads around and in the end, no one remembers where it started.
1152 BERTRAND RUSSELL/UK/ PHILOSOPHER/MATH	Many people would sooner die than think.
1153 TRAVEL/FUN/ YOUTH	Backpacking
1154 MOVIES/VIDEO	Documentaries
1155 THOMAS PAINE/USA/ PHILOSOPHER	Moderation in temper is always a virtue; but moderation in principle is always a vice.
1156 RALPH BUNCHE/USA/ POLITICAL SCIENTIST	There are no warlike people –just warlike leaders.
1157 SLOGAN/USA/FLORISTS	Say it with flowers.
1158 JAMES B. CAREY/ LABOR LEADER/USA/ THIS I BELIEVE	Man can be strong alone but not indomitable, in isolation. He has to belong to something, to realize he is not created separately or apart from the rest of mankind, whether he is an American or a Mohammedan.

NUMBER CATEGORY/CREDIT	TOPIC
1159 DAVID OGILVY/UK/ ADVERTISING/LEADER	The consumer isn't a moron; she is your wife.
1160 DR. JOYCE BROTHERS/ USA/PSYCHOLOGIST	The best proof of love is trust.
1161 J. PAUL GETTY/USA/ BILLIONAIRE/BUSINESS	Formula for success – rise early, work hard, strike oil.
1162 ALICE WALKER/USA/ NOVELIST	The animals of the world exist for their own reasons. They were not made for humans any more than black people were made for whites or women for men.
1163 PICO IYER/TRAVEL WRITER/NYTIMES	The more ways we have to connect, the more many of us seem desperate to unplug.
1164 JAMES Q. DUPONT/USA/ THIS I BELIEVE	A man may be a genius, you know, but he can still do things that practically break your heart.
1165 HELEN KELLER/ USA/ AUTHOR/LECTURER	Science may have found a cure for most evils; but it has fond no remedy for the worst of them all – the apathy of human beings.
1166 HARRY EMERSON FOSDICK/PASTOR	It is by acts and not by ideas that people live.
1167 ALEKSANDR PUSHKIN/ RUSSIA/POET	The illusion which exalts us is dearer to us than ten thousand truths.
1168 ARCHIMEDES/ANCIENT GREEK SCIENTIST	Show me the place to stand and I can move the world.
1169 CELINE DION/SINGER/ CANADA	I have become a housewife and there is no better job.
1170 STRESS	Ways of escaping stress
1171 JAMES B. CAREY/LABOR LEADER/USA/ THIS I BELIEVE	A laboring man needs bread and butter, and cash to pay the rent. But he would be a poor individual, indeed, if he were not able to furnish the vestibule of his mind and his soul with spiritual embellishment....
1172 DOUGLAS COUPLAND/ CANADIAN NOVELIST	I don't think anyone ever gets over anything in life; they merely get used to it.
1173 HARRY BROWNE/ AUTHOR	Security – it's simply the recognition that changes will take place and the knowledge that you're willing to deal with whatever happens.
1174 BEN HECHT/USA/ SCREENWRITER	Trying to determine what is going on in the world by reading newspapers is like trying to tell the time by watching the second hand of a clock.
1175 DIANNA BOOHER/ USA/AUTHOR	Physical attractiveness results in a fatter paycheck. Particularly, taller people earn more money than shorter people.
1176 ANN LANDERS/ USA/ ADVICE COLUMNIST/ CIIICAGO SUN TIMES	Some people believe holding on and hanging in there are signs of great strength. However, there are times when it takes much more strength to know when to let go and then do it.
1177 BALTASAR GRACIAN/ SPANISH/WRITER	Never compete with someone who has nothing to lose.
1178 HARRY EMERSON FOSDICK/USA/PASTOR	He who chooses the beginning of the road chooses the place it leads to. It is the means that determines the end.
1179 UK/W. SOMERSET MAUGHAM/NOVELIST	If a nation values anything more highly than freedom, it will lose its freedom; and the irony of it is that if it is comfort or money that it values more, it will lose that too.

NUMBER CATEGORY/CREDIT	TOPIC
1180 JOHN LENNON/UK/USA/ MUSICIAN/THE BEATLES	Imagine there's no countries. / It isn't hard to do. / Nothing to kill or die for. / And no religion, too. / Imagine all the people / Living life in peace.
1181 MARRIAGE/ CULTURE	Marriage and cultural differences
1182 MARK TWAIN/USA/ AUTHOR	I have never let my schooling interfere with my education.
1183 VIRGIL/ROMAN POET	Practice and thought might gradually forge many an art.
1184 VACATION/ HOME	Staycation: a vacation that is spent at home or somewhere nearby
1185 JAMES HILTON/UK/ AUTHOR/LOST HORIZON	Shangri-La: a fictional place of perpetual pleasure
1186 ALIENS/MYSTERIES	UFO's (Unidentified Flying Objects)
1187 BILL DAVENHALL/USA/ HEALTH/TED.COM	No doctor can I remember ever asking me, "Where have you lived?" They haven't asked me [about] the quality of the drinking water that I put in my mouth or the food that I ingest into my stomach.
1188 OFFICE/SKILLS	Secretaries
1189 MEN/GROOMING	Beards and moustaches
1190 ROLLS ROYCE /AUTO ADVERTISING	At 60 miles an hour the loudest noise in this new Rolls-Royce comes from the electric clock.
1191 INDIA/STREETS	Snake charmers
1192 OTTO VON BISMARK/ GERMAN STATESMAN	Anyone who has looked into the glazed eyes of a soldier dying on the battlefield will think hard before starting a war.
1193 ANNE TAYLOR FLEMING/ AUTHOR/BOOK TITLE	Motherhood Deferred
1194 ANIMAL RIGHTS	Vivisection
1195 BALTASAR GRACIAN/ SPANISH/WRITER	It is better to sleep on things beforehand than lie awake about them afterward.
1196 ALBERT EINSTEIN/ PHYSICIST/LETTER TO SYBILLE BLINOFF/1954	It is true that my parents were worried because I began to speak fairly late, so that they even consulted a doctor. I can't say how old I was – but surely not less than three.
1197 TELEVISION/DRAMA	Soap operas
1198 HELEN KELLER/ USA/ AUTHOR/LECTURER	I long to accomplish a great and noble task, but it is my chief duty to accomplish small tasks as if they were great and noble.
1199 CELEBRITY/FAME	The life of a rock star
1200 CHINA/MAO TSE TUNG	Cultural Revolution
1201 MARGARET ATWOOD/ CANADIAN NOVELIST	A divorce is like an amputation: you survive it, but there's less of you.
1202 JANNY SCOTT/DAVID LEONHARDT/SHADOWY LINES/NY TIMES	...a child's economic background is a better predictor of school performance in the United States than in Denmark, the Netherlands, or France.
1203 NEIL ARMSTRONG/ AMERICAN ASTRONAUT	I think we tried very hard not to be overconfident, because when you get overconfident, that's when something snaps up and bites you.
1204 JOEL OSTEEN/USA/ PREACHER	Somebody needs what you have to give. It may not be your money; it may be your time. It may be your listening ear.

NUMBER CATEGORY/CREDIT	TOPIC
1205 EURIPIDES/GREEK POET	When one with honeyed words but evil mind persuades the mob, great woes befall the state.
1206 RADIO/TELEVISION	Talk shows
1207 ROBERT MCCRUM/ THE OBSERVER/UK	A great novel can cost as much as a pencil and a pad of paper – or a whole life.
1208 BALTASAR GRACIAN/ SPANISH/JESUIT/ WRITER	Two kinds of people are good at foreseeing danger: those who have learned at their own expense, and the clever people who learn a great deal at the expense of others.
1209 EARTH DAY/WIKIPEDIA/ APRIL 22/SINCE 1970	Earth Day: an annual day on which events are held worldwide to increase awareness and appreciation of the Earth's natural environment.
1210 LEO BUSCAGLIA/USA	Love is life and if you miss love, you miss life.
1211 ROBERT MCCRUM/UK/ THE GUARDIAN	Two writers, alone in a room, will talk about royalties not art.
1212 COMMUNICATION	Videoconferencing
1213 LEO BUSCAGLIA/USA	Never idealize others. They will never live up to your expectations.
1214 MARGARET MEAD/ ANTHROPOLOGIST/ USA/ THIS I BELIEVE	I believe that human nature is neither intrinsically good nor intrinsically evil…and that it will depend upon how they are reared….what kind of human beings they can become.
1215 VET BILLS/READER'S DIGEST	Make a habit of checking your pet's physical condition every day.
1216 NEIL DEGRASSE TYSON/ USA/ASTROPHYSICIST	We spend the first year of a child's life teaching it to walk and talk and the rest of its life to shut up and sit down. There's something wrong there.
1217 J.P. MORGAN/USA/ FINANCIER	A man always has two reasons for doing anything: a good reason and the real reason.
1218 ALBERT CAMUS/ FRENCH/PHILOSOPHER	In the depth of winter, I found there was, within me, an invincible summer. And that makes me happy. For it says that no matter how hard the world pushes against me, within me, there's something stronger.
1219 IMAGINATION	Make-believe
1220 RELIGION	Major world religions
1221 ENGLISH PROVERB	Absence makes the heart grow fonder.
1222 ABRAHAM LINCOLN/16TH PRESIDENT/USA	Am I not destroying my enemies when I make friends of them?
1223 ALCOHOL/ ADDICTION	Alcoholism
1224 NORMALITY/ DANGER	Business as usual
1225 WOMEN/BEAUTY	*Femme fatale*
1226 N.Y. TIMES/SLOGAN	All the news that's fit to print
1227 DE BEERS/SLOGAN	A diamond is forever.
1228 SLOGAN/UNITED NEGRO COLLEGE FUND/USA	A mind is a terrible thing to waste, but a wonderful thing to invest in.
1229 SEIKO WATCH CO.	More than anything, it's your watch that shows your confidence.
1230 EURIPIDES/GREEK POET	Anger exceeding limits causes fear and excessive kindness eliminates respect.
1231 LAWRENCE CLARK POWELL/WRITER/USA	Write to be understood, speak to be heard, read to grow.

NUMBER CATEGORY/CREDIT	TOPIC
1232 FRIENDSHIP/SECRETS	What happens in Vegas stays in Vegas.
1233 BRIAN TRACY/USA/ SUCCESS COACH	Communication is a skill that you can learn. It's like riding a bicycle or typing. If you're willing to work at it, you can rapidly improve the quality of every part of your life.
1234 OSCAR WILDE/IRISH/ POET	Be yourself; everyone is already taken.
1235 ROBERT LOUIS STEVENSON/WRITER	The saints are the sinners who keep on trying.
1236 PUBLILIUS SYRUS/100 BC	A rolling stone gathers no moss.
1237 ENGLISH PROVERB	A burnt child dreads fire.
1238 ENGLISH PROVERB	A beggar can never be bankrupt.
1239 WILL ROGERS/ AMERICAN COMEDIAN	I'm not a real movie star. I've still got the same wife I started out with twenty-eight years ago.
1240 HARRY EMERSON FOSDICK/USA PASTOR	He who cannot rest, cannot work; he who cannot let go, cannot hold on; he who cannot find footing, cannot go forward.
1241 BALTASAR GRACIAN/ SPANISH/JESUIT	He that has satisfied his thirst turns his back on the well.
1242 SURGERY/IMAGE	Nose job
1243 USA/ELBERT GREEN HUBBARD/WRITER	Never explain – your friends do not need it and your enemies will not believe you anyhow.
1244 CICELY TYSON/USA/ ACTOR	I think when you begin to think of yourself as having achieved something, then there's nothing left for you to work towards. I want to believe that there is a mountain so high that I will spend my entire life striving to reach the top of it.
1245 P. T. BARNUM/USA/ CIRCUS	The noblest art is that of making others happy.
1246 U.S. ARMY/SLOGAN	Be all that you can be.
1247 MARK CUBAN/USA/ BILLIONAIRE	When you've got 10,000 people trying to do the same thing, why would you want to be number 10,001?
1248 CLAIROL/ SLOGAN	If I've only one life, let me live it as a blonde!
1249 ABRAHAM LINCOLN/ USA/16TH PRESIDENT	The better part of one's life consists of his friendships.
1250 CHRISTOPHER MORLEY/ WRITER/USA	Life is a foreign language; all men mispronounce it.
1251 ENGLISH PROVERB	A bird in the hand is worth two in the bush.
1252 TIMEX WATCH/SLOGAN	It takes a licking and keeps on ticking.
1253 YELLOW PAGES/SLOGAN	Let your fingers do the walking.
1254 PILLSBURY DOUGH/USA	Nothin' says loving' like something from the oven.
1255 AT & T/TELECOM	Reach out and touch someone.
1256 COCA COLA	The pause that refreshes.
1257 BALTASAR GRACIAN/ JESUIT/WRITER	Great ability develops and reveals itself increasingly with every new assignment.
1258 MUSIC	Lip-syncing

NUMBER CATEGORY/CREDIT	TOPIC
1259 MORAL DILEMMA	You are in a parking lot. Your car bumps another car. You look around. There's no one around. What do you do?
1260 J.P. MORGAN/USA/ FINANCIER	If you have to ask how much it costs, you can't afford it.
1261 G.K. CHESTERTON/ ENGLISH WRITER	[Feminism] is mixed up with a muddled idea that women are free when they serve their employers but slaves when they help their husbands.
1262 SPORTS	Surfing
1263 POLITICS	Political scandals
1264 USA/ARTHUR LEONARD SCHAWLOW/NOBELIST	To do successful research, you don't need to know everything; you just need to know one thing that isn't known.
1265 GEORGE BERNARD SHAW/PLAYWRIGHT	The more things a man is ashamed of, the more respectable he is.
1266 JAPANESE PROVERB	*Egao wa ikiru enerugi:* Your smile is your life force.
1267 ALBERT EINSTEIN/ SCIENTIST/NOBELIST	The value of a man resides in what he gives and not in what he is capable of receiving.
1268 THOMAS DE QUINCEY/ UK/ESSAYIST	If once a man indulges in murder, very soon he comes to think little of robbing, and from robbing he next comes to drinking and Sabbath-breaking, and from that to incivility and procrastination.
1269 E.B. WHITE/USA/ WRITER	Americans are willing to go to enormous trouble and expense defending their principles with arms, very little trouble and expense advocating them with words.
1270 CELEBRATION	Celebrating the big moments in life.
1271 LEO TOLSTOY/WRITER	What counts in making a happy marriage is not so much how compatible you are but how you deal with incompatibility.
1272 RALSTON PURINA/USA	Don't treat your puppy like a dog.
1273 J.P. MORGAN/USA	Go as far as you can see; when you get there, you'll be able to see farther.
1274 BALTASAR GRACIAN/ JESUIT/WRITER	Better mad with the rest of the world than wise alone.
1275 DEBATE	That beauty contests are harmful.
1276 MARTIN LUTHER KING JR. /USA	In the end, we will remember not the words of our enemies, but the silence of our friends.
1277 DEBATE	The use of performance-enhancing drugs in sports should be legalized.
1278 MALCOLM X/USA	The price of freedom is death.
1279 ABRAHAM LINCOLN/ USA/16TH PRESIDENT	Whatever you are, be a good one.
1280 THUCYDIDES/GREEK/ HISTORIAN	The ones who come out on top are the ones who have been trained in the hardest school.
1281 DEBATE	That government subsidy of the arts should be ended.
1282 DAVID OGILVY/UK/ ADVERTISING/BUSINESS	On advertising: If it doesn't sell, it isn't creative.
1283 ENGLISH PROVERB	Action speaks louder than words.
1284 GEORGE H. LORIMER/ EDITOR/USA	It's good to have money and the things that money can buy, but it's good, too, to check up once in a while and make sure that you haven't lost the things that money can't buy.

NUMBER CATEGORY/CREDIT	TOPIC
1285 DEBATE	That examinations should be replaced with other forms of assessment.
1286 DEBATE	That governments should always try to do the moral thing.
1287 DEBATE	That there should there be a tax on fatty foods
1288 DEBATE	That the assassination of a dictator can be justified.
1289 DAVID OGILVY/BUSINESS	Advertising is only evil when it advertises evil things.
1290 ABRAHAM LINCOLN/ 16th PRESIDENT/USA	The probability that we may be failing the struggle ought not to deter us from the support of a cause we believe to be just.
1291 BUSINESS/GOVERNMENT	Whistle-blowing
1292 DEBATE	That television advertisements for children should be banned.
1293 DEBATE	Age discrimination in the workplace is inevitable.
1294 CHINESE PROVERB	An inch of time is an inch of gold, but you can't buy that inch of time with an inch of gold.
1295 ENGLISH PROVERB	A cat may look at a king.
1296 MARTHA GRAHAM/USA	Misery is a communicable disease.
1297 BALTASAR GRACIAN/ JESUIT/WRITER	Things do not pass for what they are, but for what they seem. Most things are judged by their jackets.
1298 DEBATE	That it is morally acceptable to experiment on non-human animals to develop products and medicines that benefit human beings.
1299 HELEN KELLER/USA/ AUTHOR	Optimism is the faith that leads to achievement.
1300 OCCULT/SOCIETY	Secret societies
1301 ANNE FRANK/JEWISH AUTHOR/ DIARY OF A YOUNG GIRL	Although I'm only fourteen, I know quite well what I want, I know who is right and who is wrong. I have my opinions, my own ideas and principles, and although it may sound pretty mad from an adolescent, I feel more of a person than a child; I feel quite independent of anyone.
1302 HOBBIES/RELAXATION	Recreation clubs
1303 F. SCOTT FITZGERALD/ THE GREAT GATSBY	Let us learn to show our friendship for a man when he is alive and not after he is dead.
1304 LINDA CHAVEZ/ AMERICAN POLITICIAN	It comes as a shocking surprise to professors at Stanford, Harvard and other elite universities, but teaching immigrant children in English actually seems to help them learn the language.
1305 CONFUCIUS/CHINA/ PHILOSOPHER	Tell me and I'll forget; show me and I may remember; involve me and I'll understand.
1306 EDUCATION/YOUTH	That boarding schools are beneficial for young children.
1307 USA/WRITER/F. SCOTT FITZGERALD	It takes two to make an accident.
1308 BUSINESS/CRIME	Arms dealers
1309 ERNEST HEMINGWAY/ AMERICAN WRITER	In order to write about life, first you must live it.
1310 CHINESE PROVERB	To talk much and arrive nowhere is the same as climbing a tree to catch a fish.
1311 USA/ELBERT GREEN HUBBARD/PUBLISHER	One machine can do the work of fifty ordinary men. No machine can do the work of one extraordinary man.

NUMBER CATEGORY/CREDIT	TOPIC
1312 BEAUTY/DANGER	Cosmetic surgery
1313 POVERTY/BABIES	Abandonment of newborns
1314 HUMAN RIGHTS	Universal suffrage
1315 JAPANESE PROVERB	*Sendo uko shite fune yama ni noboru* / Too many skippers bring the boat to the mountain.
1316 WARNING/SCAMS	If it sounds too good to be true, it probably is.
1317 BALTASAR GRACIAN/ JESUIT/WRITER	Never do anything when you are in a temper, for you will do everything wrong.
1318 VIRGIL/ROMAN POET	Your descendants shall gather your fruits.
1319 BALTASAR GRACIAN/ JESUIT/WRITER	Dreams will get you nowhere; a good kick in the pants will take you a long way.
1320 PETER SALOVEY/USA	Volunteering is an act of heroism.
1321 BOXING	That boxing should be banned.
1322 JOHN WANAMAKER/ USA/AMERICAN/ MERCHANT	Any seeming deception in a statement is costly, not only in the expense of the advertising but in the detrimental effect produced upon the customer, who believes she has been misled.
1323 ULRICH BECK/ GERMAN SOCIOLOGIST	You cannot make peace with terrorists. The normal dividing lines between war and peace do not apply.
1324 JAPANESE PROVERB	*Saru mo ki kara ochiru*/Even monkeys fall from trees.
1325 DEBATE	That a police force should be fully armed.
1326 BALTASAR GRACIAN/ JESUIT/WRITER	A wise man gets more use from his enemies than a fool from his friends.
1327 ENGLISH PROVERB	A drowning man will clutch at a straw.
1328 CHINESE PROVERB	He who asks a question is a fool for five minutes; he who does not ask a question remains a fool forever.
1329 ISAAC NEWTON/ ENGLISH PHYSICIST	I can calculate the motion of heavenly bodies but not the madness of people.
1330 W. CLEMENT STONE/ USA/BUSINESS	Sales are contingent upon the attitude of the salesman, not the attitude of the prospect.
1331 ABIGAIL VAN BUREN/ USA/ADVICE COLUMNIST	Loneliness is the ultimate poverty.
1332 COCO CHANEL/FRANCE	My friends, there are no friends.
1333 MADAM C.J. WALKER/ USA/MILLIONAIRE	I got my start by giving myself a start.
1334 WILL ROGERS/ AMERICAN COMEDIAN	Even if you're on the right track, you'll get run over if you just sit there.
1335 BALTASAR GRACIAN/ JESUIT/WRITER	Keep the extent of your abilities unknown. The wise man does not allow his knowledge and abilities to be sounded to the bottom, if he desires to be honored at all.
1336 WAR/GOVERNMENT	Torture
1337 ENVIRONMENT	Protecting the forests
1338 XENOPHOBIA	Nation bashing
1339 OPINION	Creativity and discipline go hand in hand.

NUMBER CATEGORY/CREDIT	TOPIC
1340 ROBERTSON DAVIES/ CANADIAN WRITER	A truly great book should be read in youth, again in maturity and once more in old age, as a fine building should be seen by morning light, at noon and by moonlight.
1341 BALTASAR GRACIAN/ JESUIT/WRITER	Never open the door to a lesser evil, for other and greater ones invariably slink in after it.
1342 AARON COPLAND/USA/ COMPOSER	To stop the flow of music would be like the stopping of time itself, incredible and inconceivable.
1343 BELA BARTOK/ MUSICIAN/HUNGARY	Competitions are for horses, not artists.
1344 DEBATE	That the government should ban songs with violent lyrics.
1345 MAKE UP A STORY	Lucky escape
1346 ENVIRONMENT	Garbage collection in your town/city
1347 BETTE DAVIS/ AMERICAN ACTRESS	Acting should be bigger than life. Scripts should be bigger than life. It should all be bigger than life.
1348 WARREN BUFFETT/ USA/INVESTOR	It's only when the tide goes out that you learn who's been swimming naked.
1349 MOVIES/BOOKS	Batman
1350 FRANCIS BACON/UK	By indignities men come to dignities.
1351 IMPACT/INFLUENCE	Memorable people
1352 JOSEPH ADDISON/ ENGLISH WRITER	Admiration is a very short-lived passion, that immediately decays upon growing familiar with its object.
1353 DOUGLAS COUPLAND/ CANADIAN NOVELIST	I think of how the person who needs the other person the least in a relationship is the stronger member.
1354 KOREAN PROVERB	Butterflies come to pretty flowers.
1355 LINDA CHAVEZ/USA/ GOVERNMENT	We need to let the world know it is possible to celebrate long years of married life. But it doesn't happen by accident. Marriage requires commitment to something greater than ourselves. And if those of us who have succeeded at marriage aren't willing to lead the way, who will?
1356 DAVID OGILVY/UK/ ADVERTISING EXEC	Advertising reflects the mores of society, but it does not influence them.
1357 J.D. SALINGER/USA/ WRITER	People never notice anything.
1358 DAVID OGILVY/ ADVERTISING EXEC	I did not feel 'evil' when I wrote advertisements for Puerto Rico. They helped attract industry and tourists to a country which had been living on the edge of starvation for 400 years.
1359 HELEN KELLER/USA	Literature is my Utopia.
1360 JEFF DALY/USA/ ARCHITECT	Two monologues do not make a dialogue.
1361 ALBERT SCHWEITZER/ FRENCH THEOLOGIAN	Man can no longer live for himself alone. We must realize that all life is valuable and that we are united to all life. From this knowledge comes our spiritual relationship with the universe.
1362 GEORGE R.R. MARTIN/ GAME OF THRONES/US	When the snows fall and the white winds blow, the lone wolf dies but the pack survives.

NUMBER CATEGORY/CREDIT	TOPIC
1363 HEALTH/WEALTH	The Amazon jungle
1364 DIANNA BOOHER/USA/AUTHOR	Attractive criminals get lighter sentences. Attractive students get more teacher attention.
1365 MARGARET ATWOOD/CANADIAN NOVELIST	I hope that people will finally come to realize that there is only one 'race' – the human race – and that we are all members of it.
1366 GEORGE R.R. MARTIN/GAME OF THRONES/US	If a man paints a target on his chest, he should expect that sooner or later someone will loose an arrow on him.
1367 BALTASAR GRACIAN/JESUIT/WRITER	A synonym is a word you use when you can't spell the other one.
1368 BALTASAR GRACIAN/JESUIT/WRITER	Friendship multiplies the good of life and divides the evil.
1369 NOAM CHOMSKY/USA/LINGUISTICS/ACTIVIST	Our ignorance can be divided into problems and mysteries. When we face a problem, we may not know its solution, but we have insight, increasing knowledge and an inkling of what we are looking for. When we face a mystery, however, we can only stare in wonder and bewilderment, not knowing what an explanation would even look like.
1370 ANNIE DILLARD/USA/WRITER/SUCCESS	You've got to jump off cliffs all the time and build your wings on the way down.
1371 BUSINESS/GLOBAL	Sweat shops
1372 JOSEPH CAMPBELL/USA	We save the world by being alive ourselves.
1373 PERSONAL/NATIONAL	Disappointment
1374 BILL GATES/USA/ENTREPRENEUR	Television is not real life. In real life, people actually have to leave the coffee shop and go to jobs.
1375 DAVID OGILVY/ADVERTISING INDUSTRY LEADER	Much of the messy advertising you see on television today is the product of committees. Committees can criticize advertisements, but they should never be allowed to create them.
1376 NEIL ARMSTRONG/USA/ASTRONAUT	Mystery creates wonder and wonder is the basis of man's desire to understand.
1377 F. SCOTT FITZGERALD/USA/WRITER	It's a great advantage not to drink among hard drinking people.
1378 ELIZABETH BISLAND/WRITER/ADVENTURER	No ruler is ever really dethroned by his subjects. No hand but his own ever takes the crown from his head.
1379 FUN	April Fool's Day
1380 NOAM CHOMSKY/USA/LINGUISTICS/ACTIVIST	If anybody thinks they should listen to me because I'm a professor at MIT, that's nonsense. You should decide whether something makes sense by its content, not by the letters after the name of the person who says it.
1381 ANDY ROONEY/USA/JOURNALIST	Computers make it easier to do a lot of things, but most of the things they make it easier to do don't need to be done.
1382 WINSTON CHURCHILL/UK/PRIME MINISTER	I am prepared to meet my maker. Whether my maker is prepared for the great ordeal of meeting me is another matter.
1383 JENNA McCARTHY/MARRIAGE/TEDTALK	Merely watching a romantic comedy causes relationship satisfaction to plummet.
1384 GLOBALIZATION	Vanishing languages
1385 SOCIETY/FAIRNESS	Meritocracy

NUMBER CATEGORY/CREDIT	TOPIC
1386 ITALIAN/NICCOLO MACHIAVELLI/ DIPLOMAT	Everyone who wants to know what will happen ought to examine what has happened; everything in this world in any epoch has their replicas in antiquity.
1387 IDIOM/SUCCESS	Bringing down the house
1388 GEORGE S. PATTON/ USA MILITARY LEADER	A good plan, violently executed now, is better than a perfect plan next week.
1389 PARENTING	Gay foster parenting
1390 DAVID ULEVITCH/BIZ/ COMPUTER SCIENCE	Big companies will talk to you, criticize you, then copy you.
1391 DR. JAMES ROWLAND ANGELL/PRESIDENT/ YALE UNIVERSITY	Asked what his secret was for lasting so long and being sosuccessful as the president of Yale University, Dr. James R. Angell explained: "GROW ANTENNAE, NOT HORNS."
1392 MAHATMA GANDHI/ INDIAN LEADER	To call woman the weaker sex is a libel; it is man's injustice to woman.
1393 AESOP/AUTHOR	The smaller the mind the greater the conceit.
1394 USA/ELBERT GREEN HUBBARD/WRITER	No man needs a vacation so much as the man who has just had one.
1395 FAILURE	Riches to rags
1396 OPRAH WINFREY/ USA/BILLIONAIRE	Walk through life eager and open to self-improvement and that which is going to best help you evolve, because that's really why we are here: to evolve as human beings.
1397 CHINESE EXPRESSION	Pulling teeth from a tiger's mouth
1398 CORPORATIONS	Corporate greed
1399 THOMAS EDISON/USA/ INVENTOR	Many of life's failures are people who did not realize how close they were to success when they gave up.
1400 JAMES BALDWIN/ AMERICAN AUTHOR	Children have never been very good at listening to their elders, but they have never failed to imitate them.
1401 DR. PHIL McGRAW/USA/ TV/PSYCHOLOGIST	If your humor is hurting someone, it's not funny.
1402 POWER	The bully pulpit
1403 ALDO LEOPOLD/USA/ SCIENTIST/WRITER	I am glad I will not be young in a future without wilderness.
1404 SAYING	When the going gets tough, the tough go shopping.
1405 DIPLOMAT/NICCOLO MACHIAVELLI/ITALY	The vulgar crowd always is taken by appearances, and the world consists chiefly of the vulgar.
1406 ANNE HEYWOOD/ THIS I BELIEVE/USA	I believe that every human being has a special talent – something that he can do better than anyone else.
1407 POVERTY	Crumbs from the master's table
1408 EDUCATION	Lifelong learning
1409 COMPETITION	Underdogs
1410 SPORT/SPAIN	Bullfighting
1411 ADVICE	Crime doesn't pay
1412 DEBATE	That sometimes it is acceptable to pay a bribe.

NUMBER CATEGORY/CREDIT	TOPIC
1413 DORIS LESSING/WRITER/ UK	Think wrongly if you please, but in all cases, think for yourself.
1414 KINGMAN BREWSTER, JR/USA/EDUCATOR	There is no greater challenge than to have someone relying upon you; no greater satisfaction than to vindicate his expectation.
1415 AUTHOR/CHRISTOPHER HITCHENS/BRITISH	That which can be asserted without evidence, can be dismissed without evidence.
1416 NY TIMES/JANE SMILEY	The gift certificate is a giver's best friend.
1417 ROBERTSON DAVIES/ CANADIAN WRITER	Conversation in its true meaning isn't all wagging the tongue; sometimes it is a deeply shared silence.
1418 WILL ROGERS/ AMERICAN COMEDIAN	Diplomacy is the art of saying "Nice doggie" until you can find a rock.
1419 ABRAHAM LINCOLN/ USA/16th PRESIDENT	Most people are about as happy as they make up their minds to be.
1420 HELEN KELLER/ AMERICAN AUTHOR	You don't love someone for their looks, or their clothes, or for their fancy car, but because they sing a song only you can hear.
1421 USA/ELBERT GREEN HUBBARD/PUBLISHER	Every man should have a college education in order to show him how little the thing is really worth.
1422 US/THEODORE HESBURGH/ THEOLOGY	The most important thing a father can do is to love their mother.
1423 MAGGIE MASON/ FOUNDER/MIGHTY GOODS	Don't ever let anyone tell you that something is too competitive. Once you subtract the people who don't work very hard, or the people who aren't as good as you, your competition shrinks dramatically.
1424 MARRIAGE/ PREGNANCY	Shotgun wedding : a wedding that happens because the bride is pregnant
1425 C. S. LEWIS/UK/ WRITER	It may be hard for an egg to turn into a bird; it would be a jolly sight harder for it to learn to fly while remaining an egg. We are like eggs at present. And you cannot go on indefinitely being just an ordinary, decent egg. We must be hatched or go bad.
1426 RICHARD NIXON/USA/ PRESIDENT	A man is not finished when he is defeated. He is finished when he quits.
1427 ISLAM/WOMEN	Women in *chador*
1428 ELIE WIESEL/USA/ NOVELIST/PROFESSOR	When a person doesn't have gratitude, something is missing in his or her. A person can almost be defined by his or her attitude towards gratitude.
1429 MANUFACTURING	Quality control
1430 DOUBT/ SUSPICION	Something fishy
1431 ALDO LEOPOLD/USA/ SCIENTIST/WRITER	The last word in ignorance is the man who says of an animal or plant, "What good is it?"
1432 CREATE A STORY	Encounter with a kangaroo
1433 BIBLE/1 TIMOTHY 6:10	For the love of money is the root of all evil.
1434 ANNIE DILLARD/USA/ WRITER	Spend the afternoon, you can't take it with you.
1435 DEBATE	That it is better to be a living coward than a dead hero
1436 SAFETY	Walking in your city, town, or village after midnight

NUMBER CATEGORY/CREDIT	TOPIC
1437 FIXER/POLITICS/ OPERATIVES/LAW	Fixer: a person who intervenes to enable someone to circumvent the law or obtain a political favor.
1438 AESOP/AUTHOR	Familiarity breeds contempt.
1439 MILTON MELTZER/ USA/HISTORIAN	The master who recognizes no humanity in his slave loses it in himself.
1440 LEO BUSCAGLIA/ AMERICAN WRITER	Only the weak are cruel. Gentleness can only be expected from the strong.
1441 ANDY WARHOL/USA	In the future, everyone will have their fifteen minutes of fame.
1442 COLIN ALLEN/THIS I BELIEVE/USA	Disrespect for human life – any human life – is apt to be the beginning of a destructive chain reaction.
1443 SUZANNE COLLINS/USA/ WRITER	If you appeal to the crowd, either by being humorous or brutal or eccentric, you gain favor.
1444 BILL HANSTOCK/ www.sbnation.com/2012 LONDON OLYMPICS	Team USA swimmer Missy Franklin's parents spent around $100,000 a year helping her further her career in order to reach the Olympics.
1445 MAHATMA GANDHI/ INDIAN LEADER	If by strength is meant moral power, then woman is immeasurably man's superior. Has she not greater intuition, is she not more self-sacrificing, has she not greater powers of endurance, has she not greater courage.
1446 SAYING	Money is the root of all evil
1447 USA/ACTOR/ARNOLD SCHWARZENEGGER	I'll be back!
1448 BIZ STONE/ ENTREPRENEUR	Timing, perseverance, and ten years of trying will eventually make you look like an overnight success.
1449 PHIL LIBIN/USA/ ENTREPRENEUR	The easiest way to get 1 million people paying is to get 1 billion people using.
1450 MIKE BRADY/USA/TV/ THE BRADY BUNCH	A gift is only a good thing when the giver has given thought to the gift.
1451 JOSEPH P. KENNEDY/ USA/DIPLOMAT	More men die of jealousy than of cancer.
1452 WOLFGANG AMADEUS MOZART/COMPOSER	All I insist on, and nothing else, is that you should show the whole world that you are not afraid. Be silent if you choose; but when it is necessary, speak -- and speak in such a way that people will remember it.
1453 SUZANNE COLLINS/USA	You don't forget the face of the person who was your last hope.
1454 ANNE FRANK/JEWISH AUTHOR/ HOLOCAUST	I don't have much in the way of money or worldly possessions. I'm not beautiful, intelligent or clever, but I'm happy, and I intend to stay that way!
1455 SUZANNE COLLINS/USA/ THE HUNGER GAMES	Hope is the only thing stronger than fear.
1456 IDIOM/BEAUTY	A rose between two thorns
1457 JOSEPH P. KENNEDY/USA	When the going gets tough, the tough get going.
1458 THOMAS BEECHAM/ ENGLISH COMPOSER	Great music is that which penetrates the ear with facility and leaves the memory with difficulty. Magical music never leaves the memory.
1459 LEE IACOCCA/USA/ AUTO EXECUTIVE	Motivation is everything. You can do the work of two people, but you can't be two people. Instead, you have to inspire the next guy down.
1460 AESOP/GREEK AUTHOR	We would often be sorry if our wishes were gratified.

NUMBER CATEGORY/CREDIT	TOPIC
1461 PEGGY NOONAN/USA/ SPEECHWRITER	I think miracles exist in part as gifts and in part as clues that there is something beyond the flat world we see.
1462 RICHARD NIXON/USA/ PRESIDENT	If an individual wants to be a leader and isn't controversial, that means he never stood for anything.
1463 HELEN KELLER/USA/ AUTHOR	Face your deficiencies and acknowledge them; but do not let them master you. Let them teach you patience, sweetness and insight.
1464 ANDREW YOUNG/US AMBASSADOR TO UN	Influence is like a savings account. The less you use it, the more you've got.
1465 ARISTOTLE/THINKER	A flatterer is a friend who is your inferior, or pretends to be so.
1466 MAYA ANGELOU/USA/	Determine to live life with flair and laughter.
1467 CHRISTOPHER HITCHENS/ BRITISH AUTHOR	Owners of dogs will have noticed that, if you provide them with food and water and shelter and affection, they will think you are god. Whereas owners of cats are compelled to realize that, if you provide them with food and water and shelter and affection, they draw the conclusion that they are gods.
1468 BUCKMINSTER FULLER/ SCIENTIST/USA	You never change things by fighting the existing reality. To change something, build a new model that makes the existing model obsolete.
1469 PETS/ RELATIONSHIP	Sleeping in the same bed with pets
1470 NASA/SPACE/DREAMS	Space exploration
1471 TERENCE/AFRICAN SLAVE/ROME	*Homo sum, humani nihil a me alienum puto.* I am a human being; nothing human can be alien to me.
1472 FRIENDS	Childhood friends
1473 ARISTOTLE/THINKER	Education is the best provision for the journey to old age.
1474 IDIOM/TRANSIENCE	Living out of a suitcase
1475 ANDREW YOUNG/ MAYOR/USA	It is a blessing to die for a cause, because you can easily die for nothing.
1476 FEAR/AIRPLANES	Aerophobia – Fear of flying
1477 MORALITY/ETHICS	Character counts
1478 BEN LUCIEN BURMAN/ USA/WAR/THIS I BELIEVE	I believe that kindness is the natural human instinct, not cruelty.
1479 CREATE A STORY	Embraced by a bear
1480 WOODY ALLEN/USA/ ACTOR/PRODUCER	I'm astounded by people who want to 'know' the universe when it's hard enough to find your way around Chinatown.
1481 BERTRAND RUSSELL/ UK/MATHEMATICIAN	Passive acceptance of the teacher's wisdom is easy to most boys and girls... Yet the habit of passive acceptance is a disastrous one in later life.
1482 FUN/SPORTS	Cheerleading
1483 USA/ELBERT GREEN HUBBARD/PUBLISHER	I do not read a book; I hold a conversation with the author.
1484 MAYA ANGELOU/USA/ POET/WRITER	Love liberates. It doesn't just hold -- that's ego. Love liberates.
1485 LARRRY McMURTRY/ USA/NOVELIST	The older the violin, the sweeter the music.
1486 ILLEGAL/WORK	Working under the table

NUMBER CATEGORY/CREDIT	TOPIC
1487 DIPLOMAT/NICCOLO MACHIAVELLI/ITALY	I am not interested in preserving the status quo; I want to overthrow it.
1488 PHYLICIA RASHAD/ AMERICAN ACTRESS	The stubbornness I had as a child has been transmitted into perseverance. I can let go but I don't give up. I don't beat myself up about negative things.
1489 STEPHEN LEACOCK/ CANADA/HUMORIST	Advertising may be described as the science of arresting human intelligence long enough to get money from it.
1490 THOMAS JEFFERSON/ USA/FOUNDING FATHER	We should never judge a president by his age, only by his works.
1491 GENEVIEVE B. EARLE/ USA/CITIZENSHIP	The fight for good government, while a winning one, is never permanently won. It must be waged afresh each day
1492 WILL ROGERS/USA/ COMEDIAN	An onion can make people cry, but there has never been a vegetable invented to make them laugh.
1493 LEO BUSCAGLIA/ AMERICAN WRITER	The hardest battle you are ever going to have to fight is the battle to be just you.
1494 US SCHOOL OF MUSIC/ ADVERTISING	They laughed when I sat down at the Piano...but when I started to play.
1495 IDIOM	Snake in the grass
1496 TERENCE/SLAVE/ ANCIENT ROME	You can take a chance with anyone who pays his bills.
1497 TERENCE McKENNA/ USA/LECTURER	Create your own roadshow.
1498 ANDREW YOUNG/USA/ MAYOR	On the soft bed of luxury many kingdoms have expired.
1499 DIPLOMAT/NICCOLO MACHIAVELLI/ITALY	If an injury has to be done to a man it should be so severe that his vengeance need not be feared.
1500 BETTE DAVIS/ACTRESS/ USA/HOLLYWOOD	In this business, until you're known as a monster you're not a star.
1501 GOVERNMENT	Bureaucracy
1502 HENRY GEORGE/USA/ ECONOMIST	Let no man imagine that he has no influence. Whoever he may be, and wherever he may be placed, the man who thinks becomes a light and a power.
1503 ALDO LEOPOLD/USA/ SCIENTIST/WRITER	Ethical behavior is doing the right thing when no one else is watching -- even when doing the wrong thing is legal.
1504 bell hooks/US/PROFESSOR	Life-transforming ideas have always come to me through books.
1505 ALTHEA GIBSON/USA/ TENNIS	In sports, you simply aren't considered a real champion until you have defended your title successfully. Winning it once can be a fluke: winning it twice proves you are the best.
1506 PUNCTUALITY	The unforgiving alarm clock
1507 SAYING	Life is a box of chocolates.
1508 ANDREW YOUNG/USA/ AMBASSADOR TO UN	Look at those they call unfortunate and at a closer view, you'll find many of them are unwise.
1509 THOMAS PAINE/USA/ POLITICAL THINKER	The church has set up...a religion of pomp and of revenue in pretended imitation of a person whose life was humility and poverty.
1510 CREATE A STORY	Visions of wealth

NUMBER CATEGORY/CREDIT	TOPIC
1511 TERENCE McKENNA/ USA/LECTURER	Nature loves courage. You make the commitment and nature will respond to that commitment by removing impossible obstacles. Dream the impossible dream and the world will not grind you under, it will lift you up.
1512 RELIGION/SIN	Hell fire
1513 WAPO/JESSICA VALENTI/ USA	American culture can't seem to accept the fact that some women don't want to be mothers.
1514 JACKIE JOYNER-KERSEE/USA/ATHLETE	Age is no barrier. It's a limitation you put on your mind.
1515 JOAN BAEZ/SINGER/ USA	I've never had a humble opinion. If you've got an opinion, why be humble about it?
1516 ROADSIDE WARNING	Beware of falling rocks
1517 JIM COLLINS/USA/ BUSINESS CONSULTANT	The good is the enemy of the great.
1518 TERENCE McKENNA/ USA/LECTURER	Television is by nature the dominator drug par excellence. Control of content, uniformity of content, repeatability of content make it inevitably a tool of coercion, brainwashing, and manipulation.
1519 IMAGE/BEAUTY	Cosmetic dentistry
1520 TERENCE McKENNA/ USA/LECTURER	Western civilization is a loaded gun pointed at the head of this planet.
1521 ANNA JAMESON/ BRITISH WRITER	In morals, what begins in fear usually ends in wickedness; in religion, what begins in fear usually ends in fanaticism. Fear, either as a principle or a motive, is the beginning of all evil.
1522 USA/JAMES FREEMAN CLARKE/CLERGYMAN	All the strength and force of man comes from his faith in things unseen. He who believes is strong; he who doubts is weak.
1523 PERSONAL EFFORT	DIY: Do It Yourself
1524 SIGHT/TECHNOLOGY	Contact lenses
1525 PROVERB	You can't judge a book by its cover.
1526 KOREAN PROVERB	Carve the peg only after studying the hole.
1527 HEALTH/VACCINATION	Anti-vaxxers (people opposed to vaccinations)
1528 RONALD REAGAN/USA/ PRESIDENT	I've heard that hard work never killed anyone, but I say why take the chance?
1529 LORD MOUNTBATTEN/ UK/STATESMAN	My father was afraid of his father, I was afraid of my father, and I don't see why my children shouldn't be afraid of me.
1530 PROVERB	The apple does not fall far from the tree.
1531 DON MARQUIS/USA/ PHILOSOPHER	An optimist is a man who has never had much experience.
1532 TERENCE McKENNA/ USA/LECTURER	You are an explorer, and you represent our species, and the greatest good you can do is to bring back a new idea, because our world is endangered by the absence of good ideas. Our world is in crisis because of the absence of consciousness.
1533 MARRIAGE VOW	In sickness and in health
1534 MORALITY/SOCIETY	Leading a double life
1535 IDIOM	Control freak

NUMBER CATEGORY/CREDIT	TOPIC
1536 JULES VERNE/FRANCE/ WRITER	It is a great misfortune to be alone, my friends: and it must be believed that solitude can quickly destroy reason.
1537 MORALIST/MARQUIS DE VAUVENARGUES/FR.	In order to achieve great things, we must live as though we were never going to die.
1538 HARRY CREWS/USA/ NOVELIST	There is something beautiful about all scars of whatever nature. A scar means the hurt is over, the wound is closed and healed, done with.
1539 USA/ELBERT HUBBARD/ POLITICIAN	This will never be a civilized country until we expend more money for books than we do for chewing gum.
1540 JACOB BRONOWSKI/ UK/MATHEMATICS	The world can only be grasped by action, not by contemplation. The hand is more important than the eye...The hand is the cutting edge.
1541 USA/JAMES FREEMAN CLARKE/CLERGY	Strong convictions precede great actions.
1542 F. SCOTT FITZGERALD/ USA/WRITER	Whenever you feel like criticizing anyone...just remember that all the people in the world haven't had the advantages you've had.
1543 UK/CHRISTOPHER HITCHENS	Everybody does have a book in them, but in most cases that's where it should stay.
1544 HENRY BECQUES/ FRENCH DRAMATIST	The defect of equality is that we only desire it with our superiors.
1545 DANGER	Icebergs
1546 SIR RICHARD FRANCIS BURTON/UK/EXPLORER	The more I study religions the more I am convinced that man never worshipped anything but himself.
1547 EUGENE IONESCO/ PLAYWRIGHT/FRENCH	No society has been able to abolish human sadness; no political system can deliver us from the pain of living from our fear of death, our thirst for the absolute.
1548 VIN SCULLY/USA/ BASEBALL ANNOUNCER	Good is not good when better is expected.
1549 JOHN ED PEARCE/USA/ WRITER	Home is a place you grow up wanting to leave, and grow old wanting to get back to.
1550 RICHARD FEYNMAN/US/ PHYSICIST/NOBELIST	Scientific knowledge is an enabling power to do either good or bad -- but it does not carry instructions on how to use it.
1551 BILL WATTERSON/US/ AUTHOR	It's always better to leave the party early.
1552 ALBERT EINSTEIN/ NOBELIST/PHYSICIST	Unthinking respect for authority is the greatest enemy of truth.
1553 GERRY SPENCE/USA/ LAWYER	I would rather have a mind opened by wonder than one closed by belief.
1554 PROVERB	You can't judge a book by its cover.
1555 ABRAHAM JOSHUA HESCHEL/USA/JEWISH	The problem to be faced is: how to combine loyalty to one's own tradition with reverence for different traditions.
1556 ZIG ZIGLAR/USA	People don't care how much you know until they know how much you care.
1557 LARRY McMURTRY/USA/ WRITER	If you wait, all that happens is that you get older.
1558 IDIOM	Keeping an ear to the ground
1559 ANIMALS/FEAR	Snakes

NUMBER CATEGORY/CREDIT	TOPIC
1560 ALBERT EINSTEIN	Life is like riding a bicycle. To keep your balance, you must keep moving.
1561 PANDORA'S BOX/ TROUBLE/MERRIAM-WEBSTER.COM	Pandora's box: from the box, sent by the gods to Pandora, which she was forbidden to open and which loosed a swarm of evils upon humankind when she opened it out of curiosity
1562 TERENCE McKENNA/ USA/LECTURER	We have been to the moon, we have charted the depths of the ocean and the heart of the atom, but we have a fear of looking inward to ourselves because we sense that is where all the contradictions flow together.
1563 USA/ELBERT GREEN HUBBARD/BUSINESS	He who does not understand your silence will probably not understand your words.
1564 CONTRIBUTION	Making a difference
1565 DEBATE	That companies that pay bribes abroad should be prosecuted in their own countries for corruption.
1566 JANE AUSTEN/ ENGLISH AUTHOR	It is always incomprehensible to a man that a woman should refuse an offer of marriage.
1567 USA/ELBERT GREEN HUBBARD/WRITER	It is easy to get everything you want, provided you first learn to do without the things you cannot get.
1568 TERENCE McKENNA/ USA/LECTURER	Nature is not our enemy, to be raped and conquered. Nature is ourselves, to be cherished and explored.
1569 ZIG ZIGLAR/USA/ MOTIVATION/COACH	No one can go back and start a new beginning, but anyone can start today and make a new ending.
1570 FREEMAN DYSON/UK	It is better to be wrong than to be vague.
1571 BUSINESS/SOCIETY	Copycats
1572 MARVIN GAYE/USA/ SINGER	To be an artist is a blessing and a privilege. Artists must never betray their true hearts. Artists must look beneath the surface and show that there is more to this world than meets the eye.
1573 TERENCE McKENNA/USA	Only psychos and shamans create their own reality.
1574 MARTIN BUBER/ PHILOSOPHER	The real struggle is not between East and West, or capitalism and communism, but between education and propaganda.
1575 MENTAL HEALTH	Animal hoarders
1576 ALDO LEOPOLD/USA/ SCIENTIST/WRITER	When we see land as a community to which we belong, we may begin to use it with love and respect.
1577 USA/THIS I BELIEVE/ LEONARD BERNSTEIN	I believe in people...One human figure on the slope of a mountain can make the whole mountain disappear for me.
1578 CLASS MATTERS/NY TIMES/DAVID LEVINE	There is no reason to doubt the old saw that the most important decision you make is choosing your parents.
1579 EDMUND BURKE/IRISH/ STATESMAN	He that wrestles with us strenghens our nerves, and sharpens our skill. Our antagonist is our helper.
1580 ALDO LEOPOLD/USA/ BIOLOGIST/AUTHOR	We abuse land because we regard it as a commodity belonging to us. When we see land as a community to which we belong, we may begin to use it with love and respect.
1581 VOLTAIRE/FRENCH/ PHILOSOPHER	Let the punishments of criminals be useful. A hanged man is good for nothing; a man condemned to public works still serves the country, and is a living lesson.
1582 PROVERB	Silence is golden.

NUMBER CATEGORY/CREDIT	TOPIC
1583 HARRY EMERSON FOSDICK/USA/PASTOR	He who knows no hardships will know no hardihood.
1584 USA/FIRST LADY/ ELEANOR ROOSEVELT	I don't know whether I believe in a future life. I believe that all that you go through here must have some value, therefore there must be some reason.
1585 LEO BABAUTA/USA/ WRITER/MINIMALISM	Stop waiting for the right person to come into your life. Be the right person to come to someone's life.
1586 LOUISA MAY ALCOTT/ USA/NOVELIST	Women have been called queens for a long time, but the kingdom given them isn't worth ruling.
1587 TERENCE McKENNA/USA	Ideology always paves the way toward atrocity.
1588 JANE AUSTEN/ ENGLISH NOVELIST	A lady's imagination is very rapid; it jumps from admiration to love, from love to matrimony in a moment.
1589 MEDIA/POWER	Influence of the media
1590 MIRIAM MAKEBA/ S. AFRICAN SINGER	Girls are the future mothers of our society, and it is important that we focus on their well-being.
1591 ALDO LEOPOLD/USA/ SCIENTIST/WRITER	To those devoid of imagination a blank place on the map is a useless waste; to others, the most valuable part.
1592 MARY HARRIS JONES/ USA/LABOR ORGANIZER	I abide where there is a fight against wrong.
1593 HENRY FORD/ AMERICAN BUSINESSMAN	Anyone who stops learning is old, whether at twenty or eighty. Any one who keeps learning stays young. The greatest thing in life is to keep your mind young.
1594 MORTIMER ADLER/ USA/AUTHOR	The purpose of learning is growth, and our minds, unlike our bodies, can continue growing as we continue to live.
1595 USA/UK/SIR JOHN TEMPLETON/BUSINESS	It is nice to be important, but it's more important to be nice.
1596 ROBERT FROST/USA/ POET	Two roads diverged in a yellow wood. and sorry I could not travel both... Two roads diverged in a wood, and I took the one less travelled by, And that has made all the difference.
1597 PHIL McGRAW/USA	Sometimes you've got to rise above your raising.
1598 TERENCE McKENNA/ USA/LECTURER	Nothing comes unannounced, but many can miss the announcement. So it's very important to actually listen to your own intuition rather than driving through it.
1599 WILLIAM SHAKESPEARE/ UK/DRAMATIST	There's no art to find the mind's construction in the face.
1600 VOLTAIRE/ FRENCH PHILOSOPHER	Fools have a habit of believing that everything written by a famous author is admirable.
1601 DEBATE	That young people should be subjected to night-time curfews as a way to reduce crime.
1602 ALDO LEOPOLD/USA/ SCIENTIST/ WRITER	Only the mountain has lived long enough to listen objectively to the howl of the wolf.
1603 FUN/LIFESTYLE	Golfing
1604 CIVIL RIGHTS/MARY McLEOD BETHUNE/USA	We live in a world which respects power above all things. Power, intelligently directed, can lead to more freedom. Unwisely directed, it can be a dreadful, destructive force.

NUMBER CATEGORY/CREDIT	TOPIC
1605 TERENCE McKENNA/ USA/LECTURER	It's pretty simple, the ethical life. It's just demanding.
1606 SAM WALTON/USA/ ENTREPRENEUR/ WALMART/FOUNDER	The key to success is to get out into the store and listen to what the associates have to say. It's terribly important for everyone to get involved. Our best ideas come from clerks and stock-boys.
1607 RONALD REAGAN/ 40TH PRESIDENT/USA	There are no great limits to growth because there are no limits of human intelligence, imagination, and wonder.
1608 T.D. JAKES/USA/PASTOR	A setback is a setup for a comeback.
1609 TERENCE McKENNA/ USA/LECTURER	The artist's task is to save the soul of mankind; and anything less is a dithering while Rome burns.
1610 JAMES JOYCE/IRISH/ WRITER	Absence, the highest form of presence
1611 FUN/REFRESHMENT	A memorable holiday
1612 TERENCE McKENNA/USA	There's only the integrity of doing and having done.
1613 OSCAR WILDE/IRISH WRITER/POET	I choose my friends for their good looks, my acquaintances for their good characters, and my enemies for their good intellects. A man cannot be too careful in the choice of his enemies.
1614 PROVERB	One man's meat is another's poison.
1615 UK/CHRIS HITCHENS/ WRITER	Human decency is not derived from religion. It precedes it.
1616 LEO TOLSTOY/WRITER/ RUSSIA	My principal sin is doubt. I doubt everything, and am in doubt most of the time.
1617 FYODOR DOSTOEVSKY/ RUSSIAN AUTHOR	If you want to be respected by others, the great thing is to respect yourself. Only by that, only by self respect will you compel others to respect you.
1618 USA/ELIZABETH CADY STANTON/WOMEN	To deny political equality is to rob the ostracized of all self-respect; of credit in the marketplace; of recompense in the world of work.
1619 CARL SAGAN/USA/ SCIENTIST	We live in a society absolutely dependent on science and technology, and yet we have cleverly arranged things so that almost no one understands science and technology. That's a clear prescription for disaster.
1620 OSCAR WILDE/IRISH WRITER	Keep love in your heart. A life without it is like a sunless garden when the flowers are dead.
1621 WASSILY KANDINSKY/ PAINTER/THEORIST	Every work of art is the child of its age and in many cases, the mother of our emotions.
1622 SHIGERU MIYAMOTO/ VIDEO GAME DESIGNER	Games are a trigger for adults to again become primitive; primal, as a way of thinking and remembering. An adult is a child who has more ethics and morals; that's all.
1623 PAUL DIRAC/UK/ THEORETICAL PHYSICIST	If you are receptive and humble, mathematics willl lead you by the hand.
1624 CHUCK JONES/USA/ ANIMATOR	A comedian is not a person who opens a funny door -- he's a person who opens a door funny.
1625 VOLTAIRE/FRENCH/ PHILOSOPHER	Life is bristling with thorns, and I know no other remedy than to cultivate one's garden.
1626 HENRY LOUIS GATES/ PROFESSOR/USA	People are afraid, and when people are afraid, when their pie is shrinking, they look for somebody to hate. They look for somebody to blame. And a real leader speaks to anxiety and fear and allays those fears.

NUMBER CATEGORY/CREDIT	TOPIC
1627 TERENCE McKENNA/ USA/LECTURER	Alcohol is used by millions of people...how can we explain the legal toleration for alcohol, the most destructive of all intoxicants, and the almost frenzied efforts to repress nearly all other drugs?
1628 HOME/DECORATION	Coffee table books
1629 W. EDWARDS DEMING/ CONSULTANT/USA	The average American worker has fifty interruptions a day, of which seventy percent have nothing to do with work.
1630 ANTON CHEKHOV/ RUSSIAN/AUTHOR	Doctors are the same as lawyers; the only difference is that lawyers merely rob you, whereas doctors rob you and kill you too.
1631 GEORGE CLOONEY/USA/ ACTOR/ACTIVIST	In film, being a director is a dictatorship.
1632 FLORYNCE KENNEDY/US	Don't agonize, organize.
1633 JACQUELINE KENNEDY ONASSIS/US FIRST LADY	If you bungle raising your children, I don't think whatever else you do well matters very much.
1634 BERNARD M. BARUCH/ USA/BUSINESSMAN	Be who you are and say what you feel, because those who mind don't matter and those who matter don't mind.
1635 JACQUELINE KENNEDY ONASSIS/US FIRST LADY	The first time you marry for love, the second for money, and the third for companionship.
1636 SENECA/DRAMATIST	The most onerous slavery is to be a slave to oneself.
1637 MARTIN LUTHER KING JR./USA/PREACHER/ CIVIL RIGHTS ACTIVIST	Everybody can be great...because anybody can serve. You don't have to have a college degree to serve. You don't have to make your subject and verb agree to serve. You only need a heart full of grace.
1638 SAUL BELLOW/USA/ AUTHOR	I discovered that rejections are not altogether a bad thing. They teach a writer to rely on his own judgment and to say in his heart of hearts, 'To hell with you.'
1639 ABD AL-LATIF/LEGAL AND MEDICAL SCHOLAR	You should frequently distrust your nature, rather than have a good opinion of it, submitting your thoughts to men of learning and their works, proceeding with caution and avoiding haste.
1640 NEIL ARMSTRONG/ USA/ASTRONAUT	I believe that every human has a finite number of heartbeats. I don't intend to waste any of mine.
1641 TERENCE McKENNA/ USA/LECTURER	The bigger you build the bonfire, the more darkness is revealed.
1642 G.K. CHESTERTON/UK	If there were no God, there would be no atheists.
1643 BRAM STOKER/ AUTHOR/ DRACULA	No man knows till he has suffered from the night how sweet and dear to his heart and eye the morning can be.
1644 PEGGY NOONAN/USA	Part of courage is simple consistency.
1645 WILLIAM HAZLITT/UK/ WRITER	Danger is a good teacher, and makes apt scholars. So are disgrace, defeat, exposure to immediate scorn, and laughter.
1646 T.D. JAKES/USA/ PASTOR	Silence isn't golden and it surely doesn't mean consent, so start practicing the art of communication.
1647 ABD AL-LATIF/LEGAL & MEDICAL SCHOLAR	He who has not endured the stress of study will not taste the joy of knowledge.
1648 DEDICATION	Nobel prize winners
1649 PROVERB	Appearances are deceptive.
1650 T.D. JAKES/USA/ PASTOR	The art of avoiding extremes is an art that is drawn on the canvas of maturity and painted with the abstract strokes of many experiences.

NUMBER CATEGORY/CREDIT	TOPIC
1651 RICK WARREN/USA/ EVANGELICAL PASTOR	It is a myth that being beautiful will make you happy.
1652 NOAH WEBSTER/USA/ WRITER/ LEXICOGRAPHER	A pure democracy is generally a bad government. It is often the most tyrannical government on earth; for a multitude is often rash, and will not hear reason.
1653 ARNOLD H. GLASOW/USA	Nothing lasts forever -- not even your troubles.
1654 AUTHOR/CHRISTOPHER HITCHENS/ UK	Take the risk of thinking for yourself, much more happiness, truth, beauty, and wisdom will come to you that way.
1655 ST. FRANCIS OF ASSISI/ CATHOLIC FRIAR	While you are proclaiming peace with your lips, be careful to have it even more fully in your heart.
1656 JAPAN/FISH/POISON	Fugu
1657 BUSINESS	Qualities of a good boss
1658 FLORYNCE KENNEDY/US	If men could get pregnant, abortion would be a sacrament.
1659 CULTURE/BEAUTY	The Japanese garden
1660 TERENCE McKENNA/USA	The problem is not to find the answer, it's to face the answer.
1661 ADVENTURE	Mountain climbing
1662 USA/JAMES WELDON JOHNSON/AUTHOR	Every race and every nation should be judged by the best it has been able to produce, not by the worst.
1663 LOWELL THOMAS/USA	Do a little more each day than you think you possibly can.
1664 MAYA ANGELOU/USA/ WRITER	Love recognizes no barriers. It jumps hurdles, leaps fences, penetrates walls to arrive at its destination full of hope.
1665 DIETRICH BONHOFFER/ GERMANY/PASTOR	The test of the morality of a society is what it does for its children.
1666 EDGAR EVERS/USA	Freedom has never been free.
1667 RICK WARREN/USA/ EVANGELICAL PASTOR	We are all intentionally flawed to make us unique.
1668 NOAH WEBSTER/USA/ WRITER	The reasonableness of the command to obey parents is clear to children, even when quite young.
1669 APHORISM/GOD/FAITH	There are no atheists in foxholes.
1670 LORD MOUNTBATTEN/ BRITISH STATESMAN	My mother said, 'Don't worry about what people think now. Think about whether your children and grandchildren will think you've done well.'
1671 ARNOLD H. GLASOW/ USA/HUMORIST	A true friend never gets in your way unless you happen to be going down.
1672 SAMUEL JOHNSON/ UK/AUTHOR	Such seems to be the disposition of man, that whatever makes a distinction produces rivalry.
1673 ARNOLD H. GLASOW/ USA/HUMORIST	Parents can tell but never teach, unless they practice what they preach.
1674 ALBERT EINSTEIN	All religions, arts and sciences, are branches of the same tree.
1675 ALBERT HOURANI/ AUTHOR/ARAB PEOPLE	Memories grow dim, stories are changed in the telling, and not all who record them are truthful.
1676 JAPAN/HARD LIFE	*Kuroubanashi*: stories that detail the difficulties one has faced and the hard work one has done in life.
1677 JAMES JOYCE/WRITER	Shut your eyes and see.

NUMBER CATEGORY/CREDIT	TOPIC
1678 ARNOLD H. GLASOW/ USA/HUMORIST	A key to everything is patience. You get the chicken by hatching the egg, not by smashing it.
1679 PARENTING	Bringing up children
1680 HILLARY CLINTON/USA	Every moment wasted looking back, keeps us from moving forward.
1681 E.M FORSTER/NOVELIST	Death destroys a man, but the idea of death saves him.
1682 MARIE CURIE/FRENCH/ PHYSICIST/CHEMIST	You cannot hope to build a better world without improving the individuals. To that end, each of us must work for his improvement, and at the same time share a general responsibility for all humanity.
1683 BRIAN TRACY/USA/ SUCCESS COACH	One of the very worst uses of time is to do something very well that need not be done at all.
1684 MOTHER JONES/USA/ LABOR ACTIVIST	I asked a man in prison once how he happened to be there and he said he had stolen a pair of shoes. I told him if he had stolen a railroad he would have been a United States senator.
1685 BARACK OBAMA/44TH PRESIDENT/USA	Change will not come if we wait for some other person, or if we wait for some other time. We are the ones we've been waiting for.
1686 ARNOLD H. GLASOW/ USA/HUMORIST	The trouble with the future is that it usually arrives before we're ready for it.
1687 JOHN GRISHAM/USA/ WRITER	Most criminal defendants do not get adequate representation because there are not enough public defenders to represent them. There is a lot that is wrong.
1688 AGE/YOUTH	Women of a certain age
1689 THOMAS BEECHAM/ ENGLISH COMPOSER	There are two golden rules for an orchestra: start together and finish together. The public doesn't give a damn what goes on in between.
1690 USA/BERNARD M. BARUCH/BUSINESS	If all you have is a hammer, everything looks like a nail.
1691 CONFUCIUS/CHINA	He who will not economize will have to agonize.
1692 ALCUIN/ENGLISH THEOLOGIAN	Vox populi/vox dei : The voice of the people is the voice of God.
1693 USA/JAMES BRYANT CONANT/UNIV PRES.	Education is what is left after all that has been learnt is forgotten.
1694 ARNOLD H. GLASOW/ USA/HUMORIST	Success isn't the result of spontaneous combustion. You have to set yourself on fire.
1695 USA/HARRY TRUMAN/ 33RD PRESIDENT/THIS I BELIEVE	In my opinion, a man in public life must think always of the public welfare. He must be careful not to mix his private and personal interests with his public actions.
1696 BILL GATES/USA/ ENTREPRENEUR	I studied everything but never topped...But today the toppers of the best universities are my employees.
1697 PERSONAL TRAIT	Dependability
1698 PERSONAL TRAIT	Frankness
1699 RELATIONSHIP/FOOD	Breakfast in bed
1700 JUDGMENT	Knowing when to step out of a situation and when to step in.
1701 USA/HARRIET BEECHER STOWE/AUTHOR	The bitterest tears shed over graves are for words left unsaid and deeds left undone.
1702 RELATIONSHIPS	A dinner date

NUMBER CATEGORY/CREDIT	TOPIC
1703 BILL GATES/USA/ ENTREPRENEUR	I really had a lot of dreams when I was a kid, and I think a great deal of that grew out of the fact that I had a chance to read a lot.
1704 ABD AL-LATIF/LEGAL & MEDICAL SCHOLAR	...know that learning leaves a trail and a scent proclaiming its possessor; a ray of light and brightness shining on him, pointing him out.
1705 ALBERT HOURANI/ARAB	...coins are symbols of power and identity.
1706 HELEN KELLER/USA	I would rather walk with a friend in the dark, than alone in the light.
1707 NIELS BOHR/SCIENTIST/ NOBELIST/DENMARK	An expert is a person who has found out by his own painful experience all the mistakes that one can make in a very narrow field.
1708 ALBERT EINSTEIN	Intellectual growth should commence at birth and cease only at death.
1709 GEORGE ANTHEIL/ USA/THIS I BELIEVE	Laughter breaks evil spells, changes luck. Laughter is on the side of God.
1710 LOVE/MARRIAGE	The wedding anniversary band
1711 SKILL	Versatility
1712 DEATH/RITUALS	Funeral homes
1713 USA/HELEN KELLER/ AUTHOR/ACTIVIST	When one door of happiness closes, another opens; but often we look so long at the closed door that we do not see the one which has been opened for us.
1714 SINCLAIR LEWIS/USA/ WRITER/NOBEL PRIZE	It isn't what you earn but how you spend it that fixes your class.
1715 PIANIST/LUDWIG VAN BEETHOVEN/GERMAN	Beethoven can write music, thank God – but he can do nothing else on earth.
1716 WILLIAM OSLER/CANADA	The value of experience is not in seeing much, but in seeing wisely.
1717 CELEBRITY	Movie stars
1718 SOCIETY	Rumors
1719 SCHOOL	Cheating on exams
1720 J. R. R. TOLKIEN/ AUTHOR	All we have to decide is what to do with the time that is given to us.
1721 FRANCIS BACON/UK/ PHILOSOPHER	Age appears to be best in four things; old wood best to burn, old wine to drink, old friend to trust, and old authors to read.
1722 JAMES BALDWIN/USA	Be careful what you set your heart upon – for it will surely be yours.
1723 HILLARY CLINTON/ USA/POLITICIAN	I so strongly believe that the great religions of the world are stronger than any insult. They have withstood offense for centuries.
1724 SOCIETY	Living with a disability
1725 BARACK OBAMA/44TH PRESIDENT/USA	No family should have to set aside a college acceptance letter because they don't have the money.
1726 ROBERT F KENNEDY/ USA/POLITICIAN	Few are willing to brave the disapproval of their fellows, the censure of their colleagues, the wrath of their society.
1727 USA/ELBERT GREEN HUBBARD/PUBLISHER	Do not take life too seriously. You will never get out of it alive.
1728 SINCLAIR LEWIS/USA/ WRITER/NOBEL PRIZE	We'd get sick on too many cookies, but ever so much sicker on no cookies at all.
1729 WILLIAM JAMES/USA	A chain is no stronger than its weakest link.
1730 OPPRESSION	Divide and rule

NUMBER CATEGORY/CREDIT	TOPIC
1731 ARNOLD H. GLASOW/USA	Praise does wonders for our sense of hearing.
1732 SAYING	The biggest room is the room for improvement
1733 STEVE HARVEY/USA/ COMEDIAN	Real men do what they have to do to make sure their people are taken care of, clothed, housed, and reasonably satisfied, and if they're doing anything less than that, they're not men.
1734 WILLA CATHER/USA/ AUTHOR	Artistic growth is, more than anything else, a refining of the sense of truthfulness. The stupid believe that to be truthful is easy; only the artist, the great artist, knows how difficult it is.
1735 MARIO PUZO/FRANCIS FORD COPPOLA/THE GODFATHER	I don't trust society to protect us. I have no intention of placing my fate in the hands of men whose only qualification is that they managed to con a block of people to vote for them.
1736 UK/POET/WILLIAM WORDSWORTH	Poetry is the spontaneous overflow of powerful feelings; it takes its origin from emotion recollected in tranquility.
1737 ABIGAIL VAN BUREN/ ADVICE/USA	If you want children to keep their feet on the ground, put some responsibility on their shoulders.
1738 ITALY/NOBEL/RITA LEVI-MONTALCINI/SCIENTIST	Above all, don't fear difficult moments. The best comes from them.
1739 DAVE BRUBECK/USA/ COMPOSER/PIANIST	I'm beginning to understand myself. But it would have been great to be able to understand myself when I was 20 rather than when I was 82.
1740 PHIL McGRAW/USA	Kids learn what they live.
1741 THEODORE HESBURGH/ THEOLOGIAN/USA	It is easier to exemplify values than to teach them.
1742 ERLE STANLEY GARDNER USA/LAWYER/AUTHOR	I like what I like and not what I'm supposed to like because of mass rating.
1743 SIDNEY HOOK/USA/ PHILOSPHER	Everyone who remembers their own educational experience remembers teachers, not methods and techniques.
1744 PIANIST/BEETHOVEN	A great poet is the most precious jewel of a nation.
1745 STEPHEN AMBROSE/ USA/HISTORIAN	There are many more want-to-be writers out there than good editors.
1746 WRITER/SCOT/ROBERT LOUIS STEVENSON	Life is not a matter of holding good cards, but of playing a poor hand well.
1747 GRACE HOPPER/USA/ NAVY/PROGRAMMER	Humans are allergic to change. They love to say, 'We've always done it this way.' I try to fight that. That's why I have a clock on my wall that runs counterclockwise.
1748 FRENCH/MARGUERITE YOURCENAR/WRITER	There is more than one kind of wisdom, and all are essential in the world; it is not bad that they should alternate.
1749 NAPOLEON HILL/ AMERICAN AUTHOR	No accurate thinker will judge another person by that which the other person's enemies say about him.
1750 ARNOLD H. GLASOW/USA	Improvement begins with I.
1751 CITY LIFE	Noise pollution
1752 KAHLIL GIBRAN/ LEBANESE POET/ ON GOOD AND EVIL	You are good when you are one with yourself. Yet when you are not one with yourself you are not evil. For a divided house is not a den of thieves; it is only a divided house.
1753 G.K. CHESTERTON/ UK/WRITER	How you think when you lose determines how long it will be until you win.

NUMBER CATEGORY/CREDIT	TOPIC
1754 KATHY ACKER/USA/ NOVELIST	Every book, remember, is dead until a reader activates it by reading. Every time that you read you are walking among the dead, and, if you are listening, you just might hear prophecies.
1755 GEORGE ANTHEIL/USA/ THIS I BELIEVE	I believe in music…It consoles me in my hours of consternation and gives me added flight in my hours of luck.
1756 TECHNOLOGY	3D printing : for houses, body parts, products
1757 SINCLAIR LEWIS/USA/ NOBEL PRIZE/WRITER	Most troubles are unnecessary. We have Nature beaten; we can make her grow wheat; we can keep warm when she sends blizzards. So we raise the devil just for pleasure -- wars, race-hatreds, labor-disputes.
1758 DISPUTES	Caught in the crossfire
1759 ALBERT HOURANI/ARAB/ HISTORY	…in the early centuries, Judaism, Christianity, and Islam remained more open to each other than they were later to be.
1760 RONALD REAGAN/ 40TH PRESIDENT/USA	The best minds are not in government. If any were, business would hire them away.
1761 MARTIN BUBER/ PHILOSOPHER	The world is not comprehensible, but it is embraceable; through the embracing of one of its beings.
1762 PLEASURE	Life in the fast lane
1763 BILL GATES/USA/ ENTREPRENEUR	Before you were born, your parents weren't as boring as they are now. They got that way from paying your bills, cleaning your clothes and listening to you talk about how cool you thought you were.
1764 FLOWERS/JAPAN	*Ikebana* : the Japanese art of flower arranging that emphasizes form and balance
1765 NANCY L. ETCOFF/ USA/AUTHOR	Appearance is the most public part of the self. It is our sacrament, the visible self that the world assumes to be a mirror of the invisible, inner self.
1766 GEORGE ORWELL/UK/ WRITER	People sleep peaceably in their beds at night only because rough men stand ready to do violence on their behalf.
1767 USA/MADELEINE ALBRIGHT/LEADER	There is a special place in hell for women who don't help other women.
1768 HOBBY	People watching
1769 TIFFANY DUFU/CEO/ USA/WOMEN	…if little girls don't see women in public leadership, they won't always aspire to it.
1770 MIND/UNCERTAINTY	False memories
1771 SAUL BELLOW/USA/ WRITER	Everybody needs his memories. They keep the wolf of insignificance from the door.
1772 PARENTING	Overprotective parents
1773 JEAN COCTEAU/ FRENCH POET	An artist cannot speak about his art anymore than a plant can discuss horticulture.
1774 SCOTT ADAMS/BUSINESS	Luck finds the doers.
1775 SAYING	Practice makes perfect.
1776 CLAUDIA ALEXANDER/ PLANETARY SCIENTIST	I also strongly believe that science is no longer a vocation where an individual sits in a darkened lab with his instruments, tinkering away at some big question. Science is collaboration and will become even more so.
1777 NANCY L. ETCOFF/USA	Beauty ensnares hearts, captures minds, and stirs up emotional wildfires.
1778 JOHN ADAMS/US PRES.	Fear is the foundation of most governments.

NUMBER CATEGORY/CREDIT	TOPIC
1779 RELIGION/ MARRIAGE	Living together
1780 ABD AL-LATIF/LEGAL/ MEDICAL SCHOLAR	I commend you not to learn your sciences from books unaided, even though you may trust your ability to understand. Resort to professors for each science you seek to acquire; and should your professor be limited in his knowledge take all that he can offer, until you find another more accomplished than he.
1781 WILLIAM B. YEATS/POET	Education is not the filling of a pail, but the lighting of a fire.
1782 FRENCH/JULES VERNE/AUTHOR	He who is mistaken in an action which he sincerely believes to be right may be an enemy, but retains our esteem.
1783 BARACK OBAMA/ 44TH PRESIDENT/USA	Your voice can change the world.
1784 IMITATION/CHILDREN	Monkey see, monkey do.
1785 G.K. CHESTERTON/UK	Music with dinner is an insult both to the cook and the violinist.
1786 AGATHA CHRISTIE/UK/ WRITER	I don't think necessity is the mother of invention; invention, in my opinion, arises directly from idleness, possibly also from laziness. To save oneself trouble.
1787 HANDWRITING ANALYSIS/CRIME/	Graphology: the study of handwriting especially for the purpose of character analysis
1788 T. BOONE PICKENS/ USA/BUSINESSMAN	Far too many executives have become more concerned with the "four P's" - pay, perks, power and prestige – rather than making profits for shareholders.
1789 IDIOM	The handwriting on the wall
1790 BRIDE KIDNAPPING/ TRADITION/MARRIAGE/ WIKIPEDIA	Bride kidnapping, also known as marriage by abduction or marriage by capture, is a practice throughout history and around the world in which a man abducts the woman he wishes to marry.
1791 CHARLES ABRAMS/ NY/USA/THIS I BELIEVE	I'm not pretentious enough to believe that of the many hundreds of religions now functioning in the world, mine is the only true and authentic one.
1792 CARLOS RUIZ ZAFON/ SPANISH NOVELIST	Envy is the religion of the mediocre.
1793 ENGLISH PROVERB	Young men think old men fools; old men know young men to be so.
1794 RONALD REAGAN/ 40TH PRESIDENT/USA	Politics is not a bad profession. If you succeed there are many rewards, if you disgrace yourself you can always write a book.
1795 BROMANCE/MEN/ MERRIAMWEBSTER	Bromance: A close nonsexual friendship between men (blend of bro and romance)
1796 KLEENEX/SLOGAN	Our softness is our strength.
1797 PIANIST/BEETHOVEN	Love demands all, and has a right to all.
1798 NEIL ARMSTRONG/USA	Pilots take no special joy in walking: pilots like flying.
1799 HELEN KELLER/USA	The best and most beautiful things in the world cannot be seen or even touched. They must be felt with the heart.
1800 ELBERT G. HUBBARD/US	Art is not a thing; it is a way.
1801 HELEN KELLER/USA	One can never consent to creep when one feels an impulse to soar.
1802 CULTURE/PRIDE	My country's gift to the world
1803 GOALS/LIFE PATHS	The road that leads to nowhere.

NUMBER CATEGORY/CREDIT	TOPIC
1804 HILLARY CLINTON/ USA/POLITICIAN	Women have always been the primary victims of war. Women lose their husbands, their fathers, their sons in combat.
1805 J.F. KENNEDY/USA/ PRESIDENT	World peace, like community peace, does not require that each man love his neighbor -- it requires only that they live together in mutual tolerance, submitting their disputes to a just and peaceful settlement.
1806 WILL ROGERS/USA/ COMEDIAN	Advertising: The art of convincing people to buy things they do not need with money that they do not have.
1807 SALMAN RUSHDIE/UK	Fear is not susceptible to reason.
1808 JUNE JORDAN/POET/ CARIBBEAN-AMERICAN	As a child I was taught that to tell the truth was often painful. As an adult, I have learned that not to tell the truth is more painful.
1809 MICHEL DE MONTAIGNE FRENCH WRITER	Nothing is so firmly believed as what we least know.
1810 HELEN KELLER/ USA	Life is either a daring adventure or nothing at all.
1811 BOOKER WASHINGTON/ USA/EDUCATOR	In all my teaching I have watched carefully the influence of the toothbrush, and I am convinced that there are few single agencies of civilization that are more far-reaching.
1812 JON STEWART/USA/ COMEDIAN	Insomnia is my greatest inspiration.
1813 TONY DUNGY/USA FOOTBAL COACH	Things will go wrong at times…your options are to complain or to look ahead and figure out how to make the situation better.
1814 WILLIAM FAULKNER/ AMERICAN NOVELIST	Most men are a little better than their circumstances give them a chance to be.
1815 BILL GATES/USA/ BILLIONAIRE	Most people overestimate what they can do in one year and underestimate what they can do in ten years.
1816 BARACK OBAMA/44TH PRESIDENT/USA	No one is pro-abortion.
1817 EDWARD GIBBON/UK/ HISTORIAN	…gratitude is expensive.
1818 BENJAMIN DISRAELI/UK	To be conscious that you are ignorant is a great step to knowledge.
1819 FUN/FRIENDS/HOBBY	Bowling
1820 PERSONAL/PRIDE	Bragging rights
1821 NAPOLEON HILL/ AMERICAN AUTHOR	Edison failed 10,000 times before he made the electric light. Do not be discouraged if you fail a few times.
1822 USA/ELBERT GREEN HUBBARD/PUBLISHER	God will not look you over for medals, degrees or diplomas but for scars.
1823 BARACK OBAMA/44TH PRESIDENT/USA	Focusing your life solely on making a buck shows a poverty of ambition. It asks too little of yourself. And it will leave you unfulfilled.
1824 USA/THEODORE ROOSEVELT/PRESIDENT	In a moment of decision, the best thing you can do is the right thing. The worst thing is to do nothing.
1825 ERIKA ANDERSEN/USA/ BLOGGER/FORBES	I've been noticing that the people for whom I have the most respect don't hesitate to say "I was wrong" or "I'm sorry."
1826 DONNA LANGLEY/ USA/MOVIE PRODUCER	I am the only one in my family who is adopted. It always makes me feel really special. I felt like I was chosen.
1827 PERSONAL	My idea of ecstasy

NUMBER CATEGORY/CREDIT	TOPIC
1828 IGOR STRAVINSKY/ RUSSIA/COMPOSER	Just as appetite comes by eating so work brings inspiration.
1829 STEPHEN COVEY/USA/ AUTHOR	Treat a man as he is and he will remain as he is. Treat a man as he can and should be and he will become as he can and should be.
1830 RABINDRANATH TAGORE/INDIAN POET	Clouds come floating into my life, no longer to carry rain or usher storm, but to add color to my sunset sky.
1831 CULTURE	Culture shock
1832 NEIL ARMSTRONG/USA	Your library is a storehouse for mind and spirit. Use it well.
1833 NATURE/USA	The Grand Canyon
1834 TONY DUNGY/USA	I need to treat everybody fairly, but fair doesn't always mean equal.
1835 CITIES	City living
1836 BARACK OBAMA/ 44TH PRESIDENT/USA	It's only when you hitch your wagon to something larger than yourself that you realize your true potential.
1837 ANAIS NIN/USA/ AUTHOR	There are many ways to be free. One of them is to transcend reality by imagination, as I try to do.
1838 DR. DEAN FISHMAN/USA	Text neck – health issues arising from the use of smart phones
1839 NORMAN COUSINS/ EDITOR/USA/THIS I BELIEVE	As far back as the Socratic dialogues in Plato, and even before that, man has been baffled about himself. He knows he is capable of great and noble deeds, but then he is oppressed by the evidence of great wrongdoing.
1840 ROBERT KENNEDY/USA	Only those who dare greatly can ever achieve greatly.
1841 AUSTRALIA	The Australian outback
1842 UMBERTO ECO/ITALY/ PHILOSOPHER/WRITER	Not long ago, if you wanted to seize political power in a country you had merely to control the army and the police...Today a country belongs to the person who controls communication.
1843 NAOMI WOLF/ AMERICAN WRITER	A Mother who radiates self-love and self-acceptance actually vaccinates her daughter against low self-esteem.
1844 FASHION	Body piercing
1845 PROVERB/J.A. AULLS/ SPARKS AND CINDERS	He who fights and runs away, may live to fight another day.
1846 DISTRESS CALL	(S.O.S.) Save our souls
1847 MAGAZINES	My favorite magazine
1848 CHILDREN/SPIRIT	The heart of a child
1849 MODERN LIFE	Electricity
1850 JAMES BALDWIN/USA/ AUTHOR	Fires can't be made with dead embers, nor can enthusiasm be stirred by spiritless men.
1851 ZSA ZSA GABOR/USA	Husbands are like fires: They go out when unattended.
1852 SAMUEL JOHNSON/UK/ WRITER	Courage is a quality so necessary for maintaining virtue that it is always respected, even when it is associated with vice.
1853 CHALLENGE/RISK	Swimming with the sharks
1854 GEORGE CARLIN/USA/ COMEDIAN	People who see life as anything more than pure entertainment are missing the point.
1855 DR. ABDUL P. J. KALAM/ INDIA/SCIENTIST	All birds find shelter during a rain, but Eagle avoids rain by flying above the clouds.

NUMBER CATEGORY/CREDIT	TOPIC
1856 SIR THOMAS MORE/ UK/PHILOSOPHER/ LAWYER/WRITER/ UTOPIA	For if you suffer your people to be ill-educated, and their manners to be corrupted from their infancy, and then punish them for those crimes to which their first education disposed them, what else is to be concluded from this, but that you first make thieves and then punish them.
1857 ELIZABETH GURLEY BROWN /USA/EDITOR	You can have your titular recognition. I'll take money and power.
1858 MAKE UP A STORY	A letter that was never mailed
1859 NAPOLEON HILL/USA/ AUTHOR	Patience, persistence and perspiration make an unbeatable combination for success.
1860 RALPH LAUREN/USA/ DESIGNER	I've always believed one could live many lives through the way we dress and the places we travel to, even if just in our imagination. The world is open to us, and each day is an occasion to reinvent ourselves.
1861 FRANZ KAFKA/WRITER/ GERMAN	Better to have, and not need, than to need, and not have.
1862 PAT BENATAR/SINGER/ USA	Love is a battlefield.
1863 DIVERSITY/SOCIETY	Melting pot
1864 MICHAEL KRASNY/ USA/RADIO TALK SHOW HOST/AUTHOR	For the present the universe – its origins and its destiny – is unknowable, as is whether there are many universes…These are some of the fundamental reasons why I call myself an agnostic.
1865 RONALD REAGAN/ 40TH PRESIDENT/USA	People don't start wars, governments do.
1866 PARENTING/WORK	Babysitting
1867 PROVERB	Every man has his price.
1868 FREEMAN DYSON/UK-BORN/USA/PHYSICICST	We must be careful not to discourage our twelve-year olds by making them waste the best years of their lives preparing for examinations.
1869 PERSONAL	My biggest weakness
1870 FRAUD/BUSINESS	Predatory lending
1871 G.K. CHESTERTON/ UK/WRITER	The world will never starve for want of wonders, but for want of wonder.
1872 NAOMI WOLF/USA/ WRITER	Pain is real when you get other people to believe in it. If no one believes in it but you, your pain is madness or hysteria.
1873 DONALD RUMSFELD/USA	Don't blame the boss. He has enough problems.
1874 FRANCE/NAPOLEON/ POLITICAL LEADER	The greatest danger occurs at the moment of victory.
1875 HENRY FORD/USA/ BUSINESSMAN	We have most unfortunately found it necessary to get rid of a man as soon as he thinks himself an expert because no one ever considers himself expert if he really knows his job.
1876 JULES VERNE/ FRENCH WRITER	We are of opinion that instead of letting books grow moldy behind an iron grating, far from the vulgar gaze, it is better to let them wear out by being read.
1877 AGE/SPIRIT/FUN	Young at heart
1878 PROVERB	Faith can move mountains.
1879 GOSSIP	Heard through the grapevine

NUMBER CATEGORY/CREDIT	TOPIC
1880 MAURICE SENDAK/USA	It's a blessing to get old.
1881 STEVE JOBS/ APPLE/ ENTREPRRENEUR	The people who are crazy enough to think they can change the world are the ones who do.
1882 DAVID ATTENBOROUGH/ UK/NATURALIST	Human beings are good at many things, but thinking about our species as a whole is not one of our strong points.
1883 LOWELL THOMAS/ USA/PUBLIC SPEAKING	The man who can speak acceptably is usually given credit for an ability out of all proportion to what he really possesses.
1884 RESPONSIBILITY	Not in my backyard (NIMBY)
1885 RABINDRANATH TAGORE/INDIAN POET	Age considers; youth ventures.
1886 PROVERB	A man who is his own lawyer has a fool for a client.
1887 SAMUEL RICHARD-SON/UK/NOVELIST	A husband's mother and his wife had generally better be visitors than inmates.
1888 NAOMI WOLF/ AMERICAN WRITER	A cultural fixation on female thinness is not an obsession about female beauty but an obsession about female obedience.
1889 JACQUES BARZUN/ USA/WRITER	Schools are not intended to moralize a wicked world, but to impart knowledge and develop intelligence...
1890 ERNEST HEMINGWAY/ USA/NOVELIST	The world breaks everyone, and afterward, some are strong at the broken places.
1891 JUSTICE	Courtroom drama
1892 JAMES MADISON/ 4TH PRESIDENT/USA	Democracy is the right of the people to choose their own tyrant.
1893 ROBERT FULGHUM/USA	Speed and efficiency do not always increase the quality of life.
1894 ELBERT GREEN HUBBARD/USA	So long as governments set the example of killing their enemies, private individuals will occasionally kill theirs.
1895 ELDERLY/YOUNG	The generation gap
1896 SIR FRANCIS BACON/UK	A wise man will make more opportunities than he finds.
1897 HEAVEN/USA/GOSPEL	Everybody talking about heaven ain't going there.
1898 ELEANOR ROOSEVELT/ USA/ACTIVIST/1ST LADY	I think, at a child's birth, if a mother could ask a fairy godmother to endow it with the most useful gift, that gift would be curiosity.
1899 GILDA RADNER/USA/ COMEDIAN/ACTRESS	I think dogs are the most amazing creatures; they give unconditional love. For me, they are the role model for being alive.
1900 TRUST/SALES	Used-car warranties
1901 EXPERIENCE	Living with a memory
1902 REID HOFFMAN/ ENTREPRENEUR	In real estate the wisdom says 'location, location, location.' In consumer Internet, think 'distribution, distribution, distribution.
1903 DIPLOMATS/FRIENDS	Diplomatic cocktail circuit
1904 HEALTH/HEALING	Shock therapy
1905 LARRY SUMMERS/USA/ ECONOMIST/PROFESSOR	We have thousands of schools across the country where paint is chipping off the walls even as we tell our children that education is the most important thing.
1906 BEN LUCIEN BURMAN/ USA/THIS I BELIEVE	In our madly commercialized and mechanized world, we have lost our sense of the beautiful.

NUMBER CATEGORY/CREDIT	TOPIC
1907 PERSONAL	What I've learned in life to date
1908 DEREK WALCOTT/POET/ NOBEL PRIZE/WRITER	Good science and good art are always about a condition of awe…I don't think there is any other function for the poet or the scientist in the human tribe but the astonishment of the soul.
1909 PERSONAL	Your pet peeves
1910 PERSONAL	What leadership means to me
1911 JOHN H. JOHNSON/USA/ FOUNDER/EBONY	I'm convinced that the only way to get ahead in this world is to live and sell dangerously. You've got to live beyond your means. You've got to commit yourself to an act or vision that pulls you further than you want to go and forces you to use your hidden strengths.
1912 WHO IS?/OPINION	Ready, willing, and able
1913 PETER DRUCKER/ USA/BUSINESS GURU	Achievement depends less on the ability in doing research than on the courage to go after the opportunity.
1914 HEALTH/HOME/ OFFICE/ WIKIPEDIA	Sick building syndrome (SBS) is a combination of ailments (a syndrome) associated with an individuals place of work (office building) or residence.
1915 ROBERT KENNEDY/ SENATOR/USA	Few people will have the greatness to bend history, but each of us can work to change a small portion of events.
1916 PRAISE	Fishing for compliments
1917 USA/ELBERT GREEN HUBBARD/WRITER	Young women with ambitions should be very crafty and cautious, lest mayhap they be caught in the soft, silken mesh of a happy marriage, and go down to oblivion, dead to the world.
1918 T. BOONE PICKENS/USA	On a scale from 1-10, my ambition is probably 11 or 12.
1919 TED KENNEDY/US/ CONGRESSMAN	I hope for an America where no president, no public official, no individual will ever be deemed a greater or lesser American because of religious doubt – or religious belief.
1920 T. BOONE PICKENS/ USA/BUSINESSMAN	To me, emails are a little bit frustrating. I think that the telephone is much preferred because you get the sound of the voice and the interest and everything else you can't see in an email.
1921 NAOMI WOLF/ AMERICAN WRITER	What becomes of a man who acquires a beautiful woman, with her "beauty" his sole target? He sabotages himself. He has gained no friend, no ally, no mutual trust.
1922 PROVERB	Forewarned is forearmed.
1923 T. BOONE PICKENS/ USA/BUSINESSMAN	If someone I don't like gets in the crosshairs, I pull the trigger. But I don't hunt for them.
1924 USA/ELBERT GREEN/ HUBBARD/WRITER	A friend is someone who knows all about you and still loves you.
1925 JOHN GRISHAM/USA/ WRITER	One thing you really have to watch as a writer is getting on a soapbox or pulpit about anything. You don't want to alienate readers.
1926 PETER DRUCKER/USA	The best way to predict the future is to create it.
1927 PROF/JOHN KENNETH GALBRAITH/USA	We all agree that pessimism is a mark of a superior intellect.
1928 FRANZ KAFKA/GERMAN/ NOVELIST	Paths are made by walking.
1929 DALE CARNEGIE/USA/ LECTURER/AUTHOR	The way to develop self-confidence is to do the thing you fear to do and get a record of successful experiences behind you.

NUMBER CATEGORY/CREDIT	TOPIC
1930 PHYSICAL CHALLENGES	The hard of hearing
1931 DIPLOMAT/NICCOLO MACHIAVELLI/ITALY	The end justifies the means.
1932 HELEN KELLER/USA/ AUTHOR/LECTURER	We could never learn to be brave and patient if there were only joy in the world.
1933 NERVOUSNESS	Butterflies in the stomach
1934 POLICE	Undercover informants
1935 RUDYARD KIPLING/UK	A woman's guess is much more accurate than a man's certainty.
1936 BARACK OBAMA/ 44TH PRESIDENT/USA	Where you are right now doesn't have to determine where you'll end up.
1937 STEPHEN COVEY/USA / WRITER	I teach people how to treat me by what I will allow.
1938 CHARITY/HAND UP	Helping without hurting
1939 MACCHIAVELI/ITALY	Never was anything great achieved without danger.
1940 JAMES JOYCE/IRISH/ WRITER	Life is too short to read a bad book.
1941 SPORTS	Baseball
1942 ENTOMOLOGY	Insects
1943 BARACK OBAMA/ 44TH PRESIDENT/USA	A nation that can't control its energy sources can't control its future.
1944 STEVE JOBS/APPLE/USA	Real artists ship.
1945 HELEN KELLER/ USA/AUTHOR	A bend in the road is not the end of the road…Unless you fail to make the turn.
1946 WILIAM PETER BLATTY/ USA/AUTHOR	How many husbands and wives must believe they have fallen out of love because their hearts no longer race at the sight of their beloveds!
1947 HYPOCRISY	Do as I say, not as I do.
1948 SOCIETY/CRIME	Juvenile delinquents
1949 SIR THOMAS MORE/ UK/PHILOSOPHER	One man to live in pleasure and wealth, while all others weep and smart for it, that is the part not of a king, but of a jailer.
1950 RUSSELL H. CONWELL/ USA/PHILANTHROPIST	You can journey to the ends of the earth in search of success, but if you're lucky, you will discover happiness in your own backyard.
1951 BARACK OBAMA/44TH PRESIDENT/USA	The best way to not feel hopeless is to get up and do something. Don't wait for good things to happen to you.
1952 DR. ALFRED ADLER/ AUSTRIA/PSYCHIATRIST	The only worthwhile achievements of man are those which are socially useful.
1953 MAURICE SENDAK/ USA/AUTHOR	You can't get rid of evil. We can't, and I feel that so intensely. All the idiots that keep coming into the world and wrecking people's lives.
1954 MICHAEL BLOOMBERG/ USA/MAYOR/NY	I've never let planning get in the way of doing.
1955 FRANZ KAFKA/WRITER/ GERMAN LANGUAGE	Most men are not wicked…They are sleep-walkers, not evildoers.
1956 MAURICE SENDAK/ USA/WRITER	Children are tough, though we tend to think of them as fragile. They have to be tough. Childhood is not easy.

NUMBER CATEGORY/CREDIT	TOPIC
1957 SOURCE UNKNOWN	It is not wrong because it is illegal. It is illegal because it is wrong.
1958 JAMES BALDWIN/ AMERICAN AUTHOR	Hatred, which could destroy so much, never failed to destroy the man who hated, and this was an immutable law.
1959 SCOT/ROBERT LOUIS STEVENSON/WRITER	The best things are nearest: breath in your nostrils, light in your eyes, flowers at your feet, duties at your hand, the path of God just before you.
1960 PAUL ALLEN/USA/ BUSINESS	For the most part, the best opportunities now lie where your competitors have yet to establish themselves, not where they're already entrenched.
1961 STEVE WOZNIAK/USA	Artists work best alone. Work alone.
1962 DIPLOMAT/NICCOLO MACHIAVELLI/ITALY	Everyone sees what you appear to be, few experience what you really are.
1963 HAROLD S. HULBERT/ USA/EDITOR/PHYSICIAN	Children need love, especially when they don't deserve it.
1964 MENCIUS/THINKER	A real man is he whose goodness is a part of himself.
1965 BORIS BECKER/TENNIS	Tennis is a psychological sport; you have to keep a clear head. That is why I stopped playing.
1966 DECEIT/MISLEADING OTHERS/CAUTION/ WIKIPEDIA	Judas goat: A Judas goat is a trained goat used at a slaughterhouse and in general animal herding. The Judas goat is trained to associate with sheep or cattle, leading them to a specific destination.
1967 IMAGE	First impressions count.
1968 JAMES JOYCE/IRISH/ WRITER	People could put up with being bitten by a wolf but what properly riled them was a bite from a sheep.
1969 EDWARD GIBBON/UK/ HISTORIAN/POLITICIAN	Where the error is irreparable, repentance is useless.
1970 BILL GATES/USA/ ENTREPRENEUR	Our success has really been based on partnerships from the very beginning.
1971 BILL GATES/USA/ ENTREPRENEUR	Don't compare yourself with anyone in this world…if you do so, you are insulting yourself.
1972 LEADER/NAPOLEON BONAPARTE/FRENCH	Money has no fatherland,; financiers are without patriotism and without decency. Their sole object is gain.
1973 EMILY BRONTE/UK/ WRITER	Treachery and violence are spears pointed at both ends.
1974 USA/ELBERT GREEN HUBBARD/WRITER	If you cannot answer a man's argument, all is not lost; you can still call him vile names.
1975 USA/ELBERT GREEN HUBBARD/WRITER	Our admiration is so given to dead martyrs that we have little time for living heroes.
1976 GANESH DAS/ WHAT YOGA IS AND ISN'T/NY TIMES	When yoga is practiced with the right intention, it diminishes our self-centeredness, allowing us to become more aware of our responsibility towards the larger community.
1977 TONY DANZA/USA/ ACTOR	Make the most of a bad situation.
1978 SHERYL GAY STOLBERG/ REPORTER/NY TIMES	Famous people are no better than anybody else.
1979 ANSEL ADAMS/USA/ PHOTOGRAPHER	To the complaint, 'There are no people in these photographs,' I respond, 'There are always two people: the photographer and the viewer.'

NUMBER CATEGORY/CREDIT	TOPIC
1980 PROVERB	Let sleeping dogs lie.
1981 ANNE FRANK/JEWISH AUTHOR/ HOLOCAUST	Everyone has inside of him a piece of good news. The good news is that you don't know how great you can be! How much you can love! What you can accomplish! And what your potential is!
1982 USA/RABBI HAROLD KUSHNER/AUTHOR	I think of life as a good book. The further you get into it, the more it begins to make sense.
1983 VISA CARD/SLOGAN	It's everywhere you want to be.
1984 DEBATE	That voting in elections should be compulsory
1985 NY TIMES/SHERYL GAY STOLBERG/REPORTER	Newspaper reporters are notoriously nosy; they want to know everything that is going on around them.
1986 QUEEN ELIZABETH II/ UK	Diversity is a strength, not a threat.
1987 UK/PM/WINSTON CHURCHILL	Battles are won by slaughter and maneuver. The greater the general, the more he contributes in maneuver, the less he demands in slaughter.
1988 SARA BLAKELY/USA/ BUSINESS/SPANX	The smartest thing I ever did was to hire my weakness.
1989 HOWARD THURMAN/ USA/WRITER/CIVIL RIGHTS LEADER	Don't ask yourself what the world needs. Ask yourself what makes you come alive and then go do that. Becaause what the world needs is people who have come alive.
1990 MENTAL HEALTH/ PARIS/ JAPANESE TOURISTS/ WIKIPEDIA	Paris syndrome (French: *Syndrome de Paris,* Japanese:パリ症候群, *Pari shōkōgun*) is a transient psychological disorder encountered by some individuals visiting or vacationing in Paris, France.
1991 DONALD RUMSFELD/ USA/POLITICS/ LEADER	Those who made the decisions with imperfect knowledge will be judged in hindsight by those with considerably more information at their disposal and time for reflection.
1992 LEOPOLD STOKOWSKY/ CONDUCTOR/USA	A painter paints his pictures on canvas. But musicians paint their pictures on silence.
1993 J.R.R. TOLKIEN/ AUTHOR/UK	It's a dangerous business going out your front door.
1994 MICHELLE OBAMA/ US/FIRST LADY	You can't make decisions based on fear and the possibility of what might happen.
1995 DREW GILPIN FAUST/ HARVARD PRESIDENT	Look to the past to help create the future. Look to science and to poetry. Combine innovation and interpretation. We need the best of both. And it is universities that best provide them.
1996 COMMUNICATION	Gestures
1997 RELATIONSHIPS	Gift giving in your country
1998 HOTELS/TRAVEL	Dealing with porters/bellhops
1999 GEORGE BERNARD SHAW/PLAYWRIGHT	Both optimists and pessimists contribute to our society. The optimist invents the airplane and the pessimist the parachute.
2000 USA/MICHELLE WILLIAMS/SINGER	Depression is not okay, but it is okay to get help.
2001 KENJI MIYAZAWA/ JAPANESE POET	We must embrace pain and burn it as fuel for our journey.
2002 MENTAL HEALTH/ SPIRITUALITY	Jerusalem syndrome: A phenomenon in which tourists to Jerusalem become psychotic, sometimes claiming to be Jesus.

NUMBER CATEGORY/CREDIT	TOPIC
2003 LAURA HILLENBRAND/ USA/WRITER	The paradox of vengefulness is that it makes men dependent upon those who have harmed them, believing that their release from pain will come only when their tormentors suffer.
2004 AUDREY HEPBURN/USA/ ACTOR	I am proud to have been in a business that gives pleasure, creates beauty, and awakens our conscience, arouses compassion, and perhaps most importantly, gives millions a respite from our so violent world.
2005 SWAMI VIVEKANANDA/ INDIAN YOGI	All the powers in the universe are already ours. It is we who have put our hand before our eyes and cry that it is dark.
2006 TIM O'BRIEN/USA/ WRITER/WAR	A thing may happen and be a total lie; another thing may not happen and be truer than the truth.
2007 BOB WOODWARD/USA/ REPORTER/ON OBAMA	Finally the president added, 'The American people are idealists, but they also want their leaders to be realistic.'
2008 ITALY/WRITER/ NICCOLO MACHIAVELLI	It is safer to be feared than loved...
2009 PAUL ROBESON/USA	Artists are the gatekeepers of truth.
2010 STANISLAVSKI/USA	In the language of an actor, to know is synonymous with to feel.
2011 USA/FREDERICK DOUGLASS/ACTIVIST	I prefer to be true to myself, even at the hazard of incurring the ridicule of others, rather than to be false and to incur my own abhorrence.
2012 MATT DAMON/ACTOR/US CHARLIE ROSE SHOW	Judge me for how good my good ideas are, not how bad my bad ideas are.
2013 LENA DUNHAM/WRITER/ TV PRODUCER/ACTOR	Love the possible, but imagine the impossible.
2014 WHITNEY YOUNG/ USA/ACTIVIST	The hardest work in the world is being out of work.
2015 ERNEST HEMINGWAY/ USA/WRITER	There's nothing noble in being superior to your fellow men. True nobility is being superior to your former self.
2016 GOALS/ INDECISION	Going away to find oneself
2017 THOMAS CARLYLE/ SCOTTISH AUTHOR	Blessed is he who has found his work; let him ask no other blessedness.
2018 ANNIE DILLARD/ AMERICAN WRITER	The dedicated life is the life worth living. You must give with your whole heart.
2019 HENRY FORD/USA/ BUSINESSMAN	Coming together is the beginning. Keeping together is progress. Working together is success.
2020 HELEN KELLER/USA/ AUTHOR	College isn't the place to go for ideas.
2021 ITALY/WRITER/NICCOLO MACHIAVELLI	There is no other way to guard yourself against flattery than by making men understand that telling you the truth will not offend you.
2022 USA/RABBI HAROLD KUSHNER/AUTHOR/ TIME MAGAZINE Q & A	Given the unfairness that strikes so many people in life, I would rather believe in a God of limited power and unlimited love and justice, rather than the other way round.
2023 IDIOM	Flash in a pan
2024 USA/HENRY DAVID THOREAU/WRITER	I am grateful for what I am and have. My thanksgiving is perpetual. It is surprising how contented one can be with nothing definite -- only a sense of existence.

NUMBER CATEGORY/CREDIT	TOPIC
2025 MARVIN MINSKY/USA/ SCIENTIST	Every system that we build will surprise us with new kinds of flaws until those machines become clever enough to conceal their faults from us.
2026 ABRAHAM LINCOLN/ 16th PRESIDENT/USA	It is an old and true maxim that a drop of honey catches more flies than a gallon of gall.
2027 SAMUEL BUTLER/UK/ WRITER	Life is like playing a violin solo in public and learning the instrument as one goes.
2028 AUGUSTO BOAL/BRAZIL/ THEATRE/OPPRESSED	I believe in democracy, but in real democracy, not a phony democracy in which just powerful people can speak. For me, in a democracy, everyone speaks.
2029 SALMAN RUSHDIE/UK	A book is more important than a life.
2030 IDIOM	Going rogue
2031 ARABIC PROVERB	A sense of humor is the pole that adds a balance to our steps as we walk the tightrope of life.
2032 JAMAICA KINCAID/ USA/WRITER/LUCY	Why is a picture of something real eventually more exciting than the thing itself.
2033 NANCY ASTOR/UK MP WOMEN'S RIGHTS	Real education should educate us out of self into something far finer; into a selflessness which links us with all humanity.
2034 USA/HEMINGWAY	The best way to find out if you can trust somebody is to trust them.
2035 MARIE VON EBNER- ESCHENBACH/AUSTRIA/ NOVELIST	Be patient with the belligerence of the simple-minded. It is not easy to understand that one doesn't understand.
2036 ROBERT J. RINGER/ USA/WRITER	Reality isn't the way you wish things to be, nor the way they appear to be, but the way they actually are.
2037 INDIA/SRI SRI RAVI SHANKAR/PEACE	Difference between motivation and inspiration: Motivation is external and short lived. Inspiration is internal and lifelong.
2038 JAMES FRANCO/USA/ ACTOR/WRITER	Everyone pretends to be normal and be your best friend, but underneath, everyone is living some other life you don't know about…
2039 DAME JENNY SHIPLEY/ 36TH P.M./N. ZEALAND	I can't for the life of me see that by being permissive you actually assist anyone.
2040 DIPLOMAT/NICCOLO MACCHIAVELLI/ITALY	All courses of action are risky, so prudence is not in avoiding danger (it's impossible), but calculating risk and acting decisively.
2041 ELBERT G. HUBBARD/ USA/WRITER	Many a man's reputation would not know his character if they met on the street.
2042 USA/HAROLD KUSHNER	Nature is blind.
2043 SENECA/DRAMATIST	Speech is the mirror of the mind.
2044 ANNE FRANK/JEWISH AUTHOR/ HOLOCAUST	Why do some people have to starve, while there are surpluses rotting in other parts of the woRld? Oh, why are people so crazy?
2045 JAMAICA KINCAID/ ANTIGUA/US/NOVELIST	The inevitable is no less a shock just because it is inevitable.
2046 TIM O'BRIEN/US WRITER	A true war story is never moral.
2047 JACQUES BARZUN/ USA/WRITER	In teaching you cannot see the fruit of a day's work. It is invisible and remains so, maybe for twenty years.
2048 MAKE UP A STORY/ EXPERIENCE	The big scare

NUMBER CATEGORY/CREDIT	TOPIC
2049 NATURE	The power of the sea
2050 SOCIETY	Open-mindedness
2051 LYING	A person with a forked tongue
2052 JULIA GILLARD/ AUSTRALIA/P.M.	My guiding principle is that prosperity can be shared. We can create wealth together. The global economy is not a zero sum game.
2053 FAMILY/SOCIETY	Child neglect
2054 JAPAN/GAMBLING	Pachinko (pinball gaming machine)
2055 MAURICE SENDAK/ USA/WRITER	...it is through fantasy that children achieve catharsis. It is the best means they have for taming wild things.
2056 COLIN ALLEN/THIS I BELIEVE/USA	I feel that I belong to all churches. And yet I feel that I belong to no one church.
2057 SIR THOMAS MORE/UK	What is deferred is not avoided.
2058 RICHARD HORTON/ EDITOR/LANCET	Much of the scientific literature, perhaps, half, may simply be untrue.
2059 PERSONAL/TRAITS	What you like about yourself
2060 ANN LANDERS/ USA/ADVICE COLUMNIST/CHICAGO SUN TIMES	Class is an aura of confidence that is being sure without being cocky. Class has nothing to do with money. Class never runs scared. It is self-discipline. And self-knowledge. It's the sure-footedness that comes with having proved you can meet life.
2061 USA/MARIO PUZO/ GODFATHER	The man with the briefcase can steal more money than the man with the gun.
2062 EMILE ZOLA/FRENCH	The artist is nothing without the gift, but the gift is nothing without work.
2063 BARACK OBAMA/USA/ PRESIDENT	What makes a man is not the ability to make a child but the courage to raise one.
2064 GRACE HOPPER/ CO-INVENTOR/COBOL	The most dangerous phrase in the language is, "We've always done it this way."
2065 CLASS MATTERS/NY TIMES/USA/2005	If you're certified and licensed, nobody can take that away from you.
2066 KAHLIL GIBRAN/ LEBANESE POET	I have learned silence from the talkative, toleration from the intolerant, and kindness from the unkind; yet, strange, I am ungrateful to those teachers.
2067 PETER JENNINGS/USA/ CANADA/JOURNALIST	I was raised with the notion that it was OK to ask questions, and that it was OK to say, I'm not sure.
2068 DEBATE/SOCIETY	Cell phones – blessing or curse?
2069 SIR THOMAS MORE/ UK/PHILOSOPHER	If the lion knew his own strength, hard were it for any man to rule him.
2070 USA/WRITER/ERNEST HEMINGWAY	Never think that war, no matter how necessary, nor how justified, is not a crime.
2071 MARY AUGUSTA WARD/ UK/NOVELIST	Truth has never been, can never be, contained in any one creed.
2072 USA/WILIAM PETER BLATTY/AUTHOR/ THE EXORCIST	Would you like to hear a nice definition of jealousy? It's the feeling that you get when someone you absolutely detest is having a wonderful time without you.

NUMBER CATEGORY/CREDIT	TOPIC
2073 COURT/LAW/ JUSTICE	Expert witness
2074 HENRY FORD/USA/ BUSINESSMAN	If money is your hope for independence, you will never have it. The only real security that a man can have in this world is a reserve of knowledge, experience and ability.
2075 PROSPERITY/PLACE	A land of milk and honey
2076 SIR THOMAS MORE/ UK/PHILOSOPHER	You wouldn't abandon ship in a storm just because you couldn't control the winds.
2077 STEVE WOZNIAK/ APPLE COMPUTERS/ CO-FOUNDER	Our first computers were born not out of greed or ego, but in the revolutionary spirit of helping common people rise above the most powerful institutions.
2078 ELBERT G. HUBBARD/ USA/PUBLISHER	The object of teaching a child is to enable him to get along without a teacher.
2079 LAWRENCE KRAUS/ THEORETICAL PHYSICIST	The universe doesn't care about our common sense.
2080 TIM O'BRIEN/USA/ WRITER	Stories are for eternity, when memory is erased, when there is nothing to remember except the story.
2081 DANIEL J. BOORSTIN/ LIBRARIAN/US WRITER	Trying to plan for the future without a sense of the past is like trying to plant cut flowers.
2082 RICHARD LOVELACE/ UK/POET	Stone walls do not a prison make, Nor iron bars a cage.
2083 CHARLES LAMB/UK	I always arrive late at the office, but I make up for it by leaving early.
2084 NICHOLAS KRISTOF/ NY TIMES	...jailing juveniles leads them to be more likely to commit crimes as adults.
2085 USA/RUTH DAVIS KONIGSBERG/TIME.COM	Catherine Steiner-Adair: Kids say, 'My parents are hypocrites. They say no phones at the dinner table ad then they take a call. '
2086 ROBERT J. RINGER/ USA/WRITER	People say they love truth, but in reality they want to believe that which they love is true.
2087 JASON CALACANIS/USA/ ENTREPRENEUR	People's reputations are made in the bad times more than the good times.
2088 SOCIETY/FAIRNESS	Affirmative action
2089 WILL/PRESSURE	My way or the highway
2090 LIFE/CHANCES	Everyone needs a second chance.
2091 HENRY WADSWORTH LONGFELLOW/USA	Every man has his secret sorrows which the world knows not; and often times we call a man cold when he is only sad.
2092 MICHELLE OBAMA/ US/FIRST LADY	Good relationships feel good. They feel right. They don't hurt. They're not painful.
2093 LOWELL THOMAS/USA	After the age of 80, everything reminds you of something else.
2094 HELEN KELLER/USA/ AUTHOR/LECTURER	No pessimist ever discovered the secrets of the stars or sailed an uncharted land, or opened a new doorway for the human spirit.
2095 ANNE FRANK/JAUTHOR	No one has ever become poor by giving.
2096 SAM. RICHARDSON/UK	A stander-by is often a better judge of the game than those that play.
2097 JOHN H. JOHNSON/ USA/FOUNDER/EBONY	Every day I run scared. That's the only way I can stay ahead.

NUMBER CATEGORY/CREDIT	TOPIC
2098 YO-YO MA/USA/ MUSICIAN	My passion is not really for music...my passion is actually for people.
2099 USA/MURIEL STRODE/ POET	Do not follow where the path may lead. Go instead where there is no path and leave a trail.
2100 BUSINESS	Accounting fraud
2101 JRR TOLKIEN/WRITER	All that is gold does not glitter; not all those that wander are lost.
2102 SPIRO T. AGNEW/USA	If you've seen one city slum you've seen them all.
2103 USA/KONSTANTIN STANISLAVSKY/ACTING COACH/RUSSIA	In the creative process, there is the father, the author of the play; the mother, the actor pregnant with the part; and the child, the role to be born.
2104 LL COOL J/RAPPER/ ACTOR/2013/USA	A Grammy isn't just a shiny trophy to hold on to. A Grammy is a dream come true.
2105 GEORGE ANTHEIL/USA/ MOZART COULD LAUGH/ THIS I BELIEVE	I was once asked what I would most deeply wish for my young son, could I bestow but one quality upon him. Without hesitation, I wrote back, "a sense of humor."
2106 POWER/ INFLUENCE	Movers and shakers
2107 AUSTRALIA	Australian Aborigines
2108 DANTE ALEGHIERI/ ITALIAN POET	The devil is not so black as he is painted.
2109 MIKE MYERS/FORBES/US	Make your goals known to those that can help you.
2110 ELVIS PRESELEY/USA	I never expected to be anybody important.
2111 GANESH DAS/NY TIMES	Yoga is just a fitness craze.
2112 USA/THEODORE HESBURGH/RELIGION	The very essence of leadership is that you have vision. You can't blow an uncertain trumpet.
2113 CHARLES LAMB/ ENGLISH ESSAYIST	'Tis the privilege of friendship to talk nonsense, and to have her nonsense respected.
2114 DEBATE/SCHOOL	That homework is hazardous to life.
2115 JOHN H. JOHNSON/ USA/FOUNDER/EBONY	When I see a barrier, I cry and I curse, and then I get a ladder and climb over it.
2116 TONY HSIEH/USA/ CEO/ZAPPOS.COM	Taking risks and making mistakes is how you grow, on both a business and personal level.
2117 JIM ROHN/USA/ BUSINESSMAN/WRITER	We must all suffer one of two things: the pain of discipline or the pain of regret.
2118 BARBARA BUSH/USA/ FIRST LADY	Cherish your human connections: your relationships with friends and family.
2119 LOUIS L'AMOUR/USA/ WRITER	No man ever raised a monument to a cynic or wrote a poem about a man without faith.
2120 MIA BIRDSONG/USA/ ACTIVIST/REFORMER	Everywhere I go, I see people who are broke but not broken.
2121 FRENCH/GEORGES CLEMENCEAU/P.M.	War is too serious a matter to entrust to military men.
2122 STEPHEN JAY GOULD/ AMERICAN SCIENTIST	Nothing is more dangerous than a dogmatic worldview – nothing more constraining, more blinding to innovation, more destructive of openness to novelty.

NUMBER CATEGORY/CREDIT	TOPIC
2123 WEALTH/IDIOM	Fat cats
2124 MARQUIS DE SADE/ FRENCH ARISTOCRAT	Destruction, hence like creation, is one of Nature's mandates.
2125 ELBERT G. HUBBARD/ USA/WRITER	Every man is a damn fool for at least five minutes a day. Wisdom consists of not exceeding the limit.
2126 ADAM JOHNSON/USA/ ORPHAN MASTER'S SON	All the lessons you need to learn in life...will be taught to you by your enemy.
2127 MICHELLE OBAMA/ US/FIRST LADY	The arts are not just a nice thing to have or to do if there is free time or if one can afford it. Rather, paintings and poetry, music and fashion, design and dialogue, they all define who we are as a people and provide an account of our history for the next generation.
2128 RICHARD NIXON/USA/ PRESIDENT	If you want to make beautiful music, you must play the black and white notes together.
2129 POWER/MONEY/ SOCIETY/MERRIAM-WEBSTER.COM	Oligarchy: a government in which a small group exercises control especially for corrupt and selfish purposes; *also* : a group exercising such control
2130 MURPHY'S LAW	If anything can go wrong, it will.
2131 EDWARD WARD/USA	Death and Taxes, they are certain.
2132 MAJ. GEN. SMEDLEY BUTLER/USA/MARINE	War is a racket. It is the only one international in scope. It is the only one in which the profits are reckoned in dollars and the losses in lives.
2133 SUMO IIJIMA/JAPAN/ PHYSICIST	Research can be undertaken in any environment as long as you have the interest. I believe that true education means fostering the ability to be interested in something.
2134 FRED WILSON/ ENTREPRENEUR	Entrepreneurs don't need degrees like lawyers and doctors do. They are credentialed by virtue of their track record.
2135 HENRY WADSWORTH LONGFELLOW/POET	For after all, the best thing one can do when it's raining is to let it rain.
2136 NAPOLEON HILL/USA/ AUTHOR	Desire is the starting point of all achievement, not a hope, not a wish, but a keen pulsating desire which transcends everything.
2137 STEPHEN JAY GOULD/ USA/SCIENTIST	I am, somehow, less interested in the weight and convolutions of Einstein's brain than in the near certainly that people of equal talent have lived and died in cotton fields and sweatshops.
2138 JESSICA VALENTI/WAPO	...love isn't shown by force or coercion. It's based on respect.
2139 OUSMANE SEMBENE/ SENEGAL/WRITER	However long it stays in the river the tree trunk will never turn into a crocodile.
2140 PUBLILIUS SYRUS/100 BC	You should not live one way in private, another in public.
2141 EDWIGE DANTICAT/USA	They say behind mountains are mountains.
2142 JOHN EDWARDS/USA/ POLITICIAN	There are two Americas – one for the powerful and the privileged and one for everybody else.
2143 DONNA TARTT/USA/ THE SECRET HISTORY	Beauty is terror. Whatever we call beautiful, we quiver before it.
2144 BUSINESS/ACADEMIA	Research and development
2145 DONNA TARTT/USA/ THE GOLDFINCH	Caring too much for objects can destroy you.

NUMBER CATEGORY/CREDIT	TOPIC
2146 CHARLES LAMB/ ENGLISH ESSAYIST	Don't introduce me to that man! I want to go on hating him, and I can't hate a man whom I know.
2147 ERICA JONG/USA	Solitude is un-American.
2148 KATHERINE BOO/USA	Never trust anyone who tells you how people come to trust him.
2149 ELBERT G. HUBBARD/ USA/WRITER	If there is any better way to teach virtue than by practicing it, I do not know it.
2150 REV. PETER J. GOMES/ USA/COMMENCE MENT ADDRESS	I invite you into the realm of reflection, especially when you don't get the job, you don't get the promotion, you don't get the guy or you don't get the girl.
2151 ELBERT G. HUBBARD/ USA/WRITER	Folks who never do any more than they get paid for, never get paid for any more than they do.
2152 COCO CHANEL/ FRENCH DESIGNER	Fashion is made to become unfashionable.
2153 ANONYMOUS	The average woman would rather have beauty than brains because the average man can see better than he can think.
2154 CHARLES LAMB/ ENGLISH ESSAYIST	The greatest pleasure I know is to do a good action by stealth, and to have it found out by accident.
2155 HELEN KELLER/USA	Life is a succession of lessons which must be lived to be understood.
2156 PROPERTY/FAMILY	Property rights
2157 SWAMI VIVEKANANA/ INDIAN YOGI	Condemn none; if you can stretch out a helping hand, do so. If you cannot, fold your hands, bless your brothers, and let them go their own way.
2158 MOTHER JONES/USA	No matter what the fight, don't be ladylike.
2159 JAMES DYSON/UK/ INVENTOR	There is no such thing as a quantum leap. There is only dogged persistence – and in the end you make it look like a quantum leap.
2160 OPPORTUNITY	Missing the boat
2161 LORD CHESTERFIELD/ UK/ADVICE	Be wiser than other people if you can; but do not tell them so.
2162 USA/NATHANIEL HAWTHORNE/WRITER	Happiness is like a butterfly which, when pursued, is always beyond our grasp, but, if you will sit down quietly, may alight upon you.
2163 HARRY TRUMAN/USA/ 33RD PRESIDENT/THIS I BELIEVE	The ethics of a public man must be unimpeachable. He must learn to reject unwise or imprudent requests from friends and associates without losing their friendship or loyalty.
2164 DR. CORNEL WEST/ PROFESSOR/WRITER/ PHILOSOPHER	You've got to be a thermostat rather than a thermometer. A thermostat shapes the climate of public opinion; a thermometer just reflects it.
2165 KATE CHOPIN/USA/ WRITER	There are some people who leave impressions not so lasting as the imprint of an oar upon the water.
2166 ARABIC PROVERB	A wise man associating with the vicious becomes an idiot; a dog traveling with good men becomes a rational being.
2167 UK/POET/WILLIAM WORDSWORTH	Pictures deface walls more often than they decorate them.
2168 USA/NATHANIEL HAWTHORNE/WRITER	Easy reading is damn hard writing.

NUMBER CATEGORY/CREDIT	TOPIC
2169 SWAMI VIVEKANANDA/ INDIAN YOGI	Take up one idea. Make that one idea your life – think of it, dream of it, live on that idea. Let the brain, muscles, nerves, every part of your body, be full of that idea, and just leave every other idea alone. This is the way to success.
2170 LOUIS L'AMOUR/ AMERICAN WRITER	Knowledge is like money: to be of value it must circulate, and in circulating it can increase in quantity and, hopefully, in value.
2171 DR. SAMUEL BEST/ BUSINESS/USA/THIS I BELIEVE/CANADA	If we are to be successful in every aspect of the word, if we are to live truly full lives, we must share ourselves, as well as our material gain, with our fellow men.
2172 SUCCESS	Virtuous circle
2173 SEXUALITY/PEOPLE	Sexual orientation
2174 LIEUTENANT COL. JOHN McCRAE/CANADA/WAR	We are the Dead. Short days ago / We lived, felt dawn, saw sunset glow, Loved and were loved, and now we lie in Flanders Fields.
2175 ABRAHAM LINCOLN/US/ 16TH PRESIDENT	As I would not be a slave, so I would not be a master.
2176 DEBATE/LAW	That working hours should be controlled by legislation.
2177 ANONYMOUS	Another advantage of being rich is that all your faults are called eccentricities.
2178 CHARLES LAMB/ ENGLISH ESSAYIST	Think of what you would have been now, if instead of being fed with tales and wives' fables in childhood, you had been crammed with geography and natural history!
2179 DAVID BRINKLEY/ USA/TV JOURNALIST	A successful person is one who can lay a firm foundation with the bricks others have thrown at him.
2180 JOEL OSTEEN/USA/ PREACHER	Keep in mind, just because you don't know the answer doesn't mean that one does not exist.
2181 MALTBIE BABCOCK/ USA/CLERGY	Business is religion, and religion is business. The man who does not make a business of his religion has a religious life of no force, and the man who does not make a religion of his business has a business life of no character.
2182 INSTRUCTIONS	Rules of the road
2183 SOPHOCLES/THINKER	If you try to cure evil with evil you will add more pain to your fate.
2184 SUSAN B. ANTHONY/ USA/SOCIAL REFORMER	People, always casting about to preserve their reputation and social standing, never can bring about a reform.
2185 COCO CHANEL/FRENCH	Elegance is refusal.
2186 ELBERT G. HUBBARD/ USA/ PUBLISHER	If your religion does not change you, then you had better change your religion.
2187 TIM O'BRIEN/USA/ WRITER/THE THINGS THEY CARRIED	...when a nation goes to war it must have reasonable confidence in the justice and imperative of its cause. You can't fix your mistakes. Once people are dead, you can't make them undead.
2188 PRESSURE	Hot seat
2189 ELIE WIESEL/USA	Which is worse? Killing with hate or killing without hate.
2190 USA/NATHANIEL HAWTHORNE/WRITER	To do nothing is the way to be nothing.
2191 COCO CHANEL/FRENCH	A fashion that does not reach the streets is not fashion.
2192 SOPHOCLES/THINKER	One must wait until the evening to see how splendid the day has been.

NUMBER CATEGORY/CREDIT	TOPIC
2193 HERACLITUS/ THINKER	No man ever steps in the same river twice, for it's not the same river and he's not the same man.
2194 DAVID OGILVY/AD INDUSTRY LEADER	I avoid clients for whom advertising is only a marginal factor in their marketing mix. They have an awkward tendency to raid their advertising appropriations whenever they need cash for other purposes.
2195 SAYING	Only in bad times do we know who our friends are.
2196 OVERSEAS/WORK	Expatriates
2197 BILL BOWERMAN/ NIKE/USA/BUSINESS	I wasn't thinking about markets or fortunes. I was making better shoes a foot at a time.
2198 PETER USTINOV/UK	The habit of religion is oppressive, an easy way out of thought.
2199 HERACLITUS/THINKER	The unlike is joined together, and from differences results the most beautiful harmony.
2200 ENGLISH PROVERB	You never know till you have tried.
2201 ERIC BURDON/UK/ SINGER/SONGWRITER	Don't sing the same song twice.
2202 ELIE WIESEL/USA/ NOVELIST	There is divine beauty in learning...To learn means to accept the postulate that life did not begin at my birth. Others have been here before me, and I walk in their footsteps.
2203 USA/STEVE JOBS/ CO-FOUNDER/APPLE COMPUTERS/ ENTREPRENEUR	I hate it when people call themselves 'entrepreneurs' when what they're really trying to do is launch a startup and then sell or go public, so they can cash in and move on. They're unwilling to do the work it takes to build a real company, which is the hardest work in business.
2204 ANNE BRONTE/UK/ WRITER	But he who dares not grasp the thorn should never crave the rose.
2205 ELIE WIESEL/USA	One person of integrity can make a difference.
2206 G.K. CHESTERTON/UK/ WRITER	One sees great things from the valley, only small things from the peak.
2207 ART BUCHWALD/USA/ HUMOR/COLUMNIST	The best things in life aren't things.
2208 JASON MRAZ/USA/ MUSICIAN	For me to create an album of 12 songs I got to write about 80 songs.
2209 ANTON CHEKHOV/ RUSSIAN WRITER	Love, friendship and respect do not unite people as much as a common hatred of something.
2210 JANE YOLEN/USA/ WRITER	Exercise the writing muscle every day, even if it is only a letter, notes, a title list, a character sketch, a journal entry. Writers are like dancers, like athletes. Without that exercise, the muscles seize up.
2211 HENRY FORD/USA/ BUSINESSMAN	Thinking is the hardest work there is, which is probably the reason so few engage in it.
2212 J.B. PRIESTLEY/UK	Be yourself is about the worst advice you can give some people.
2213 JAMES BALDWIN/ USA/AUTHOR	Enthusiasm in our daily work lightens effort and turns even labor into pleasant tasks.
2214 FYODOR DOSTOEVSKY	The darker the night, the brighter the stars.
2215 KATE CHOPIN/USA/ WRITER	The bird that would soar above the level plain of tradition and prejudice must have strong wings.

NUMBER CATEGORY/CREDIT	TOPIC
2216 PEARL S. BUCK/ NOVELIST/USA	Our society must make it right and possible for old people not to fear the young or be deserted by them, for the test of a civilization is the way that it cares for its helpless members.
2217 ENGLISH PROVERB	You cannot teach an old dog new tricks.
2218 GUSTAVE FLAUBERT/ FRENCH	Travel makes one modest. You see what a tiny place you occupy in the world.
2219 JAY HANNA DEAN/WAPO	It ain't braggin' if you can do it.
2220 MARQUIS DE SADE/FR.	It is always by way of pain one arrives at pleasure.
2221 BILL McDERMOTT/USA/ BUSINESS	I've always tried to prioritize my marriage, my children, my family above everything else because in the end, those are the things that will be here when everything else is long gone.
2222 USA/ANNE MORROW LINDBERGH/WRITER	A note of music gains significance from the silence on either side.
2223 AMBROSE BIERCE/ WRITER	Money, n. a blessing that is of no advantage to us excepting when we part with it.
2224 JAPAN	Narita *rikon* (Narita divorce) -- a very short marriage
2225 OTTO VON BISMARK/GM.	Politics is the art of the possible.
2226 ELBERT G. HUBBARD/US	All good men are anarchists.
2227 GEORGE ORWELL/UK/ WRITER	If liberty means anything at all, it means the right to tell people what they do not want to hear.
2228 CLARENCE THOMAS/US	Good manners will open doors that the best education cannot.
2229 SALMAN RUSHDIE/UK/ WRITER	A book is a version of the world. If you do not like it, ignore it; or offer your own version in return.
2230 EMPLOYMENT	Occupational hazards
2231 GOVERNMENT/USA	Separation of church and state
2232 GRATITUDE	Counting one's blessings
2233 VIKTOR FRANKL/ AUSTRIAN PSYCHIATRIST/ AUTHOR	Our generation is realistic, for we have come to know man as he really is. After all, man is that being who invented the gas chambers of Auschwitz, however, he is also that being who entered those gas chambers upright, with the Lord's prayer or the Shema Yisrael on his lips.
2234 ROGER EBERT/USA/FILM CRITIC	The problem with being sure that God is on your side is that you can't change your mind, because God sure isn't going to change His.
2235 ENGLISH PROVERB	You cannot shoe a running horse.
2236 SIR THOMAS MORE/ UK/PHILOSOPHER/ LAWYER/WRITER	[How can anyone] be silly enough to think himself better than other people, because his clothes are made of finer woolen thread than theirs. After all, those fine clothes were once worn by a sheep...
2237 ELBERT G. HUBBARD/ WRITER/ PUBLISHER	Do not dump your woes upon people – keep the sad story of your life to yourself. Troubles grow by recounting them.
2238 SOCIETY/PEOPLE	Albinism
2239 DEMOCRACY	One person, one vote
2240 ZORA NEALE HURSTON/ USA/ANTHROPOLOGIST	Bitterness is the coward's revenge on the world for having been hurt.
2241 FUN/MONEY	Best shopping experience

NUMBER CATEGORY/CREDIT	TOPIC
2242 HERACLITUS/GREEK/ PHILOSOPHER	The only thing that is constant is change.
2243 ARTHUR MILLER/ USA/WRITER	Just remember, kid, you can quicker get a back a million dollars that was stolen than a word that you gave away.
2244 SOPHOCLES/THINKER	The keenest sorrow is to recognize ourselves as the sole cause of all our adversities.
2245 CUISINE	French food
2246 EVERYDAY/MUNDANE	Doing laundry
2247 CESAR CHAVEZ/USA/ ACTIVIST	All my life, I have been driven by one dream, one goal, one vision: to overthrow a farm labor system in this nation that treats farmworkers as if they were not important human beings. Farmworkers are not agricultural implements; they are not beasts of burden to be used and discarded.
2248 MAHATMA GANDHI	Hate the sin, love the sinner.
2249 CLARENCE THOMAS/USA SUPREME COURT	It really bugs me that someone will tell me, after I spent 20 years being educated, how I'm supposed to think.
2250 IDIOM	Wearing your heart on your sleeve
2251 CARRIE CHAPMAN CATT/USA/WOMEN'S SUFFRAGE LEADER	This world taught woman nothing skillful and then said her work was valueless. It permitted her no opinions and said she did not know how to think. It forbade her to speak in public, and said the sex had no orators.
2252 SIGMUND FREUD/ AUSTRIA/PSYCHIATRIST	I could not point to any need in childhood as strong as that of a father's protection.
2253 LIFESTYLE	The need for speed
2254 ROBERT FULGHUM/USA	Play fair
2255 TOURISM/TRAVEL	Favorite sightseeing spots
2256 NICHOLAS KRISTOF/ NY TIMES	California devotes $179, 400 to keep a juvenile in detention for a year, and spends less than $20,000 per student in its schools.
2257 TIM O'BRIEN/USA	War makes you a man; war makes you dead.
2258 GLOBAL CUISINE	Japanese restaurants
2259 OTTO VON BISMARK	When you want to fool the world, tell the truth.
2260 SOCIETY	Fresh start
2261 IDIOM	It's in the bag.
2262 STEPHEN COVEY/USA	The main thing is to keep the main thing the main thing.
2263 S. I. HAYAKAWA/USA/ SENATOR	Cultural and intellectual cooperation is the great principle of human life.
2264 SOCIETY/LIFE	Fire fighters
2265 US/HENRY WADSWORTH LONGFELLOW/POET	Music is the universal language of mankind.
2266 CAPITALISM/SOCIETY	Exploitation
2267 GEORGE SAND/FRENCH/ NOVELIST	One is happy as a result of one's own efforts once one knows the necessary ingredients of happiness: simple tastes, a certain degree of courage, self denial to a point, love of work, and above all, a clear conscience.
2268 JACK LONDON/USA/ NOVELIST	Affluence means influence.

NUMBER CATEGORY/CREDIT	TOPIC
2269 ARTHUR MILLER/US/ PLAYWRIGHT	A small man can be just as exhausted as a great man.
2270 HEALTH/RELIGION	Near-death experience
2271 JULIE TAYMOR/USA/ THEATRE/DIRECTOR	Limitations force you to find the essence of what you want to say, which is one of the most important things to know for an artist.
2272 OTTO VON BISMARK	Never believe anything in politics until it has been officially denied.
2273 FASHION	Eye wear
2274 AUTOMOBILES	Parking problems
2275 JULIA CAMERON/USA/ ARTIST/AUTHOR	The creative process is a process of surrender, not control. Mystery is at the heart of creativity. That, and surprise.
2276 ENGLISH PROVERB	You cannot get blood out of a stone.
2277 PERSONAL	My greatest fear
2278 ANNE BRONTE/ ENGLISH NOVELIST	All our talents increase in the using, and every faculty, both good and bad, strengthens by exercise.
2279 PERFUME/ETIQUETTE	Perfume is to be discovered, never announced.
2280 JANE YOLEN/ AMERICAN WRITER	Literature is a textually transmitted disease, normally contracted in childhood.
2281 SUCCESS/SAYING	The race is not always to the strong.
2282 SCOT/ROBERT LOUIS STEVENSON/WRITER	The difficulty of literature is not to write, but to write what you mean; not to affect your reader, but to affect him precisely as you wish.
2283 ANAIS NIN/US/ AUTHOR	The role of a writer is not so say what we all can say, but what we are unable to say.
2284 MICHELLE OBAMA/USA	Do not bring people in your life who weigh you down.
2285 USA/KONSTANTIN STANISLAVSKY/ ACTING COACH	Do not try to push your way through to the front ranks of your profession; do not run after distinctions and rewards, but do your utmost to find an entry into the world of beauty.
2286 USA/JOURNALIST/ CHRISTIANE AMANPOUR	Don't seek to be liked.
2287 PROVERB	Death is the great leveler.
2288 ROBERT FULGHUM/USA	Don't hit people.
2289 HEMINGWAY/USA	There is no friend as loyal as a book.
2290 LOUIS L'AMOUR/USA	To disbelieve is easy; to scoff is simple; to have faith is harder.
2291 JAMES BALDWIN/USA/ WRITER	The paradox of education is precisely this -- that as one begins to become conscious, one begins to examine the society in which he is being educated.
2292 COMPUTERS	Ubiquitous computing
2293 G.K. CHESTERTON/UK/ WRITER	Love means to love that which is unlovable; or it is no virtue at all.
2294 IDIOM	Being spoilt for choice
2295 ENGLISH PROVERB	You cannot eat your cake and have it.
2296 SOPHOCLES/THINKER	All men make mistakes, but a good man yields when he knows his course is wrong, and repairs the evil.
2297 HERACLITUS/THINKER/ GREECE	Even a soul submerged in sleep is hard at work and helps make something of the world.

NUMBER CATEGORY/CREDIT	TOPIC
2298 MEISTER ECKHART/ GERMAN/HUMANIST	If the only prayer you say in your life is "Thank You," then that will be enough.
2299 SAYING	Work to live, not live to work.
2300 HENRY L. DOHERTY/ USA/BUSINESS	The man who will neither play nor do business unless everything is just to his liking and notions, retards rather than contributes to progress.
2301 USA/MARGARET HEFFERNAN/BUSINESS	It's the mortar, not the just the bricks that makes a building strong.
2302 REST	Siesta
2303 DANGER/PEOPLE	Natural disasters
2304 ANNIE DILLARD/USA	How we spend our days is, of course, how we spend our lives.
2305 MALCOLM X/USA	If you don't stand for something you will fall for anything.
2306 SPIRIT/AIRPLANE	Flying solo
2307 MALCOLM X/ AMERICAN ACTIVIST	A wise man can play the part of a clown, but a clown can't play the part of a wise man.
2308 WEATHER/LIFE	Cold weather
2309 PAUL FRAMPTON/ NY TIMES	People who are socially inept can nevertheless be the most creative people.
2310 COCO CHANEL/ FRENCH DESIGNER	How many cares one loses when one decides not to be something but to be someone.
2311 MALCOLM X/ AMERICAN ACTIVIST	To have once been a criminal is no disgrace. To remain a criminal is the disgrace.
2312 HOWARD SCHULTZ/ USA/STARBUCKS	The best words are never big or complicated, but are packed with emotion and meaning, leaving no question of what I expect of myself and others.
2313 WAR/RESCUE/FUN	Helicopters
2314 STEVE BIKO/S. AFRICA	The most potent weapon of the oppressor is the mind of the oppressed.
2315 LESSONS	A teachable moment
2316 ELIE WIESEL/USA	Only the guilty are guilty. Their children are not.
2317 NICHOLAS KRISTOF/ NY TIMES/USA	Boys aare more likely to get into trouble without a dad at home.
2318 KING JAMES BIBLE/ ECCLESIASTES 11:1	Cast your bread upon the waters, For you will find it after many days.
2319 DONALD WOODS/ S. AFRICA/AUTHOR	It is a joy to be hidden, and disaster not to be found.
2320 INTERNATIONAL	Balance of power
2321 GUSTAVE FLAUBERT/ FRENCH/WRITER	Pleasure is found first in anticipation, later in memory.
2322 COCO CHANEL/FRENCH	Luxury must be comfortable, otherwise it is not luxury.
2323 REVENGE	Payback time
2324 SAYING	Different strokes for different folks

NUMBER CATEGORY/CREDIT	TOPIC
2325 HANNAH ARENDT/ POLITICAL THEORIST	To think and to be fully alive are the same.
2326 FAMILY/HEALTH	Caregivers
2327 ENTERTAINMENT	Online games
2328 MALCOLM X/ AMERICAN ACTIVIST	I have often reflected upon the new vistas that reading has opened to me. I knew right there in prison that reading had changed forever the course of my life. As I see it today, the ability to read awoke inside me some long dormant craving to be mentally alive.
2329 INTERNATIONAL	Bilateral military relations
2330 ITALIAN/NICCOLO MACHIAVELLI/ DIPLOMAT	Men are driven by two principal impulses, either by love or by fear.
2331 INVESTIGATOR	Private eye
2332 TELL A STORY/TAXI	Honest cabbie
2333 VOLATILE TEMPER	Walking on eggshells
2334 CELEBRATION/CLASH	Fireworks
2335 GAVIN NEWSOM/USA	Most people are local optimists.
2336 SKILL/AIR/DANGER	Aerobatics
2337 GAVIN NEWSOM/ USA/AUTHOR/ POLITICIAN	The jobs in the greatest demand in the future don't yet exist and will require workers to use technologies that have not yet been invented to solve problems that we don't yet even know are problems.
2338 BUSINESS	IPO (Initial Public Offering)
2339 CITIES/GROWTH	Urbanization
2340 SWAMI VIVEKANANDA/ INDIAN YOGI	The world is the great gymnasium where we come to make ourselves strong.
2341 BERNARD M. BARUCH/ USA/BUSINESS	We can't cross that bridge until we come to it, but I always like to lay down a pontoon ahead of time.
2342 EMOTION/ATTITUDE	Drama queen
2343 MALCOLM X/ AMERICAN ACTIVIST	To me, the thing that is worse than death is betrayal. You see, I could conceive death, but I could not conceive betrayal.
2344 AFRICAN PROVERB	It takes a village to raise a child.
2345 COUNTRY/SELF	National pride
2346 ENGLISH PROVERB	Whom the gods love die young.
2347 JANE YOLEN/US WRITER	How often is the passing of one storm only a prelude to another.
2348 COWARDICE	A person with no backbone
2349 SAYING/EXPERIENCE	A new broom sweeps clean but the old one knows the corners.
2350 RESPONSIBILITY	Practice what you preach.
2351 UGANDAN PROVERB	The "medicine" for winning a woman's attention is having another woman.
2352 HARD WORK	Backbreaking work
2353 STEVE JOBS/APPLE/ USA/BUSINESSMAN	Some people think design means how it looks. But of course, if you dig deeper, it's really how it works.

NUMBER CATEGORY/CREDIT	TOPIC
2354 MALCOLM X/ AMERICAN ACTIVIST	If you're not ready to die for it, take the word 'freedom' out of your vocabulary.
2355 GENDER/LEADERS	Difference between male and female managers
2356 WRITER/USA/ZORA NEALE HURSTON	There are years that ask questions and there are years that answer.
2357 SOCIETY/CHILDREN	Missing children
2358 DALAI LAMA XIV	Peace does not mean an absence of conflicts; differences will always be there. Peace means solving these differences through peaceful means; through dialogue, education, knowledge; and through humane ways.
2359 ENGLISH PROVERB	Who judges others condemns himself.
2360 IDIOM	Rubbing salt in the wound
2361 BARBARA JORDAN/ USA/CONGRESS	What the people want is very simple – they want an America as good as its promise.
2362 SIR SERETSE KHAMA/ BOTSWANA/PRESIDENT	A people withou a past is a poeple without a soul.
2363 BERTRAND RUSSELL/ UK/MATHEMATICIAN/ PHILOSOPHER	I believe in using words, not fists.
2364 ELIE WIESEL/ USA/ PROFESSOR	Write only if you cannot live without writing. Write only what you alone can write.
2365 DIVORCE/CHILDREN	Custody battles
2366 EZRA POUND/USA/ POET	There is no reason why the same man should like the same books at eighteen and at forty-eight.
2367 USA/ZORA NEALE HURSTON/WRITER	It is hard to apply oneself to study when there is no money to pay for food and lodging. I almost never explain these things when folks are asking me why I don't do this or that.
2368 JULIA WARD HOWE/ AMERICAN MUSICIAN	Any religion which sacrifices women to the brutality of men is no religion.
2369 CRIME	Fingerprinting
2370 RELATIONHIPS	Personal rivalries
2371 ABIGAIL VAN BUREN/ COLUMNIST/USA	Religion, like water, may be free, but when they pipe it to you, you've got to help pay for piping. And the Piper!
2372 MALCOLM X/USA	Truth is on the side of the oppressed.
2373 HILLARY CLINTON/ USA/POLITICIAN	…as long as there are those who would take innocent life in the name of God, the world will never know a true and lasting peace.
2374 PERSONAL/BUSINESS	Off and on relationships
2375 FUN/MONEY/DESIRE	Buying a new car
2376 USA/ZORA NEALE HURSTON/WRITER	No matter how far a person can go the horizon is still way beyond you.
2377 SECRETS/OBSCURITY	Living in the shadows
2378 WEALTH/FREEDOM	Golden cage
2379 STEPHEN HAWKING/ BRITISH SCIENTIST	Although I cannot move and I have to speak through a computer, in my mind I am free.

NUMBER CATEGORY/CREDIT	TOPIC
2380 PROVERB	Let bygones be bygones.
2381 ROBERT FULGHUM/USA	Share everything.
2382 PAUL ENGLSH/ KAYAK/WISDOM/ ENTREPRENEUR	The only way 100 people can ever build a larger company that one that has more than 8,000 people – that's what Expedia has – is by hiring Olympic-quality, unbelievable all stars of technology. My favorite metric is revenue per employee.
2383 PROVERB	Give credit where credit is due.
2384 PROVERB	Circumstances alter cases.
2385 MYSTERY/ KNOWING	Sixth sense
2386 JULIA WARD HOWE/USA	Marriage, like death, is a debt we owe to nature.
2387 ANIMALS	Dolphins
2388 CAVEAT EMPTOR	Let the buyer beware.
2389 FANNIE HURST/ USA/NOVELIST	Some people think they are worth a lot of money just because they have it.
2390 FRANTZ FANON/WRITER	To speak a language is to take on a world, a culture.
2391 MADAME DE STAEL/ SWISS AUTHOR	Courage of soul is necessary for the triumphs of genius.
2392 DATING/FRIENDS	Wingmen and women
2393 WILLIAM LEAST HEAT-MOON/TRAVEL WRITER	When you're traveling, you are what you are right there and then. People don't have your past to hold against you.
2394 PROVERB	Do not cross the bridge till you come to it.
2395 PHILIP ZIMBARDO/USA/ PSYCHOLOGY/PROF.	Human behavior is incredibly pliable, plastic.
2396 BACKGROUND	Humble origins
2397 SUSAN FALUDI/USA	Women are enslaved by their own liberation.
2398 BARBARA JORDAN/USA	Do not call for black power or green power. Call for brain power.
2399 CARLO DOSSI/ITALY/ AUTHOR/ DIPLOMAT	The best way to be more free is to grant more freedom to others.
2400 LIFESTYLE	Healthy habits
2401 ANNE BRONTE/UK	The end of Religion is not to teach us how to die, but how to live.
2402 ROBERT A. HEINLEIN/ AUTHOR/USA	It is a truism that almost any sect, cult, or religion will legislate its creed into law if it acquires the political power to do so.
2403 MEN/BEHAVIOR	Men and shopping
2404 KATHLEEN NORRIS/US/ NOVELIST/COLUMNIST	In any free society, the conflict between social conformity and individual liberty is permanent, unresolvable, and necessary.
2405 CZESLAW MILOSZ/POET/ NOVELIST	Not that I want to be a god or a hero. Just to change into a tree, grow for ages, not hurt anyone.
2406 USA/ZORA NEALE HURSTON/WRITER	Learning about wisdom is a load of books on a donkey's back.
2407 MADAME DE STAEL/ SWISS AUTHOR	Politeness is the art of choosing among your thoughts.
2408 ANNE FRANK/AUTHOR	Look at how a single candle can both defy and define the darkness.

NUMBER CATEGORY/CREDIT	TOPIC
2409 JAPAN	*Oyabaka*/Overindulgent parents
2410 AN AHA MOMENT/ MERRIAMWEBSTER.COM	Aha moment: a moment of sudden realization, inspiration, insight, recognition, or comprehension.
2411 ITALY/WRITER/NICCOLO MACHIAVELLI	There is no avoiding war; it can only be postponed to the advantage of your enemy.
2412 WORK/PRESSURE	Bringing work home from the office
2413 CHILDREN/SCHOOL	School buses
2414 PERSONAL	Milestones in ife
2415 NOBEL/WOLE SOYINKA/ NIGERIAN PLAYWRIGHT	Well, some people say I'm pessimistic because I recognize the eternal cycle of evil. All I say is, look at the history of mankind right to this moment and what do you find?
2416 HANNAH SENESH/ JEWISH POET/ PARATROOPER	There are stars whose radiance is visible on Earth though they have long been extinct. There are people whose brilliance continues to light the world though they are no longer among the living.
2417 USA/ELIZABETH KUBLER-ROSS/SWISS/ PSYCHIATRIST/AUTHOR	People are like stained glass windows: they sparkle and shine when the sun is out, but when the darkness sets in their true beauty is revealed only if there is a light within.
2418 MATERNITY	Postpartum blues
2419 CHINESE GENERAL/ AUTHOR/THE ART OF WAR	Now the reason the enlightened prince and the wise general conquer the enemy whenever they move and their achievements surpass those of ordinary men is foreknowledge.
2420 EDWIN LAND/USA/ INVENTOR/POLAROID	Every significant invention must be startling, unexpected, and must come into a world that is not prepared for it. If the world were prepared for it, it would not be much of an invention.
2421 BILL GATES/USA/ ENTREPRENEUR	Technology is just a tool. In terms of getting the kids working together and motivating them, the teacher is the most important.
2422 JANE YOLEN/ USA/ WRITER	Time may heal all wounds, but it does not erase the scars.
2423 PARENTHOOD	New parents
2424 ENGLISH PROVERB	Wash your dirty linen at home.
2425 KARL POPPER/THINKER/ AUSTRIAN/BRITISH	The notion that one can begin anything at all from scratch, free from the past, or unindebted to others, could not conceivably be more wrong.
2426 PROVERB	The grass is always greener on the other side of the fence.
2427 SAYING	Don't throw the baby out with the bathwater.
2428 CORITA KENT/ARTIST/ SISTERS OF THE IMMACULATE HEART	Creativity belongs to the artist in each of us. To create means to relate. The root meaning of the word art is "to fit together" and we all do this every day. Not all of us are painters but we are all artists. Each time we fit things together we are creating – whether it is to make a loaf of bread, a child, a day.
2429 USA/ELBERT HUBBARD/ POLITICIAN/THINKER	The supernatural is the natural not yet understood.
2430 SELF-RELIANCE	Paddle your own canoe
2431 PROVERB	All's well that ends well.

NUMBER CATEGORY/CREDIT	TOPIC
2432 JESUS/BIBLE/LUKE 6:31	Do unto others as you would have others do unto you.
2433 ENGLISH PROVERB	Waste not, want not.
2434 ELLA WHEELER WILCOX/USA/POET	Laugh and the world laughs with you; weep, and you weep alone
2435 HART CRANE/POET/USA	One must be drenched in words, literally soaked in them, to have the right ones form themselves into the proper patterns at the right moment.
2436 RACHEL CARSON/ USA/SCIENTIST/ AUTHOR/SILENT SPRING	If I had influence with the good fairy who is supposed to preside over the christening of all children, I should ask that her gift to each child in the world be a sense of wonder so indestructible that it would last throughout life.
2437 WILLIAM MAKEPEACE THACKERAY/NOVELIST	People hate as they love, unreasonably.
2438 ELIE WIESEL/USA/ NOVELIST/HOLOCAUST	No human race is superior; no religious faith is inferior. All collective judgments are wrong. Only racists make them.
2439 PROVERB	One swallow does not make a summer
2440 PROVERB	The hot coal burns; the cold one blackens.
2441 WILLA CATHER/ AMERICAN AUTHOR	I like trees because they seem more resigned to the way they have to live than other things do.
2442 USA/MALCOLM X/ LEADER	The media's the most powerful entity on earth. They have the power to make the innocent guilty and to make the guilty innocent, and that's power. Because they control the minds of the masses.
2443 PROVERB	Don't count your chickens before they are hatched.
2444 ELIE WIESEL/USA/ PROFESSOR	Whoever survives a test, whatever it may be, must tell the story. That is his duty.
2445 MORTIMER ADLER/ USA/PHILOSOPHER	Not to engage in the pursuit of ideas is to live like ants instead of like men.
2446 SAYING	Wisdom lies in waiting
2447 ACTION/SUCCESS	Carpe Diem: Seize the day
2448 OGDEN NASH/POET	To keep your marriage brimming, With love in the loving cup, Whenever you're wrong, admit it; whenever you're right, shut up.
2449 JOHN CAGE/USA/ COMPOSER	I can't understand why people are frightened of new ideas. I'm frightened of the old ones.
2450 CARRIE CHAPMAN CATT/ LEADER/USA/WOMEN	The vote is the emblem of your equality, women of America, the guarantee of your liberty.
2451 PROVERB	Vows made in storms are forgotten in calm.
2452 PROVERB	He who pays the piper can call the tune.
2453 ANTI-WAR SLOGAN/ AMERICA/1960's	Make love – not war!
2454 GERMAN PROVERB	The morning hour has gold in the mouth.
2455 GERMAN PROVERB	He who digs a pit for others falls in himself.
2456 PROVERB	Blood is thicker than water.
2457 SAYING	Chickens come home to roost
2458 PROVERB	Business before pleasure

NUMBER CATEGORY/CREDIT	TOPIC
2459 WILLA CATHER/USA/ WRITER	All the intelligence and talent in the world can't make a singer.
2460 CLASS MATTERS/ NY TIMES/USA/2005	The more education and income people have, the less likely they are to have and die of heart disease, strokes, diabetes, and many types of cancer.
2461 PROVERB	One rotten apple can spoil the whole barrel.
2462 WILLIAM SHAKESPEARE	The course of true love never did run smooth.
2463 POET/WILLIAM WORDSWORTH	The child is father to the man.
2464 JAMES ALLEN/AUTHOR/ AS A MAN THINKETH	Circumstances do not make the man; they reveal a man to himself.
2465 SAYING	Children should be seen and not heard
2466 WILLIAM SHAKESPEARE	Words without thoughts never to heaven go.
2467 TIM ELMORE/USA	The best man for the job may be a woman!
2468 SAYING	Early to bed, early to rise; and your girl goes out with other guys.
2469 SAYING	Seeing is believing.
2470 SAYING	A sound mind in a sound body
2471 FEAR	Panic
2472 LAO TZU/CHINA	New beginnings are often disguised as painful endings.
2473 ROALD DAHL/UK/ WRITER	...if you are interested in something, no matter what it is, go at it full speed ahead. Embrace it with both arms, hug it, love it, and above all become passionate about it. Lukewarm is no good. Hot is no good either. White hot is the only thing to be.
2474 MALCOLM X/ AMERICAN ACTIVIST	Usually when people are sad, they don't do anything. They just cry over their condition. But when they get angry, they bring about a change.
2475 ELIE WIESEL/USA/ NOVELIST/PROFESSOR	Ultimately, the only power to which man should aspire is that which he exercises over himself.
2476 SAYING	Easy come, easy go.
2477 PHILIP ADAMS/ AUSTRALIAN FILM DIRECTOR	Fame often comes to those who are thinking about something else, while celebrity comes to those who think of nothing else. Celebrity ia a forgery of fame: it has the form but lacks the content.
2478 IDIOM	Comin' in on a wing and a pray'r
2479 MICHAEL DIRDA/ BOOK COLUMNIST/ WASHINGTON POST	Without a knowledge of the Greek myths, the Bible, ancient history, the world's folktales and fairy tales, one can never fully understand the visual arts, most opera, and half the literature of later ages....The classics are important not because they are old but because they are always being renewed.
2480 BIBLE/JOHN 8:32	...the truth shall set you free.
2481 JULIUS NYERERE/ PRESIDENT/ KENYA	[A] man is developing himself when he grows, or earns, enough to provide decent conditions for himself and his family; he is not being developed if someone gives him these things.
2482 HEALTH	Germs
2483 ANTHONY TROLLOPE/ UK/AUTHOR	The habit of reading is the only enjoyment in which there is no alloy; it lasts when all other pleasures fade.

NUMBER CATEGORY/CREDIT	TOPIC
2484 JAMES JOYCE/IRISH/ WRITER	You can still die when the sun is shining.
2485 MUHAMMAD ALI/USA/ BOXER/ACTIVIST	Float like a butterfly; sting like a bee.
2486 e.e. cummings/POET/ USA	To be nobody but myself -- in a world which is doing its best, night and day, to make you everybody else -- means to fight the hardest battle which any human being can fight, and never stop fighting.
2487 ENGLISH PROVERB	What belongs to everybody belongs to nobody.
2488 DAPHNE DU MAURIER/ WRITER	Women want love to be a novel. Men, a short story.
2489 MARTIN AMIS/UK	Weapons are like money; no one knows the meaning of enough.
2490 MAYA ANGELOU/USA	As human beings we're more alike than we're unalike.
2491 LYNN ANDREWS/UK/ AUTHOR	Power lies in individuality and the ability to see yourself through your own eyes not the eyes of another.
2492 EDNA FERBER/USA/ NOVELIST	If American politics are too dirty for women to take part in, there's something wrong with American politics.
2493 TOKUGAWA IEYASU/ JAPAN	When ambitious desires arise in your heart, recall the days of extremity you have passed through. Forbearance is the root of all quietness and assurance forever.
2494 SUZANNE KEEN/ USA/PROFESSOR	Novel reading is not a team sport.
2495 ENGLISH PROVERB	We never miss the water till the well runs dry.
2496 SWAMI VIVEKANANDA/ INDIAN YOGI	We are what our thoughts have made us; so take care about what you think. Words are secondary. Thoughts live; they travel far.
2497 OPRAH WINFREY/USA HARVARD ADDRESS	...there is no such thing as failure. Failure is just life trying to move us in a different direction.
2498 NEIL ARMSTRONG/USA MOON LANDING	That's one small step for a man, one giant leap for mankind.
2499 IBM/SLOGAN	No manager ever got fired for buying IBM.
2500 AVIS/CAR RENTAL	We're number two; we work harder.
2501 HEALTH/RELIGION	Blood transfusions
2502 MACHO	Manly men
2503 USA/ACTOR/ARNOLD SCHWARZENEGGER	Girly men
2504 CLIFTON FADIMAN/ AMERICAN WRITER	When you read a classic, you do not see more in the book than you did before; you see more in you than there was before.
2505 MARTIN GARDNER/ MATHEMATICIAN/USA	Biographical history, as taught in our public schools, is still largely a history of boneheads: ridiculous kings and queens, paranoid political leaders, compulsive voyagers, ignorant generals, the flotsam and jetsam of historical currents. The men who radically altered history, the great creative scientists and mathematicians, are seldom mentioned if at all.
2506 CHILDREN/TOYS	Barbie doll
2507 POPULATION	Falling birthrate in developed nations

NUMBER CATEGORY/CREDIT	TOPIC
2508 TRANSPORTATION	Traffic problems
2509 RELATIONSHIPS	Love-hate relationship
2510 ART BUCHWALD/ AMERICAN HUMORIST	Every time you think television has hit its lowest ebb, a new program comes along to make you wonder where you thought the ebb was.
2511 JANE YOLEN/US WRITER	If you love a waist, you waste a love.
2512 FUN/DANGER	Playing pranks
2513 ENGLISH PROVERB	What can't be cured must be endured.
2514 MONEY/CRIME	Tax evasion
2515 KIDNAPPING/CRIME	Paying a ransom for hostages
2516 SONGS/FESTIVITY	Christmas carols
2517 AUSTRALIAN SAYING	Out in the bush, the tarred road always ends just after the house of the local mayor.
2518 PLAYWRIGHT/WILLIAM SHAKESPEARE	Love is blind and lovers cannot see the pretty follies that themselves commit.
2519 DIET	If it tastes good, it's bad for you.
2520 NANCY ASTOR/ BRITISH M.P.	One reason why I don't drink is because I wish to know when I'm having a good time.
2521 PEOPLE/NATIONS	Wasted effort
2522 HECTOR BOLITHO/ UK/THIS I BELIEVE	There's too much adulation for the man who swims the channel and not enough for the man who sits on the beach and contemplates the waters before him.
2523 MEDICINE/DOCTORS	Medical malpractice
2524 CONFLICT	War of words
2525 BUSINESS	Conflict of interest
2526 USA/FRANKLIN D. ROOSEVELT/PRESIDENT	I ask you to judge me by the enemies I have made.
2527 DORIS LESSING/NOBEL LAUREATE/NOVELIST	All one's life as a young woman one is on show, a focus of attention, people notice you. You set yourself up to be noticed and admired. And then, not expecting it, you become middle-aged and anonymous. No one notices you. You achieve a wonderful freedom. It's a positive thing. You can move about unnoticed and invisible.
2528 TIM O'BRIEN/USA/ WRITER/SOLDIER	In any war story, but especially a true one, it's difficult to separate what happened from what seemed to happen.
2529 ENGLISH PROVERB	Who chatters to you will chatter of you.
2530 ROBERTO CLEMENTE/ BASEBALL/USA	Any time you have an opportunity to make a difference in this world and you don't, then you are wasting your time on Earth.
2531 PAUL GRAHAM/USA/ ENTREPRENEUR	In a startup, things seem great one moment and hopeless the next. And by next, I mean a couple hours later.
2532 YEHUDA BAUER/ HOLOCAUST SCHOLAR	Thou shalt not be a perpetrator; Thou shalt not be a victim; thou shalt never, but never be a bystander.
2533 ATTITUDE	If it isn't fun then it isn't worth doing.
2534 IDIOM	Falling through the cracks
2535 IDIOM	Mind your own business (MYOB)

NUMBER CATEGORY/CREDIT	TOPIC
2536 JAPAN/SCAM	*Atari-ya* (professional traffic accident victim)
2537 CHINA	*Fubai Jie:* Corruption Street
2538 MADAME DE STAEL/ SWISS AUTHOR	Love is the whole history of a woman's life; it is but an episode in a man's.
2539 JAPAN/FOOD	Sushi
2540 WILLIAM WORDSWORTH	Wisdom is oft-times nearer when we stoop than when we soar.
2541 STEPHEN HAWKING/ UK/SCIENTIST	Government works best under the glare of public scrutiny. Absent such scrutiny, abuses occur.
2542 BARBARA JORDAN/ CONGRESSWOMAN/ USA	I believe that women have a capacity for understanding and compassion which man structurally does not have, does not have it because he cannot have it. He's just incapable of it.
2543 CRIME/WAR	Mass graves
2544 IDIOM/BACKGROUND	White noise
2545 BUSINESS/MONEY	Oil
2546 USA/IMMIGRATION	U.S. Visa lottery
2547 RACHEL CARSON/ USA/SCIENTIST/AUTHOR	The control of nature is a phrase conceived in arrogance, born of the Neanderthal age of biology and philosophy, when it was supposed that nature exists for the convenience of man.
2548 SAMUEL JOHNSON/UK	A writer only begins a book. A reader finishes it.
2549 POVERTY PIMPS/ USA/ WIKIPEDIA	Poverty pimp or "professional poverty pimp" is a pejorative label used to convey that an individual or group is benefiting unduly by acting as an intermediary on behalf of the poor, the disadvantaged, or some other "victimized" groups.
2550 BERTRAND RUSSELL/ NOBELIST	Every advance in civilization has been denounced as unnatural when it was recent.
2551 INSIGHT/TIME	The wisdom of hindsight
2552 WALTER LIPPMAN/USA	Where all think alike, no one thinks very much
2553 CORRUPTION	Cronyism
2554 ENGLISH PROVERB	Where there's a will, there's a way.
2555 JANE AUSTEN/ ENGLISH AUTHOR/ PRIDE & PREJUDICE	There is a stubbornness about me that never can bear to be frightened at the ill of others. My courage always rises at every attempt to intimidate me.
2556 MICHAEL DIRDA/ BOOK COLUMNIST/ WASHINGTON POST/ USA	People sometimes ask teachers or critics, "Which books should I read to become educated?" The short answer is either 'AS many as you can' or 'A small handful that you study to pieces.' But a better question might be this one: "Which books should I read first?"
2557 JOHN KEATS/POET	There is a budding morrow in midnight.
2558 ACTIVIST/FREDERICK DOUGLASS/USA	If there is no struggle there is no progress.
2559 IDIOM	Minding one's P's and Q's
2560 ANNE SULLIVAN/USA/ TEACHER	Children require guidance and sympathy far more than instruction.
2561 SIR FRANCIS BACON/ UK/ESSAYIST	Natural abilities are like natural plants: they need pruning by study.

NUMBER CATEGORY/CREDIT	TOPIC
2562 IDIOM/FOOD	(Something that) makes the mouth water
2563 FRENCH PROVERB	A father is a banker provided by nature.
2564 SUCCESS/NATIONS	Asian tigers
2565 WARNING/ADVICE	Safety first
2566 HISTORIAN/NICCOLO MACHIAVELLI	Men are so simple of mind, and so much dominated by their immediate needs, that a deceitful man will always find plenty who are ready to be deceived.
2567 PLATO	Wise men talk because they have something to day; fools, because they have to say something.
2568 MAYA ANGELOU/USA/ WRITER	When you know better you do better.
2569 ELBERT GREEN HUBBARD/USA	The recipe for perpetual ignorance is: Be satisfied with your opinions and content with your knowledge.
2570 PEARL BAILEY/USA/ ACTRESS/SINGER	A crown, if it hurts us, is not worth wearing.
2571 GERRY SPENCE/USA/ LAWYER/AUTHOR/GIVE ME LIBERTY	Children should become the role models for us, their parents, for they are coated with the spirit from which they came – out of the ether, clean, innocent, brimming with the delight of life, aware of the beauty of the simplest thing: a snail, a bud....
2572 ENGLISH PROVERB	When the cat's away the mice will play.
2573 IDEA/FEELING	Born too late
2574 ELLA W. WILCOX/POET/ USA	To sin by silence when they should protest makes cowards of men.
2575 JAMES BALDWIN/USA	The price one pays for pursuing any profession or calling is to know its ugly side
2576 LUCILLE BALL/USA/ ACTOR	I have an everyday religion that works for me. Love yourself first and everything else falls into line.
2577 EDUCATOR/BOOKER T. WASHINGTON/USA	Success is to be measured not so much by the position that one has reached in life as by the obstacles which he has overcome.
2578 USA/1ST PRESIDENT/ GEORGE WASHINGTON	Be courteous to all, but intimate with few, and let those few be well tried before you give them your confidence.
2579 MEDICINE/ SURGERY	Medical operations
2580 MARIE CURIE/ FRENCH-POLISH PHYSICIST/CHEMIST	We must not forget that when radium was discovered no one knew that it would prove useful in hospitals. The work was one of pure science. And this is a proof that scientific work must not be considered from the point of view of the direct usefulness of it.
2581 FEELING	Superiority complex
2582 ROBERT GATES/USA/ SEC./DEFENSE	Leadership: The ability to stand in the shadow and let others receive attention and accolades.
2583 SAMUEL JOHNSON/UK	What is written without effort is in general read without pleasure.
2584 WALTER BAGEHOT/UK/ JOURNALIST	The greatest pleasure in life is doing what people say you cannot do.
2585 PEARL BAILEY/USA/ ACTRESS/SINGER	A man without ambition is dead.

NUMBER CATEGORY/CREDIT	TOPIC
2586 OPRAH WINFREY/USA	Become the change you want to see!
2587 IDIOM	Pull someone's leg
2588 IDIOM	Looking down one's nose on others
2589 RALPH NADER/USA/ LAWYER	Cognition is not ignition.
2590 IDIOM	Close-fisted
2591 WAR/FRENCH/ERICH MARIA REMARQUE	Modesty and conscientiousness receive their reward only in novels. In life they are exploited and then shoved aside.
2592 IDIOM	Can't make heads or tails of something
2593 VIKTOR FRANKL/ AUSTRIAN/AUTHOR	Happiness can't be pursued; it must ensue.
2594 JOHN STEINBECK/ USA/WRITER	If you're in trouble, or hurt or need – go to the poor people. They're the only ones that'll help – the only ones.
2595 GEORGE SAND/WRITER	Admiration and familiarity are strangers.
2596 GROWING DISBELIEF/ ECONOMIST.COM	Over 40% of Americans say they would never vote for an atheist presidential candidate.
2597 RELATIONSHIPS	Getting along with others
2598 IDIOM	Gaining ground
2599 IDIOM	Fly off on a tangent
2600 IDIOM	Putting an end to one's misery
2601 IDIOM	Paying through the nose
2602 FRENCH/EMILE-AUGUST CHARTIER/POET	Nothing is more dangerous than an idea, when you have only one idea.
2603 JOHN STEINBECK/ USA/WRITER	I have never smuggled anything in my life. Why, then, do I feel an uneasy sense of guilt on approaching a customs barrier?
2604 IDIOM	Making one's mark
2605 JOHN STEINBECK/US/ WRITER	Ideas are like rabbits. You get a couple and learn how to handle them, and pretty soon you have a dozen.
2606 ENGLISH PROVERB	When in Rome, do as the Romans do.
2607 JOHN LE CARRE/USA	A desk is a dangerous place from which to view the world.
2608 NEW LITERACY	Technology is the new literacy.
2609 FAMILY	Next of kin
2610 ENGLISH PROVERB	When poverty comes in at the door loves flies out of the window.
2611 IDIOM	Making ends meet
2612 MUSINGS/JAPAN/ DAILY YOMIURI	It is a fact that the human world, where people are surrounded by the same species, is full of loneliness.
2613 IDIOM	Beating about the bush
2614 POET/WILLIAM WORDSWORTH/UK	The best portion of a good man's life: his little, nameless unremembered acts of kindness and love.
2615 IDIOM	Working behind the scenes
2616 PEARL BAILEY/USA/ ACTRESS/SINGER	You never find yourself until you face the truth.

NUMBER CATEGORY/CREDIT	TOPIC
2617 GABRIEL LEGOUVE/ FRENCH/POET	A brother is a friend given by nature.
2618 MICHAEL DIRDA/WAPO/ COLUMNIST	Throughout history the exemplary teacher has never been just an instructor in a subject; he is nearly always its living advertisement.
2619 USA/ALEXANDER HAMILTON/WRITER	A national debt, if it is not excessive, will be to us a national blessing.
2620 IDIOM	Blow one's trumpet
2621 ARABIC PROVERB	Ask the experienced rather than the learned.
2622 AUTHOR/ERICH MARIA REMARQUE/FRENCH	No soldier outlives a thousand chances. But every soldier believes in Chance and trusts his luck.
2623 IDIOM	Cutting corners
2624 ENGLISH PROVERB	When a man is going down the hill, everyone will give him a push.
2625 ANTHONY TROLLOPE/ UK/AUTHOR	A small daily task, if it be really daily, will beat the labors of a spasmodic Hercules.
2626 USA/ELBERT GREEN HUBBARD/WRITER	It's a fine thing to have ability, but the ability to discover ability in others is the true test.
2627 USA/ALEXANDER HAMILTON/WRITER	The passions of a revolution are apt to hurry even good men into excesses.
2628 TIM O'BRIEN/US WRITER	You're never more alive than when you're almost dead.
2629 DIPLOMAT/NICCOLO MACHIAVELLI/ITALY	The lion cannot protect himself from traps, and the fox cannot defend himself from wolves. One must therefore be a fox to recognize traps, and a lion to frighten wolves.
2630 HELEN KELLER/ USA/AUTHOR	So much has been given to me I have not time to ponder over that which has been denied.
2631 IDIOM	A Spartan life
2632 IDIOM	A storm in a teacup
2633 WHAT DO YOU THINK?	A teacup in a storm
2634 IDIOM	A white elephant
2635 IDIOM	Pooh-pooh an idea
2636 OPRAH WINFREY/USA	The right to choose your own path is a sacred privilege.
2637 IDIOM	Cut the ground from under someone's feet
2638 IDIOM	Pick someone's brains
2639 FUN/OUTDOORS	Camping out
2640 IDIOM	A nine days' wonder
2641 IDIOM	Armed to the teeth
2642 VIKTOR FRANKL/ AUTHOR/AUSTRIAN PSYCHIATRIST	We who lived in concentration camps can remember the men who walked through the huts comforting others, giving away their last piece of bread.
2643 USA/ELBERT GREEN HUBBARD/WRITER	The world is moving so fast these days that the man who says it can't be done is generally interrupted by someone doing it.
2644 SAMUEL RICHARDSON/ ENGLISH NOVELIST	If the education and studies of children were suited to their inclinations and capacities, many would be made useful members of society that otherwise would make no figure in it.

NUMBER CATEGORY/CREDIT	TOPIC
2645 IDIOM	At the eleventh hour
2646 GEORGE SAND/ FRENCH NOVELIST	Charity degrades those who receive it and hardens those who dispense it.
2647 ADDICTION	Doctor shopping
2648 JOSS WHEDON/USA/ SCREENWRITER	I write to give myself strength. I write to be the characters that I am not. I write to explore all the things I'm afraid of.
2649 ANTHONY TROLLOPE/ UK/WRITER	Never think that you're not good enough yourself...Nobody holds a good opinion of a man who holds a low opinion of himself.
2650 LOU REED/UK/USA	Those who hate the nine-to-five regime do not know the blessing that it holds.
2651 HENRY VAN DYKE/POET/ USA/NOVELIST	Use the talents you possess, for the woods would be a very silent place if no birds sang except the best.
2652 IDIOM	Put one's shoulders to the wheel
2653 IDIOM	Pull strings to achieve a goal
2654 IDIOM	Go off the deep end
2655 IDIOM	Give a piece of one's mind
2656 ANNE FRANK/JEWISH AUTHOR/ HOLOCAUST	Why should millions be spent daily on the war and yet there's not a penny available for medical services, artists, or for poor people?
2657 RONALD REAGAN/ 40TH PRESIDENT/USA	No arsenal...is so formidable as the will and moral courage of free men and women.
2658 IDIOM	Go bananas
2659 IDIOM	Draw a blank
2660 IDIOM	Fall on deaf ears
2661 ENGLISH PROVERB	What the eye does not admire, the heart does not desire.
2662 IDIOM	Down to earth
2663 IDIOM	Get into hot water
2664 BARBARA JORDAN/USA	Life is too large to hang out a sign: "For Men Only."
2665 IDIOM	Wear a long face
2666 ROYALTY/LAW	Lèse majesté
2667 IDIOM	Go at it hammer and tongs
2668 SAMUEL JOHNSON/UK	It is necessary to hope...for hope itself is happiness.
2669 IDIOM	Face the music
2670 IDIOM	Get hold of the wrong end of the stick
2671 USA/AMOS BRONSON ALCOTT/EDUCATOR	To be ignorant of one's ignorance is the malady of the ignorant.
2672 SAMUEL JOHNSON/ ENGLISH AUTHOR	What we hope ever to do with ease, we must first learn to do with diligence.
2673 IDIOM	Go Dutch
2674 IDIOM	Eat one's words
2675 MATT HARDING/USA/ WORLD TRAVELLER	I don't need to travel to influence lives on the other side of the globe. All I have to do is buy a cup of coffee or a tank of gas.

NUMBER CATEGORY/CREDIT	TOPIC
2676 USA/1st PRES./GEORGE WASHINGTON	If the freedom of speech is taken away, then dumb and silent we may be led, like sheep to the slaughter.
2677 SAMUEL JOHNSON/ ENGLISH AUTHOR	To keep your secret is wisdom, but to expect others to keep it is folly.
2678 IDIOM	Caught on the wrong foot
2679 SAYING	Who will bell the cat?
2680 AMY TAN/USA/WRITER	You see what fear is -- holding someone else's fear in your hand and showing it to them.
2681 THICH NHAT HANH/ VIETNAM/BUDDHIST	In every one of us, there are good seeds and there are bad seeds.
2682 IDIOM	A cock-and-bull story
2683 IDIOM	Get away with murder
2684 HELEN KELLER/AUTHOR	My friends have made the story of my life.
2685 IDIOM	Go by the book
2686 SAMUEL JOHNSON/ ENGLISH AUTHOR	Knowledge is of two kinds. We know a subject ourselves, or we know where we can find information on it.
2687 GERRY SPENCE/ USA/LAWYER	Skepticism, not cleanliness, is next to godliness. Skepticism is the father of freedom. It is like the pry that holds open the door for truth to slip in.
2688 IDIOM	In the nick of time
2689 ENGLISH PROVERB	What is worth doing at all is worth doing well.
2690 IDIOM	In one ear and out the other
2691 GEORGE SAND/ FRENCH NOVELIST	Don't walk in front of me, I may not follow. Don't walk behind me, I may not lead. There is only one happiness in life, to love and be loved.
2692 IDIOM	Rest on one's laurels
2693 VIKTOR FRANKL/ AUSTRIAN PSYCHIATRIST	...man is ultimately self-determining. What he becomes – within the limits of endowment and environment – he has made out of himself.
2694 IDIOM	Hard and fast rules
2695 IDIOM	Lose one's head
2696 BENJAMIN FRANKLIN/ USA/FOUNDING FATHER	Necessity never made a good bargain.
2697 IDIOM	Living from hand to mouth
2698 IDIOM	Hold one's tongue
2699 WILLIAM SHAKESPEARE/ PLAYWRIGHT/MACBETH	What's done cannot be undone.
2700 LOU REED/MUSICIAN	Life is like Sanskrit read to a pony.
2701 JOSS WHEDON/USA	Recognizing power in another does not diminsh your own.
2702 LOU REED/MUSICIAN	I don't like nostalgia unless its's mine.
2703 PAULO COELHO/BRAZIL	If you want to control someone, all you have to do is to make them feel afraid.
2704 KATHLEEN PARKER/ WAPO/USA	Studies have confirmed what all successfully married men know: The correct answer to any question is "Yes, dear."
2705 IDIOM	Hitting below the belt

NUMBER CATEGORY/CREDIT	TOPIC
2706 MICHAEL DIRDA/USA/ COLUMNIST/WAPO	Order and surprise: these are two interwoven elements that make for any great library or collection.
2707 STACY JOHNSON/USA/ MONEY TALKS NEWS	Life affords you the opportunity to either *look* rich or *be* rich.
2708 SAMUEL JOHNSON/ ENGLISH AUTHOR	Read over your compositions, and wherever you meet with a passage which you think is particularly fine, strike it out.
2709 PANASONIC/SLOGAN	Ideas for life
2710 GERRY SPENCE/ USA/LAWYER	The old saw that 'sticks and stones can break my bones but words will never harm me' does not, in fact, hold true.
2711 IDIOM	Have one's heart in one's mouth
2712 IDIOM	Have one's hands full
2713 IDIOM	A chip off the old block
2714 IDIOM	Bury the hatchet
2715 USA/ALEXANDER HAMILTON/WRITER/ POLITICIAN/ LAWYER	It is a maxim deeply ingrafted in that dark system, that no character, however upright, is a match for constantly reiterated attacks...however false.
2716 FRANTZ FANON/ MARTINIQUE- BORN FRENCH- ALGERIAN/ PSYCHIATRIST	Sometimes people hold a core belief that is very strong. When they are presented with evidence that works against that belief, the new evidence cannot be accepted. It would create a feeling that is extremely uncomfortable, called cognitive dissonance.
2717 BARBARA JORDAN/ USA/CONGRESS	One thing is clear to me; We, as human beings, must be willing to accept people who are different from ourselves.
2718 HELEN KELLER/USA/ AUTHOR/LECTURER	Self-pity is our worst enemy and if we yield to it, we can never do anything good in the world.
2719 IDIOM	In black and white
2720 IDIOM	Red-letter day
2721 IDIOM	Like water off a duck's back
2722 IDIOM	Lose face
2723 LEO BUSCAGLIA/ AMERICAN WRITER	Life lived for tomorrow will always be just a day away from being realized.
2724 IDIOM	In the same boat
2725 FRANCE/NAPOLEON BONAPARTE/LEADER	Never ascribe to malice that which can adequately be explained by incompetence.
2726 IDIOM	Put the cart before the horse
2727 IDIOM	Have an axe to grind
2728 IDIOM	Keep a straight face
2729 IDIOM	Hit the nail on the head
2730 ALBERT CAMUS/ WRITER/PHILOSOPHER	Too many have dispensed with generosity in order to practice charity.
2731 COMPETITION	Bitter rivals
2732 T. BOONE PICKENS/ USA/BUSINESSMAN	Work eight hours and sleep eight hours and make sure that they are not the same hours.

NUMBER CATEGORY/CREDIT	TOPIC
2733 USA/ALEXANDER HAMILTON/WRITER/ POLITICIAN/ LAWYER	Let us recollect that peace or war will not always be left to our option; that however moderate or unambitious we may be, we cannot count upon moderation, or hope to extinguish the ambition of others.
2734 USA/RUSSELL BAKER/ AUTHOR/COLUMNIST	By the age of six the average child will have completed basic American education...From television, the child will have learned how to pick a lock, commit a fairly elaborate bank holdup, prevent wetness all day long, get the laundry twice as white, and kill people with a variety of sophisticated armaments.
2735 EXCUSE/EVIL	Just following orders
2736 SAYING	Blind leading the blind
2737 SAMUEL JOHNSON/ ENGLISH AUTHOR	This is one of the disadvantages of wine; it makes a man mistake words for thoughts.
2738 PERSUASION	Winning hearts and minds
2739 EDUCATION	Prestigious qualifications
2740 JOHNNY CASH/USA	You're so heavenly minded, you're no earthly good.
2741 IDIOM/WISDOM	An old soul
2742 IDIOM	Head over heels in love
2743 IDIOM	A flash in the pan
2744 IDIOM	Keep the ball rolling
2745 ENGLISH PROVERB	What costs nothing is worth nothing.
2746 SAMUEL JOHNSON/ ENGLISH AUTHOR	The chains of habit are too weak to be felt until they are too strong to be broken.
2747 IDIOM	Keep one's head above water
2748 USA/ELBERT GREEN HUBBARD/WRITER	Happiness is a habit – cultivate it.
2749 UK/NANCY ASTOR/ WOMEN'S RIGHTS	Women have got to make the world safe for men since men have made it so darned unsafe for women.
2750 USA/GEORGE WASHINGTON/ 1ST PRESIDENT	Experience teaches us that it is much easier to prevent an enemy from posting themselves that it is to dislodge them after they have got possession.
2751 IDIOM	Picking up the pieces
2752 GANGS/LAW	Protection money
2753 GINA PAROSA/FARMER/ USA/THIS I BELIEVE	The architectural term "pathways of desire" refers to dirt ruts in the grass that people make when they want a shortcut between prescribed routes.
2754 LAW/POLICE	Police crackdown
2755 FRANCE/NAPOLEON BONAPARTE/LEADER	He who knows how to flatter also knows how to slander.
2756 BERTRAND RUSSELL/ BRITISH AUTHOR	Not to be absolutely certain is, I think, one of the essential things in rationality.
2757 ENGLISH PROVERB	What can't be cured must be endured.
2758 DISEASE/GREED	There is no profit in a cure
2759 IDIOM	Break the ice

NUMBER CATEGORY/CREDIT	TOPIC
2760 IDIOM	Burn the candle at both ends
2761 PHILIP ZIMBARDO/ PSYCHOLOGIST/USA	Heroes are those who can somehow resist the power of the situation and act out of noble motives, or behave in ways that do not demaean others when they easily can.
2762 IDIOM	Building castles in the air
2763 ENGLISH PROVERB	What the eyes don't see the heart does not grieve for.
2764 JORGE LUIS BORGES/ WRITER	All that happens to us, including our humiliations, our misfortunes, our embarrassments, all is given to us as raw material, as clay, so that we may shape our art.
2765 IDIOM	Come to one's senses
2766 IDIOM	A hard nut to crack
2767 ENGLISH PROVERB	The road to hell is paved with good intentions.
2768 IDIOM/METAPHOR	Hail Mary pass: last ditch pass in an attempt to win a game
2769 UK/JULIAN TREASURE/ SPEAKING/TEDTALK	We spend roughly 60 percent of our communication time listening, but we're not very good at it. We retain just 25 percent of what we hear.
2770 STEFANO MANCUSO: PLANTS/TEDTALK	Plants are not just able to live; they are able to sense.
2771 BILL JOY/TEDTALK/USA/ COMPUTER SCIENTIST	Today scientists, technologists, businessmen, engineers don't have any personal responsibility for the consequences of their actions.
2772 LEO BUSCAGLIA/USA	Those who think they know it all have no way of finding out they don't.
2773 DR. DAPHNE KOLLER/ COURSERA/US/TEDTALK	High-quality education will move from being something that is a privilege of the few to being a basic human right.
2774 LEO BUSCAGLIA/ AMERICAN WRITER	If you don't like the scene you're in, if you're unhappy, if you're lonely, if you don't feel that things are happening, change your scene. Paint a new backdrop.
2775 NICHOLAS KRISTOFF/ USA/NY TIMES/WRITER	People are less willing to contribute to save kids from cancer if the same amount of money is going to save not one life but eight lives.
2776 ANIMALS/SKILL	Taming of a wild animal
2777 USA/ISAAC BASHEVIS SINGER/WRITER	People often say that humans have always eaten animals, as if this is a justification for continuing the practice.
2778 LEO BUSCAGLIA/USA	Life is a paradise for those who love many things with a passion.
2779 USA/TITLE/JAMES H. BILLINGTON	Fire in the minds of men
2780 CHINESE SAYING	As if the chickens tried talking with the ducks
2781 IDIOM	A good Samaritan
2782 ARTHUR MILLER/ USA/PLAYWRIGHT	Don't be seduced into thinking that that which does not make a profit is without value.
2783 NATIONAL SECURITY	Traitors
2784 ANTHONY TROLLOPE/UK	For there is no folly so great as keeping one's sorrows hidden.
2785 HERBERT SPENCER/UK/ PHILOSOPHER	The great aim of education is not knowledge but action.
2786 IDIOM	Have something at one's fingertips
2787 INDIAN PROVERB	He who does not climb will not fall either.

NUMBER CATEGORY/CREDIT	TOPIC
2788 CIGARETTES	Second-hand smoke
2789 ALBERT EINSTEIN/ PHYSICIST/NOBELIST	If a cluttered desk is a sign of a cluttered mind, what are we to think of an empty one?
2790 MARCEL PROUST/ FRENCH NOVELIST	Happiness is beneficial for the body, but it is grief that develops the powers of the mind.
2791 LOUISA MAY ALCOTT/US/ WRITER	Christmas won't be Christmas without any presents.
2792 IDIOM	A feather in one's cap
2793 SAMUEL JOHNSON/ ENGLISH AUTHOR	He who waits to do a great deal of good at once will never do anything.
2794 NIKKI GIOVANNI/ AMERICAN POET/ WRITER	I resent people who say writers write from experience. Writers don't write from experience, though many are hesitant to admit that they don't. I want to be clear about this. If you wrote from experience, you'd get maybe one book, maybe three poems. Writers write from empathy.
2795 HOME/NATURE/ JOY	Gardening
2796 LOUISA MAY ALCOTT/US	Stay is a charming word in a friend's vocabulary.
2797 CHILDREN/DEATH	The death of a child
2798 DESPAIR	Feeling of helplessness
2799 CHINESE PROVERB	Joy when shared doubles; sorrow when shared, halves.
2800 NOBEL/WOLE SOYINKA/ NIGERIAN WRITER	The hand that dips into the bottom of the pot will eat the biggest snail.
2801 HUMAN CONDITION	Feeling of isolation
2802 NOSTALGIA/PEOPLE	The old familiar faces
2803 SAMUEL JOHNSON/ ENGLISH AUTHOR	In order that all men may be taught to speak truth, it is necessary that all likewise should learn to hear it.
2804 ALDO LEOPOLD/USA	The modern dogma is comfort at any cost.
2805 SUSAN GLASPELL/USA/ PLAYWRIGHT/ACTRESS	Seems nothing draws men together like killing other men.
2806 FRANTZ FANON/WRITER	What matters is not to know the world but to change it.
2807 BILL CLINTON/USA/ PRESIDENT	In earlier history, wealth was measured in land, in gold, in oil, in machines. Today, the principal measure of our wealth is information: its quality, its quantity and speed with which we acquire it and adapt to it.
2808 RELATIONSHIPS	A sense of belonging
2809 USA/ELBERT GREEN HUBBARD/WRITER	The sculptor produces the beautiful statue by chipping away such parts of the marble block as are not needed – it is a process of elimination.
2810 ACHIEVEMENT	Self-motivation
2811 SOCIETY/SUCCESS	An affluent society
2812 MARIO PUZO/WRITER	Never get angry. Never make a threat. Reason with people.
2813 JEAN-PAUL MARAT/ SWISS/SCIENTIST	Man has the right to deal with his oppressors by devouring their palpitating hearts.
2814 ROBERT FULGHUM/ USA/WRITER/TRUE LOVE	We are all a little weird. And life is a little weird. And when we find someone whose weirdness is compatible with ours, we join up with them and fall into mutually satisfying weirdness – and call it love – true love.

NUMBER CATEGORY/CREDIT	TOPIC
2815 USA/WILLIAM S. BURROUGHS/WRITER	A paranoid is someone who knows a little of what's going on.
2816 WILLIAM SHAKESPEARE	Action is eloquence.
2817 N. ZEALAND/KATHERINE MANSFIELD/AUTHOR	I always felt that the great high privilege, relief and comfort of friendship was that one had to explain nothing.
2818 EDUCATION/LOANS	Student loans
2819 CHINESE PROVERB	Men have their say, but women have their way
2820 HERBERT SPENCER/UK/ PHILOSOPHER	Before he can remake his society, his society must make him.
2821 DEREK WALCOTT/POET/ ST. LUCIA/NOBELIST	What are men? Children who doubt.
2822 SUSAN GLASPELL/USA	Be the most you can be, so life will be more because you were.
2823 EMMA GOLDMAN/ RUSSIAN/ ANARCHIST	Someone has said that it requires less mental effort to condemn than to think.
2824 WASHINGTON IRVING/USA/ AUTHOR/ESSAYIST/ HISTORIAN	A mother is the truest friend we have, when trials heavy and sudden fall upon us; when adversity takes the place of prosperity; when friends desert us; when trouble thickens around us, still will she cling to us, and endeavor by her kind precepts and counsels to dissipate the clouds of darkness, and cause peace to return to our hearts.
2825 EDUCATION	Gifted students
2826 V. S. NAIPAUL/WRITER/ INDO-TRINIDADIAN	Life is a helluva thing. You can see trouble coming and you can't do a damn thing to prevent it coming. You just go to sit and watch and wait.
2827 DR. PHIL McGRAW/USA	Every situation needs a hero.
2828 USA/GEORGE WASHINGTON/ 1ST PRESIDENT/USA	True friendship is a plant of slow growth, and must undergo and withstand the shocks of adversity, before it is entitled to the appellation.
2829 SAYING	Don't sweat the small stuff.
2830 ELVIS PRESLEY/USA/ MUSICIAN	I have no use for bodyguards, but I have very specific use for two highly trained certified public accountants.
2831 DR. PHIL/USA/TV	The best protection is self-protection.
2832 EMMA GOLDMAN/ ANARCHIST/CANADA	I'd rather have roses on my table than diamonds on my neck.
2833 MEDICINE/CHARITY	Medicins sans frontiere / Doctors without borders
2834 ANN LANDERS/USA/ CHICAGO SUN TIMES/ ADVICE COLUMNIST	Love is friendship that has caught fire. It is quiet understanding, mutual confidence, sharing and forgiving. It is loyalty through good and bad times. It settles for less than perfection and makes allowances for human weaknesses.
2835 GEORGE SAND/ FRENCH NOVELIST	Guard well within yourself that treasure, kindness. Know how to give without hesitation, how to lose without regret, how to acquire without meanness.
2836 JEFFREY ARCHER/UK ONLY TIME WILL TELL/ UK/AUTHOR	I have discovered with advancing years that few things are entirely black or white, but more often different shades of grey.

NUMBER CATEGORY/CREDIT	TOPIC
2837 JIM CARREY/USA/CANADA/ACTOR	You can fail at what you don't want, so you might as well take a chance on doing what you love.
2838 CORRUPTION	Influence peddling
2839 ISAAC BASHEVIS SINGER/WRITER	When I was a little boy, they called me a liar, but now that I am grown up, they call me a writer.
2840 ISAIAH BERLIN/UK/MUSICIAN/RUSSIA	To understand is to perceive patterns.
2841 LOU REED/UK/USA	The most important part of my religion is to play the guitar.
2842 USA/WASHINGTON IRVING/AUTHOR	A kind heart is a fountain of gladness, making everything in its vicinity freshen into smiles
2843 ISLAM	*Fatwa* – a religious edict
2844 POLITICS/ PRESSURE	Taking political heat
2845 USA/WILLIAM S. BURROUGHS/WRITER	Nobody owns life, but anyone who can pick up a frying pan owns death.
2846 GERRY SPENCE/USA	The way people move is their autobiography in motion.
2847 USA/WILLIAM S. BURROUGHS/WRITER	Silence is only frightening to people who are compulsively verbalizing.
2848 SAM WALTON/USA/ENTREPRENEUR/WALMART/FOUNDER	I probably have traveled and walked into more variety stores than anybody in America. I am just trying to get ideas, any kind that will help our company. Most of us don't invent ideas. We take the best ideas from someone else..
2849 CHANDRA NAIR/CEO/GLOBAL INSTITUTE	5 billion Asians in 2050 cannot live like Americans. You don't need to be a rocket scientist to know that.
2850 EXPRESSION OF HATE	Hate mail
2851 USA/WILLIAM S. BURROUGHS/WRITER	I don't care if people hate my guts…The important question is whether they are in a position to do anything about it.
2852 PERSONAL/NATIONAL	Feeling of responsibility
2853 ISAIAH BERLIN/UK/POLITICAL THEORIST	Freedom for the wolves has often meant death to the sheep.
2854 IDIOM	Betting the ranch
2855 JEAN M. TWENGE/USA/AUTHOR/PROFESSOR	The purpose of school is for children to learn, not for them to feel good about themselves all the time.
2856 USA/WILLIAM S. BURROUGHS/WRITER	Your mind will answer most questions if you learn to relax and wait for an answer.
2857 GEORGE SAND/FRANCE/WRITER	No human creature can give orders to love.
2858 NUCLEAR/AXIOM OF PROLIFERATION	As long as any country has nuclear weapons other countries will seek to get them.
2859 PERSPECTIVE/INSIGHT	The big picture
2860 HATE/PREJUDICE	A poisoned mind
2861 P.J. O'ROURKE/WRITER	No drug, not even alcohol, causes the fundamental ills of society. If we're looking for the source of our troubles, we shouldn't test people for drugs, we should test them for stupidity, ignorance, greed, and love of power.

NUMBER CATEGORY/CREDIT	TOPIC
2862 LOU REED/UK/USA/ ROCK STAR	The music is all. Poeple should die for it. People are dying for everything else, so why not the music?
2863 SAMUEL JOHNSON/ ENGLISH AUTHOR	Life is not long, and too much of it must not pass in idle deliberation how it shall be spent.
2864 LIFE/CONSEQUENCES	Domino effect
2865 STEREOTYPE	Bungling bureaucrats
2866 ACTOR/MOLIERE/ PLAYWRIGHT	It is not only what we do, but also what we do not do, for which we are accountable.
2867 PUNISHMENT	Turning the screws on someone
2868 ISAIAH BERLIN/ BRITISH/ESSAYIST	Out of the crooked timber of humanity, nothing completely straight was ever made.
2869 POWER	Totalitarianism
2870 FRANTZ FANON/ PSYCHIATRIST	A man who has a language consequently possesses the world expressed and implied by that language..
2871 CHARITY	NGO's (Non Governmental Organizations)
2872 SAM WALTON/USA/ ENTREPRENEUR	The two most important words I ever wrote were on that first Wal-Mart sign, 'Satisfaction Guaranteed'.
2873 USA/THEODORE HESBURGH/CLERGYMAN	All of us are experts at practicing virtue at a distance.
2874 ISAIAH BERLIN/ BRITISH/ESSAYIST	...to be free to choose, and not to be chosen for, is an inalienable ingredient in what makes human beings human.
2875 IDIOM	A tall order
2876 IDIOM	Breathing space
2877 GERRY SPENCE/ AMERICAN LAWYER/ AUTHOR	Children, as persons, are entitled to the greatest respect. Children are given to us as free-flying souls, but then we clip their wings like we domesticate the wild mallard.
2878 USA/WILLIAM S. BURROUGHS/ ESSAYIST/WRITER	The question is frequently asked: Why does a man become a drug addict? The answer is that he usually does not intend to become an addict. You don't wake up one morning and decide to be a drug addict.
2879 PHILIP ZIMBARDO/ USA/PSYCHOLOGIST	The line between good and evil is permeable and almost anyone can be induced to cross it when pressured by situational forces.
2880 JAPAN/TRADITION	Bonsai trees
2881 MADELEINE LEVINE/US/ CLINICAL PSYCHOLOGIST	The most toxic part of over-parenting, I think, is when we confuse our own needs with our children's needs.
2882 STYLE/CULTURE	Nose rings
2883 JEFFREY ARCHER/UK/ A PRISONER OF BIRTH	Are parents always more ambitious for their children than they are for themselves?
2884 ST. FRANCIS DE SALES/ BISHOP OF GENEVA	When you encounter difficulties and contradictions, do not try to break them, but bend them with gentleness and time.
2885 GUSTAVE FLAUBERT/ FRENCH NOVELIST	Anything becomes interesting if you look at it long enough.
2886 LOUISA MAY ALCOTT/ US/NOVELIST	Housekeeping ain't no joke.

NUMBER CATEGORY/CREDIT	TOPIC
2887 LOUISA MAY ALCOTT/ USA/NOVELIST	I want to do something splendid...Something heroic or wonderful that won't be forgotten after I'm dead...I think I shall write books.
2888 MARLO THOMAS/ USA/ACTRESS	My father said there were two kinds of people: givers and takers. The takers may eat better, but the givers sleep better.
2889 HECTOR BOLITHO/ UK/ COMPETITION IS A SIN/THIS I BELIEVE	I believe that history should be re-written for children so that they may comprehend the motives behind action. They should be taught that actions do not speak louder than words if the words are audible expressions of thought.
2890 WORKPLACE/IMAGE	White-collar workers
2891 PERSISTENCE	Going from strength to strength
2892 HENRY WADSWORTH LONGFELLOW/USA/POET	Talk not of wasted affection; affection never was wasted.
2893 TEACHERS/GLOBAL	Gurus
2894 J C PENNEY/USA/ BUSINESS/VALUES	I would never have amounted to anything were it not for adversity. I was forced to come up the hard way.
2895 ACTOR/MOLIERE/ PLAYWRIGHT	Life is a tragedy to those who feel and a comedy to those who think.
2896 PERSONAL	I'm good at...
2897 JOHNNY CASH/USA	You build on failure. You use it as a stepping stone.
2898 USA/POET/HENRY W. LONGFELLOW	Perseverance is a great element of success. If you only knock long enough at the gate, you are sure to wake up somebody.
2899 WASHINGTON IRVING/USA/HISTORIAN	There is in every true woman's heart a spark of heavenly fire, which lies dormant in the broad daylight of prosperity; but which kindles up, and beams and blazes in the dark hour of adversity.
2900 PERFORMANCE	The role of a lifetime
2901 TAVIS SMILEY/USA/ BROADCASTER	Too many children are forced to surrender their life's choices before they ever know their life's chances.
2902 JOHNNY CASH/USA	My arms are too short to box with God.
2903 PROCRASTINATION	Dilly-dallying
2904 MANNERS/CHIVALRY	Ladies first
2905 FAIRNESS/SOCIETY	First come first served
2906 LOUISA MAY ALCOTT/US	I'm not afraid of storms, for I'm learning how to sail my ship.
2907 USA/ELBERT GREEN HUBBARD/WRITER	Parties who want milk should not seat themselves on a stool in the middle of the field in hope that the cow will back up to them.
2908 SAMUEL JOHNSON/ ENGLISH AUTHOR	The two most engaging powers of an author are to make new things familiar and familiar things new.
2909 MOLIERE/FRENCH	Trees that are slow to grow bear the best fruit.
2910 R.S. LAWRENCE/AUTHOR	To speak well in public you must think well in private.
2911 JAPAN/OLD FEMININE IDEAL	Yamatonadeshiko : Traditional image of long-suffering Japanese woman
2912 JAPAN/MODERN GIRLS	YamatonadeGucci: Brand-name obsessed modern Japanese girls
2913 CEREMONY	Honored guests

NUMBER CATEGORY/CREDIT	TOPIC
2914 JEFFREY ARCHER/UK/ ONLY TIME WILL TELL	I find I don't learn a lot while I'm talking.
2915 ALDO LEOPOLD/USA/ SCIENTIST/WRITER	Non-conformity is the highest evolutionary attainment of social animals.
2916 IDIOM	A basket case
2917 IDIOM	A work in progress
2918 USA/WASHINGTON IRVING/AUTHOR	There is a sacredness in tears. They are not the mark of weakness, but of power. They speak more eloquently than ten thousand tongues.
2919 PSYCHOLOGY	Inferiority complex
2920 BOOKS	Detective stories
2921 COMFORT/ FASHION	Wearing sensible shoes
2922 JOSS WHEDON/USA/ SCREENWRITER	If you can't run, you crawl. If you can't crawl, you find someone to carry you.
2923 BOOKS	Thrillers
2924 FRANK McCOURT/USA	You might be poor, your shoes might be broken, but your mind is a palace.
2925 SAMUEL JOHNSON/UK	Men more frequently require to be reminded than informed.
2926 DEANNE D. SELLNOW/ USA/PROFESSOR	Looking like a professional tends to improve speaker credibility.
2927 JOSS WHEDON/USA	Half of writing history is hiding the truth.
2928 LOUISA MAY ALCOTT/ AMERICAN NOVELIST/ LITTLE WOMEN	Have regular hours for work and play: make each day both useful and pleasant, and prove that you understand the worth of time by employing it well. Then youth will bring few regrets, and life will become a beautiful success.
2929 SAMUEL JOHNSON/UK/ AUTHOR/POET/ESSAYIST	I hate mankind, for I think myself one of the best of them, and I know how bad I am.
2930 ARABIC SAYING	A thousand knocks at the door, but no invitation from within.
2931 PERSONAL/EFFORT	Personal best
2932 MOLIERE/FRENCH	The greater the obstacle, the more glory in overcoming it.
2933 USA/ANN LANDERS/USA	Problems are inevitable. Misery is a choice.
2934 LAO TZU/CHINESE PHILOSOPHER	The best [man] is like water. Water is good; it benefits all things and does not compete with them. It dwells in [lowly] places that all disdain. This is why it so near to Tao.
2935 TRADE/PERSONAL	Barter
2936 ASPIRATIONS/FRAUD	Get rich quick schemes
2937 CELINE DION/ CANADIAN SINGER	I often buy myself presents. Sometimes I will spend $100,000 in one day in a posh boutique.
2938 LEWIS CARROLL/UK	If you don't know where you are going, any road will get you there.
2939 H.L. MENCKEN/WRITER	Any man who afflicts the human race with his ideas must be prepared to see them misunderstood.
2940 JIM CARREY/USA/ CANADA/ACTOR	I hope everybody could get rich and famous and have everything they ever dreamed of, so they will know that it's not the answer.
2941 MENCIUS/CHINESE PHILOSOPHER	Every duty is a charge, but the charge of oneself is the root of all others.

NUMBER CATEGORY/CREDIT	TOPIC
2942 STEPHEN RUSSELL/ BAREFOOT DOCTOR'S GUIDE TO THE TAO	You can trust everyone to be human, with all the quirks and inconsistencies we humans display, including disloyalty, dishonesty and downright treachery.
2943 TED TURNER/USA/BIZ	If only I had a little humility, I'd be perfect.
2944 LAO TZU/CHINESE PHILOSOPHER	Knowing others is intelligence; knowing yourself is true wisdom. Mastering others is strength; mastering yourself is true power.
2945 ST. FRANCIS DE SALES/BISHOP/GENEVA	A quarrel between friends, when made up, adds a new tie to friendship.
2946 EMMA GOLDMAN/ RUSSIAN/ANARCHIST	Women need not always keep their mouths shut and their wombs open.
2947 CHARACTER/RESPECT	Fulfilling a promise
2948 ST. FRANCIS DE SALES/BISHOP/GENEVA	Nothing is so strong as gentleness, nothing so gentle as real strength.
2949 INDIAN PROVERB	Pearls are of no value in a desert.
2950 ARABIC SAYING	A thousand cranes in the air are not worth one sparrow in the fist.
2951 RALPH WALDO EMERSON	A good indignation brings out all one's powers.
2952 CULTURE/TV	Reality TV
2953 JOSS WHEDON/USA/ TELEVISION PRODUCER	Don't give people what they want. Give them what they need.
2954 CELINE DION/ CANADIAN SINGER	Golf is a search for perfection, for balance. It's about meditation and concentration. You have to use hand and brain.
2955 BARACK OBAMA/ 44TH PRESIDENT/USA/ U.N. SPEECH/2012	The future must not belong to those who bully women – it must be shaped by girls who go to school, and those who stand for a world where our daughters can live their dreams just like our sons.
2956 JOAN BAEZ/USA/SINGER	The only thing that's been a worse flop than the organization of nonviolence has been the organization of violence.
2957 BLESSING	Windfall
2958 ADVICE	You are what you eat.
2959 ARABIC SAYING	If a worthless fellow be with you, do not let him go, or else one worse will come to you.
2960 RELATIONSHIPS	Cougar – an older woman dating a younger man
2961 MYSTERY/SURPRISE	Wonders shall never cease.
2962 PROSPECTS	Moving to higher ground
2963 EMMA GOLDMAN/USA/ POLITICAL ACTIVIST	Every society has the criminals it deserves.
2964 SAYING/SOCIETY	Rules are meant to be broken.
2965 CHARACTER	Stubborn streak
2966 PARENTING	Quality time
2967 COLIN ALLEN/THIS I BELIEVE/USA	I have never known anyone who was happier for breaking the Ten Commandments or the Golden Rule.
2968 ARABIC SAYING	If your neighbor dislikes you, change the gate of your home.
2969 H. P. LOVECRAFT/USA/ WRITER	The oldest and strongest emotion of mankind is fear, and the oldest and strongest kind of fear is fear of the unknown.

NUMBER CATEGORY/CREDIT	TOPIC
2970 DAVID LYNCH/USA/ FILM MAKER	Ideas are like fish. If you want to catch little fish you can stay in the shallow water. But if you want to catch the big fish, you've got to go deeper.
2971 DOLLY PARTON/USA/ MUSICIAN/BUSINESS	A bird and a fish can fall in love but where do they make a home?
2972 EXERCISE	Exertainment
2973 LOUIS STEVENSON/SCOT NOVELIST/ESSAYIST	Don't judge each day by the harvest you reap, but by the seeds you plant.
2974 J C PENNEY/USA/ BUSINESS/ VALUES	When this business was founded, it sought to win public confidence through service for it was my conviction then, as it is now, that nothing else than right service to the public results in mutual understanding and satisfaction between customer and merchant.
2975 THE GREATER FOOL THEORY	Greater fool theory: the notion that even if you paid a ridiculously high amount of money for something, eventually, a greater fool (than you) will come along and pay an even more ridiculous amount for the privilege of taking the item off your hands.
2976 RESPONSIBILITY	Missing in action (MIA)
2977 ARABIC SAYING	If you see a wall inclining, run from under it.
2978 ABD AL-LATIF/LEGAL & MEDICAL SCHOLAR/ 1162/3-1231/A. HOURANI	When you read a book, make every effort to learn it by heart and master its meaning. Imagine the book to have disappeared and that you can dispense with it, unaffected by its loss.
2979 MISTAKES/CHANGE	Change of heart
2980 SIR KINGSLEY AMIS/ ENGLISH NOVELIST	If you can't annoy somebody, there is little point in writing.
2981 RICHARD NIXON/ USA/PRESIDENT	When the president does it, that means that it's not illegal.
2982 ALICE MUNRO/ CANADIAN WRITER	There is a limit to the amount of misery and disarray you will put up with, for love, just as there is a limit to the amount of mess you can stand around a house. You can't know the limit beforehand, but you will know when you've reached it.
2983 LEWIS CARROLL/ ENGLISH AUTHOR	One of the deep secrets of life is that all that is really worth the doing is what we do for others.
2984 ARABIC SAYING	The beetle is a beauty in the eyes of its mother.
2985 ANGER/CONFLICT	Road rage
2986 CLIMATE/WEATHER	Snowstorms
2987 JAMES BALDWIN/ USA/AUTHOR	It is certain, in any case, that ignorance, allied with power, is the most ferocious enemy justice can have.
2988 ACHIEVEMENT	Participating in contests
2989 JACQUES COUSTEAU/ FRENCH/EXPLORER	What is a scientist after all? It is a curious person looking through a keyhole, the keyhole of nature, trying to know what's going on.
2990 SUCCESS/IDIOM	Hitting the bull's eye
2991 IDIOM/COWARDICE	A person without spine
2992 BOXING/MONEY	Prize fight: a boxing match with a cash prize for the winner
2993 ALBERT SCHWEITZER GERMAN/THEOLOGIAN	The greatest evil is to destroy life, to injure life, to repress life that is capable of development

NUMBER CATEGORY/CREDIT	TOPIC
2994 EMMA GOLDMAN/ USA/ ANARCHIST	Give us what belongs to us in peace, and if you don't give it to us in peace, we will take it by force.
2995 ISAAC BASHEVIS SINGER/WRITER	There are 500 reasons I write for children...Children read books, not reviews.
2996 MAUREEN DOWD/USA/ COLUMNIST	Deceive, you're golden; tell the truth, you're gone.
2997 USA/POET/HENRY W. LONGFELLOW	If you must hit the mark, you must aim a little bit above it. Every arrow that flies feels the pull of the earth.
2998 ARABIC SAYING	Throw him into the river and he will emerge with a fish in his mouth.
2999 USA/POET/HENRY W. LONGFELLOW	For age is opportunity no less than youth itself, though in another dress. And as the evening twilight fades away, the Sky is filled with stars, invisible by day.
3000 MEDITATION	Buddhist chants
3001 JILL BOLTE TAYLOR/ SCIENTIST/AUTHOR	Unfortunately, we do not teach children that they need to tend carefully the garden of their minds.
3002 MENCIUS/THINKER	If the king loves music, there is little wrong in the land.
3003 ANNE FRANK/WRITER	Laziness may appear attractive, but work gives satisfaction.
3004 USA/POET/HENRY W. LONGFELLOW	The heights by great men reached and kept. Were not attained by sudden flights. But they, while their companions slept, they were toiling upwards in the night.
3005 MEDICINE	Medical specialists
3006 CHRIS COLE/USA/ SKATEBOARDER	A skateboarder's way of thought is so different that I feel if somebody had some sort of dilemma in their life you could ask a skateboarder for an outside opinion. You may get something that is absolutely ridiculous or you could get something that's absolutely brilliant.
3007 USA/POET/HENRY W. LONGFELLOW	Most people would succeed in small things if they were not troubled with great ambitions.
3008 FOOD/HEALTH	Seafood
3009 MENCIUS/THINKER	In abundance prepare for scarcity.
3010 FAILURE/POWER	Feeling of defeat
3011 JILL BOLTE TAYLOR/ STROKE OF INSIGHT	When we are being compassionate, we consider another's circumstance with love rather than judgment.
3012 COURAGE/DANGER	A person with guts
3013 JOHN 4:44/KJ BIBLE	...a prophet hath no honor in his own country.
3014 RELATIONSHIPS	The way to a man's heart is through his stomach.
3015 PEOPLE	Lifespan
3016 CICELY TYSON/ AMERICAN ACTRESS	When I told my mother that I wanted to be an actress, she said, you can't live here and do that, and so I moved out. I was determined to prove her wrong because she was so sure that I was going to go astray. And that's the juice that kept me going.
3017 ALBERT EINSTEIN/ NOBEL LAUREATE	Insanity: doing the same thing over and over again and expecting different results
3018 LOUISA MAY ALCOTT/ USA/NOVELIST	What do girls do who haven't any mother to help them through their troubles?

NUMBER CATEGORY/CREDIT	TOPIC
3019 JEFFREY ARCHER/UK/ POLITICIAN	...we all suffer in our different ways from being prisoners of birth.
3020 U.S. POSTAL SYSTEM	No living person shall be honored by portrayal on U.S. postage.
3021 NATION/STRIFE	Civil war
3022 PEOPLE/CITIES	Name change
3023 JAMES FREY/USA/ WRITER	Addiction is a decision. An individual wants something, whatever that something is, and makes a decision to get it.
3024 MEDICINE	Online drug sales
3025 MEN/GROOMING	Metrosexuals
3026 JACQUES COUSTEAU/ CONSERVATIONIST	For most of history, man has had to fight nature to survive; in this century he is beginning to realize that, in order to survive, he must protect it.
3027 USA/J C PENNEY/ BUSINESSMAN/ BUSINESS VALUES	The friendly smile, the word of greeting, are certainly something fleeting and seemingly insubstantial. You can't take them with you. But they work good beyond your power to measure their influence. It is the service we are not obliged to give that people value most.
3028 DENG XIAOPING/ CHINESE LEADER	It does not matter the color of the cat as long as it can catches mice.
3029 PRINCE CHARLES/UK	I learned the way a monkey learns – by watching its parents.
3030 PEGGY NOONAN/USA/ SPEECHWRITER	Don't' fall in love with politicians, they're all a disappointment. They can't help it, they just are.
3031 STEPHEN HUNT/UK	Even a broken clock is right twice a day.
3032 PROVERB	A word to the wise is enough.
3033 LAW/PERSISTENCE	Tentacles of the law
3034 PEGGY NOONAN/USA/ SPEECHWRITER	Cynicism is not realistic and tough. It's unrealistic and kind of cowardly because it means you don't have to try.
3035 ST FRANCIS DE SALES/BISHOP/GENEVA	There was never an angry man that thought his anger unjust.
3036 CELEBRITY	Being famous for being famous
3037 JILL BOLTE TAYLOR/ STROKE/TED.COM	Just like children, emotions heal when they are heard and validated
3038 KAITLIN QUISTGAARD/ YOGA/NY TIMES	The real value of yoga...is the opportunity it offers to know yourself.
3039 ST FRANCIS DE SALES/ BISHOP OF GENEVA	Those who love to be feared fear to be loved.
3040 WEIGHT LOSS	Fat farms
3041 DALE CARNEGIE/USA	How to win friends and influence people
3042 MALCOLM S. FORBES/US	Education's purpose is to replace an empty mind with an open one.
3043 DALE CARNEGIE/BOOK	How to Stop Worrying and Start Living
3044 LOVE/SYMBOLS	The perfect symbol of love
3045 ARABIC SAYING	Don't pray for the destruction of the house from which you eat.
3046 INDIA	*Dalit* / Untouchables
3047 BEAUTY	Anti-aging medicine/efforts
3048 ARABIC SAYING	The wise with a wink, the fool with a kick, are taught to understand.

NUMBER CATEGORY/CREDIT	TOPIC
3049 JOSEPH CAMPBELL/USA	The cave you fear to enter holds the treasure you seek.
3050 MALCOLM S. FORBES/US	Everybody has to be somebody to somebody to be anybody.
3051 SALLY RIDE/USA/ ASTRONAUT	The world and our perceptions have changed a lot, even since the '70s, but there are lingering stereotypes. If you ask an 11-year-old to draw a scientist, she's likely to draw a geeky guy with a pocket protector. That's just not an image an 11-year-old girl aspires to.
3052 SAM WALTON/USA	Capitalism isn't scarce; vision is.
3053 JACQUES COUSTEAU/ FRENCH/EXPLORER	Water and air, the two essential fluids on which all life depends, have become global garbage cans.
3054 BIBLE/MATTHEW 7:7	Ask and it will be given to you.
3055 DELICACY	Snake soup
3056 AFRICA/ASIA/HEALTH	Bleaching of skin
3057 SOCIETY	Science and progress
3058 GERRY SPENCE/ AMERICAN LAWYER	To bargain freedom for security is the devil's bargain. Having made the bargain, one enjoys neither freedom nor security.
3059 AFRICA	The Sahara Desert
3060 FINANCE	Being in debt
3061 JILL BOLTE TAYLOR/USA	Peace is only a thought away.
3062 JAPANESE PROVERB	If you stop at a place, better get in the shade of a big tree.
3063 DECISIONMAKING	Groupthink
3064 STEVE JOBS/ ENTREPRRENEUR/ APPLE COMPUTERS	When I was 17, I read a quote that went something like: "If you live each day as if it was your last, someday you'll most certainly be right." It made an impression on me...
3065 POET/RALPH WALDO EMERSON/USA	There are many things of which a wise man might wish to be ignorant.
3066 ARABIC SAYING	A single spark can burn the whole quarter.
3067 HEALTH	Cigars
3068 MALCOLM S. FORBES/US	Failure is success if we learn from it.
3069 ISAAC BASHEVIS SINGER/US WRITER	Doubt is part of all religion. All the religious thinkers were doubters.
3070 FRENCH/NAPOLEON	Never interrupt your enemy when he is making a mistake.
3071 ARABIC SAYING	At the narrow passage there is no brother and no friend.
3072 ARABIC SAYING	Poverty and anger do not go together.
3073 JAPANESE PROVERB	A country may go to ruin, but its mountains and streams remain.
3074 RELATIONSHIPS	Master-servant relationship
3075 MALCOLM S. FORBES/US	If you have a job without any aggravations, you don't have a job.
3076 ARABIC SAYING	If my friend is wrong, I reproach him in secret, but praise him in the company of others.
3077 FAILURE/IDIOM	Licking your wounds
3078 ARABIC SAYING	If kindness will not change a person, neither will bad treatment.
3079 FAILURE/PRIDE	When glory turns to ashes
3080 CONFUCIUS/CHINA	Only the wisest and stupidest of men never change.

NUMBER CATEGORY/CREDIT	TOPIC
3081 BUSINESS/BOYCOTT	Voting with your feet
3082 FAILURE/PRIDE	Too proud to admit defeat
3083 PRIDE/COMPETITION	Showing off
3084 STORIES/CULTURE	Folk tales
3085 JAPANESE SAYING	As though a bird had flown up from under your feet
3086 MALCOLM S. FORBES	If you never budge, don't expect a push.
3087 SAM WALTON/USA/ENTREPRENEUR	High expectations is the key to everything.
3088 SOCIETY/JUSTICE	Exposure of an injustice
3089 WILLIAM COWPER/UK	Variety is the spice of life.
3090 MALCOLM S. FORBES/PUBLISHER	Executives who get there and stay suggest solutions when they present the problems.
3091 USA/BEN LUCIEN BURMAN/ANTIDOTE FOR WAR/THIS I BELIEVE	I believe we need beauty in our lives just as much as we need food on our dining room tables. A world where beauty flourishes is a happy world, a world at peace.
3092 STEVE JOBS/APPLE COMPUTERS/USA	We think basically you watch television to turn your brain off, and you work on your computer when you want to turn your brain on.
3093 FESTIVAL/BRAZIL	Carnival
3094 JACQUES COUSTEAU/FRENCH/EXPLORER	We are living in an interminable succession of absurdities imposed by the myopic logic of short-term thinking.
3095 IYANLA VANZANT/USA/LIFE COACH	Unfortunately pain gets your attention, and as human beings the fastest way we learn is when we are in pain.
3096 IDIOM	Fool's paradise
3097 SOCIETY/PEOPLE	Decision by consensus
3098 THOMAS MANN/GERMAN NOVELIST	We do not fear being called meticulous, inclining as we do to the view that only the exhaustive can be truly interesting.
3099 MALCOLM S. FORBES/US	Let your children go if you want to keep them.
3100 POTTER STEWART/USA/SUPREME COURT	Ethics is knowing the difference between what you have a right to do and what is right to do.
3101 SIR KEN ROBINSON/UK	Very many people go through their whole lives having no real sense of what their talents may be, or if they have any to speak of.
3102 CORETTA SCOTT KING/USA/	Hate is too great a burden to bear. It injures the hater more than it injures the hated.
3103 ARABIC SAYING	He who eats alone coughs alone.
3104 COMMUNICATION	Euphemisms
3105 PLATO/THINKER	A work well begun is half-ended.
3106 JAMES ALLEN/AUTHOR	They who have conquered doubt and fear have conquered failure.
3107 JAPANESE SAYING/CLASS DIFFERENCES	I would like to break off the flower, but the branch is too high.
3108 FRENCH SAYING	A throne is only a bench covered with velvet.
3109 ANN LANDERS/USA/ADVICE COLUMNIST	Don't accept your dog's admiration as conclusive evidence that you are wonderful.

NUMBER CATEGORY/CREDIT	TOPIC
3110 KOREAN PROVERB	The bad calligrapher is choosy about his brushes.
3111 KOREAN PROVERB	When there are no tigers, a wild cat is very self-important.
3112 WILLIAM JAMES/ USA	If you care enough for a result, you will most certainly attain it.
3113 GERMAN SAYING	Anger without power is folly.
3114 USA/MARIO PUZO	Many young men started down a false path to their true destiny. Time and fortune usually set them aright.
3115 JULIETTE BINOCHE/ FRENCH ACTRESS	Being a famous actress may give you a sense of being important, but believe me, it's just an illusion.
3116 OSCAR WILDE/IRISH WRITER	It is a curious fact that people are never so trivial as when the take themselves seriously.
3117 MARGARET HEFFERNAN/ USA/BUSINESS/TED.COM	Humans do not have enough mental capacity to do all the things we think we can do. As attentional load increases, attentional capacity gradually diminishes.
3118 FRENCH SAYING	An old rat is a brave rat.
3119 GERMAN SAYING	A teacher is better than two books.
3120 ETHICS/MORALITY	Would you allow someone to take responsibility for a crime you inadvertently committed?
3121 ARABIC SAYING	Only the person in the bath knows how hot it is in there.
3122 WILLIAM SHAKESPEARE/ COMEDY OF ERRORS	He must have a long spoon that must eat with the devil.
3123 FAMILY	Causes of divorce
3124 MARGARET ATWOOD/ CANADIAN NOVELIST	Potential has a shelf life.
3125 LAW/FRIENDSHIP	Will you commit perjury to defend your best friend?
3126 ANN LANDERS/USA/ ADVICE COLUMNIST	Make somebody happy today, and mind your own business.
3127 GERRY SPENCE/USA/ LAWYER	Is there anyone I wouldn't take as a client? Well, I'd never represent a banker.
3128 MALCOLM S. FORBES/US	Men who never get carried away should be.
3129 ALEISTER CROWLEY/ ENGLISH OCCULTIST	Paganism is wholesome because it faces the facts of life.
3130 LIFE/EXPERIENCE	Street smarts
3131 POLITICS	Lame-duck leader
3132 USA/BOOKER T. WASHINGTON	No race can prosper till it learns that there is as much dignity in tilling a field as in writing a poem.
3133 RICHARD SCARRY/ USA/CHILDREN'S BOOK WRITER	I'm not interested in creating a book that is read once and then placed on the shelf and forgotten. I am very happy when people have worn out my books, or that they're held together by Scotch tape.
3134 PEGGY NOONAN/ SPEECHWRITER/USA	Boundaries aren't all bad. That's why there are walls around mental institutions.
3135 USA/RICHARD P. FEYNMAN/PHYSICIST	For a successful technology, reality must take precedence over public relations, for nature cannot be fooled.
3136 MAUREEN DOWD/ USA/COLUMNIST	The minute you settle for less than you deserve, you get even less than you settled for.

NUMBER CATEGORY/CREDIT	TOPIC
3137 JOHNNY CASH/USA/ MUSICIAN	Close the door on the past. You don't try to forget the mistakes, but you don't dwell on it. You don't let it have any of your energy, or any of your time, or any of your space.
3138 THOMAS MANN/ GERMAN NOVELIST/ NOBEL LAUREATE	I have always been an admirer; I regard the gift of admiration as indispensable if one is to amount to something. I don't know where I would be without it.
3139 FRENCH SAYING	When a doctor succeeds in curing a patient, the sun sees it; but if he kills a patient, the earth hides it.
3140 HARRY BROWNE/USA/ AUTHOR/	Everyone will experience the consequences of his own acts. If his acts are right, he'll get good consequences; if they're not, he'll suffer for it.
3141 MALCOLM S. FORBES/ USA/PUBLISHER	People who matter are most aware that everyone else does too.
3142 INJUSTICE	A petition to the emperor
3143 FRANCE/NAPOLEON BONAPARTE/LEADER	Show me a family of readers, and I will show you the people who move the world.
3144 STEVE JOBS/USA/ BUSINESS	We have always been shameless about stealing great ideas.
3145 MALCOLM S. FORBES/ USA/BUSINESS	Presence is more than just being there.
3146 SAFETY/CELEBRITY	Body guards
3147 SUGGESTION	Fishing is unfair to fish
3148 MILITARY/HONOR	Stolen valor
3149 FRENCH SAYING	A hedge between keeps friendship green.
3150 MARCEL PROUST/ FRENCH NOVELIST	Everything we think of as great has come to us from neurotics. It is they and they alone who found religions and create great works of art.
3151 SPORTS/RISK	Extreme sports
3152 JOSEPH CAMPBELL/USA	The hero's journey always begins with a call.
3153 ARABIC SAYING	The mother of a coward has nothing to worry about.
3154 HARRIET TUBMAN/USA/ ABOLITIONIST	I was the conductor of the Underground Railway for eight years, and I can say what most conductors can't say -- I never ran my train off the track and I never lost a passenger.
3155 PYTHAGORAS/THINKER	Do not say a little in many words but a great deal in a few.
3156 MARGARET ATWOOD/ CANADIAN NOVELIST	An eye for an eye only leads to more blindness.
3157 CHALLENGE/IDIOM	Rising to the occasion
3158 FAILURE	Rebuilding one's confidence
3159 USA/CHARLES LINDBERGH/AVIATOR	Real freedom lies in wildness, not in civilization.
3160 UNITED NATIONS	Peacekeeping
3161 HARRY BROWNE/ AUTHOR/USA	You don't have to buy from anyone. You don't have to work at any particular job. You don't have to participate in any given relationship. You can choose.
3162 INNOVATION/IDIOM	Pushing the envelope

NUMBER CATEGORY/CREDIT	TOPIC
3163 SELF-APPRECIATION	Self-gifting
3164 PHYSICIAN/ALBERT SCHWEITZER	If you love something so much let it go. If it comes back it was meant to be; if it doesn't it never was.
3165 JOHN GOTTI/ AMERICAN GANGSTER	I never lie because I don't fear anyone. You only lie when you're afraid.
3166 PEGGY NOONAN/USA/ SPEECHWRITER	As we have become more open minded (tolerant) in society we have become more closed hearted.
3167 CREATE A STORY/FUN	Lying in a hammock is serious business.
3168 DEMOCRACY	People power
3169 FRENCH SAYING	Friends are lost by calling them too often and by seldom calling.
3170 MICHAEL ONDAATJE/ CANADA/WRITER	All I ever wanted was a world without maps.
3171 MALCOLM S. FORBES	The best vision is insight.
3172 CRIME	Public enemy number one
3173 USA/STEVE JOBS/ ENTREPRENEUR	It's really hard to design products by focus groups. A lot of times, people don't know what they want until you show it to them.
3174 THOMAS MANN/WRITER	War is only a cowardly escape from the problems of peace.
3175 COMMUNICATION	English provides a global link.
3176 JOHN M. GOTTMAN/ PSYCHOLOGIST	If you think your boss is stupid, remember: you woun't have a job if he was any smarter.
3177 GERRY SPENCE/USA LAWYER/WRITER	The function of the law is not to provide justice or to preserve freedom. The function of the law is to keep those who hold power, in power.
3178 PSYCHOLOGY	Co-dependency
3179 ARABIC SAYING	A well is not to be filled with dew.
3180 UK/SIR WINSTON CHURCHILL	Personally I'm always ready to learn, although I do not always like being taught.
3181 FRENCH/ALBERT SCHWEITZER/CLERGY	Sometimes our light goes out, but is blown again into instant flame by an encounter with another human being.
3182 INDIRA GANDHI/INDIA/ PRIME MINISTER	To be liberated, woman must feel free to be herself, not in rivalry to man but in the context of her own capacity and her personality.
3183 BENJAMIN DISRAELI/ UK/PRIME MINISTER	Tobacco is the tomb of love.
3184 ENGLISH PROVERB	One of these days is none of these days.
3185 ENGLISH PROVERB	An empty purse frightens away friends.
3186 ORGANIZATIONS	Code of ethics
3187 GERRY SPENCE/USA	Money in doses disproportionate to our needs enslaves.
3188 PERSONAL	Self-control
3189 PERSONAL	False hope
3190 ARAB SAYING	He caused his bird to run away, and then went running after it.
3191 LADY GAGA/USA/MUSIC	Trust is like a mirror. You can fix it if it's broken, but you can still see the crack in [the] reflection.
3192 SAYING/CAUTION	What goes up must come down.

NUMBER CATEGORY/CREDIT	TOPIC
3193 MALCOLM S. FORBES/ USA/BUSINESS	The biggest mistake people make in life is not trying to make a living at doing what they most enjoy.
3194 MICHAEL JACKSON/ AMERICAN MUSICAN	Lies run sprints, But the truth runs marathons!
3195 RELATIONSHIPS	Need for personal space
3196 HANS CHRISTIAN ANDERSEN/DANISH	Where words fail, music speaks.
3197 WILLIAM SHAKESPEARE	The devil can cite scripture for his purpose.
3198 JEREMY BENTHAM	Nonsense on stilts
3199 JAPAN/TRADITION	Sumo wrestling
3200 LAW/JUSTICE	Supreme court
3201 SAYING	Every house has its treasure
3202 MARGARET ATWOOD/ CANADIAN NOVELIST	A ratio of failures is built into the process of writing. The wastebasket has evolved for a reason.
3203 CRIME/HISTORY	Theft of cultural relics
3204 STEVIE WONDER/USA	Heaven help the roses if the bombs begin to fall.
3205 HARPER LEE/USA/ NOVELIST	You never really understand a person until you consider things from his point of view...Until you climb inside of his skin and walk around in it.
3206 JERRY SEINFELD/USA/ COMEDIAN	A bookstore is one of the only pieces of evidence we have that people are still thinking.
3207 ALICE MUNRO/ CANADIAN WRITER	Always remember that when a man goes out of the room, he leaves everything in it behind...When a woman goes out she carries everything that happened in the room along with her.
3208 ENGLISH PROVERB	Age can be a bad travelling companion.
3209 RELATIONSHIPS	False smiles
3210 FRANCIS BACON/UK	A prudent question is one-half of wisdom.
3211 RELATIONSHIPS	Secrets of a happy marriage
3212 CONFUCIUS/CHINA	I hear and I forget. I see and I remember. I do and I understand.
3213 STEVIE WONDER/USA	You can't base your life on other people's expectations.
3214 DEBATE	Employers should not bar employees from sharing payroll information with colleagues.
3215 NEIL ARMSTRONG/ USA/ASTRONAUT	I guess we all like to be recognized not for one piece of fireworks, but for the ledger of our daily work.
3216 STEPHEN COLBERT/ AMERICAN COMEDIAN	If our Founding Fathers wanted us to care about the rest of the world, they wouldn't have declared their independence from it.
3217 NOSTALGIA	Reminiscing about the good old days
3218 CRIME	Destroying evidence
3219 HANS CHRISTIAN ANDERSON/DENMARK	"Just living is not enough," said the butterfly, "one must have sunshine, freedom, and a little flower."
3220 CONFUCIUS/CHINESE PHILOSOPHER	He who learns but does not think, is lost! He who thinks but does not learn is in great danger.
3221 SUCCESS JOURNEY	Starting off on the right foot

NUMBER CATEGORY/CREDIT	TOPIC
3222 DANE/HANS CHRISTIAN ANDERSON/WRITER	To travel is to live.
3223 JONAS SALK/US/SCIENTIST	Our greatest responsibility is to be good ancestors.
3224 JEFFREY KLUGER/USA/AUTHOR	Even our greatest and most humble people, Mahatma Gandhi, Martin Luther King, had to have narcissism components to their personality. They gravitated toward attention...but they were equally humble men.
3225 RELATIONSHIPS	Active listening
3226 LIFE	Problem solving
3227 CHRISTOPHER REEVE/USA/ACTOR	I think a hero is an ordinary individual who finds the strength to persevere and endure in spite of overwhelming obstacles. They are the real heroes, and so are the families and friends who have stood by them.
3228 REBBE NACHMAN	Whoever is able to write a book and does not, it is as if he has lost a child.
3229 MALCOLM S. FORBES	Diversity: the art of thinking independently together.
3230 DAVID OGILVY/ADVERTISING INDUSTRY LEADER	If each of us hires people who are smaller than we are, we shall become a company of dwarfs. But if each of us hires people who are bigger than we are, we shall become a company of giants.
3231 MAX BEERBOHM/UK	Some people are born to lift heavy weights, some are born to juggle golden balls.
3232 ZIG ZIGLAR/USA	Your attitude, not your aptitude, will determine your altitude.
3233 DIZZY GILLESPIE / AMERICAN MUSICIAN	I always try to teach by example and not force my ideas on a young musician.
3234 SAYING/JUSTICE	Justice must be seen to be done.
3235 CONFUCIUS/THINKER	Faced with what is right, to leave it undone shows a lack of courage.
3236 VIGILANTE JUSTICE	Taking the law into one's own hands
3237 CHINA/MAO TSE TUNG	The Four Olds: Old customs, Old culture, Old habits, Old Ideas
3238 CONFLICT	Cooler heads must prevail.
3239 MALCOLM S. FORBES/US	By the time we've made it, we've had it.
3240 PAULO COELHO/BRAZIL	When someone leaves, it's because someone else is about to arrive.
3241 JORGE LUIS BORGES/WRITER/ARGENTINA	After a while you learn the subtle difference / Between holding a hand and chaining a soul.
3242 ROHINTON MISTRY/INDIA/CANADA	What an unreliable thing is time -- when I want it to fly, the hours stick to me like glue.
3243 ERICH FROMM/GERMAN PSYCHOLOGY	Love is a decision, it is a judgment, it is a promise. If love were only a feeling, there would be no basis for the promise to love each other forever.
3244 ATUL GAWANDE/USA/MEDICINE	We look for medicine to be an orderly field of knowledge and procedure. but it is not. It is an imperfect science, an enterprise of constantly changing knowledge, uncertain information, fallible individuals, and at the same time lives on the line.
3245 JOHN DEWEY/USA	Every great advance in science has issued from a new audacity of imagination.
3246 EUGEN HERRIGEL/ZEN/GERMANY/JAPAN	In the case of archery, the hitter and the hit are no longer two opposing objects, but are one reality.
3247 CONFUCIUS/THINKER	An oppressive government is more to be feared than a tiger.

NUMBER CATEGORY/CREDIT	TOPIC
3248 ATUL GAWANDE/USA/ MEDICINE	The important question isn't how to keep bad physicians from harming patients; it's how to keep good physicians from harming patients.
3249 SHUNRYU SUZUKI/ ZEN/JAPAN/USA	In the beginner's mind there are many possibilities, but in the expert's mind there are few.
3250 URSULA LE GUIN/USA/ WRITER	When you light a candle, you also cast a shadow.
3251 STEPHEN RUSSELL/ ACTOR/USA/WRITER	We are all capable of the entire range of human behavior, given the circumstances, from absolute saintliness to abject depravity.
3252 ANDY WARHOL/USA/ ARTIST	An artist is somebody who produces things that people don't need to have.
3253 PAULO COELHO/BRAZIL/ EDUCATOR	We can never judge the lives of others, because each person knows only their own pain and renunciation.
3254 JOHN DEWEY/USA	The self is not something ready-made, but something in continuous formation through choice of action.
3255 LAO TZU/CHINA	A scholar who cherishes the love of comfort is not fit to be deemed a scholar.
3256 ANDY WARHOL/USA	Don't pay any attention to what they write about you. Just measure it in inches.
3257 ERROL FLYNN/ACTOR/ USA/AUSTRALIA	Any man who has $10,000 left when he dies is a failure.
3258 WAR/ERICH MARIA REMARQUE/FRENCH	That is the remarkable thing about drinking: it brings people together so quickly, but between night and morning it sets an interval again of years.
3259 CHARLES KINGSLEY/UK/ HISTORIAN/PROFESSOR	We act as though comfort and luxury were the chief requirements of life, when all that we need to make us really happy is something to be enthusiastic about.
3260 DANIEL DEFOE/UK/ TRADER/WRITER	Today we love what tomorrow we hate, today we seek what tomorrow we shun, today we desire what tomorrow we fear...
3261 ANNE SULLIVAN/USA/ TEACHER	...obedience is the gateway through which knowledge, yes, and love, too, enter the mind of the child.
3262 UPTON SINCLAIR/USA/ WRITER	It is difficult to get a man to understand something, when his salary depends on his not understanding it.
3263 THOMAS CARLYLE/SCOT	Books are a triviality. Life alone is great.
3264 JORGE LUIS BORGES/ WRITER/ARGENTINA	...you learn to build all your roads on today / Because tomorrow's ground is too uncertain for plans.
3265 JOHN DEWEY/USA/ PHILOSOPHER	No man's credit is as good as his money.
3266 ANDY ROONEY/USA	I've learned that no matter how serious your life requires you to be, everyone needs a friend to act goofy with.
3267 ANDY WARHOL/USA	Employees make the best dates. You don't have to pick them up and they're always tax-deductible.
3268 UPTON SINCLAIR/USA	It is paradoxical that the idea of living a long life appeals to everyone, but the idea of getting old doesn't appeaL to anyone.
3269 JERRY SEINFELD/USA/ COMEDIAN	Dogs are the leaders of the planet. If you see two life forms, one of them's making a poop, the other one's carrying it for him. Who would you assume is in charge?

NUMBER CATEGORY/CREDIT	TOPIC
3270 JOHN DEWEY/USA	Anyone who has begun to think, places some portion of the world in jeopardy.
3271 WAR/ERICH MARIA REMARQUE/FRENCH	...death is not an adventure to those who stand face to face with it.
3272 SHUNRYU SUZUKI/ ZEN/JAPAN/USA	When you do something, you should burn yourself up completely, like a good bonfire, leaving no trace of yourself.
3273 DANIEL DEFOE/UK	The best of men cannot defend their fate: the good die early, the bad die late.
3274 LAO TZU/CHINA	An ant on the move does more than a dozing ox.
3275 JOHN DEWEY/USA	One lives with so many bad deeds on one's conscience and some good intentions in one's heart.
3276 ERROL FLYNN/ACTOR	My problem lies in reconciling my gross habits with my net income.
3277 ROGER ROSENBLATT/US	A library should be like a pair of open arms.
3278 SOJOURNER TRUTH/ USA	If the first woman God ever made was strong enough to turn the world upside down all alone...women together ought to be able to turn it back, and get it right side up again!
3279 ANNE SULLIVAN/USA	The truth is not wonderful enough to suit the newspapers; so they enlarge upon it, and invent ridiculous embellishments.
3280 ERICH FROMM/GERMAN PSYCHOLOGY	If other people do not understand our behavior -- so what? Their request that we must only do what they understand is an attempt to dictate to us.
3281 ANDY ROONEY/USA	The best classroom in the world is at the feet of an elderly person.
3282 SIR FRANCIS BACON/UK	Discretion in speech is more than eloquence.
3283 PAULO COELHO/BRAZIL	Choosing a path means having to miss out on others.
3284 SIR FRANCIS BACON/UK	He of whom many are afraid ought to hear many.
3285 ROHINTON MISTRY/ INDIA/CANADA	The whole quilt is much more important than any single square.
3286 ARISTOTLE/THINKER	Evil draws men together.
3287 SIR FRANCIS BACON/UK	Read not to contradict and confute, nor to find talk and discourse, but to weigh and consider.
3288 SIR FRANCIS BACON/UK	Some books are to be tasted, others to be swallowed, and some few to be chewed and digested...
3289 PAULO COELHO/BRAZIL	God hides the fires of hell within paradise.
3290 JORGE LUIS BORGES/ WRITER/ARGENTINA	After a while, you learn...That even sunshine burns if you get too much.
3291 ANDY ROONEY/USA	I'm always on the lookout for something good about people. Often months go by.
3292 DAVE BARRY/USA/ HUMOR/WRITER	I can win an argument on any topic, against any opponent. People know this and steer clear of me at parties. Often, as a sign of their great respect, they don't even invite me.
3293 HARPER LEE/USA/ NOVELIST/ATTICUS FINCH CHARACTER	I wanted you to see what real courage is, instead of getting the idea that courage is a man with a gun in his hand. It's when you know you're licked before you begin but you begin anyway and see it through no matter what.
3294 DANIEL DEFOE/UK/ NOVELIST	Expect nothing and you'll always be surprised.

NUMBER CATEGORY/CREDIT	TOPIC
3295 SHINICHI SUZUKI/ MUSIC/JAPAN	Teaching music is not my main purpose. I want to make good citizens. If children hear fine music from the day of their birth and learn to play it, they develop sensitivity, discipline and endurance.
3296 ROGER ROSENBLATT/ USA/ESSAYIST	Do not keep company with people who speak of careers. Not only are such people uninteresting in themselves; they also have no interest in anything interesting.
3297 WILLIAM ROPER/UK	Where there is no malice there can be no offense.
3298 PAUL EKMAN/USA	Can you tell when a politician is lying? When he moves his lips!
3299 JOHN DEWEY/USA/ PHILOSOPHER	Education is not preparation for life; education is life itself.
3300 ERICH FROMM/GERMAN PSYCHOLOGY	Paradoxically, the ability to be alone is the condition for the ability to love.
3301 DANIEL DEFOE/UK/ NOVELIST	Fear of danger is ten thousand times more terrifying than danger itself.
3302 PAUL EKMAN/USA/ PSYCHOLOGY	Emotions can override...People will not eat if they think the only food available is disgusting...Emotion triumphs over the hunger drive.
3303 JERRY SEINFELD/USA/ COMEDIAN	What I don't understand is how women can pour hot wax on their bodies, let it dry, then rip out every single hair by its root and still be scared of spiders.
3304 PAUL EKMAN/USA/ PSYCHOLOGY	Public opinion polls time and again show that honesty is among the top five characteristics people want in a leader, friend, or lover.
3305 JOHN DEWEY/USA	The belief that all genuine education comes about through experience does not mean that all experiences are genuinely or equally educative.
3306 PAUL EKMAN/USA/ PSYCHOLOGY	Terror is harder to conceal than worry, just as rage is harder to conceal than annoyance.
3307 NATSUO KIRINO/JAPAN/ WRITER/REAL WORLD	Brains and talent will never stand up against a girl who is clearly physically attractive.
3308 ERICH FROMM/GERMAN	Creativity requires the courage to let go of certainties.
3309 DANIEL DEFOE/UK/ TRADER	For I cannot think that GOD Almighty made [women] so delicate, so glorious creatures; and furnished them with such charms, so agreeable and so delightful to mankind; with souls capable of the same accomplishments with men: and all, to be only Stewards of our Houses, Cooks, and Slaves.
3310 PAUL EKMAN/USA/ PSYCHOLOGIST	A broken promise is not a lie.
3311 NATSUO KIRINO/JAPAN/ WRITER/REAL WORLD	A woman who does not know herself has no choice other than to live with other people's evaluations.
3312 FRANCOISE GILOT/ LIFE WITH PICASSO	You have to admit that most women who do something with their lives have been disliked by almost everyone.
3313 NATSUO KIRINO/JAPAN/ WRITER/REAL WORLD	Let's face it: the world is twisted. And rotten.
3314 EXPERIENCE	Making the wrong choices
3315 FRANCOISE GILOT/ LIFE WITH PICASSO	No one is indispensable to anyone else.
3316 JORGE LUIS BORGES/ WRITER/ARGENTINA	Nothing is built on stone: All is built on sand, but we must build as if the sand were stone.

NUMBER CATEGORY/CREDIT	TOPIC
3317 DAVE BARRY/USA/ HUMOR	Skiing combines outdoor fun with knocking down trees with your face.
3318 LOIS McMASTER BUJOLD/USA/WRITER	Reputation is what other people know about you. Honor is what you know about yourself.
3319 GEORGE W. BUSH/USA/ PRESIDENT/UN SPEECH	The desire for freedom resides in every human heart. And that desire cannot be contained forever by prison walls, or martial laws, or secret police.
3320 GEORGE CARLIN/USA/ COMEDIAN	As a matter of principle, I never attend the first annual anything.
3321 UK/PM/SIR WINSTON CHURCHILL	A fanatic is one who can't change his mind and won't change the subject.
3322 LOIS McMASTER BUJOLD/USA/WRITER	My home is not a place, it is people.
3323 GEORGE CARLIN/USA	Some national parks have long waiting lists for camping reservations. When you have to wait a year to sleep next to a tree, something is wrong.
3324 UK/PM/SIR WINSTON CHURCHILL	History will be kind to me for I intend to write it.
3325 LOIS McMASTER BUJOLD/USA/WRITER	A good friend of my son's is a son to me.
3326 ERICH FROMM/ GERMAN/PSYCHOLOGIST	Modern man thinks he loses something - time - when he does not do things quickly. Yet he does not know what to do with the time he gains, except to kill it.
3327 LOIS McMASTER BUJOLD/USA/WRITER	Good soldiers never pass up a chance to eat or sleep. They never know how much they'll be called on to do before the next chance.
3328 LOIS McMASTER BUJOLD/USA/WRITER	What you are is a question only you can answer.
3329 UK/PM/SIR WINSTON CHURCHILL	If we open a quarrel between the past and the present, we shall find that we have lost the future.
3330 DAVE BARRY/USA/ HUMORIST/COLUMNIST	What I look forward to is continued immaturity followed by death.
3331 ERICH FROMM/ GERMAN/PSYCHOLOGIST	Freedom does not mean license.
3332 LOIS McMASTER BUJOLD/USA/WRITER	If you can't do what you want, do what you can.
3333 GEORGE W. BUSH/USA/ PRESIDENT/UN SPEECH	Armies and missiles are not stopped by stiff notes of condemnation. They are held in check by strength and purpose and the promise of swift punishment.
3334 GEORGE CARLIN/USA/ COMEDIAN	I think it's the duty of the comedian to find out where the line is drawn and cross it deliberately.
3335 JERRY SEINFELD/USA/ COMEDIAN	According to most most studies, people's number one fear is public speaking. Number two is death. Death is number two. Does that sound right? This means to the average person, if you go to a funeral, you're better off in the casket than doing the eulogy.
3336 MIYAMOTO MUSASHI/ JAPANESE WRITER	You win battles by knowing the enemy's timing, and using a timing which the enemy does not expect.

NUMBER CATEGORY/CREDIT	TOPIC
3337 MAYA ANGELOU/USA/ WRITER	Perhaps travel cannot prevent bigotry, but by demonstrating that all peoples cry, laugh, eat, worry and die, it can introduce the idea that if we try and understand each other, we may even become friends.
3338 SAMURAI MAXIM	The angry man will defeat himself in battle as well as in life.
3339 CHALLENGE	Sink or swim
3340 LOIS McMASTER BUJOLD/USA/WRITER	An honor is not diminished for being shared.
3341 ALANIS MORISSETTE/ SINGER	I see my body as an instrument, rather than an ornament.
3342 LOIS McMASTER BUJOLD/USA/WRITER	Never...ever suggest they don't have to pay you. What they pay for, they'll value. What they get for free, they'll take for granted, and then demand as a right.
3343 ENTERTAINMENT	Feel-good movie
3344 USA/ELBERT GREEN HUBBARD/WRITER	An idea that is not dangerous is not worthy of being called an idea at all.
3345 EXPERIENCE	If only I had known then what I know now.
3346 MALCOLM S. FORBES/US	The purpose of education is to replace an empty mind with an open one.
3347 REBBE NACHMAN/RABBI	Always wear a smile. The gift of life will then be yours to give.
3348 BAHA U'LLAH	The earth is but one country and mankind its citizens.
3349 IAN McEWAN/ ENGLISH NOVELIST	That love which does not build a foundation on good sense is doomed.
3350 GURU NANAK/ FOUNDER/SIKHISM	Alone let him constantly meditate in solitude on that which is salutary for his soul, for he who meditates in solitude attains supreme bliss.
3351 USA/ERLE STANLEY GARDNER /WRITER	Dear Editor: It's a damn good story. If you have any comments, write them on the back of a check.
3352 HOLIDAY	Your getaway fantasy
3353 HEALTH	Blood donations
3354 REBBE NACHMAN/ JEWISH LEADER	Worldly riches are like nuts; many a tooth is broken in cracking them, but never is the stomach filled with eating them.
3355 THOUGHT	Good ideas are always too advanced for their time.
3356 LOVE	Whirlwind romance
3357 RUDYARD KIPLING/ ENGLISH WRITER	If history were taught in the form of stories it would never be forgotten.
3358 FRANCE/NAPOLEON BONAPARTE/LEADER	Religion is excellent stuff for keeping common people quiet. Religion is what keeps the poor from murdering the rich.
3359 USA/ISAAC BASHEVIS SINGER/WRITER	If you believe in God, then He exists.
3360 CELINE DION/SINGER	It's the moment you think you can't that you realize you can.
3361 MEN/ACCESSORIES	Cufflinks
3362 RONALD REAGAN/ 40TH PRESIDENT/USA	I have left orders to be awakened at any time in case of national emergency, even if I'm in a cabinet meeting.
3363 FRENCH/NAPOLEON BONAPARTE/LEADER	Courage isn't having the strength to go on – it is going on when you don't have strength.

NUMBER CATEGORY/CREDIT	TOPIC
3364 REBBE NACHMAN/ JEWISH LEADER	If you won't be better tomorrow than you were today, then what do you need tomorrow for?
3365 VIKTOR FRANKL/ AUTHOR/AUSTRIAN	In some way suffering ceases to be suffering at the moment it finds meaning, such as the meaning of a sacrifice.
3366 INTERNET/SECURITY	Catfish: a phenomenon on the Internet where a scam artist creates a fake identity and uses that to trick people into relationships, romantic or otherwise.
3367 SIR KINGSLEY AMIS/ ENGLISH NOVELIST	Death has this much to be said for it: You don't have to get out of bed for it. Wherever you happen to be / They bring it to you – free.
3368 ALICE MUNRO/ CANADIAN WRITER	Why is it a surprise to find that people other than ourselves are able to tell lies?
3369 OG MANDINO/ AMERICAN AUTHOR	I seek constantly to improve my manners and graces, for they are the sugar to which all are attracted.
3370 ENGLISH PROVERB	Experience teaches fools.
3371 YOMIURI/JAPAN/ YOSHIKO MIKASHIMA	Nothing makes parents feel happier than the sleeping faces of their children.
3372 TRAVEL	Bitten by the travel bug
3373 MALCOLM S. FORBES/US	Being right half the time beats being half-right all the time.
3374 BOB WOODWARD/ AMERICAN REPORTER	A reporter's ability to keep the bond of confidentiality often enables him to learn the hidden or secret aspects of government.
3375 CONFUCIUS/CHINA	Better a diamond with a flaw than a pebble without.
3376 OG MANDINO/AUTHOR	Always do your best. What you plant now, you will harvest later.
3377 EDWARD SNOWDEN/ USA/WHISTLEBLOWER	Arguing that you don't care about the right to privacy because you have nothing to hide is no different than saying you don't care about free speech because you have nothing to say.
3378 DIPLOMAT/NICCOLO MACHIAVELLI/ITALY	War should be the only study of a prince. He should consider peace only as a breathing-time, which gives him leisure to contrive, and furnishes as ability to execute, military plans.
3379 PRINCESS DIANA/ UK/ROYAL FAMILY	I have a woman's instinct and it's always a good one.
3380 CONFUCIUS	A journey of a thousand miles begins with a single step.
3381 CONSERVATION	Preserving historic buildings
3382 CONFUCIUS/ CHINESE SAGE	In a country well governed, poverty is something to be ashamed of. In a country badly governed, wealth is something to be ashamed of.
3383 GERRY SPENCE/ AMERICAN LAWYER	Nearly everyday on the television set the hero cop breaks into the bad guy's home and beats a confession out of him and we cheer on the cop.
3384 CORRUPTION	Transparency International
3385 JUSTICE/MERCY	Throwing oneself on the mercy of the court
3386 THUCYDIDES/ HISTORIAN	Most people, in fact, will not take the trouble in finding out the truth, but are much more inclined to accept the first story they hear.
3387 MARCUS AURELIUS/ ROMAN EMPEROR	The true worth of a man is to be measured by the objects he pursues.
3388 HANGOUT/PLEASURE	A home away from home

NUMBER CATEGORY/CREDIT	TOPIC
3389 PAULO FREIRE/ THINKER/SOCIETY	No one is born fully-formed: it is through self-experience in the world that we become what we are.
3390 TIME MAGAZINE	A man who believes he was born to make history shouldn't expect a quiet life.
3391 ART BUCHWALD/USA/ HUMORIST	Whether it's the best of times or the worst of times, it's the only time we've got.
3392 PAOLO FREIRE/ BRAZIL/WRITER	Knowledge emerges only through invention and re-invention, through the restless, impatient, continuing, hopeful inquiry human beings pursue in the world, with the world, and with each other.
3393 CREATE A STORY	Sold out
3394 LIFE/UNCERTAINTIES	Just one moment can change everything.
3395 TRAVEL	Travelling around the world
3396 HENRY FORD/USA BUSINESSMAN	The man who thinks he can and the man who thinks he can't are both right. Which one are you?
3397 IMAGE	Glamour
3398 HARPER LEE/USA/ NOVELIST	Sometimes the Bible in the hand of one man is worse than a whisky bottle in the hand of (another)...There are just some kind of men who -- who're so busy worrying about the next world they've never learned to live in this one, and you can look down the street and see the results.
3399 NAPOLEON HILL/USA	Whatever the mind of man can conceive and believe, it can achieve.
3400 JUDY GARLAND/USA/ ACTOR	I can live without money, but I cannot live without love.
3401 USA/ELBERT GREEN IIUBBARD/WRITER	If men could only know each other, they would neither idolize nor hate.
3402 PAULO FREIRE/ THINKER/SOCIETY	If the structure does not permit dialogue the structure must be changed.
3403 CHANGE/SEASONS	Season's colours
3404 DE BEERS/SLOGAN	Diamonds are forever.
3405 JUDY GARLAND	If I'm such a legend, then why am I so lonely?
3406 OG MANDINO/USA/ AUTHOR/SALES	Always render more and better service than is expected of you, no matter what your task may be.
3407 HENRY FORD/USA/ BUSINESSMAN	When everything seems to be going against you, remember that the airplane takes off against the wind, not with it.
3408 SOCIETY/INEQUALITY	Gap between rich and poor
3409 WILLIAM SHAKESPEARE	There's no art to find the mind's construction in the face.
3410 GOVERNMENT	Hawks and doves
3411 ARABIC PROVERB	Ask thy purse what you ought to buy.
3412 JORGE LUIS BORGES/ WRITER	I have always imagined that Paradise will be a kind of a library.
3413 ROBERT GREEN INGERSOLL/LAWYER	The true civilization is where every man gives to every other every right that he claims for himself.
3414 ALFRED HITCHCOCK/ USA/MOVIE DIRECTOR	Drama is life with the dull bits cut out.

NUMBER CATEGORY/CREDIT	TOPIC
3415 ADMIRATION	Starstruck
3416 IAN McEWAN/ ENGLISH NOVELIST	A person is, among all else, a material thing, easily torn and not easily mended.
3417 TED FORBES/ART OF PHOTOGRAPHY	Your mind is what makes you a photographer, not your camera.
3418 GAME/LIFE	Solitaire
3419 SHUNRYU SUZUKI/ ZEN MIND/JAPAN	Treat every moment as your last. It is not preparation for something else.
3420 FUN/CELEBRATION	Balloons
3421 SOCCER/FANS	Soccer fans
3422 CHILDREN	Bedwetting
3423 TELL A STORY	A snake on the 14th floor!
3424 BOB WOODWARD/USA OBAMA'S WARS	Obama said, 'I welcome debate among my team, but I won't tolerate division.'
3425 ENDURANCE/FAITH	The patience of Job
3426 GOVERNMENT	Government secrecy
3427 EXCUSES	Pleading ignorance
3428 DANE/HANS CHRISTIAN ANDERSEN/WRITER	To be of use to the world is the only way to be happy.
3429 OVERCONFIDENCE	Delusions of grandeur
3430 DALE CARNEGIE/ USA/WRITER	Let's keep a record of the fool things we have done and criticize ourselves.
3431 GERRY SPENCE/USA/ LAWYER	To freely bloom – that is my definition of success.
3432 UK/INVICTUS/WILLIAM EVERETT HENLEY/POET	It matters not how strait the gate, How charged with punishments the scroll, I am the master of my fate, I am the captain of my soul.
3433 LOVE/FRIENDSHIP	Someone you'd like to surprise
3434 DE BEERS/SLOGAN	Diamonds are a girl's best friend
3435 FRENCH/ALBERT SCHWEITZER	Until he extends the circle of his compassion to all living things, man will not himself find peace.
3436 IDIOM	Black sheep of the family
3437 IDIOM/UK	All talk and no trousers
3438 IDIOM/UK	Champagne tastes, beer wages
3439 IDIOM/UK	Fair crack of the whip
3440 IDIOM/UK	Make a song and dance about something
3441 IDIOM/UK	Rake over old coals
3442 IDIOM/UK	Teething problems
3443 IDIOM/UK	You do not get a dog and bark yourself.
3444 IDIOM/UK	Stiff upper lip
3445 ZHUANGZI/CHINESE PHILOSOPHER	The wise man knows that it is better to sit on the banks of a remote mountain stream than to be emperor of the whole world.
3446 GOOD FORTUNE	Double happiness

NUMBER CATEGORY/CREDIT	TOPIC
3447 IBN BATTUTA/ MUSLIM EXPLORER	Traveling – it leaves you speechless, then turns you into a storyteller.
3448 WOMEN/DREAMS	Knight in shining armor
3449 GOLDA MEIR/ ISRAELI POLITICIAN/ PRIME MINISTER	Women's Liberation is just a lot of foolishness. It's the men who are discriminated against. They can't bear children. And no one's likely to do anything about that.
3450 SELF-ABSORPTION/ MERRIAMWEBSTER	Navel gazing : useless or excessive self-contemplation
3451 CHINESE PROVERB	The finger that points to the moon is not the moon.
3452 RONALD REAGAN/ 40TH PRESIDENT/USA	I don't believe in a government that protects us from ourselves.
3453 JERRY SEINFELD/USA/ COMEDIAN	Sometimes the road less traveled is less traveled for a reason.
3454 SCIENCE	Astronomy
3455 ANN LANDERS/USA/ ADVICE COLUMNIST	The naked truth is always better than the best-dressed lie.
3456 RITA MAE BROWN/ FEMINIST	I believe in a lively disrespect for most forms of authority.
3457 ANN LANDERS/USA/ ADVICE COLUMNIST	Hanging onto resentment is letting someone you despise live rent-free in your head.
3458 JAMES JOYCE/IRISH	Let my country die for me.
3459 CURIOSITY/WONDER	Childlike wonderment
3460 PARTY/WORKPLACE	Year-end bash
3461 RUDYARD KIPLING/ ENGLISH WRITER	If you can keep your wits when all about you are are losing theirs, and blaming it on you. If you can trust yourself when all men doubt you but make allowance for their doubting too....Yours is the earth. And which is more, you'll be a man, my son.
3462 MODERN LIFE	Today's woman
3463 SUSAN ORLEAN/USA/ WRITER/ADVICE	Anything that can be fixed with money isn't worth crying over.
3464 LADY GAGA/USA	People will always talk so let's give them something to talk about.
3465 SUCCESS	Personal breakthroughs
3466 STEVE IRWIN/ AUSTRALIA	Crocodiles are easy. They try to kill and eat you. People are harder. Sometimes they pretend to be your friend first.
3467 SALMAN RUSHDIE/UK/ NOVELIST	What is freedom of expression? Without the freedom to offend, it ceases to exist.
3468 HENRY FORD/USA/ BUSINESSMAN	It has been my observation that most people get ahead during the time that others waste.
3469 PAUL DIRAC/PHYSICS	Pick a flower on earth and you move the farthest star.
3470 LADY GAGA/USA	I'm obsessively opposed to the typical.
3471 HARPER LEE/USA/ NOVELIST	When a child asks you something, answer him, for goodness sake. But don't make a production of it. Children are children, but they can spot an evasion faster than adults, and evasion simply muddles 'em.
3472 CELEBRATION	High fives

NUMBER CATEGORY/CREDIT	TOPIC
3473 OG MANDINO/USA/ AUTHOR	I have never heard anything about the resolutions of the apostles, but a good deal about their acts.
3474 RITA MAE BROWN	Lead me not into temptation; I can find the way myself.
3475 PERSONALITY	Doing something out of character
3476 RELTIONSHIPS	Unrequited love (one-sided love)
3477 HOBBY	Bird watching
3478 RITA MAE BROWN/USA	Morals are private. Decency is public.
3479 ENVIRONMENT	Ecological footprints
3480 BIRTH/MEDICAL	Caesarean birth
3481 SALMAN RUSHDIE/ NOVELIST	We are described into corners, and then we must describe ourselves out of corners.
3482 PETS/LUXURY	Spending lots of money on household pets
3483 ARTS/COMMUNITY	Taxpayer support of the arts
3484 LUXURY/HOTELS	Five star hotels
3485 UK/LEADER/LORD MOUNTBATTEN	Never feel that a piece of criticism or advice is too much trouble to give, or that it exceeds your province.
3486 CULTURE/TRAVEL	Italy
3487 QURAN	There is no compulsion in religion.
3488 RELIGION	Faith healing
3489 ANSEL ADAMS/USA/ PHOTOGRAPHER	When words become unclear, I shall focus with photographs. When images become inadequate, I shall be content with silence.
3490 WILLIAM FAULKNER/ AMERICAN NOVELIST	All of us have failed to match our dream of perfection. I rate us on the basis of our splendid failure to do the impossible...This is the healthiest condition for an artist. That's why he keeps working, trying again; he believes each time that this time he will do it, bring it off. Of course he won't.
3491 JERRY SEINFELD/USA/ COMEDIAN	Keep your head up in failure, and your head down in success.
3492 FAMILY	Single parenthood
3493 G.K. CHESTERTON/ ENGLISH WRITER	No man who worships education has got the best out of education... Without a gentle contempt for education no man's education is complete.
3494 OPINION MAKERS	Think tanks
3495 BEAUTY/MERRIAM- WEBSTER.COM	Eye candy: something superficially attractive to look at.
3496 FRENCH/ALBERT SCHWEITZER	Man is a clever animal who behaves like an imbecile.
3497 PERFECTIONISM	Quest for perfection
3498 GUY DE MAUPASSANT/ FRENCH/NOVELIST	Patriotism is a kind of religion; it is the egg from which wars are hatched.
3499 TIME.COM/SCIENTIFIC ILLITERACY/JEFFREY KLUGER	...an Italian court sentenced six scientists and a government official to six years in prison on manslaughter charges, for failing to predict a 2009 earthquake that killed 300 people in the town of l'Aquila.
3500 MATCH/MARRIAGE	Marriage and socioeconomic background

NUMBER CATEGORY/CREDIT	TOPIC
3501 JIM ROHN/USA/ WRITER/MOTIVATION	Learn how to be happy with what you have while you pursue all that you want.
3502 BOB WOODWARD/ USA/REPORTER	The central dilemma in journalism is that you don't know what you don't know.
3503 JOHANN SEBASTIAN BACH/GERMAN/MUSIC	I was obliged to be industrious. Whoever is equally industrious will succeed equally.
3504 SOCIETY	Religion and war
3505 JORGE LUIS BORGES/ PATRIOTISM	I thought that a man can be an enemy of other men, of the moments of other men, but not of a country: not of fireflies, words, gardens, streams of water, sunsets.
3506 YU HUA/AUTHOR/ TO LIVE	Your life is given to you by your parents. If you don't want to live, you have to ask them first.
3507 DAI SIJIE/AUTHOR	In Chinese love stories the one who loves always starts by borrowing a book from the beloved.
3508 JAMES BALDWIN/ USA/WRITER	Not everything that is faced can be changed, but nothing can be changed until it is faced.
3509 FRENCH/MICHEL DE MONTAIGNE/THINKER	A wise man never loses anything, if he has himself.
3510 ALEXANDER SMITH/ SCOTTISH POET	A man gazing on the stars is proverbially at the mercy of the puddles in the road.
3511 ERASMUS/DUTCH	Don't give your advice before you are called upon.
3512 ISAAC NEWTON/UK	No great discovery was ever made without a bold guess.
3513 MICHEL DE MONTAIGNE	A good marriage would be between a blind wife and a deaf husband.
3514 SHUNRYU SUZUKI/ ZEN MIND	If your mind is empty, it is always ready for anything; it is open to everything.
3515 ALTERNATIVE MED	Chinese traditional medicine
3516 ANSEL ADAMS/USA	You don't take a photograph, you make it.
3517 CELIBACY/SLOGAN/USA	True love waits
3518 STEVE JOBS/USA/APPLE	Your time is limited, so don't waste it living someone else's.
3519 HARPER LEE/USA/ NOVELIST	We know all men are not created equal in the sense some people would have us believe -- some people are smarter than others, some people have more opportunity because they're born with it, some men make more money than others, some ladies make better cakes than others..
3520 HERMAN MELVILLE/ USA/WRITER	Of all the preposterous assumptions of humanity over humanity, nothing exceeds most of the criticisms made on the habits of the poor by the well-housed, well-warmed, and well-fed.
3521 J.K. ROWLING/UK/ WRITER	It takes a great deal of bravery to stand up to our enemies, but just as much to stand up to our friends.
3522 AUTHOR/C. NORTHCOTE PARKINSON/HISTORIAN	The man who is denied the opportunity of taking decisions of importance begins to regard as important the decisions he is allowed to take.
3523 HARPER LEE/USA/ NOVELIST	...there is one way in this country in which all men are created equal -- there is one human institution that makes a pauper the equal of a Rockefeller, the stupid man the equal of an Einstein, and the ignorant man the equal of any college president. That institution, gentlemen, is a court.

NUMBER CATEGORY/CREDIT	TOPIC
3524 HENRY FORD/USA	Nothing is particularly hard if you divide it into small jobs.
3525 HARVEY MACKAY/ USA/BUSINESSMAN	A dream is just a dream. A goal is a dream with a plan and a deadline.
3526 SÉANCE/WIKIPEDIA	A séance or seance is an attempt to communicate with spirits.
3527 ENTERTAINMENT	Pay-per-view TV
3528 ISAAC NEWTON/UK/ PHYSICIST	We need to build fewer walls and more bridges.
3529 NANCY YI FAN/AUTHOR	Birds are born to have wings; wings are symbols of freedom.
3530 JAPAN/RYUNOSUKE AKUTAGAWA/WRITER	A man sometimes devotes his life to a desire which he is not sure will ever be fulfilled. Those who laugh at this folly are, after all, no more than mere spectators of life.
3531 HENRY FORD/USA	Chop your own wood and it will warm you twice.
3532 GOLDA MEIR/ISRAELI POLITICIAN/PRIME MINISTER	Let me tell you something that we Israelis have against Moses. He took us 40 years through the desert in order to bring us to the one spot in the Middle East that has no oil!
3533 CRIME	Vandalism
3534 ANNE FRANK/JEWISH AUTHOR/HOLOCAUST	Human greatness does not lie in wealth or power, but in character and goodness. People are just people, and all people have faults and shortcomings, but all of us are born with a basic goodness.
3535 PARANORMAL	ESP (Extra Sensory Perception)
3536 ART/VANDALISM	Graffiti
3537 IDIOM	Being a good sport
3538 ROALD DAHL/UK NOVELIST	A writer of fiction lives in fear. Each new day demands new ideas and he can never be sure whether he is going to come up with them or not.
3539 SAYING	Time is money.
3540 WATER/BEAUTY	Venice
3541 RELATIONSHIPS	Age differences in relationships
3542 SECURITY/PERSONAL	Internet and privacy
3543 JULIAN BARNES/UK	Memory is identity.
3544 CULTURE/RELIGION	Polygamy
3545 US 1ST LADY/JACKIE KENNEDY ONNASIS	There are many little ways to enlarge your child's world. Love of books is the best of all.
3546 CARL SAGAN/ AMERICAN SCIENTIST	In science it often happens that scientists say, 'You know that's a really good argument; my position is mistaken,' and then they would actually change their minds and you never hear that old view from them again.
3547 KENZABURO OE/ JAPANESE WRITER	...please allow me to say that the fundamental style of my writing has been to start from my personal matters and then link it up with society, the state and the world.
3548 HARPER LEE/USA/ NOVELIST	Bad language is a stage all children go through, and it dies with time when they learn they're not attracting attention with it.
3549 JAPANESE PROVERB	Better than a thousand days of diligent study is one day with a great teacher.
3550 HUMANITY	Adopting babies from another race

NUMBER CATEGORY/CREDIT	TOPIC
3551 KENZABURO OE/WAR/ JAPANESE WRITER	The Japanese chose the principle of eternal peace as the basis of morality for our rebirth after the War.
3552 VINCE LOMBARDI/ USA/ COACH	If it doesn't matter who wins or loses, then why do they keep the score?
3553 VIVEK WADHWA/INDIA/ USA/PROFESSOR	When you have critical mass of women (guiding companies), the companies produce better performance. So you have more innovation, you have better financial management, you have greater success rate by having more women. Why leave them out?
3554 SHUNRYU SUZUKI/ ZEN MIND...	Each of you is perfect the way you are...and you can use a little improvement.
3555 CULTURE/FAMILY	Multigenerational families under one roof
3556 RUDYARD KIPLING/ ENGLISH WRITER	Words are, of course, the most powerful drug used by mankind.
3557 BHAGAVAD GITA/ INDIA/SPIRITUALITY	The mind is restless and difficult to restrain, but it is subdued by practice.
3558 ANIMAL WELFARE	Wearing of fur
3559 VINCE LOMBARDI/USA	Winning isn't everything. It's the only thing.
3560 PERSONAL	Shyness
3561 RUDYARD KIPLING/ ENGLISH WRITER	We have forty million reasons for failure, but not a single excuse.
3562 WOMEN/JEAN KERR/ IRISH-AMERICAN/ AUTHOR	The only thing worse than a man you can't control is a man you can.
3563 HARVEY MACKAY/USA	If you fail to plan, then you plan to fail.
3564 BUSINESS	Outsourcing
3565 ISAAC NEWTON/UK	Live your life as an Exclamation rather than an Explanation.
3566 HENRY FORD/USA	Vision without execution is just hallucination.
3567 SIR KINGSLEY AMIS/ ENGLISH NOVELIST	One of the great benefits of organized religion is that you can be forgiven your sins, which must be a wonderful thing.
3568 MALCOLM S. FORBES/US	When you cease to dream you cease to live.
3569 CARL SAGAN/USA	It pays to keep an open mind, but not so open your brains fall out.
3570 HARVEY MACKAY/ USA/BUSINESSMAN	Good habits are as addictive as bad habits, and a lot more rewarding.
3571 DOUGLAS STONE/ USA/AUTHOR/ DIFFICULT CONVERSATIONS	Remind yourself that if you think you already understand how someone feels or what they are trying to say, it is a delusion. Remember a time when you were sure you were right and then discovered one little fact that changed everything. There is always more to learn.
3572 PEGGY NOONAN/ SPEECHWRITER FOR PRESIDENT REAGAN	Here's an old tradition badly in need of return; You have to earn your way into politics. You should go have a life, build a string of accomplishments, then enter public service.
3573 SPORTS	Kinesthetic intelligence
3574 IDIOM	Playing the devil's advocate
3575 MARK CUBAN/USA/ BUSINESS	Money is a scoreboard where you can rank how you're doing against other people.

NUMBER CATEGORY/CREDIT	TOPIC
3576 CORMAC McCARTHY/ USA/NOVELIST	Nothing wounded goes uphill.
3577 PETER SINGER/USA/ PHILOSOPHER	It should be seen as a serious moral failure when those with ample income do not do their fair share toward relieving global poverty.
3578 USA/MARGARET HEFFERNAN/BUSINESS	When we care about people, we care less about money, and when we care about money, we care less about people.
3579 FRANZ KAFKA/AUTHOR	Evil is whatever distracts.
3580 LADY GAGA/MUSICIAN	They can't scare me if I scare them first.
3581 PAULO COELHO/ WRITER/ALCHEMIST	Everyone seems to have a clear idea of how other people should lead their lives, but none about his or her own.
3582 BALDNESS/HUMOR	Hair today gone tomorrow
3583 MARK CUBAN/USA/ BUSINESS	I hate politics. It's slimy. Any job where people pander for votes, I don't like.
3584 MATERNITY/ DEPRESSION/ WIKIPEDIA	Baby blues: a transient condition that 75-80% of mothers could experience shortly after childbirth with a wide variety of symptoms which generally involve mood [instability], tearfulness, and some mild anxiety and depressive symptoms.
3585 E.M FORSTER/UK	Either life entails courage, or it ceases to be life.
3586 ANNE FRANK/JEWISH AUTHOR/ HOLOCAUST	People can tell you to keep your mouth shut, but that doesn't stop you from having your own opinion.
3587 FUN/MARINE LIFE	Whale watching
3588 E.M. FORSTER/WRITER/ ENGLISH	How can I know what I think till I see what I say?
3589 COMPETITION	It's okay to lose sometimes.
3590 DOUGLAS STONE/USA	The urge to blame is based...on the fear of being blamed.
3591 JULIAN BARNES/ ENGLISH NOVELIST	Books are where things are explained to you; life is where things aren't. I'm not surprised some people prefer books.
3592 WORLD OF WORK	Trade Unions
3593 PICO AYER/GLOBAL NOMAD/WRITER	I've always felt that the beauty of being surrounded by the foreign is that it slaps you awake; you can't take anything for granted.
3594 ART/HOBBY	Calligraphy
3595 FUTURE/JOB	Tree planting
3596 JAPANESE PROVERB	Fall seven times, stand up eight.
3597 USA/WRITER/ERNEST HEMINGWAY/	Happiness in intelligent people is the rarest thing I know.
3598 BELIEF	Life after death
3599 JAPAN	Cherry blossoms
3600 HENRI MATISSE/ART/ FRENCH	An artist must never be a prisoner of himself, prisoner of style, prisoner of reputation, prisoner of success, etc.
3601 BABY/PREGNANCY	Ultrasound
3602 RAY BRADBURY/USA/ WRITER	You have to know how to accept rejection and reject acceptance.
3603 ENGLISH PROVERB	Every tide has its ebb.

NUMBER CATEGORY/CREDIT	TOPIC
3604 HENRY FORD/USA	You can't build a reputation on what you are going to do.
3605 MILTON FRIEDMAN/ USA/ECONOMIST	The government solution to a problem is usually as bad as the problem.
3606 RANDY PAUSCH/PROF/ THE LAST LECTURE/USA	Fundamentals, fundamentals, fundamentals. You've got to get the fundamentals down because otherwise the fancy stuff isn't going to work.
3607 CARL SAGAN/ AMERICAN SCIENTIST	Frederick Douglass taught that literacy is the path from slavery to freedom. There are many kinds of slavery and many kinds of freedom, but reading is still the path.
3608 GOVERNMENT	Civil servants
3609 MARK CUBAN/ AMERICAN BILLIONAIRE	Wherever I see people doing something the way it's always been done, the way it's 'supposed' to be done, following the same old trends, well, that's just a big red flag to me to go look somewhere else.
3610 SMOKEY ROBINSON/ AMERICAN MUSICIAN	We're very physical creatures, and we worry about how we look sometimes more than our spiritual selves.
3611 THOMAS SOWELL/USA/ THINK TANK	You will never understand bureaucracies until you understand that for bureaucrats procedure is everything and outcomes are nothing.
3612 PROFESSION/FUN	Bartenders
3613 WAR/CASUALTIES	Journalists and danger
3614 GREATEST OF ALL TIME	GOAT: Greatest Of All Time -- Muhammad Ali
3615 SENSATION/YELLOW JOURNALISM	Yellow journalism, or the yellow press, is a type of journalism that presents little or no legitimate well-researched news and instead uses eye-catching headlines to sell more newspapers.
3616 USA/PRESIDENCY	The White House
3617 EDUCATION/HISTORY	Oxford University
3618 RANCE ALLEN GROUP/US	Ain't no need of crying when it's raining.
3619 JAPAN/BULLET TRAIN	*Shinkansen*
3620 WILL ROGERS/USA/ COMEDIAN	There's no trick to being a humorist when you have the whole government working for you.
3621 CARL SAGAN/ AMERICAN SCIENTIST	It is of interest to note that while some dolphins are reported to have learned English – up to 50 words used in correct context – no human being has been reported to have learned dolphinese.
3622 MARIE CURIE/SCIENCE	Be less curious about people and more curious about ideas.
3623 INTERNET/PERSONAL LOSS/BUSINESS	Computer viruses
3624 DOUGLAS STONE/USA	People almost never change without first feeling understood.
3625 ISAMU NAGUCHI/JAPAN	We are a landscape of all we have seen.
3626 EDWARD R. MURROW/ USA/BROADCASTER	We must not confuse dissent with disloyalty.
3627 DEBBIE ALLEN/USA/ ACTRESS/DIRECTOR	But out of limitations comes creativity.
3628 JOHN MAXWELL/USA	Tend to the people and they will tend to the business.
3629 ANIMAL CRUELTY	Dog fighting
3630 MUSIC/AUSTRALIA	Didgeridoo

NUMBER CATEGORY/CREDIT	TOPIC
3631 JAPANESE PROVERB	The reputation of a thousand years may be determined by the conduct of one hour.
3632 ROBERT M. GATES/USA	Leadership is a rare and precious commodity.
3633 TRAUMA	Flashbacks
3634 BRIAN TRACY/USA/ SUCCESS COACH	Leaders think and talk about the solutions. Followers think and talk about the problems.
3635 MARK CUBAN/USA/ BILLIONAIRE	The number-one job of the hedge-fund manager is not to make sure that you can retire with a smile on your face – it's for him to retire with a smile on his face.
3636 ATTENTION	Being fashionably late
3637 FRANZ KAFKA/AUTHOR	God gives the nuts, but he does not crack them.
3638 JAPANESE PROVERB	One kind word can warm three winter months.
3639 ECOLOGY	The food chain
3640 NATIONS/WAR	Warmongering
3641 SCOT/ROBERT LOUIS STEVENSON/WRITER	To know what you prefer instead of humbly saying Amen to what the world tells you you ought to prefer, is to have kept your soul alive.
3642 SAYING	Talent is not enough
3643 MILITARY	AWOL (Absent Without Leave)
3644 SELF	Personal rituals
3645 WILLIAM BEVERIDGE/ UK/ECONOMIST	The object of government in peace and in war is not the glory of rulers or of race, but the happiness of the common man.
3646 CONCERTS	Live music
3647 G.K. CHESTERTON/ ENGLISH WRITER	A dead thing goes with the stream, but only a living thing can go against it.
3648 BENJAMIN DISRAELI/UK	A precedent embalms a principle.
3649 G.K. CHESTERTON/ ENGLISH WRITER	There is a great deal of difference between an eager man who wants to read a book and a tired man who wants to read.
3650 V.S. NAIPAUL/ BRITISH NOVELIST	The only lies for which we are truly punished are those we tell ourselves.
3651 PICO AYER/GLOBAL NOMAD/USA/JAPAN	Home is not just the place you happen to be born. It's the place where you become yourself.
3652 MARK VAN DOREN/ AMERICAN POET	Bring ideas in and entertain them royally, for one of them may be the king.
3653 URSULA K. LeGUIN/USA	The creative adult is the child who has survived.
3654 F. SCOTT FITZGERALD	Show me a hero and I'll write you a tragedy.
3655 GAVIN KENNEDY/UK/	Don't just complain, propose a remedy.
3656 JRR TOLKIEN/UK	Many that live deserve death. And some die that deserve life.
3657 ISAAC ASIMOV/USA/ WRITER	Science fiction writers foresee the inevitable, and although problems and catastrophes may be inevitable...solutions are not.
3658 MARGARET ATWOOD/ CANADA/WRITER	Wanting to meet an author because you like his work is like wanting to meet a duck because you like pâté.
3659 VIKTOR FRANKL/ PSYCHIATRIST/AUTHOR	The point is not what we expect from life, but rather what life expects from us.

NUMBER CATEGORY/CREDIT	TOPIC
3660 FRENCH/NAPOLEON	You don't reason with intellectuals. You shoot them.
3661 E.M FORSTER/ ENGLISH NOVELIST	I am sure that if the mothers of various nations could meet, there would be no more wars.
3662 CHARITY	Habitat for Humanity
3663 FRENCH/NAPOLEON	If you want a thing done well, do it yourself.
3664 MICHAEL JACKSON/ AMERICAN MUSICIAN	I'm never pleased with anything. I'm a perfectionist; it's part of who I am.
3665 HOMELESSNESS	Hobo : a homeless, usually penniless vagabond
3666 RELIGION	Merry Christmas versus Happy Holidays
3667 WORK/FULFILLMENT	The rat race
3668 PRINCE CHARLES/ ROYAL FAMILY/UK	I sometimes wonder if two thirds of the globe is covered in red carpet.
3669 MIDDLE EAST	Belly dancing
3670 LADY GAGA/USA/ MUSICIAN	Some women choose to follow men, and some women choose to follow their dreams. If you're wondering which way to go, remember that your career will never wake up and tell you that it doesn't love you anymore.
3671 IMMIGRANTS	Astronaut husbands: husbands who live away from their families in order to earn a good living to support the family
3672 FOOD/CULTURE/ASIA	Chopsticks
3673 BUSINESS/ASIA	Year-end bonus
3674 CAMBODIA/ TOURISM	Angkor Wat
3675 VIKTOR FRANKL/ AUSTRIA/WRITER	I recommend that the Statue of Liberty on the East Coast be supplemented by a Statue of Responsibility on the West Coast.
3676 CANDY CHANG/TED.COM	Preparing for death is one of the most empowering things you can do. Thinking about death clarifies your life.
3677 VIKTOR FRANKL/ PSYCHIATRIST	When we are no longer able to change a situation, we are challenged to change ourselves.
3678 MARIE CURIE/ PHYSICIST/CHEMIST	Nothing in life is to be feared, it is only to be understood. Now is the time to understand more, so that we may fear less.
3679 COLIN ALLEN/THIS I BELIEVE/USA	I believe that every human wants to be respected.
3680 KONRAD ADENAUER/ GERMAN/LEADER	In view of the fact that God limited the intelligence of man, it seems unfair that he did not also limit his stupidity.
3681 CHALLENGE	Learning another language
3682 SOCIETY	The working poor
3683 WRITER/MALCOLM DE CHAZAL/PAINTER	The sun is pure communism everywhere except in cities, where it's private property.
3684 PSYCHIC/PHYSICAL	War wounds
3685 MICHAEL JACKSON/USA/ MUSICIAN	Children show me in their playful smiles the divine in everyone.
3686 THEODOR ADORNO/ PSYCHOLOGY	The most powerful person is he who is able to do least himself and burden others most with the things for which he lends his name and pockets the credit.

NUMBER CATEGORY/CREDIT	TOPIC
3687 JOSEPH ADDISON/ ENGLISH WRITER	What sunshine is to flowers, smiles are to humanity.
3688 JEAN RHYS/UK	It's so easy to make a person who hasn't got anything seem wrong.
3689 MURIEL SPARK/UK	It is impossible to persuade a man who does not disagree but smiles.
3690 JOSEPH ADDISON/UK	He who hesitates is lost.
3691 MURIEL SPARK/UK	I never trust the airlines from those countries where the pilots believe in the afterlife. You are safer when they don't.
3692 SIMONE DE BEAUVOIR/ FRENCH WRITER	Society cares about the individual only in so far as he is profitable. The young know this. Their anxiety as they enter in upon social life matches the anguish of the old as they are excluded from it.
3693 ELON MUSK/USA/ S. AFRICA/BUSINESS	It's worth looking at industries which a lot of people think are impossible or think you can't succeed at -- that's usually where there's opportunity.
3694 IDIOM	Sticking to one's guns
3695 JOSEPH ADDISON/UK	A misery is not to be measured from the nature of the evil, but from the temper of the sufferer.
3696 TIMOTHY LEARY/USA/ WRITER	In the information age, you don't teach philosophy as they did after feudalism. You perform it. If Aristotle were alive today he'd have a talk show.
3697 MAYA ANGELOU/ AMERICAN AUTHOR	At fifteen life had taught me undeniably that surrender, in its place, was as honorable as resistance, especially if one had no choice.
3698 NIKE/SLOGAN/USA	Just Do It
3699 ANN LANDERS/USA/ ADVICE COLUMNIST	If you have love in your life it can make up for a great many things you lack. If you don't have it, no matter what else there is, it's not enough.
3700 USA/F. SCOTT FITZGERALD/WRITER	Vitality shows in not only the ability to persist but the ability to start over.
3701 ELIZABETH KUBLER-ROSS/PSYCHIATRIST	Guilt is perhaps the most painful companion to death.
3702 GLOBAL/RIGHTS	Human rights groups
3703 KNOWLEDGE	Public Intellectuals
3704 IDIOM	Standing one's ground
3705 FRAUD	Rigged elections
3706 AGRICULTURE	Pesticides
3707 PERSUASION	Advertising forces people to buy products they don't need
3708 FOOD	National self-sufficiency
3709 JOHN WESLEY/UK/ CLERGY	Think not the bigotry of another is any excuse for your own.
3710 FAMILY	Sibling rivalry
3711 PARENTING	Public tantrums
3712 PRESERVATION	Irradiated food – to stay longer
3713 LINGUA FRANCA	Esperanto
3714 EXPRESSION	Steely discipline
3715 JOSEPH ADDISON/UK/ ESSAYIST	An empty desk is a sign of a cluttered desk drawer.

NUMBER CATEGORY/CREDIT	TOPIC
3716 ZADIE SMITH/UK/ NOVELIST	Any woman who counts on her face is a fool.
3717 JOHN CHEEVER/USA/ WRITER	I can't write without a reader. It's precisely like a kiss -- you can't do it alone.
3718 HENRY VAN DYKE/ WRITER/USA	There is a loftier ambition than to stand high in the world. It is to step down and lift mankind a little higher.
3719 M. SCOTT PECK/USA/ PSYCHOLOGIST	Until you value yourself, you won't value your time. Until you value your time, you will not do anything with it.
3720 KAHLIL GIBRAN/POET	No man can reveal to you aught but that which already lies half asleep in the dawning of your knowledge.
3721 RANDY PAUSCH/USA/ THE LAST LECTURE	There's a lot of talk these days about giving children self-esteem. It's not something you can give; it's something they have to build.
3722 SYDNEY J. HARRIS/USA/ JOURNALIST	Don't take advice from someone who hasn't had your kind of trouble.
3723 EVAN KIRKPATRICK/ USA/ENTREPRENEUR	Do what you are uniquely qualified to do, and outsource the rest.
3724 SYDNEY J. HARRIS/USA/ JOURNALIST	The three hardest tasks in the world are neither physical feats nor intellectual achievements, but moral acts: to return love for hate, to include the excluded, and to say, 'I was wrong.'
3725 IDIOM	Burning one's bridges
3726 NISA CHITAKASEM/USA/ FORBES	Even people who are relatively happy at work go through periods when they hate their jobs -- for days, weeks, or even months at a time.
3727 HEALING	Hypnotherapy
3728 SYDNEY J. HARRIS/USA	Sometimes the best, and only effective, way to kill an idea is to put it into practice.
3729 SYDNEY J. HARRIS/USA/ JOURNALIST	The most important thing in an argument, next to being right, is to leave an escape hatch for your opponent, so that he can gracefully swing over to your side without too much apparent loss of face.
3730 KAHLIL GIBRAN/POET	The teacher...if he is indeed wise does not bid you enter the house of his wisdom, but rather leads you to the threshold of your own mind.
3731 HEALTH & HEALING	The placebo effect
3732 KWAME ANTHONY APPIAH/PHILOSOPHER	...globalization can produce homogeneity. But globalization is also a threat to homogeneity.
3733 M. SCOTT PECK/USA/ PSYCHIATRIST	Share our similarities; celebrate our differences.
3734 SYDNEY J. HARRIS/USA/ JOURNALIST	There's no point in burying the hatchet if you're going to put up a marker on the site.
3735 GERMAN SAYING	*Und willst du nicht mein Bruder sein, So schlag' ich Dir den Schadedl ein.* If you don't want to be my brother, then I'll smash your skull in.
3736 M. SCOTT PECK/USA/ PSYCHOLOGIST	Evil is that which kills spirit...Thus we may "break" a horse or even a child without harming a hair on its head.
3737 SYDNEY J. HARRIS/USA	The whole purpose of education is to turn mirrors into windows.
3738 MARK VAN DOREN/USA/ POET	To fail to love is not to exist at all.

NUMBER CATEGORY/CREDIT	TOPIC
3739 NORMAN MAILER/USA/ WRITER	The mark of mediocrity is to look for precedent.
3740 MARRIAGE	Serial monogamy
3741 RITA F. PIERSON/USA/ TED.COM/EDUCATOR	Every child deserves a champion -- an adult who will never give up on them, who understands the power of connection, and insists that they become the best that they can possibly be.
3742 RANDY PAUSCH/USA/ PROFESSOR/THE LAST LECTURE	Want to have a short phone call with someone? Call them at 11:55 a.m., right before lunch. They'll talk fast. You may think you are interesting, but you are not more interesting than lunch.
3743 TRADITION	Men as breadwinners
3744 ALTERNATIVE MEDICINE	Aromatherapy/massage
3745 OG MANDINO/USA/ AMERICAN AUTHOR	I will love the light for it shows me the way, yet I will endure the darkness because it shows me the stars.
3746 MARRIAGE	Trial marriage
3747 FLORYNCE KENNEDY/ USA/LAWYER/ACTIVIST	Freedom is like taking a bath: You got to keep doing it every day.
3748 JACK ABRAMOFF/USA	You can't unring the bell.
3749 MUTUAL SUPPORT	Men's movement
3750 HAROLD BLOOM/USA	Real reading is a lonely activity.
3751 ASKING QUESTIONS	Socratic method
3752 RONALD REAGAN/ 40TH PRESIDENT/USA	Coercion, after all, merely captures man. Freedom captivates him.
3753 KAHLIL GIBRAN/POET	Your friend is your needs answered.
3754 DOUGLAS ADAMS/UK/ WRITER	We don't have to save the world. The world is big enough to look after itself. What we have to be concerned about is whether or not the world we live in will be capable of sustaining us in it.
3755 FLORYNCE KENNEDY/US	...if you're not living on the edge, then you are taking up space.
3756 DAVID O. McKAY/ MORMON LEADER	Motherhood is the greatest potential influence either for good or ill in human life. The mother's image is the first that stamps itself on the unwritten page of the young child's mind.
3757 GREED/SPOUSE	What is yours is mine; what is mine is mine.
3758 TED RHEINGOLD/USA	Spend at least 50% of your time selling.
3759 VIKTOR FRANKL/ AUSTRIAN PSYCHIATRIST	Ultimately, man should not ask what the meaning of life is, but rather must recognize that it is he who is asked. In a word, each man is questioned by life, and he can only answer by answering for his own life; to life he can only respond by being responsible.
3760 WAR/RELIGION	Conscientious objection
3761 FREEMAN HRABOWSKI/ COLLEGE PRESIDENT/US	It's hard work that makes the difference. I don't care how smart you are or how smart you think you are. Smart simply means you are ready to learn.
3762 ADM. THAD ALLEN/USA	Great leaders are great learners.
3763 HARRY TRUMAN/USA/ 33RD PRESIDENT/NPR	There can be no justifiable reason for discrimination because of ancestry, or religion, or race, or color.
3764 KWAME ANTHONY APPIAH/PHILOSOPHER	In India, thousands of wives are burned to death each year for failing to make their dowry payments.

NUMBER CATEGORY/CREDIT	TOPIC
3765 STEPHEN COVEY/USA	Seek first to understand, then to be understood.
3766 INDIAN PROVERB	Good people, like clouds, receive only to give away.
3767 SCIENCE	Artificial diamonds
3768 EXPLORATION	Intelligent life on other planets
3769 INDIA/PAKISTAN	The Kashmir issue
3770 URSULA K. LeGUIN/ AMERICAN WRITER	There have been great societies that did not use the wheel, but there have been no societies that did not tell stories.
3771 SAFETY	Contingency planning
3772 RANDY PAUSCH/USA/ THE LAST LECTURE	Never lose the childlike wonder. It's just too important. It's what drives us.
3773 DEATH	Cremation
3774 URSULA K. LeGUIN/ AMERICAN WRITER	While we read a novel, we are insane – bonkers. We believe in the existence of people who aren't there, we hear their voices...Sanity returns (in most cases) when the book is closed.
3775 ROBERT MCCRUM/UK	There are probably just 100 novels you really must read.
3776 NEW DIRECTIONS	Breaking from tradition
3777 DEATH/LOVE	Life-diamond (made from remains of loved one)
3778 SETH GODIN/ USA/ ENTREPRENEUR	Being the dumbest partner in a room of smart people is exactly where you want to be.
3779 THOMAS J. WATSON/ AMERICAN BUSINESSMAN/ FOUNDER/IBM	Would you like me to give you a formula for success? It's quite simple, really. Double your rate of failure. You're thinking of failure as the enemy of success. But it isn't at all...you can be discouraged by failure or you can learn from it. So go ahead and make mistakes.
3780 FUN/SINGING	Karaoke
3781 JULIUS NYERERE/ PRESIDENT/KENYA	To measure a country's wealth by its gross national product is to measure things, not satisfactions.
3782 MOLIERE/FRENCH ACTOR/PLAYWRIGHT	The more we love someone, the less we flatter them; it is by excusing nothing that true love shows itself.
3783 SHANE KOYCZAN/POET/ TED.COM	If you can't see anything beautiful about yourself, get a better mirror.
3784 TILLET WRIGHT/ TEDTALK/ARTIST/ DIRECTOR	Familiarity really is the gateway drug to empathy. Once an issue pops up in your own backyard or amongst your own family, you're more likely to... explore a new perspective on it.
3785 JUSTICE	Wrongful conviction
3786 MOLIERE/FRENCH	...unbroken happiness is a bore: it should have ups and downs.
3787 JULIUS NYERERE/ PRESIDENT/KENYA	Capitalism means that the masses will work, and a few people – who may not labor at all – will benefit from that work. The few will sit down to a banquet, and the masses will eat whatever is left over.
3788 OG MANDINO/USA/ AUTHOR	Love doesn't sit there like a stone, it has to be made, like bread; remade all the time, made new.
3789 SETH GODIN/USA/ ENTREPRENEUR	Starting a business is far easier than making it successful.
3790 DAVID O. McKAY/ MORMON LEADER	It is glorious when you can lie down at night with a clear conscience that you have done your best not to offend anyone and have injured no one.

NUMBER CATEGORY/CREDIT	TOPIC
3791 BALANCE	Yin and yang
3792 ECOLOGY/NATURE	Reduced habitat for various animal species
3793 RELATIONSHIPS	Noisy neighbors
3794 J.K. ROWLING/UK	It does not do to dwell on dreams and forget to live.
3795 RELATIONSHIPS	Nosey neighbors
3796 FOOD/SCIENCE	Genetically modified food
3797 EDUCATION	Three R's: Reading, 'riting, 'rithmetic
3798 ETHICS	Cosmetics and animal testing
3799 NATIONAL/PROBLEM	Brain drain
3800 URSULA K. LeGUIN/USA	In war everybody is a prisoner.
3801 PEARL BUCK/USA	Hunger makes a thief of any man.
3802 HEALTH/BLOOD	Bloodless surgery
3803 MONEY	Lottery winners
3804 BILL NYE/USA/ SCIENTIST	Everybody in the space program, everybody who's a doctor, got interested in science when he or she was seven or eight years old, not when they were 16 or 18. That's where you spend your money: science education in elementary levels.
3805 EDDIE OBENG/UK/ PROFESSOR	We spend our time responding rationally to a world which we understand and recognize, but which no longer exists.
3806 PAUL RAND/ AMERICAN DESIGNER	You will learn most things by looking, but reading gives understanding. Reading will make you free.
3807 VIKTOR FRANKL	What is to give light must endure burning.
3808 PEARL BUCK/ AMERICAN NOVELIST	The person who tries to live alone will not succeed as a human being.
3809 NEIL DE GRASSE TYSON/ ASTRONOMER/USA	I'm often asked by parents what advice can I give them to help get kids interested in science? And I have only one bit of advice: get out of their way. Kids are born curious. Period.
3810 FAITH JEGEDE/TED.COM AUTISTIC BROTHERS	The chance for greatness, for progress and for change dies the moment we try to be like someone else.
3811 STEPHEN COVEY/ USA/AUTHOR	Sow a thought, reap an action; sow an action, reap a habit; sow a habit, reap a character; sow a character, reap a destiny.
3812 ADVERTISING	Sex sells
3813 MYSTERY	Occultism
3814 INTERNET	Social networking
3815 GOVERNMENT/CRIME	Presidential pardons
3816 DEBBIE MACOMBER/ WRITER/USA	If the grass is greener on the other side of the fence, you can bet the water bill is higher.
3817 BILL NYE/USA/ SCIENTIST	Science is the key to our future, and if you don't believe in science, then you're holding everybody back.
3818 WINSTON CHURCHILL	We make a living by what we get. We make a life by what we give.
3819 CHRISTA McAULIFFE/US	I touch the future; I teach.
3820 SLOVAKIAN PROVERB	Anger is the only thing to put off till tomorrow.

NUMBER CATEGORY/CREDIT	TOPIC
3821 LOU HOLTZ/COACH	Ability is what you're capable of doing. Motivation determines what you do. Attitude determines how well you do it.
3822 AUTHOR UNKNOWN	To the world you might be just one person, but to just one person, you might be the world.
3823 WILLIAM JAMES/USA/ PHILOSOPHER	The deepest principle in human nature is the craving to be appreciated.
3824 FREDERICK DOUGLASS/ USA/ABOLITIONIST	It is easier to build strong children than to repair broken men.
3825 ERASMUS/DUTCH PHILOSOPHER	When I get a little money, I buy books; and if any is left, I buy food and clothes.
3826 LEO J. BURKE/USA/ PSYCHOLOGIST	People who say they sleep like a baby usually don't have one.
3827 USA/GROUCHO MARX/ COMEDIAN	Speak when you're angry and you'll make the best speech you'll ever regret.
3828 USA/THEODORE ROOSEVELT/ PRESIDENT	People ask the difference between a leader and a boss. The leader works in the open, and the boss in covert. The leader leads and the boss drives.
3829 ZSA ZSA GABOR/USA	Macho does not prove mucho.
3830 USA/WRITER/MARY WOLLSTONECRAFT	No man chooses evil because it is evil; he only mistakes it for happiness, the good he seeks.
3831 BILL NYE/USA/ SCIENTIST	Everybody's dream is to be able to fly...I can see how people get hooked on that. And I think space exploration would be the same deal.
3832 SENECA/ROMAN DRAMATIST	One hand washes the other. (Manus Manum Lavet)
3833 YANN MARTEL/ CANADIAN WRITER	To choose doubt as a philosophy of life is akin to choosing immobility as a means of transportation.
3834 FAYE WATTLETON/USA	The only safe ship in a storm is leadership.
3835 BEYONCE KNOWLES/ USA/SINGER	When you love and accept yourself, when you know who really cares about you, and when you learn from your mistakes, then you stop caring about what people who don't know you think.
3836 ABRAHAM LINCOLN/ 16TH PRESIDENT/USA	Nearly all men can stand adversity, but if you want to test a man's character, give him power.
3837 KOFI ANNAN/GHANA/ UNITED NATIONS/ SECRETARY GENERAL	We need to create a world that is equitable, that is stable and a world where we bear in mind the needs of others, and not only what we need immediately. We are all in the same boat.
3838 RONALD REAGAN/ 40TH PRESIDENT/USA	All great change in America begins at the dinner table.
3839 IMPERIALISM	Neo-colonialism
3840 ALEXANDER GRAHAM BELL/SCIENTIST	The achievement of one goal should be the starting point of another.
3841 JONATHAN WINTERS/US	If your ship doesn't come in, swim out to it!
3842 LYNDON B. JOHNSON/ PRESIDENT/USA	At the desk where I sit, I have learned one great truth. The answer for all our national problems -- the answer for all the problems of the world -- comes to a single word. That word is EDUCATION.
3843 DIFFERENCE	Tribalism

NUMBER CATEGORY/CREDIT	TOPIC
3844 CHARLES SCHWAB/ USA/ENTREPRENEUR	The way to develop the best in a person is by appreciation and encouragement.
3845 DEREK BOK/US/ WRITER/EDUCATION	If you think education is expensive, try ignorance.
3846 STEPHEN COVEY/ USA/AUTHOR	Most people do not listen with the intent to understand; they listen with the intent to reply.
3847 KURT COBAIN/MUSICIAN	The duty of youth is to challenge corruption.
3848 PEARL BUCK/ AMERICAN NOVELIST	Praise out of season, or tactlessly bestowed, can freeze the heart as much as blame.
3849 EVANGELICAL CHRISTIANITY	The rapture - Idea that some Christians will one day be caught up in the air to meet Jesus Christ
3850 FRANCIS BACON/ UK/WRITER	If we are to achieve results never before accomplished, we must expect to employ methods never before attempted.
3851 GUSTAVE FLAUBERT/ FRENCH NOVELIST	Artists who seek perfection in everything are those who cannot attain it in anything.
3852 FRANCIS BACON/ ENGLISH THINKER	A man must make his opportunity, as oft as find it.
3853 HEALTH	Organic food
3854 PAMELA ANDERSON/ CANADIAN ACTRESS	It's great being blond. With such low expectations, it's easy to impress.
3855 TAYLOR BRANCH/ USA/AUTHOR	Truth requires a maximum effort to see through the eyes of strangers, foreigners, and enemies.
3856 ELON MUSK/USA ENTREPRENEUR	I think that's the single best piece of advice: constantly think about how you could be doing things better and questioning yourself.
3857 HENRY FORD/USA/ BUSINESSMAN	Failure is simply an opportunity to be begin again, this time more intelligently.
3858 HEALTH/HEART	Pacemaker
3859 HENRY FORD/USA/ BUSINESSMAN	My best friend is the one who brings out the best in me.
3860 ANN LANDERS/USA/ ADVICE COLUMNIST	When life's problems seem overwhelming, look around and see what other people are coping with. You may consider yourself fortunate.
3861 ANONYMOUS	Professionals are people who can do their job when they don't feel like it. Amateurs are people who can't do their job when they do feel like it.
3862 CHRISTIANITY	Christian fundamentalism
3863 ANN LANDERS/USA/ ADVICE COLUMNIST	Opportunities are usually disguised as hard work, so most peple don't recognize them.
3864 HISTORY	Jewish pogroms
3865 T. S. ELIOT/POET/ ESSAYIST/USA	The years between fifty and seventy are the hardest. You are always being asked to do more, and you are not yet decrepit enough to turn them down.
3866 ANN LANDERS/USA/ ADVICE COLUMNIST	It is not what you do for your children, but what you have taught them to do for themselves that will make them successful human beings.
3867 GEORGE WASHINGTON CARVER/USA/SCIENTIST	Fear of something is at the root of hate for others, and hate within will eventually destroy the hater. Keep your thoughts free from hate, and you need have no fear from those who hate you.

NUMBER CATEGORY/CREDIT	TOPIC
3868 HERMANN HESSE/ GERMAN/SWISS/WRITER	Learn what is to be taken seriously and laugh at the rest.
3869 EUGENE IONESCO/ FRENCH PLAYWRIGHT	Ideologies separate us. Dreams and anguish bring us together.
3870 CYRIL CONNOLY/UK/ WRITER	There is no pain equal to that which two lovers can inflict on one another.
3871 JAPAN/TRADITIONAL THEATER	Kabuki : traditional Japanese popular drama performed with highly stylized singing and dancing
3872 GOVERNMENT/DRUGS	War on drugs
3873 RESPONSIBILITY	Drinking and driving
3874 CYRIL CONNOLY/UK	Literature is the art of writing something that will be read twice.
3875 MAYA ANGELOU/USA/ AUTHOR/POET	Bitterness is like cancer. It eats the host. But anger is like fire. It burns it all clean.
3876 PIERRE CORNEILLE/ FRENCH DRAMATIST	A liar is always lavish of oaths.
3877 CYRIL CONNOLY/ WRITER	Better to write for yourself and have no public, than to write for the public and have no self.
3878 HISTORIAN/NICCOLO MACHIAVELLI	Where the willingness is great, the difficulties cannot be great.
3879 J.R.R. TOLKIEN/UK	Faithless is he that says farewell when the road darkens.
3880 EUGENE IONESCO/ PLAYWRIGHT	Explanation separates us from astonishment, which is the only gateway to the incomprehensible.
3881 THOMAS BEECHAM/ ENGLISH COMPOSER	I have just been all round the world and have formed a very poor opinion of it.
3882 SOCIETY	Respect for others' feelings
3883 BEAUTY	Facial treatments
3884 GUSTAVE FLAUBERT/ FRENCH NOVELIST	O do not read, as children do, to amuse yourself, or like the ambitious, for the purpose of instruction. No, read in order to live.
3885 PEARL S. BUCK/ AMERICAN NOVELIST	The young do not know enough to be prudent, and therefore they attempt the impossible - and achieve it, generation after generation.
3886 RANDY PAUSCH/USA	No job is beneath you.
3887 FAMILY	House husbands
3888 JAPAN/SHUT-INS	*Hikikomori* - people who prefer to remain perpetually indoors
3889 HABIT/PERSONAL	Procrastination
3890 PERSONAL/SOCIETY	Weight loss programs
3891 KWAME ANTHONY APPIAH/PHILOSOPHER	...we should learn about people in other places, take an interest in their civilizations, their arguments, their errors, their achievements, not because that will bring us to agreement but because it will help us get used to one another...
3892 PIERRE CORNEILLE/ FRENCH/TRAGEDIAN	A victory without danger is a triumph without glory.
3893 CHINA/LEARNERS DICTIONARY.COM	*Feng shui* : a Chinese system for positioning a building and the objects within a building in a way that is thought to agree with spiritual forces and to bring health and happiness

NUMBER CATEGORY/CREDIT	TOPIC
3894 ROBERT MCCRUM/ THE OBSERVER/UK	You don't have to read every book you buy, and you certainly don't have to finish the book you've started.
3895 HENRY FORD/USA	A business that makes nothing but money is a poor business.
3896 SUCCESS/MARRIAGE	Trophy wives
3897 LOVE/FOOD	Candle light dinner
3898 GUSTAVE FLAUBERT/ FRENCH NOVELIST	I believed that if one always looked at the skies, one would end up with wings.
3899 MARTIN BUBER/ PHILOSOPHER	All journeys have secret destinations of which the traveler is unaware.
3900 JOHN LE CARRE/ AMERICAN WRITER	Americans believe that if you know something, you should do something about it.
3901 ARTHUR ASHE/ USA/TENNIS PLAYER	The best way to judge a life is to ask yourself, "Did I make the best use of the time I had?"
3902 CYRIL CONNOLLY/ UK/WRITER	There are many who dare not kill themselves for fear of what the neighbours will say.
3903 MAHATMA GANDHI/ INDIAN LEADER	Like the bee gathering honey from different flowers, the wise person accepts the essence of the different scriptures, and sees only the good in all religions.
3904 PERSONAL/SOCIETY	Accident by design
3905 PIERRE CORNEILLE/FR.	Desire increases when fulfillment is postponed.
3906 OG MANDINO/US / AUTHOR/THE GREATEST SALESMAN IN THE WORLD	The person who knows one thing and does it better than anyone else, even if it only be the art of raising lentils, receives the crown he merits. If he raises all his energy to that end, he is a benefactor of mankind and is rewarded as such.
3907 PUBLIUS TERENCE/ SLAVE/ROME	If you're right, I'll do what you do. If you're wrong, I'll set you straight.
3908 ALEXANDER DUMAS/ FRENCH WRITER	A person who doubts himself is like a man who would enlist in the ranks of his enemies and bear arms against himself. He makes his failure certain by himself being the first person to be convinced of it.
3909 HONORE DE BALZAC/ FRENCH/NOVELIST	A flow of words is a sure sign of duplicity.
3910 ANN LANDERS/USA/ ADVICE COLUMNIST	Some women have the best husbands. Others make the best of the husbands they have.
3911 MARIO PUZO/FRANCIS FORD COPPOLA/USA	Power isn't everything. It's the only thing.
3912 CHARLES BOLDEN/ NASA/TAVISTALKS/USA	Just because you're having difficulty in one area doesn't mean that you can't cooperate and collaborate and do great things in other areas.
3913 CHINESE PROVERB	Light a candle instead of cursing the darkness.
3914 DEVON FRANKLIN/USA/ MOTIVATION	Star in your own movie.
3915 GOD COMPLEX/ INSANITY/WIKIPEDIA	A god complex is an unshakable belief characterized by consistently inflated feelings of personal ability, privilege, or infallibility.
3916 HORACE M. KALLEN/ USA/PHILOSOPHER	Cultural pluralism

NUMBER CATEGORY/CREDIT	TOPIC
3917 CYRIL CONNOLLY/ WRITER	….art is made by the alone for the alone…The reward of art is not fame or success but intoxication…
3918 MUSINGS/DAILY YOMIURI/JAPAN/ PRINCE TOMOHITO OF MIKASA/CANDOR	I am Prince Tomohito and am known as an alcoholic. As I have enjoyed drinking since I was a university student, I would feel quite unhappy if you think I became an alcoholic all of a sudden. I hope you'll understand that I'm a lifetime alcoholic.
3919 H.V. ADOLT/FORBES/ WRITER/BUSINESS	We are all manufacturers – making good, making trouble or making excuses.
3920 USA/SAYING	Never trouble trouble until trouble troubles you.
3921 H.L. MENCKEN/USA/ JOURNALIST	God must love the rich or he wouldn't divide so much among so few of them.
3922 JUSTICE/COURTS	Judicial activism
3923 USA/THURGOOD MARSHALL/JUDGE/	In recognizing the humanity of our fellow beings, we pay ourselves the highest tribute.
3924 USA/DOMINIQUE BROWNING/NY TIMES	Long hair is not the appropriate choice of grown-ups. It says rebellion.
3925 P.T. BARNUM/USA	I don't care what you say about me, just spell my name right.
3926 DAVID HANNUM/ P.T. BARNUM/USA	There's a sucker born every minute.
3927 NEGOTIATION	Win-lose
3928 DONALD SADOWAY/ TEDTALK/CANADA/USA	In a battery, I strive to maximize electrical potential. When mentoring, I strive to maximize human potential.
3929 REGINA DUGAN/FROM MACII-20/TED.COM	If you don't already have a nerd in your life, you should get one.
3930 FRANK WARREN/ HALF A MILLION SECRETS	Secrets can take many forms. They can be shocking or silly or soulful. They can connect us with our deepest humanity, or with people we'll never meet.
3931 LUCY McRAE/TED.COM/ TECH/HUMAN BODY	I created a swallowable perfume…The fragrance comes out through the skin's surface when you perspire.
3932 STEFON HARRIS/ TEDTALK	Every 'mistake' is an opportunity in jazz.
3933 QUYEN NGUYEN/ COLOR-CODED SURGERY/TED.COM	Our society loves to romanticize the idea of the single, solo inventor who, working late in the lab one night, makes an earthshaking discovery, and voila, overnight everythings's changed. That's a very appealing picture; however, it's just not true. Medicine today is a team sport.
3934 WILLIAM SAFIRE/ USA/AUTHOR	If you re-read your work, you can find on re-reading a great deal of repetition can be avoided by re-reading and editing.
3935 BILLY COLLINS/USA/ TEDTALK/POET LAUREATE	It's a good thing to get poetry off the shelves and more into public life.
3936 P.T. BARNUM/USA/ PROMOTER	Nobody lost a dollar by underestimating the taste of the American public.
3937 LYNN TOLER/USA/ JUDGE	Fear is a fatal leader.

NUMBER CATEGORY/CREDIT	TOPIC
3938 T. S. ELIOT/POET/ ESSAYIST/USA	For last year's words belong to last year's language. And next year's words await another voice.
3939 MARTHA NUSSBAUM/ USA/PHILOSOPHER	You cannot really change the heart without telling a story.
3940 KWAME ANTHONY APPIAH/PHILOSOPHER	My philosophy is that everything is more complicated than you thought.
3941 PAUL BLOOM/NY TIMES/ USA	You don't solve moral problems with a show of hands..
3942 PRO-CHOICE SLOGAN/US	If you don't like abortions, don't have one.
3943 KWAME ANTHONY APPIAH/PHILOSOPHER	A value is like a fax machine. It's not much use if you're the only one who has one.
3944 PEARL S. BUCK/ NOBELIST/WRITER	I enjoy life because I am endlessly interested in people and their growth.
3945 PAUL SNELGROVE/ OCEAN/TED.COM	Marine organisms do not care about international boundaries; they move where they will.
3946 UNEMPLOYMENT/ FAMILY/PRIVACY	Boomerang children: young adults who return to live with their parents because of difficulty surviving on their own
3947 J.R.R. TOLKIEN/UK/ WRITER	Courage is found in unlikely places.
3948 PAVAN SUKHDEV/PUT A VALUE ON NATURE!/ TEDTALK	When we measure corporate performance, we don't include our impacts on nature and what our business costs society. That has to stop.
3949 KWAME ANTHONY APPIAH/PHILOSOPHER	…a person of honor cares first of all not about being respected but about being worthy of respect.
3950 SAYING	Dead men tell no tales.
3951 PAUL SNELGROVE/ OCEAN/TED.COM	We know more about the surface of the Moon and about Mars than we do about [the deep sea floor]…
3952 SUSAN CAIN/THE INTROVERTS/TED.COM	There's zero correlation between being the best talker and having the best ideas.
3953 T. S. ELIOT/POET/ ESSAYIST/USA	Only those who will risk going too far can possibly find out how far one can go.
3954 ANDREW STANTON/ GREAT STORY/TEDTALK/ USA/FILM DIRECTOR	Change is fundamental in story. If things go static, stories die.
3955 STEPHEN COVEY/USA/ AUTHOR	Trust is the glue of life. It's the most essential ingredient in effective communication. It's the foundational principle that holds all relationships.
3956 HANNAH ARENDT/ POLITICAL THEORIST	The sad truth is that most evil is done by people who never make up their minds to be good or evil.
3957 BENJAMIN FRANKLIN USA/AUTHOR/DIPLOMAT	Remember not only to say the right thing in the right place, but far more difficult still, to leave unsaid the wrong thing at the tempting moment.
3958 SELF/SPIRITUALITY	Why I pray (or not)
3959 REINHARD BONNKE/ GERMAN EVANGELIST	Don't accept the applause of men, and you won't be destroyed by their criticism.

NUMBER CATEGORY/CREDIT	TOPIC
3960 SHERRY TURKLE/ CONNECTED/TED.COM	The feeling that 'no one is listening to me' make us want to spend time with machines that seem to care about us.
3961 JAPANESE PROVERB	Time spent laughing is time spent with the gods.
3962 JANE GOODALL/UK/ PRIMATOLOGIST	Anyone who tries to improve the lives of animals invariably comes in for criticisms from those who believe such efforts are misplaced in a world of suffering humanity.
3963 ALAIN DE BOTTON/ AUTHOR/TED.COM	We may not agree with what religions are trying to teach us, but we can admire the institutional way in which they're doing it.
3964 SHLOMO BENARTZI/ SAVING/TEDTALK	When you get your driving license [in Austria], you check the box if you do not want to donate your organ. Nobody checks boxes. That's too much effort. One percent check the box.
3965 ARABIC PROVERB	Believe what you see and lay aside what you hear.
3966 STEDMAN GRAHAM/ USA/AUTHOR/ MOTIVATIONAL SPEAKER	People who control their own lives are like those cities of the future you have seen with huge bubbles covering them. Like those futuristic cities, these people are self-contained. It doesn't matter what goes on around them, they are in control.
3967 SCOTT RAFER/ ENTREPRENEUR WISDOM	With VCs [venture capitalists], if you want money, ask for advice – and vice versa. When they offer money, make sure you get advice. When they go out of their way to offer advice, watch your wallet.
3968 KAHLIL GIBRAN/POET/ ON GOOD AND EVIL	You are good when you strive to give of yourself. Yet you are not evil when you seek gain for yourself.
3969 JAMES HANSEN/ CLIMATE CHANGE/ TEDTALK	Imagine a giant asteroid on a direct collision course with Earth. That is the equivalent of what we face now [with climate change], yet we dither.
3970 SIR THOMAS MORE/ UK/WRITER	In no victory do they glory so much as in that which is gained by dexterity and good conduct without bloodshed.
3971 LEO TOLSTOY/WRITER/ RUSSIA	Wrong does not cease to be wrong because the majority share in it.
3972 SAMMY DAVIS JR./ MUSICIAN/USA	You don't swing where you sleep.
3973 CHIP KIDD/TEDTALK/ GRAPHIC DESIGNER/USA	A book cover is a distillation. It is a haiku of the story.
3974 ALAN ALDA/WRITER/ USA	Here's my Golden Rule for a tarnished age: Be fair with others, but keep after them until they're fair with you.
3975 USA/JOHN KENNETH GALBRAITH/ECONOMIST	All successful revolutions are the kicking in of a rotten door.
3976 STEDMAN GRAHAM/USA	You must move from your history to your imagination.
3977 BILL GATES/USA/ ENTREPRENEUR	Success is a lousy teacher. It seduces smart people into thinking they can't lose.
3978 BRYAN STEVENSON/US/ INJUSTICE/TEDTALK	The opposite of poverty is not wealth…In too many places, the opposite of poverty is justice.
3979 ROBERT REDFORD/ USA/ACTOR	I think the environment should be put in the category of our national security. Defense of our resources is just as important as defense abroad. Otherwise what is there to defend?

NUMBER CATEGORY/CREDIT	TOPIC
3980 RESEARCH/MIND	Positive psychology
3981 SAMMY DAVIS JR./MUSICIAN/USA	I have to be a star like another man has to breathe.
3982 PUBLIC OWNERSHIP	Government ownership of utilities
3983 ANAIS NIN/US/AUTHOR	The only abnormality is the incapacity to love.
3984 LAO-TZU/CHINA	There is no greater guilt than discontentment.
3985 PUBLISHING/WRITERS	Self-publishing
3986 USA/JOHN KENNETH GALBRAITH/ECONOMIST	Economics is extremely useful as a form of employment for economists.
3987 ALAN ALDA/USA/WRITER	Be smart as you can, but remember that it is always better to be wise than to be smart.
3988 MARGARET FULLER/USA	If you have knowledge, let others light their candles at it.
3989 PAUL GRAHAM/WISDOM ENTREPRENEUR	If you're worried about threats to the survival of your company, don't look for them in the news. Look in the mirror.
3990 W. CLEMENT STONE/USA/BUSINESSMAN	Have the courage to say no. Have the courage to face the truth. Do the right thing because it is right. These are the magic keys to living your life with integrity.
3991 MARC CUBAN/AMERICAN BILLIONAIRE/ENTREPRENEUR	Taking money from someone else kills more start-ups than anything else does. Do everything you can to avoid taking money. If you must, your best prospects are potential customers. You have something they want, so if they invest in you, it can be a win-win situation.
3992 MOTHER TERESA/CATHOLIC NUN	The hunger for love is much more difficult to remove than the hunger for bread.
3993 NATIVE AMERICANS/FIRST NATIONS	The longhouse: a long communal dwelling of some North American Indians (as the Iroquois)
3994 T. S. ELIOT/POET/ESSAYIST/USA	It is not wise to violate the rules until you know how to observe them.
3995 STEPHEN COVEY/USA/AUTHOR	Most of us spend too much time on what is urgent and not enough time on what is important.
3996 ELIZABETH BARRETT BROWNING/UK/POET	If you desire faith, then you have faith enough.
3997 PAT RILEY/USA/COACH/BASKETBALL	There's no such thing as coulda, shoulda, or woulda. If you shoulda and coulda, you woulda done it.
3998 JENNIFER PAHLKA/CODING/TED	[The Internet generation is] not fighting that battle about who gets to speak; they all get to speak.
3999 ALAN ALDA/USA/WRITER	If you know what you're looking for, that's all you get -- what's previously known. But when you're open to what's possible, you get something new -- that's creativity.
4000 RANDY PAUSCH/USA/THE LAST LECTURE	All my adult life I've felt drawn to ask long-married couples how they were able to stay together. All of them said the same thing: "We worked hard at it."
4001 ALAN ALDA/USA/WRITER	It isn't necessary to be rich and famous to be happy. It's only necessary to be rich.
4002 FUN	An amusement park visit

NUMBER CATEGORY/CREDIT	TOPIC
4003 WILLIAM SAFIRE/USA/ WRITER	Never assume the obvious is true.
4004 ROBERT FULGHUM/ USA/WRITER	Wash your hands before you eat.
4005 INDIAN PROVERB	A doctor is only a doctor when he has killed one or two patients.
4006 B.F. SKINNER/USA	The mob rushes in where individuals fear to tread.
4007 URSULA LeGUIN/ USA/WRITER	We are volcanoes. When we women offer our experience as our truth, as human truth, all the maps change. There are new mountains.
4008 ROBERT FULGHUM/USA	Say you're sorry when you hurt somebody.
4009 ALAN DERSHOWITZ/ LAWYER/PROFESSOR/ HARVARD	I came from a poor family, so working and going to school at the same time was natural. It taught me multi-tasking although we didn't call it that back then. I learned I could never be idle.
4010 SELMA LAGERLOF/ SWEDISH WRITER	There isn't much that tastes better than praise from those who are wise and capable.
4011 TALI SHAROT/THE OPTIMISM BIAS/TED	Optimists are people who expect more kisses in their future, more strolls in the park. And that anticipation enhances their well-being.
4012 ROBIN WILLIAMS/USA/ COMEDIAN	You're only given one little spark of madness. You mustn't lose it.
4013 NANCY LUBLIN/ TEXTING/TED.COM	We're finding [texting] 11 times more powerful than email [for communicating with kids.
4014 HORACE MANN/USA/ EDUCATION	Be ashamed to die until you have scored some victory for humanity.
4015 ALAN ALDA/USA	Loneliness is everything it's cracked up to be.
4016 USA/JOHN KENNETH GALBAITH/ECONOMIST	Faced with the choice between changing one's mind and proving that there is no need to do so, almost everyone gets busy on the proof.
4017 USA/RALPH WALDO EMERSON/ESSAYIST	Most of the shadows of this life are caused by our standing in our own sunshine.
4018 CYRIL CONNOLLY/UK/ WRITER	Always be nice to those younger than you, because they are the ones who will be writing about you.
4019 ALAN DERSHOWITZ/ LAWYER/PROFESSOR/ HARVARD	I think most defense attorneys honestly believe the principle that says, 'Better 10 guilty go free than even one possibly innocent person be convicted."
4020 B.F. SKINNER/USA/ WALDEN TWO	Fame is...won at the expense of others. Even the well-deserved honors of the scientist or man of learning are unfair to many persons of equal achievement.
4021 ALEXANDER GRAHAM BELL/INVENTOR	Concentrate all your thoughts upon the work at hand. The sun's rays do not burn until brought to a focus.
4022 MUSINGS/DAILY YOMIURI/JAPAN	There is a saying that businesspeople and folding screens cannot stand without bending.
4023 ARIEL GARTEN/KNOW THYSELF/TED.COM/ CANADA	Imagine if you had access to data that allowed you to rank on a scale of overall happiness which people in your life made you the happiest...Would you make more time for those people?
4024 W. CLEMENT STONE/ US/BUSINESS/WRITER	Aim for the moon. If you miss, you may hit a star.

NUMBER CATEGORY/CREDIT	TOPIC
4025 ANIMALS	Lessons animals teach
4026 ALBERT EINSTEIN	An empty stomach is not a good political adviser.
4027 WRITER/ROBERT LOUIS STEVENSON/SCOTTISH	There is no duty we so much underrate as the duty of being happy. By being happy we sow anonymous benefits upon the world.
4028 WILLIAM BLAKE/POET/UK	Excessive sorrow laughs. Excessive joy weeps.
4029 PUBLILIUS SYRUS	The end always passes judgment on what has gone before.
4030 HENRY FORD/USA	You can't learn in school what the world is going to do next year.
4031 MADONNA/USA/SINGER	A lot of people are afraid to say what they want. That's why they don't get what they want.
4032 QUYEN NGUYAN/COLOR-CODED SURGERY/TED.COM	Successful innovation is not a single breakthrough. It is not a sprint. It is not an event for the runner. Successful innovation is a team sport, it's a relay race.
4033 W. CLEMENT STONE/USA/BUSINESSMAN/PHILANTHROPIST	There is little difference in people, but that little difference makes a big difference. The little difference is attitude. The big difference is whether it is positive or negative.
4034 DAG HAMMARSKJOLD/UN SEC. GENERAL	Never, for the sake of peace and quiet, deny your own experience or convictions.
4035 JOAN BAEZ/USA/FOLK SINGER	The easiest kind of relationship is with ten thousand people, the worst is with one.
4036 INDIRA GANDHI/INDIA	Martyrdom does not end something, it is only a beginning.
4037 FAME/PAIN/JOY	The price of fame
4038 DENG MING-DAO/EVERYDAY TAO	Those who don't know how to suffer are the worst off. There are times when the only correct thing we can do is to bear our troubles until a better day.
4039 DR. MARTIN LUTHER KING JR./USA/LEADER	I submit to you that if a man hasn't discovered something he will die for, he isn't fit to live.
4040 CHINA/RELATIONSHIPS/WIKIPEDIA	Guanxi : At its most basic, *guanxi* describes a personal connection between two people in which one is able to prevail upon another to perform a favor or service, or be prevailed upon.
4041 OLGA KORBUT/SOVIET GYMNAST/ GOLD MEDALIST/OLYMPICS	Don't be afraid if things seem difficult in the beginning. That's only the initial impression. The important thing is not to retreat; you have to master yourself.
4042 BENJAMIN BARBER/USA/WRITER/ JIHAD vs. MCWORLD	I don't divide the world into the weak and the strong, or the successes and the failures, those who make it or those who don't. I divide the world into learners and non-learners.
4043 ZIG ZIGLAR/US/SPEAKER	A goal properly set is halfway reached.
4044 VERNON JORDAN/USA/BUSINESS/SUCCESS	My mother was the president of the PTA at every school I attended.
4045 ABIGAIL VAN BUREN/ADVICE COLUMNIST/USA	Wisdom doesn't automatically come with old age. Nothing does – except wrinkles. It's true, some wines improve with age. But only if the grapes were good in the first place.
4046 USA/DR. ARTHUR CALIANDRO/PRIEST	That which every human being, every one of us, needs and wants more than anything else is to be in a relationship, or in relationships, where we feel safe.

NUMBER CATEGORY/CREDIT	TOPIC
4047 TED KOPPEL/USA/ BROADCASTER/TED.COM	We can learn from history how past generations thought and acted, how they responded to the demands of their time and how they solved their problems.
4048 ATUL GAWANDE/ MEDICINE?/TED.COM	[In medicine,] we have trained, hired and rewarded people to be cowboys, but it's pit crews that we need.
4049 USA/MARY MCLEOD BETHUNE/EDUCATOR	Next to God we are indebted to women, first for life itself, and then for making it worth living.
4050 JEREMY RIFKIN/USA/ ECONOMIST	We are already producing enough food to feed the world. We already have technology in place that allows us to produce more than we can find a market for.
4051 ISLAM/LAW	Sharia : the religious laws rooted in the Koran/followed by Muslims
4052 WILLIAM BLAKE/ ENGLISH POET	The man who never alters his opinions is like standing water, and breeds reptiles of the mind.
4053 STEDMAN GRAHAM/ USA/ AUTHOR	People who let events and circumstances dictate their lives are living reactively. That means they don't act on life, they only react to it.
4054 THOMAS JEFFERSON/ USA/3RD PRESIDENT	All tyranny needs to gain a foothold is for people of good conscience to remain silent.
4055 JOSEPH NYE/USA/ HARVARD/PROFESSOR	America rests on shared values rather than shared ethnicity.
4056 RANDY PAUSCH/USA	You can always change your plan, but only if you have one.
4057 DORIS LESSING/WRITER	Some people obtain fame, others deserve it.
4058 OG MANDINO/ USA	There is an immeasurable distance between late and too late.
4059 PRIME MINISTER/GRO HARLEM BRUNDTLAND/ NORWAY	It is simple, really. Human health and the health of ecosystems are inseparable.
4060 ABRAHAM LINCOLN/USA	I don't like that man. I need to get to know him better.
4061 FRENCH/NAPOLEON BONAPARTE/LEADER	Nothing is more difficult, and therefore more precious, than to be able to decide.
4062 WORKERS/RIGHTS	The right to strike
4063 MADONNA/US/SINGER	I always thought I should be treated like a star.
4064 RESPONSIBILITY	Age of majority in your country
4065 USA/MARY CATHERINE BATESON/RESEARCH	Most higher education is devoted to affirming the traditions and origins of an existing elite and transmitting them to new members.
4066 BEAUTY/DANGER	Tanning
4067 OG MANDINO/USA/ AUTHOR	To be always intending to make a new and better life but never to find time to set about it is as to put off eating and drinking and sleeping from one day to the next until you're dead.
4068 PETER VAN UHM/ WHY I CHOSE A GUN/ TEDTALK	I hope that one day armies can be disbanded and humans will find a way of living together without violence and oppression. But until that day comes, we will have to make ideals and human failure meet somewhere in the middle.
4069 DR. CARL SAGAN/USA/ SCIENTIST	Absence of evidence is not evidence of absence.
4070 FRENCH/NAPOLEON	It is the cause, not the death, that makes the martyr.

NUMBER CATEGORY/CREDIT	TOPIC
4071 THICH NHAT HANH/ VIETNAM/BUDDHISM	Walk as if you are kissing the Earth with your feet.
4072 ABIGAIL VAN BUREN/ USA/COLUMNIST	The best index to a person's character is how he treats people who can't do him any good, and how he treats people who can't fight back.
4073 ABRAHAM MASLOW/ USA/PSYCHOLOGIST	If the essential core of the person is denied or suppressed, he gets sick sometimes in obvious ways, sometimes in subtle ways, sometimes immediately, sometimes later.
4074 SINGAPORE	Ban on chewing gum
4075 STATISTICS/LYING	Lies, damned lies, and statistics
4076 CONFUCIANISM/ CHINA/WOMEN	Three forms of Obedience: Father, Husband, Son
4077 US/ABRAHAM LINCOLN	The emancipation proclamation
4078 USA/MARIO PUZO/USA	Falling in love is great but being in love is a disaster.
4079 TRAVEL/SAFETY	Travel insurance
4080 GOVERNMENT	Compulsory education
4081 EDUCATION	Senior citizens and education
4082 PUBLIC FACILITIES	Public access and the disabled
4083 RELATIONSHIPS	Love at first sight
4084 SELF ESTEEM	Body image/Anorexia nervosa
4085 ROBERT FULGHUM/ USA/WRITER	Live a balanced life – learn some and think some and draw some and paint some and sing and dance and play and work everyday some.
4086 SOCIETY	Television and violence
4087 LATIN PROVERB	Where there's smoke, there's fire
4088 T. S. ELIOT/POET/ ESSAYIST/USA	We read so many books, because we cannot know enough people.
4089 SAYING	Life is a bowl of cherries
4090 MOTHER TERESA/ CATHOLIC NUN	Kind words can be short and easy to speak, but their echoes are truly endless.
4091 OPINION/DEBATE	Art is necessary in life
4092 CHILDREN/FUN	Toy guns
4093 DEBATE	Technology will save the day
4094 CREATE A STORY	Love at first bite
4095 WOODY ALLEN/USA/ FILMMAKER	I took a speed reading course and read *War and Peace* in twenty minutes. It involves Russia.
4096 WRITER/GABRIEL GARCÍA MÁRQUEZ	Words are not created by the academics in universities and such like; rather, it is the man in the street who does so.
4097 JOHN K. GALBRAITH/ USA/ECONOMIST	If wrinkles must be written upon our brows, let them not be written upon the heart. The spirit should never grow old.
4098 PAUL ZAK/TRUST/ TEDTALK	[You need] eight hugs a day. You'll be happier and the world will be a better place.
4099 LIFE	Suffering in silence
4100 CONTRIBUTION	Community service

NUMBER CATEGORY/CREDIT	TOPIC
4101 PUBLILIUS SYRUS	We simply rob ourselves when we make presents to the dead.
4102 DORIS LESSING/UK/ S. AFRICA/WRITER	Any human anywhere will blossom in a hundred unexpected talents and capacities simply by being given the opportunity to do so.
4103 BARBARA BUSH/USA/ FIRST LADY	At the end of your life, you will never regret not having passed one more test, winning one more verdict, or not closing one more deal. You will regret time not spent with a husband, a child, a friend, or a parent.
4104 SALVADOR DALI/ARTIST/ SPAIN	At the age of six I wanted to be a cook. At seven I wanted to be Napoleon. And my ambition has been growing steadily ever since.
4105 SERVICE/GLOBAL	Volunteering overseas
4106 SOCIETY	The metric system
4107 DR. CORNEL WEST/USA/ PHILOSOPHER	You can't move forward until you look back.
4108 US/UK/MARGARET HEFFERMAN/BUSINESS	I regularly take my entrepreneurship students out walking because I want to get them in the habit of noticing and thinking about what they notice.
4109 AUTHOR/ERICH MARIA REMARQUE/FRENCH	Keep things at arm's length...If you let anything come too near you want to hold on to it. And there is nothing a man can hold on to.
4110 FRAUD/SAFETY	Dangers lurking in cyberspace
4111 ENGLISH PROVERB	Every cloud has a silver lining.
4112 USA/MARY CATHERINE BATESON/RESEARCHER	Fear is not a good teacher. The lessons of fear are quickly forgotten.
4113 STEPHEN COVEY/USA AUTHOR	We are free to choose our actions...but we are not free to choose the consequence of these actions.
4114 LAO TZU/CHINA	Leadership is the ability to hide your panic from others.
4115 LIFE/DEATH/SOCIETY	Euthanasia
4116 SALVADOR DALI/ARTIST	Have no fear of perfection - you'll never reach it.
4117 BUDDHISM	Buddhist monks
4118 ELIZABETH BARRETT BROWNING/UK/POET	What is genius but the power of expressing a new individuality?
4119 GLOBALIZATION	Globalization and developing countries
4120 JOE MARTI/CUBA/HERO	A knowledge of different literatures is the best way to free one's self from the tyranny of any of them.
4121 BEN LUCIEN BURMAN/ USA/WAR/THIS I BELIEVE	When all the peoples of the world remember to laugh, particularly at themselves, there will be no more dictators and no more wars.
4122 MULTI-TALENTED	Triple threat
4123 DORIS LESSING/UK/ S. AFRICA/WRITER	What's really terrible is to pretend that the second-rate is the first rate.
4124 SAYING	Beware of the tyranny of the obvious.
4125 THICH NHAT HANH/ VIETNAM/BUDDHIST	When another person makes you suffer, it is because he suffers deeply within himself, and his suffering is spilling over.
4126 JOHN LE CARRE/ AMERICAN WRITER	Having your book turned into a movie is like seeing your oxen turned into bouillon cubes.
4127 ACHIEVEMENT/LOSS	Fall from grace
4128 KAHLIL GIBRAN/POET	It is well to give when asked, but it is better to give unasked.

NUMBER CATEGORY/CREDIT	TOPIC
4129 INDIAN PROVERB	Poverty destroys all virtues.
4130 DR. CORNEL WEST/USA	Never forget that justice is what love looks like in public.
4131 USA/AMELIA J. BLOOMER	When you find a burden in belief or apparel, cast it off.
4132 PERSONAL	Ideal job
4133 TRAFFIC/SAFETY	Cycle lanes for cyclists
4134 MADONNA/USA/SINGER	I have the same goal I've had ever since I was a girl. I want to rule the world.
4135 PERSONAL	Jobs you wouldn't do even for a million bucks
4136 SATIRE/JAPAN/POEM/EDO PERIOD	Stranded at riverside / Even more infuriating / A clear view of Mt. Fuji
4137 ENVIRONMENT	Forest conservation
4138 BALANCE	Work versus leisure
4139 PERSONAL	Most interesting job held
4140 USA/GWENDOLYN BROOKS/POET	Art hurts. Art urges voyages – and it is easier to stay at home.
4141 SOCIETY/WELFARE	Unemployment benefits
4142 ABRAHAM MASLOW/PSYCHOLOGY	Let people realize clearly that every time they threaten someone or humiliate or unnecessarily hurt or dominate or reject another human being, they become forces for the creation of psychopathology, even if these be small forces. Let them recognize that every person who is kind, helpful, decent, psychologically democratic, affectionate, and warm, is a psychotherapeutic force, even though a small one.
4143 USA/AD COUNCIL	Friends don't let friends drive drunk.
4144 AMBITION/CHINA	Migrant workers
4145 SUCCESS	Rags to riches
4146 ETHICS/BUSINESS	Ethical business practices
4147 BEAUTY/YOUTH	Peter Pan mothers : mothers who try to stay young, often dressing like young people and competing with their children for attention
4148 ISLAM	Halal : food considered fit for eating based on Muslim law
4149 DORIS LESSING/UK	You only learn to be a better writer by actually writing.
4150 THICH NHAT HANH/VIETNAM/BUDDHIST	Sometimes your joy is the source of your smile, but sometimes your smile can be the source of your joy.
4151 RITA MAE BROWN/USA	I finally figured out the only reason to be alive is to enjoy it.
4152 MADONNA/USA/SINGER	Poor is the man whose pleasures depend on the permission of another.
4153 JOSH KOPELMAN/ENTREPRENEUR	There is a big difference between uncertainty and risk. Great entrepreneurs tackle great uncertainty while intelligently reducing risk.
4154 NATURAL/ARTIFICIAL	Artificial Christmas trees
4155 PADDY ASHDOWN/THE GLOBAL POWER SHIFT/TED.COM	The multinational corporations now developing budgets often bigger than medium-sized countries -- these live in a global space which is largely unregulated, not subject to the rule of law, and in which people may act free of constraint.
4156 HONORE DE BALZAC/FRENCH NOVELIST	A good husband is never the first to go to sleep at night or the last to awake in the morning.

NUMBER CATEGORY/CREDIT	TOPIC
4157 SLAVERY/USA	Reparations to descendants of African slaves
4158 SALVADOR DALI/ARTIST	There are some days when I think I'm going to die from an overdose of satisfaction.
4159 CONCEPT CAR/ WIKIPEDIA DEFINITION	Concept car: A concept vehicle or show vehicle is a car made to showcase new styling and or new technology. They are often shown at motor shows to gauge customer reaction to new and radical designs which may or may not have a chance of being produced.
4160 EZRA POUND/USA	A slave is one who waits for someone to come and free him.
4161 SCOTTISH PROVERB	Confession is good for the soul.
4162 MICHEL DE MONTAIGNE/ FRENCH/WRITER	I quote others only in order to better express myself.
4163 PERSONAL	Magic moments in my life
4164 STEPHEN COVEY/USA	Start with the end in mind.
4165 THICH NHAT HANH/ VIETNAM/BUDDHIST	To be beautiful means to be yourself. You don't need to be accepted by others. You need to accept yourself.
4166 CHRISTOPHER NOLAN/ UK/FILM DIRECTOR	Superheroes fill a gap in the pop culture psyche similar to the role of Greek mythology. There isn't really anything else that does the job in modern terms. For me, Batman is the one that can clearly be taken seriously.
4167 BUSINESS/DEBATE	It is dangerous for a business to grow too fast.
4168 MALCOLM S. FORBES	Victory is sweetest when you've known defeat.
4169 CONFUCIUS/CHINA	When anger rises, think of the consequences.
4170 MENCIUS/CHINA	The great man is he who does not lose his child-heart.
4171 MOTHER TERESA	It is a kingly act to assist the fallen.
4172 CONFUCIUS	Wherever you go, go with all your heart.
4173 MENCIUS	Friendship is one mind in two bodies.
4174 MOTHER TERESA	Do not wait for leaders; do it alone, person to person.
4175 ALAN ALDA/USA/ACTOR	Originality is unexplored territory. You get there by carrying a canoe - you can't take a taxi.
4176 MALCOLM S. FORBES	To measure the man, measure his heart.
4177 ENGLISH PROVERB	Every dog has its day.
4178 PEOPLE/ENCOUNTERS	Memorable characters I've known
4179 DENG MING-DAO/ EVERYDAY TAO	The moon does not fight. It attacks no one. It does not worry. It does not try to crush others. It keeps to its course, but by its very nature, it gently influences. What other body could pull an entire ocean from shore to shore?
4180 FRENCH/NAPOLEON	Music is what tells us that the human race is greater than we realize.
4181 W. CLEMENT STONE/ USA/BUSINESSMAN	Tell everyone what you want to do and someone will want to help you do it.
4182 MADONNA/USA/ SINGER	When I'm hungry, I eat. When I'm thirsty, I drink. When I feel like saying something, I say it.
4183 JANE FONDA/USA/ THIRD ACT/TED.COM	We are living on average today 34 years longer than our great-grandparents did.
4184 GET CREATIVE/STORY	Face to face with a python!

NUMBER CATEGORY/CREDIT	TOPIC
4185 STEPHEN JAY GOULD/ USA/SCIENTIST	Science is an integral part of culture. It's not this foreign thing, done by an arcane priesthood. It's one of the glories of the human intellectual tradition.
4186 LAO TZU/CHINESE PHILOSOPHER	Shape clay into a vessel; It is the space within that makes it useful.
4187 MADONNA/USA/ SINGER	I want to be like Gandhi, and Martin Luther King, and John Lennon…but I want to stay alive.
4188 THICH NHAT HANH/ VIETNAM/BUDDHIST	The seed of suffering in you may be strong but don't wait until you have no more suffering before allowing yourself to be happy.
4189 JEFF BEZOS/FOUNDER AMAZON.COM	If you want to be a pioneer, you have to be comfortable being misunderstood.
4190 RITA MAE BROWN/ FEMINIST	Any woman whose I.Q. hovers above her body temperature must be a feminist.
4191 STEDMAN GRAHAM/ USA/AUTHOR	Isolating yourself is not healthy spiritually, mentally, or physically, and it is certainly not the way to achieve a better life.
4192 ABRAHAM MASLOW/ USA/PSYCHOLOGY	If you plan on being anything less than you are capable of being, you will probably be unhappy all the days of your life.
4193 GARY ZUKAV/USA/ SPIRITUAL TEACHER/ AUTHOR	If you want to have the kind of relationship that your heart yearns for, you have to create it. You can't depend on somebody else creating it for you.
4194 NATAN SHARANSKY/ ISRAELI POLITICIAN	Fear societies are societies in which dissent is banned.
4195 DORIS LESSING/UK S. AFRICA/WRITER	I don't know much about creative writing programs. But they're not telling the truth if they don't teach, one, that writing is hard work, and, two, that you have to give up a great deal of life, your personal life, to be a writer.
4196 FAMILY	Latchkey kids
4197 RANDY PAUSCH/PROF/ LAST LECTURE	Be good at something. It makes you valuable. Have something to bring to the table, because that will make you more welcome.
4198 WILMA MANKILLER/ 1ST FEMALE CHIEF/ CHEROKEE/USA	In Iroquois society, leaders are encouraged to remember seven generations in the past and consider seven generations in the future when making decisions.
4199 GET CREATIVE/STORY	The blind tourist guide
4200 AUTHOR/FRENCH/ ERICH M. REMARQUE	Life did not intend to make us perfect. Whoever is perfect belongs in a museum.
4201 ELIZABETH BARRETT BROWNING/UK/POET	The devil is most devilish when respectable.
4202 FRENCH/NAPOLEON	Glory is fleeting but obscurity is forever.
4203 DEREK SIVERS/USA	A balanced diet is a cookie in each hand
4204 SAVINGS/FUTURE	Nest egg
4205 NATIONALISM	Arms race
4206 SOCIETY	Elderly residential care homes
4207 ABRAHAM MASLOW/ USA/PSYCHOLOGY	One's only rival is one's own potentialities. One's only failure is failing to live up to one's own possibilities. In this sense, every man can be a king, and must therefore be treated like a king.

NUMBER CATEGORY/CREDIT	TOPIC
4208 SOCIETY/PEOPLE	Slippery slope
4209 ANNA PAVLOVA/ CLASSICAL BALLET/	When a small child, I thought that success spelled happiness. I was wrong, happiness is like a butterfly which appears and delights us for one brief moment, but soon flits away.
4210 THICH NHAT HANH/ VIETNAM/BUDDHIST	Hope is important because it can make the present moment less difficult to bear.
4211 STEPHEN JAY GOULD/ AMERICAN SCIENTIST	Life is short, and potential studies infinite. We have a much better chance of accomplishing something significant when we follow our passionate interests and work in areas of deepest personal meaning.
4212 LAO TZU/CHINESE PHILOSOPHER	Cut doors and windows for a room / It is the holes which make it useful. Therefore, benefit comes from what is there; Usefulness from what is not there.
4213 PROVERB	A man is known by the company he keeps.
4214 ABRAHAM MASLOW/ USA/PSYCHOLOGY	The most stable, and therefore, the most healthy self-esteem is based on deserved respect from others rather than on external fame or celebrity and unwarranted adulation.
4215 DORIS LESSING/WRITER	Trust no friend without faults, and love a woman, but no angel.
4216 THICH NHAT HANH/ VIETNAM/BUDDHIST	My actions are my only true belongings.
4217 LONELINESS	Empty nest syndrome
4218 HENRIK IBSEN/WRITER	Public opinion is an extremely mutable thing.
4219 EDITH WHARTON/USA/ NOVELIST	There are two ways of spreading light: to be the candle or to be the mirror that reflects it.
4220 SALVADOR DALI/ ARTIST/SPAIN	Those who do not want to imitate anything, produce nothing.
4221 ABRAHAM MASLOW/ PSYCHOLOGY/USA	We fear our highest possibilities. We are generally afraid to become that which we can glimpse in our most perfect moments, under conditions of great courage. We enjoy and even thrill to godlike possibilities we see in ourselves in such peak moments. And yet we simultaneously shiver with weakness, awe, and fear before these very same possibilities.
4222 BILL BRADLEY/USA/ POLITICIAN/SPORTS	Ambition is the path to success. Persistence is the vehicle you arrive in.
4223 PEGGY NOONAN/USA/ SPEECHWRITER	Candor is a compliment; it implies equality. It's how true friends talk.
4224 NATAN SHARANSKY/ ISRAELI POLITICIAN	Free societies are societies in which the right of dissent is protected.
4225 WOMEN/EMMELINE PANKHURST/RIGHTS	We have to free half of the human race, women, so that they can free the other half.
4226 DOROTHY PARKER/US	I don't care about what is written about me so long as it isn't true.
4227 ALICE PAUL/USA EQUAL RIGHTS	When you put your hand to the plow, you can't put it down until you get to the end of the row.
4228 UK/CHRISTABEL PANKHURST/RIGHTS	Ability is sexless.
4229 ANN LANDERS/USA/ ADVICE COLUMNIST	There are really only three types of peple: those who make things happen, those who watch things happen, and those who say, "What happened?"

NUMBER CATEGORY/CREDIT	TOPIC
4230 SOCIETY	Characteristics of a good citizen
4231 JASON FRIED/USA/BIZ	The fastest way to burn money: Lawyers
4232 THOMAS JEFFERSON/ USA	Do you want to know who you are? Don't ask. Act! Action will delineate and define you.
4233 SALVADOR DALI/ARTIST/ SPAIN	There is only one difference between a madman and myself. The madman thinks he is sane. I know I am mad.
4234 DOROTHY PARKER/USA/ POET	Women and elephants never forget.
4235 PROVERB/T. HYDE	You can't make bricks without straw.
4236 HENRIK IBSEN/NORWAY	The strongest men are the most alone.
4237 NOLAN BUSHNELL/USA	The true entrepreneur is a doer, not a dreamer.
4238 BARBARA JORDAN/USA	I never intended to become a run-of-the-mill person.
4239 WILLIAM JAMES/USA/ SCHOLAR	The greatest discovery of any generation is that human beings can alter their lives by altering the attitudes of their minds.
4240 ROBERT FULGHUM/USA	Take a nap every afternoon.
4241 RANDY PAUSCH/ PROF/ LAST LECTURE	A good apology is like an antibiotic; a bad apology is like rubbing salt in the wound.
4242 AVIATION	Black box
4243 THICH NHAT HANH/ VIETNAM/BUDDHIST	Many people think excitement is happiness…But when you are excited you are not peaceful. True happiness is based on peace.
4244 DORIS LESSING/UK SOUTH-AFRICA/WRITER	It is the mark of great people to treat trifles as trifles and important matters as important.
4245 SAYING	Always a bridesmaid, never a bride.
4246 RANDY PAUSCH/ USA	When there's an elephant in the room, introduce him.
4247 LAZINESS	Couch potatoes
4248 ROALD DAHL/UK	Those who don't believe in magic will never find it.
4249 USA/H. MARTINEAU	Readers are plentiful: thinkers are rare.
4250 MILTON FRIEDMAN/ USA/ECONOMIST/ NOBEL LAUREATE	The greatest advances of civilization, whether in architecture or painting, in science and literature, in industry or agriculture, have never come from centralized government.
4251 THOMAS PAINE/USA	Character is much easier kept than recovered.
4252 USA/WILMA MANKILLER/FEMALE CHIEF/CHEROKEE	I don't think anybody anywhere can talk about the future of their people or of an organization without talking about education. Whoever controls the education of our children controls our future
4253 BRUCE VAN HORN/USA	One of the most important trips a man can make is that involved in meeting the other fellow halfway.
4254 CHRISTINA ROSETTI/ POET	Can anything be sadder than work left unfinished? Yes, work never begun.
4255 NOVELIST/LOUIS DE BERNIERES/UK	The real index of civilization is when people are kinder than they need to be.
4256 MARRIAGE	Traditional wedding in your country

NUMBER CATEGORY/CREDIT	TOPIC
4257 BERTRAND RUSSELL/ UK/PHILOSOPHER	Fear is the main source of superstition, and one of the main sources of cruelty. To conquer fear is the beginning of wisdom.
4258 NAPOLEON HILL/USA/ AUTHOR	Great achievement is usually born of great sacrifice, and is never the result of selfishness.
4259 GIANNI VERSACE/ ITALIAN DESIGNER	I have a fantastic relationship with money. I use it to buy my freedom.
4260 LOUISE FILI/USA/ DESIGNER/ITALY	A designer is nothing without great collaborators.
4261 SPENCER JOHNSON/ USA/AUTHOR	The fear you let build up in your mind is worse than the situation that actually exists.
4262 ELSA MAXWELL/USA/ WOMEN/COLUMNIST	I make enemies deliberately. They are the sauce piquante to my dish of life.
4263 SIMON WIESENTHAL/ AUSTRIA/ACTIVIST	Humour is the weapon of unarmed people: it helps people who are oppressed to smile at the situation that pains them.
4264 DORIS LESSING/UK/ WRITER/NOBELIST	What is a hero without love for mankind?
4265 ROBERT FULGHUM/ USA/WRITER	Be aware of wonder. Remember the little seed in the Styrofoam cup. The roots go down and the plant goes up and nobody really knows how or why, but we are all like that.
4266 JOE LOUIS/USA/BOXER	You can run but you can't hide.
4267 HISTORY	Favorite period in history
4268 SIMON WIESENTHAL/ AUSTRIA/ACTIVIST	Violence is like a weed - it does not die even in the greatest drought.
4269 ROALD DAHL/UK	A little nonsense now and then is relished by the wisest men.
4270 KAHLIL GIBRAN/POET/ ON WORK	Always you have been told that work is a curse and labor a misfortune. But I say to you that...keeping yourself with labor you're loving life.
4271 SAM HARRIS/USA/ SCIENTIST/WRITER	Consider it: every person you have ever met, every person will suffer the loss of his friends and family. All are going to lose everything they love in this world. Why would one want to be anything but kind to them in the meantime?
4272 THOMAS CARLYLE/ SCOTTISH AUTHOR	What we become depends on what we read after all of the professors have finished with us. The greatest university of all is a collection of books.
4273 DENISE LEVERTOV/ BRITISH-BORN POET/ USA	Very few people really see things unless they've had someone in early life who made them look at things. And name them too. But the looking is primary, the focus.
4274 THAILAND	Elephant foot massage
4275 ERNEST HEMINGWAY/ USA/WRITER	I like to listen. I have learned a great deal from listening carefully. Most people never listen.
4276 ANGELA CARTER/ ENGLISH NOVELIST	A book is simply the container of an idea -- like a bottle; what is inside the book is what matters.
4277 PAT RILEY/COACH/ USA	To have long-term success as a coach or in any position of leadership, you have to be obsessed in some way.
4278 CHRISTINA ROSSETI/ POET	For there is no friend like a sister / In calm or stormy weather; / To cheer one on the tedious way, / To fetch one if one goes astray, / To lift one if one totters down, / To strengthen whilst one stands.

NUMBER CATEGORY/CREDIT	TOPIC
4279 SAM HARRIS/USA/ SCIENTIST/WRITER	We have a choice. We have two options as human beings. We have a choice between conversation and war. That's it. Conversation and violence. And faith is a conversation stopper.
4280 DUSTIN HOFFMAN/US/ ACTOR	Blame is for God and small children.
4281 THOMAS JEFFERSON/ USA/3RD PRESIDENT	My reading of history convinces me that most bad government results from too much government.
4282 MICHAEL JORDAN/ NBA/USA/ BASKETBALL	To be successful you have to be selfish, or else you never achieve. And once you get to your highest level, then you have to be unselfish. Stay reachable. Stay in touch. Don't isolate.
4283 ALBERT SCHWEITZER/ FRENCH/PHYSICIAN	In the hopes of reaching the moon men fail to see the flowers that blossom at their feet.
4284 SAM HARRIS/USA/ SCIENTIST/WRITER	If someone doesn't value evidence, what evidence are you going to provide to prove that they should value it? If someone doesn't value logic, what logical argument could you provide to show the importance of logic?
4285 ITALIAN/DONATELLA VERSACE/DESIGNER	Fashion is all about happiness. It's fun. It's important. But it's not medicine.
4286 UNKNOWN	Every job is a self-portrait of the person who did it. Autograph your work with excellence.
4287 DOROTHY PARKER/ USA/WRITER	Four be the things I'd have been better without: Love, curiosity, freckles and doubt.
4288 ANNA PAVLOVA/RUSSIA	Master technique and then forget about it and be natural.
4289 LAO TZU/CHINESE PHILOSOPHER	A leader is best when people barely know he exists, when his work is done, his aim fulfilled, they will say: we did it ourselves.
4290 AUTHOR/YOSHIMOTO BANANA/JAPAN	Sometimes people put up walls, not to keep others out, but to see who cares enough to break them down.
4291 ARISTOTLE/ PHILOSOPHER	Even when laws have been written down, they ought not always to remain unaltered.
4292 MARY CATHERINE BATESON/USA	Of any stopping place in life, it is good to ask whether it will be a good place from which to go on as well as a good place to remain.
4293 ANN LANDERS/ USA/ADVICE COLUMNIST	Expect trouble as an inevitable part of life, and when it comes, hold your head high. Look it squarely in the eye, and say, 'I will be bigger than you. You cannot defeat me.'
4294 GIANNI VERSACE/ ITALIAN DESIGNER	In the past, people were born royal. Nowadays, royalty comes from what you do.
4295 KOREAN PROVERB	Cast no dirt into the well that gives you water.
4296 BUSINESS/LIFE	Timing is everything
4297 NOVELIST/LOUIS DE BERNIERES	Women only nag when they feel unappreciated.
4298 DORIS LESSING/ SOUTH-AFRICA/ ENGLAND/WRITER	With a library you are free, not confined by temporary political climates. It is the most democratic of institutions because no one -- but no one at all -- can tell you what to read and when and how.

NUMBER CATEGORY/CREDIT	TOPIC
4299 THOMAS EDISON/USA	To have a great idea, have a lot of them.
4300 WILLIAM CONGREVE/ UK/POET	Music has charms to soothe the savage breast, to soften rocks, or bend a knotted oak.
4301 ANDY GROVE/CEO/ INTEL	Leaders have to act more quickly today. The pressure comes much faster.
4302 AMBROSE BIERCE/USA/ AUTHOR	Acquaintance: A person whom we know well enough to borrow from, but not well enough to lend to.
4303 KARL MARX/GERMANY/ PHILOSOPHER	Religion is the opium of the masses.
4304 SENECA/DRAMATIST	All art is an imitation of nature.
4305 UK/CHRISTABEL PANKHURST/ACTIVIST/	Never lose your temper with the Press or the Public is a major rule of political life.
4306 DOROTHY PARKER/ USA/WRITER	Take care of luxuries and the necessities will take care of themselves.
4307 USA/ANNE MORROW LINDBERGH/WRITER	One cannot collect all the beautiful shells on the beach.
4308 ANNA PAVLOVA/ RUSSIAN/BALLET	No one can arrive from being talented alone; work transforms talent into genius.
4309 JAPAN/YOSHIMOTO BANANA/JAPAN	People aren't overcome by situations or outside forces. Defeat comes from within.
4310 JANE AUSTEN/UK/ WRITER	The person, be it gentleman or lady, who has not pleasure in a good novel, must be intolerably stupid.
4311 B.C. FORBES/USA/ PUBLISHER	The man who is smugly content that he has arrived is ripe for the return trip.
4312 HENRIK IBSEN/ NORWAY/WRITER	Money may be the husk of many things but not the kernel. It brings you food, but not appetite; medicine, but not health; acquaintance, but not friends; servants, but not loyalty; days of joy, but not peace or happiness.
4313 LIZ CLARKE/USA/ WAPO/TENNIS	...being perceived as a loner, cold or even unfriendly is hardly a character flaw for an athlete trying to become No. 1 in the world.
4314 AUTHOR/PATRICK LENCIONI/	Trust is knowing that when a team member does push you, they're doing it because they care about the team.
4315 WILLIAM MAXWELL/ USA/EDITOR	A gentleman doesn't have one set of manners for the house of a poor man and another for the house of someone with an income incomparable to his own.
4316 WILSON MIZNER/ USA/SCREENWRITER	If you steal from one author, it's plagiarism; if you steal from many, it's research.
4317 ZIG ZIGLAR/USA/ MOTIVATION/SPEAKER	Never make a promise without a plan.
4318 GERMANY/ARTHUR SCHOPENHAUER	I've never known any trouble than an hour's reading didn't assuage.
4319 OCTAVIA BUTLER/USA/ WRITER	All that you touch, you change. All that touches you change, changes you.
4320 JOSEPH CAMPBELL/ AMERICAN AUTHOR	Your life is the fruit of your own doing. You have no one to blame but yourself.

NUMBER CATEGORY/CREDIT	TOPIC
4321 BILL COSBY/ USA/ COMEDIAN	Human beings are the only creatures on earth that allow their children to come back home.
4322 DOROTHY PARKER/ USA/WRITER	Money cannot buy health, but I'd settle for a diamond-studded wheelchair.
4323 YOSHIMOTO BANANA/JAPAN/ AUTHOR	This world of ours is piled high with farewells and goodbyes of so many different kinds, like the evening sky renewing itself again and again.
4324 USA/ANNE MORROW LINDBERGH/WRITER	Good communication is as stimulating as black coffee, and just as hard to sleep after.
4325 ITALY/DONATELLA VERSACE/DESIGNER	Creativity comes from a conflict of ideas.
4326 JIM LEHRER/USA/ BROADCASTER	There's only one interview technique that matters…Do your homework so you can listen to the answers and react to them and ask followups. Do your homework, prepare.
4327 LOUIS L'AMOUR/ AMERICAN WRITER	It is often said that one has but one life to live, but that is nonsense. For one who reads, there is no limit to the number of lives that may be lived…
4328 MALCOLM X/USA/ ACTIVIST	I don't even call it violence when it's in self-defense; I call it intelligence.
4329 BANKING	Switzerland
4330 ELSA MAXWELL/USA	Most rich people are the poorest people I know.
4331 NAPOLEON HILL/ AMERICAN AUTHOR	All the breaks you need in life wait within your imagination. Imagination is the workshop of your mind, capable of turning mind energy into accomplishment and wealth.
4332 SPORTS	Gymnastics
4333 MALCOLM X/USA	The future belongs to those who prepare for it today.
4334 WILLIAM CONGREVE/ UK/POET	Heaven has no rage like love to hatred turned, nor hell a fury like a woman scorned.
4335 PAUL RAND/USA/ART	Don't try to be original; just try to be good.
4336 USA/DR. MARTIN LUTHER KING JR.	Injustice anywhere is a threat to justice everywhere.
4337 ADAM SMITH/SCOT	Individual ambition serves the common good.
4338 PEGGY NOONAN/ SPEECHWRITER/USA	TV gives everyone an image, but radio gives birth to a million images in a million brains.
4339 CANADA	Multiculturalism
4340 JIM ROHN/USA/ BUSINESSMAN/SPEAKER	Don't wish it was easier, wish you were better. Don't wish for less problems, wish for more skills. Don't wish for less challenge, wish for more wisdom.
4341 AFRICA	African Union
4342 HENRY BROOKS ADAMS/ USA/WRITER	What one knows is, in youth, of little moment; they know enough who know how to learn.
4343 FRIEDRICH NIETZSCHE/ GERMAN/PHILOSOPHER	The doer alone learneth.
4344 WOMEN/EMMELINE PANKHURST/RIGHTS	Justice and judgment lie often a world apart.

NUMBER CATEGORY/CREDIT	TOPIC
4345 WILLIAM CONGREVE/ UK/POET	He who closes his ears to the views of others shows little confidence in the integrity of his own voice.
4346 MARGE PIERCY/USA/ POET/SOCIAL ACTIVIST	In an elitist world, it's always "women and children last."
4347 WILLIAM MAXWELL/ USA/EDITOR	My father represented authority, which meant -- to me -- that he could not also represent understanding.
4348 MARY ASTELL/UK	An opinion's age is no guide to its truth.
4349 FRENCH/MICHEL DE MONTAIGNE/AUTHOR	We must reserve a little back-shop, all our own, entirely free, wherein to establish our true liberty and principal retreat and solitude.
4350 STEDMAN GRAHAM/ DIVERSITY/LEADERS NOT LABELS / SUCCESS MAGAZINE	To succeed in the 21st century, you must: 1. Invest in yourself 2. See beyond the labels 3. See yourself as a citizen of the world
4351 MARIA GOEPPERT MAYER/NOBEL/USA/ PHYSICIST	Mathematics began to seem too much like puzzle solving. Physics is puzzle solving, too, but of puzzles created by nature, not by the mind of man.
4352 STEVE JOBS/ CO-FOUNDER/ APPLE COMPUTERS	Your work is going to fill a large part of your life, and the only way to be truly satisfied is to do what you believe is great work. And the only way to do great work is to love what you do.
4353 ROALD DAHL/ BRITISH NOVELIST	A person who has good thoughts cannot ever be ugly. You can have a wonky nose and a crooked mouth and a double chin and stick-out teeth, but if you have good thoughts they will shine out of your face like sunbeams and you will always look lovely.
4354 MARILYN MONROE/ ACTRESS/USA	I learned...that the best way to keep out of trouble was by never complaining or asking for anything.
4355 CHARLES DARWIN/UK/ NATURALIST	Darwin's theory of evolution
4356 LARRY KRAMER/USA/ PLAYWRIGHT	When you get money, you immediately meet people with a lot more money.
4357 LOUIS NIZER/USA/ LAWYER	True religion is the life we lead, not the creed we profess.
4358 DEBATE	Virtual meetings are no less effective than face-to-face meetings.
4359 DEBATE	Everyone should have a chance to earn a university degree.
4360 DOROTHY PARKER/USA/ POET	Scratch a lover and find a foe.
4361 JAPAN/YOSHIMOTO BANANA/AUTHOR	Truly great people emit a light that warms the hearts of those around them. When that light has been put out, a heavy shadow of despair descends.
4362 ELSA MAXWELL/USA/ WOMEN	Under pressure, people admit to murder, setting fire to the village church or robbing a bank, but never to being bores.
4363 JAPAN/YOSHIMOTO BANANA/JAPAN	People who are going to get along really well know it almost as soon as they meet.
4364 NEIL DEGRASSE TYSON/ USA/ASTROPHYSICIST	Scientific inquiry shouldn't stop just because a reasonable explanation has apparently been found.
4365 STEDMAN GRAHAM/ USA/AUTHOR/	People who consider themselves victims of their circumstances will always remain victims unless they develop a greater vision for their lives.

NUMBER CATEGORY/CREDIT	TOPIC
4366 HENRIK IBSEN/ NORWAY/WRITER	You should never wear your best trousers when you go out to fight for freedom and truth.
4367 MALCOLM X/USA/ ACTIVIST	In fact, once he is motivated no one can change more completely than the man who has been at the bottom. I call myself an example of that.
4368 JUSTICE/GLOBAL	Crimes against humanity
4369 RANDY PAUSCH/USA/ USA/COMPUTER SCIENTIST/THE LAST LECTURE	Too many people go through life complaining about their problems. I've always believed that if you took one-tenth the energy you put into complaining and applied it to solving the problem, you'd be surprised by how well things can work out.
4370 FRENCH/ALBERT SCHWEITZER/ THEOLOGIAN	The thinking (person) must oppose all cruel customs, no matter how deeply rooted in tradition and surrounded by a halo. When we have a choice, we must avoid bringing torment and injury into the life of another.
4371 THOMAS JEFFERSON/ USA/3RD PRESIDENT	The glow of one warm thought is to me worth more than money.
4372 MARGE PIERCY/USA/ POET/ SOCIAL ACTIVIST	If you want to be listened to, you should put in time listening.
4373 ADVENTURE/SAFETY	Hitchhiking
4374 SOCIETY/VALUE	National treasures
4375 MARTIN BUBER/ PHILOSOPHER	All real living is meeting.
4376 DUSTIN HOFFMAN/ USA/ACTOR	I envy people who can just look at a sunset. I wonder how you can shoot it. There is nothing more grotesque to me than a vacation.
4377 LOUIS L'AMOUR/USA/ WRITER	If you want the law to leave you alone, keep your hair trimmed and your boots shined.
4378 MAO TSETUNG/CHINA	The differences between friends cannot but reinforce their friendship.
4379 DR PHIL McGRAW/ USA/PSYCHOLOGIST	When you allow a person's words to upset you, you are giving away your power.
4380 MARGE PIERCY/USA	My idea of Hell is to be young again.
4381 MARILYN MONROE/USA	I think that when you are famous every weakness is exaggerated.
4382 JAPAN/YOSHIMOTO BANANA/AUTHOR	No one can survive childhood without being wounded.
4383 ROBERT FULGHUM/ USA/WRITER	Goldfish and hamster and white mice and even the little seed in the Styrofoam cup – they all die. So do we.
4384 WILLIAM STYRON/ USA/NOVELIST	A great book should leave you with many experiences, and slightly exhausted at the end. You live several lives while reading.
4385 WILLIAM MAXWELL/ USA/EDITOR	The nail doesn't choose the time or the circumstance in which it is drawn to the magnet.
4386 JOSEPH E. STIGLITZ/ USA/ECONOMIST/NY TIMES	Despite rhetoric about the land of opportunity, a young American's life prospects are more dependent on the income and education of his parents than in almost any other advanced country.
4387 DORIS LESSING/ SOUTH-AFRICA	It is terrible to destroy a person's picture of himself in the interests of truth or some other abstraction.
4388 PAUL RAND/USA/ ART DIRECTOR/DESIGN	Everything is design. Everything!

NUMBER CATEGORY/CREDIT	TOPIC
4389 DOROTHY PARKER/USA	The only ism Hollywood believes in is plagiarism.
4390 MARTIN BUBER/ AUSTRIAN-BORN ISRAELI PHILOSOPHER	If I had been asked in my early youth whether I preferred to have dealings only with men or only with books, my answer would certainly have been in favor of books. In later years this has become less and less the case..the many bad experiences with men have nourished the meadow of my life as the noblest book could not do, and the good experiences have made the earth into a garden for me.
4391 ALBERT SCHWEITZER/ FRENCH/GERMAN	A man does not have to be an angel to be a saint.
4392 NAPOLEON HILL/ USA/AUTHOR	Before success comes in any man's life, he's sure to meet with much temporary defeat and, perhaps some failures. When defeat overtakes a man, the easiest and the most logical thing to do is to quit. That's exactly what the majority of men do.
4393 WILLIAM CONGREVE/ UK/POET	Fear comes from uncertainty. When we are absolutely certain, whether of our worth or worthlessness, we are almost impervious to fear.
4394 A.A. MILNE/UK/AUTHOR	If the person you are talking to doesn't appear to be listening, be patient. It may simply be that he has a small piece of fluff in his ear.
4395 JIM LEHRER/USA/ BROADCASTER	I wanted to be a bus driver when I was a kid. I look at bus driving through the eyes of a little boy. I see it as glamorous.
4396 WILLIAM CONGREVE/UK	Never go to bed angry. Stay up and fight.
4397 NANCY DITOMASO/USA/ SOCIAL NETWORKS	Getting an inside edge by using help from family and friends is a powerful, hidden force driving inequality in the United States.
4398 RABINDRANATH TAGORE/INDIAN POET	A mind all logic is like a knife all blade. It makes the hand bleed that uses it.
4399 ARABIC PROVERB	Call someone your lord and he'll sell you in the slave market.
4400 JOHN ADAMS/USA	Genius is sorrow's child.
4401 SYLVIA PLATH/POET/ WRITER	There must be quite a few things a hot bath won't cure, but I don't know many of them.
4402 WRITER/ANNE MORROW LINDBERGH/USA	By and large, mothers and housewives are the only workers who do not have regular time off. They are the great vacationless class.
4403 WILLIAM STYRON/ USA/NOVELIST	The good writing of any age has always been the product of someone's neurosis, and we'd have a mighty dull literature if all the writers that came along were a bunch of happy chuckleheads.
4404 USA/ANNE MORROW LINDBERGH	I feel we are all islands -- in a common sea.
4405 THOMAS JEFFERSON/US	Honesty is the first chapter in the book of wisdom.
4406 CLARE BOOTH LUCE/US	Male supremacy has kept woman down. It has not knocked her out.
4407 NEIL DEGRASSE TYSON/ USA/ASTROPHYSICIST	The atoms of our bodies are traceable to stars that manufactured them in their cores and exploded these enriched ingredients across our galaxy, billions of years ago. For this reason, we are biologically connected to every other living thing in the world...We are not figuratively, but literally, sttardust.
4408 KYUNG-SOOK SHIN/ S. KOREAN/WRITER	People say that when a baby is crying the paternal grandmother will say, "The baby is crying, you should feed her," and the maternal grandmother will say, "Why is that baby crying so much, making her mother so tired?"

NUMBER CATEGORY/CREDIT	TOPIC
4409 PEARL S. BUCK/USA/WRITER	I feel no need for any other faith than my faith in human beings.
4410 CLAUDE MONET/ARTIST/FRENCH	It's on the strength of observation and reflection that one finds a way. So we must dig and delve unceasingly.
4411 NAPOLEON HILL/USA/AUTHOR	Any idea, plan, or purpose may be placed in the mind through repetition of thought.
4412 FRENCH/NAPOLEON BONAPARTE/LEADER	Men are more easily governed through their vices than through their virtues.
4413 A. A. MILNE/UK/WRITER	People say nothing is impossible, but I do nothing every day.
4414 LOUIS L'AMOUR/USA/WRITER	Anger is a killing thing; it kills the man who angers, for each rage leaves him less than he had been before – it takes something from him.
4415 MAHATMA GANDHI/INDIAN LEADER	Intolerance is itself a form of violence and an obstacle to the growth of a true democratic spirit.
4416 LAO TZU/PHILOSOPHER	Doing nothing is better than being busy doing nothing.
4417 SILAS HOUSE/USA/WRITER/PROFESSOR	People will drive miles and miles to go jump in a cool swimming hole, but when it rains, they scatter.
4418 DOROTHY PARKER/USA/WRITER	Misfortune, and recited misfortune especially, may be prolonged to that point where it ceases to excite pity and arouses only irritation.
4419 BEATRIX POTTER/WRITER/BRITISH	I hold an old-fashioned notion that a happy marriage is the crown of a woman's life.
4420 CLARE BOOTH LUCE/CONGRESSWOMAN/USA/WRITER	Because I am a woman, I must make unusual efforts to succeed. If I fail, no one will say, "She doesn't have what it takes." They will say, "Women don't have what it takes."
4421 SILAS HOUSE/USA	Sometimes just being still is the best thing you can do for yourself.
4422 FRENCH/NAPOLEON BONAPARTE/LEADER	If we could read the past histories of all our enemies we would disregard all hostility for them.
4423 ELIZABETH ARDEN/USA/CANADA	I only want people around me who can do the impossible.
4424 DR PHIL McGRAW/USA	Take the high road; there's a lot less traffic up there.
4425 JAMES DYSON/UK/INVENTOR/WISDOM	Stumbling upon the next great invention in an "ah ha!" moment is a myth. It is only by learning from mistakes that progress is made.
4426 LOUIS L'AMOUR/USA/WRITER	Too often I would hear men boast of the miles covered that day, rarely of what they had seen.
4427 SALVADOR DALI/ARTIST/SPAIN	The reason some portraits don't look true to life is that some people make no effort to resemble their pictures.
4428 RICHARD BRANSON/BRITISH BILLIONAIRE	I have always lived my life by making lists: list of people to call, lists of ideas, lists of companies to set up, lists of people who can make things happen.
4429 USA/DR. CHESTER KARRASS/NEGOTIATION	In business you don't get what you deserve; you get what you negotiate.
4430 FRANCIS BACON/ENGLISH THINKER	A bachelor's life is a fine breakfast, a flat lunch, and a miserable dinner.
4431 ROBERT FULGHUM/USA/WRITER	When you go out into the world, watch out for traffic, hold hands, and stick together.

NUMBER CATEGORY/CREDIT	TOPIC
4432 FRANK STRONACH/ CANADA/BUSINESS	Helping people, feeding and shelter, that's the easy part. The challenging part is what do we do to get them back on their feet again.
4433 WILLIAM CONGREVE/ UK/POET	Grief walks upon the heels of pleasure; married in haste, we repent at leisure.
4434 T.J. LEYDEN/ ACTIVIST/ WAPO/USA	Treat someone normal like a winner and he'll fight for you, but treat a loser like a winner and he'll kill for you.
4435 HILARY MANTEL/UK WRITER/WOLF HALL	It is the absence of facts that frightens people: the gap you open, into which they pour their fears, fantasies, desires.
4436 LORRIE MOORE/USA/ WRITER	A short story is a love affair, a novel is a marriage.
4437 CHARLOTTE PERKINS GILMAN/WRITER/USA	The women who do the most work get the least money, and the women who have the most money do the least work.
4438 CLARE BOOTH LUCE/USA	No good deed goes unpunished.
4439 SILAS HOUSE/USA/ WRITER/PROFESSOR	I have come to understand that sometimes the best families of all are those we create ourselves, the people we choose to be with.
4440 FERNANDO PESSOA/ PORTUGUESE/WRITER	Literature is the most agreeable way of ignoring life.
4441 DR. PHIL McGRAW/USA/ PSYCHOLOGIST/TV	For every rat you see, there are fifty you don't see.
4442 ITALIAN PROVERB	You can't have the barrel full of wine and your wife drunk.
4443 NATIONAL HONOR	The national anthem
4444 GILLIAN FLYNN/ USA/AUTHOR/GONE GIRL	There is an unfair responsibility that comes with being an only child -- you grow up knowing you aren't allowed to disappoint, you're not even allowed to die.
4445 DAN BROWN/USA/ AUTHOR/FICTION	Men go to far greater lengths to avoid what they fear than to obtain what they desire.
4446 SHERYL SANDBERG/USA	Done is better than perfect.
4447 SALVADOR DALI/ARTIST/ SPAIN	Intelligence without ambition is a bird without wings.
4448 KEVIN PLANK/USA/ BUSINESSMAN	Great brands are like great stories. And every story has a beginning, a middle, and an end.
4449 REED HASTINGS/USA/ FOUNDER/NETFLIX	Companies rarely die from moving too fast, and they frequently die from moving too slowly.
4450 MARILYN MONROE/USA	I don't know who invented high heels, but all women owe him a lot.
4451 ROSIE ALISON/UK/ FILMMAKER/WRITER	A true lover of books knows no time.
4452 PROVERBS 29:18	Where there is no vision, the people perish.
4453 ANTON CHEKHOV/ RUSSIAN WRITER	Let us learn to appreciate that there will be times when the trees will be bare, and look forward to the time when we may pick the fruit.
4454 ARISTOTLE/GREEK PHILOSOPHER	In a democracy the poor will have more power than the rich, because there are more of them, and the will of the majority is supreme.
4455 NANCY LUBLIN/ TEDTALK	The parents in the room know that texting is actually the best way to communicate with your kids. It might be the only way to communicate with your kids.

NUMBER CATEGORY/CREDIT	TOPIC
4456 FRENCH/ALBERT SCHWEITZER/ THEOLOGIAN	Anyone who proposed to do good must not expect people to roll stones out of his way, but must accept his lot calmly if they even roll a few more upon it.
4457 ACTOR/DENZEL WASHINGTON/USA	I've worked in a factory. I was a garbage man. I worked in a post office. It's not that long ago. I like to think that I'm just a regular guy.
4458 ROSA PARKS/USA/ CIVIL RIGHTS ACTIVIST	I have learned over the years that when one's mind is made up, this diminishes fear; knowing what must be done does away with fear.
4459 CLARE BOOTH LUCE/ USA/AUTHOR	Love is a verb.
4460 NEIL DEGRASSE TYSON/ USA/ASTROPHYSICIST	Dinosaurs are extinct today because they lacked opposable thumbs and the brainpower to build a space program.
4461 WILLIAM STYRON/ USA/NOVELIST	The query: "At Auschwitz, tell me, where was God?" And the answer: "Where was man?"
4462 GILLIAN FLYNN/USA	The face you give the world tells the world how to treat you.
4463 DAVID SEDARIS/USA/ WRITER	If you aren't cute, you may as well be clever.
4464 USA/AUTHOR/LAURA HILLENBRAND	Without dignity, identity is erased.
4465 ABRAHAM LINCOLN/ USA/16TH PRESIDENT	Things may come to those who wait. But only the things left by those who hustle.
4466 KEVIN PLANK/USA/ BUSINESS LEADER	The companies that win are the ones that communicate the best.
4467 SALLY HOGSHEAD/ USA/COPYWRITER	Messages that fail to fascinate will become irrelevant. It's that simple.
4468 ANNE FRANK/ JEWISH AUTHOR/ HOLOCAUST	Ever since I was a little girl and could barely talk, the word 'why' has lived and grown along with me. It's a well-known fact that children ask questions about anything and everything, since almost everything is new to them. That is especially true of me, and not just as a child. Even when I was older, I couldn't stop asking questions.
4469 DAVID SEDARIS/USA/ HUMORIST	Real love amounts to withholding the truth, even when you'r eoffered the perfect opportunity to hurt someone's feelings.
4470 DIANE AIRBUS/ PHOTOGRAPHER/ PROFESSOR/ USA	Regardless of how you feel inside, always try to look like a winner. Even if you are behind, a sustained look of control and confidence can give you a mental edge that results in victory.
4471 LORRIE MOORE/USA/ FICTION WRITER	If one publishes, then one is creating a public record of Learning to Write.
4472 ROALD DAHL/ BRITISH NOVELIST	A person is a fool to become a writer. His only compensation is absolute freedom. He has no master except his own soul, and that, I am sure, is why he does it.
4473 USA/BARBARA KINGSOLVER/ESSAYIST	If you want sweet dreams, you've got to live a sweet life.
4474 HARRY EMERSON FOSDICK/PASTOR	Hating people is like burning down your own house to get rid of a rat.
4475 RANDY PAUSCH/USA/ PROFESSOR	When we're connected to others, we become better people.

NUMBER CATEGORY/CREDIT	TOPIC
4476 FERNANDO PESSOA/ PORTUGUESE POET	No intelligent idea can gain general acceptance unless some stupidity is mixed in with it.
4477 GILLIAN FLYNN/ USA/AUTHOR	I just think some women aren't made to be mothers. And some women aren't made to be daughters.
4478 DAN BROWN/USA	Google is not a synonym for research.
4479 DR PHIL McGRAW/USA	Pain is the price you pay for resisting life.
4480 SHERYL SANDBERG/ USA/FACEBOOK	In the future, there will be no female leaders. There will just be leaders.
4481 ABRAHAM LINCOLN/ USA/16TH PRESIDENT	Always bear in mind that your own resolution to succeed, is more important than any other one thing.
4482 BENJAMIN DISRAELI/UK	I must follow the people. Am I not their leader?
4483 SALLY HOGSHEAD/USA/ SOCIAL MEDIA	The world is not changed by people who sort of care.
4484 HILARY MANTEL/UK	...there is an art to being in a hurry but not showing it.
4485 USA/MARILYNNE ROBINSON/WRITER	Memory can make a thing seem to have been much more than it was.
4486 ENDURANCE/IDIOM	Down but not out
4487 KURT COBAIN/USA	I'd rather be hated for who I am, than loved for who I am not.
4488 USA/FRIDAY NIGHT LIGHTS/TV/PETER BERG	Clear eyes; full hearts; can't lose.
4489 JIM LEHRER/USA/ BROADCASTER	If you go to the ball game, you don't need to read the game story.
4490 MARIA MONTESSORI/ EDUCATION/ITALY	The greatest sign of success for a teacher is to be able to say, "the children are now working as if I did not exist."
4491 CHARLOTTE PERKINS GILMAN/WRITER/USA	To be surrounded by beautiful things has much influence upon the human creature; to make beautifl things has more.
4492 WILLIAM STYRON/ USA/NOVELIST	Writing for me is the hardest thing in the world, but also a thing which, once completed, is the most satisfying.
4493 GILLIAN FLYNN/USA/ SCREENWRITER	Sleep is like a cat: It only comes to you if you ignore it.
4494 SHERYL SANDBERG/ USA/BUSINESS LEADER	If you're offered a seat on a rocket ship, don't ask what seat! Just get on.
4495 CARL JUNG/SWISS/ PSYCHOLOGIST	There can be no transforming of darkness into light and of apathy into movement without emotion.
4496 MARIA MONTESSORI/ EDUCATION/ITALY	...the task of the educator lies in seeing that the child does not confound good with immobility and evil with activity.
4497 USA/MARILYNNE ROBINSON/WRITER	Loneliness is an absolute discovery.
4498 REAR ADMIRAL GRACE M. HOPPER/USA	You manage things; you lead people.
4499 LAW	Stupid laws
4500 ANNA PAVLOVA/BALLET	To follow without halt, one aim; there is the secret of success.
4501 THICH NHAT HANH	Our own life has to be our message.
4502 DOROTHY PARKER/USA	Men seldom make passes at girls who wear glasses.

NUMBER CATEGORY/CREDIT	TOPIC
4503 ALFRED NORTH WHITEHEAD/UK/ MATHEMATICIAN	Religion carries two sorts of people in two entirely opposite directions: the mild and gentle people it carries toward mercy and justice; the persecuting people it carries into fiendish sadistic cruelty.
4504 DAN BROWN/USA/ AUTHOR/THRILLER	To live in the world without becoming aware of the meaning of the world is like wandering about in a great library without touching the books.
4505 YVON CHOUINARD/ USA/MANUFACTURER	I purposely try to hire people who are really self-motivated and good at what they do, and then I just leave them alone.
4506 ANDY GROVE/USA/CEO	The most powerful tool of all is the word no.
4507 HENRIK IBSEN/NORWAY	Cage an eagle and it will bite at the wires, be they iron or gold.
4508 ELIE WIESEL/USA/ NOVELIST	Indifference is the sign of sickness, a sickness of the soul more contagious than any other.
4509 ROBERT FULGHUM/ USA/WRITER	Remember the Dick-and-Jane books and the first words you learned – the biggest word of all – LOOK.
4510 JACKSON POLLOCK/USA	Every good artist paints what he is.
4511 LAW	Frivolous lawsuits
4512 THE ELDERLY	Gray power
4513 ATOMIC BOMB/USA	Bombing of Hiroshima and Nagasaki (Japan)
4514 PUBLILIUS SYRiUS	T'is foolish to fear what you cannot avoid.
4515 AUTHOR/DR. ELLEN KREIDMAN/USA	If two people agree on everything, then one of them is really not necessary in the relationship.
4516 HONORE DE BALZAC/FR.	Behind every great fortune lies a great crime.
4517 FAIRNESS/SOCIETY	Level-playing field
4518 MAXWELL MALTZ/ SURGEON/USA	Your nervous system cannot tell the difference between an imagined experience and a 'real' experience.
4519 MARIANNE WIGGINS/US	...what you can't see is always what you should be frightened of.
4520 LAW	Malpractice suits
4521 INDIRA GANDHI/INDIA	You cannot shake hands with a clenched fist.
4522 MAX DE PREE/USA/ WRITER/BUSINESS	The first responsibility of a leader is to define reality. The last is to say thank you. In between, the leader is a servant.
4523 CLARE BOOTH LUCE/ USA/WRITER	A man's home may seem to be his castle on the outside; inside, it is more often his nursery.
4524 AUTHOR/PATRICK LENCIONI/THE FIVE DYSFUNCTIONS...	Great teams do not hold back with one another. They are unafraid to air their laundry. They admit their mistakes, their weaknesses, and their concerns without fear of reprisal.
4525 GILLIAN FLYNN/ USA/AUTHOR	People want to believe they know other people. Parents want to believe they know their kids. Wives want to believe they know thier husbands.
4526 SHERYL SANDBERG/ USA/LEADER/BIZ	The reason I don't have a plan is because if I have a plan I'm limited to today's options.
4527 GILLIAN FLYNN/USA/ AUTHOR/TV CRITIC	Friends see most of each other's flaws. Spouses see every awful last bit.
4528 OG MANDINO/USA/ AUTHOR	Tomorrow is only found in the calendar of fools.
4529 A.A. MILNE/WRITER/UK	To the uneducated, an A is just three sticks.

NUMBER CATEGORY/CREDIT	TOPIC
4530 USA/HEALTH	Centers for Disease Control
4531 SHERYL SANDBERG/USA	Careers are a jungle gym, not a ladder.
4532 DR. PHIL McGRAW/ US/PSYCHOLOGIST	My dad used to tell me, "Boy, don't ever miss a good chance to shut up."
4533 ANGELA CARTER/UK	A day without an argument is like an egg without salt.
4534 MAGIC/FRAUD/ MERRIAMWEBSTER	Levitation: the rising or lifting of a person or thing by means held to be supernatural
4535 HONG KONG/SLOGAN	Hong Kong: Live It. Love It.
4536 ARABIC PROVERB	Do not buy either the moon or the news, for in the end they will both come out.
4537 DR. MARTIN LUTHER KING JR./USA	All progress is precarious, and the solution of one problem brings us face to face with another problem.
4538 COLONEL SANDERS/ KFC/USA	There's no reason to be the richest man in the cemetery. You can't do any business from there.
4539 MATERIALISM	Conspicuous consumption
4540 PERSONAL SUCCESS	Making your mark
4541 RACISM/REVERSE	Reverse racism
4542 THE OCEAN	Freak waves
4543 A.A. MILNE/ENGLISH AUTHOR	When you see someone putting on his Big Boots, you can be pretty sure that an Adventure is going to happen.
4544 DR PHIL McGRAW/USA	I would rather be healthy alone than sick with someone else.
4545 FERNANDO PESSOA/ PORTUGAL/WRITER	I bear the wounds of all the battles I avoided.
4546 DAN BROWN/USA/	Religion is flawed but only because man is flawed.
4547 DAVID SEDARIS/USA/ HUMORIST	"College is the best thing that can ever happen to you," my father used to say, and he was right, for it was there that I discovered drugs, drinking, and smoking.
4548 SHERYL SANDBERG/ USA/FACEBOOK	I have never met a woman, or man, who stated emphatically, "Yes, I have it all."
4549 YVON CHOUINARD/ USA/ROCK CLIMBER	For me, adventure is when everything goes wrong -- that's when the adventure starts.
4550 PHIL KNIGHT/ FOUNDER/NIKE/USA	A brand is something that has a clear-cut identity among consumers, which a company creates by sending out a clear, consistent message over a period of years until it achieves a critical mass of marketing.
4551 USA/MARILYNNE ROBINSON/WRITER	Love is holy because it is like grace -- the worthiness of its object is never really what matters.
4552 WARREN BENNIS/USA	Leadership is the capacity to translate vision into reality.
4553 REACTIONS/PEOPLE	Mixed feelings
4554 MOTHERHOOD	Prenatal screening
4555 ISAAC ASIMOV/USA/ WRITER	The saddest aspect of life right now is that science gathers knowledge faster than society gathers wisdom.
4556 HONORE DE BALZAC/ FRENCH NOVELIST	A husband who submits to his wife's yoke is justly held an object of ridicule. A woman's influence ought to be entirely concealed.

NUMBER CATEGORY/CREDIT	TOPIC
4557 HENRY FORD/USA	The only real mistake is the one from which we learn nothing.
4558 ANTON CHEKHOV/ RUSSIAN WRITER	Love, friendship and respect do not unite people as much as a common hatred for something.
4559 NAPOLEON HILL/ AMERICAN AUTHOR	Every adversity, every failure, every heartache carries with it the seed of an equal or greater benefit.
4560 BILL MOGGRIDGE/ BRITISH DESIGNER/ LAPTOP INVENTOR	Few people think about it or are aware of it. But there is nothing made by human beings that does not involve a design decision somewhere.
4561 USA/MARILYNNE ROBINSON/WRITER	Having a sister or a friend is like sitting at night in a lighted house.
4562 LIONEL BARRYMORE/ ACTOR/USA/THIS I BELIEVE	The thing to be careful in choosing a model is: don't aim too high for your capacity...Shoot a little closer to home..If you keep aiming at an attainable target, you can always raise your sights on another and more difficult one. But if you start off for the impossible, you're foredoomed to eternal failure.
4563 DAVID SEDARIS/USA	...there's a reason regular people don't appear on TV: we're boring.
4564 CLARE BOOTH LUCE/ SOCIALITE/USA	Lying increases the creative faculties, expands the ego, and lessens the frictions of social contacts.
4565 FERNANDO PESSOA/ PORTUGUESE POET	We worship perfection because we can't have it; if we had it, we would reject it.
4566 DAN BROWN/AUTHOR	Everyone loves a conspiracy.
4567 SHERYL SANDBERG/ USA/BUSINESS LEADER	Give us a world where half our homes are run by men, and half our institutions are run by women. I'm pretty sure that would be a better world.
4568 DR PHIL McGRAW/USA	The most you get is what you ask for.
4569 YVON CHOUINARD/ USA/ROCK CLIMBER/ MANUFACTURER	Evil doesn't have to be an overt act; it can be merely the absence of good. If you have the ability, the resources, and the opportunity to do good and you do nothing, that can be evil.
4570 PHIL KNIGHT/NIKE/USA	Play by the rules but be ferocious.
4571 T.J. LEYDEN/ ACTIVIST/WAPO	When you ask a kid to abandon his violence and his gang, you're asking him to give up his identity, his sense of self.
4572 WANGARI MAATHAI/ KENYA/NOBEL PRIZE WINNER	The privilege of higher education, especially outside Africa, broadened my original horizon and encouraged me to focus on the environment, women and development in order to improve the quality of life of people in my country in particular and in the African region in general.
4573 POWER/WEALTH	Old money
4574 USA/ABRAHAM LINCOLN/PRESIDENT	When you've got an elephant by the hind leg, and he is trying to run way, it's best to let him go.
4575 DAN BROWN/USA/ AUTHOR/THRILLER FICTION	History is always written by the winners. When two cultures clash, the loser is obliterated, and the winner writes the history books - books which glorify their own cause and disparage the conquered foe.
4576 MILTON FRIEDMAN/ USA/ECONOMIST	The power to do good is also the power to do harm.
4577 ANDY GROVE/USA/CEO	Your career is your business, and you are its CEO.
4578 KHALED HOSSEINI/USA/ PHYSICIAN/AFGHAN	...But better to get hurt by the truth than comforted with a lie.

NUMBER CATEGORY/CREDIT	TOPIC
4579 WALT WHITMAN/USA	I sing myself and celebrate myself.
4580 USA/DR PHIL McGRAW	You're only lonely if you are not there for yourself.
4581 GENERAL GEORGE S. PATTON/USA	Lead me, follow me, or get out of my way.
4582 FERNANDO PESSOA/ PORTUGUESE POET	If after I die, people want to write my biography, there is nothing simpler. they only need two dates: the date of my birth and the date of my death. Between one and another, every day is mine.
4583 ROBERT KING MERTON/ USA/ SOCIOLOGIST	Most institutions demand unqualified faith but the institution of science makes skepticism a virtue.
4584 GILLIAN FLYNN/USA	Daydreams can be dangerous.
4585 DAN BROWN/USA	God answers all prayers but sometimes his answer is 'no. '
4586 DAVID SEDARIS/USA/ HUMORIST	In other parts of the country people tried to stay together for the sake of the children. In New York they tried to work things out for the sake of the apartment.
4587 SHERYL SANDBERG/ USA/BUSINESS	The promise of equality is not the same as true equality.
4588 ANDY GROVE/USA/ INTEL/CEO	Success breeds complacency. Complacency breeds failure. Only the paranoid survive.
4589 USA/MARILYNNE ROBINSON/WRITER	There are a thousand thousand reasons to live this life, everyone of them sufficient.
4590 FRENCH/ALBERT SCHWEITZER/THINKER	Soldiers' graves are the greatest preachers of peace.
4591 USA/ANTI- DRUG/USA	Friends don't let friends do drugs.
4592 WEALTH	Nouveau riche
4593 PUBLILIUS SYRUS	Hares can gambol over the body of a dead lion.
4594 ROBERT FROST/USA/ POET	The best way out is always through.
4595 CHARLOTTE BRONTE/UK	I would always rather be happy than dignified.
4596 L.M. MONTGOMERY/ CANADA/WRITER	Tomorrow is always fresh, with no mistakes in it.
4597 KHALED HOSSEINI/ WRITER/AFGHAN	It may be unfair, but what happens in a few days, sometimes even in a single day, can change the course of a whole lifetime.
4598 AYN RAND/THINKER	Honor is self-esteem made visible in action.
4599 MAURICE SENDAK/USA	There must be more to life than having everything
4600 YVON CHOUINARD/ USA/ROCK CLIMBER/ MANUFACTURER	If you want to understand the entrepreneur, study the juvenile delinquent. The delinquent is saying with his actions, "This sucks, I'm going to do my own thing."
4601 HARVARD BUSINESS SCHOOL/DEFINITION	Leadership is about making others better as a result of your presence and making sure that impact lasts in your absence.
4602 DAVID SEDARIS/USA	If you read someone else's diary, you get what you deserve.
4603 DAN BROWN/USA	Great minds are always feared by lesser minds.
4604 MARIA MONTESSORI/ ITALY	Never help a child with a task at which he feels he can succeed.

NUMBER CATEGORY/CREDIT	TOPIC
4605 SHERYL SANDBERG/ USA/FACEBOOK/ BUSINESS LEADER	Success and likeability are positively correlated for men and negatively for women. When a man is successful, he is liked by both men and women. When a woman is successful, people of both genders like her less.
4606 ANDY GROVE/USA/ INTEL/CEO	People who have no emotional stake in a decision can see what needs to be done sooner.
4607 USA/MARILYNNE ROBINSON/WRITER	It's not a man's working hours that is important, it is how he spends his leisure time.
4608 BEN HOROWITZ/USA/ ENTREPRENEUR	...learning to be a CEO through classroom training would be like learning to be an NFL quarterback through classroom training.
4609 NANCY REAGAN/USA/ FIRST LADY/ANTI-DRUG	Just say No
4610 USA/REV. JESSE LEE PETERSON/LEADER	Everyone who turns over his life to a leader is a fool.
4611 INDIA/GLORY	The Taj Mahal
4612 JOHN RUSKIN/ ENGLISH ART CRITIC	All books are divisible into two classes: the books of the hours, and the books of all time.
4613 RANDY PAUSCH/USA/ THE LAST LECTURE	A lot of people want a shortcut. I find the best shortcut is the long way, which is basically two words: work hard.
4614 USA/BERNARD M. BARUCH/BUSINESS	Most of the successful people I've known are the ones who do more listening than talking.
4615 HONORE DE BALZAC/ FRENCH	A mother who is really a mother is never free.
4616 ENGLISH PROVERB	Every ass loves to hear himself bray.
4617 JAPANESE PROVERB	*Kappa no kawa nagare.* -- Even professionals fail sometimes.
4618 DEBATE	That universities should be judged by their graduates' pay.
4619 ROBERT GATES/USA/ SEC. OF DEFENSE/WAPO	A leader is able to make decisions, but then, delegate and trust others to make things happen.
4620 CASSANDRA CLARE/US/ AUTHOR	One must be careful of books, and what is inside them, for words have the power to change us.
4621 KHALED HOSSEINI/ AFGHAN/USA/WRITER	Beauty is an enormous, unmerited gift given randomly, stupidly.
4622 W.B. YEATS/POET/ IRISH/NOBEL LAUREATE	I have spread my dreams under your feet. Tread softly because you tread on my dreams.
4623 KHALED HOSSEINI	Marriage can wait, education cannot.
4624 DR PHIL McGRAW/USA	We teach people how to treat us.
4625 JACK WELCH/USA/ BUSINESS LEADER	Before you are a leader, success is all about growing yourself. When you become a leader, success is all about growing others.
4626 FERNANDO PESSOA	The inventor of the mirror poiisoned the human heart.
4627 DAN BROWN/USA	Sooner or later we've all got to let go of the past.
4628 DAVID SEDARIS/USA/ HUMORIST	It's safe to assume that by 2085 guns will be sold in vending machines but you won't be able to smoke anywhere in America.
4629 DEBATE	That physical education must be compulsory in schools
4630 GHANA/EXPRESSION	*Konongo kaya:* A clumsy person who will not allow more competent people to handle a task.

NUMBER CATEGORY/CREDIT	TOPIC
4631 MARISHA PESSL/USA/ WRITER	Always live your life with your biography in mind.
4632 JULES H. POINCARE/FR. MATHEMATICIAN	Science is built up with facts, as a house is with stones. But a collection of facts is no more a science than a heap of stones is a house.
4633 RITA MAE BROWN/USA/ WRITER	A life of reaction is a life of slavery, intellectually and spiritually. One must fight for a life of action, not reaction.
4634 NOVELIST/LOUIS DE BERNIERES	Love is a temporary madness. It erupts like an earthquake and then subsides.
4635 DEBATE	That formal prayer in schools must be prohibited.
4636 EZRA POUND/USA/POET	The sum of human wisdom is not contained in any one language…
4637 DEBATE	That the state should provide free nursery education for all children
4638 ELIE WIESEL/USA	No human being is illegal.
4639 BUSINESS	Mergers and acquisitions
4640 ANTON CHEKHOV/ RUSSIAN WRITER	If you are afraid of loneliness, do not marry.
4641 CHINESE SAYING	When you have only two pennies left in the world, buy a loaf of bread with one, and a lily with the other.
4642 ARABIC PROVERB	Eat whatever you like, but dress as others do.
4643 DR PHIL McGRAW/USA	If you need a miracle, be a miracle.
4644 NAPOLEON BONAPARTE	A leader is a dealer in hope.
4645 KHALED HOSSEINI/ AUTHOR/AFGHAN	Like a compass needle that points north, a man's accusing finger always finds a woman. Always.
4646 MARIA BARTIROMO/ USA/BROADCASTER	Don't ever, ever believe anyone who tells you that you can just get by, by doing the easiest thing possible. Because there's always somebody behind you who really wants to do what you're doing.
4647 DR PHIL McGRAW/ USA/PSYCHOLOGIST	Sometimes you just got to forgive yourself what you wish someone else would forgive you.
4648 UNKNOWN	You don't need a title to be a leader.
4649 FERNANDO PESSOA/ PORTUGUESE POET	Travel is the traveler. What we see isn't what we see but what we are.
4650 MARIA MONTESSORI/ EDUCATION/ITALY	Establishing lasting peace is the work of education; all politics can do is keep us out of war.
4651 GILLIAN FLYNN/USA	Love should require both partners to be their very best at all times.
4652 MELINDA GATES/USA/ PHILANTHROPIST	If you are successful, it is because somewhere, sometime, someone gave you a life or an idea that started you in the right direction. Remember also that you are indebted to life until you help someone less fortunate.
4653 DAVID SEDARIS/USA/ HUMORIST	As bad a dresser as I am, anything beats being judged by my character.
4654 SHERYL SANDBERG/ USA/BUSINESS LEADER	When a woman works outside the home and shares breadwinning duties, couples are more likely to stay together.
4655 ANDY GROVE/USA/ INTEL/CEO	Businesses fail either because they leave their customers or because their customers leave them.
4656 USA/MARILYNNE ROBINSON/WRITER	It is possible to know the great truths without knowing the truth of them.

NUMBER CATEGORY/CREDIT	TOPIC
4657 DEBATE	Parents must be held morally and legally responsible for the actions/needs of their children.
4658 SHERYL SANDBERG/ USA/BUSINESS LEADER	The more women help one another, the more we help ourselves. Acting like a coalition truly does produce results.
4659 LEARNING	Language exchange
4660 JAPANESE PROVERB	*Mochi wa mochi ya:* Leave it in the hands of a professional.
4661 USA/JOHN JAMES AUDUBON/SCIENTIST	A true conservationist is a man who knows that the world is not given by his fathers, but borrowed from his children.
4662 DEBATE	Should children be given sex education in schools, or should this be the responsibility of the parents?
4663 PERSONAL	Secret pleasures
4664 ANTON CHEKHOV/ RUSSIAN WRITER	A fiance is neither this nor that; he's left one shore, but not yet reached the other.
4665 UK/ALFRED NORTH WHITEHEAD/MATH	A science that hesitates to forget its founders is lost.
4666 BROCK BASTIAN/ AUSTRALIA/PSYCH.	Pain is a kind of shortcut to mindfulness.
4667 CARL SAGAN/USA/ SCIENTIST	The universe is a pretty big place. If it's just us, it seems like an awful waste of space.
4668 REAL ESTATE	Serviced apartments
4669 ENGLISH PROVERB	Empty vessels make the most noise.
4670 STEVE JOBS/USA	Innovation distinguishes between a leader and a follower.
4671 HEALTH	Eating disorders
4672 ELBERT HUBBARD/USA	Positive anything is better than negative nothing.
4673 THUCYDIDES/ HISTORIAN	It is useless to attack a man who could not be controlled even if conquered, while failure would leave us in an even worse position.
4674 USA/GILLIAN FLYNN	People have to do awful things for money.
4675 JOSEPH HAYDN/MUSIC	There was no one near to confuse me, so I was forced to become original.
4676 RACHEL CARSON/USA/ SCIENTIST/WRITER	The real wealth of the Nation lies in the resources of the earth -- soil, water, forests, minerals, and wildlife. To utilize them for present needs while insuring their preservation for future generations requires a delicately balanced and continuing program, based on the most extensive research.
4677 KHALED HOSSEINI/ AFGHAN/WRITER	Children aren't coloring books. You don't get to fill them with your favorite colors.
4678 DR PHIL McGRAW/ USA/PSYCHOLOGIST	People have the right to think and say whatever they want to. But you have the right not to take it to heart, and not to react.
4679 USA/TONI MORRISON/ NOBEL PRIZE WINNER	"What difference do it make if the thing you scared of is real or not?"
4680 EDMUND BURKE/IRISH	To read without reflecting is like eating without digesting.
4681 JOHN MAXWELL/USA	A leader is one who knows the way, goes the way, and shows the way.
4682 ABRAHAM LINCOLN/ USA/16TH PRESIDENT	You have to do your own growing no matter how tall your grandfather was.
4683 HERB KELLEHER/USA	A company is stronger if it is bound by love rather than by fear.

NUMBER CATEGORY/CREDIT	TOPIC
4684 J. F. KENNEDY/USA/PRESIDENT	I look forward to a great future for America -- a future in which our country will match its military strength with our moral restraint, its wealth with our wisdom, its power with our purpose.
4685 SHERYL SANDBERG/USA/BUSINESS	Aggressive and hard-charging women violate unwritten rules about acceptable social conduct.
4686 LADY MARGARET THATCHER/PM/UK	Being powerful is like being a lady. If you have to tell people you are, you aren't.
4687 ROBERT FULGHUM/USA/WRITER	You may never have proof of your importance but you are more important than you think. There are always those who couldn't do without you. The rub is that you don't always know who.
4688 AA/ADDICTION	Alcoholics Anonymous
4689 ANGELA CARTER/UK/NOVELIST	Comedy is tragedy that happens to other people.
4690 HOWARD WHITE/USA/NIKE/BUSINESS	I speak to everyone I see, no matter where I am. I've learned that speaking to people creates a pathway into their world, and it lets them come into mine, too.
4691 AMY CUDDY/HARVARD/USA/PROFESSOR	Our bodies change our minds, and our minds can change our behavior, and our behavior can change our outcomes.
4692 LIONEL BARRYMORE/ACTOR/ACTOR?/THIS I BELIEVE	I believe the difference between an eminently successful person and one whose life is just mediocre is the difference between a person who had an aim, a focus, a model upon which he superimposed his own life and one who didn't.
4693 DELINQUENCY	Pickpockets
4694 FERNANDO PESSOA	Whether or not they exist we are slaves to our gods.
4695 AUTHOR/PATRICK LENCIONI	Politics is when people choose their words and actions based on how they want others to react rather than based on what they really think.
4696 MARISHA PESSL/USA	Sometimes it takes more courage not to let yourself see.
4697 DAN BROWN/USA/AUTHOR	Religion is like language or dress. We gravitate toward the practices with which we were raised.
4698 KHALED HOSSEINI/WRITER/AFGHAN	…it always hurts more to have and lose than to not have in the first place.
4699 DR PHIL McGRAW/USA/PSYCHOLOGIST	The difference between winners and losers is that winners do things losers don't want to do.
4700 FERNANDO PESSOA	Life is full of paradoxes, as roses are of thorns.
4701 USA/HENRY DAVID THOREAU/WRITER	The greatest compliment that was ever paid me was when one asked me what I thought, and attended to my answer.
4702 DAN BROWN/USA	The decisions of our past are the architects of our present.
4703 SHERYL SANDBERG/USA/BUSINESS LEADER	We need to stop telling women, "Get a mentor and you will excel." Instead, we need to tell them, "Excel and you will get a mentor."
4704 USA/MARILYNNE ROBINSON/WRITER	You never know when you might be seeing someone for the last time.
4705 JOHN UPDIKE/USA/NOVELIST	A leader is one who, out of madness or goodness, volunteers to take upon himself the woes of the people.
4706 RICHARD BRANSON/UK/BILLIONAIRE	I had never been interested in being in business. I've been interested in creating things.

NUMBER CATEGORY/CREDIT	TOPIC
4707 DR PHIL McGRAW/ USA/PSYCHOLOGIST	Sometimes you make the right decision; sometimes you make the decision right.
4708 MARRIAGE/MONEY	Prenuptial agreements
4709 JAPANESE PROVERB	A good husband is one who is healthy and absent!
4710 RABBI SHMULEY BOTEACH/USA	You need to show humanity at home, not righteousness.
4711 DEBATE	That material success is a false happiness.
4712 HERB KELLEHER/ USA/FOUNDER/ S.W. AIRLINES	We will hire someone with less experience, less education, and less expertise, than someone who has more of those things and has a rotten attitude.
4713 KYUNG-SOOK SHIN/ SOUTH KOREA/WRITER	If you only do what you like, who's going to do what you don't like?
4714 JOHN STUART MILL/ UK/PHILOSOPHER	A person may cause evil to others not only by his actions but by his inaction, and in either case he is justly accountable to them for the injury.
4715 UK/GENERAL MONTGROMERY	My own definition of leadership is this: The capacity and the will to rally men and women to a common purpose and the character which inspires confidence.
4716 LADY MARGARET THATCHER/PM/UK	In politics, if you want anything said, ask a man. If you want anything done, ask a woman.
4717 MARISHA PESSL/ WRITER/USA	Not returning phone calls is the severest form of torture in the civilized world.
4718 SHERYL SANDBERG/ USA/BUSINESS LEADER	...intelligence and success are not clear paths to popularity at any age.
4719 USA/MARILYNNE ROBINSON/WRITER	To crave and to have are as like a thing and its shadow.
4720 T. BOONE PICKENS/ USA/BUSINESS MAGNATE	Chief executives, who themselves own few shares of their companies, have no more feeling for the average stockholder than they do for baboons in Africa.
4721 EDUCATION	University should be open to all who want to attend.
4722 LUCRETIA MOTT/USA/ WOMEN'S RIGHTS	I have no idea of submitting tamely to injustice inflicted either on me or on the slave...I am no advocate of passivity.
4723 HOUSING	Renting a house versus buying
4724 JAPANESE PROVERB	*Kaiinu ni te wo kamareru:* Your own dog bites your hand.
4725 IDIOM	Having one's head in the clouds
4726 ENGLISH PROVERB	Easier said than done.
4727 NAPOLEON HILL/USA	Action is the real measure of intelligence.
4728 RELATIONSHIPS	Mind games
4729 USA/MARGARET HEFFERNAN/BUSINESS	Silence is the language of inertia.
4730 MARIA BARTIROMO/ USA/BROADCASTER	Most women outlive their spouses. Divorce remains at record rates. It's important for a woman to be able to control her finances.
4731 GOALS/CHOICES	Path of least resistance
4732 H.L. MENCKEN/USA/ EDITOR	Archbishop – A Christian ecclesiastic of a rank superior to that attained by Christ.

NUMBER CATEGORY/CREDIT	TOPIC
4733 ARABIC PROVERB	Every ambitious man is a captive and every covetous one a pauper.
4734 NORMAN COUSINS/ USA/EDITOR	...man is a creature of dualism. He is both good and evil, both altruistic and selfish.
4735 BULGARIAN PROVERB	A tree falls the way it leans.
4736 JONAS SALK/SCIENTIST	I feel that the greatest reward for doing is the opportunity to do more.
4737 FRENCH/MOLIERE	A wise man is superior to any insults which can be put upon him, and the best reply to unseemly behavior is patience and moderation.
4738 DR PHIL McGRAW/ USA/PSYCHOLOGIST	You wouldn't care so much about what people think about you if you knew how little they did.
4739 DEBATE	Women make better leaders.
4740 MARISHA PESSL/USA	It's hard in America not to equate 'happiness' with 'things.'
4741 DAN BROWN/USA	Time is a river and books are boats.
4742 DAVID PACKARD/USA/ HP/CO-FOUNDER	The greatest success goes to the person who is not afraid to fail in front of even the largest audience.
4743 FRANK GEHRY/USA/ ARCHITECT	Ninety-eight percent of buildings are boxes, which tells me that a lot of people are in denial. we live and work in boxes.
4744 RENE DESCARTES/ FRENCH PHILOSOPHER	I think, therefore, I am.
4745 ANNA FREUD/AUSTRIA/ PYSCHOANALYST	Creative minds have always been known to survive any kind of bad training.
4746 FRANKLIN P. ADAMS/ COLUMNIST/USA	You can learn many things from children. How much patience you have, for instance.
4747 JAPANESE PROVERB	*Ishi bashi o tataete wataru* Checking for the strength of a stone bridge before crossing
4748 JOHN RUSKIN/UK	A man wrapped up in himself makes a very small parcel.
4749 DEBATE/SOCIETY	It's a man's world.
4750 ADOLF HITLER/NAZI LEADER/MEIN KAMPF	Any alliance whose purpose is not the intention to wage war is senseless and useless.
4751 CHINESE PROVERB	A courtyard common to all will be swept by none.
4752 IRISH PROVERB	A friend's eye is a good mirror.
4753 AKIRA KUROSAWA/ JAPAN/FILM MAKER	There is nothing that says more about its creator than the work itself.
4754 FRANKLIN P. ADAMS/ COLUMNIST/USA	Nothing is more responsible for the good old days than a bad memory.
4755 PHILIP JOHNSON/ ARCHITECT	I hate vacations. If you can build buildings, why sit on the beach?
4756 GERMAN PROVERB	A clear conscience is a soft pillow.
4757 SAYING	Knowing the price of everything but the value of nothing
4758 CARL SAGAN/USA	Nature is unsentimental.
4759 J. C. PENNEY/USA	Courteous treatment will make a customer a walking advertisement.
4760 YIDDISH PROVERB	A table is not blessed if it has fed no scholars.
4761 HAPPINESS/FLEETING	The Chinese character for happiness means "short-lived."
4762 POLISH PROVERB	Better no doctor at all than three.

NUMBER CATEGORY/CREDIT	TOPIC
4763 CONFUCIUS/CHINA/ SAGE	Riches and honors acquired by unrighteousness are to me as a floating cloud.
4764 DEBATE	That parenthood is a right, not a privilege
4765 SUCCESS/MEANING	There's more to life than career success
4766 DEBATE	That nature will take care of the population explosion
4767 HAROLD E. WAGONER/ ARCHITECT	The great thing about being an architect is that you can walk into your dream.
4768 MARGARET MEAD/ USA/ANTHROPOLOGIST	Never doubt that a small group of thoughtful, concerned citizens can change the world. Indeed it is the only thing that ever was.
4769 FERNANDO PESSOA	Everything interests me, but nothing holds me.
4770 MARISHA PESSL/ WRITER/USA	Some people are as fragile as butterflies and sensitive and it's your responsibility not to destroy them.
4771 DAN BROWN/USA	One does not need to have cancer to analyze its symptoms.
4772 ENGLISH PROVERB	Don't cut off your nose to spite your face.
4773 GERMAN PROVERB	A little too late, is much too late.
4774 LOUIS KAHN/ARCHITECT	Form follows function.
4775 JOHN CUSSACK/USA/ FILM MAKER	I force people to have coffee with me, just because I don't trust that a friendship can be maintained without any other senses besides a computer or cell phone screen.
4776 DAVID PACKARD/USA/ HEWLETT-PACKARD	Set out to build a company and make a contribution, not an empire and a fortune.
4777 FRENCH PROVERB	A lie travels round the world while truth is putting her boots on.
4778 MARIA MONTESSORI/ EDUCATION/ITALY	One test of the correctness of educatianal procedure is the happiness of the child.
4779 HUNGARY/PROVERB	A prudent man does not make the goat his gardener.
4780 YIDDISH PROVERB	If rich people could hire other people to die for them, the poor could make a wonderful living.
4781 DANISH PROVERB	It is hard to pay for bread that has been eaten.
4782 MICHAEL JORDAN/USA	There is no "I" in team but there is in win.
4783 CHINESE PROVERB	Give a man a fish, and he'll eat for a day. Teach him how to fish and he'll eat forever.
4784 CHINESE PROVERB	He who rides a tiger is afraid to dismount.
4785 ENGLISH PROVERB	Don't put all your eggs in one basket.
4786 J. F. KENNEDY/USA/ 35TH PRESIDENT	A nation reveals itself not only by the men it produces but also by the men it honors, the men it remembers.
4787 DEBATE	Teachers should be paid according to how much their students learn.
4788 DEBATE	That museum entry should be free
4789 ABRAHAM LINCOLN/ 16th PRESIDENT/USA	Whenever I hear anyone arguing for slavery, I feel a strong impulse to see it tried on him personally.
4790 DISRAELI/BRITISH PRIME MINISTEER	Bore: one who has the power of speech but not the capacity for conversation.
4791 BENJAMIN DISRAELI/ BRITISH PM	You know who the critics are? The men who have failed in literature and art.

NUMBER CATEGORY/CREDIT	TOPIC
4792 TINA SEELIG/USA/PROF	Quitting is actually incredibly empowering.
4793 ROBERT VENTURI/ ARCHITECT	Less is a bore.
4794 LUCRETIA MOTT/USA	We too often bind ourselves by authorities rather than by truth.
4795 LADY MARGARET THATCHER/PRIME MINISTER/UK	Look at a day when you are supremely satisfied at the end. It's not a day when you lounge around doing nothing; it's a day you've had everything to do and you've done it.
4796 DAN BROWN/USA	Fear cripples faster than any implement of war.
4797 DAVID PACKARD/USA/ HEWLETT-PACKARD	The biggest competitive advantage is to do the right thing at the worst time.
4798 CHINESE PROVERB	If you are planning for a year, sow rice; if you are planning for a decade, plant trees; if you are planning for a lifetime, educate people.
4799 FRENCH PROVERB	In love, there is always one who kisses and one who offers the cheek.
4800 J. F. KENNEDY/USA/ 35TH PRESIDENT	Do not pray for easy lives. Pray to be stronger men.
4801 JAMES ALLEN/ AUTHOR	All that you accomplish or fail to accomplish with your life is the direct result of your thoughts.
4802 DEBATE	Parents should be jailed when their children commit a crime.
4803 CARL SAGAN/ AMERICAN SCIENTIST	The cure for a fallacious argument is a better argument, not the suppression of ideas.
4804 ALAN LAKEIN/USA	It's not worthwhile to make a big effort for a task of little value.
4805 PERSONAL	Hunger for praise
4806 DEBATE	That the number of women in the legislature should be raised through a quota
4807 DEBATE	Playing a game is only fun when you win
4808 ENGLISH PROVERB	Distance lends enchantment to the view.
4809 DEBATE	That advertising persuades people to buy things that they do not need
4810 CANTONESE PROVERB	Brothers are like arms and legs; husband and wife are like clothing.
4811 DEBATE	Zoos must be banned.
4812 HARRY TRUMAN/ 33RD PRESIDENT/ USA/A PUBLIC MAN/ THIS I BELIEVE	A public man should not worry constantly about the verdict of history or what future generations will say about him. He must live in the present; make his decisions for the right on the facts as he sees them, and history will take care of itself.
4813 RUDYARD KIPLING/ ENGLISH WRITER	Borrow trouble for yourself, if that's your nature, but don't lend it to your neighbors.
4814 WILLIAM JENNINGS BRYAN/USA/LAWYER	The parents have a right to say that no teacher paid by their money shall rob their children of faith in God and send them back to their homes skeptical, or infidels, or agnostic, or atheists.
4815 HENRIK IBSEN/ NORWAY/WRITER	A thousand words leave not the same deep impression as does a simple deed.
4816 MARISHA PESSL/ WRITER/USA	Just when you think you've hit rock bottom, you realize you're standing on another trapdoor.
4817 HENRY W. LONG- FELLOW/USA/POET	We judge ourselves by what we feel capable of doing, while others judge us by what we have already done.

NUMBER CATEGORY/CREDIT	TOPIC
4818 JAPANESE PROVERB	*Neko wo kaburu (to wear the cat)* - deceptive behaviour
4819 GILLIAN FLYNN/USA/ AUTHOR/TV CRITIC/ GONE GIRL	My mother had always told her kids: if you're about to do something, and you want to know if it's a bad idea, imagine seeing it printed in the paper for all the world to see.
4820 DAVID PACKARD/ HEWLETT-PACKARD	A frustrated employee is a greater threat than a merely unhappy one.
4821 ENGLISH PROVERB	Cut your coat according to your cloth.
4822 WARREN BENNIS/ USA/CONSULTANT	The most dangerous leadership myth is that leaders are born -- that there is a genetic factor to leadership. That's nonsense; in fact, the opposite is true. Leaders are made rather than born.
4823 LEE CHILD/UK/WRITER	I am not a vagrant. I am a hobo. Big difference.
4824 MARISHA PESSL/USA/ WRITER	People don't realize how easy life is to change. You just get on the bus.
4825 USA/TENNIS/MARTINA NAVRATILOVA	It is easier to do a job right than to explain why you didn't.
4826 DAN BROWN/US/ WRITER	Even brilliant scientists Google themselves.
4827 PERSONAL	What you would do if your government granted you 40 acres and a mule.
4828 EDWARD HOPPER/US	If you could say it in words, there would be no reason to paint.
4829 HANK PAULSON/USA/ BUSINESS	Big, ugly, messy problems don't have neat perfect answers.
4830 TENNIS/MARTINA NAVRATILOVA	The mark of great sportsmen is not how good they are at their best, but how good they are at their worst.
4831 EDUCATION	Listening to lectures versus interactive learning
4832 JAMES ALLEN/AUTHOR	Good thoughts bear good fruit, bad thoughts bear bad fruit.
4833 FRANK GEHRY/USA/ ARCHITECT	Architecture should speak of its time and place, but yearn for timelessness..
4834 OSCAR WILDE/IRISH WRITER/POET	Thirty-five is a very attractive age. London society is full of women of the very highest birth who have, of their own free choice, remained thirty-five for years.
4835 USA/RALPH WALDO EMERSON/ESSAYIST	The only way to have a friend is to be one.
4836 AUTHOR/JOÃO UBALDO RIBEIRO/BRAZIL	The way you ask a question chooses its answer.
4837 ALICE MUNRO/ CANADIAN WRITER	In twenty years I've never had a day when I didn't have to think about someone else's needs. And this means the writing has to be fitted around it.
4838 HENRIK IBSEN/ NORWAY/WRITER	You see, there are some people that one loves and others that perhaps one would rather be with.
4839 FERNANDO PESSOA/ PORTUGUESE POET	Some people have big dreams in life which they never fulfill. Others don't have any dreams in life, and they don't fulfill those either.
4840 FERNANDO PESSOA/ PORTUGUESE WRITER/POET	The value of things is not the time they last, but the intensity with which they occur. That is why there are unforgettable moments and unique people.
4841 SALLY HOGSHEAD/USA/ SOCIAL MEDIA	Mistakes are tuition.

NUMBER CATEGORY/CREDIT	TOPIC
4842 PERSONAL	Differences between your generation and your parents' generation
4843 HENRIK IBSEN/ NORWAY/WRITER	What is the difference in being alone with another and being alone by one's self?
4844 DAVID PACKARD/ HEWLETT-PACKARD	The best business decisions are the most humane decisions.
4845 DEBATE	That drivers be prohibited from using mobile phones
4846 JAPANESE PROVERB	*Rei mo sugireba burei.* / More than polite is rude.
4847 DEBATE	That the minimum voting age should be 16
4848 MARTIN LUTHER KING JR./USA/CIVIL RIGHTS	Whatever your life's work is, do it well. A man should do his job so well that the living, the dead, and the unborn could do it no better.
4849 DAN BROWN/USA	Sometimes a change in perspective is all it takes to see the light.
4850 MARISHA PESSL/USA	Everyone smiles for a photograph.
4851 COCO CHANEL/FRANCE	A girl should be two things: who and what she wants.
4852 DAN BROWN/USA/ WRITER	Everything is possible. The impossible just takes longer.
4853 BOB HOPE/USA/ACTOR	I like politicians who pray a lot. It keeps their hands up where we see them.
4854 ENGLISH PROVERB	Courtesy costs nothing.
4855 FRENCH/ALBERT SCHWEITZER	If a man loses his reverence for any part of life, he will lose his reverence for all of life.
4856 UK/ALFRED NORTH WHITEHEAD/MATH	All of Western philosophy is but a footnote to Plato.
4857 UNIVERSITIES	Grade inflation
4858 J C PENNEY/USA/ BUSINESS VALUES	Give me a stock clerk with a goal and I'll give you a man who will make history. Give me a man with no goals and I'll give you a stock clerk.
4859 DIPLOMAT/NICCOLO MACHIAVELLI/ITALY	A man who is used to acting in one way never changes; he must come to ruin when the times, in changing, no longer are in harmony with his ways.
4860 WILLIAM BOYD/UK/ NOVELIST	Enthusiasm is the match that lights the candle of achievement
4861 HEROES/'SHEROES'	If you could name a day for an important person, who would it be and why?
4862 MARRIAGE	That women should have the right to retain their maiden name after marriage
4863 ENGLISH PROVERB	Charity begins at home but should not end there.
4864 D. P. MOYNIHAN/USA	Everyone is entitled to his own opinion, but not his own facts.
4865 ITALIAN/NICCOLO MACHIAVELLI/ DIPLOMAT/ HISTORIAN	It must be remembered that there is nothing more difficult to plan, more doubtful of success, nor more dangerous to manage than a new system. For the initiator has the enmity of all who would profit by the preservation of the old institution and merely lukewarm defenders in those who gain by the new ones.
4866 YVON CHOUINARD/ USA/ROCK CLIMBER	No young kid growing up dreams of someday becoming a businessman. He wants to be a fireman, a sponsored athlete or a forest ranger.
4867 DR PHIL McGRAW/USA	You can't put feathers on a dog and call it a chicken.
4868 CLARE BOOTH LUCE/ USA/WRITER	All autobiographies are alibi-ographies.

NUMBER CATEGORY/CREDIT	TOPIC
4869 CHARLOTTE PERKINS GILMAN/WRITER/USA	In our steady insistence on proclaiming sex-distinctions we have grown to consider most human attributes as masculine attributes, for the simple reason that they were allowed for men and forbidden to women.
4870 TENNIS/MARTINA NAVRATILOVA/USA	Labels are for filing. Labels are for clothing. Labels are not for people.
4871 JOHN LOCKE/ PHILOSOPHER	New opinions are always suspected, and usually opposed, without any other reason but because they are not already common.
4872 ANDRE MALRAUX/ FRENCH/NOVELIST	To command is to serve, nothing more and nothing less.
4873 DAN BROWN/USA/ AUTHOR/THRILLER	When a question has no correct answer, there is only one honest response. The gray area between yes and no. Silence.
4874 RELATIONSHIPS	Secrets of a successful marriage
4875 OPINION	What's your view of adults who live with their parents?
4876 ENGLISH PROVERB	Care killed the cat.
4877 RELATIONSHIP	Handling difficult people
4878 WORK/SOCIETY	Two-career families
4879 US/CHARLES LINDBERG/ AVIATOR	If I had to choose, I would rather have birds than airplanes.
4880 CHILDREN	Daycare facilities in your country or community
4881 SIR THOMAS MORE/ UK/PHILOSOPHER	Pride thinks its own happiness shines the brighter by comparing it with the misfortunes of others.
4882 E.B. WHITE/USA	The time not to become a father is eighteen years before a war.
4883 DEBATE	That a farmer is more important than a doctor
4884 USA/ANTHONY P. CARNEVALE/COLLEGE	"...getting a degree matters, but what you take matters more."
4885 ROBERT LOUIS STEVENSON/ SCOT	To be what we are, and to become what we are capable of becoming, is the only end of life.
4886 FRANCIS BACON/ UK/PHILOSOPHER	A little philosophy inclineth man's mind to atheism, but depth in philosophy bringeth men's minds about to religion.
4887 PETER DRUCKER/ MANAGEMENT/USA	The aim of marketing is to know and understand the customer so well the product or service fits him and sells itself.
4888 NORMAN MAILER/USA	You don't know a woman until you've met her in court.
4889 HENRY GEORGE/USA/ ECONOMIST	There is danger in reckless change, but greater danger in blind conservatism.
4890 JOHN UPDIKE/USA/ WRITER	America is a vast conspiracy to make you happy.
4891 LEE CHILD/BRITISH NOVELIST	Never forget a Favor. Never forgive a Slight!
4892 ARISTOTLE/THINKER	He who has never learned to obey cannot be a good commander.
4893 LEE CHILD/BRITISH NOVELIST	Nothing ever works like you predict it. All plans fall apart as soon as the first shot is fired.
4894 RENE DESCARTES/ FRENCH PHILOSOPHER	Bad books engender bad habits, but bad habits engender good books.
4895 GRATITUDE	What are you grateful for in life?

NUMBER CATEGORY/CREDIT	TOPIC
4896 FAMILY/ROLES	Who wears the pants in your family?
4897 DEBATE	A pleasant voice contributes to success
4898 IMAGE	Dressing for success
4899 FRIENDSHIP/RESPONSIBILITY	What do you think of taking time off from work to show a friend around town?
4900 ENGLISH PROVERB	Birds of a feather flock together.
4901 SUCCESS	Memory training
4902 US/ANTI-RAPE SLOGAN	No means no
4903 W. CLEMENT STONE/USA/BUSINESSMAN/PHILANTHROPIST	You are the product of your environment. So choose the environment that will best develop you toward your objective. Analyze your life in terms of its environment. Are the things around you helping you toward success – or are they holding you back?
4904 G.K. CHESTERTON/ENGLISH WRITER	It is absurd for the Evolutionist to complain that it is unthinkable for an admittedly unthinkable God to make everything out of nothing, and then pretend that it is more thinkable that nothing should turn itself into everything.
4905 BENJAMIN DISRAELI/UK/PRIME MINISTER	A majority is always better than the best repartee.
4906 F. MOLLY IVINS/USA/COLUMNIST	The first rule of holes: when you're in one, stop digging.
4907 ENGLISH PROVERB	Everyone thinks his own burden the heaviest.
4908 WARREN G. BENNIS/USA/PSYCHOLOGIST	Trust is the lubrication that makes it possible for organizations to work.
4909 LAO-TZU/THINKER/CHINA	There is no calamity greater than lavish desires.
4910 ANTON CHEKHOV/WRITER/RUSSIA	Knowledge is of no value unless you put it into practice.
4911 MITCH ALBOM/USA/WRITER	Death ends a life, not a relationship.
4912 PERSONAL	What do you love?
4913 PATRICIA ANDERSON/USA/THIS I BELIEVE	I live simply so others may simply live.
4914 LADY THATCHER/UK/PRIME MINISTER	You may have to fight a battle more than once to win it.
4915 TENNIS/OUT/MARTINA NAVRATILOVA/USA	The moment of victory is much too short to live for that and nothng else.
4916 HENRIK IBSEN/NORWAY/WRITER	Was the majority right when they refused to believe that the earth moved around the sun and let Galileo be driven to his knees like a dog?
4917 RELIGION/CHRISTIANITY	Women and the priesthood
4918 MADAME de STAEL/WRITER	Search for the truth is the noblest occupation of man; its publication is a duty.
4919 NIZAR QABBANI/SYRIAN POET	We wear the cape of civilization but our soul lives in the stone age.

NUMBER CATEGORY/CREDIT	TOPIC
4920 BRIAN TRACY/USA/ SUCCESS COACH	Become the kind of leader that people would follow voluntarily; even if you had no title or position.
4921 RALPH NADER/USA/ POLITICIAN/ACTIVIST	I start with the premise that the function of leadership is to produce more leaders, not more followers.
4922 LADY MARGARET THATCHER/UK	If you just set out to be liked, you will be prepared to compromise on anything at anytime, and would achieve nothing.
4923 LEE CHILD/BRITISH	Nothing of value was ever achieved in the morning.
4924 DAN BROWN/USA/ AUTHOR/THRILLER	Life is filled with difficult decisions, and winners are those who make them.
4925 BILL CLINTON/USA/ PRESIDENT	Some are in prison who shouldn't be, others are in for too long, and without a plan to educate, train and reintegrate them into our community, we all suffer.
4926 MARTIN L. KING JR./USA	A riot is the language of the unheard.
4927 EDUCATION	What do you think about people who pay their way through college or university?
4928 USA/ELBERT GREEN HUBBARD/WRITER	Anyone who idolized you is going to hate you when he discovers that you are fallible.
4929 ROBERT ALLMAN/ USA/THIS I BELIEVE	I find strength in the friendship and interdependence of people.
4930 PERSONAL	What would you do if you had only 24 hours to live?
4931 ANAIS NIN/US/AUTHOR	People living deeply have no fear of death.
4932 RENE DESCARTES/ FRENCH PHILOSOPHER	It is useful to know something of the names of different nations, that we may be enabled to form a more correct judgment regarding our own, and be prevented from thinking that everything contrary to our customs is ridiculous and irrational, a conclusion usually come to by those whose experience has been limited to their own country.
4933 ALBERT EINSTEIN/ USA/PHYSICIST	Any man who can drive safely while kissing a pretty girl is simply not giving the kiss the attention it deserves.
4934 ARABIC PROVERB	Give a man some cloth and he'll ask for some lining.
4935 HARRY COHN/USA	I don't have ulcers. I give them.
4936 ABIGAIL VAN BUREN/ COLUMNIST/USA	In Biblical times, a man could have as many wives as he could afford. Just like today.
4937 MITCH ALBOM/US	All endings are also beginnings. We just don't know it at the time.
4938 PETER DRUCKER/ USA/MANAGEMENT GURU	Leadership is lifting a person's vision to high sights, the raising of a person's performance to a higher standard, the building of a personality beyond its normal limitations.
4939 STEVE IRWIN/ AUSTRALIA	I have no fear of losing my life – if I have to save a crocodile or a kangaroo or a snake, mate, I will save it.
4940 JAMES ALLEN/UK/ AUTHOR/SELF-HELP	Whether you be man or woman you will never do anything in this world without courage. It is the greatest quality of the mind next to honor.
4941 JAPANESE PROVERB	*Kabe ni mimi ari, shoji ni me:* Walls have ears; doors have eyes.
4942 PERSONAL	How do your friends see you?
4943 DR. MARTIN L KING JR/ USA	The quality, not the longevity, of one's life is what is important.

NUMBER CATEGORY/CREDIT	TOPIC
4944 PETER DRUCKER/ USA/PROFESSOR	Effective leadership is not about making speeches or being liked; leadership is defined by results, not attributes.
4945 RENE DESCARTES/ FRENCH PHILOSOPHER	Whenever anyone has offended me, I try to raise my soul so high that the offense cannot reach it.
4946 DAN BROWN/USA/ AUTHOR/THRILLER FICTION	In my mind, the men and women of NASA are history's modern pioneers. They attempt the impossible, accept failure, and then go back to the drawing board while the rest of us stand back and criticize.
4947 PERSONAL	How important is job security to you?
4948 PERSONAL	How do you take criticism from your colleagues?
4949 ROBERT FULGHUM/ USA/WRITER	Don't worry that children never listen to you; worry that they are always watching you.
4950 BEN HOOWITZ/ ENTREPRENEUR	There is no such thing as a great executive. There is only a great executive for a specific company at a specific point in time.
4951 ENGLISH PROVERB	Brevity is the soul of wit.
4952 CHINESE/GAMBLING	When the money is gone a person feels at ease
4953 LEADERSHIP	What do you think about delegating work?
4954 USA/ELBERT GREEN HUBBARD/ WRITER	A genius is a man who takes the lemons that Fate hands him and starts a lemonade stand with them.
4955 ROBERT ALLMAN/USA/ THIS I BELIEVE	Life, I believe, asks a continuous series of adjustments to reality. The more readily a person is able to make these adjustments, the more meaningful his own private world becomes.
4956 MITCH ALBOM/USA WRITER	When someone is in your heart, they're never truly gone. They can come back to you, even at unlikely times.
4957 SCOT/ROBERT L. STEVENSON/WRITER	I am in the habit of looking not so much to the nature of a gift as to the spirit in which is it is offered.
4958 MAIMONIDES/SCHOLAR	You must accept the truth from whatever source it comes.
4959 MOTHERHOOD	Single motherhood
4960 G.K. CHESTERTON/ ENGLISH WRITER	A good novel tells us the truth about its hero; but a bad novel tells us the truth about its author.
4961 JOSEPH CAMPBELL/USA	Every religion is true one way or another.
4962 MARY PICKFORD/USA/ CANADA/ACTRESS	You may have a fresh start any moment you choose, for this thing that we call 'failure' is not the falling down, but the staying down.
4963 VIRGINIA WOOLF/UK	Humor is the first of the gifts to perish in a foreign tongue.
4964 BID RIGGING/FRAUD/ WIKIPEDIA	Bid rigging is a form of fraud in which a commercial contract is promised to one party even though for the sake of appearance several other parties also present a bid.
4965 USA/KAREEM ABDUL-JABBAR/BASKETBALL	I'm not comfortable being preachy, but more people need to start spending as much time in the library as they do on the basketball court.
4966 ARABIC PROVERB	Every day of your life is a page of your history.
4967 DEBATE/BUSINESS	People before profits
4968 HEALTH	The importance of yearly physical checkups
4969 LEGACY/EPITAPH	What would you like your headstone to say?
4970 ELEANOR ROOSEVELT/ USA/FIRST LADY	When you are genuinely interested in one thing, it will always lead to something else.

NUMBER CATEGORY/CREDIT	TOPIC
4971 DEBATE/SOCIETY	Hospitals before hotels
4972 PERSONAL INTRODUCTION	How would you describe yourself to someone you've just met on the Internet?
4973 SELF-REFLECTION	How well do you control your temper?
4974 SELF-REFLECTION	Do you speak up if your viewpoint differs from those of others?
4975 JUSTICE/TRUTH	What do you think about taking a lie detector test?
4976 INDIRA GANDHI/ INDIA/PRIME MINISTER	To bear many children is considered not only a religious blessing but also an investment. The greater their number, some Indians reason, the more alms they can beg.
4977 DEBATE	It makes no sense to be afraid of ghosts.
4978 USA/MALCOLM GLADWELL/AUTHOR	The key to good decision making is not knowledge. It is understanding.
4979 RENE DESCARTES/ FRENCH PHILOSOPHER	It is not enough to have a good mind; the main thing is to use it well.
4980 INDIAN PROVERB	Rather be a slave to a rich man than the spouse of a poor man.
4981 CHILDREN/ COMFORT	Teddy bears
4982 DAN BROWN/USA	Language can be very adept at hiding the truth.
4983 PUBLILIUS SYRUS/100 BC	You should go to a pear tree for pears, not to an elm.
4984 FRANCIS BACON/UK	Wife and children are a kind of discipline of humanity.
4985 BENJAMIN DISRAELI/ UK/PRIME MINISTER	I have climbed on the top of the greasy pole.
4986 WRITER/WILLIAM SHAKESPEARE	Be not afraid of greatness; some are born great, some achieve greatness, and others have greatness thrust upon them.
4987 JANE AUSTEN/UK/ NOVELIST	It is a truth universally acknowledged, that a single man in possession of a good fortune must be in want of a wife.
4988 BENJAMIN DISRAELI/UK	Talk to a man about himself and he will listen for hours.
4989 G.K. CHESTERTON/ ENGLISH WRITER	To have a right to do a thing is not at all the same as to be right in doing it.
4990 SUN TZU/CHINA/ AUTHOR/THE ART OF WAR	The art of war is of vital importance to the State. It is a matter of life and death, a road either to safety or to ruin. Hence it is a subject of inquiry that can on no account be neglected.
4991 BETTY FRIEDAN/ USA/FEMINIST	It is easier to live through someone else than to become complete yourself.
4992 DEBATE/BEST MAN/ MARRIAGE	Being chosen best man is both a blessing and a curse
4993 JAMES A. MICHENER/US	Character consists of what you do on the third and fourth tries.
4994 NAPOLEON HILL/USA	Think and grow rich.
4995 J C PENNEY/USA/ BUSINESS VALUES	A merchant who approaches business with the idea of serving the public well has nothing to fear from the competition.
4996 MADAME de STAEL/ WRITER/FRENCH	The desire of the man is for the woman, but the desire of the woman is for the desire of the man.
4997 MARTIN LUTHER KING JR./USA/CIVIL RIGHTS	The time is always right to do the right thing.

NUMBER CATEGORY/CREDIT	TOPIC
4998 NIZAR QABBANI/ SYRIAN WRITER	Light is more important than the lantern; The poem more important than the notebook.
4999 LADY THATCHER/UK/PM	Don't follow the crowd. Let the crowd follow you.
5000 SCOT/ROBERT LOUIS STEVENSON/WRITER	We are all travelers in the wilderness of this world, and the best we can find in our travels is an honest friend.
5001 TEAMWORK	What do you think about working with other people?
5002 JOHN K. GALBRAITH/ ECONOMIST	The process by which banks create money is so simple that the mind is repelled.
5003 EDUCATION	What was the most important lesson you learned in school?
5004 DAN BROWN/USA/ AUTHOR/FICTION	Force a hand, and it will fight you. But convince a mind to think as you want it to think, and you have an ally.
5005 COMMUNICATION	The importance of oral communication
5006 COMMENCEMENT	Your advice to high school students about to graduate
5007 STEPHEN COVEY/USA/ AUTHOR	People simply feel better about themselves when they're good at something.
5008 FRENCH/NAPOLEON	He who fears being conquered is sure of defeat.
5009 BALTHUS/FRENCH/ART/ POLISH	Painting is a source of endless pleasure, but also of great anguish.
5010 SENECA/DRAMATIST	Nothing deters a good man from doing what is honorable.
5011 R.L. STEVENSON	Wine is bottled poetry.
5012 HOME/SAFETY	Child-proofing a home
5013 DEBATE	Role models can be the death of budding talent.
5014 JOHN K. GALBRAITH/ ECONOMIST	Under capitalism, man exploits man. Under communism, it's just the opposite.
5015 RICHARD STEELE/UK	That man never grows old who keeps a child in his heart.
5016 bell hooks/USA/ WRITER/ PROFESSOR	Our hearts connect with lots of folks in a lifetime but most of us will go to our graves with no experience of true love.
5017 BENJAMIN DISRAELI/ UK/STATESMAN	An author who speaks about his (or her) own books is almost as bad as a mother who speaks about her own children.
5018 MARTIN LUTHER KING JR./LEADER/USA	Whatever your life's work is, do it well. A man should do his job so well that the living, the dead, and the unborn child could do it no better.
5019 MACCHIAVELI/ITALY	There is nothing more important than appearing to be religious.
5020 E.B. WHITE/USA	Don't write about Man; write about a man.
5021 TIM O'BRIEN/USA/'NAM	I was a coward. I went to the war.
5022 JOHANN WOLFGANG VON GOETHE	A great person attracts great people and knows how to hold them together.
5023 ROBIN WILLIAMS/USA/ COMEDIAN	I think the saddest people always try their hardest to make people happy. Because they know what it's like to feel absolutely worthless and they don't want anybody else to feel like that.
5024 DAN BROWN/USA	If a hippo ever wants to fight, just walk away.
5025 LADY MARGARET THATCHER/PM/UK	To wear your heart on your sleeve isn't a very good plan; you should wear it inside, where it functions best.
5026 OSCAR WILDE/POET	Always forgive your enemies; nothing annoys them so much.

NUMBER CATEGORY/CREDIT	TOPIC
5027 USA/THEODORE ROOSEVELT/ PRESIDENT	The best executive is the one who has sense enough to pick good men to do what he wants done, and the self-restraint enough to keep from meddling with them while they do it.
5028 MOHANDAS K. GANDHI/ LEADER/INDIA	I will not let anyone walk through my mind with their dirty feet.
5029 HENRY JAMES/USA/UK/ WRITER	Live all you can; it's a mistake not to.
5030 DEBATE	Social services before space research
5031 DONALD WINNICOTT/ UK/PEDIATRICIAN	Creativity makes life worth living.
5032 USA/ELBERT GREEN HUBBARD/WRITER	If you want the work well done, select a busy man; the other kind has no time.
5033 TARA PARKER-POPE/ USA/AUTHOR	The road to better health is paved with the small decisions we make every day.
5034 USA/ALAN LAKEIN/ AUTHOR	Horror stories abound of men who work so hard that they hardly ever see their families and who end up with ulcers and heart trouble.
5035 VINCE LOMBARDI/ USA/FOOTBALL	If you aren't fired with enthusiasm, you will be fired with enthusiasm.
5036 PUBLILIUS SYRUS/100 BC	While we stop to think, we often miss our opportunity.
5037 HUFFPO/ HEADLINE	Cat Divorce: Israeli Man Divorces Wife Over Her 550 Cats
5038 ROBERT GATES/USA/ WAPO/LEADERSHIP	While many people witness history, those who step forward to serve in a time of crisis have a place in history.
5039 RAPHAEL DE LEON/ TRINIDAD/CALYPSO	If you want to be happy living a king's life Never make a pretty woman your wife.
5040 CHARLES DARWIN/ SCIENTIST/UK	If I had my life to live over again, I would have made a rule to read some poetry and listen to some music at least once a week.
5041 NIC ROBERTS/UK/ JOURNALIST	No story is worth dying for.
5042 MARTIN LUTHER KING JR./LEADER/USA	We must build dikes of courage to hold back the flood of fear.
5043 JOHN DEWEY/USA/	A problem well stated is a problem half solved.
5044 LEONARDO DA VINCI/ ARTIST/ITALY	Everything connects to everything else.
5045 STEPHEN AMBROSE/ USA/HISTORIAN	I'm an historian who has learned through a lifetime of studying that nothing in the world beats universal education.
5046 DALE CARNEGIE/ USA/WRITER	Many people think that if they were only in some other place, or had some other job, they would be happy.
5047 BETTY FRIEDAN/USA FEMINIST	In almost every professional field, in business and in the arts and sciences, women are still treated as second-class citizens. It would be a great service to tell girls who plan to work in society to expect this subtle, uncomfortable discrimination--tell them not to be quiet, and hope it will go away, but fight it.
5048 LOUIS PASTEUR/ FRENCH/SCIENTIST	Science knows no country, because knowledge belongs to humanity, and is the torch which illuminates the world.

NUMBER CATEGORY/CREDIT	TOPIC
5049 USA/CHARLES LINDBERGH/USA	In wilderness I sense the miracle of life, and behind it our scientific accomplishments fade to trivia.
5050 ENGLISH PROVERB	Books and friends should be few and good.
5051 US/AFRICAN-AMERICANS	Ebonics (Black English)
5052 JOHN K. GALBRAITH/ ECONOMIST	There's a certain part of the contented majority who love anybody who is worth a million dollars.
5053 KEN KESEY/USA/ AUTHOR	You don't lead by pointing and telling people some place to go. You lead by going to that place and making a case.
5054 DAN BROWN/USA	Religion has always persecuted science.
5055 DANICA PATRICK/USA FORMULA 1 RACER	Success doesn't just happen. You have to go out there and make it happen. If you sit around waiting for success, it'll never come.
5056 DRUG COMPANIES	Generic drugs
5057 LOUISE NEVELSON/USA	I think all great innovations are built on rejection.
5058 CHARISMA	Larger-than-life figures
5059 RELATIONSHIPS	Informed consent
5060 PERSONAL ANALYSIS	Do you consider yourself innovative?
5061 JOACHIM KRUEGER/USA CNN/OCT 18, 2011/PROF.	As humans, we are horrified when we learn that a person in distress is not helped.
5062 ROBERT KENNEDY/USA	I believe as long as there is plenty, poverty is evil.
5063 THE WRITTEN WORD	The importance of spelling
5064 CARL SAGAN/USA/ SCIENTIST	If you wish to make an apple pie from scratch, you must first invent the universe.
5065 STEVE IRWIN/ AUSTRALIA	One crowded hour of glorious life is worth more than an age without a name.
5066 SAUL BELLOW/USA	When we ask for advice, we are usually looking for an accomplice.
5067 ABDOULAYE WADE/ PRESIDENT/SENEGAL	When one compensates, one erases.
5068 PUBLILIUS SYRUS/100 BC	He is a despicable sage whose wisdom does not profit himself.
5069 JAMES CONE/USA/ PROFESSOR	If you are a human being, you cannot realize your potential if other human beings cannot realize their potential.
5070 H.L. MENCKEN/USA/ EDITOR	Democracy is the theory that the common people know what they want and deserve to get it good and hard.
5071 MAIMONIDES/SCHOLAR	The physician should not treat the disease but the patient who is suffering from it.
5072 COMMUNICATION	The importance of written communication
5073 INDIAN PROVERB	Regularity is the best medicine.
5074 NAPOLEON HILL/ USA/AUTHOR	Think twice before you speak, because your words and influence will plant the seed of either success or failure in the mind of another.
5075 VOICE/IMAGE	Voice training
5076 PETER USTINOV/UK	Never confuse the size of your paycheck with the size of your talent.
5077 JIM ROHN/USA/SPEAKER	Motivation is what gets you started. Habit is what keeps you going.
5078 ENGLISH PROVERB	Better late than never.

NUMBER CATEGORY/CREDIT	TOPIC
5079 CHRISTY TURLINGTON/ SUPERMODEL/USA	I would rather go naked than wear fur.
5080 DESIGNER/DIANE von FURSTENBURG/USA	I didn't really know what I wanted to do, but I knew the woman I wanted to become.
5081 MAYA ANGELOU/USA/ AUTHOR & POET	How important it is for us to recognize and celebrate our heroes and she-roes!
5082 LUCIUS SENECA/ PHILOSOPHER	We are always complaining that our days are few, and acting as though there would be no end to them.
5083 KURT COBAIN/USA/ MUSICIAN	Drugs are a waste of time. They destroy your memory and your self-respect and every thing that goes along with your self-esteem. They're no good at all.
5084 MAGIC JOHNSON/ NBA BASKETBALL/USA	All kids need is a little help, a little hope and somebody who believes in them.
5085 INDIAN PROVERB	Something done at the wrong time should be regarded as not done.
5086 USA/ALEXANDER HAMILTON/LEADER	There is a certain enthusiasm in liberty, that makes human nature rise above itself, in acts of bravery and heroism.
5087 MORTIMER ADLER/ USA/PHILOSOPHER	There is only one situation I can think of in which men and women make an effort to read better than they usually do. It is when they are in love and reading a love letter.
5088 MOTHER JONES/USA/ ACTIVIST	Pray for the dead and fight like hell for the living.
5089 DEBATE	A recession is not as bad as people make it out to be.
5090 USA/RALPH WALDO EMERSON/POET	Ideas must work through the brains and the arms of good and brave men, or they are no better than dreams.
5091 CHINA	Naked marriage – "luo hun" / No house, no car, no ring, no wedding, no ceremony, no honeymoon kind of marriage.
5092 HEALTH/GREED	Food fraud – the sale of food products that are misrepresented in quality or substance
5093 McDONALD'S/USA	Hamburger University
5094 DR. MARTIN L. KING JR.	War is a poor chisel to carve out tomorrow.
5095 FRENCH/NAPOLEON BONAPARTE/LEADER	When I give a minister an order, I leave it to him to find the means to carry it out.
5096 JOHN K. GALBRAITH/US	War remains the decisive human failure.
5097 ITALY/NICCOLO MACHIAVELLI/WRITER	The new ruler must determine all the injuries that he will need to inflict. He must inflict them once and for all.
5098 LEADER/DR. MARTIN LUTHER KING JR.	We must learn to live together as brothers or perish together as fools.
5099 GEORGE SANTAYANA/US	There is no cure for birth and death save to enjoy the interval.
5100 ROBERT GUPTA/USA/ TEDTALK	Music is medicine, music is sanity.
5101 DAN BROWN/USA/ WRITER	I am a fan of the truth...even if it's painfully hard to accept.
5102 SOCIETY/POVERTY	Guns versus butter issue
5103 J. F. KENNEDY/USA	Leadership and learning are indispensable to each other.

NUMBER CATEGORY/CREDIT	TOPIC
5104 MOLIERE/FRENCH/ WRITER	Perfect reason avoids all extremes.
5105 HARRY S. TRUMAN/ USA/PRESIDENT	Men make history and not the other way around. In periods where there is no leadership, society stands still.
5106 JOHN K. GALBRAITH/ ECONOMIST	Wealth is not without its advantages and the case to the ontrarry, although it has often been made, has never proved widely persuasive.
5107 ALAN WATTS/USA/ WRITER	The only way to make sense of change is to plunge into it, move with it, and join the dance.
5108 DAN BROWN/USA/ AUTHOR/FICTION	Every generation's breakthroughs are proven false by the next generation's technology.
5109 ARNOLD PALMER/USA/ PROFESSIONAL GOLF	I never rooted against an opponent, but I never rooted for him either.
5110 USA/MARTIN LUTHER KING JR./CIVIL RIGHTS	Hate cannot drive out hate; only love can do that.
5111 STEPHEN COVEY/ USA/AUTHOR	Effective leadership is putting first things first. Effective management is discipline, carrying it out.
5112 MICHAEL JORDAN/ NBA/USA/BASKETBALL	The game is my wife. It demands loyalty and responsibility, and it gives me back fulfillment and peace.
5113 JACQUES BARZUN/ USA/WRITER	There was a time when Mr. Einstein was not quite sure what eight times nine came to. He had to learn and he had to be taught.
5114 KOREAN PROVERB	Catch not at the shadow and lose the substance.
5115 ALAN WATTS/USA/ WRITER	Zen does not confuse spirituality with thinking about God while one is peeling potatoes. Zen spirituality is just to peel the potatoes.
5116 ARABIC PROVERB	Meaningless laughter is a sign of ill-breeding.
5117 LI PEN/CHINA	Western-style elections are nothing but a game for the rich.
5118 CHARLES KETTERING/ USA/INVENTOR	Every time you tear a leaf off a calendar you present a new place for new ideas and progress.
5119 ST. AUGUSTINE	Great is the power of memory, a fearful thing.
5120 DR. BOYCE WATKINS/US	Even if you are a high-paid slave, you are still a slave.
5121 W.E.B. DU BOIS/USA	The problem of the 20th century is the problem of the color line.
5122 SOUTH AFRICA	Truth and Reconciliation Commission
5123 ANAIS NIN/WRITER/	Life shrinks or expands according to one's courage.
5124 ARTHUR ASHE/USA/ TENNIS PLAYER	True heroism is remarkably sober, very undramatic. It is not the urge to surpass all others at whatever cost, but the urge to serve others at whatever cost.
5125 MONITORING/SPYING	An electronic leash
5126 PETER THIEL/USA/ BUSINESS	All failed companies are the same: they failed to escape competition.
5127 KATHRYN BIGELOW/ DIRECTOR/USA	I suppose I like to think of myself as a filmmaker – not a female filmmaker.
5128 WRITER/MALCOLM GLADWELL/USA	Practice isn't the thing you do once you're good. It's the thing you do that makes you good.
5129 INDIA	The river Ganges
5130 MOLIERE/FRENCH	There is no protection against slander.

NUMBER CATEGORY/CREDIT	TOPIC
5131 CHARLES SWINDOLL/US	Life is 10% what happens to you and 90% how you react to it.
5132 KURT COBAIN/USA	A friend is nothing but a known enemy.
5133 YOSHIDA KENKO/ ESSAYS IN IDELENESS	As a rule the tales that get abroad in the world are false. People always exaggerate things.
5134 MATTHEW CHILDS/ TED.COM	Fear really sucks because what it means is you're not focusing on what you're doing.
5135 MAXWELL MALTZ/USA/ SURGEON	If you make friends with yourself, you'll never be alone.
5136 INDIAN PROVERB	That which blossoms must also decay.
5137 MACBETH/WILLIAM SHAKESPEARE	T'is safer to be that which we destroy Than by destruction dwell in doubtful joy.
5138 OSCAR WILDE/IRISH WRITER/POET	What is a cynic? A man who knows the price of everything and the value of nothing.
5139 GEORGE SANTAYANA/US	Those who cannot remember their past are condemned to repeat it.
5140 DR. BOYCE WATKINS/US/ FINANCE/PODCAST	George Fraser: We don't need more Ph.D's; we need more Ph.Do's.
5141 ANAIS NIN/WRITER	Living never wore out one so much as the effort not to live.
5142 PROTEST METHOD	Hunger strike
5143 MARTIN JACQUES/ TED.COM	The Chinese view the state, not just as an intimate member of the family… but as the head of the family.
5144 USA/J. F. KENNEDY	Mankind must put an end to war or war will put an end to mankind.
5145 PUBLILIUS SYRUS/ ANCIENT ROME/WRITER	What is left when honor is lost?
5146 DR. JOYCE BROTHERS/ USA/PSYCHOLOGIST	The world at large does not judge us by who we are and what we know; it judges us by what we have.
5147 ENGLISH PROVERB	Be not the first to quarrel, nor the last to make it up.
5148 USA/W.O. DOUGLAS	Common sense often makes good law.
5149 OSCAR WILDE/IRISH WRITER	Anyone who lives within their means suffers from a lack of imagination.
5150 SAVING/EDUCATION	Digital textbooks/e-textbook rental
5151 ENGLISH PROVERB	Better half a loaf than no bread.
5152 LOUISE NEVELSON/ USA/SCULPTOR	The freer that women become, the freer men will be. Because when you enslave someone, you are enslaved.
5153 TIM O'BRIEN/WAR/USA	War is hell, but that's not the half of it, because war is also mystery and terror and adventure and courage and holiness and pity and despair and longing and love.
5154 MALCOLM X/USA/ ACTIVIST	My alma mater was books, a good library…I could spend the rest of my life reading, just satisfying my curiosity.
5155 SAYING/NAIVETE	Bringing a knife to a gunfight.
5156 HISTORY	The past continues to speak to the present.
5157 PEOPLE/SOCIETY	Social awkwardness
5158 BILL GATES/USA	Life is not fair; get used to it.
5159 PUBLILIUS SYRUS/LATIN	We desire nothing so much as what we ought not to have.

NUMBER CATEGORY/CREDIT	TOPIC
5160 DAN BROWN/USA/ AUTHOR/FICTION	I consider myself a student of many religions. The more I learn, the more questions I have. For me, the spiritual quest will be a life-long work in progress.
5161 USA/BERNARD M. BARUCH/BUSINESS	The greatest blessing of our democracy is freedom. But in the last analysis, our only freedom is the freedom to discipline ourselves.
5162 PETER DRUCKER/USA/ MANAGEMENT GURU	So much of what we call management consists in making it difficult for people to work.
5163 YEVGENY ZAMYATIN/ SOVIET UNION/WRITER	A person is like a novel: Up to the very last page you don't know how it's going to end. Otherwise, there'd be no point in reading.
5164 ENVIRONMENT/TREES	Before you cut down a tree, think about how long it took to grow.
5165 ANAIS NIN/WRITER/ FEMINIST THINKER	I have the right to love many people at once and to change my prince often.
5166 RALPH ELLISON/USA/ WRITER/INVISIBLE MAN	Power doesn't have to show off. Power is confident, self-assuring, self-starting, and self-stopping, self-warming and self-justifying. When you have it, you know it.
5167 HARUKI MURAKAMI/ JAPAN/WRITER	If you're young and talented, it's like you have wings.
5168 JAPANESE PROVERB	Sitting on a stone for three years. / *Ishi no ue nimo sannen.*
5169 NATSUME SOSEKI/ JAPAN/WRITER	Under normal conditions, everybody is more or less good, or, at least, ordinary. But tempt them and they may suddenly change. That is what is so frightening about men.
5170 INDIAN PROVERB	Smiles that you broadcast will always come back to you.
5171 KATHRYN SCHULZ/USA/ TED.COM/REGRET	The point isn't to live without any regrets,. The point is to not hate ourselves for having them.
5172 ALAN WATTS/USA/ WRITER	When we attempt to exercise power or control over someone else, we cannot avoid giving that person the very same power or control over us.
5173 ALAN WATTS/USA/ WRITER	Muddy water is best cleared by leaving it alone.
5174 WILLIAM SAFIRE/USA	Don't overuse exclamation marks!!!
5175 GEORGE BURNS/USA/ COMEDIAN	Happiness is having a large, loving, caring, close-knit family in another city.
5176 JOHN K. GALBRAITH/ ECONOMIST	There are times in politics when you must be on the right side and lose.
5177 CONFUCIUS/CHINA/ PHILOSOPHER	When we see men of worth, we should think of equaling them; when we see men of a contrary character, we should turn inwards and examine ourselves.
5178 MADAME de STAEL/ FRENCH/WRITER	As we grow in wisdom, we pardon more freely.
5179 JAMES CLAVELL/USA/ WRITER	Wars are fought by teenagers, you realize that. They really ought to be fought by the politicians and old people who start these wars.
5180 SHOPPING/THRIFT	Impulse buying
5181 YOUTHFULNESS	The Peter Pan Syndrome
5182 MARTIN LUTHER KING JR./CIVIL RIGHTS/USA	The moral arc of the universe bends towards justice.

NUMBER CATEGORY/CREDIT	TOPIC
5183 ELEANOR HOLMES NORTON/USA	The only way to make sure people you agree with can speak is to support the rights of people you don't agree with.
5184 TONY BLAIR/UK/ PRIME MINISTER	The art of leadership is saying no, not saying yes. It is very easy to say yes.
5185 PETER THIEL/USA/ BUSINESS	The best entrepreneurs know this: every great business is built around a secret that's hidden from the outside. A great company is a conspiracy to change the world; when you share your secret, the recipient becomes a fellow conspirator.
5186 DAN BROWN/USA	Compassion is a universal language.
5187 EUGENE IONESCO/ FRENCH/PLAYWRIGHT	Why do people always expect authors to answer questions? I am an author because I want to ask questions. If I had answers, I'd be a politician.
5188 CHINESE PROVERB	Jade requires chiselling before becoming a gem.
5189 LOUISE ERDRICH/ WRITER/OJIBWE/USA	We do know that no one gets wise enough to really understand the heart of another, though it is the task of our life to try.
5190 MAXWELL MALTZ/USA	The most delightful surprise in life is to suddenly recognize your own worth.
5191 WEALTH/POVERTY	The digital divide
5192 DEBATE	It is better to value some employees over others because of differences in work
5193 JACQUES BARZUN/USA	Simple English is no one's mother tongue. It has to be worked for.
5194 FEAR	Acrophobia – Fear of heights
5195 EMINEM/USA/HIP HOP	I might talk about killing people, but that doesn't mean I'd do it.
5196 MAXINE HAIRSTON/ USA/WRITER/ADVICE	Whenever you can, write about people. In fact, adding people to your sentences may do more to make them clear than any other writing habit you could develop.
5197 AYN RAND/USA	A gun is not an argument.
5198 ARCHAEOLOGY/HISTORY	Cave drawings
5199 USA/W. E DEMING/ JAPAN/QUALITY	Any manager can do well in an expanding market.
5200 R.P. WARREN/USA/POET	Americans love a tragedy as long as it has a happy ending.
5201 ALAN FEUER/NY TIMES	The Monkey Theory: the higher you climb in life the more you are exposed.
5202 JAPAN/PROVERB	The nail that sticks out will be hammered down. (*Deru kui wa utareru*)
5203 LOUISE ERDRICH/USA	Things which do not grow and change are dead things.
5204 RADICAL/MERRIAM-WEBSTER.COM	Game Changer: a newly introduced element or factor that changes an existing situation or activity in a significant way.
5205 HARRY RATHBURN/USA	Everyone has a religion, whether he/she knows it or not.
5206 PETER THIEL/USA/ BUSINESS	Higher education is the place where people who had big plans in high school get stuck in fierce rivalries with equally smart peers over conventional careers like management consulting and investment banking.
5207 MONEY/LIFE/ HEALTH	Oxygen
5208 USA/TEDTALK/STANLEY McCHRYSTAL/ARMY	Leaders can let you fail and yet not let you be a failure.
5209 MARRIAGE/ABUSE	Women who hit their spouses/partners

NUMBER CATEGORY/CREDIT	TOPIC
5210 JOHN STEINBECK/ USA/WRITER	It is a common experience that a problem difficult at night resolves itself in the morning after the committee of sleep has worked on it.
5211 MICHIO KAKU/USA/ PHYSICIST/HYPERSPACE	Beyond work and love, I would add two other ingredients that give meaning to life. First, to fulfill whatever talents you were born with. ... second, we should try to leave the world a better place than when we entered it.
5212 JAMES THURBER/USA	He who hesitates is sometimes rear-ended.
5213 ALAN WATTS/USA/ WRITER	Problems that remain persistently insoluble should always be suspected as questions asked in the wrong way.
5214 VINCE LOMBARDI/USA	If you can accept losing, you can't win.
5215 USA/ALEXANDER HAMILTON	When the sword is once drawn, the passions of men observe no bounds of moderation.
5216 AMBROSE BIERCE/USA	Politeness: The most acceptable hypocrisy.
5217 DEVELOPMENT/KIDS	Blank slate
5218 STANLEY CROUCH/USA	Empathy is the strongest force between human beings.
5219 E.H. NORTON/USA	There is no reason to repeat bad history.
5220 MIDRASH/JEWISH COMMENTARY	When you arrive in the world, your hands are clenched, as though to say, "Everything is mine. I will inherit it all." When you depart from the world, your hands are open, as though to say, "I have acquired nothing from the world."
5221 ENGLISH PROVERB	Barking dogs seldom bite.
5222 RENE DESCARTES/ FRENCH PHILOSOPHER	...it is a mark of prudence never to place our complete trust in those who have deceived us even once.
5223 ALAN WATTS/USA/ WRITER	But I'll tell you what hermits realize. If you go off into a far, far forest and get very quiet, you'll come to understand that you're connected with everything.
5224 ANAIS NIN/WRITER/ FEMINIST THINKER	The final lesson a writer learns is that everything can nourish the writer. The dictionary, a new word, a voyage, an encounter, a talk on the steet, a book, a phrase learned.
5225 WAR/CHOICE/JUST WAR	War of necessity
5226 JOHN MAXWELL/USA	People buy into the leader before they buy into the vision.
5227 DAVID SHIELDS/USA	Anything processed by memory is false.
5228 JOHN WESLEY/ FOUNDER/ METHODIST CHURCH	Do all the good that you can, by all the means that you can, in all the ways that you can, in all the places that you can, at all the times that you can, to all the people you can, as long as ever you can.
5229 TECHNOLOGY	Web Luddites (people who refuse to use the Internet)
5230 HENRY GEORGE/ USA/ECONOMIST	What has destroyed every previous civilization has been the tendency to the unequal distribution of wealth and power.
5231 EDUCATION/CHOICE	Home-schooling
5232 DALE CARNEGIE/USA/ LECTURER/WRITER	You can't win an argument, because if you lose, you lose it; and if you win it you lose it.
5233 URSULA LeGUIN/ USA/WRITER	The power of the harasser, the abuser, the rapist depends above all on the silence of women.
5234 PARENTING	Time-out

NUMBER CATEGORY/CREDIT	TOPIC
5235 MILTON FRIEDMAN/ USA/ECONOMIST/ NOBEL LAUREATE	The great achievements of civilization have not come from government bureaus. Einstein didn't construct his theory under order from a bureaucrat.
5236 HARVEY MACKAY/ USA/BUSINESSMAN/ AUTHOR	Time is free, but it's priceless. You can't own it, but you can use it. You can't keep it, but you can spend it. Once you've lost it you can never get it back.
5237 JEAN BAPTISTE HENRI LACORDAIRE/ACTIVIST/ PREACHER/JOURNALIST	Neither genius, fame, nor love show the greatness of the soul. Only kindness can do that.
5238 EUGENE IONESCO/FRNC	The end of childhood is when things cease to astonish us.
5239 EMINEM/USA/HIP HOP	I need drama in my life to keep making music.
5240 BELLA ABZUG/USA/ POLITICIAN/US NEWS & WORLD REPORT	We don't want so much to see a female Einstein become an assistant professor. We want a woman schlemiel to get promoted as quickly as a male schlemiel.
5241 EDUCATION	Is there a difference between education and training?
5242 USA/MARIAN WRIGHT EDELMAN/ACTIVIST	Don't feel entitled to anything you didn't sweat and struggle for.
5243 US/HARRY EMERSON FOSDICK/PREACHER	A person wrapped up in himself makes a small package.
5244 ERASMUS/DUTCH	In the country of the blind, the one-eyed man is king.
5245 JIM ROHN/USA/ BUSINESS	Whoever renders service to many puts himself in line for greatness: great wealth, great return, great satisfaction, great reputation, and great joy.
5246 MILTON FRIEDMAN/USA	There's no such thing as a free lunch.
5247 INDIAN PROVERB	The hands of a lawyer are always in someone's pocket.
5248 BERTRAND RUSSELL/ UK/AUTHOR	Almost everything that distinguishes the modern world from earlier centuries is attributable to science.
5249 TUPAC SHAKUR/USA	Is it a crime to fight, for what is mine?
5250 GEORGE SANTAYANA/ SPANISH-AMERICAN	The young man who has not wept is a savage, and the old man who will not laugh is a fool.
5251 PUBLILIUS SYRUS	Ready tears are a sign of treachery, not of grief.
5252 MAHATMA GANDHI/ INDIAN LEADER	You must not lose faith in humanity. Humanity is an ocean; if a few drops of the ocean are dirty, the ocean does not become dirty.
5253 PETER GABRIEL/ MUSICIAN	I have always believed that if I can do it, anyone can. I think talent is overrated.
5254 LYING	Pathological liars
5255 DAN BROWN/USA/ AUTHOR/FICTION	Since the beginning of time, spirituality and religion have been called to fill in the gaps that science did not understand.
5256 ENGLISH PROVERB	A wise man changes his mind sometimes, a fool never.
5257 URSULA LeGUIN/USA/ WRITER	Morning comes whether you set the alarm or not.
5258 ENGLISH PROVERB	A wild goose never laid a tame egg
5259 HARUKI MURAKAMI/ (1Q 84)/JAPAN/WRITER	If you can love someone with your whole heart, even one person, then there's salvation in life. Even if you can't get together with that person.
5260 KAHLIL GIBRAN/POET	Your house shall be not an anchor but a mast.

NUMBER CATEGORY/CREDIT	TOPIC
5261 CARL HIASSEN/USA/ JOURNALIST	...fighting is for people who can't fight with their brains.
5262 ERASMUS/DUTCH	He who allows oppression shares the crime.
5263 LORD ACTON/UK	Power tends to corrupt and absolute power corrupts absolutely.
5264 N.D. KRISTOF/NY TIMES	Talent is universal, but opportunity is not.
5265 JOHN MAXWELL/USA/ CONSULTANT	A great leader's courage to fulfill his vision comes from passion, not position.
5266 THUCYDIDES/HISTORY	Of all manifestations of power, restraint impresses men the most.
5267 KANAE MINATO/JAPAN/ WRITER	Weak people find even weaker people to be their victims. And the victimized often feel that they have only two choices: put up with the pain or end their suffering in death. But they're wrong.
5268 RUSSIA/ALEKSANDR SOLZHENITSYN/WRITER	You only have power over people as long as you don't take everything away from them. But when you've robbed a man of everything, he's no longer in your power -- he's free again.
5269 DEBATE/SOCIAL WELFARE	Children in troubled homes should be placed only with extended family members, not foster parents unconnected to the children.
5270 MAHATMA GANDHI/ INDIAN LEADER	Nonviolence is the first article of my faith. It is also the last article of my creed.
5271 ALBERT EINSTEIN/ NOBEL WINNER/ PHYSICIST/NY TIMES	I believe in Spinoza's God who revelas Himself in the orderly harmony of what exists, not in a God who concerns himself with fates and actions o human beings.
5272 POLYBIUS/HISTORIAN	A good general not only sees the way to victory; he also knows when victory is impossible.
5273 J.D. SALINGER/USA/ AUTHOR	I am sick of just liking people. I wish to God I could meet somebody I could respect.
5274 MICHAEL JORDAN/USA	Talent wins games, but teamwork and intelligence wins championships.
5275 INDIAN PROVERB	Stolen sugar is the sweetest.
5276 J.K. ROWLING/UK/ AUTHOR	Youth cannot know how age thinks and feels. But old men are guilty if they forget what it was to be young.
5277 J.D. SALINGER/USA/ AUTHOR/THE CATCHER IN THE RYE	What really knocks me out is a book that, when you're all done reading it, you wish the author that wrote it was a terrific friend of yours and you could call him up on the phone whenever you felt like it. That doesn't happen much, though.
5278 CARL von CLAUSEWITZ/ PRUSSIAN GENERAL	Everything in war is very simple, but the simplest thing is difficult.
5279 ALAN WATTS/USA/ WRITER	The art of living...is neither careless drifting on the one hand nor fearful clinging to the past on the other. It consists in being sensitive to each moment, in regarding it as utterly new and unique, in having the mind open and wholly receptive.
5280 UK/WINSTON CHURCHILL	Courage is rightly esteemed the first of human qualities...because it is the quality which guarantees all others.
5281 ROSALYNN CARTER/ USA/FIRST LADY	A leader takes people where they want to go. A great leader takes people where they don't necessarily want to go, but ought to be.
5282 DEAN ACHESON/USA/ STATESMAN	A memorandum is written not to inform the reader but to protect the writer.

NUMBER CATEGORY/CREDIT	TOPIC
5283 MADELEINE L'ENGLE/ USA/WRITER	Inspiration usually comes during work.
5284 ELBERT GREEN HUBBARD/USA	If men will not act for themselves, what will they do when the benefit of their effort is for all?
5285 STEPHEN COVEY/ USA/AUTHOR	The ability to subordinate an impulse to a value is the essence of the proactive person.
5286 INDIAN PROVERB	The heart at rest sees a feast in everything.
5287 KAHLIL GIBRAN/POET	Work is love made visible.
5288 URSULA LeGUIN/USA	To light a candle is to cast a shadow.
5289 DEBATE	That formal schooling is a waste of time.
5290 ENGLISH PROVERB	A thing begun is half done.
5291 BERNARD M. BARUCH	Never follow the crowd.
5292 ROLE PLAY	Change of plans – need to call off attending a friend's party
5293 CHARLES DE GAULLE/ FRANCE/PRESIDENT	I have come to the conclusion that politics are too serious a matter to be left to the politicians.
5294 PUBLILIUS SYRUS	Treat your friend as if he might become an enemy.
5295 OPINION/DEBATE	Students' evaluation of teachers
5296 JANET EVANOVICH/ USA/WRITER	There is no such thing as a call at 7 AM. It's been my experience that all calls between the hours of 11 PM and 9 AM are disaster calls.
5297 ENGLISH PROVERB	As you sow, so you shall reap
5298 MAO TSETUNG/CCP/ CHAIRMAN/CHINA	We think too small, like the frog at the bottom of the well. He thinks the sky is only as big as the top of the well. If he surfaced, he would have an entirely different view.
5299 WHO/HEALTH/RISK	Mobile phone radiation poses possible cancer risk.
5300 DEBATE/PERSONAL	University students should not be forced to attend classes.
5301 CODE OF SILENCE/ WIKIPEDIA	A code of silence is a condition in effect when a person opts to withhold what is believed to be vital or important information voluntarily or involuntarily.
5302 WOMEN/SUCCESS	Is having a family the enemy of female achievement?
5303 ROLES	Wearing many hats
5304 KEIKO HIGUCHI/ DAILY YOMIURI/JAPAN	Divorce can be 'the end of unhappiness' for couples, but 'the start of unhappiness' for their children.
5305 BARBARA JORDAN/ USA/CONGRESS	If you're going to play the game properly, you'd better know every rule.
5306 REINHOLD NIEBUHR/ USA/THEOLOGIAN	The tendency to claim God as an ally for our partisan value and ends is the source of all religious fanaticism.
5307 DEBORAH TANNEN/USA	Silence can be a matter of saying nothing and meaning something.
5308 CICERO/ROMAN ORATOR	The shifts of Fortune test the reliability of friends.
5309 HARRY EMERSON FOSDICK/USA	God is not a cosmic bellboy for whom we can press a button to get things.
5310 MADELEINE L'ENGLE/ USA/WRITER	We tend to think things are new because we've just discovered them.

NUMBER CATEGORY/CREDIT	TOPIC
5311 DAVID LIVINGSTONE/UK	Sympathy is no substitute for action.
5312 USA/ISAAC BASHEVIS SINGER/WRITER	I believe in God but people are liars. It's those people who say they are appointed by God who I don't believe in.
5313 SAM WALTON/USA/ FOUNDER/WALMART	Outstanding leaders go out of their way to boost the self-esteem of their personnel. If people believe in themselves, it's amazing what they can accomplish.
5314 JOHN RUSKIN/UK/ ART CRITIC	Taste is the only morality. Tell me what you like and I'll tell you what you are.
5315 MAHATMA GANDHI/ INDIAN LEADER	SEVEN SOCIAL SINS: 1) Politics without principles
5316 DEBATE	That we should we pay attention to what celebrities have to say
5317 OPINION/DEBATE	Contributions of artists versus those of scientists
5318 GERMAN/FRIEDRICH NIETZSCHE/THINKER	He who fights with monsters might take care lest he thereby become a monster.
5319 HAITIAN PROVERB	Behind the mountains are more mountains.
5320 LEO TOLSTOY/ RUSSIAN NOVELIST	Everyone thinks of changing humanity and nobody thinks of changing himself.
5321 LATIN PROVERB	Peace is the best medicine.
5322 STEPHEN COVEY/ USA/AUTHOR	At sometime in your life, you probably had someone believe in you when you didn't believe in yourself.
5323 PERSONAL SPACE/ PREFERENCE	If you could change one thing about your living place, what would it be and why?
5324 HARUKI MURAKAMI/ JAPAN/WRITER	Most runners run not because they want to live longer, but because they want to live life to the fullest.
5325 ADVICE/ EDUCATION	Advice for a student who wants to get good grades
5326 JOHN GODFREY SAXE/ AMERICAN POET	I love vast libraries; yet there is a doubt, / If one be better with them or without, / Unless he use them wisely, and, indeed, / Knows the high art of what and how to read
5327 DEBATE/PEOPLE	War is good for the economy.
5328 DEBATE	Unhappy couples should stay married for the sake of their children.
5329 ABUSE	Physical scars versus mental scars
5330 TEACHERS	Student evaluation of teachers
5331 EASY TARGET	Low hanging fruit
5332 SMOKING/HEALTH	Anti-smoking movement
5333 CHARLES SCHULZ/USA	Happiness is a warm puppy.
5334 CALVIN COOLIDGE/USA	I have never been hurt by what I have not said.
5335 HARVEY McKAY/USA/ BUSINESS	Unless you work in demolition, don't burn bridges.
5336 HARVEY MACKAY/ USA/WRITER	One sure-fire way to stay creative; force yourself to learn something new.
5337 DEBATE	That governments should censor material on the World Wide Web.
5338 MITCH ALBOM/USA/ WRITER	Don't let go too soon, but don't hold on too long.

NUMBER CATEGORY/CREDIT	TOPIC
5339 J.D. SALINGER/USA	I'm sick of not having the courage to be an absolute nobody.
5340 EDVARD MUNCH/ NORWAY/PAINTER	My fear of life is necessary to me, as is my illness. Without anxiety and illness, I am a ship without a rudder. My art is grounded in reflections over being different from others.
5341 ANN LANDERS/ USA/ADVICE	Nobody gets to live life backward. Look ahead, that is where your future lies.
5342 MILITARY/DOUGLAS MacARTHUR/USA/ LEADER	A true leader has the confidence to stand alone, the courage to make tough decisions, and the compassion to listen to the needs of others. He does not set out to be a leader, but becomes one by the equality of his actions and the integrity of his intent.
5343 MARIAN WRIGHT EDELMAN/USA	Children don't vote but adults who do must stand up and vote for them.
5344 JOHN BARRYMORE/USA	A man is not old until regrets take the place of dreams.
5345 QUEEN ELIZABETH I/UK	A clean and innocent conscience fears nothing.
5346 USA/SANDRA DAY O'CONNOR/JUDGE	The power I exert on the court depends on the power of my arguments, not on my gender.
5347 W. CLEMENT STONE/ USA/BUSINESSMAN	We have a problem. 'Congratulations.' But it's a tough problem. 'Then double congratulations.'
5348 STEVE IRWIN/THE CROCODILE HUNTER	If we can teach people about wildlife, they will be touched. Share my wildlife with me. Because humans want to save things that they love.
5349 JOHN ADAMS/USA/ PRESIDENT	Great is the guilt of an unnecessary war.
5350 BENJAMIN DISRAELI/UK	Everyone likes flattery.
5351 BUSINESS	Family-run businesses
5352 DELAY/DECISIONS	Analysis paralysis
5353 POLITICAL TACTIC	Filibuster
5354 SCHOOL/SOCIETY	Uniform expectations
5355 STEVE JOBS, APPLE CO-FOUNDER	The benefit of death is you know not to waste life living someone else's choices.
5356 JOHN KENNETH GALBRAITH/ ECONOMIST	The salary of the chief executive of a large corporation is not a market award for achievement. It is frequently in the nature of a warm personal gesture by the individual to himself.
5357 DR. BOYCE WATKINS/ USA/PROFESSOR	You can't look to someone who hates you to tell you that you are worthy.
5358 INSULARITY/ ISOLATION	Galapagos syndrome (e.g., Japanese companies' fixation on the Japanese market, etc)
5359 CHARLES LAMB/UK/ CRITIC	I love to lose myself in other men's minds. When I am not walking, I am reading.
5360 MADAME de STAEL/FR.	The greatest happiness is to transform one's feelings into action.
5361 PAULO COELHO/BRAZIL	Beauty is the greatest seducer of man.
5362 TIMOTHY FERRIS / AUTHOR/USA	"Someday" is a disease that will take your dreams to the grave with you.
5363 JOHN K. GALBRAITH/ ECONOMIST	Wealth, in even the most improbable cases, manages to convey the aspect of intelligence.

NUMBER CATEGORY/CREDIT	TOPIC
5364 JIM ROHN/USA/ MOTIVATIONAL SPEAKER/SUCCESS	The challenge of leadership is to be strong, not rude; be kind, not weak; be bold, but not bully; be thoughtful, but not lazy; be humble, but not timid; be proud, but not arrogant; have humor, but without folly.
5365 J.D. SALINGER/USA	Mothers are all slightly insane.
5366 SAYING	You can't ride two horses with one arse.
5367 ELEANOR HOLMES NORTON/USA/LAWYER/ EDUCATOR	Affirmative action is the most important modern anti-discrimination technique ever instituted in the United States. It is the one tool that has had a demonstrable effect on discrimination.
5368 FLANNERY O'CONNOR/USA/ WRITER	Everywhere I go I'm asked if I think the university stifles writers. My opinion is that they don't stifle enough of them. There's many a best-seller that could have been prevented by a good teacher.
5369 ALAN WATTS/WRITER/ USA	How is it possible that a being with such sensitive jewels as the eyes, such enchanted musical instruments as the ears, and such fabulous arabesque of nerves as the brain, can experience itself as anything less than a god.
5370 IRISH/WILLIAM BUTLER YEATS/POET/NOBEL LAUREATE	I have believed the best of every man. And find that to believe is enough to make a bad man show him at his best, or even a good man swing his lantern higher.
5371 W. CLEMENT STONE/USA	Definitiveness of purpose is the starting point of all achievement.
5372 JOHN RUSKIN/UK/ ENGLISH ART CRITIC	You should read books like you take medicine, by advice, and not by advertisement.
5373 ALAN WATTS/WRITER/ USA	The menu is not the meal.
5374 MADELEINE L'ENGLE/ USA/WRITER	Artistic temperament sometimes seems a battleground, a dark angel of destruction and a bright angel of creativity wrestling.
5375 VICTORIA BECKHAM/ UK/DESIGNER	If you haven't got it. Fake it! Too short? Wear big high heels, but do practice walking!
5376 HARRY BELAFONTE/USA	You can cage the singer but not the song.
5377 MACBETH/WILLIAM SHAKESPEARE	Things without all remedy should be without regard: what's done is done.
5378 SENECA/DRAMATIST	No one can wear a mask for very long.
5379 WORKPLACE	Importance of one's relationship with one's co-workers
5380 FUN/WASTE	The Ig Nobel Prize: honors research that cannot or should not be reproduced
5381 DEBATE	Corporations have no heart.
5382 EUGENE IONESCO/ ROMANIA/FRENCH	A writer never has a vacation. For a writer, life consists of either writing or thinking about writing.
5383 E.M. REMARQUE/FRNC	To forget is the secret of eternal youth. One grows old only through memory.
5384 SAMUEL SMILES/SCOT	Hope...is the companion of power, and the mother of success; for who so hopes has within him the gift of miracles.
5385 SAMUEL SMILES/SCOT	A place for everything, and everything in its place.
5386 DEBATE	That school prepares us for life.
5387 OVID/ROMAN POET	A leader should be slow to punish and swift to reward.
5388 POLITICS/USA	Bipartisanship

NUMBER CATEGORY/CREDIT	TOPIC
5389 ANN LANDERS/ USA/ADVICE	Too many people know the price of everything and the value of nothing.
5390 HARVEY MACKAY/ USA/WRITER	A mediocre person tells. A good person explains. A superior person demonstrates. A great person inspires others to see for themselves.
5391 BRUCE BARTON/USA/ AUTHOR	If you can give your son or daughter only one gift, let it be enthusiasm.
5392 USA/BERNARD M. BARUCH/FINANCIER	Millions saw the apple fall, but Newton was the one who asked why.
5393 MARIAN WRIGHT EDELMAN/USA/ WRITER/ACTIVIST	When Jesus Christ asked little children to come to him, he didn't say only rich children, or White children, who didn't have a mental or physical handicap. He said, "Let all children come unto me."
5394 DEBATE	That patience is overrated
5395 PARENTING	Some things your parents did but you would never think of doing to your children
5396 JOHN BARRYMORE/ USA/ACTOR	In Genesis, it says that it is not good for a man to be alone; but sometimes it is a great relief.
5397 GEORGE ELIOT/UK/ AUTHOR	I am open to conviction on all points except dinner and debts. I hold that the one must be eaten and the other paid. Those are my only prejudices.
5398 ROBERT GATES/USA/ DEFENSE/WAPO	A self-confident leader doesn't cast a large shadow that no one else can grow.
5399 USA/RABBI SHMULEY BOTEACH	Every politician is a narcissist.
5400 LAO-TZU/CHINESE PHILOSPHER	The softest things in the world overcome the hardest things in the world.
5401 PETER THIEL/USA/ BUSINESS	Selling your company to the media is an essential part of selling it to everyone else.
5402 DANIEL J. BOORSTIN/ LIBRARIA /US CONGRESS	It is not skeptics or explorers but fanatics and ideologues who menace decency and progress.
5403 HARVEY MACKAY/USA	For the real winners, there are no finish lines.
5404 ANDREW CARNEGIE/ USA/BUSINESS	No man will make a great leader who wants to do it all himself, or to get all the credit for doing it.
5405 J.D. SALINGER/USA	People are always ruining things for you.
5406 CHARLES BARKLEY/ USA/BASKETBALL	You know it's going to hell when the best rapper out there is white and the best golfer is black.
5407 ROSEANNE BARR/ USA/ACTRESS	The thing women have yet to learn is nobody gives you power. You just take it.
5408 MADELEINE L'ENGLE/ USA/WRITER	Truth is eternal. Knowledge is changeable. It is disastrous to confuse them
5409 JOSEPH CONRAD/UK; WRITER	It's only those who do nothing that make no mistakes, I suppose.
5410 HARVEY MACKAY/ USA/WRITER	Anyone too busy to say thank you will get fewer and fewer chances to say it.
5411 RUSSIA/ALEKSANDR SOLZHENITSYN/WRITER	As the 2000 year old saying goes, 'You can have eyes and still not see." But a hard life improves vision.

NUMBER CATEGORY/CREDIT	TOPIC
5412 SPENCER JOHNSON/USA	What would you do if you weren't afraid?
5413 SANDRA DAY O'CONNOR/JUDGE/ USA/SUPREME COURT	The courts of this country should not be the places where resolution of disputes begins. They should be the places where the disputes end after alternative methods of resolving disputes have been considered and tried.
5414 STANISLAW LEM/POLISH WRITER/SCI-FICTION	When smashing monuments, save the pedestals. They always come in handy.
5415 SAMUEL JOHNSON/ UK/AUTHOR	We do not always find visible happiness in proportion to visible virtue.
5416 GEORGE ELIOT/UK	There are glances of hatred that stab, and raise no cry of murder.
5417 GEORGE S. CLASON/ UK/AUTHOR	Advice is one thing that is freely given away, but watch that you only take what is worth having.
5418 BETTY FRIEDAN/ USA/WRITER	Chosen motherhood is the real liberation. The choice to have a child makes the whole experience of motherhood different...
5419 ETHEL BARRYMORE/USA	The best time to make friends is before you need them.
5420 ANTHONY ROBBINS/USA	Awaken the giant within
5421 ENGLISH PROVERB	A small leak will sink a great ship.
5422 MORTIMER ADLER/ USA/PHILOSOPHER	The ultimate end of education is happiness or a good human life, a life enriched by the possession of every kind of good, by the enjoyment of every type of satisfaction.
5423 LEO TOLSTOY/WRITER	The best stories don't come from "good vs. bad" but "good vs good."
5424 BARRY DILLER/USA/ ENTREPRENEUR	The only thing anyone should pay attention to, entrepreneur or not, is what intrigues them, what they're passionate about.
5425 BEVERAGE/SLOGAN	Red Bull gives you wings.
5426 CHARLIE CHAPLIN/USA	Life could be wonderful if people would leave you alone.
5427 NATALIE GOLDBERG/ USA/WRITER	Write what disturbs you, what you fear, what you have not been willing to speak about.
5428 CHALLENGE	Upsetting the status quo
5429 ANGER	Losing control
5430 ANN LANDERS/USA/ ADVICE COLUMNIST	Anyone who believes the competitive spirit in America is dead has never been in a supermarket when the cashier opens another check-out line.
5431 MORTIMER ADLER/ USA/ PHILOSOPHER	...always keep in mind that an article of faith is not something that the faithful assume. Faith, for those who have it, is the most certain form of knowledge, not a tentative opinion.
5432 HARD WORK	Burning the candle at both ends
5433 PETER THIEL/USA/ BUSINESS	People who sell advertising are called "account executives." People who sell customers work in "business development." People who sell companies are "investment bankers." And people who sell themselves are called "politicians." There's a reason for these redescriptions: none of us wants to be reminded when we're being sold.
5434 ERIN CASEY/MARIA SHRIVER-IT'S TIME	When women are happy, healthy, strong and financially stable, their families and communities reap the benefits.
5435 ODETTA/USA/ SINGER/GUITARIST	Human beings have language skills other than just verbal: we read each other. When performing, there is true communication. I get energy from the audience, and they get energy from me.

NUMBER CATEGORY/CREDIT	TOPIC
5436 GENERAL DWIGHT EINSENHOWER/USA/	Leadership is the art of getting someone else to do something you want done because he wants to do it.
5437 STANISLAW LEM/SCIFI	The only writers who have any peace are the ones who don't write.
5438 JOYCE CAROL OATES/ USA/NOVELIST	When people say there is too much violence in my books, what they are saying is there is too much reality in life.
5439 DR. WAYNE DYER/ USA/WRITER	My goal is not to be better than anyone else, but to be better than I used to be.
5440 CHINESE PROVERB	A spark can start a fire that burns the entire prairie.
5441 SAYING	Hindsight is always 20-20.
5442 LATIN PROVERB	If you want peace, prepare for war.
5443 CARL von CLAUSEWITZ/ PRUSSIAN GENERAL	The conqueror is always a lover of peace; he would prefer to take over our country unopposed.
5444 DEBATE	This house believes in fighting fire with fire.
5445 FANTASY/MARRIAGE	Happily ever after
5446 MARK TWAIN/USA/ WRITER	Twenty years from now you will be more disappointed by the things you didn't do than by the ones you did. So throw off the bowlines, sail away from the safe harbor. Catch the trade winds in your sails. Explore. Dream.
5447 ALAN TURING/UK/ SCIENTIST	Sometimes it is the people who no one imagines anything of who do the things no one can imagine.
5448 VOLUNTEERING	Raising money for disaster relief
5449 ALAN WATTS/USA/ WRITER	A scholar tries to learn something everyday; a student of Buddhism tries to unlearn something daily.
5450 JOSEPH SMITH JR/USA	If my life is of no value to my friends it is of none to myself.
5451 RUSSIA/ALEKSANDR SOLZHENITSYN/WRITER	The salvation of mankind lies only in making everything the concern of all.
5452 JILL BECKER/ SUCCESS MAGAZINE	When it comes to building a business, small steps can make the biggest impact.
5453 KANAE MINATO/ JAPAN/WRITER/ CONFESSIONS	The world you live in is much bigger than that. If the place in which you find yourself is too painful, I say you should be free to seek another, less painful place of refuge. There is no shame in seeking a safe place. I want you to believe that somewhere in this wide world there is a place for you, a safe haven.
5454 PLATO/THE REPUBLIC	He who is of calm and happy nature will hardly feel the pressure of age, but to him who is of an opposite disposition youth and age are equally a burden.
5455 RELATIONSHIPS	Learning how to compromise is an important social skill.
5456 HEALTH	Music therapy
5457 ZIG ZIGLAR/USA	Build a foundation of pure trust through communication and love.
5458 COURAGE	Speaking truth to power
5459 JAPAN/SAMURAI CODE	Rather die than disgrace yourself.
5460 NICHOLAS D. KRISTOF/ NY TIMES/USA	Education is the grandest accelerant for human potential.
5461 STANISLAW LEM/ POLISH WRITER	We have no need of other worlds. We need mirrors...A single world, our own, suffices us; but we can't accept it for what it is.

NUMBER CATEGORY/CREDIT	TOPIC
5462 MURIEL RUKEYSER/ USA/POET	The universe is made of stories, not of atoms.
5463 GEORGIA O'KEEFFE/ USA/ARITST	I've been absolutely terrified every moment of my life -- and I've never let it keep me from doing a single thing I wanted to do.
5464 ERIC HOFFER/USA/ MORAL PHILOSOPHER	The leader has to be practical and a realist yet must talk the languaage of the visionary and the idealist.
5465 STANISLAW LEM/ POLISH WRITER	A writer should not run around with a mirror for his countrymen; he should tell his society and his times things no one ever thought before.
5466 COST OF LIVING	Retiring overseas
5467 LEADERSHIP	Speechwriting
5468 J.D. SALINGER/USA/ AUTHOR	An artist's only concern is to shoot for some kind of perfection, and on his own terms, not anybody else's.
5469 CHINESE PROVERB	One never so much needs his wit, as when he argues with a fool.
5470 INDECISION	Flip-flopping
5471 SELF-PITY/CALAMITY	Why me?
5472 DEBATE	That humanity has lost its way.
5473 LATIN PROVERB	Viewed from a distance, everything is beautiful.
5474 CHINESE SAYING	Covering one's ear when pilfering a bell.
5475 HUMAN RIGHTS	Human rights activists
5476 PREDICTION	Changes you expect in the 21st century
5477 HONOR/HOLIDAYS	If you could create a new holiday for whom or what would it be for?
5478 MAXWELL MALTZ/ SURGEON/USA	Our self-image and our habits tend to go together. Change one and you will automatically change the other.
5479 ARABIC PROVERB	No cure, no pay.
5480 AYN RAND/THINKER	A culture is made – or destroyed – by its articulate voices.
5481 ELIA KAZAN/USA/ WRITER/ACTOR	I question the value of stars. I think they're overrated. They get too much money, too much praise.
5482 AMY GOODMAN/USA	Go to where the silence is and say something.
5483 DAVID J. SCHWARTZ/US	The mind is what the mind is fed.
5484 ALAN WATTS/USA/ WRITER	The meaning of life is just to be alive. It is so plain and so obvious and so simple. And yet, everybody rushes around in a great panic as if it were necessary to achieve something beyond themselves.
5485 MARIA SHRIVER/USA	Life changes can bring opportunities.
5486 HARVEY MACKAY/USA	Failures don't plan to fail; they fail to plan.
5487 GEORGIA O'KEEFFE/ USA/ARTIST	The days you work are the best days.
5488 MAX LUCADO/USA/ PREACHER	A man who wants to lead the orchestra must turn his back on the crowd.
5489 BETTY FRIEDAN/ USA/WRITER/	A girl should not expect special privileges because of her sex, but neither should she "adjust" to prejudice and discrimination.
5490 USA/HOLIDAY	Kwanzaa
5491 HARVEY MACKAY/USA	Be like a postage stamp. Stick to it until you get there.

NUMBER CATEGORY/CREDIT	TOPIC
5492 BRIAN TRACY/USA/ SUCCESS COACH	Leaders think and talk about the solutions. Followers think and talk about the problems.
5493 STANISLAW LEM/ POLISH WRITER/ SCIENCE FICTION	The fate of a single man can be rich with significance, that of a few hundred less so, but the history of thousands and millons of men does not mean anything at all, in any adequate sense of th world.
5494 PROVERB	The noblest vengeance is to forgive.
5495 CLASSROOM	Interactive classroom versus lectures
5496 EXPERIENCE	Experience of being in a new school or workplace
5497 CHOICE	You have money to buy either a business or a house
5498 YOSHIMOTO BANANA/ JAPAN/WRITER/ASLEEP	I really believe that no matter how old people get, they tend to change in certain ways depending on how people treat them - they change their colors.
5499 RANDY PAUSCH/ USA/COMPUTER SCIENTIST/THE LAST LECTURE	Wait long enough and people will surprise and impress. When you're pissed off at someone and you're angry at them, you just haven't given them enough time. Just give them a little more time and they almost always will impress you.
5500 OPINION	Creationism versus evolution
5501 LEADERSHIP/GLOBAL	World leaders
5502 JEWISH HOLIDAYS	Hanukkah
5503 MORTIMER ADLER/ USA/PHILOSOPHER	One of the most embarrassing problems for the nineteenth-century champions of the Christian faith was that not one of the first six Presidents of the United States was an orthodox Christian.
5504 YOSHIMOTO BANANA/ JAPAN/WRITER	There is no reason anyone would want a computer in their home.
5505 EDUCATION	Distance learning
5506 E.B. WHITE/USA/ WRITER	Humor can be dissected, as a frog can, but the thing dies in the process and the innards are discouraging to any but the pure scientific mind.
5507 bell hooks/USA/ WRITER/ PROFESSOR	It is necessary to remember, as we think critically about domination, that we all have the capacity to act in ways that oppress, dominate, wound (whether or not that power is institutionalized).
5508 JOHN GRISHAM/USA/ WRITER	All students enter law school with a certain amount of idealism and desire to serve the public, but after three years of brutal competition we care for nothing but the right job with the right firm, where we can make partner in seven years and earn big bucks.
5509 FLANNERY O'CONNOR/ USA/WRITER	The truth does not change according to our ability to stomach it.
5510 AMY GOODMAN/USA	The media – stenographers to power.
5511 TINA SEELIG/USA/ PROFESSOR	One of the things that people do to get in their own way is to take on way too many responsibilities.
5512 MAIMONIDES/THE GUIDE FOR THE PERPLEXED	We naturally like what we have been accustomed to, and are attracted towards it. The same is the case with those opinions of man to which he has been accustomed from his youth; he likes them, defends them, and shuns the opposite views.
5513 ENGLISH PROVERB	An ounce of prevention is worth a pound of cure.

NUMBER CATEGORY/CREDIT	TOPIC
5514 HARVEY MACKAY/USA	Believe in yourself even when no one else does.
5515 J.D. SALINGER/USA/ AUTHOR/FRANNY & ZOOEY	I'm just sick of ego, ego. My own and everybody else's. I'm sick of everybody that wants to get somewhere, do something distinguished and all, be somebody interesting. It's digusting.
5516 STANISLAW LEM/ POLISH WRITER	I never read to kill time. Killing time is like killing somone's wife or a child. There is nothing more precious to me than time.
5517 DEBATE	Childhood is the most important part of life.
5518 DEBATE	It is useless to read fiction.
5519 PETER THIEL/USA/ BUSINESS/INVESTOR	The lawyers I worked with ran a valuable business, and they were impressive individuals one by one. But the relationships between them were oddly thin. They spent all day together, but few of them seemed to have much to say to each other outside the office. Why work with a group of people who don't even like each other?
5520 DEBATE	Only people who make big money can be considered truly successful.
5521 TRAVEL/ASPIRATION	A foreign country you must visit
5522 D.H. LAWRENCE/UK/ NOVELIST	All our troubles, says somebody wise, come upon us because we cannot be alone.
5523 PARENTS/NEGLECT	Parents who leave young children alone in a car for extended periods.
5524 JOEL A. BARKER/USA/ FUTURIST/WRITER	A leader is a person you will follow to a place you wouldn't go by yourself.
5525 TYRA BANKS/USA/ MODEL/BUSINESS	I love the confidence that makeup gives me.
5526 WORK/FULFILLMENT	Giving 110%
5527 TAMMY F. BAKKER/USA	I always say shopping is cheaper than a psychiatrist.
5528 ROGER BANNISTER/UK/ PHYSICIAN/ATHLETE	The man who can drive himself further once the effort gets painful is the man who will win.
5529 CAMILLE PAGLIA/ USA/FEMINIST	It is woman's destiny to rule men. Not to serve them, flatter them, or hang on them for guidance. Nor to insult them, demean them, or stereotype them as oppressors.
5530 JOHN ADAMS/USA/ PRESIDENT	Because power corrupts, society's demands for moral authority and character increase as the importance of the position increases.
5531 RELIGION/SOCIAL ENCAPSULATION/CULT	Social encapsulation – when people live their lives in a community or in relation to one another but remain separate from the general society
5532 JULES VERNE/FRENCH/ AUTHOR/	Great robbers always resemble honest folk. Fellows who have rascally faces have only one course to take, and that is to remain honest; otherwise, they would be arrested off-hand.
5533 MARIA SHRIVER/USA	Success is being...the kind of woman that I would want as a friend.
5534 STANISLAW LEM/ POLISH WRITER/ SCIENCE FICTION	There are friends with whom we share neither interests nor any particular experiences, friends with whom we never correspond, whom we seldom meet and then only by chance, but whose existence nonetheless has for us a special if uncanny meaning.
5535 PROVERB	He who waits for dead men's shoes may go barefoot.
5536 HEALTH	Psychological wounds
5537 PEOPLE	Extroverts

NUMBER CATEGORY/CREDIT	TOPIC
5538 D.H. LAWRENCE/UK/ WRITER	Here's to the thorn in the flower.
5539 GENERAL GEORGE PATTON/USA/LEADER	Never tell people how to do things. Tell them what to do and they will surprise you with their ingenuity.
5540 STANISLAW LEM/SCIFI	Is a mountain only a huge stone?
5541 GERMAN PROVERB	More are drowned in the bottle than in the ocean.
5542 JOEL A. BARKER/USA	Your successful past will block your visions of the future.
5543 DEBATE	Young people have nothing to teach their elders.
5544 DEBATE	Children must receive gifts from time to time.
5545 ABUSE/DISCIPLINE	Corporal punishment
5546 ENGLISH PROVERB	An idle brain is the devil's workshop.
5547 SANTA CLAUS/XMAS	Bringing Christmas cheer to children
5548 CAMILLE PAGLIA/ USA/FEMINIST	If civilization had been left in female hands, we would still be living in grass huts.
5549 CUSTOMS/TRADITION	Customs in your country that you feel are outdated
5550 INDIRA GANDHI/INDIA/ O. FALLACI INTERVIEW	There exists no politician in India daring enough to attempt to explain to the masses that cows can be eaten.
5551 JOAN BAEZ/USA/ FOLK SINGER	If it's natural to kill, how come men have to go into training to learn how?
5552 PERSONAL/OPINION	If you could go back, what you would change about your education.
5553 JOSEPHINE BAKER/ USA/SINGER	A violinist had a violin, a painter his palette. All I had was myself. I was the instrument that I must care for.
5554 ROBERT GATES/USA/ DEFENSE/WAPO	A further quality of leadership is courage; not just the physical courage of the seas, of the skies and of the trenches, but moral courage.
5555 SERVICE/QUALITY	Making complaints about a product or service
5556 ABRAHAM LINCOLN/ 16th PRESIDENT/USA	When I do good, I feel good; when I do bad, I feel bad, and that is my religion.
5557 REBUILDING	Post-disaster reconstruction
5558 TINA SEELIG/USA/ PROFESSOR/BUSINESS	Never miss an opportunity to be fabulous.
5559 WILLIAM SHAKESPEARE/ UK/PLAYWRIGHT	The eyes are the windows to the soul.
5560 NEGOTIATION	"Nice to have" versus "Must have"
5561 ZHUANGZI/ CHINESE PHILOSOPHER	If a man crosses a river and an empty boat collides with his own skiff, Even though he be a bad tempered man / He will not become very angry. But if he sees a man in the boat, He will shout at him to steer clear. If the shout is not heard, he will shout again, and yet again, and begin cursing. And all because someone is in the boat. Yet if the boat were empty, He would not be shouting, and not be angry.
5562 C. H. DUELL/ DIR./US PATENT OFFICE/1899	Everything that can be invented has already been invented.
5563 HARVEY MACKAY/USA/ BUSINESS	When you're thirsty, it's too late to think about digging a well.

NUMBER CATEGORY/CREDIT	TOPIC
5564 D.H. LAWRENCE/UK/ POET/NOVELIST	The dead don't die. They look on and help.
5565 JARED DIAMOND/ USA/AUTHOR/GUNS, GERMS AND STEEL	History followed different courses for different peoples because of differences among people's environments, not because of biological diffences among peoples themselves.
5566 ANTHONY BOURDAIN/ CHEF/AUTHOR	Vegetarians are the enemy of everything good and decent in the human spirit, an affront to all I stand for, the pure enjoyment of food.
5567 J.D. SALINGER/USA/ AUTHOR	The mark of the immature man is that he wants to die nobly for a cause, while the mark of the mature man is that he wants to live humbly for one.
5568 STANISLAW LEM/ POLISH WRITER	When you jump for joy, beware that no one moves the ground from beneath your feet.
5569 PROVERB	Little strokes fell great oaks.
5570 CLAUS von CLAUSEWITZ/ PRUSSIAN GENERAL	There are cases in which the greatest daring is the greatest wisdom.
5571 YOSHIMOTO BANANA/ JAPAN/WRITER	I wonder what it felt to move to a country where you didn't grow up. I had thought about that often since my sister got married. Do you become a character in a story native to that land, or do you, somewhere in your heart, want to return to your homeland.
5572 JAMES BALDWIN/ USA/WRITER	The most dangerous creation of any society is the man who has nothing to lose.
5573 LUCILLE BALL/USA/ COMEDIAN/ACTRESS	The secret of staying young is to live honestly, eat slowly, and lie about your age.
5574 JACK WELCH/USA/ BUSINESS	Change before you have to.
5575 G.K. CHESTERTON/ UK/WRITER	Religious liberty might be supposed to mean that everybody is free to discuss religion. In practice it means that hardly anybody is allowed to mention it.
5576 WILLIAM JENNINGS BRYAN/USA/LAWYER	The humblest citizen of all the land, when clad in the armor of a righteous cause, is stronger than all the hosts of error.
5577 WEDDING/MONEY	Large wedding versus small wedding
5578 GLENN LLOPIS/CUBA/ USA/ENTREPRENEUR	Self-promotion creates division in the workplace.
5579 EXCELLENCE	Memorable airport facilities
5580 WILLIAM JENNINGS BRYAN/USA/LAWYER	I believe the fundamental basis for a happy life with family and friends is to treat others as you would like to be treated, speak truthfully, act honorably, and keep commitments to the letter.
5581 H.L. MENCKEN/ AMERICAN EDITOR	A church is a place in which gentlemen who have never been to heaven brag about it to persons who will never get there.
5582 B.F. SKINNER/USA/ PSYCHOLOGIST	We shouldn't teach great books; we should teach a love of reading.
5583 DONALD RUMSFELD/ USA/DEFENCE	Don't necessarily avoid sharp edges. Occasionally they are necessary to leadership.
5584 USA/ALEXANDER WOOLLCOTT/CRITIC	Many of us spend half our time wishing for things we could have if we didn't spend half our time wishing.
5585 NEGOTIATIONS	Playing hardball

NUMBER CATEGORY/CREDIT	TOPIC
5586 WENDELL WILKIE/USA/LAWYER	Education is the mother of leadership.
5587 PROVERB	Out of debt, out of danger.
5588 PAUL McCARTNEY/MUSICIAN	Imagination grows by exercise and, contrary to common belief, is more powerful in the mature than in the young.
5589 CHOICE	Working with a team versus working independently
5590 DEBATE	Modern technology is creating a single world culture.
5591 JEFFREY JACOB ABRAMS/USA/MOVIE DIRECTOR	Opportunity creates opportunty.
5592 RECOMMENDATION	The must-see place in your country or city.
5593 PETER THIEL/USA/BUSINESS/INVESTOR	If you've invented something new but you haven't invented an effective way to sell it, you have a bad business -- no matter how good the product.
5594 TIME TRAVEL	A time in the past you would like to visit
5595 INTERNET	Information overload
5596 RUSSIA/ALEKSANDR SOLZHENITSYN/WRITER	Should one point out that from ancient times decline in courage has been considered the beginning of the end?
5597 DEBATE	All children should learn at least one foreign language.
5598 ZHUANGZI/THINKER	If you don't realize the source, you stumble in confusion and sorrow.
5599 SCHOOL	Teacher's pet
5600 RAY CHARLES/USA	I never wanted to be famous. I only wanted to be great.
5601 CULTURE	Courtship in your country
5602 ARTHUR MILLER/USA	Betrayal is the only truth that sticks.
5603 RUDYARD KIPLING/UK/WRITER	Down to Gehenna or up to the Throne, He travels the fastest who travels alone.
5604 AMY REITER/US/WRITER	Disagreeable men tend to earn more than agreeable men.
5605 SUSANNAH MEADOWS/USA/JOURNALIST	You shouldn't give in to your child's tantrum.
5606 ABRAHAM LINCOLN/USA	You cannot escape the responsibility of tomorrow by evading it today.
5607 THOMAS SOWELL/USA/ECONOMIST	It takes considerable knowledge just to realize the extent of your own ignorance.
5608 WOMEN/ADVANCEMENT	Gender equality index
5609 IDIOM	A thankless job
5610 LATIN EXPRESSION	*Abnormis sapiens* -- Wise without instruction
5611 D.H. LAWRENCE/UK/NOVELIST/POET	I never saw a wild thing sorry for itself. A small bird will drop frozen dead from a bough without ever having felt sorry for itself.
5612 ENGLISH PROVERB	A penny saved is a penny gained.
5613 LATIN EXPRESSION	*Absens haeres non erit* -- He who is at a distance will not be the heir.
5614 FRANCIS BACON/UK/PHILOSOPHER	All rising to a great place is by a winding stair.
5615 DEBATE	Grades encourage students to learn.
5616 JOHN UPDIKE/USA/NOVELIST	Americans have been conditioned to respect newness, whatever it costs them.

NUMBER CATEGORY/CREDIT	TOPIC
5617 B.F. SKINNER/USA/ PSYCHOLOGIST	A failure is not always a mistake; it may simply be the best one can do under the circumstances. The real mistake is to stop trying.
5618 CARL von CLAUSEWITZ/ PRUSSIAN GENERAL	The backbone of surprise is fusing speed with secrecy.
5619 SAYING	He would fall on his back and break his nose.
5620 VICKI MYRON/DEWEY: THE SMALL TOWN LIBRARY CAT WHO TOUCHED THE WORLD	A great library doesn't have to be big or beautiful. It doesn't have to have the best facilities or the most efficient staff or the most users…A great library is one nobody notices because it is always there and always has what people need.
5621 OPRAH WINFREY/USA/ MEDIA ENTREPRENEUR	Create the highest, grandest vision possible for your life, because you become what you believe.
5622 PERSONAL/CULTURAL	Favorite baby name
5623 IDIOM	Crying wolf
5624 B.F. SKINNER/USA/ PSYCHOLOGIST	Education is what survives when what has been learned has been forgotten.
5625 DEBATE	Telephones and email have made communication less personal.
5626 INVENTIONS	Which discovery is the most beneficial to humans?
5627 PERSONAL	A famous entertainer you would like to meet
5628 LUCILLE BALL/USA/ COMEDIAN/ACTRESS	A man who correctly guesses a woman's age may be smart, but he's not very bright.
5629 PETER DRUCKER/ MANAGEMENT	Rank does not confer privilege or give power. It imposes responsibility.
5630 CHINESE SAYING	When you want to test the depths of a stream, don't use both feet.
5631 JOEL OSTEEN/USA/ PREACHER	You cannot expect victory and plan for defeat.
5632 DEBATE	That every country should have national paid maternity leave
5633 AMOS BRONSON ALCOTT/USA/WRITER	Our ideals are our better selves.
5634 ARTHUR MILLER/ USA/PLAYWRIGHT	The two most common elements in the world are hydrogen and stupidity.
5635 STEVE JOBS/USA APPLE FOUNDER	Remembering that I'll be dead soon is the most important tool I've ever encountered to help me make the big choices in life.
5636 WILLIAM JAMES/USA/ PHILOSOPHER	To study the abnormal is the best way of understanding the normal.
5637 TYLER PERRY/USA/ PLAYWRIGHT	It doesn't matter if a million people tell you what you can't do, or if ten million tell you no. If you get one yes from God that's all you need.
5638 CHINESE SAYING	When planning for a year, plant corn. When planning for a decade, plant trees. When planning for life, train and educate people.
5639 HILLARY CLINTON/ USA/POLITICIAN	When Christians are subject to insults to their faith, and that certainly happens, we expect them not to resort to violence.
5640 JIM ROHN/SUCCESS MAGAZINE/DARREN HARDY	There are some people who you can spend three hours with, but not three days. Others you can spend three minutes with, but not three hours.

NUMBER CATEGORY/CREDIT	TOPIC
5641 GENERAL COLIN POWELL/USA/LEADER	Great leaders are almost always great simplifiers, who can cut through argument, debate, and doubt to offer a solution everybody can understand.
5642 WALTER RUSSELL/USA/ POLYMATH	Mediocrity is self-inflicted and genius is self-bestowed.
5643 DEBATE	Computers have made life more stressful.
5644 CARL von CLAUSEWITZ/ PRUSSIAN GENERAL	Of all the passions that inspire a man in a battle, none, we have to admit, is so powerful and so constant as the longing for honor and renown.
5645 ENGLISH PROVERB	An empty bag will not stand upright.
5646 DEBATE	That we are lucky to live in the 21st century.
5647 GIFTS/NATIONAL	A product or custom from your country the world should know about
5648 D.H. LAWRENCE/UK/ NOVELIST	My great religion is a belief in the blood, the flesh, as being wiser than the intellect. We can go wrong in our minds. But what our blood feels and says, is always true.
5649 PERSONAL	A historical personality you would have liked to meet
5650 B.F. SKINNER/USA/ PSYCHOLOGIST	Chaos breeds geniuses. It ofers a man something to be a genius about.
5651 JOHN WANAMAKER/ USA/MERCHANT/	Half the money I spend on advertising is wasted; the trouble is, I don't know which half.
5652 DIANE AIRBUS/USA/ PHOTOGRAPHER	There are things which nobody would see unless I photographed them.
5653 ARTHUR MILLER/ USA/PLAYWRIGHT	What am I doing in an office, making a contemptuous, begging, fool of myself, when all I want is out there, waiting for me the minute I say I know who I am!
5654 KEVIN RUDD/PM/ AUSTRALIA/ HUMOR	By way of personal instinct, I have an inherent distaste for grandiose rhetorical statements, which don't have any substantive dimension to them.
5655 WRITER/MARIO VARGAS LLOSA/PERUVIAN	Memory is a snare, pure and simple; it alters, it subtly rearranges the past to fit the present.
5656 J.K. ROWLING/UK/ WRITER/HARRY POTTER	Climbing out of poverty by your own efforts, that is something on which to pride yourself, but poverty itself, is romanticized only by fools.
5657 CHARLIE CHAPLIN/USA	Laughter is the tonic, the relief, the surcease for pain.
5658 IMMANUEL KANT/ PHILOSOPHER	He who is cruel to animals becomes hard also in his dealings with men. We can judge the heart of a man by his treatment of animals.
5659 EDUCATION/CHANGE	Finance should be taught to elementary school pupils.
5660 ARABIC PROVERB	Seek counsel of him who makes you weep, and not of him who makes you laugh.
5661 ARTHUR MILLER/USA/ USA/PLAYWRIGHT	Maybe all one can do is hope to end up with the right regrets.
5662 HONOR	A statue to honor a famous person in your city
5663 LATIN EXPRESSION	Approach this fire, and you will soon be too warm.
5664 JERRY COYNE/BIOLOGY/ PROFESSOR/USA	In religion, faith is a virtue. In science, faith is a vice.
5665 LATIN EXPRESSION	Zealous at the commencement, careless towards the conclusion.

NUMBER CATEGORY/CREDIT	TOPIC
5666 JOHN ZENGER/USA/ GERMAN/PRINTER	Great leaders are not defined by the absence of weakness, but rather by the presence of clear strengths.
5667 LEE IACOCCA/USA/ BUSINESS EXECUTIVE	I have found that being honest is the best technique I can use. Right upfront, tell people what you're trying to accomplish and what you're willing to sacrifice to accomplish it.
5668 B.F. SKINNER/USA/ PSYCHOLOGIST	No one asks how to motivate a baby. A baby naturally explores everything it can get at, unless restraining forces have already been at work.
5669 PERSONAL	What you would say about the building of a factory next to your house
5670 THOUGHT	Parents are the best teachers.
5671 THOUGHT/DEBATE	Not everything that is learned is contained in books.
5672 RAY CHARLES/USA/ MUSICIAN	There's nothing written in the Bible, Old or New Testament, that says, "If you believe in Me, you ain't going to have no troubles."
5673 SUSAN B. ANTHONY/ WOMEN'S RIGHTS	I always distrust people who know so much about what God wants them to to do because I notice it always coincides with their own desires.
5674 ENGLISH PROVERB	An apple a day keeps the doctor away.
5675 FANNIE HURST/USA	A woman has to be twice as good as a man to go half as far.
5676 BENJAMIN FRANKLIN/US	Keep thy shop, and thy shop will keep thee.
5677 ARTHUR MILLER/USA	The jungle is dark but full of diamonds.
5678 ARABIC PROVERB	The sinning is the best part of repentance.
5679 MALCOLM X/USA/ ACTIVIST	We cannot think of being acceptable to others until we have first proven acceptable to ourselves.
5680 MARIO V. LLOSA/PERU	One can't fight with oneself, for this battle has only one loser.
5681 ST. FRANCIS OF ASSISI	A single sunbeam is enough to drive away many shadows.
5682 SHARON SASSLER/USA	Marriage is an economic arrangement.
5683 MYTHS/ COMMUNITY	Collective memory
5684 FREEDOM SOFTWARE	Software that disables the Internet for up to 8 hours to help people who think they are addicted to the Internet
5685 PLATO/THE REPUBLIC	Knowledge which is acquired under compulsion obtains no hold on the mind.
5686 LATIN EXPRESSION/ DURESS	An act done by me against my will, is not my act.
5687 B.F. SKINNER/USA/ PSYCHOLOGIST	Society attacks early, when the individual is helpless. It enslaves him almost before he has tasted freedom.
5688 MICHAEL JORDAN/USA	Earn your leadership everyday.
5689 HENRY KAISER/USA	Trouble is only opportunity in work clothes.
5690 MARIAN WRIGHT EDELMAN/USA	If we don't stand up for children, then we don't stand for much.
5691 ALLAN WATTS/USA/ WRITER	Money is a way of measuring wealth but is not wealth in itself. A chest of gold coins or a fat wallet of bills is of no use whatsoever to a wrecked sailor alone on a raft. He needs real wealth, in the form of a fishing rod, a compass, an outboard motor with gas,, and a female companion.
5692 B.F. SKINNER/USA/ PSYCHOLOGIST	We are only just beginning to understand the power of love because we are just beginning to understand the weakness of force and aggression.

NUMBER CATEGORY/CREDIT	TOPIC
5693 ENGLISH PROVERB	Among the blind the one-eyed man is king.
5694 WILLIAM FAULKNER/US	If a story is in you, it has to come out.
5695 STEPHEN COVEY/ USA /AUTHOR	If the ladder is not leaning against the right wall, every step we take just gets us to the wrong place faster.
5696 JOHN WANAMAKER/ USA/MERCHANT	People who cannot find time for recreation are obliged sooner or later to find time for illness.
5697 DEBATE	That the Olympic Games bring out the best in humanity.
5698 LATIN PROVERB	Good health is worth more than the greatest wealth.
5699 JEAN COCTEAU/POET	Be yourself. The world worships the original.
5700 USA/PRESIDENT/D. EISENHOWER	You don't lead by hitting people over the head -- that's assault, not leadership.
5701 HANS CHRISTIAN ANDERSEN/WRITER	The whole world is a series of miracles, but we're so used to them we call them ordinary things.
5702 JEAN COCTEAU/FRENCH	What the public criticizes in you, cultivate. It is you.
5703 ENGLISH PROVERB	A miss is as good as a mile.
5704 OTTO VON BISMARK/ PRUSSIA/LEADER	The main thing is to make history, not to write it.
5705 USA/ELBERT GREEN/ HUBBARD/WRITER	I believe that no one can harm you but yourself.
5706 ARTHUR MILLER/ USA/PLAYWRIGHT	If a person measures his spiritual fulfillment in terms of...enjoying a sunrise, being warmed by a child's smile, or being able to help someone have a better day, then he is likely to know much spiritual fulfillment.
5707 ERASMUS/DUTCH	Great abundance of riches cannot be gathered and kept by any man without sin.
5708 MAO TSE TUNG/CHINA	Political power grows out of the barrel of a gun.
5709 USA/B.M. BARUCH/USA	To me, old age is always fifteen years older than I am.
5710 BUDDHISM/JAPAN (DAILY YOMIURI)	*Omizutori* (Month-long retreat for abbots/priests to practice asceticism for penitence)
5711 RAY CHARLES/USA/ MUSICIAN	Affluence separates people. Poverty knits 'em together. You got some sugar and I don't; I borrow some of yours. Next month you might not have any flour; well, I'll give you some of mine.
5712 LATIN EXPRESSION	Every rumor is believed when directed against the unfortunate.
5713 BENJAMIN FRANKLIN/ USA/FOUNDING FATHER	Keep your eyes wide open before marriage, half shut afterwards.
5714 JOHN IRVING/ WRITER/A PRAYER FOR OWEN MEANY	If you care about something you have to protect it -- if you're lucky enough to find a way of life you love, you have to find the courage to live it.
5715 PEARL S. BUCK/ WRITER/USA	The common sense of people will surely prove to them someday that mutual support and cooperation are only sensible for the security and happiness of all.
5716 D. H. LAWRENCE/UK/ NOVELIST	It is far, far better to read one book six times at intervals, than to read six several books.

NUMBER CATEGORY/CREDIT	TOPIC
5717 ALAN WATTS/USA/ WRITER	We seldom realize, for example, that our most private thoughts and emotions are not actually our own. For we think in terms of languages and images which we did not invent, but which were given to us by our society.
5718 H. G. WELLS/UK/WRITER	Losing your way on a journey is unfortunate. But, losing your reason for the journey is a fate more cruel.
5719 RUSSIA/ALEKSANDR SOLZHENITSYN/WRITER	I leaf through the ancient philosophers and find my newest discoveries there.
5720 MARK TWAIN/USA/ WRITER	Keep away from people who try to belittle your ambitions. Small people do that, but the really great make you feel that you, too, can become great.
5721 A. N. WHITEHEAD/UK	Religion is what an individual does with his solitariness.
5722 FRANK LLOYD WRIGHT/ USA/ARCHITECT	A doctor can bury his mistakes, but an architect can only advise his clients to plant vines.
5723 ALAN WATTS/USA/ WRITER	The morning glory which blooms for an hour differs not at heart from the great pine, which lives for a thousand years.
5724 H. G. WELLS/UK/WRITER	The crisis of today is the joke of tomorrow.
5725 DEREK SIVERS/USA	Every complaint is an opportunity.
5726 JEAN DE LA FONTAINE/ FRENCH/POET	A person often meets his destiny on the road he took to avoid it.
5727 D. H. LAWRENCE/UK	The human soul needs beauty more than bread.
5728 FRANK LLOYD WRIGHT/ USA/ARCHITECT	Early in my career I had to choose between an honest arrogance and a hypocritical humility…I deliberately chose an honest arrogance, and I've never been sorry.
5729 D. H. LAWRENCE/UK/ POET/ESSAYIST	Be a good animal, true to your instincts.
5730 JEAN DE LA FONTAINE/ FRENCH POET	Every newspaper editor owes tribute to the devil.
5731 ROBERT LOUIS STEVENSON/SCOT	You cannot run away from a weakness, you must sometimes fight it out or perish. And if that be so, why not now and where you stand?
5732 H. G. WELLS/UK/WRITER	States organized for war will make war as surely as hens will lay eggs.
5733 ALAN WATTS/WRITER	The mystery of life is not a problem to be solved but a reality to be experienced.
5734 FRANK L. WRIGHT/USA	If it sells, it's art.
5735 SUSAN POWTER/USA/ AUTHOR	My father instilled in me that if you don't see things happening the way you want them to, you get out there and make them happen.
5736 NICHOLAS KRISTOF/ WRITER/USA	Since the beginning of the 1990's, China has succeeded in overcoming a great deal of poverty by empowering women.
5737 DEBORAH L. JACOBS/ FORBES/USA	…self-employment can be a bit of an emotional roller coaster, with higher highs and lower lows than you're probably used to.
5738 STEVE JOBS/APPLE/ ENTREPRENEUR/USA/ CO-FOUNDER	When you are young, you look at television and think, 'There's a conspiracy.' The networks have conspired to dumb us down. But when you get a little older, you realize that's not true. The networks are in business to give people exactly what they want.
5739 WILLIAM JAMES/USA/ PHILOSOPHER	The greatest weapon against stress is our ability to choose one thought over another.

NUMBER CATEGORY/CREDIT	TOPIC
5740 B.F. SKINNER/USA/ PSYCHOLOGIST	Some of us learn control more or less by accident. The rest of us go all our lives not even understanding how it is possible, and blaming our failure on being born the wrong way.
5741 LAO TZU/PHILOSOPHER	He who rushes ahead doesn't go far.
5742 RANDY PAUSCH/ USA/COMPUTER	When you are screwing up and nobody says anything to you anymore, that means they've given up on you.
5743 GERRY SPENCE/USA/ LAWYER	There are only two races (and they are not distinguished by color): those who are free and those who are not.
5744 RAY CHARLES/USA/ MUSICIAN	Love is a special word, and I use it only when I mean it. You say the word too much and it becomes cheap.
5745 NAPOLEON HILL/USA/ AUTHOR	It is literally true that you can succeed best and quickest by helping others succeed.
5746 LAUREN BACALL/USA	Imagination is the highest kite that one can fly.
5747 BENJAMIN FRANKLIN/ USA/FOUNDING FATHER	Well done is better than well said.
5748 RICHARD BACH/WRITER	A professional writer is an amateur who didn't quit.
5749 ISAAC NEWTON/UK/ MATHEMATICIAN	Gravity explains the motions of the planets, but it cannot explain who sets the planet in motion.
5750 MALCOLM X/ AMERICAN ACTIVIST	Why am I as I am? To understand that any of any person, his whole life, from birth must be reviewed. All of our experiences fuse into our personality. Everything that ever happened to us is an ingredient.
5751 ENGLISH PROVERB	A man's house is his castle.
5752 ARTHUR MILLER/USA	A good newspaper, I suppose, is a nation talking to itself.
5753 ROBERT ALLMAN/USA THIS I BELIEVE	Perhaps a man without sight is blinded less by the importance of material things than other men are.
5754 WILLIAM O. DOUGLAS/ USA/JUDGE/SUPREME COURT	Free speech is not to be regulated like disease cattle and impure butter. The audience that hissed yesterday may applaud today, even for the same performance.
5755 SAMUEL GOLDWYN/ MOVIE PRODUCER	I don't want any yes-men around me. I want everybody to tell me the truth even if it costs them their jobs.
5756 WARREN BUFFETT/ TAXATION/USA	My friends and I have been coddled long enough by a billionaire-friendly Congress. It's time for our government to get serious about shared sacrifice.
5757 WILLIAM SHAKESPEARE/ PLAYWRIGHT	He who has injured thee was either stronger or weaker than thee. If weaker, spare him; if stronger, spare thyself.
5758 JAPANESE PROVERB	Vision without action is a daydream. Action without vision is a nightmare.
5759 MARGARET ATWOOD/ CANADA/NOVELIST	Little girls are cute and small only to adults. To one another they are not cute. They are life-sized.
5760 THOMAS CARLYLE/SCOT	The history of the world is but the biography of great men.
5761 ALAN WATTS/WRITER/ USA	We have untold stacks of recorded music from every age and culture, and the most superb means of playing it. But who actually listens? Maybe a few pot smokers.
5762 B.F. SKINNER/USA/ PSYCHOLOGIST	A scientist may not be sure of the answer, but he's often sure he can find one.

NUMBER CATEGORY/CREDIT	TOPIC
5763 GEORGE T. ANGELL/USA/ REFORMER/LAWYER	I'm sometimes asked "Why do you spend so much of your time and money talking about kindness to animals when there is so much cruelty to men?" I answer: "I am working at the roots."
5764 JAY WALKER/USA/ PRICELINE FOUNDER	There are only four ways to create value (in a digital economy): information, entertainment, convenience, and savings.
5765 ROBERT A. HEINLEIN/ AUTHOR/USA	Women and cats will do as they please, and men and dogs should relax and get used to the idea.
5766 PERSONAL/FRIEND	Qualities you seek most in a friend
5767 JEAN DE LA FONTAINE/ FRENCH/POET	The best laid plot can injure its maker, and often man's perfidy will rebound on himself.
5768 ENTERTAINMENT	Movies should always make people think.
5769 BENJAMIN FRANKLIN/ USA/STATESMAN	Experience keeps a dear school, but fools will learn in no other.
5770 LATIN EXPRESSION	The act does not make the crime, unless the intention is criminal.
5771 PROS AND CONS	Attending a large university versus a small university
5772 ROBERT A. HEINLEIN/ AUTHOR/USA	Never attempt to teach a pig to sing; it wastes your time and annoys the pig.
5773 LAO TZU/PHILOSOPHER	The flame that burns twice as bright burns half as long.
5774 TOURISM/BUSINESS	What you would do to attract more people to your town/city
5775 DEBATE	The most important aspect of a job is the money one earns.
5776 BENJAMIN FRANKLIN/ USA/STATESMAN	If you would not be forgotten / As soon as you are dead and rotten, Either write things worth reading, Or do things worth the writing.
5777 OPRAH WINFREY/ USA/BUSINESSWOMAN	Everyday brings a chance for you to draw a breath, kick off your shoes, and dance.
5778 ARTHUR MILLER/USA	Sometimes, it's better for a man to just walk away.
5779 DEBATE	Drinking age should be raised to 25 all over the world.
5780 CARROLL BINDER/ USA/ABOUT SECRETS AND FALLING TILES/ THIS I BELIEVE	One of the best ways I know of fortifying oneself to withstand the vicissitudes of this insecure and unpredictable era is to school oneself to require relatively little in the way of material possessions, physical satisfactions, or the praise of others.
5781 JOHN UPDIKE/USA/ WRITER	By the time a partnership dissolves, it has dissolved.
5782 USA/RALPH WALDO EMERSON/ESSAYIST	The louder he talked of his honor, the faster we counted our spoons.
5783 JACK KEVORKIAN/USA/ ASSISTED SUICIDE	Dying is not a crime.
5784 HEALTH/WORK	Ergonomics
5785 PROS AND CONS	Working in a large company versus a small company
5786 CARROLL BINDER/ USA/THIS I BELIEVE	I learned one of the great secrets of friendship early in life – to regard each person with whom one associates as an end in himself, not a means to one's own ends.
5787 ARTHUR MILLER/ USA/PLAYWRIGHT	A character is defined by the kinds of challenges he cannot walk away from. And by those he has walked away from that cause him remorse.

NUMBER CATEGORY/CREDIT	TOPIC
5788 B.F. SKINNER/USA/ PSYCHOLOGIST	Men build society and society builds men.
5789 STEPHEN KING/USA/ WRITER	A cowardly leader is the most dangerous of men.
5790 JOHN IRVING/USA/ WRITER	You've got to be obsessed and stay obsessed.
5791 LATIN EXPRESSION	No expectation can allure a good man to the commission of evil.
5792 DEBATE	Businesses should do anything possible to make a profit.
5793 WAR/FRENCH/ERICH MARIA REMARQUE/ AUTHOR	I am young, I am twenty years old; yet I know nothing of life but despair, death, fear, and fatuous superficiality cast over an abyss of sorrow. I see how peoples are set against one another, and in silence, unknowingly, foolishly, obediently, innocently, slay one another.
5794 DEBATE	That sports stars deserve our admiration.
5795 FRANK LLOYD WRIGHT/ USA/ARCHITECT	Many wealthy people are little more than janitors of their possessions.
5796 DEBATE	A person should never make an important decision alone.
5797 ENGLISH PROVERB	All work and no play makes Jack a dull boy; all play and no work makes Jack a mere toy.
5798 PROS AND CONS	Waking up early versus sleeping in
5799 STEPHEN COLBERT/ USA/COMEDIAN	They say that the only people who tell the truth are drunkards and children.
5800 ARTHUR MILLER/ USA/PLAYWRIGHT	Immortality is like trying to carve your initiials in a block of ice in the middle of July.
5801 CONFUCIUS/CHINA/ PHILOSOPHER	What the superior man seeks is in himself. What the mean man seeks is in others.
5802 JEAN DE LA FONTAINE/ FRENCH/POET	Never sell the bear's skin before one has killed the beast.
5803 ARABIC PROVERB	The wound that bleedeth inwardly is the most dangerous.
5804 WRITER/MARIO VARGAS LLOSA/PERU	No matter how ephemeral it is, a novel is something, while despair is nothing.
5805 WORKPLACE/ WOMEN	Equal pay for equal work
5806 NIKKI GIOVANNI/ POET/USA	If I'm not dead, then I should be alive, and if I'm alive then I should tell the truth.
5807 HEALTH	Epidemics
5808 DEBATE	Games are as important for adults as they are for children.
5809 DEBATE	Always being in a hurry is a good sign
5810 CHINESE PROVERB	When a tree falls, the monkeys scatter.
5811 LAUREN BACALL/USA	I am not a has-been. I am a will be.
5812 DAVE BARRY/USA/ HUMORIST	Experts agree that the best type of computer for your individual needs is one that comes on the market about two days after you actually purchase some other computer.
5813 JOHN WANAMAKER/ USA/BUSINESS	When a customer enters my store, forget me. He is king.

NUMBER CATEGORY/CREDIT	TOPIC
5814 DEE DEE MYERS/USA/ POLITICAL ANALYST	I am endlessly fascinated that playing football is considered a training ground for leadership, but raising children isn't.
5815 ROBERT A. HEINLEIN/ AUTHOR/USA	A human being should be able to change a diaper, plan an invasion, butcher a hog, conn a ship, design a building, write a sonnet, balance accounts, build a wall, set a bone, comfort the dying, take orders, give orders, cooperate, act alone, solve equations, analyze a new problem, pitch manure, program a computer, cook a tasty meal, fight efficiently, die gallantly. Specialization is for insects.
5816 PROS AND CONS	Traveling alone versus traveling with a companion
5817 MARIE CURIE/FRENCH/ POLISH/SCIENTIST	One never notices what has been done; one can only see what remains to be done.
5818 GENERAL GEORGE S. PATTON/USA/	Don't tell people how to do things; tell them what to do and let them surprise you with their results.
5819 LATIN EXPRESSION	Speak not against the sun.
5820 LAO TZU/PHILOSOPHER	He who stands on tiptoe doesn't stand firm.
5821 DEBATE	Technology such as the Internet has made teachers redundant
5822 RUSSIA/ALEKSANDR SOLZHENITSYN/WRITER	The belly is an ungrateful wretch; it never remembers past favors. It always wants more tomorrow.
5823 FRANK LLOYD WRIGHT/ USA/ARCHITECT	Imitation is always insult -- not flattery.
5824 BEN FRANKLIN/USA	When the well's dry, we know the worth of water.
5825 DAVE BARRY/USA/ HUMOUR COLUMNIST	Cigarette sales would drop to zero overnight if the warning said: CIGARETTES CONTAIN FAT.
5826 DEBATE/DISCUSSION	Watching an event live versus watching it on television
5827 ARTHUR MILLER/ USA/PLAYWRIGHT/ DEATH OF A SALESMAN	To suffer fifty weeks of the year for the sake of a two-week vacation, when all you really desire is to be outdoors, with your shirt off. and always to have to get ahead of the next fella. And still -- that's how you build a future.
5828 ALBERT EINSTEIN/ PHYSICIST/NOBEL LAUREATE	When a man sits with a pretty girl for an hour, it seems like a minute. But let him sit on a hot stove for a minute – and it's longer than any hour. That's relativity.
5829 ARABIC PROVERB	When a door opens that you did not knock, consider your reputation.
5830 JOHN UPDIKE/USA/ WRITER	Creativity is merely a plus name for regular activity. Any activity becomes creative when the doer cares about doing it right, or better.
5831 DEBATE	Government should provide subsidies for nannies to care for children of people in the work force.
5832 FRANK SINATRA/USA	Alcohol may be man's worst enemy, but the bible says love your enemy.
5833 USA/MIKE MYATT/ FORBES	Great leaders are never satisfied with traditional practice, static thinking, conventional wisdom, or common performance.
5834 PARENTING	Attachment parenting
5835 PLATO/THE REPUBLIC	Necessity is the mother of invention.
5836 TERRY PRATCHETT/ UK/AUTHOR	Build a man a fire, and he'll be warm for a day. Set a man on fire, and he'll be warm for the rest of his life.
5837 GEORGE BEST/SOCCER/ NORTHERN IRELAND	I spent 90% of my money on women and drink. The rest I wasted.

NUMBER CATEGORY/CREDIT	TOPIC
5838 JOHN MAXWELL/USA/ BUSINESS	A good leader is a person who takes a little more than his share of the blame and a little less than his share of the credit.
5839 WILLIAM MAXWELL/USA	A writer is a reader who is moved to emulation.
5840 JOHN F. KENNEDY/US PRESIDENT	A man does what he must -- in spite of personal consequences, in spite of obstacles and dangers and pressures.
5841 ABRAHAM JOSHUA HESCHEL/USA	Self-respect is the fruit of discipline; and the sense of dignity grows with the ability to say no to oneself.
5842 ROBERT A. HEINLEIN/ AUTHOR/USA	A prude is a person who thinks that his own rules of propriety are natural laws.
5843 BENJAMIN FRANKLIN	Who has deceiv'd thee so oft as thy self?
5844 EMPLOYMENT	Lifetime employment
5845 ENGLISH PROVERB	All that glitters is not gold.
5846 DEBATE	Television destroys communication among friends and family members.
5847 PROS AND CONS	Living in a small town versus living in a city
5848 TOM WAITS/BEASTIE BOYS/US SINGER	Artists who take money for ads poison and pervert their songs. It reduces them to the level of a jingle.
5849 CULTURE	The importance of museums
5850 I. M. PEI/ARCHITECT/ CHINESE-AMERICAN	Success is as collection of problems solved.
5851 CARING	Qualities of a good neighbor
5852 MAYA ANGELOU/USA	The most called-upon prerequisite of a friend is an accessible ear.
5853 BUSINESS/JACK WELCH/BUSINESS/ LEADER	Strong managers who make tough decisions to cut jobs provide the only true job security in today's world. Weak managers are the problem. Weak managers destroy jobs.
5854 THUCYDIDES/ HISTORIAN	When one is deprived of one's liberty, one is right in blaming not so much the man who puts the shackles on as the one who had the power to prevent him, but did not use it.
5855 AYN RAND/RUSSIAN-AMERICAN WRITER	The man who does not value himself, cannot value anything or anyone.
5856 INDIRA GANDHI/INDIA	The power to question is the basis of all human progress.
5857 R.L. STEVENSON/SCOT	Our business in life is not to succeed, but to fail in good spirits.
5858 I. M. PEI/ARCHITECT/ CHINESE-AMERICAN	Great artists need great clients.
5859 EXTRA WORK	Moonlighting
5860 PATRICK HENRY/USA	Give me liberty, or give me death.
5861 DEBATE	Peer pressure versus parents' influence
5862 NAPOLEON/FRANCE	Men are moved by two levers only: fear and self interest.
5863 B.F. SKINNER/USA/ PSYCHOLOGIST	A fourth-grade reader may be a sixth-grade mathematician. The grade is an administrative device which does violence to the nature of the developmental process.
5864 USA/D. EISENHOWER	The supreme quality of leadership is integrity.
5865 HERODOTUS	Of all possessions a friend is the most precious.
5866 PATRIOTISM	Saluting the flag

NUMBER CATEGORY/CREDIT	TOPIC
5867 USA/T. ROOSEVELT/26TH PRESIDENT	The most important single ingredient in the formula of success is knowing how to get along with people.
5868 ENTERTAINMENT	Concerts you have seen or would like to see
5869 ESSAYIST/BARBARA KINGSOLVER/USA	Everything you're sure is right can be wrong in another place.
5870 PAUL McCARTNEY/UK/USA/MUSICIAN	If slaughterhouses had glass walls, everyone would be a vegetarian.
5871 ADAM SMITH/SCOT	Mercy to the guilty is cruelty to the innocent.
5872 WOMEN/NOVELS	Chick-lit
5873 ANN LANDERS/USA/ADVICE COLUMNIST	...at every party there are two kinds of people – those who want to go home and those who don't. The trouble is, they are usually married to each other.
5874 WILLIAM FAULKNER/USA/NOVELIST	You don't love because: you love despite; not for the virtues, but despite the faults.
5875 G.B. SHAW/PLAYWRIGHT	Lack of money is the root of all evil.
5876 GEORGE S. CLASON/USA	It costs nothing to ask wise advice from a good friend.
5877 WILLIAM FAULKNER/US	War and drink are the two things man is never too poor to buy.
5878 ARTHUR MILLER/USA/PLAYWRIGHT	Great drama is great questions or it is nothing but technique. I could not imagine a theater worth my time that did not want to change the world.
5879 AN INDIAN PROVERB	A cat in a cage becomes a lion.
5880 FRANK LLOYD WRIGHT/USA/ARCHITECT	The measure of a man's culture is the measure of his appreciation. We are ourselves what we appreciate and no more.
5881 ALAN WATTS/USA/WRITER	No one is more dangerously insane than the one who is sane all the time; he is like a steel bridge without flexibility, and the order of his life is rigid and brittle.
5882 MARIO VARGAS LLOSA/PERU/SPANISH WRITER/POLITICIAN	You cannot teach creativity – how to become a good writer. But you can help a young writer discover within himself what kind of writer he would like to be.
5883 LEE IACOCCA/USA/CHRYSLER/CEO/LEADERSHIP	No matter what you've done for yourself or for humanity, if you can't look back on having given love and attention to your own family, what have you really accomplished?
5884 JAMES THURBER/USA	He who hesitates is sometimes saved.
5885 OSCAR WILDE/IRISH	We are all in the gutter, but some of us are looking at the stars.
5886 TINA SEELIG/USA/PROFESSOR/BUSINESS	Father's advice: You shouldn't take yourself too seriously nor judge others too harshly.
5887 JOHN J. PERSHING/USA/MILITARY/LEADER	A competent leader can get efficient service from poor troops, while on the contrary an incapable leader can demoralize the best of troops.
5888 PLATO/PHIOSOPHER	Good people do not need laws to tell them to act responsibly, while bad people will find a way around the laws.
5889 JULIUS NYERERE/PRESIDENT/KENYA/CHANGE IN AFRICA	If a door is shut, attempts should be made to open it; if it is ajar, it should be pushed until it is wide open. In neither case should the door be blown up at the expense of those inside.
5890 WALTER LIPPMAN/USA/WRITER	The final test of a leader is that he leaves behind him in other men, the conviction and the will to carry on.
5891 JOURNALISM	Investigative journalism

NUMBER CATEGORY/CREDIT	TOPIC
5892 EMPLOYMENT/JOB	The job interview
5893 FRANK GEHRY/USA/ ARCHITECT	I don't know why people hire architects and then tell them what to do.
5894 RANDY PAUSCH/USA/ PROFESSOR	If I only had three words of advice, they would be, 'Tell the truth.' If I got three more words, I'd add, 'all the time.'
5895 USA/EDUCATION/ BOOKER T. WASHINGTON	If you can't read, it's going to be hard to realize your dreams.
5896 DAVID O. McKAY/USA/ MORMON	No other success can compensate for failure in the home.
5897 JAPANESE PROVERB	*Amarimono ni wa fuku ga aru.* Fortunes exist among leftovers
5898 CHOICE	A battle between head and heart
5899 GERRY SPENCE/USA/ LAWYER	Teach the child to respect that which is not respectable and you teach the child the first requisite of slavery: subjection to unjust authority.
5900 HENRY FORD/USA/ BUSINESSMAN	Obstacles are those frightful things you see when you take your eyes off your goals.
5901 BENJAMIN FRANKLIN/ USA/FOUNDING FATHER	The worst wheel of a cart makes the most noise.
5902 HUMOR	Money can't buy happiness, but it can help you look for it quicker, in a convertible.
5903 ENGLISH PROVERB	A good name is better than riches.
5904 ARTHUR MILLER/ USA/PLAYWRIGHT	Self-realization and self-fulfillment are the *sine qua non* for human existence.
5905 BILL GATES/USA/ ENTREPRENEUR	Information technology and business are becoming inextricably interwoven. I don't think anybody can talk meaningfully about one without the talking about the other.
5906 MARIO VARGAS LLOSA/PERUVIAN-SPANISH WRITER/ POLITICIAN	I learned to read at the age of five, in Brother Justiniano's class at the De la Salle Academy in Cochabamba, Bolivia. It is the most important thing that has ever happened to me. Almost seventy years later I remember clearly how the magic of translating the words in books into images enriched my life, breaking the barriers of time and space.
5907 IMMANUEL KANT/ GERMAN	If man makes himself a worm he must not complain when he is trodden on.
5908 CHARLIE CHAPLIN/ FILM DIRECTOR	I went into the business for the money, and the art grew out of it. If people are disillusioned by that remark, I can't help it. It's the truth.
5909 CEO/LEE IACOCCA/USA/ LEADERSHIP	My father always used to say that when you die, if you've got five real friends, then you've had a great life.
5910 EDWARD DE BONO/ UK/AUTHOR/	Unhappiness is best defined as the difference between our talents and our expectations.
5911 MARIO VARGAS LLOSA/PERU	It isn't true that convicts live like animals: animals have more room to move around.
5912 ARNOLD GLASOW/USA/ BUSINESS	One of the tests of leadership is the abiity to recognize a problem before it becomes an emergency.
5913 CROWFOOT/NATIVE AMERICAN WARRIOR/ORATOR	What is life? It is the flash of a firefly in the night. It is the breath of a buffalo in the wintertime. It is the little shadow which runs across the grass and loses itself in the sunset.

NUMBER CATEGORY/CREDIT	TOPIC
5914 GIAN LORENZO BERNINI/ ITALY/SCULPTOR	Three things are needed for success in painting and sculpture: to see beauty when young and accustom oneself to it, to work hard, and to obtain good advice.
5915 OSCAR NIEMEYER/ ARCHITECT/BRAZIL	Surprise is key in all art.
5916 JAPAN/RELIGION	Visiting shrines
5917 JIM ROHN/USA/SPEAKER	Make rest a necessity, not an objective.
5918 ZAHA HADID/UK/IRAQ/ ARCHITECT	When I taught, all my best students were women.
5919 MEDIA	Press freedom
5920 AVIATOR/CHARLES LINDBERGH/WRITER/ NY TIMES/1971	Our ideals, laws and customs should be based on the proposition that each generation, in turn, becomes the custodian rather than the absolute owner of our resources and each generation has the obligation to pass this inheritance on to the future.
5921 ENGLISH PROVERB	After a storm comes a calm.
5922 USA/BEN FRANKLIN	Fish and visitors stink after three days.
5923 ALEXANDER DUMAS/FR.	All for one, one for all.
5924 EMILY DICKINSON/POET	We turn not older with years, but newer every day.
5925 D. H. LAWRENCE/UK/ NOVELIST	A man could no longer be private and withdrawn. The world allows no hermits.
5926 ARTHUR MILLER/USA	I only ask you one thing -- don't trust nobody.
5927 VICTOR ANDRADE/ USA/A LIVE WIRE/ THIS I BELIEVE	I believe that happiness is rooted in the soul and in the subjective appreciation of the state of mind; therefore, it is false to seek that happiness in the satisfaction of appetite, ambitions, and sensual pleasures.
5928 COLLEGE/CHEATING	Academic dishonesty
5929 DERRICK BELL/ HARVARD/LAW	We live in a system that espouses merit, equality, and a level playing field, but exalts those with wealth, power, and celebrity, however gained.
5930 ALEXANDER BLOCH/ USA/THE HIGH PRICE OF MONEY/THIS I BELIEVE	When I broke away from business it was against the advice of practically all my friends and family. So conditioned are most of us to the association of success with money that the thought of giving up a good salary for an idea seemed little short of insane. If so, all I can say is "Gee, it's great to be crazy."
5931 TRAGEDY	Loss of innocence
5932 MEDICINE	Misdiagnosis
5933 ENGLISH PROVERB	A hungry man is an angry man.
5934 LINDA RONSTADT/ USA/MUSICIAN	Art is for healing ourselves and everybody needs their personal art to heal their problems.
5935 CHOICE/DEBATE	Living in one place versus living in different places
5936 IDIOM	Cash cow
5937 CHINESE PROVERB	Not the cry, but the flight of a wild duck, leads the flock to fly and follow.
5938 JOY	What gives me the greatest joy
5939 WALTER E. COLE/USA WAR HERO	We must look for the opportunity in every difficulty, instead of being paralyzed at the thought of the difficulty in every opportunity.

NUMBER CATEGORY/CREDIT	TOPIC
5940 MIYAMOTO MUSASHI/ JAPANESE WARRIOR	Respect Buddha and the gods without counting on their help.
5941 SHOPPINGADDICTION	Shopaholics
5942 JOHN WANAMAKER/USA	Courtesy is the one coin you can never have too much of or be stingy with.
5943 CHANGE/HOMETOWN	What you would change about your hometown
5944 AFRICAN PROVERB	Two small antelopes beat a big one.
5945 YOSHIMOTO BANANA/ JAPAN/WRITER	Recognizing how totally ignorant you are is the only honest way to deal with people who've been through something traumatic.
5946 ROBERT A. HEINLEIN/ AUTHOR/USA	Do not confuse 'duty' with what other people expect of you; they are utterly different. Duty is a debt you owe to yourself to fulfill obligations you have assumed voluntarily. Paying that debt can entail anything from years of patient work to instant willingness to die. Difficult it may be, but the reward is self-respect.
5947 ECOLOGY/TOURISM	Eco-tourism
5948 FRIENDSHIP	Study groups
5949 FRENCH/NAPOLEON	The best way to keep one's word is not to give it.
5950 GERRY SPENCE/USA	When you are faced with prejudice, logic and justice are important.
5951 PROVERB	Experience is the best teacher.
5952 LATIN EXPRESSION	It is fair that he who expects forgiveness, should, in his turn, extend it to others.
5953 FOOD/POVERTY	Dumpster diving
5954 W. EDWARDS DEMING/ QUALITY/USA/JAPAN	If you can't describe what you are doing as a process, you don't know what you are doing.
5955 CARROLL BINDER/ USA/THIS I BELIEVE	I believe the quest for a better life is the most satisfying pursuit of men and nations.
5956 BILL MOYERS/USA/ JOURNALIST	Secrecy is the freedom tyrants dream of.
5957 SCIENCE	The big bang theory
5958 IRRESPONSIBILITY	Financial abuse of elderly people
5959 PAUL GILDING/WRITER/ TEDTALK/USA	It takes a good crisis to get us going. When we feel fear and we fear loss we are capable of quite extraordinary things.
5960 USA/BARBARA KINGSOLVER/	The most important thing about a person is the thing you don't know.
5961 BENJAMIN FRANKLIN/ USA/STATESMAN	Does thou love life? Then do not squander time; for that's the stuff life is made of.
5962 LATIN EXPRESSION	A trifling debt makes a man your debtor; a more weighty one, your enemy.
5963 PROS AND CONS	Movie theaters in residential neighborhoods
5964 DEBATE	The media focus too much on the personal lives of celebrities.
5965 DEBATE	No one country should control the Internet.
5966 NORMAN COUSINS/ EDITOR/THIS I BELIEVE	The problem confronting us today is far more serious than the destiny of any political system or even of any nation. The problem is the destiny of man: first, whether we can make this planet safe for man; second, whether we can make it fit for man.

NUMBER CATEGORY/CREDIT	TOPIC
5967 DEBATE	Enjoying your money now versus saving for the future.
5968 JOHN LENNON/UK/ SINGER/THE BEATLES	Being honest may not get you many friends, but it will always get you the right ones.
5969 MERRIAMWEBSTER	La-la land: A euphoric dreamlike state detached from the harsher realities of life.
5970 GENERAL DOUGLAS MacARTHUR/USA	Never give an order that can't be obeyed.
5971 RELATIONSHIPS	Workplace harassment
5972 BENJAMIN FRANKLIN	He that lieth down with Dogs, shall rise up with Fleas.
5973 ENGLISH PROVERB	A friend is easier lost than found.
5974 NIGERIAN PROVERB	A boisterous horse needs a boisterous bridle.
5975 ASHANTI PROVERB	He is a fool whose sheep runs away twice.
5976 AFRICAN PROVERB	One string joined to another can bind the leopard.
5977 FRENCH/NAPOLEON BONAPARTE/LEADER	Ten people who speak make more noise than ten thousand who are silent.
5978 ROBERT A. HEINLEIN/ USA/WRITER	Always listen to experts. They'll tell you what can't be done, and why. Then do it.
5979 KENYAN PROVERB	One who relates with a corrupt person likewise gets corrupted.
5980 MALIAN PROVERB	No matter how long a log stays in the water, it doesn't become a crocodile.
5981 LEADER/DR. KWEGYIR AGGREY/GHANA	If you educate a man you educate an individual, but if you educate a woman you educate a family.
5982 UGANDAN PROVERB	The person who has not traveled widely thinks his or her mother is the only cook (the best cook).
5983 ANTON CHEKHOV/ RUSSIAN WRITER	It is easier to write about Socrates than about a young woman or a cook.
5984 BILL GATES/USA/ ENTREPRENEUR	Just in terms of allocation of time resources, religion is not every efficient. There's a lot more I could be doing on a Sunday morning.
5985 MARILYN MONROE/USA	A career is wonderful, but you can't curl up with it on a cold night.
5986 USA/ABRAHAM LINCOLN/16th PRESIDENT	Quarrel not at all. No man resolved to make the most of himself can spare time for personal contention.
5987 DOLLY PARTON/USA/ SINGER	If your actions create a legacy that inspires others to dream more, learn more, do more and become more, then, you are an excellent leader.
5988 DOROTHY DIX/USA/ JOURNALIST	So many persons think divorce a panacea for every ill, who find out, when they try it, that the remedy is worse than the disease.
5989 JOAN DIDION/USA/ WRITER	Children are by nature unprotectable.
5990 DEBATE	Having a nuclear power plant in your country is no different from having easily accessible bombs in your territory.
5991 HARUKI MURAKAMI/ JAPAN/WRITER	Mediocrity is like a spot on your shirt, it never comes off.
5992 STEPHEN COVEY/USA/ AUTHOR	Management is efficiency in climbing the ladder of success; leadership determines whether the ladder is leaning against the right wall.
5993 ENGLISH PROVERB	A friend in need is a friend indeed.

NUMBER CATEGORY/CREDIT	TOPIC
5994 BENJAMIN FRANKLIN	The cat in gloves catches no mice.
5995 H. G. WELLS/UK/ NOVELIST	The path of social advancement is, and must be, strewn with broken friendships.
5996 TONY DORSETT/USA/ FOOTBALL PAYER	To succeed, you need to find something to hold on to, something to motivate you, something to inspire you.
5997 URSULA LeGUIN/USA	There are no right answers to wrong questions.
5998 UNIVESITY/COLLEGE	University admissions process in your country
5999 D. H. LAWRENCE/UK/ POET/WRITER	Men fight for liberty and win it with hard knocks. Their children, brought up easy, let it slip away again, poor fools. And their grandchildren are once more slaves.
6000 HUMOR	If only the good die young then what does that say about senior citizens?
6001 ENGLISH PROVERB	Rome was not built in a day.
6002 CHINESE PROVERB	Hit a dog with a meat bun, it does not return.
6003 ANNE FRANK/JEWISH AUTHOR/HOLOCAUST	We all live with the objective of being happy; our lives are all different and the same.
6004 BENJAMIN FRANKLIN	T'is easy to see, hard to foresee.
6005 HUMOR/ENGINEERING	You might be an engineer if you spent more on your calculator than on your wedding ring.
6006 HUMOR	Men are like bank accounts. Without a lot of money, they don't generate much interest.
6007 BARBARA KINGSOLVER/ USA/WRITER	Morning always comes.
6008 NORMAN MAILER/ USA/WRITER	The writer can grow as a person or he can shrink...His curiosity, his reaction to life must not diminish.
6009 JOHN ADAMS/USA/ PRESIDENT	I must study politics and war that my sons may have liberty to study mathematics and philosophy.
6010 LATIN EXPRESSION	Over a distant realm, sovereignty is insecure.
6011 NY TIMES/S. MEADOWS	French parents don't set foot in playgrounds.
6012 G. SANTAYANA/POET	The wise mind has something yet to learn.
6013 BLAISE PASCAL/ PHILOSOPHER	Distraction is the only thing that consoles us for our miseries...and yet it is itself the greatest of our miseries.
6014 N. KRISTOF/USA	Get involved in a cause larger than one's self.
6015 ARTHUR MILLER/USA	The world is an oyster but you don't crack it open on a mattress.
6016 HUMOR/EXERCISE	If God Had Wanted Me to Touch My Toes, He Would Have Put Them on My Knees.
6017 ANAIS NIN/USA/ AUTHOR	Age does not protect you from love. But love, to some extent, protects you from age.
6018 SENECA/ROMAN	Many things have fallen only to rise higher.
6019 JAMES THURBER/USA	It is better to know some of the questions than all of the answers.
6020 KIERKEGAARD/DANISH PHILOSOPHER	Once you label me you negate me.
6021 USA/GEN. NORMAN SCHWARZKOPF	Leadership is a potent combination of strategy and character. But if you must be without one, be without the strategy.

NUMBER CATEGORY/CREDIT	TOPIC
6022 LEE IACOCCA/USA/ AUTO EXECUTIVE	Motivation is everything. You can do the work of two people, but you can't be two people. Instead, you have to inspire the next guy down the line and get him to inspire his people.
6023 T-SHIRT SLOGAN	Be Nice to Your Children -- They'll Pick Your Nursing Home"
6024 GENERAL COLIN POWELL/USA/ SECRETARY OF STAT	Leadership is solving problems. The day soldiers stop bringing you their problems is the day you have stopped leading them. They have either lost confidence that you can help or concluded you do not care. Either case is a failure of leadership.
6025 HUMOR/POT SMOKING	If You Remember the '60s, You Weren't Really There.
6026 BENJAMIN FRANKLIN/ USA/STATESMAN	Work as if you were to live a hundred years; Pray as if you were to die tomorrow.
6027 AKAN/GHANAIAN PROVERB	The old woman looks after the child to grow its teeth and the young one in turn looks after the old woman when she loses her teeth.
6028 IDIOM	Not the sharpest tool in the shed.
6029 JOSEPH CONRAD/UK/ WRITER/HUMOR	Being a woman is a terribly difficult trade, since it consists principally of dealing with men.
6030 TANZANIAN PROVERB	The hen with baby chicks doesn't swallow the worm.
6031 E. AFRICAN PROVERB	If you refuse the advice of an elder you will walk until sunset.
6032 WOLOF PROVERB	Words are like bullets; if they escape, you can't catch them again.
6033 ENGLISH PROVERB	A fool and his money are soon parted.
6034 BARBARA KINGSOLVER/ USA/WRITER	Love weighs nothing.
6035 SWAHILI PROVERB	Hot water does not burn down the house.
6036 EDWARD COKE/ ENGLISH JUDGE	The house of every one is to him as his castle and fortress, as well for his defense against injury and violence, as for his repose.
6037 ROBERT MCCRUM/UK	Everything is fiction.
6038 JOHN UPDIKE/ AMERICAN WRITER	Dreams come true; without that possibility, nature would not incite us to have them.
6039 H. G. WELLS/UK/ NOVELIST	Jesus was a penniless teacher who wandered about the dirty sun-bit country of Judea, living upon casual gifts of food; yet he is always represented clean, combed, and sleek, in spotless raiment, erect with something motionless about him as though he was gliding through the air.
6040 ELMER BOBST/USA/ THIS I BELIEVE	Two of the hardest things to accomplish in this world are to acquire wealth by honest effort and, having gained it, to learn how to use it properly.
6041 FOOD/COST/VALUE	All-you-can eat restaurants
6042 LATIN - ALIBI	When a person that is accused of an offence tries to prove that he or she was absent while the crime was committed, the person is said to have an alibi.
6043 OCTAVIA BUTLER/USA/ WRITER	Civilization is the way one's own people live. Savagery is the way foreigners live.
6044 JULIUS NYERERE PRESIDENT/KENYA	No nation has the right to make decisions for another nation; no people for another people.
6045 SAYING/SUCCESS	Success is just a matter of luck, just ask any failure.
6046 JAPANESE PROVERB	*Nana korobi ya oki.* / Fall down seven times, get up eight.

NUMBER CATEGORY/CREDIT	TOPIC
6047 WOODROW WILSON/ USA/PRESIDENT	Leadership does not always wear the harness of compromise.
6048 LATIN EXPRESSION	Vice is nourished and lives by concealment.
6049 BEN FRANKLIN/USA	Three may keep a secret, if two of them are dead.
6050 JAPANESE PROVERB	*Chiri mo tsumoreba yama to naru.* Even dust amassed will grow into a mountain.
6051 JOHN NAISBITT/USA/ AUTHOR	The new source of power is not money in the hands of a few, but information in the hands of many.
6052 ENGLISH PROVERB	A fault confessed is half redressed.
6053 CLOUD COMPUTING/ MERRIAMWEBSTER	Cloud computing: the practice of storing regularly used computer data on multiple servers that can be accessed through the Internet.
6054 TIMOTHY FERRIS /USA/ WRITER	If someone isn't making you stronger, they are making you weaker.
6055 EVAN WILLIAMS/ TEDTALK/TWITTER	When you give people better ways to share information great things happen.
6056 WRITER/M. GLADWELL	Who we are cannot be separated from where we're from.
6057 MILTON FRIEDMAN/ USA/ECONOMIST/ NOBEL LAUREATE	Universities exist to transmit knowledge and understanding of ideas and values to students, not to provide entertainment for spectators or employment for athletes.
6058 MAYA ANGELOU/USA	I believe that every person is born with talent.
6059 INDIAN PROVERB	The man who has mounted an elephant will not fear the bark of a dog.
6060 BERTRAND RUSSELL/UK	Anything you're good at contributes to happiness.
6061 USA/ROY GARLAND BOGER/LOVE/THIS I BELIEVE	Hate and fear do the greatest damage to the person who hates and fears. So we have stomach ulcers and people who are emotionally upset. Love does the opposite to the lover, who is healthy and happy.
6062 WRITER/ROBERT LOUIS STEVENSON/SCOTTISH	It is perhaps a more fortunate destiny to have a taste for collecting shells than to be born a millionaire.
6063 DR. ARTHUR S. ABRAMSON/USA	I believe that human beings grow up with aspirations and hopes for joy and sorrow, and by contrast appreciate each the more.
6064 J. F. KENNEDY/USA/ 35TH PRESIDENT	Our problems are man-made, therefore they may be solved by man. And man can be as big as he wants. No problem of human destiny is beyond human beings.
6065 DEBATE	The Internet is the best place to find love in the modern world.
6066 CHILDREN/PARENTS	Fertility clinics
6067 CHINESE SAYING	Adding legs when painting a snake. (Ruining work by unnecessary additions)
6068 NEW YEAR/GOALS	New Year's resolution
6069 FOOD/EXOTIC	The most unusual food you have ever eaten.
6070 GHANAIAN PROVERB	If God breaks your leg, He will teach you how to limp.
6071 CHARLES M. SCHULZ/ USA/WRITER	Don't worry about the world coming to an end today. It is already tomorrow in Australia.
6072 JESSE JACKSON/USA/ CIVIL RIGHTS LEADER	Leadership cannot just go along to get along. Leadership must meet the moral challenge of the day.

NUMBER CATEGORY/CREDIT	TOPIC
6073 JOHN WOODEN/USA	It is what you learn after you know it all that counts.
6074 JAMES ALLEN/ AUTHOR/AS A MAN THINKETH	As in the rankest soil the most beautiful flowers are grown, so in the dark soil of poverty the choicest flowers of humanity have developed and bloomed.
6075 R.M. KANTER/USA	A great idea is not enough.
6076 CHINESE SAYING	You can't expect both sides of the sugar cane to have the same sweetness.
6077 MAHATMA GANDHI/ INDIAN LEADER	The weak can never forgive. Forgiveness is the attribute of the strong.
6078 THORSTEIN VEBLEN/ USA/ECONOMIST	The chief use of servants is the evidence they afford of the master's ability to pay.
6079 BUSINESS	Executive perks
6080 J.K. ROWLING/ BRITISH AUTHOR	Indifference and neglect often do much more damage than outright dislike.
6081 G. GREER/AUSTRALIA	Revolution is the festival of the oppressed.
6082 CHARLES SWINDOLL/ USA/CLERGYMAN	The difference between something good and something great is attention to detail.
6083 INDIAN PROVERB	The pain is sometimes preferable to the treatment.
6084 ANDREW CARNEGIE/ USA/PHILANTHROPIST	Every act you have ever performed since the day you were born was performed because you wanted something.
6085 AUTHOR/YOSHIMOTO BANANA/JAPAN	There are many, many difficult times, god knows. If a person wants to stand on her own two feet, I recommend undertaking the care and feeding of something. It could be children, or it could be house plants, you know? By doing that you come to understand your own limitations. That's where it starts.
6086 BILL GATES/USA/ PHILANTHROPIST	If you can't make it good, at least make it look good.
6087 VICTOR ANDRADE/ USA/A LIVE WIRE/ THIS I BELIEVE	I believe that the control over instincts and the absence of fear are much more indicative of human superiority than is the possession of physical power.
6088 GLENN LLOPIS/USA/ FORBES	Adversity is very big when it's all you can see. But it's very small when it's surrounded by opportunity.
6089 WILLIAM PITT THE ELDER/BRITISH STATESMAN	The poorest man may in his cottage bid defiance to all the forces of the Crown. It may be frail, its roof may shake, the wind may blow through it, the storm may enter, the rain may enter – but the King of England cannot enter, all his force dares not cross the threshold of the ruined tenement.
6090 BILL CLINTON/USA	Follow the trend lines, not the headlines.
6091 MAN CAVE/MEN/ MERRIAM WEBSTER	Man cave: a room or space (as a basement) designed according to the taste of the man of the house to be used as his personal area for hobbies and leisure activities.
6092 BRIAN MULRONEY/ CANADA/PM	If everything is important, then nothing is important.
6093 TANZANIAN PROVERB	When elephants fight the grass (reeds) gets hurt.
6094 ENGLISH PROVERB	A fool may give a wise man counsel.
6095 ROSS PEROT/USA/ BUSINESS LEADER	Lead and inspire people. Don't try to manage and manipulate people.

NUMBER CATEGORY/CREDIT	TOPIC
6096 PROVERB	Many hands make light work.
6097 USA/ARETHA FRANKLIN/ INAUGURATION HAT	... sometimes you could search for something long and hard, until you realize that what you're looking for is right at home.
6098 DAVID CAMERON/UK/ PRIME MINISTER	Violence against women is an iceberg under the surface of society.
6099 EMILY DICKINSON/USA/ WRITER	Dogs are better than human beings because they know but do not tell.
6100 TIMOTHY FERRIS/USA	What we fear doing most is usually what we most need to do.
6101 WILLIAM JAMES/ USA/PHILOSOPHER	To be a real philosopher all that is necessary is to hate someone else's type of thinking.
6102 WILLIAM BLAKE/UK	A fool sees not the same tree that a wise man sees.
6103 SAMUEL JOHNSON/ ENGLISH AUTHOR	Few things are impossible to diligence and skill. Great works are performed not by strength, but perseverance.
6104 VINCE LOMBARDI/ USA/COACH	Individual commitment to a group effort – that is what makes a team work, a company work, a society work, a civilization work.
6105 IMMANUEL KANT/ PHILOSOPHER	Immaturity is the incapacity to use one's intelligence without the guidance of another.
6106 INDIAN PROVERB	The thief that is not caught is a king.
6107 YOSHIDA KENKO/ ESSAYS IN IDELENESS	The pleasantest of all diversions is to sit alone under the lamp, a book spread out before you, and to make friends with people of a distant past you have never known.
6108 SAMUEL JOHNSON/ UK/AUTHOR/POET	The true measure of a man is how he treats someone who can do him absolutely no good.
6109 PAUL SAMUELSON/USA/ ECONOMIST/NOBELIST L	Investing should be more like watching paint dry or watching grass grow. If you want excitement, take $800 and go to Las Vegas.
6110 MARIO VARGAS LLOSA/PERUVIAN-SPANISH WRITER/ POLITICIAN	Reading good literature is an experience of pleasure...but it is also an experience of learning what and how we are, in our human integrity and our human imperfection, with our actions, our dreams, and our ghosts, alone and in relationships that link us to others, in our public image and in the secret recesses of our consciousness.
6111 COMPOSER/LEONARD BERNSTEIN/USA	I believe that man's noblest endowment is his capacity to change.
6112 MAYA ANGELOU/ USA/POET	It is my intention to treat every person I meet as a brother, a sister, a daughter, a son, a grandson, a great grand-daughter of mine.
6113 INDIRA GANDHI/INDIA	There is not love where there is no will.
6114 ARTHUR ASHE/USA/ TENNIS	Start where you are. Use what you have. Do what you can.
6115 ALAN WATTS/USA/ WRITER	If the universe is meaningless, so is the statement that it is so. If this world is a vicious trap, so is its accuser, and the pot is calling the kettle black.
6116 ROSABETH MOSS KANTER/BUSINESS	Ambivalence about family responsibilities has a long history in the corporate world.
6117 CHINESE SAYING	Given time and patience, the mulberry leaf becomes a silk gown.
6118 INDIAN PROVERB	The voice of the poor has no echo.
6119 ILLUMINATION	Holiday related light display

NUMBER CATEGORY/CREDIT	TOPIC
6120 ANDREW CARNEGIE/ USA/BUSINESS LEADER	People who are unable to motivate themselves must be content with mediocrity, no matter how impressive their other talents.
6121 VINCE LOMBARDI/USA	Confidence is contagious. So is lack of confidence.
6122 CHARLES SWINDOLL/ USA/CLERGYMAN	We are all faced with a series of great opportunities brilliantly disguised as impossible situations.
6123 BOB HOPE/USA/ COMEDIAN	A sense of humor is good for you. Have you ever heard of a laughing hyena with a heartburn?
6124 ENGLISH PROVERB	Union is strength.
6125 EMILE ZOLA/ FRENCH NOVELIST	If I cannot overwhelm with my quality, I will overwhelm with my quantity.
6126 JOHN F. KENNEDY/USA	Forgive your enemies, but never forget their names.
6127 MARRIAGE	The popularity of "white weddings"
6128 INDIAN PROVERB	The world flatters the elephant and tramples on the ant.
6129 SAMUEL JOHNSON/UK	If you are idle, be not solitary; if you are solitary, be not idle.
6130 JOHN F. KENNEDY/ 35TH PRESIDENT/USA	I would rather be accused of breaking precedents than breaking promises.
6131 MILTON FRIEDMAN/ USA/ECONOMIST	We have a system that increasingly taxes work and subsidizes non-work.
6132 MIYAMOTO MUSASHI/ JAPANESE WARRIOR	Never let yourself be saddened by a separation.
6133 USA/BILLY BOB THORNTON/MUSICIAN	I don't have a fear of flying; I have a fear of crashing.
6134 AUSTRALIA/WISDOM OF A CONVICT	To plunder is at first as natural as to eat. How readily children lay their little hands upon every tempting article they see, until taught that it is not proper to do so.
6135 TAHAR DJAOUT/ ALGERIAN WRITER	Silence is death / And if you say nothing you die, / And if you speak you die. So speak and die.
6136 MEISTER ECKHART/ HUMANIST	Do exactly what you would do if you felt most secure.
6137 UK/PM/WINSTON CHURCHILL	Speeches should be like a lady's skirt, long enough to be appropriate, short enough to keep their attention.
6138 CHARLES DE GAULLE/ FRANCE/PRESIDENT	Since a politician never believes what he says, he is quite surprised to be taken at his word.
6139 MAGIC JOHNSON/USA/ FORMER NBA BASKETBALL PLAYER	Research your idea. See if there's a demand. A lot of people have great ideas, but they don't know if there's a need for it. You also have to research your competition.
6140 ROBERT MCCRUM/UK	Ebooks are not the end of the world.
6141 THOMAS JEFFERSON/ USA	In matters of style, swim with the current; in matters of principle, stand like a rock.
6142 DEBATE	Gambling is a personal matter.
6143 PAUL BOESE/USA/ BUSINESS/WRITER	Forgiveness does not change the past, but it does enlarge the future.
6144 DR. JOYCE BROTHERS/ USA/PSYCHOLOGIST	There is such a thing as bad publicity.

NUMBER CATEGORY/CREDIT	TOPIC
6145 UK/KATHERINE WHITEHORN	Find out what you like doing best and get someone to pay you for doing it.
6146 CHARLES SCHULTZ/USA/ CARTOONIST	Life is like a 10-speed bike. Most of us have gears we never use.
6147 CLASS MATTERS/NY TIMES/USA/2005	An old joke that Harvard's idea of diversity is putting a rich kid from California in the same room as a rich kid from New York is truer today than ever.
6148 GEOFF MULGAN/ STUDIO SCHOOL/ TED.COM	Teenagers learn best by doing things, they learn best in teams and they learn best by doing things for real – all the opposite of what mainstream schooling actually does.
6149 SAMUEL JOHNSON/ UK/AUTHOR/POET	Hope is itself a species of happiness, and, perhaps, the chief happiness which this world affords.
6150 PATRICIA RYAN/ TED.COM	Languages are dying at an unprecedented rate. A language dies every 14 days!
6151 BOB HOPE/USA/ COMEDIAN	I do benefits for all religions – I'd hate to blow the hereafter on a technicality.
6152 WARREN G. BENNIS/ USA/PSYCHOLOGIST	Becoming a leader is synonymous with becoming yourself. It is precisely that simple, and it is also that difficult.
6153 AUTHOR/YOSHIMOTO BANANA/JAPAN	As I grow older, much older, I will experience many things, and I will hit rock bottom again and again. Again and again I will suffer; again and again I will get back on my feet. I will not be defeated. I won't let my spirit be destroyed.
6154 INDIAN PROVERB	There is nothing noble in being superior to some other person. True nobility lies in being superior to your previous self.
6155 OPINION/BUSINESS	Criteria for promotion of employees
6156 VIKTOR FRANKL/ AUSTRIAN/AUTHOR/ PSYCHIATRIST	The one thing you can't take away from me is the way I choose to respond to what you do to me. The last of one's freedoms is to choose one's attitude in any given circumstance.
6157 HECTOR BOLITHO/ UK/THIS I BELIEVE	I believe that one should learn the difference between being lonely and being alone.
6158 R.L. STEVENSON/ SCOTTISH WRITER	Books are good enough in their own way but they are a mighty bloodless substitute for life.
6159 BUSINESS/EMPLOYEES	Disenchanted employees
6160 IMMANUEL KANT/ GERMAN PHILOSOPHER	Seek not the favor of the multitude; it is seldom got by honest and lawful means. But seek the testimony of few; and number not voices, but weigh them.
6161 WILLIAM JAMES/ USA/ PHILOSOPHER	What every genuine philosopher (every genuine man, in fact) craves most is praise although the philosophers generally call it recognition!
6162 CHRISTINE OVERAL/ NY TIMES/USA	In fact, people are still expected to provide reasons *not* to have children, but no reasons are required to have them.
6163 DR. JOYCE BROTHERS/ USA/PSYCHOLOGIST	If Shakespeare had to go on an author tour to promote Romeo and Juliet, he never would have written Macbeth.
6164 ELLEN GOODMAN/USA/ MEDIA/JOURNALIST	The millions of women who have had abortions do not regard them as a victory. For most they were failures – whether of contraception or relationships – accompanied by mixed feelings of regret and relief.

NUMBER CATEGORY/CREDIT	TOPIC
6165 USA/RALPH WALDO EMERSON/STATESMAN	Big jobs usually go to the men who prove their abiity to outgrow small ones.
6166 DR. RANJANA BIRD/ CANADA	A smart person can generate new knowledge. A wise person will recognize the virtue of that knowledge.
6167 THOMAS SOWELL/USA/ ECONOMIST	There are only two ways of telling the complete truth -- anonymously or posthumously.
6168 JAMES ALLEN/UK	Dream lofty dreams, and as you dream, so you shall become.
6169 TIMOTHY FERRIS/USA	People will choose unhappiness over uncertainty.
6170 SONIA SOTOMAYOR/ USA/JUDGE	Although I grew up in very modest and challenging circumstances, I consider my life to be immeasurably rich.
6171 MICHAEL JORDAN/ USA/BASKETBALL	My attitude is that if you push me towards something that you think is a weakness, then I will turn that perceived weakness into a strength.
6172 ANNA QUINDLEN/ USA/AUTHOR	Nothing important, or meaningful, or beautiful, or interesting, or great ever came out of imitations.
6173 CHINESE SAYING	You can't catch a cub without entering the tiger's den.
6174 MIYAMOTO MUSASHI	Do not let yourself be guided by the feeling of lust or love.
6175 ROBERT A. HEINLEIN/ USA/WRITER	Secrecy is the keystone to all tyranny. Not force, but secrecy and censorship. When any government or church for that matter, undertakes to say to its subjects, "This you may not read, this you must not know," the end result is tyranny and oppression, no matter how holy the motives.
6176 MANAGEMENT	Delegation
6177 JOHN JAY/USA/ JUDGE	No power on earth has a right to take our property from us without our consent.
6178 JAMES THURBER/ USA/AUTHOR	The paths of glory at least lead to the grave, but the paths of duty may not get you anywhere.
6179 MARIO VARGAS LLOSA/PERU	If you are killed because you are a writer, that's the maximum expression of respect, you know.
6180 AMBROSE BIERCE/ USA/AUTHOR	Painting: The art of protecting flat surfaces from the weather and exposing them to the critic.
6181 USA/LEONARD BERNSTEIN/COMPOSER	I believe in the potential of people. I cannot rest passively with those who give up in the name of "human nature."
6182 CANADA	Graphic anti-smoking images on cigarette boxes
6183 JONATHAN SACKS/UK	A world without values quickly becomes a world without value.
6184 JAMES CONNOLLY/ IRISH NATIONALIST	The worker is the slave of the capitalist society, the female worker is the slave of that slave.
6185 HENRY FORD/USA/ BUSINESS LEADER	It is not the employer who pays wages -- he only handles the money. It is the product that pays wages.
6186 URSULA LeGUIN/ USA/WRITER	It is good to have an end to journey towards; but it is the journey that matters in the end.
6187 ABRAHAM LINCOLN/ USA/16TH PRESIDENT	I will prepare, and someday my chance will come.
6188 PAT RILEY/USA/SPORTS/ BASKETBALL COACH	A champion needs a motivation above and beyond winning.

NUMBER CATEGORY/CREDIT	TOPIC
6189 DATING/VALUES	A perfect gentleman
6190 NAPOLEON HILL/USA/ WRITER	Do not wait; the time will never be "just right." Start where you stand, and work with whatever tools you may have at your command, and better tools will be found as you go along.
6191 TED.COM/KEVIN BREEL/ CONFESSIONS OF A DEPRESSED COMIC/USA	The world I believe in is one where I can look someone in the eye and say, "I'm going through hell," and they can look back at me and go, "Me too," and that's okay.
6192 USA/MIRIAM/THIS I BELIEVE/JURY DUTY	I suppose to some the only time a lie is not a lie is when it is given as an excuse to escape jury duty.
6193 BOB HOPE/USA/ COMEDIAN	I don't feel old. I don't feel anything till noon. That's when it's time for my nap.
6194 USA/DORIS KEARNS GOODWIN/HISTORIAN	Good leadership requires you to surround yourself with people of diverse perspectives who can disagree with you without fear of retaliation.
6195 GREED	When need turns to greed
6196 USA/ROSABETH MOSS KANTER/PROFESSOR	Cheap labor is not going to be the way we compete in the United States. It's going to be brain power.
6197 ELEANOR GORDON/ USA/MINISTER	Real sympathy with human life is the secret of the minister's success. When a young man or woman confides in me his or her desire to be a minister, I always ask first: 'Do you like people?' If not, stay away until you do.
6198 J.K. ROWLING/UK/ AUTHOR	You sort of start thinking anything's possible if you've got enough nerve.
6199 KAHLIL GIBRAN/ LEBANESE POET	Friendship is always a sweet responsibility, never an opportunity.
6200 SAYING/USA	Going to jail is not a rite of passage or a badge of honor.
6201 LUIS ALBERTO URREA/USA/THIS I BELIEVE	Many writing instructors will tell you that to be a great writer, you must be attentive. Shamans will tell you the same thing: If you want to be a good person, a whole person, wake up. Pay attention.
6202 ANONYMOUS	Before you criticize someone, you should walk a mile in their shoes. That way, when you criticize them, you're a mile away and have their shoes.
6203 USA/PAUL LAWRENCE DUNBAR/WRITER	There is no reward in being daring where courage is commonplace.
6204 FAMILY/LEARNING	Living with grandparents
6205 PUBLILIUS SYRUS/ LATIN WRITER	It is a consolation to the wretched to have companions in misery.
6206 JOSEPH CONRAD/UK	One writes only half the book; the other half is with the reader.
6207 GEORGE ORWELL/UK/ WRITER	All animals are equal, but some animals are more equal than others.
6208 CHRISTOPHER F. SCHUETZE/WRITER/ INTERNATIONAL NY TIMES	Laura Vincens (college counselor/American School of Paris): Choosing a college is like choosing a spouse – you want to be attracted to the person you marry, but at the same time there has to be more than physical attraction.
6209 ANATOLE FRANCE/ WRITER	History books that contain no lies are extremely dull.

NUMBER CATEGORY/CREDIT	TOPIC
6210 WILLIAM JAMES/USA/ PHILOSOPHER	Man can alter his life by altering his thinking.
6211 INDIAN PROVERB	To the mediocre, mediocrity seems great.
6212 CICERO/ROMAN ORATOR	We should measure affection, not like youngsters by the ardor of the passion, but by its strength and constancy.
6213 ROBERT A. HEINLEIN/ USA/WRITER	Never attribute to malice that which can be adequately explained by stupidity.
6214 USA/R.W. EMERSON	Every artist was once an amateur.
6215 MIYAMOTO MUSASHI	In all things have no preferences.
6216 BOB HOPE/USA/ COMEDIAN	I grew up with six brothers. That's how I learned to dance waiting for the bathroom.
6217 OLIVER WENDELL HOLMES, SR./USA	Beware how you take away hope from any human being.
6218 DEBATE	Biological parenthood is not necessarily the best kind of parenthood.
6219 EMILY DICKINSON/USA/ WRITER	We never know how high we are. Till we are called to rise. Then, if we are true to form, our statures touch the skies.
6220 MONI BASU/POVERTY TOURS/NYTIMES/USA	Kennedy Odede: (Executive Director of Shining Hope for Communicianes) 'Slum tourism turns poverty into entertainment, something that can be momentarily experienced and then escaped from.'
6221 AIMEE MULLINS/ THE OPPORTUNITY OF ADVERSITY/TEDTALK	Adversity isn't an obstacle that we need to get around in order to resume living our life. It's part of our life. I think of it like my shadow – sometimes I see a lot of it, sometimes there's very little, but it is always with me.
6222 CHARLES DE GAULLE/ FRANCE/PRESIDENT	The graveyards are full of indispensable men.
6223 DAN HURLEY/NY TIMES/ USA	Tiger Mothers generally expect only higher grades will come from their children's diligence – not better brains.
6224 UK/WRITER/MARY WOLLSTONECRAFT	Independence I have long considered as the grand blessing of life, the basis of every virtue; and independence I will ever secure by contracting my wants, though I were to live on a barren heath.
6225 IMMANUEL KANT/ GERMAN/PHILOSOPHER	To be is to do.
6226 GEORGE WASHINGTON CARVER/USA/SCIENTIST	Anything will give up its secrets if you love it enough.
6227 SAMUEL BUTLER/UK/ WRITER	A friend who cannot at a pinch remember a thing or two that never happened is as bad as one who does not know how to forget.
6228 CASSANDRA WILSON/US	Coca Cola will always outsell champagne.
6229 WILLIAM JAMES/USA/ PHILOSOPHER	The one who thinks over his experiences most, and weaves them into systematic relations with each other, will be the one with the best memory.
6230 HECTOR BOLITHO/ UK/THIS I BELIEVE	I believe it is wrong to wish to be one-up on the Joneses, and it's a sin to plant this notion in the minds of the young.
6231 OPRAH WINFREY/ USA/MEDIA MOGUL	Real integrity is doing the right thing, knowing that nobody's going to know whether you did it or not.
6232 BILL GATES/USA/ ENTREPRENEUR	It's fine to celebrate success but it is more important to heed the lessons of failure.

NUMBER CATEGORY/CREDIT	TOPIC
6233 COLIN POWELL/USA/ STATESMAN	Experts often possess more data than judgment.
6234 HAROLD H. GREENE/ USA/JUDGE	Every one of the world's dictatorships can and does claim to be acting in the name of the people.
6235 USA/MALCOLM GLADWELL/AUTHOR	No one who can rise before dawn three hundred sixty days a year fails to make his family rich.
6236 JOHN F. KENNEDY/ USA/35TH PRESIDENT	Change is the law of life. And those who look only to the past or present are certain to miss the future.
6237 CLINT EASTWOOD/USA	If you want a guarantee, buy a toaster.
6238 DEBATE	That aliens exist somewhere in the universe
6239 LOUIS NIZER/USA/ LAWYER	I know of no higher fortitude than stubbornness in the face of overwhelming odds.
6240 DR. ANDREW WEIL/ TIME MAGAZINE	Don't be afraid to leave the digital world behind, even for extended periods.
6241 ISAAC NEWTON/UK/ SCIENTIST	If I have seen further it is by standing on the shoulders of giants.
6242 INDIAN PROVERB	Though the snake be small, it is still wise to hit it with a big stick.
6243 WARREN G. BENNIS/USA	Failing organizations are usually over-managed and under-led.
6244 EMILY DICKINSON/USA/ WRITER	The truth I do not dare to know I muffle with a jest.
6245 SAMUEL JOHNSON/UK	It is better to live rich than to die rich.
6246 DR. JOYCE BROTHERS/ USA/PSYCHOLOGIST	Anger repressed can poison a relationship as surely as the cruelest words.
6247 SAMUEL JOHNSON/ UK/AUTHOR/POET	People need to be reminded more often than they need to be instructed.
6248 BRETT KENNY/SOCCER/ AUSTRALIA	I say to the young blokes, when you get asked for an autograph, don't knock it back because there'll be a time when no one will ask you.
6249 MAO TSETUNG/ CHAIRMAN/CHINA/	Weapons are an important factor in war, but not the decisive one; it is man and not materials that counts.
6250 ADVICE	Don't let anyone else tell you who you are. You decide who you are.
6251 JAPAN/ELDERLY	70 year-olds taking care of their 90-year-old parents
6252 SUCCESS/EFFORT	Turning setbacks into comebacks
6253 ROBERT A. HEINLEIN/ USA/WRITER	Being right too soon is socially unacceptable.
6254 SHLOMO BENARTZZI/ TED.COM	Self-control is not a problem in the future. It's only a problem now when the chocolate is next to us.
6255 ROBERT A. HEINLEIN/ USA/WRITER	Whenever women have insisted on absolute equality with men, they have invariably wound up with the dirty end of the stick. What they are and what they can do makes them superior to men, and their proper tactic is to demand special privileges, all the traffic will bear. They should never settle merely for equality. For women, "equality" is a disaster.
6256 ARISTOTLE ONASSIS/ SHIPPING MAGNATE	If women didn't exist, all the money in the world would have no meaning.
6257 AESOP/GREEK SLAVE	Beware lest you lose the substance by grasping at the shadow.

NUMBER CATEGORY/CREDIT	TOPIC
6258 MIYAMOTO MUSASHI/ JAPAN/WARRIOR	To know ten thousand things, know one well.
6259 MEDICINE/SURGERY	Conjoined twins
6260 ZIG ZIGLAR/USA/ MOTIVATION	Some of us learn from other people's mistakes and the rest of us have to be other people.
6261 ISAAC NEWTON/UK	To every action there is always opposed an equal reaction.
6262 C.K. PRAHALAD/ BUSINESS/AUTHOR	If your aspirations are not greater than your resources, you're not an entrepreneur.
6263 YOSHIDA KENKO/ ESSAYS IN IDLENESS	It is a great error to be superior to others…It is such pride as this that makes a man appear a fool, makes him abused by others, and invites disaster.
6264 DEBATE	That good fences make good neighbors.
6265 TIM WENDEL/NY WORLD-TELEGRAM - SUN	After [Martin Luther] King's assassination, riots broke out in more than 100 U.S. cities – the worst destruction since the Civil War.
6266 JAMES ALLEN/NEW ZEALAND/AUTHOR	Your vision is the promise of what you shall one day be; your ideal is the prophecy of what you shall at last unveil.
6267 INDIAN PROVERB	Undeserved punishment is better than that which is deserved.
6268 THOMAS SOWELL/USA	Capitalism knows only one color: that color is green.
6269 UN SEC. GEN. KOFI ANNAN/NATIONAL SOVEREIGNTY	Humanitarian intervention: military or other intervention in the affairs of another country where people are being subject to inhumane treatment
6270 FRANK SINATRA/USA/ SINGER/HUMOR	Basically, I'm for anything that gets you through the night – be it prayer, tranquilizers or a bottle of Jack Daniels.
6271 ABRAHAM LINCOLN/ 16th PRESIDENT/USA	Character is like a tree and reputation like its shadow. The shadow is what we think of it; the tree is the real thing.
6272 AMOS BRONSON ALCOTT/USA	A true teacher defends his students against his own personal influences.
6273 USA/W. EDWARDS DEMING/QUALITY	It is not enough to do your best; you must know what to do, and then do your best.
6274 ADVICE/BABZEE VEE/ TWITTER	Marriage isn't a 50-50 partnership – more like 90-10. Sometimes you're the 90, sometimes you're the 10.
6275 IMMANUEL KANT/ PHILOSOPHER	It is not God's will merely that we should be happy, but that we should make ourselves happy.
6276 SOCIETY	Civil disobedience
6277 GERMAN/ARTHUR SCHOPENHAUER	We forfeit three-quarters of ourselves in order to be like other people.
6278 JOSEPH P. KENNEDY/ USA/DIPLOMAT/ CONFIDENCE	Whenever you're sitting across from some important person, always picture him sitting there in a suit of long red underwear. That's the way I always operated in business.
6279 ARAB PROVERB	Write bad things that are done to you in sand, but write the good things that happen to you on a piece of marble.
6280 DRUGS	Use of medication to calm children down

NUMBER CATEGORY/CREDIT	TOPIC
6281 ELIZABETH GURLEY BROWN/USA	Beauty can't amuse you, but brainwork – reading, writing, thinking – can.
6282 LANGUAGE/SPEECH	Slip of tongue
6283 PUBLILIUS SYRUS	The poor man is ruined as soon as he begins to ape the rich.
6284 UK/WINSTON CHURCHILL/PM	No one pretends that democracy is perfect or all-wise. Indeed, it has been said that democracy is the worst form of Government except all those other forms that have been tried from time to time.
6285 SIR ARTHUR CONAN DOYLE/UK	Mediocrity knows nothing higher than itself, but talent instantly recognizes genius.
6286 GEORGIA O'KEEFE/ USA/ARTIST	I hate flowers – I paint them because they're cheaper than models and they don't move.
6287 JOHN DRYDEN/ UK/POET/ PLAYWRIGHT	The famous rules, which the French call *Des Trois Unites*, or, the Three Unities, which ought to be observed in very regular play: namely, of Time, Place, and Action.
6288 PUBLILIUS SYRUS/ LATIN WRITER	He who is bent on doing evil can never want occasion.
6289 HEALTH/GEOGRAPHY	Common health problems in your part of the world
6290 INDIAN PROVERB	He who works like a slave, eats like a king.
6291 CHARLES BUKOWSKI/ USA/POET/NOVELIST	Some people never go crazy. What truly horrible lives they must lead.
6292 ELIZABETH GURLEY BROWN/USA/EDITOR	After you're older, two things are possibly more important than any others: health and money.
6293 JONATHAN SACKS/ RABBI/ THE DIGNITY OF DIFFERENCE	Peace can be agreed around the conference table, but unless it grows in ordinary hearts and minds, it does not last. It may not even begin.
6294 SABATINA JAMES/USA/ THE DAILY BEAST	According to the United Nations, 5,000 women and girls are murdered around the world each year for "shaming" the family by acting in ways deemed disobedient or immodest.
6295 JAMES ALLEN/AS A MAN THINKETH	You will become as small as your controlling desire; as great as you dominant aspiration.
6296 MALCOLM X/USA/ MINISTER/ACTIVIST	You show me a capitalist, and I will show you a blood sucker.
6297 PUBLILIUS SYRUS	Never promise more than you can perform.
6298 JOHN UPDIKE/USA/ WRITER	Four years was enough of Harvard. I still had a lot to learn, but had been given the liberating notion that now I could teach myself.
6299 AYN RAND/RUSSIAN-AMERICAN WRITER	The most depraved type of human being is the man without a purpose.
6300 GUY KAWASAKI/ AUTHOR/USA	You should always try to be a 'mensch.' A mensch helps people who can't necessarily help them back.
6301 CHARLES BUKOWSKI/ USA/POET/NOVELIST	Do you hate people? I don't hate them...I just feel better when they're not around.
6302 WARREN G. BENNIS/USA	Leaders keep their eyes on the horizon, not just on the bottom line.
6303 J.K. ROWLING/ UK/WRITER/	Poverty entails fear and stress and sometimes depression. It means a thousand petty humiliations and hardships.

NUMBER CATEGORY/CREDIT	TOPIC
6304 PHILIPPE NERICAULT DESTOUCHES/FRENCH	Those not present are always wrong.
6305 PUBLILIUS SYRUS	The anger of lovers renews the strength of love.
6306 SONIA SOTOMAYOR/ USA/SUPREME COURT	We apply law to facts. We don't apply feelings to facts.
6307 DOROTHY HEIGHT/ USA/CIVIL RIGHTS	If you worry about who is going to get credit, you don't get much work done.
6308 ACHIEVEMENT	There is intelligence in motion.
6309 ADAM SMITH/SCOT	No complaint …is more common than that of a scarcity of money.
6310 J.M. COETZEE/S. AFRICA/ NOVELIST	The secret of happiness is not doing what we like but in liking what we do.
6311 JOHN F. KENNEDY/ 35TH PRESIDENT/USA	The great French Marshall Lyautey once asked his gardener to plant a tree. The gardener objected that the tree was slow growing and would not reach maturity for 100 years. The Marshall replied, 'In that case, there is no time to lose; plant it this afternoon!
6312 FRANCE/ARMAND JEAN DU PLESSIS	To know how to dissimulate is the knowledge of kings.
6313 P. JENNINGS/CAN/USA	I'm a reporter. I'm not a scholar.
6314 ADAM SMITH/ SCOTTISH	No society can surely be flourishing and happy, of which the greater part of the members are poor and miserable.
6315 BERTRAND RUSSELL/ UK/PHILOSOPHER	It's easy to fall in love. The hard part is finding someone to catch you.
6316 JOHN STUART MILL/ UK/PHILOSOPHER	Education: the inculcation of the incomprehensible into the indifferent by the incompetent.
6317 PERSONAL/ HOLIDAYS	Favorite holidays
6318 OSCAR WILDE/POET	Experience is the name everyone gives to their mistakes.
6319 PETER DRUCKER/ MANAGEMENT WRITER/PROFESSOR	Checking the results of a decision against its expectations shows executives what their strengths are, where they need to improve, and where they lack knowledge or information.
6320 DEBORAH L. JACOBS/ FORBES/USA	These days if people can't find you on Google, they might decide you don't exist.
6321 ZHUANGZI/CHINA	The use of reward and punishment is the lowest form of education.
6322 JIM ROHN/USA	Decide the quality of life you want to have, and then surround yourself with the people who represent and support that vision.
6323 LISA KRISTINE/US PHOTOGRAPHER	There are more than 27 million people enslaved in the world today – that's double the amount of people taken from Africa during the entire trans-Atlantic slave trade.
6324 STEVE JOBS/USA/ ENTREPRRENEUR	You can't just ask customers what they want and then try to give that to them. By the time you get it built, they'll want something new.
6325 MORTIMER ADLER/ USA/PHILOSOPHER	The telephone book is full of facts, but it doesn't contain a single idea.
6326 GERMAINE GREER/ AUSTRALIAN FEMINIST/WRITER	All societies on the verge of death are masculine. A society can survive with only one man; no society will survive a shortage of women.

NUMBER CATEGORY/CREDIT	TOPIC
6327 JOHN F. KENNEDY/ USA/35th PRESIDENT	Let us never negotiate out of fear. But let us never fear to negotiate.
6328 PAULO COELHO/ BRAZILIAN NOVELIST	Love can consign us to hell or to paradise, but it always takes us somewhere.
6329 LOUIS L'AMOUR/USA/ WRITER	The trail is the thing, not the end of the trail. Travel too fast, and you miss all you are traveling for.
6330 PUBLILIUS SYRUS	The judge is condemned when the criminal is absolved.
6331 POET/RALPH WALDO EMERSON/USA	A man builds a fine house; and now he has a master, and a task for life; he is to furnish, watch, show it, and keep it in repair, the rest of his days.
6332 UK/PM/WINSTON CHURCHILL/MY EARLY LIFE	It is a good thing for an uneducated man to read books of quotations…The quotations when engraved upon the memory give you good thoughts. They also make you anxious to read the authors and look for more.
6333 INDIAN PROVERB	I have lanced many boils, but none pained like my own.
6334 WRITER/WILLIAM SHAKESPEARE	How poor are they who have not patience / What wound did ever heal but by degrees
6335 DR. ALEXANDER FORBES/THIS I BELIEVE	The notion that science and religion are antagonistic and incompatible seems, to me, utterly false.
6336 MIYAMOTO MUSASHI/ JAPANESE WARRIOR	You may abandon your own body but you must preserve your honor.
6337 PAUL THEROUX/TRAVEL WRITER	Fiction gives us a second chance that life denies us.
6338 ROBERT GATES/USA/ DEFENSE/WAPO	For everyone who would become a leader, the time will inevitably come when you must stand alone.
6339 STEVEN WRIGHT/USA	Everywhere is walking distance if you have the time.
6340 ROBERT LOUIS STEVENSON/WRITER	Perpetual devotion to what a man calls his business, is only sustained by perpetual neglect of many other things.
6341 JONATHAN SWIFT/ IRISH/WRITER	Better belly burst than good liquor be lost.
6342 ANNE SULLIVAN/USA/ INSTRUCTOR/HELEN KELLER	It's a great mistake, I think, to put children off with falsehoods and nonsense, when their growing powers of observation and discrimination excite in them a desire to know about things.
6343 IMMANUEL KANT/ PHILOSOPHER	It is not necessary that whilst I live I live happily; but it is necessary that so long as I live I should live honorably.
6344 HERODOTUS/HISTORY	Men trust their ears less than their eyes.
6345 ADOPTION/ HONESTY	Open adoption
6346 CHARLES M. BLOW/USA/ NYTIMES/COLUMNIST	Just because a person is soft-spoken doesn't mean he is well-spoken.
6347 ERNEST HEMINGWAY/US	A man can be destroyed but not defeated.
6348 JOAN CRAWFORD/USA/ ACTOR	If you've earned a position, be proud of it. Don't hide it.
6349 MESSAGE IN A BOTTLE/ OCEAN/FUTURE	What message you would write and put in a bottle if you were trapped on an island.
6350 J.M. COETZEE/ S. AFRICA/NOVELIST	We must cultivate, all of us, a certain ignorance, a certain blindness, or society will not be tolerable.

NUMBER CATEGORY/CREDIT	TOPIC
6351 TOM PETERS/USA/AUTHOR	Only those who constantly retool themselves stand a chance of staying employed in the years ahead.
6352 BUDDY DESYLVA/USA/SONGWRITER	So always look for the silver lining /And try to find the sunny side of life.
6353 AESOP/GREEK SLAVE	Never trust the advice of a man in difficulties.
6354 JOSEPH CONRAD/UK/POLISH-BORN/NOVELIST	A work that aspires, however humbly, to the condition of art should carry its justification in every line.
6355 EDUCATION	Academic bridge programs
6356 MIKE MYATT/FORBES/USA	Desire and determination can work around or overcome most of life's challenges.
6357 ANNA QUINDLEN/USA/AUTHOR	When you really want to say no, say no. You can't do everything—or at least not well.
6358 WILKIE COLLINS /THE WOMAN IN WHITE/WRITER	No sensible man ever engages, unprepared, in a fencing match of words with a woman.
6359 MICHAEL JORDAN/USA/BASKETBALL	I play to win, whether during practice or a real game. And I will not let anything get in the way of me and my competitive enthusiasm to win.
6360 THE TALMUD	The highest form of wisdom is kindness.
6361 J.K. ROWLING/UK/AUTHOR	It is our choices...that show what we truly are, far more than our abilities.
6362 PAULO COELHO/BRAZILIAN NOVELIST	Love is a trap. When it appears, we see only its light, not its shadows.
6363 WILLIAM SHAKESPEARE	The empty vessel makes the greatest sound.
6364 ELMER BOBST/USA/THIS I BELIEVE	When a fruit tree ceases to bear fruit, it is dying. And it is even so with man.
6365 SENECA/DRAMATIST	Laws do not persuade just because they threaten.
6366 CONFUCIUS/CHINESE/TR.WING-TSIT CHAN	By nature men are alike. Through practice they have become far apart.
6367 GEORGE SANTAYANA/PHILOSOPHER	To delight in war is a merit in the soldier, a dangerous quality in the captain, and a positive crime in the statesman.
6368 OSCAR WILDE/POET	I am not young enough to know everything.
6369 WORK/HOME/BUSINESS	Homepreneur
6370 ROBERT MCCRUM/UK/THE GUARDIAN	Writing can't be taught; better reading can.
6371 LOUIS L'AMOUR/USA/WRITER	Once you have read a book you care about, some part of it is always with you.
6372 KRISTA TIPPETT/USA/JOURNALIST	[Kindness] is a most edifying form of instant gratification.
6373 MARILYN MONROE/USA	Dreaming about being an actress is more exciting than being one.
6374 PUBLILIUS SYRUS	Learn to see in another's calamity the ills which you should avoid.
6375 ANWAR SADAT/EGYPTIAN PRESIDENT	Fear is, I believe, a most effective tool in destroying the soul of an individual – and the soul of a people.
6376 WINSTON CHURCHILL/UK/PRIME MINISTER	We are all worms. But I do believe that I am a glow-worm.

NUMBER CATEGORY/CREDIT	TOPIC
6377 MAYA ANGELOU/ USA/AUTHOR & POET	I've learned that people will forget what you said…but people will never forget how you made them feel.
6378 UK/WINSTON CHURCHILL/PM	In war: resolution. In defeat, defiance. In victory; magnanimity. In peace; goodwill.
6379 INDIAN PROVERB	If a man from humble beginnings gets rich, he will carry his umbrella at midnight.
6380 STEVE WILKOS/USA/ TALK SHOW HOST	The first time a man hits you should be the last time he hits you.
6381 HAROLD H. GREENE/USA	People are intimidated in court, and I try to make them comfortable.
6382 EMILY DICKINSON/USA/ WRITER	A wounded deer jumps the highest.
6383 ELLEN GOODMAN/USA/ JOURNALIST	Normal is getting dressed in clothes that you buy for work and driving through traffic in a car that you are still paying for – in order to get to the job you need to pay for the clothes and the car, and the house you leave vacant all day so you can afford to live in it.
6384 LOUIS NIZER/USA/ LAWYER	Words of comfort, skillfully administered, are the oldest therapy known to man.
6385 HAMLET/WILLIAM SHAKESPEARE	I must be cruel only to be kind; Thus bad begins, and worse remains behind.
6386 NATHAN WOLFE/ TED.COM	Don't assume that what we currently think is out there is the full story. Go after the dark matter, in whatever field you choose to explore.
6387 UMBERTO ECO/WRITER	When you are on the dance floor, there is nothing to do but dance.
6388 KAHLIL GIBRAN/ LEBANESE POET	If the other person injures you, you may forget the injury; but if you injure him you will always remember.
6389 JOHN McENROE/USA/ TENNIS CHAMPION	The important thing is to learn a lesson every time you lose.
6390 US/THIS I BELIEVE/ ARTHUR S. ABRAMSON	I believe that experience counts most heavily in the construction of the house of life, and not how we are told to build.
6391 LEE IACOCCA/USA/CEO	Management is nothing more than motivating other people.
6392 WAR ON TERROR/USA	No-fly list
6393 GEORGE SANTAYANA/ USA/WRITER	To be interested in the changing seasons is a happier state of mind than to be hopelessly in love with spring.
6394 ALBERT EINSTEIN/ PHYSICIST/NOBELIST	The intuitive mind is a sacred gift and the rational mind its faithful servant. We have created a society that honors the servant and has forgotten the gift.
6395 BLAISE PASCAL/ FRENCH THINKER	All of man's problems come from his inability to sit quietly in a room alone.
6396 GHANA/DR. KWAME NKRUMAH/LEADER	We prefer self-government with danger to servitude in tranquility.
6397 GROUCHO MARX/USA	She got her looks from her father. He's a plastic surgeon.
6398 ABDUL KALAM/ INDIA/PRESIDENT	As a child of God, I am greater than anything that can happen to me.
6399 THE TALMUD	A person who seeks help for a friend, while needy himself, will be answered first.

NUMBER CATEGORY/CREDIT	TOPIC
6400 WILLIAM SHAKESPEARE	Ill deeds are doubled with an evil word.
6401 SATORU IWATA/ JAPAN/NINTENDO	I sincerely doubt that employees who fear they may be laid off will be able to develop software titles that could impress people around the world.
6402 ANNIE POTTS/USA/ ACTRESS	Satire is good for society.
6403 NATALIE GOLDBERG/ USA/WRITER	This is your life. You are responsible for it. You will not live forever. Don't wait.
6404 KAHLIL GIBRAN/ON TEACHING	The teacher who walks in the shadow of the temple, among his followers, gives not of his wisdom but rather of his faith and his lovingness.
6405 PAULO COELHO/ BRAZILIAN NOVELIST	We have to stop and be humble enough to understand that there is something called mystery.
6406 LONGINES/SLOGAN	Elegance is an attitude.
6407 WILLIAM JAMES/USA/ PHILOSOPHER	Compared to what we ought to be, we are half awake.
6408 EDITH HAMILTON/ AMERICAN EDUCATOR WRITER/CLASSICIST	It has always seemed strange to me that in our endless discussions about education, so little stress is laid on the pleasure of becoming an educated person, the enormous interest it adds to life. To be able to be caught up into the world of thought – that is to be educated.
6409 RUSSIA/ALEKSANDR SOLZHENITSYN/WRITER	A genius does not adjust his treatment of a theme to a tyrant's taste.
6410 AESOP/GREEK SLAVE	The gods help them that help themselves.
6411 DEBATE	People change for the worse after getting married.
6412 COLIN POWELL/USA/ STATESMAN	Giving back involves a certain amount of giving up.
6413 EDUCATION	High school education is not enough to get a good job.
6414 MIYAMOTO MUSASHI/ JAPAN/WARRIOR	To become the enemy, see yourself as the enemy.
6415 CONFUCIUS/CHINA/ SAGE	To go beyond is as wrong as to fall short.
6416 DEBATE	Drug addicts should have access to medical care, not jail
6417 NORMAN COUSINS/USA/ EDITOR/A GAME OF CARDS/THIS I BELIEVE	This I believe – that man today has all the resources to shatter his fears and go on to the greatest golden age in history, an age which will provide the conditions for human growth and for the development of the good that resides within man, whether in his individual or his collective being.
6418 EMILY DICKINSON/USA/ WRITER	The truth must dazzle gradually or every man be blind.
6419 JOSEPH CAMPBELL/ USA/AUTHOR	We must be willing to let go of the life we have planned, so as to accept the one that is waiting for us.
6420 JOSEPH CAMPBELL/USA/ WRITER	The privilege of a lifetime is being who you are.
6421 SCIENCE/RESEARCH	Scientific fraud
6422 CHINUA ACHEBE/ NIGERIA/WRITER	Storytellers are a threat. They threaten all champions of control, they frighten usurpers of the right-to-freedom of the human spirit -- in state, in church or mosque, in party congress, in the university or wherever.

NUMBER CATEGORY/CREDIT	TOPIC
6423 ACTRESS/KATHARINE HEPBURN/USA	Life is to be lived. If you have to support yourself, you had bloody well find some way that is going to be interesting. And you don't do that by sitting around wondering about yourself.
6424 CHARLES DICKENS/ UK/NOVELIST	Subdue your appetites, my dears, and you've conquered human nature.
6425 FANNIE LOU HAMER/US	We serve God by serving our fellow man.
6426 JOSEPH CONRAD/ POLISH-BORN ENGLISH NOVELIST	The conquest of the earth, which mostly means the taking it away from those who have a different complexion or slightly flatter noses than ourselves, is not a pretty thing when you look into it.
6427 ANATOLE FRANCE/FR.	If a million people say a foolish thing it is still a foolish thing..
6428 ENGLISH IDIOM	The devil is in the details.
6429 PAULO COELHO/ BRAZILIAN NOVELIST	When a person really desires something, all the universe conspires to help that person to realize his dream.
6430 SAYING	If you don't go away, they'll never miss you.
6431 JOHN DRYDEN/ UK/PLAYWRIGHT	Happy the man, and happy he alone / He, who can call today his own; / He who, secure within, can say / Tomorrow do thy worst, for I have lived today.
6432 UK/WINSTON CHURCHILL/PM	I would say to the House, as I said to those who have joined this Government: "I have nothing to offer but blood, toil, tears, and sweat."
6433 PUBLILIUS SYRUS	He who helps the guilty, shares the crime.
6434 JEAN DE LA FONTAINE/ FRENCH WRITER	To hell with pleasure that's haunted by fear.
6435 JONATHAN SACKS/ RABBI/THE DIGNITY OF DIFFERENCE	Nowadays... deals are transactional rather than personal. Instead of placing your faith in a person, you get lawyers to write safeguards into the contract. This is an historic shift from a trust economy to a risk economy.
6436 GEORGE MARDIKIAN/ USA/THIS I BELIEVE	I believe that true humility is a basic need of mankind today.
6437 THOMAS CARLYLE/SCOT ESSAYIST	The best effect of any book is that it excites the reader to self-activity.
6438 MARIO VARGAS LLOSA/WRITER	Writing a book is a very lonely business. You are totally cut off from the rest of the world, submerged in your obsessions and memories.
6439 J.P. DONLEAVY/USA	Writing is turning one's worst moments into money.
6440 IMMANUEL KANT/ GERMAN/PHILOSOPHER	Live your life as though your every act were to become a universal law.
6441 CLOTHING	Wearing fashionable clothes
6442 NELSON MANDELA/ S. AFRICA/PRESIDENT	It always seems impossible until it's done.
6443 TAVIS SMILEY/USA/ BROADCASTER	Even hope needs help.
6444 NELSON MANDELA/ SOUTH AFRICA	There is no passion to be found playing small -- in settling for a life that is less than the one you are capable of living.
6445 CHINESE PROVERB	The palest ink is better than the best memory.
6446 KARL MARX/GERMAN PHILOSOPHER	Revolutions are the locomotives of history.

NUMBER CATEGORY/CREDIT	TOPIC
6447 GERTRUDE STEIN/ USA/WRITER/POET	Everybody knows if you are too careful you are so occupied in being careful that you are sure to stumble over something.
6448 EDWARD DE BONO/ UK/AUTHOR/ PSYCHOLOGIST	An expert is someone who has succeeded in making decisions and judgments simpler through knowing what to pay attention to and what to ignore.
6449 ANN LANDERS/ USA/ADVICE COLUMNIST	Inside every seventy-year-old is a thirty-five-year-old asking, 'What happened?'
6450 WILLIAM FAULKNER/ USA/NOVELIST	Given the choice between the experience of pain and nothing, I would choose pain.
6451 KENNETH PATCHEN/ USA/POET	The one who comes to question himself cares for mankind.
6452 SATORU IWATA/CEO/ JAPAN/NINTENDO	On my business card, I am a company president. In my mind, I am a game developer. But in my heart, I am a gamer.
6453 PLATO/GREEK PHILOSOPHER	The punishment suffered by the wise who refuse to take part in the government is to live under the government of bad men.
6454 JOHANN WOLFGANG VON GOETHE/ GERMAN DRAMATIST	Beware of dissipating your powers; strive constantly to concentrate them. Genius thinks it can do whatever it sees others doing, but is sure to repent of every ill-judged outlay.
6455 BUSINESS/FUN	Auctions
6456 TRANSPORTATION	Electric vehicles
6457 WILLIAM FAULKNER/ USA/NOVELIST	A bus station is where a bus stops. A train station is where a train stops. On my desk, I have a work station…
6458 ROBERT BROWNING/ UK/POET	Measure your mind's height by the shade it casts.
6459 USA/LEONARD BERNSTEIN/COMPOSER	We must not enslave ourselves to dogma.
6460 ADOLFO BIOY CASARES/ARGENTINA	Life has now taught me that love for things, like all unrequited love, takes its toll in the long run.
6461 MALCOLM X/USA/ LEADER/ACTIVIST	If you have no critics you'll likely have no success.
6462 PAUL FARMER/USA	I believe in health care as a human right.
6463 CHINUA ACHEBE/ NIGERIA/WRITER	It is only the story…that saves our progeny from blundering like blind beggars into the spikes of the cactus fence. The story is our escort; without it, we are blind.
6464 CULTURE/TABOOS/ RESTRICTION	Cultural restrictions
6465 WALTER H. PAGE/USA/ UP FROM SLAVERY	Every student does not profit by a great teacher…
6466 WOMEN/CHILDREN	Biological clock
6467 RUSSIA/ALEKSANDR SOLZHENITSYN/WRITER	Every man always has a dozen glib little reasons why he is right not to sacrifice himself.
6468 BOB MARLEY/ MUSICIAN/JAMAICA	The winds that sometimes take something we love, are the same that bring us something we learn to love.
6469 TUPAC SHAKUR/USA/ MUSICIAN	I just don't know how to deal with so many people giving me that much affection. I never had that in my life.

NUMBER CATEGORY/CREDIT	TOPIC
6470 UK/WINSTON CHURCHILL/ STATESMAN	There comes a special moment in everyone's life; a moment for which that person was born. That special opportunity, when he seizes it, will fulfill his mission -- a mission for which he is uniquely qualified. In that moment, he finds greatness. It is his finest hour.
6471 J.M. COETZEE/S. AFRICA/ WRITER	Our lies reveal as much about us as our truths.
6472 W.E.B. DU BOIS/USA/ REFORMER/WRITER	To be a poor man is hard, but to be a poor race in a land of dollars is the very bottom of hardships.
6473 LOUIS L'AMOUR/ AMERICAN WRITER	Up to a point a person's life is shaped by environment, heredity, and changes in the world about them. Then there comes a time when it lies within their grasp to shape the clay of their life into the sort of thing they wish it to be. Only the weak blame parents, their race, their times, lack of good fortune or the quirks of fate. Everyone has the power to say, "This I am today. That I shall be tomorrow."
6474 MOTHER TERESA/ CATHOLIC NUN	Every time you smile at someone, it is an action of love, a gift to that person, a beautiful thing.
6475 PAT RILEY/AMERICAN COACH	Being a part of success is more important than being personally indispensable.
6476 WILLIAM JAMES/USA/ PHILOSOPHER	Do something everyday for no other reason than you would rather not do it, so that when the hour of dire need draws nigh, it may find you not unnerved and untrained to stand the test.
6477 ARAB PROVERB	If you have much, give of your wealth; if you have little, give of your heart.
6478 VINCE LOMBARDI/ USA/FOOTBALL COACH	Leaders are made, they are not born. They are made by hard effort, which is the price which all of us must pay to achieve any goal that is worthwhile.
6479 WILLIAM SHAKESPEARE	In a false quarrel there is no true valor.
6480 GEORGE WHITMAN/ FRANCE/PROPRIETOR	The book business is the business of life.
6481 MRS JOHN G. LEE/USA/ THIS I BELIEVE	I learned that each one of us has a right to his own beliefs, that prejudice perverts truth and that violence in the long run gains us nothing.
6482 J.R LABBE/MOTHERLY ADVICE/TWITTER	When you break off an engagement (or get divorced) give back the ring – but keep the stone.
6483 GEORGE ELIOT/UK	Breed is stronger than pasture.
6484 RORY SUTHERLAND/ TED.COM/ADVERTISING	The circumstances of our lives actually matter less to our happiness than the sense of control we feel over our lives.
6485 SAMUEL JOHNSON/ UK/AUTHOR	Self-confidence is the first requisite to great undertakings.
6486 ROBERT KIYOSAKI/ AUTHOR/USA	The employee mindset: Schools teach children to be compliant, to do as they're told, to be good employees – or face the consequences.
6487 TIA CARRERE/USA/ ACTRESS/CELEBRITY	People want me to do the strangest things. They want to me to sign their arms or chests.
6488 DEBATE	You cannot legislate morality.
6489 ALLEN KLEIN/ BUSINESSMAN	I contend that not only can you laugh at adversity, but it is essential to do so if you are to deal with setbacks without defeat.
6490 PERSONAL DESIRE	The most important wish for your life.
6491 FAILURE	Fear of failure

NUMBER CATEGORY/CREDIT	TOPIC
6492 G.K. CHESTERTON/UK/ WRITER	There is but an inch of difference between the cushioned chamber and the padded cell.
6493 MURIEL RUKEYSER/ USA/POET	Breathe-in experience; breathe-out poetry.
6494 ECKHART TOLLE/ GERMAN/CANADA	You can only lose something that you have, but you cannot lose something that you are.
6495 NORMAN BORLAUG/ NOBEL LAUREATE/ FATHER OF THE GREEN REVOLUTION	The forgotten world is made up primarily of the developing nations, where most of the people, comprising more than fifty percent of the total world population live in poverty, with hunger as a constant companion and fear of famine a continual menace.
6496 THE TALMUD	You can educate a fool, but you cannot make him think.
6497 WILLIAM SHAKESPEARE	In time we hate that which we often fear.
6498 EDWARD EVERETT/USA	Education is a better safeguard of liberty than a standing army.
6499 LANCE ITO/USA/ JUDGE	If you take the cameras out of the courtroom, then you hide a certain measure of truth from the public.
6500 WILKIE COLLINS/UK/ WRITER	Silence is safe.
6501 HOSPITALS	Intensive care unit (ICU)
6502 FAVORITE/CITY	Favorite city in the world
6503 BUSINESS/JACK WELCH/FORMER CEO	Number one, cash is king...number two, communicate...number three, buy or bury the competition.
6504 ALBERT EINSTEIN/ PHYSICIST/NOBEL	Nationalism is an infantile sickness. It is the measles of the human race.
6505 FRANK LLOYD WRIGHT/ USA/ARCHITECT	I'm all in favor of keeping dangerous weapons out of the hands of fools. Let's start with typewriters.
6506 WINSTON CHURCHILL/ UK/PRIME MINISTER	The empires of the future are the empires of the mind.
6507 ROBERT LOUIS STEVENSON/SCOT/ WRITER	In each of us, two natures are at war – the good and the evil. All our lives the fight goes on between them, and one of them must conquer. But in our own hands lies the power to choose – what we want most to be we are.
6508 ANONYMOUS	The real measure of your wealth is how much you'd be worth if you lost all your money.
6509 HORATIO NELSON/ UK/LEADER	My character and good name are in my own keeping. Life with disgrace is dreadful. A glorious death is to be envied.
6510 JOHN NAISBITT/USA/ AUTHOR	Don't get so far in front of the parade that no one knows you're in the parade.
6511 DEBATE	That paparazzi are dangerous.
6512 DANISH/SOREN KIERKEGAARD/THINKER	Prayer does not change God, but it changes him who prays.
6513 USA/HENRY BROOKS ADAMS/WRITER	A friend in power is a friend lost.
6514 JULIA MORGAN/USA/ ARCHITECT	Never turn down a job because you think it's too small. You don't know where it can lead.
6515 THE TALMUD	Learning is achieved only in company.

NUMBER CATEGORY/CREDIT	TOPIC
6516 FAMILY	Family pressure
6517 ROGER BABSON/ BUSINESS/MONEY	More people should learn to tell their dollars where to go instead of asking them where they went.
6518 KAHLIL GIBRAN/POET	There are those among you who seek the talkative through fear of being alone.
6519 MOTHER TERESA/ CATHOLIC NUN	Give the world the best you have and you may get hurt. Give the world your best anyway.
6520 KEVIN STONE/TED.COM/ PHYSICIAN	Cancer may kill you, but when you look at the numbers, arthritis ruins more lives.
6521 AESOP/GREEK	Self-conceit may lead to self-destruction.
6522 INDIAN PROVERB	If they don't exchange a few words, father and son will never know each other.
6523 USA/THOMAS SOWELL/ECONOMIST	Talkers are usually more articulate than doers, since talk is their specialty.
6524 EDWARD DE BONO/ UK/PSYCHOLOGIST	An idea that is developed and put into action is more important than an idea that exists only as an idea.
6525 BUDDY DESYLVA/ USA/SONGWRITER	Though April showers may come your way. They bring the flowers that bloom in May.
6526 ANONYMOUS	A truly happy person is the one who can enjoy the scenery on a detour.
6527 NADINE GORDIMER/ AUTHOR/S. AFRICA	Books don't need batteries.
6528 HORACE MANN/USA/ EDUCATION	A teacher who is attempting to teach without inspiring the pupil with a desire to learn is hammering on cold iron.
6529 ANTON CHEKHOV/ RUSSIAN WRITER	I promise to be an excellent husband, but give me a wife who, like the moon, will not appear every day in my sky.
6530 MAYA ANGELOU/USA/ WRITER	Forgiveness is the greatest gift you can give yourself.
6531 GERMAN/ARTHUR SCHOPENHAUER	Treat a work of art like a prince. Let it speak to you first.
6532 CHARLES DICKENS/ ENGLISH NOVELIST	Annual income twenty pounds, annual expenditure nineteen six, result happiness. Annual income twenty pounds, annual expenditure twenty pound ought and six, result misery.
6533 AMBROSE BIERCE/ USA/AUTHOR	Admiration: Our polite recognition of another's resemblance to ourselves.
6534 HERODOTUS/HISTORIAN	A man calumniated is doubly injured – first by him who utters the calumny, and then by him who believes it.
6535 PAULO COELHO/ BRAZIL/MUSICIAN	You drown not by falling into a river, but by staying submerged in it.
6536 UK/PM/WINSTON CHURCHILL	If you love somebody, let them go, for if they return, they were always yours. And if they don't, they never were.
6537 PUBLILIUS SYRUS	The fear of death is more to be dreaded than death itself.
6538 PARENTING/ TWINS	Twins: burden or a blessing
6539 STEVE JOBS/ ENTREPRRENEUR	What a computer is to me is the most remarkable tool that we have ever come up with. It's the equivalent of a bicycle for our minds.

NUMBER CATEGORY/CREDIT	TOPIC
6540 LEE J. COLAN/USA/ BUSINESS CONSULTANT	I felt as if I were walking with destiny, and that all my past life had been but a preparation for this hour and this trial.
6541 OLIVER WENDELL HOLMES JR./USA	Any two philosophers can tell each other all they know in two hours.
6542 NATION	What you wish for your country
6543 FYODOR DOSTOEVSKY/ RUSSIA/WRITER	If there is no God, everything is permitted.
6544 CHARLES BUKOWSKI/ USA/POET/NOVELIST	Sometimes you climb out of bed in the morning and you think, I'm not going to make it, but you laugh inside – remembering all the time you've felt that way.
6545 AKIRA KUROSAWA/ JAPAN/FILMMAKER	In order to write scripts, you must first study the great novels and dramas of the world. You must consider why they are great. Where does the emotion come from that you feel as you read them? What degree of passion did the author have to have, what level of meticulousness did he have to command, in order to portray the characters and events as he did?... If your goal is to become a film director, you must master screenwriting.
6546 AUTHOR UNKNOWN	Without a compelling cause, our employees are just putting in time. Their minds might be engaged, but their hearts are not. Meaning precedes motivation.
6547 BORIS PASTERNAK/ RUSSIAN NOVELIST	At the moment of childbirth, every woman has the same aura of isolation, as though she were abandoned, alone.
6548 CHARLES BUKOWSKI/ USA/NOVELIST	We are all going to die, all of us, what a circus! That alone should make us love each other but it doesn't. We are terrorized and flattened by trivialities, we are eaten up by nothing.
6549 NORTHROP FRYE/ CRITIC/CANADA	Americans like to make money; Canadians like to audit it. I know no other country where accountants have a higher social and moral status.
6550 NATIONAL SECURITY/ ESPIONAGE	When an intelligence officer smells flowers, he looks around for the coffins.
6551 JAPAN/W. EDWARDS DEMING/QUALITY/USA	Profit in business comes from repeat customers, customers that boast about your project or service, and that bring friends with them.
6552 BERTRAND RUSSELL/ UK/AUTHOR	So far as I can remember, there is not one word in the Gospels in praise of intelligence.
6553 JOSEPH STIGLITZ/ USA/ECONOMIST	I grew up in a family in which political issues were often discussed, and debated intensely.
6554 TUPAC SHAKUR/ USA/MUSICIAN	I think I am a natural born leader. I know how to bow down to authority if it's authority that I respect.
6555 BOB MARLEY/MUSIC/ JAMAICA	Who are you to judge the life I live? Before you start pointing fingers, make sure your hands are clean.
6556 DEREK SIVERS/HOW TO START A MOVEMENT/ TEDTALK/USA	If you really care about starting a movement, have the courage to follow and show others how to follow. And when you find a lone nut doing something great, have the guts to be first one to stand up and join in.
6557 DENIS DIDEROT/ FRANCE/THINKER	Only passions, great passions, can elevate the soul to great things.
6558 ARISTOTLE/THINKER	All paid jobs absorb and degrade the mind.

NUMBER CATEGORY/CREDIT	TOPIC
6559 BORIS PASTERNAK/ RUSSIAN NOVELIST	I don't like people who have never fallen or stumbled. Their virtue is lifeless and it isn't of much value. Life hasn't revealed its beauty to them.
6560 IDEAS/CITY LIFE	Your ideas for improving city life
6561 JONATHAN SACKS/ RABBI/THE DIGNITY OF DIFFERENCE	We know – it has been measured in many experiments – that children with strong impulse control grow to be better adjusted, more dependable, achieve higher grades in school and college and have more success in their careers than others.
6562 WOODY ALLEN/USA/ MOVIE PRODUCER	If only God would give me some clear sign! Like making a large deposit in my name at a Swiss bank.
6563 JOSEPH CONRAD/ NOVELIST	I don't like work – no man does – but I like what is in work – the chance to find yourself.
6564 J. K. ROWLING/UK/ AUTHOR/HARRY POTTER	It takes a great deal of courage to stand up to your enemies, but even more to stand up to your friends.
6565 JOSEPH CONRAD/ NOVELIST/UK/POLAND	No fear can stand up to hunger, no patience can wear it out; disgust simply does not exist where hunger is.
6566 MAYA ANGELOU/USA/ WRITER/POET	I have found that among its other benefits, giving liberates the soul of the giver.
6567 WILLIAM SHAKESPEARE/ UK/PLAYWRIGHT	It is not enough to help the feeble up, but to support him after.
6568 J.M. COETZEE/ S. AFRICA/NOVELIST	Live like a hero. That's what the classics teach us. Be a main character. Otherwise what is life for?
6569 JOHN ADAMS/USA/ PRESIDENT	In politics the middle way is none at all.
6570 GIL PENCHINA/CEO/ WIKIA	If you throw gasoline on a log, all you get is a wet log. But if you throw gasoline on a small flame, you get an inferno.
6571 HARUKI MURAKAMI/ JAPAN/NOVELIST	No matter how far you travel, you can never get away from yourself.
6572 J. F. KENNEDY/USA/ 35TH PRESIDENT	For in the final analysis, our most basic common link, is that we all inhabit this small planet, we all breathe the same air, we all cherish our children's futures, and we are all mortal.
6573 SUN TZU/CHINA/ GENERAL/AUTHOR	To win one hundred victories in one hundred battles is not the acme of skill. To subdue the enemy without fighting is the acme of skill.
6574 NORTHROP FRYE/ CANADA/CRITIC	Many students in university cannot write or speak prose. The smear word 'elitist' is near to being applied to anyone who does.
6575 GAY TALESE/WRITER/ USA	News, if unreported, has no impact. It might as well have not happened at all.
6576 ANTHONY HOPKINS/ ACTOR/HUMOR	I have a punishing workout regimen. Every day I do 3 minutes on a treadmill, then, I lie down, drink a glass of vodka and smoke a cigarette.
6577 USA/BOOKER T. WASHINGTON/ EDUCATOR	Success in life is founded upon attention to the small things rather than to the large things; to the every day things nearest to us rather than to the things that are remote and uncommon.
6578 RUSSIA/ALEKSANDR SOLZHENITSYN/WRITER	If only there were evil people somewhere insidiously committing evil deeds, and it were necessary only to separate them from the rest of us and destroy them. But the line dividiing good and evil cuts through the heart of every human being. And who is willing to destroy a piece of his own heart?

NUMBER CATEGORY/CREDIT	TOPIC
6579 TV/SKILL	Makeover television programs
6580 CICERO/THINKER	To each his own.
6581 MARTIN HANCZYC/ TED.COM	If we went to another planet and though there might be life there, how could we even recognize it as life?
6582 SOJOURNER TRUTH/ USA/ACTIVIST	If women want any rights more than they's got, why don't they just take them, and not be talking about it.
6583 ADAM SMITH/ SCOTTISH ECONOMIST	It is not from the benevolence of the butcher, the brewer, or the baker that we expect our dinner, but from their regard to their own self interest.
6584 DR. DANIEL KRAFT/USA/ INNOVATOR/TED.COM	As a cancer doctor, I'm looking forward to being out of a job.
6585 ABIGAIL WASHBURN/ US-CHINA RELATIONS/ BANJO/TEDTALK	Outside your door, the world is waiting. Inside your heart, a voice is calling. The four corners of the world are watching. So travel, daughter, travel. Go get it, girl.
6586 GERMAN/FRIEDRICH NIETZSCHE/THINKER	But thus do I counsel you, my friends: distrust all in whom the impulse to punish is powerful.
6587 NUTRITION	Nutrition needs of athletes
6588 AKIRA KUROSAWA/ JAPAN/FILMMAKER	Something that you should take particular notice of is the fact that the best scripts have very few explanatory passages.
6589 FEAR/MEN	Androphobia: Fear of men
6590 MOTHER TERESA/ CATHOLIC NUN	Honesty and transparency make you vulnerable. Be honest and transparent anyway.
6591 NORTHROP FRYE/ CANADA/BOOK CRITIC	A person who knows nothing about literature may be an ignoramus, but many people do not mind being that.
6592 JEAN-BAPTISTE COLBERT/FRENCH	The art of taxation consists in so plucking the goose as to procure the greatest quantity of feather with the least possible amount of hissing.
6593 INDIA/JAWAHARLAL NEHRU/PM	The best and noblest gifts of humanity cannot be the monopoly of a particular race or country.
6594 ALAN GREENSPAN/ ECONOMIST/USA	I guess I should warn you, if I turn out to be particularly clear, you've probably misunderstood what I've said.
6595 NORTHROP FRYE/ CANADA/BOOK CRITIC	Literature encourages tolerance -- bigots and fanatics seldom have any use for the arts, because they're so preoccupied with their beliefs and actions that they can't see them also as possibilities.
6596 SKILL/SECURITY	Don't quit your day job!
6597 RUSSIA/ALEKSANDR SOLZHENITSYN/WRITER	Beat a dog once and you only have to show him the whip.
6598 ACTRESS/KATHERINE HEPBURN/USA	Death will be a great relief. No more interviews.
6599 GEORGE SANTAYANA/ WRITER	Fanaticism consists of redoubling your effort when you have forgotten your aim.
6600 DR. WILLIAM OSLER/ CANADA	Medicine is a science of uncertainty and an art of probability.
6601 SIR FRANCIS BACON/UK	The worst solitude is to be destitute of sincere friendship.
6602 JOANN THOMAS	Sometimes the best helping hand you can get is a good, firm push.

NUMBER CATEGORY/CREDIT	TOPIC
6603 FOOD/CULTURE	Typical food in your country.
6604 YOSHIDA KENKO/ ESSAYS IN IDELENESS	If you must take care that your opinions do not differ in the least from those of the person with whom you are talking, you might just as well be alone.
6605 C. NORTHCOTE PARKINSON/WRITER	Expenditure rises to meet income.
6606 RONALD REAGAN/ 40TH PRESIDENT/USA	A people free to choose will always choose peace
6607 DEBATE	Parents must help their children with homework.
6608 PAT RILEY/USA/COACH	The Ten Commandments were not a suggestion.
6609 MIYAMOTO MUSASHI/ JAPANESE WARRIOR	The only reason a warrior is alive is to fight, and the only reason a warrior fights is to win.
6610 BENJAMIN BRITTEN/ ENGLISH COMPOSER	The old idea of a composer suddenly having a terrific idea and sitting up all night to write it is nonsense. Nighttime is for sleeping.
6611 EMPLOYMENT	Hiring new employees
6612 AKIRA KUROSAWA/ JAPAN/FILMMAKER	With a good script a good director can produce a masterpiece; with the same script a mediocre director can make a passable film. But with a bad script even a good director can't possibly make a good film.
6613 ELIZABETH GURLEY BROWN/USA/EDITOR	Good girls go to heaven; bad girls go everywhere.
6614 AKIRA KUROSAWA/ JAPAN/FILMMAKER	Have the courage to follow your heart and intuition.
6615 MICHELE GOODWIN/ USA	Why does Cuba, an incredibly poor nation, have a higher literacy rate than the U.S.?
6616 AUTOMOBILE	Car air bags
6617 BILL GATES/USA	Be nice to nerds. Chances are you'll end up working for one.
6618 GEORGE SANTAYANA	The highest form of vanity is love of fame.
6619 CHRONICLE/NANCY SCHEPER- HUGHES/USA	Universities are meant to produce skepticism as well as knowledge
6620 PETER DRUCKER/ MANAGEMENT/USA	Company cultures are like country cultures. Never try to change one. Try, instead, to work with what you've got.
6621 NATALIE GOLDBERG/US	Anything we fully do is an alone journey.
6622 USA/PRES. DWIGHT D. EISENHOWER	What counts is not necessarily the size of the dog in the fight – it's the size of the fight in the dog.
6623 KARL MARX/GERMAN	The rich will do anything for the poor but get off their backs.
6624 SUSAN CAIN/AUTHOR/ TED.COM/LECTURER/US	Don't think of introversion as something to be cured.
6625 ANA IVANOVIC/SERBIA/ TENNIS PROFESSIONAL	A smile is a curve that can straighten out a lot of problems.
6626 RUSSIA/FYODOR DOSTOYEVSKY/ NOVELIST	The man who lies to himself and listens to his own lie comes to a point that he cannot distinguish the truth within him, or around him, and so loses all respect for himself and for others.
6627 RUSSIA/ALEKSANDR SOLZHENITSYN/WRITER	Talent is always conscious of its own abundance, and does not object to sharing.

NUMBER CATEGORY/CREDIT	TOPICoi9
6628 RUSSIA/ALEKSANDR SOLZHENITSYN/WRITER	Do not pursue what is illusory -- property and position: all that is gained at the expense of your nerves decade after decade and can be confiscated in one fell night.
6629 WILLIAM SHAKESPARE/UK/PLAYWRIGHT	Love looks not with the eyes, but with the mind.
6630 BRENE BROWN/WAPO	In fact, I often call perfectionism the 20-ton shield.
6631 DEBATE	Marriage for life is a recipe for boredom.
6632 INDIAN PROVERB	If you are up to your knees in pleasure, then you are up to your waist in grief.
6633 MICHAEL JORDAN/USA BASKETBALL	I can accept failure, everyone fails at something. But I can't accept not trying.
6634 PAUL THEROUX/USA/TRAVEL WRITER	Travel is glamorous only in retrospect.
6635 RICHARD POSNER/USA/JUDGE	As a social good, I think privacy is greatly overrated because privacy basically means concealment. People conceal things in order to fool other people about them.
6636 GEORGE ALLEN/USA/FOOTBALL COACH	People of mediocre ability sometimes achieve outstanding success because they don't know when to quit.
6637 JOSEPH CONRAD/ENGLISH NOVELIST	I remember my youth and the feeling that will never come back any more – the feeling that I could last for ever, outlast the sea, the earth, and all men....
6638 JANE GOODALL/UK/PRIMATOLOGIST	We can't leave people in abject poverty, so we need to raise the standard of living for 80% of the world's people, while bringing it down considerably for the 20% who are destroying our natural resources.
6639 LOUIS L'AMOUR/AMERICAN WRITER	A book is less important for what it says than for what it makes you think.
6640 BORIS PASTERNAK/RUSSIAN NOVELIST	Literature is the art of discovering something extraordinary about ordinary people, and saying with ordinary words something extraordinary.
6641 PAT RILEY/USA/COACH/BASKETBALL	Discipline is not a nasty word.
6642 ERNEST HEMINGWAY/AMERICAN NOVELIST	About morals, I know only that what is moral is what you feel good after and what is immoral is what you feel bad after.
6643 USA/RALPH WALDO EMERSON/ESSAYIST	None of us will ever accomplish anything excellent or commanding except when he listens to this whisper which is heard by him alone.
6644 LAO-TZU/CHINA/PHILOSOPHER	People are difficult to govern because they have too much knowledge.
6645 FELIX FRANKFURTER/USA/SUPREME COURT	Freedom of the press is not an end in itself but a means to the end of achieving a free society.
6646 AKIRA KUROSAWA/JAPAN/FILMMAKER	Human beings share the same common problems. A film can only be understood if it depicts these properly.
6647 BOB MARLEY/MUSICIAN/	Better to die fighting for freedom than be a prisoner all the days of your life.
6648 HORATIO NELSON/UK/ OFFICER	Time is everything; five minutes make the difference between victory and defeat.

NUMBER CATEGORY/CREDIT	TOPIC
6649 ANNE FRANK/WRITER	Parents can only give good advice, but the final forming of a person's character lies in their own hands.
6650 AKIRA KUROSAWA/ JAPAN/FILMMAKER	The characters in my films try to live honestly and make the most of the lives they've been given. I believe you must live honestly and develop your abilities to the full. People who do this are the real heroes.
6651 EDWARD DE BONO/UK	Argument is meant to reveal the truth, not to create it.
6652 ANDREW J. CHERLIN/ SOCIOLOGIST/WAPO	In the 1950s, if you weren't married, people thought you were mentally ill.
6653 REV. OTIS MOSS III/USA	Family is rooted in love, not blood.
6654 WILKIE COLLINS/UK/ MOONSTONE/WRITER	Your tears come easy, when you're young, and beginning the world. Your tears come easy, when you're old, and leaving it.
6655 DEBATE	All children must do chores at home.
6656 USA/R.W. EMERSON	The reward of a thing well done is to have done it.
6657 ALAN LAKEIN/USA	Lakein's question: "What is the best use of my time right now?"
6658 WILLIAM SHAKESPEARE	Nothing emboldens sin so much as mercy.
6659 INDIAN PROVERB	If you can't give any sugar, then speak sweetly.
6660 R. MOSS KANTER/USA/ PROFESSOR	To stay ahead, you must have your next idea waiting in the wings.
6661 WINSTON CHURCHILL/ UK/PRIME MINISTER	To jaw-jaw is always better than to war-war.
6662 USA/GENERAL LUCIUS D. CLAY/THIS I BELIEVE	In my view, to be a good citizen, does not require the holding of public office, the achievement of either political or financial success.
6663 MARILYN MONROE/USA	Dogs never bite me. Just humans.
6664 USA/ABRAHAM LINCOLN/16th PRESIDENT	I have always found that mercy bears richer fruits than strict justice.
6665 OSCAR WILDE/IRISH WRITER/POET	I was working on the proof of one of my poems all the morning, and took out a comma. In the afternoon I put it back again.
6666 USA/DR. MARTIN LUTHER KING JR.	Faith is taking the first step, even when you don't see the whole staircase.
6667 JOHN F. KENNEDY/ 35TH PRESIDENT/USA	The great enemy of truth is very often not the lie – deliberate, contrived and dishonest, but the myth, persistent, persuasive, and unrealistic.
6668 INTERNET	Cyber-bullying
6669 MERYL STREEP/ USA/ACTRESS	Every single decision I make about what material I do, what I'm putting out in the world, is because of my children.
6670 OSCAR WILDE/IRISH WRITER/POET	The aim of life is self-development. To realize one's nature perfectly – that is what each of us is here for.
6671 CONNIE PODESTA/ SUCCESS MAGAZINE	Children who can manipulate their parents soon learn to enjoy feelings of power and control over others.
6672 GERMAN/ARTHUR SCHOPENHAUER/	Great men are like eagles, and build their nest on some lofty solitude.
6673 LOUIS D. BRANDEIS/ USA/JUDGE/ SUPREME COURT	Our government...teaches the whole people by its example. If the government becomes the lawbreaker, it breeds contempt for law; it invites every man to become a law unto himself; it invites anarchy.

NUMBER CATEGORY/CREDIT	TOPIC
6674 JACOB RIIS/ PHOTOGRAPHER/ JOURNALIST	When nothing seems to help, I go and look at a stonecutter hammering away at his rock perhaps a hundred times without as much as a crack showing in it. Yet at the hundred and first blow it will split in two, and I know it was not that blow that did it -- but all that had gone before.
6675 GEORGE ORWELL/WAR/ BRITISH AUTHOR	As I write, highly civilized human beings are flying overhead, trying to kill me.
6676 AKIRA KUROSAWA/ JAPAN/FILM MAKER	I like unformed characters. This may be because, no matter how old I get, I am still unformed myself.
6677 KAREN TSE/TEDTALK/ LAWYER/USA	Ninety-five percent of torture today is not for political prisoners; it is for people who are in broken-down legal systems.
6678 PUBLILIUS SYRUS	Speech is a mirror of the soul; as a man speaks, so is he.
6679 JANE AUSTEN/UK/ NOVELIST	I do not want people to be agreeable, as it saves me the trouble of liking them.
6680 WILLIAM SHAKESPEARE	Praising what is lost makes the remembrance dear.
6681 JOSEPH CONRAD/UK/ WRITER	The terrorist and the policeman both come from the same basket.
6682 THOMAS JEFFERSON/US	Never trouble another for what you can do for yourself.
6683 INDIAN PROVERB	If you live in the river, you should make friends with the crocodile.
6684 THE TALMUD	If silence is good for the wise, how much better for fools.
6685 ZIG ZIGLAR/USA/ MOTIVATION	If you can dream it, then you can achieve it. You will get all you want in life if you help enough other people get what they want.
6686 ANAND AGARAWALA/ TEDALK/US/DESIGNER	We're in the 'cave-painting' era of computer interfaces.
6687 UK/PM/WINSTON CHURCHILL/SPEECH/ HOUSE OF COMMONS	You ask, what is our aim? I can answer in one word: It is victory, victory at all costs, victory in spite of all terror, victory, however long and hard the road may be; for without victory, there is no survival.
6688 JORGE AMADO/ BRAZILIAN WRITER	It is a very risky thing for anyone to go about proclaiming the truth simply because he finds himself in possession of concrete documentary proofs or on the evidence of his own eyes, which is always overestimated.
6689 REV. OTIS MOSS III/USA	The family is the community and the community is the family.
6690 SENECA/ROMAN/ DRAMATIST	It should be our care not so much to live a long life as a satisfactory one.
6691 LEO TOLSTOY/WRITER/ RUSSIA	The strongest warriors are these two...time and patience.
6692 T.E. LAWRENCE/UK/ OFFICER/WRITER	The printing press is the greatest weapon in the armory of the modern commander.
6693 MARGARET MEAD/USA/ ANTHROPOLOGIST	Instead of needing lots of children, we need high-quality children.
6694 MARGARET ATWOOD/ CANADIAN NOVELIST	Love blurs your vision; but after it recedes, you can see more clearly than ever.
6695 HEALTH	Bone marrow transplants
6696 HARVARD UNIVERSITY/ USA	Every application is reviewed as a whole package. We are admitting candidates with personalities, not scores.
6697 BUSINESS/LIFE/DEBATE	Ethics are nonnegotiable.

NUMBER CATEGORY/CREDIT	TOPIC
6698 USA/MICHAEL ALTSHULER/THERAPIST	The bad news is time flies. The good news is you're the pilot.
6699 CHARLES BUKOWSKI/ AMERICAN POET	An intellectual says a simple thing in a hard way. An artist says a hard thing in a simple way.
6700 THE TALMUD	Never expose yourself unnecessarily to danger; a miracle may not save you...and if it does, it will be deducted from your share of luck or merit.
6701 BORIS PASTERNAK/ RUSSIAN NOVELIST	Man is born to live and not to prepare to live.
6702 OLIVER WENDELL HOLMES/USA	A person is always startled when he hears himself seriously called an old man for the first time.
6703 ZIG ZIGLAR/ SPEAKER	If you don't see yourself as a winner, then you cannot perform as a winner.
6704 RUSSIA/ALEKSANDR SOLZHENITSYN/WRITER	...intolerance is the first sign of an inadequate education. An ill-educated person behaves with arrogant impatience whereas truly profound education breeds humility.
6705 EDWARD DE BONO/UK	If you never change your mind why have one?
6706 JANE AUSTEN/ ENGLISH NOVELIST	Where so many hours have been spent in convincing myself that I am right, is there not some reason to fear I may be wrong?
6707 MOTHER TERESA/ CATHOLIC NUN	I have found the paradox that if I love until it hurts, then there is no hurt, but only more love.
6708 KATHRYN SCHULZ/ TED.COM	The inability to experience regret is one of the diagnostic characteristics of sociopaths.
6709 FLORYNCE KENNEDY/US	The biggest sin is sitting on your ass.
6710 SAINT AUGUSTINE/ LATIN PHILOSOPHER & THEOLOGIAN	Do you wish to be great? Then begin by being. Do you desire to construct a vast and lofty fabric? Think first about the foundations of humility. The higher your structure is to be, the deeper must be its foundation.
6711 USA/MR & MRS OLIVER HALE/THIS I BELIEVE	We believe that the achievements of man are greater than his failures.
6712 CONFUCIUS/CHINA/ PHILOSOPHER	The superior man is modest in his speech, but exceeds in his actions.
6713 TAVIS SMILEY/USA	Poverty is a matter of national security.
6714 THOMAS MORE/UK/ POLITICIAN	Anticipated spears wound less.
6715 JAMES FRANCO/USA	Fear of embarrassment can be extremely stifling.
6716 E.B. WHITE/USA/ WRITER	I am reminded of the advice of my neighbor, "Never worry about your heart till it stops beating."
6717 UK/PM/WINSTON CHURCHILL	Courage is what it takes to stand up and speak; courage is also what it takes to sit down and listen.
6718 AKIRA KUROSAWA/ JAPAN/FILM MAKER	Being an artist means not having to avert one's eyes.
6719 RUSSIAN/FYODOR DOSTOYEVSKY	I think the devil doesn't exist, but man has created him, he has created him in his own image and likeness.
6720 MATSUO BASHO/JAPAN/ POET	The journey itself is my home.

NUMBER CATEGORY/CREDIT	TOPIC
6721 USA/RALPH WALDO EMERSON/ESSAYIST	Common sense is genius dressed up in work clothes.
6722 ALBERT EINSTEIN/ SCIENTIST	Logic will get you from A to B. Imagination will take you everywhere.
6723 RUSSIA/ALEKSANDR SOLZHENITSYN/WRITER	Own only what you can always carry with you: know languages, know countries, know people. Let your memory be your travel bag.
6724 KAHLIL GIBRAN/ LEBANESE POET	If you reveal your secrets to the wind, you should not blame the wind for revealing them to the trees.
6725 EDITOR/ARIANNA HUFFINGTON/USA	The essence of leadership is being able to see the iceberg before it hits the Titanic.
6726 OPRAH WINFREY/ USA/BILLIONAIRE	Every right decision I have ever made has come from my gut. Every wrong decision I've made was the result of me not listening to the greater voice of myself.
6727 THE TALMUD	Until a child is one year old it is incapable of sin.
6728 BOOKS/FEAR	Bibliophobia: Fear of books
6729 CHARLES BUKOWSKI/US	You begin saving the world by saving one man at a time.
6730 JARED DIAMOND/ WHY SOCIETIES COLLAPSE/TED.COM	Our biggest threat is not an asteroid about to crash into us, something we can do nothing about. Instead, all the major threats facing us today are problems entirely of our own making. And since we made the problems, we can also solve the problems.
6731 UMBERTO ECO/ESSAYIST	Nothing gives a fearful man more courage than another's fear.
6732 CARL SAGAN/USA/ SCIENTIST	I am often amazed at how much more capability and enthusiasm for science there is among elementary school youngsters than among college students.
6733 BUDDY DESYLVA/USA/ SONGWRITER	The moon belongs to ev'ryone. The best things in life are free.
6734 HECTOR BOLITHO/ UK/COMPETITION IS A SIN/THIS I BELIEVE	Children are taught that they must do something. The heroes in their school books are men of action, not thinkers. And children are haunted by too many examinations that prove nothing of their capacity to think. They, thus, develop a false sense of the value of action, as opposed to the value of thought and of motives.
6735 DR. SEUSS/USA/ WRITER/THE LORAX	Unless someone like you cares a whole awful lot, Nothing is going to get better. It's not.
6736 USA/J. F. KENNEDY/ 35TH PRESIDENY	The Chinese use two brush strokes to write the word 'crisis.' One brush stroke stands for danger; the other for opportunity. In a crisis, be aware of the danger – but recognize the opportunity.
6737 RUSSIA/ALEKSANDR SOLZHENITSYN/WRITER	If one is forever cautious, can one remain a human being?
6738 JOSEPH CAMPBELL/USA	Where there is a way or path, it is someone else's path.
6739 JOHN F. KENNEDY/ 35TH PRESIDENT/USA	So, let us not be blind to our differences – but let us also direct attention to our common interest and to the means by which those differences can be resolved.
6740 ANITA BAKER/USA/ MUSICIAN	I don't let people use me. That's why I like a small number of people in my life. The more people in my life, the more complex it becomes, so I just try to keep it at a minimum.

NUMBER CATEGORY/CREDIT	TOPIC
6741 RENE DESCARTES/ PHILOSOPHER	Divide each difficulty into as many parts as is feasible and necessary to resolve it.
6742 INDIRA GANDHI/PM/ INDIA	Opportunities are not offered. They must be wrested and worked for. And this calls for perseverance...and courage. "
6743 NORTHROP FRYE/ CANADA/BOOK CRITIC	I soon realized that a student of English literature who does not know the Bible does not understand a good deal of what is going on in what he reads: the most conscientious student will be continually misconstruing the implications, even the meaning.
6744 J.M. COETZEE/ NOVELIST	The one who comes to teach learns the keenest of lessons, while those who come to learn, learn nothing.
6745 USA/POET/LAWRENCE FERLINGHETTI	If you're too open-minded, your brains will fall out.
6746 WILLIAM SHAKESPEARE	Strong reasons make strong actions.
6747 ISAAC BASHEVIS SINGER/USA	I did not become a vegetarian for my health, I did it for the health of the chickens.
6748 CICERO/ROMAN	To be content with what one has is the greatest and truest of riches.
6749 JACK GILBERT/USA/ POET	The heart lies to itself because it must.
6750 EVE ENSLER/WRITER/ SECURITY/TED.COM	Real security is contemplating death, not pretending it does not exist.
6751 JOSEPH CONRAD/ NOVELIST	A man's real life is that accorded to him in the thoughts of other men by reason of respect or natural love.
6752 USA/RALPH WALDO EMERSON/ESSAYIST	It is easy in the world to live after the world's opinion; it is easy in solitude to live after our own; but the great man is he who in the midst of the crowd keeps with perfect sweetness the independence of solitude.
6753 KAORU KURIMOTO/ JAPAN/WRITER/THE BATTLE OF NOSPHERUS	A weapon is merely a weapon, nothing more. What matters is how you use it.
6754 NELSON MANDELA/ PRESIDENT/S. AFRICA	If you talk to a man in a language he understands, that goes to his mind. If you talk to him in his language, that goes to his heart.
6755 USA/DR. ARTHUR S. ABRAMSON/THIS I BELIEVE	Wise men and cynics alike continue to propound that old bromide that happiness is a goal impossible of attainment. But the wisest men can be wrong, and I believe that despite the sorrows and disappointments and frustrations that all men must endure, happiness is attainable.
6756 DAPHNE ZUNIGA/ USA/ACTRESS	People feel powerless and useless in the world. But they can buy something. It can give them a sense of value, of power.
6757 JAMES FREY/AUTHOR USA	Sometimes skulls are thick. Sometimes hearts are vacant. Sometimes words won't work.
6758 THE INTERNET	Cyberphobia: fear of computers.
6759 LES BROWN/USA	Live full. Die empty.
6760 GERMAN/ARTHUR SCHOPENHAUER	It is with trifles, and when he is off guard, that a man best reveals his character.
6761 BURGER KING/FOOD/US	Have it your way.
6762 GEORGE SANTAYANA/ WRITER	For a man who has done his duty, death is as natural as sleep.

NUMBER CATEGORY/CREDIT	TOPIC
6763 JISHO NI NORANAI NIHONGO/YASUO KITAHARA/YOMIURI	..."CHIIGESA" means "talking about serious events as if they were small matters."
6764 HIROMI KAWAKAMI/ JAPAN/WRITER	Everyone causes trouble for someone at some point in their lives.
6765 USA/POET/LAWRENCE FERLINGHETTI	We have seen the best minds of our generation destroyed by boredom at poetry readings.
6766 UK/C. NORTHCOTE PARKINSON/WRITER	Delay is the deadliest form of denial.
6767 JAMES EARL JONES/USA/ ACTOR	If you live in an oppressive society, you've got to be resilient. You can't let each little thing crush you. You have to take every encounter and make yourself larger, rather than allow yourself to be diminished by it.
6768 CLINT EASTWOOD/ USA/ACTOR	I've never met a genius. A genius to me is someone who does well at something he hates.
6769 HOWARD COSSELL/ USA/LAWYER	The importance that our society attaches to sport is incredible. After all, is football a game or a religion? The people of this country have allowed sports to get completely out of hand.
6770 SERGEI RACHMANINOV/ RUSSIA/MUSICIAN	Music is enough for a lifetime, but a lifetime is not enough for music.
6771 GORE VIDAL/USA/ AUTHOR	Today's public figures can no longer write their own speeches or books, and there is some evidence that they can't read them either.
6772 JOHN MARSHALL HARLAN/USA/JUDGE	Our constitution is color-blind, and neither knows nor tolerates classes among citizens.
6773 BRENE BROWN/USA	We look confident on the outside and feel scared on the inside.
6774 ALBERT CAMUS/ FRENCH/AUTHOR	I shall tell you a great secret, my friend. Do not wait for the last judgment, it takes place every day.
6775 AN INDIAN PROVERB	A buffalo does not feel the weight of his own horns.
6776 PAUL FARMER/ PARTNERS IN HEALTH/ THIS I BELIEVE	The fight for health as a human right with real promise, has so far been plagued by failures. Failure because we are chronically short of resources. Failure because we are too often at the mercy of those with the power and money to decide the fates of hundreds of millions.
6777 JOHN DONNE/ ENGLISH POET	No man is an island, entire of itself; everyman is a piece of the Continent, a part of the main.
6778 DOLLY PARTON/ AMERICAN SINGER	If you don't like the road you're walking, start paving another one.
6779 RUDYARD KIPLING/ ENGLISH WRITER	Gardens are not made by singing "Oh, how beautiful," and sitting in the shade.
6780 WILLIAM JAMES/USA/ PHILOSOPHER	We have to live today by what truth we can get today and be ready tomorrow to call it falsehood.
6781 LOUIS D. BRANDEIS/ USA/ JUDGE	The greatest dangers to liberty lurk in the insidious encroachment by men of zeal, well meaning but without understanding.
6782 JONATHAN SACKS/ ENGLISH RABBI/THE DIGNITY OF DIFFERENCE	Success depends on the ability to delay gratification, which is precisely what a consumerist culture undermines. At every stage, the emphasis is on the instant gratification of instinct. In the words of the pop group Queen, "I want it all and I want it now." A whole culture is being infantilized.

NUMBER CATEGORY/CREDIT	TOPIC
6783 TRAFFIC/CITIES	Traffic congestion
6784 OPRAH WINFREY/USA/ BUSINESS/ COMMUNICATION	Difficulties come when you don't pay attention to life's whisper. Life always whispers to you first, but if you ignore the whisper, sooner or later you'll get a scream.
6785 HIROMI KAWAKAMI/ JAPAN/WRITER	...even a cracked pot has a lid that fits.
6786 JANE AUSTEN/UK	A large income is the best recipe for happiness I ever heard of.
6787 YOSHIDA KENKO/JAPAN	It cannot be in reason to know others and not to know oneself.
6788 CHARLES BUKOWSKI/ USA/POET/NOVELIST	If you want to know who your friends are, get yourself a jail sentence.
6789 NALINI NADKARNI/ CONSERVING THE CANOPY/TED.COM	People tend to compartmentalize themselves into IT people, and movie star people, and scientists, but when we share our perspectives about nature, we find a common denominator.
6790 LES BROWN/USA/ MOTIVATIONAL SPEAKER	Align yourself with people that you can learn from, people who want more out of life, people who are stretching and searching and seeking some higher ground in life.
6791 GEORGE AYITTEY/ GHANA/TEDTALK/USA	Back in the 1960s, Africa not only fed itself, it also exported food. Not anymore.
6792 ADAM SMITH/SCOT	Science is the great antidote to the poison of enthusiasm and superstition.
6793 MOTHER TERESA/ CATHOLIC NUN	I know God will not give me anything I can't handle. I just wish he didn't trust me so much.
6794 HOWARD COSSELL/ USA/LAWYER	What's right isn't always popular. What's popular isn't always right.
6795 SOREN KIERKEGAARD	One can advise comfortably from a safe port.
6796 USA/ACTOR/DENZEL WASHINGTON	I'm not in the loop; I don't know any actors, really, just the ones I work with.
6797 ERNEST HEMINGWAY/ USA/NOVELIST	All my life I've looked at words as though I were seeing them for the first time.
6798 CONFUCIUS/CHINA	Be not ashamed of mistakes and thus make them crimes.
6799 RUSSIA/ALEKSANDR SOLZHENITSYN/WRITER	Unlimited power in the hands of limited people always leads to cruelty.
6800 THOMAS J. WATSON/US	A manager is an assistant to his men.
6801 LOUIS D. BRANDEIS/ USA/JUDGE	Publicity is justly commended as a remedy for social and industrial diseases. Sunlight is said to be the best of disinfectants; electric light the most efficient policeman.
6802 SCHOPENHAUER	Friends and acquaintances are the surest passport to fortune.
6803 ANDREW CARNEGIE/ INDUSTRIALIST/USA	I resolved to stop accumulating and begin the infinitely more serious and difficult task of wise distribution.
6804 BEVERLY SILLS/USA/ OPERA/SOPRANO	There are no shortcuts to anywhere worth going.
6805 HUMANITY/PEOPLE	False modesty
6806 HITOMI KANEHARA/ JAPAN/WRITER	God has to be a sadist to give people life.

NUMBER CATEGORY/CREDIT	TOPIC
6807 DRIVING	Automatic shift versus Manual shift cars
6808 USA/DOUGLAS MacARTHUR/LEADER	Age wrinkles the body. Quitting wrinkles the soul.
6809 WILLIAM SHAKESPEARE	We know what we are, but not what we may be.
6810 JANE GOODALL/UK PRIMATOLOGIST	Lasting change is a series of compromises. And compromise is all right, as long as your values don't change.
6811 RUSSIA/ALEKSANDR SOLZHENITSYN/WRITER	One drop of truth can outweigh an ocean of lies.
6812 DMITRI SHOSTAKOVICH/ RUSSIA/COMPOSER	If they cut off both hands, I will compose music anyway holding the pen in my teeth.
6813 CARL SAGAN/USA/ SCIENTIST	Imagination will often carry us to worlds that never were. But without it we go nowhere.
6814 J.K. ROWLING/UK/ AUTHOR	I just write what I wanted to write. I write what amuses me. It's totally for myself.
6815 INDIAN PROVERB	If you throw a handful of stones, one at least will hit.
6816 JOSEPH CONRAD/UK/ WRITER	A belief in a supernatural source of evil is not necessary; men alone are quite capable of every wickedness.
6817 ROBERT GREEN INGERSOLL/USA	Colleges are places where pebbles are polished and diamonds are dimmed.
6818 UK/WILLIAM SHAKESPEARE	When we are born, we cry, that we are come / To this great stage of fools.
6819 GABRIEL GARCÍA MÁRQUEZ/COLOMBIA	No medicine cures what happiness cannot.
6820 HARVEY VAN CLIBURN/ USA/MUSICIAN	If you hold onto the beauty and inspiration and the clarity that is music, you will have an anchor, you will not be too far swayed by what the world is.
6821 JAMES FREY/USA/ WRITER	If you care about what others think of you, then you will always be their slave.
6822 MAO TSE TUNG/CHINA	In time of difficulties, we must not lose sight of our achievements.
6823 AYN RAND/WRITER/ USA/RUSSIA	I will never live for the sake of another man, nor ask another man to live for mine.
6824 BEAUTY/CONFIDENCE	Wearing jewelry
6825 LAO-TZU/CHINA/CHINA	He who knows does not speak. He who speaks does not know.
6826 EDUCATION	Learning at your own pace
6827 ANDREW CARNEGIE/ INDUSTRIALIST	I shall argue that strong men, conversely, know when to compromise and that all principles can be compromised to serve a greater principle.
6828 OSCAR WILDE/IRISH WRITER/POET	The only thing to do with good advice is pass it on. It is never any use to oneself.
6829 USA/RALPH WALDO EMERSON/ESSAYIST	We boil at different degrees.
6830 OG MANDINO/ WRITER/USA	The only certain means of success is to render more and better service than is expected of you, no matter what your task may be.
6831 ECONOMY/PLANNING	Economic bubble

NUMBER CATEGORY/CREDIT	TOPIC
6832 THE TALMUD	When you teach your son, you teach your son's son.
6833 WILKIE COLLINS/UK/ AUTHOR	Where is the faultless human creature who can persevere in a good resolution, without sometimes failing and falling back?
6834 ADAM SMITH/ SCOTTISH ECONOMIST	People of the same trade seldom meet together, even for merriment and diversion, but the conversation ends in a conspiracy against the public, or in some contrivance to raise prices.
6835 URSULA LeGUIN/ USA/WRITER	Love doesn't just sit there like a stone; it has to be made, like bread, remade all the time, made new.
6836 RUSSIA/ALEKSANDR SOLZHENITSYN/WRITER	What is the most precious thing in the world? I see now that is the knowledge that you have no part in injustice. Injustice is stronger than you; it always was and always will be. But let it not be done through you.
6837 CHARLES BUKOWSKI/ POET/NOVELIST	The difference between a democracy and a dictatorship is that in a democracy you vote first and take orders later; in a dictatorship you don't have to waste your time voting.
6838 B. PASTERNAK/RUSSIA	Surprise is the greatest gift which life can grant us.
6839 RUSSIA/ALEKSANDR SOLZHENITSYN/WRITER	If you live in a graveyard, you can't weep for everyone.
6840 HARVEY VAN CLIBURN/ USA/MUSICIAN	An artist can only be evaluated after he's dead. At the 11th hour he might do something that will eclipse everything else.
6841 DEBATE	Stomach stapling is the best way to lose weight.
6842 ROBERT GATES/USA/ DEFENSE/WAPO	We read of too many successful and intelligent people in and out of government who succumb to the easy wrong rather than the hard right.
6843 GABRIEL GARCÍA MÁRQUEZ/NOVELIST	What matters in life is not what happens to you but what you remember and how you remember it.
6844 FRANK SINATRA/USA	I'm very fond of women; but like all men, I don't understand them.
6845 GROUCHO MARX/ USA/COMEDIAN	Age is not a particularly interesting subject. Anyone can get old. All you have to do is live long enough.
6846 MICHAEL GATES GILL/AUTHOR/USA	...nobody at Starbucks ever ordered anyone to do anything. It was always: "Would you do me a favor?"
6847 GEORGE SANTAYANA/ SPANISH-AMERICAN	To know what people really think, pay regard to what they do, rather than what they say.
6848 JAMES FREY/USA/ WRITER	Even a second of freedom is worth more than a lifetime of bondage.
6849 NINA SIMONE/USA/ JAZZ SINGER	There's no excuse for the young people not knowing who the heroes and heroines are or were.
6850 ROBERT KIYOSAKI/ USA/WRITER	It's a kindness to speak honestly and say what you feel is right. Only cowards let fear keep them from making tough decisions.
6851 BOB MARLEY/MUSICIAN/ JAMAICA	Free speech carries with it some freedom to listen.
6852 ANITA BAKER/USA/ MUSICIAN	You leave home to seek your fortune and, when you get it, you go home and share it with your family.
6853 TONY ROBBINS/WHY WE DO WHAT WE DO/ TED.COM/ROSA PARKS	The history of our world is these decisions. When a woman stands up and says, 'No, I won't go to the back of the bus,' she didn't just affect her life. That decision shaped our culture.

NUMBER CATEGORY/CREDIT	TOPIC
6854 MITSUYO KAKUTA/ JAPAN/WRITER/WOMAN ON THE OTHER SHORE	Every country's different. All that happy talk you hear about understanding one another and people everywhere being basically the same, it's all a bunch of crap. Everybody's different. And if you don't realize that, you're never going to experience anything truly new.
6855 VACLAV HAVEL/ CZECH LEADER	Even a purely moral act that has no hope of any immediate and visible political effect can gradually and indirectly, over time, gain in political significance.
6856 HELEN FISHER/] TEDTALK/ ANTHROPOLOGIST	Romantic love is an obsession. It possesses you. You lose your sense of self. You can't stop thinking about another human being.
6857 CHINESE SAYING	When eating bamboo sprouts, keep in mind the person who planted them.
6858 SCOT/THOMAS ROBERT DEWAR/DISTILLER	Minds are like parachutes; they only function when open.
6859 GORE VIDAL/USA	Every time a friend succeeds, I die a little.
6860 R.G. INGERSOLL/USA	Courage without conscience is a wild beast.
6861 BLAISE PASCAL/MATH/ FRENCH	I have made this letter longer than usual, only because I have not had the time to make it shorter.
6862 KEN ROBINSON/TED. COM/CREATIVITY	There isn't an education system on the planet that teaches dance everyday to children the way we teach them mathematics. Why?
6863 THOMAS PAINE/USA/ PHILOSOPHER	Government, even in its best state, is but a necessary evil; in its worst state, an intolerable one.
6864 FUMIKO ENCHI/ JAPAN/WRITER/MASKS	A woman's love is quick to turn into a passion for revenge--an obsession that becomes an endless river of blood, flowing on from generation to generation.
6865 BILL GATES/USA/ ENTREPRENEUR	As we look ahead into the next century, leaders will be those who empower others.
6866 LEE IACOCCA/CEO/ CHRYSLER/USA	In times of great stress or adversity, it's always best to keep busy to plow your anger and your energy into something positive.
6867 HORACE MANN/USA/ POLITICIAN/REFORMER	To pity distress is but human; to relieve it is Godlike.
6868 JONATHAN SWIFT/IRISH	A tavern is a place where madness is sold by the bottle.
6869 BOB MARLEY/MUSICIAN	None but ourselves can free our minds.
6870 MIYAMOTO MUSASHI/ JAPANESE WARRIOR	In battle, if you make your opponent flinch, you have already won.
6871 HEALTH	Chronic fatigue syndrome
6872 KEN ROBINSON/TED. COM/UK/US/EDUCATOR	If you're not prepared to be wrong, you'll never come up with anything original.
6873 NICHOLAS KRISTOF/ SHERYL WUDUNN/USA	Female empowerment is one of the most effective tools for eradicating poverty and extremism.
6874 ETHICS/TRUST	Don't trust the person who tells you that her lawyer says something is legal.
6875 PUBLILIUS SYRUS	Everything is worth what its purchaser will pay for it.
6876 ABDUL KALAM/ INDIA/PRESIDENT	Let us sacrifice our today so that our children can have a better tomorrow.

NUMBER CATEGORY/CREDIT	TOPIC
6877 MARIA CALLAS/SINGER/ ITALY/OPERA	When my enemies stop hissing, I shall know I'm slipping.
6878 KATHRYN SCHULZ/ TEDTALK/WRITER	Thirty-three percent of all of our regrets pertain to decisions we made about education.
6879 LES BROWN/USA/ MOTIVATION	Make sure when you fall you land on your back; if you can see you can get up.
6880 ROBERT GREEN INGERSOLL/USA	Every man is dishonest who lives upon the labor of others, no matter if he occupies a throne.
6881 CARL SAGAN/USA	Science is a way of thinking much more than it is a body of knowledge.
6882 JONATHAN SACKS/ ENGLISH RABBI/ DIFFERENCE	God has given us many faiths but only one world in which to co-exist. May your work help all of us to cherish our commonalities and feel enlarged by our differences.
6883 J.M. COETZEE/ S. AFRICA/NOVELIST	If we are going to be kind, let it be out of simple generosity, not because we fear guilt or retribution.
6884 USA/WHOOPIE GOLDBERG/ACTRESS	An actress can only play a woman. I'm an actor, I can play anything.
6885 STEVEN PINKER/USA/ TED.COM/PROFESSOR	We are probably living in the most peaceful time in our species' existence.
6886 RUSSIA/ALEKSANDR SOLZHENITSYN/WRITER	Only those who decline to scramble up the career ladder are interesting as human beings. Nothing is more boring than a man with a career.
6887 ELLEN GOODMAN/USA/ JOURNALIST	The central struggle of parenthood is to let our hopes for our children outweigh our fears.
6888 JANE AUSTEN/UK	Friendship is certainly the finest balm for the pangs of disappointed love.
6889 MIYAMOTO MUSASHI/ JAPANESE WARRIOR	Never be jealous.
6890 ANONYMOUS	The guy who wrote "A job well done never needs doing again" never weeded a garden.
6891 GABRIEL GARCÍA MÁRQUEZ/COLOMBIA	Nobody deserves your tears, but whoever deserves them will not make you cry.
6892 OPRAH WINFREY/MEDIA	The biggest adventure you can ever take is to live the life of your dreams.
6893 P. L. ANDARR/USA/ BUSINESS/FORBES	Most of us never recognize opportunity until it goes to work in our competitor's business.
6894 BERTRAND RUSSELL/ UK/PHILOSOPHER	The time you enjoy wasting is not wasted time.
6895 SERGEI PROKOFIEV/ RUSSIA/COMPOSER	My chief virtue (or if you like, defect) has been a tireless lifelong search for an original, individual musical idiom. I detest imitation. I detest hackneyed devices.
6896 TIA CARRERE/USA/ SINGER/HAWAII	Doors open because you're beautiful, but I wouldn't cultivate beauty to the exclusion of brains.
6897 CALVIN COOLIDGE/USA/ PRESIDENT	If you see ten troubles coming down the road, you can be sure that nine will run into the ditch before they reach you.
6898 THICH NHAT HANH/ VIETNAM/BUDDHISM	If you love someone but rarely make yourself available to him or her, that is not true love.
6899 CAMILLE SAINT-SAENS/ FRENCH/COMPOSER	There is nothing more difficult than talking about music.

NUMBER CATEGORY/CREDIT	TOPIC
6900 BERTRAND RUSSELL/ UK/PHILOSOPHER	Three passions, simple but overwhelmingly strong have governed my life: the longing for love, the search for knowledge, and unbearable pity for the suffering of mankind.
6901 OPRAH WINFREY/USA/ BILLIONAIRE	Feelings are really your GPS system for life. When you're supposed to do something, or not supposed to do something, your emotional guidance system lets you know.
6902 OLIVER WENDELL HOLMES/USA	It is the province of knowledge to speak and it is the privilege of wisdom to listen.
6903 BARRY SCHWARTZ/USA/ PSYCHOLOGIST	The secret to happiness is low expectations.
6904 MAXIM GORKY/ RUSSIAN NOVELIST	Everybody, my friend, everybody lives for something better to come. That's why we want to be considerate of every man – Who knows what's in him, why he was born and what he can do?
6905 TOM CLANCY/USA/ NOVELIST	I was one of the first generations to watch television. TV exposes people to news, to information, to knowledge, to entertainment. How is it bad?
6906 PREFERENCE	Teacher-assigned seats versus personal choice of seats
6907 WRITER/FRANCOIS DE LA ROCHEFOUCAULD	However brilliant an action it should not be esteemed great unless the result of a great motive.
6908 OLIVER WENDELL HOLMES/USA	Man's mind, once stretched by a new idea, never regains its original dimensions.
6909 USA/WHOOPIE GOLDBERG/ACTRESS	I am the American Dream. I am the epitome of what the American Dream basically said. It said, you could come from anywhere and be anything you want in this country. That's exactly what I've done.
6910 ALVIN TOFFLER/USA/ WRITER	If you don't have a strategy, you're part of someone else's strategy.
6911 AMERICAN FOLK SAYING	Every politician, when he leaves office, ought to go straight to jail and serve his time.
6912 CLAUDE DEBUSSY/ FRENCH/COMPOSER	To complete a work is just like being present at the death of someone you love.
6913 WAR/GANGS/GUNS	Traumatic brain injury
6914 DAPHNE KOLLER/ TEDTALK/PROFESSOR	We should spend less time at universities filling our students' minds with content by lecturing at them, and more time igniting their creativity...by actually talking with them.
6915 AYN RAND/RUSSIAN-AMERICAN WRITER/ PHILOSOPHER	A government is the most dangerous threat to man's rights; it holds legal monopoly on the use of physical force against legally disarmed victims.
6916 CALVIN COOLIDGE/USA/ PRESIDENT	If you don't say anything, you won't be called on to repeat it.
6917 AYN RAND/WRITER/ PHILOSOPHER	Do not ever say that the desire to "do good" by force is a good motive.
6918 TAVIS SMILEY/USA/ BROADCASTER	The choices we make about the lives we live determine the kinds of legacies we leave.
6919 ALAN GREENSPAN/ ECONOMIST/USA	Whatever you tax, you get less of.
6920 DEFINITION	Simple does not necessarily mean easy..

NUMBER CATEGORY/CREDIT	TOPIC
6921 HERODOTUS/HISTORIAN	In peace, sons bury their fathers. In war, fathers bury their sons
6922 JOSEPH CONRAD/UK/WRITER	Reality, as usual, beats fiction out of sight.
6923 MAXIM GORKY/RUSSIA	The most beautiful words in the English language are "not guilty."
6924 UK/WINSTON CHURCHILL/PM	We shall fight on the beaches, we shall fight on the landing grounds, we shall fight in the fields and in the streets. We shall fight in the hills; we shall never surrender…
6925 VINOD KHOSLA/INDIA/USA/BUSINESS	The bigger the problem, the bigger the opportunity. Nobody will pay you to solve a non-problem.
6926 THOMAS SOWELL/USA/ECONOMIST	There are few things more dishonorable than misleading the young.
6927 MOTHER TERESA CATHOLIC NUN	I would rather make mistakes in kindness and compassion than work miracles in unkindness and hardness.
6928 E.O. WILSON/USA/BIOLOGIST/TED.COM	In the attempt to make scientific discoveries, every problem isn't an opportunity – and the more difficult the problem, the greater will be the importance of the solution.
6929 ALAN RUSSELL/TEDTALK/MEDICINE/REGENERATIVE	One of the challenges is that the richer we are, the longer we live. And the longer we live, the more expensive it is to take care of our diseases as we get older.
6930 ALBERT CAMUS/FRENCH	But in the end one needs more courage to live than to kill himself.
6931 PETER THE GREAT/RUSSIA	It is my great desire to reform my subjects, and yet I am ashamed to confess that I am unable to reform myself.
6932 JOHN ADAMS/USA/PRES.	Liberty cannot be preserved without general knowledge among the people.
6933 USA/E. HEMINGWAY	All things truly wicked start from innocence.
6934 LEE IACOCCA/CHRYSLER/CEO	In the end, all business operations can be reduced to three words: people, product, and profits.
6935 PETER DRUCKER/USA/MANAGEMENT	Plans are only good intentions unless they immediately degenerate into hard work.
6936 USA/RALPH WALDO EMERSON/ESSAYIST	Conversation is an art in which a man has all mankind for his competitors, for it is that which all are practicing every day while they live.
6937 CLINT EASTWOOD/AMERICAN ACTOR	The less secure a man is, the more likely he is to have extreme prejudice.
6938 DEBATE	Anger should never be shown in public.
6939 CONFUCIUS/CHINESE PHILOSOPHER	The superior man, when resting in safety, does not forget that danger may come.
6940 HANNAH ARENDT/GERMAN/THINKER	War has become a luxury that only small nations can afford.
6941 MIYAMOTO MUSASHI/JAPANESE WARRIOR	Think lightly of yourself and deeply of the world.
6942 GERMAN/KARL MARX/PHILOSOPHER	The writer must earn money in order to be able to live and to write, but he must by no means live and write for the purpose of making money.
6943 WOMEN/ABUSE	Female genital mutilation
6944 HEALTH/RELIGION	Parents denying medical care to their children because of religion.

NUMBER CATEGORY/CREDIT	TOPIC
6945 STEWART BRAND/USA/ TEDTALK/WRITER	If all of your electricity in your lifetime came from nuclear [energy], the waste from that lifetime of electricity would go in a Coke can.
6946 ROBERT GREEN INGERSOLL/USA/ LAWYER	Few nations have been so poor as to have but one god. Gods were made so easily, and the raw material cost so little, that generally the god market was fairly glutted and heaven crammed with these phantoms.
6947 CONSUMER RISKS	Risks faced by consumers
6948 WHOOPIE GOLDBERG/ AMERICAN ACTRESS	It's being willing to walk away that gives you strength and power – if you're willing to accept the consequences of doing what you want to do.
6949 GAYLE TZEMACH LEMMON/WOMEN	[Women] are not a special interest group. We are the majority.
6950 VINCE LOMBARDI/USA	Once you learn to quit, it becomes a habit.
6951 J.M. COETZEE/ S. AFRICA/NOVELIST	I want to find a way of speaking to fellow human beings that will be cool rather than heated.
6952 ACTRESS/WHOOPIE GOLDBERG/USA	That's the thing about Mother Nature; she really doesn't care what economic bracket you're in.
6953 TINA SEELIG/USA/ STANFORD/ PROFESSOR	T-shaped people: those with a depth of knowledge in at least one discipline and a breadth of knowledge about innovation and entrepreneurship that allows them to work effectively with professionals in other disciplines.
6954 KOFI ANNAN/GHANA/ UNITED NATIONS	.as a young man in high school one of the professors came in and put a broad white sheet on the board with a dot in the right hand corner and said, "Boys, what do you see?" And we all shouted, a black dot. He stood back and said, "Not a single one of you saw the broad white sheet; you all saw the black dot."
6955 PAUL FARMER/ PARTNERS IN HEALTH/HUMAN RIGHT/ THIS I BELIEVE	[Ill health], as we have learned again and again, is more often than not a symptom of poverty and violence and inequality – and we do little to fight those when we provide just vaccines, or only treatment for one disease or another.
6956 MAHATMA GANDHI/ INDIA/LEADER	To give pleasure to a single heart by a single act is better than a thousand heads bowing in prayer.
6957 GABRIEL GARCÍA MÁRQUEZ/NOVELIST	It's not true that people stop pursuing their dreams because they grow old, they grow old because they stop pursuing dreams.
6958 GERMAN/ARTHUR SCHOPENHAUER/ PHILOSOPHER	To live alone is the fate of all great souls.
6959 GEORGE ELIOT/UK/ AUTHOR	Blessed is the man, who having nothing to say, abstains from giving wordy evidence of the fact.
6960 TEMPLE GRANDIN/ USA/EDUCATOR	People are always looking for the single magic bullet that will totally change everything. There is no single magic bullet.
6961 HARVEY FIRESTONE/US	You get the best out of others when you get the best out of yourself.
6962 KURT VONNEGUT/ USA/WRITER	Who is more to be pitied, a writer bound and gagged by policemen or one living in perfect freedom who has nothing more to say?
6963 RICK TATE/USA/ PUBLIC SPEAKER	Feedback is the breakfast of champions.
6964 MIYAMOTO MUSASHI/ JAPANESE WARRIOR	You must understand that there is more than one path to the top of the mountain.

NUMBER CATEGORY/CREDIT	TOPIC
6965 CATHERINE THE GREAT/ RUSSIA	I like to praise and reward loudly, to blame quietly.
6966 KAHLIL GIBRAN/POET	If your heart is a volcano, how shall you expect flowers to bloom?
6967 CICERO/THINKER	There is no duty more obligatory than the repayment of kindness.
6968 LEONTYNE PRICE/USA/ OPERA SINGER	You must learn to say no when something is not right for you.
6969 GORE VIDAL/USA/ WRITER	To be perfect for television is all a President has to be these days.
6970 GHOSTS	Haunted houses
6971 WILKIE COLLINS/THE WOMAN IN WHITE	The fool's crime is the crime that is found out and the wise man's crime is the crime that is not found out.
6972 ROSABETH MOSS KANTER/AUTHOR/USA	Too many people let others stand in their way and don't go back for one more try.
6973 EDUCATION	Education is the great equalizer.
6974 MIKE MYATT/LIFE ISN'T FAIR – DEAL WITH IT/FORBES/USA	It doesn't matter whether you are born with a silver spoon, plastic spoon, or no spoon at all. It's not the circumstances by which you come into this world, but what you make of them once you arrive that matter.
6975 JAMES EARL JONES/ USA/ACTOR	One of the hardest things in life is having words in your heart that you can't utter.
6976 MIKE FLACY/YAHOO NEWS	...children that text or talk on a cell phone while walking near or on a street are 40 percent more likely to get hit by an automobile.
6977 PUBLILIUS SYRUS/ LATIN WRITER	Look to be treated by others as you have treated others.
6978 MORTIMER ADLER/ USA/PHILOSOPHER	The philosopher ought never to try to avoid the duty of making up his mind.
6979 EXPERIENCE/STORY	A cautionary tale
6980 THOMAS MANN/ GERMAN NOVELIST/ NOBEL LAUREATE	Solitude gives birth to the original in us, to beauty unfamiliar and perilous – to poetry. But also, it gives birth to the opposite: to the perverse, the illicit, the absurd.
6981 FINANCE/THRIFT	Why should one save in a country where it's easy to borrow?
6982 MATT CUTTS/TRY SOMETHING NEW FOR 30 DAYS/TEDTALK	The next 30 days are going to pass whether you like or not, so why not think about something you have always wanted to try and give it a shot for the next 30 days.
6983 MARILYN MANSON/ AMERICAN MUSICIAN	Part of me is afraid to get close to people because I'm afraid that they're going to leave.
6984 GERMAN/ARTHUR SCHOPENHAUER	Almost all of our sorrows spring out of our relations with other people.
6985 BOOKS/EXPERIENCE	Not everything useful is learned from books.
6986 SIMON SINEK/TEDTALK/ BUSINESS/USA	If you hire people just because they can do a job, they'll work for your money. But if you hire people who believe what you believe, they'll work for you with blood and sweat and tears.
6987 USA/KATHERINE HEPBURN/ACTOR	As for me, prices are nothing. My price is my work.
6988 BOB EIDEM/USA/THIS I BELIEVE	Those who fish are more optimistic than people who don't.

NUMBER CATEGORY/CREDIT	TOPIC
6989 OG MANDINO/SALES/ AMERICAN AUTHOR	I determine to render more and better service, each day, than I am being paid to render. Those that reach the top are the ones who are not content with doing only what is required of them.
6990 KEVIN ALLOCCA/ TEDTALK/VIRAL VIDEOS	On YouTube no one has to green-light your idea.
6991 GORE VIDAL/USA/ WRITER	It is not enough to succeed. Others must fail.
6992 LAWRENCE BLOCK/ USA/CRIME WRITER	Serendipity. Look for something, find something else, and realize that what you've found is more suited to your needs than what you thought you were looking for.
6993 JACQUES CHIRAC/ FRANCE/PRESIDENT	One can go to war alone, but you can't build peace alone.
6994 OLIVER REED/UK	Awe and respect are two different things.
6995 ISABEL ALLENDE/ TALES OF PASSION/ TED.COM	For real change, we need feminine energy in the management of the world. We need a critical number of women in positions of power, and we need to nurture the feminine energy in men.
6996 WILLIAM FAULKNER/ USA/NOVELIST	The saddest thing about love, Joe, is that not only the love cannot last forever, but even the heartbreak is soon forgotten.
6997 CAMILLE PAGLIA/ USA/WRITER/CRITIC	Woman is the dominant sex. Men have to do all sorts of stuff to prove they are worthy of woman's attention.
6998 INDIAN PROVERB	A thief thinks everybody else is a thief.
6999 GEN. L.D. CLAY/USA	Like all precious possessions, freedom must be guarded.
7000 NOVELIST/FYODOR DOSTOYEVSKI/ RUSSIA	The degree of civilization in a society can be judged by entering its prisons.
7001 ANNE FRANK/JEWISH AUTHOR/ HOLOCAUST	Where there's hope, there's life. It fills us with fresh courage and makes us strong again.
7002 OPRAH WINFREY/USA	It's always wonderful being underestimated.
7003 DR. MARTIN LUTHER KING JR..USA/NOBELIST	Human salvation lies in the hands of the creatively maladjusted.
7004 WILLIAM PITT/UK	Poverty of course is no disgrace, but it is damn annoying.
7005 B. BROWN/TED.COM	Vulnerability is our most accurate measurement of courage.
7006 JOHN F. KENNEDY/ 35TH PRESIDENT/USA	The ancient Greek definition of happiness was the full use of your powers along lines of excellence.
7007 TALI SHAROT/THE OPTIMISM BIAS/ TED.COM	Whatever happens, whether you succeed or you fail, people with high expectations always feel better, because how we feel – when we get dumped or we win employee of the month – depends on how we interpret that event.
7008 MAYA ANGELOU/USA	No human being can be more human than another human being.
7009 MIYAMOTO MUSASHI/ JAPANESE WARRIOR/ THE BOOK OF FIVE RINGS	You should not have any special fondness for a particular weapon, or anything else, for that matter. Too much is the same as not enough. Without imitating anyone else, you should have as much weaponry as suits you.
7010 CALVIN COOLIDGE/ USA/PRESIDENT	No person was ever rewarded for what he received. Honor has been the reward for what he gave.

NUMBER CATEGORY/CREDIT	TOPIC
7011 USA/MALCOLM GLADWELL/WRITER	In the act of tearing something apart, you lose its meaning.
7012 JOAN CRAWFORD/ USA/ACTRESS	Hollywood is like life, you face it with the sum total of your equipment.
7013 R.G. INGERSOLL/USA/	Few rich men own their property; their property owns them.
7014 RONALD REAGAN/ 40TH PRESIDENT/USA	Democracy is worth dying for, because it's the most deeply honorable form of government ever devised by man.
7015 PUBLILIUS SYRUS	Pardon one offense, and you encourage the commission of many.
7016 JOHN CONSTABLE/ UK/PAINTER	There is nothing ugly; I never say an ugly thing in my life: for let the form of an object be what it may – light, shade, and perspective will always make it beautiful.
7017 CLINT EASTWOOOD/USA	Men must know their limitations.
7018 WARREN G. BENNIS/ USA/PSYCHOLOGIST	Leaders must encourage their organizations to dance to forms of music yet to be heard.
7019 GERMAINE GREER/ AUSTRALIA/WRITER	The housewife is an unpaid employee in her husband's house in return for the security of being a permanent employee.
7020 SRIKUMAR RAO/LEADER	Most large companies are toxic places.
7021 ALBERT SCHWEITZER/ PHILOSOPHER/ GERMAN/FRENCH	I don't know what your destiny will be, but one thing I do know: the only ones among you who will be really happy are those who have sought and found how to serve.
7022 SUN TZU/CHINA/ AUTHOR/THE ART OF WAR	It is essential to seek out enemy agents who have come to conduct espionage against you and to bribe them to serve you. Give them instructions and care for them. Thus double agents are recruited and used.
7023 WILLIAM O. DOUGLAS/ USA/SUPREME COURT	Since when have we Americans been expected to bow submissively to authority and speak with awe and reverence to those who represent us?
7024 W. B. YEATS/IRISH POET	Be not inhospitable to strangers, lest they be angels in disguise.
7025 ANONYMOUS	Some mistakes are too much fun to only make once.
7026 RUDOLF NUREYEV/ RUSSIA/BALLET	When I miss class for one day, I know it. When I miss class for two days, my teacher knows it. When I miss class for three days, the audience knows it.
7027 NADINE GORDIMER/ S. AFRICA/AUTHOR	The truth isn't always beauty, but the hunger for it is.
7028 GLENN LLOPIS/USA FORBES	The farmer sows many seeds knowing that not every seed will grow into full bloom.
7029 JONATHAN SWIFT/ IRISH WRITER	Blessed is he who expects nothing, for he shall never be disappointed.
7030 BORIS BECKER/ GERMAN/TENNIS	I love the winning. I can take the losing, but most of all I love to play.
7031 LOUIS ARMSTRONG/USA	All music is folk music. I ain't never heard no horse sing a song.
7032 MARGARET MEAD/ USA/ ANTHROPOLOGIST	Life in the twentieth century is like a parachute jump; you have to get it right the first time.
7033 ANDREW CARNEGIE/US	I would as soon leave my son a curse as the almighty dollar.
7034 BOB EIDEM/USA/THIS I BELIEVE	Catching a fish is a peek of heaven without the commitment.

NUMBER CATEGORY/CREDIT	TOPIC
7035 CARL SAGAN/USA/ SCIENTIST	The universe is not required to be in perfect harmony with human ambition.
7036 DAVID COPPERFIELD/ USA/THIS I BELIEVE	In the movies, the hero never kills the bad guy with kindness.
7037 JOHN DEWITT/USA/ ARMY OFFICER/FEB. 14, 1992/INTERNMENT/ JAPANESE AMERICANS	There are indications that the [Japanese Americans] are organized and ready for concerted action at a favorable opportunity. The very fact that no sabotage has taken place to date is a disturbing and confirming indication that such action will be taken.
7038 VIVIENNE WALT/NEW YORK TIMES	Snack and soda machines are banned from school buildings in France.
7039 VACLAV HAVEL/POET/ CZECH REPUBLIC	Hope is a feeling that life and work have meaning.
7040 WRITER/WILLIAM SHAKESPEARE	All the world's a stage, And all the men and women players. They have their exits and their entrances; And one man in his time plays many parts...
7041 WILKIE COLLINS/UK	Crimes cause their own detection.
7042 THE TALMUD	Do not decide that someone is good until you see how he or she acts at home.
7043 MOTHER TERESA/ CATHOLIC NUN	If we have no peace, it is because we have forgotten that we belong to each other.
7044 RUMI/PERSIAN POET	Drunkards vaunt their bravery when you speak of war. But in the blaze of battle they scatter like mice.
7045 CICERO	My precept to all who build, is, that the owner should be an ornament to the house, and not the house to the owner.
7046 MAO TSETUNG/CHINA	Women hold up half the sky.
7047 GROUCHO MARX/USA/ COMEDIAN	I find television very educating. Every time somebody turns on the set, I go into the other room and read a book.
7048 TYLER PERRY/USA/ MOVIE PRODUCER	Never despise small beginnings.
7049 FELIX FRANKFURTER/ USA/JUDGE	I don't like a man to be too efficient. He's likely to be not human enough.
7050 FYODOR DOSTOEVSKY/ RUSSIA/WRITER	Beauty will save the world.
7051 WILLIAM OSLER/ CANADIAN SCIENTIST	It is much simpler to buy books than to read them and easier to read them than to absorb their contents.
7052 PETER DRUCKER/ WRITER/PROFESSOR	My greatest strength as a consultant is to be ignorant and ask a few questions.
7053 USA/BERNARD M. BARUCH/BUSINESS	During my eighty-seven years I have witnessed a whole succession of technological revolutions. But none of them has done away with the need for character in the individual or the ability to think.
7054 ELIZABETH WARREN/ USA/POLITICIAN	Everybody in this room knows the basic rule: if you don't have a seat at the table, you are probably on the menu.
7055 THE TALMUD	Hold no man responsible for what he says in his grief.
7056 OG MANDINO/ AMERICAN AUTHOR	There are two kinds of discontented in the world, the discontented that works and the discontented that wrings its hands. The first gets what it wants and the second loses what it has.

NUMBER CATEGORY/CREDIT	TOPIC
7057 CONSTITUTION OF THE UNITED STATES	Congress shall make no law respecting an establishment of religion...
7058 USA/ELBERT GREEN HUBBARD/WRITER	A retentive memory may be a good thing, but the ability to forget is the true token of greatness.
7059 OLIVER WENDELL HOLMES, JR./USA/ JUDGE	Life is action and passion; therefore, it is required of man that he should share the passion and action of the time, at peril of being judged not to have lived.
7060 ISAAC STERN/USA/ VIOLINIST/RUSSIA	A man possesses talent; genius possesses the man.
7061 BLAISE PASCAL/FRENCH MATHEMATICIAN	How vain painting is, exciting admiration by its resemblance to things of which we do not admire the originals.
7062 WRITER/WILLIAM SHAKESPEARE	Neither a borrower nor a lender be; For loan oft loses both itself and friend.
7063 SPORTS/PSYCHOLOGY	The importance of mental preparation
7064 EDWARD DE BONO/ UK/AUTHOR/ PSYCHOLOGIST	Many highly intelligent people are poor thinkers. Many people of average intelligence are skilled thinkers. The power of a car is separate from the way the car is driven.
7065 KAHLIL GIBRAN/ON PAIN	Even as the stone of the fruit must break, that its heart may stand in the sun, so must you know pain.
7066 JACEK UTKO/DESIGNS TO SAVE NEWSPAPERS	There is no reason – no practical reason – for newspapers to survive.
7067 TEDTALK/DR. ABRAHAM VERGHESE/USA	We know the average American physician interrupts their patient in 14 seconds.
7068 DIANA/ PRINCESS OF WALES/UK	I'd like to be a queen in people's hearts but I don't see myself being Queen of this country.
7069 CHINESE SAYING	We are not so concerned if you are slow but our concern grows when you come to a halt.
7070 GABRIEL GARCÍA MÁRQUEZ/COLOMBIA NOVELIST	Human beings are not born once and for all on the day their mothers give birth to them, but...life obliges them over and over again to give birth to themselves.
7071 STEVE JOBS, APPLE CO-FOUNDER	Don't let the noise of others' opinions drown out your own inner voice.
7072 GEORGE SANTAYANA/US	Only the dead have seen the end of war.
7073 CHARLIE CHAPLIN/USA	A day without laughter is a day wasted.
7074 THOMAS J. WATSON/ IBM CEO	Don't make friends who are comfortable to be with. Make friends who will force you to lever yourself up.
7075 ABDUL KALAM/ INDIA/PRESIDENT	Man needs his difficulties because they are necessary to enjoy success.
7076 WILLIAM OSLER/ CANADIAN SCIENTIST	He who studies medicine without books sails an uncharted sea, but he who studies medicine without patients does not go to sea at all.
7077 MEDIA/ CELEBRITIES	Celebrities and right to privacy
7078 ALFRED HITCHCOCK/ MOVIE PRODUCER	There's nothing to winning really. That is if you happen to be blessed with a keen eye, an agile mind, and no scruples whatsoever.
7079 ISAAC STERN/USA/ VIOLINIST	Whoever controls the media, controls the mind.

NUMBER CATEGORY/CREDIT	TOPIC
7080 BRIAN GREENE/USA/ PHYSICIST/COLUMBIA UNIVERSITY	I believe the process of going from confusion to understanding is a precious, even emotional experience that can be the foundation of self-confidence.
7081 SPORTS/CHILDREN	Sports that are too dangerous for children
7082 CHARLES DICKENS/UK	I will honor Christmas in my heart, and try to keep it all the year.
7083 JOHN STEINBECK/ AMERICAN WRITER	I hold that a writer who does not passionately believe in the perfectibility of man has no dedication nor any membership in literature.
7084 CLINT EASTWOOOD/ USA/ACTOR	Sometimes if you want to see a change for the better, you have to take things into your own hands.
7085 DAILY YOMIURI/JAPAN	Politicians are always sensitive to popularity.
7086 LORD CHESTERFIELD/ UK/STATESMAN	Wear your learning, like your watch, in a private pocket, and do not pull it out and strike it merely to show you have one. If you are asked what o'clock it is, tell it, but do not proclaim it hourly and unasked, like the watchman.
7087 WALT WHITMAN/POET	Be curious, not judgmental.
7088 RUSSIA/ALEKSANDR SOLZHENITSYN/WRITER	When you are cold, don't expect sympathy from someone who's warm.
7089 COLIN POWELL/USA/ STATESMAN	Have fun in your command. Don't always run at a breakneck pace. Take a leave when you've earned it, spend time with your families.
7090 JOHN STUART MILL/ UK/PHILOSOPHER	Eccentricity has always bounded when and where strength of character had abounded; and the amount of eccentricity in a society has generally been proportional to the amount of genius, mental vigor, and courage which it contained.
7091 JAMES SUROWIECKI/ USA/JOURNALIST	The problem is that groups are only smart when people in them are as independent as possible. This is the paradox of the wisdom of crowds.
7092 RUSSIA/ALEKSANDR SOLZHENITSYN/WRITER	We always pay dearly for chasing after what is cheap.
7093 ROBBINS MILBANK/USA/ THIS I BELIEVE	I noticed something: you may notice something quite wonderful in most everybody you meet, even in those who annoy you or frighten you.
7094 RELIGION/WILLIAM J.H.BOETCKER/LEADER	If your business keeps you so busy that you have no time for anything else, there must be something wrong, either with you or with your business.
7095 OLIVER WENDELL HOLMES JR./USA	A moment's insight is worth a life's experience.
7096 PETER DRUCKER//USA	Management is doing things right; leadership is doing the right things.
7097 THINKER/ARTHUR SCHOPENHAUER	It is a clear gain to sacrifice pleasure in order to avoid pain.
7098 DJIMON HONSOU/ ACTOR/BENIN/FRENCH/ NY DAILY NEWS	School bored me. Being educated and being intelligent are two different things. I thought I was smart enough and I wanted to be an entertainer. I stopped going to school as a way of saying I was mature, a way of saying I was going to choose who I was going to become.
7099 SENECA/ROMAN DRAMATIST	Be silent as to services you have rendered, but speak of favors you have received.
7100 RUSSIA/ALEKSANDR SOLZHENITSYN/WRITER	If a person can build a fence around himself, he is bound to do it.
7101 MARIAN ANDERSON/ AMERICAN SINGER	Everyone has a gift for something, even if it is the gift of being a good friend.

NUMBER CATEGORY/CREDIT	TOPIC
7102 LAO TZU/CHINA	A good traveler has no fixed plans, and is not intent on arriving.
7103 MATTHEW ARNOLD/UK/ POET	Life is not a having and a getting, but a being and becoming.
7104 BRENE BROWN/USA/ WAPO	Vulnerability is indeed the center of difficult experiences like fear, disappointment and shame.
7105 JOHN F. KENNEDY/ 35TH PRESIDENT/USA	If we cannot end now our differences, at least we can help make the world safe for diversity.
7106 JOAN CRAWFORD/USA	I believe in the dollar. Everything I earn, I spend!
7107 ROBERT G. INGERSOLL/ USA/LAWYER	Give to every human being every right that you claim for yourself.
7108 UK/WRITER/WILLIAM SHAKESPEARE	To thine own self be true; And it must follow, as the night the day Thou canst not be false to any man.
7109 RIC ELIAS/TED.COM	I no longer try to be right; I choose to be happy.
7110 MATTHEW ARNOLD/UK/ POET	We are here on earth to do good to others. What the others are here for, I do not know.
7111 ELIZABETH KUBLER-ROSS/USA/ PSYCHIATRIST	The most beautiful people I've known are those who have known trials, have known struggles, have known loss, and have found their way out of the depths.
7112 CHINESE SAYING	When you are poor, neighbors close by will not visit; when you become rich, don't be surprised that you will have far more relatives than you imagined.
7113 LIFE CHANCES	Children at risk
7114 ROBERT GATES/USA/ DEFENSE/WAPO	An acid test of leadership is how you treat those you outrank, or as President Truman once said, "how you treat those who can't talk back."
7115 ANAIS NIN/USA/ AUTHOR	Each contact with a human being is so rare, so precious, one should preserve it.
7116 ERNEST HEMINGWAY/ USA/NOVELIST	As you get older it is harder to have heroes, but it is sort of necessary.
7117 USA/MARGARET MITCHELL/WRITER	How wonderful to know someone who was bad and dishonorable and a cheat and a liar, when all the world was filled with people who would not lie to save their souls and who would rather starve than do a dishonorable deed.
7118 SHADOW WORK	Unpaid work in a wage-based economy such as doing house chores, deleting spam email, or walking to the bank to pay your bills
7119 AMELIA EARHART/ USA/AVIATION	Never do things others can do and will do, if there are things others cannot do or will not do.
7120 ECONOMIST/FEB 24/ 2010/DISTANCE-LEARNING	...there will always be a demand for Harvard MBAs in the boardrooms of McKinsey and Barclays. But business education is fundamentally about personal betterment.
7121 USA/DWIGHT D. EISENHOWER/ PRESIDENT	Farming looks mighty easy when your plow is a pencil, and you're a thousand miles from the cornfield.
7122 JANE AUSTEN/UK/ WRITER	Happiness in marriage is entirely a matter of chance.
7123 THE TALMUD	Who can protest and does not, is an accomplice in the act.

NUMBER CATEGORY/CREDIT	TOPIC
7124 GILBERT HIGHET/ SCOTTISH WRITER	These are not books, lumps of lifeless paper, but minds alive on the shelves.
7125 J.M. COETZEE/ SOUTH AFRICA	One thought alone preoccupies the submerged mind of Empire: how not to end, how not to die, how to prolong its era.
7126 CHILDREN/CRIME	Children and shoplifting
7127 GLORIA STEINEM/USA/ THIS I BELIEVE	My parents thought that travelling in a house trailer was as enlightening as sitting in a classroom.
7128 ALBERT CAMUS/ FRENCH AUTHOR	You know what charm is: a way of getting the answer yes without having asked any clear question.
7129 OLIVER WENDELL HOLMES/USA	Speak clearly, if you speak at all; carve every word before you let it fall.
7130 JOHN RAWLS/USA/ EDUCATOR	Certainly it is wrong to be cruel to animals and the destruction of a whole species can be a great evil.
7131 ANNA JULIA COOPER/ USA/EDUCATOR	I constantly felt (as I suppose many an ambitious girl has felt) a thumping from within unanswered by any beckoning from without.
7132 BARBARA McCLINTOCK/ SCIENTIST/NOBELIST/ USA/BIOLOGIST	The [Nobel] prize is such an extraordinary honor. It might seem unfair, however, to reward a person for having so much pleasure over the years, asking the maize plant to solve problems and then watching its responses.
7133 WARREN BUFFETT/USA	Price is what you pay. Value is what you get.
7134 HARUKI MURAKAMI/ JAPAN	Whiskey, like a beautiful woman, demands appreciation.
7135 TINA SEELIG/USA/ PROFESSOR	Father's advice: You should not define yourself by your current position nor believe all your own press.
7136 DR. MARTIN LUTHER KING JR./USA/ CIVIL RIGHTS LEADER	I submit that an individual who breaks a law that conscience tells him is unjust, and who willingly accepts the penalty of imprisonment in order to arouse the conscience of the community over its injustice, is in reality expressing the highest respect for the law.
7137 NATALIE GOLDBERG/ USA/WRITER	Stress is an ignorant state. It believes that everything is an emergency. Nothing is that important. Just lie down.
7138 SUN TZU/CHINESE PHILOSOPHER	What the ancients called a clever fighter is one who not only wins, but excels in winning with ease.
7139 AGATHA CHRISTIE/ ENGLISH WRITER	But surely for everything you have to love you have to pay some price.
7140 MARGARET ATWOOD/ CANADIAN NOVELIST	The only way you can write the truth is to assume that what you set down will never be read. Not by any other person, and not even by yourself at some later date.
7141 REBECCA WEST/UK/ WRITER	That shows how impossible it is to be a woman. One's whole life depends on one's looks but one mayn't speak of one's own beauty,
7142 SIR FRANCIS BACON/UK	Knowledge is power.
7143 USA/BOOKER T. WASHINGTON	One man cannot hold another man down in the ditch without remaining down in the ditch with him.
7144 RUSSIA/ALEKSANDR SOLZHENITSYN/WRITER	A great writer is, so to speak, a second government in his country. And for that reason no regime has ever loved great writers, only minor ones.
7145 GEORGE SANTAYANA/ WRITER	For gold is tried in the fire and acceptable men in the furnace of adversity.

NUMBER CATEGORY/CREDIT	TOPIC
7146 PAUL ZAK/TRUST/ TEDTALK	Countries with a higher proportion of trustworthy people are more prosperous.
7147 TAN LE/TEDTALK/ RESEARCHER/BUSINESS	I am afraid of privilege, of ease, of entitlement.
7148 S. ACHOR/TED.COM	If we study what is merely average, we will remain merely average.
7149 JAPAN/LETHARGY	May sickness (*Gogatsubyo*)
7150 KAREN ARMSTRONG/ LET'S REVIVE THE GOLDEN RULE	Look into your own heart, discover what it is that gives you pain and then refuse, under any circumstance whatsoever, to inflict that pain on anybody else.
7151 WILLIAM SHAKESPEARE	A custom more honored in the breach than the observance
7152 OLIVER WENDELL HOLMES/USA	To be 70 years young is sometimes far more cheerful and hopeful than to be 40 years old.
7153 TRAVEL/PETS/ CARE	Travelling with pets
7154 JANE AUSTEN/UK/ NOVELIST/PRIDE AND PREJUDICE	Vanity and pride are different things, though the words are often used synonymously...Pride relates more to our opinion of ourselves, vanity to what we would have others think of us.
7155 MOTHER TERESA/ CATHOLIC NUN	If we want a love message to be heard, it has to be sent out. To keep a lamp burning, we have to keep putting oil in it.
7156 TIERNEY THYS/MARINE BIOLOGIST/TED.COM	Being a loner is a great thing, especially in today's seas, because schooling used to be salvation for fishes, but it's suicide for fishes now.
7157 SANJIT "BUNKER" ROY/TEDTALK	I had a very elitist, snobbish, expensive education in India, and that almost destroyed me.
7158 WILL THOMAS/THIS I BELIEVE	Love of country, I found, can be very deep, very strong.
7159 CONUNDRUM/ORIGINS	Chicken and egg question
7160 OSCAR WILDE/POET	I can resist anything but temptation.
7161 POWER/WORK	Sexual harassment
7162 GERMAN/FRIEDRICH NIETZSCHE	To live is to suffer, to survive is to find some meaning in the suffering.
7163 PAMELA MEYER/USA/ LIES/TEDTALK	If you're in an average married couple, you're going to lie to your spouse in one out of every 10 interactions.
7164 PUBLILIUS SYRUS	How unhappy is he who cannot forgive himself.
7165 LAO-TZU/CHINESE PHILOSPHER	I have three treasures. Guard and keep them: The first is deep love, The second is frugality, And the thirds is not to dare to be ahead of the world.
7166 PAMELA MEYER/USA/ TED.COM	Lying is a cooperative act. Think about it. A lie has no power whatsoever by its mere utterance; its power emerges when someone else agrees to believe the lie.
7167 MBA/VALUE	The value of taking an MBA (Master of Business Administration) course is in the network you build from classmates and alumni.
7168 CHILDREN/TRUTH	Punishment of children for telling lies
7169 QUINQUE AVILES/ POET/USA	I believe that addiction can kill me, but that writing and performing will save me.

NUMBER CATEGORY/CREDIT	TOPIC
7170 R.G. INGERSOLL/USA	Hope is the only bee that makes honey without flowers.
7171 BLAISE PASCAL/FRENCH/ MATHEMATICIAN	Man is only a reed, the weakest in nature, but he is a thinking reed.
7172 JOAN CRAWFORD/USA/ ACTRESS	I never go outside unless I look like Joan Crawford the movie star. If you want to see the girl next door, go next door.
7173 CONSTITUTION OF THE UNITED STATES	The right of the people to be secure in their persons, houses, papers, and effects, against unreasonable searches and seizures, shall not be violated....
7174 MUSIC/HEAVY METAL	Listening to heavy metal music
7175 TOM CLANCY/USA/ WRITER	I've made up stuff that's turned out to be real, that's the spooky part.
7176 ROBERT GREEN INGERSOLL/USA/	If a man would follow, today, the teachings of the Old Testament, he would be a criminal. If he would follow strictly the teachings of the New, he would be insane.
7177 ALAIN DE BOTTON/ ATHEISM 2.0	Let's say you went to Harvard or Oxford or Cambridge, and you said, "I've come here because I'm in search of morality, guidance and consolation; I want to know how to live," – they would show you the way to the insane asylum.
7178 JANE GOODALL/UK/ PRIMATOLOGIST	The greatest danger to our future is apathy.
7179 CULTURE/COLOR	Different cultures assign different meanings to color.
7180 WILLIAM SHAKESPEARE	There is nothing either good or bad, but thinking makes it so.
7181 OPRAH WINFREY/USA/ COMMUNICATION	Whatever you fear has no power – it is your fear that has the power.
7182 D. D.EISENHOWER/ 39TH PRESIDENT/ USA	Leadership is the ability to get a person to do what you want, when you want it done, in the way you want it done, because they want to.
7183 SIR COLIN DAVIS/ CONDUCTOR/UK	Conducting is like holding a small bird in your hand. If you hold it too tightly, you crush it. If you hold it too loosely, it flies away.
7184 GABRIEL GARCÍA MÁRQUEZ/COLOMBIA	There is always something left to love.
7185 NATIONAL RIFLE ASSOCIATION/USA	I'll give up my gun when they pry it from my cold dead hand.
7186 USA/RALPH WALDO EMERSON/ESSAYIST	Children are all foreigners.
7187 OPRAH.COM/USA	Make peace with imperfection.
7188 ALAN WATTS/USA/ WRITER	For the trouble with our rich and powerful people is not so much that they are wicked, but that they do not enjoy themselves.
7189 PUBLILIUS SYRUS/ LATIN/WRITER	Count not him among your friend who will retail your privacies to the world.
7190 GHANA/S. AFRICA/FRED SWANICKER/AFRICAN LEADERSHIP ACADEMY	I believe that you don't learn leadership through theory, you learn leadership by leading...
7191 THICH NHAT HANH/ VIETNAM/BUDDHISM	My actions are my only true belongings.
7192 JACK WELCH/USA/ BUSINESS	An organization's ability to learn, and translate that learning into action rapidly, is the ultimate competitive advantage.

NUMBER CATEGORY/CREDIT	TOPIC
7193 THE TALMUD	Sin is sweet in the beginning, but bitter in the end.
7194 ELLEN GOODMAN/USA/ JOURNALIST	I have never been especially impressed by the heroics of people who are convinced they are about to change the world. I am more awed by those who struggle to make one small difference after another.
7195 WILKIE COLLINS/ POOR MISS FINCH	You may scold your carpenter, when he has made a bad table, though you can't make a table yourself.
7196 MAXIM GORKY/WRITER	When work is a pleasure, life is a joy! When work is a duty, life is slavery.
7197 PUBLILIUS SYRUS	Nothing can be done at once hastily and prudently.
7198 TOM CLANCY/USA	Life is about learning; when you stop learning, you die.
7199 KAHLIL GIBRAN/POET	Much of your pain is self-chosen.
7200 BERTRAND RUSSELL/ UK/PHILOSOPHER	Men are born ignorant, not stupid. They are made stupid by education.
7201 LES BROWN/USA/ MOTIVATION	A friend who is far away is sometimes much nearer than one who is at hand.
7202 MARRIAGE	Ideal location for a honeymoon
7203 COLIN POWELL/USA	I don't want to spend the rest of my life giving speeches.
7204 LES BROWN/USA	Forgive yourself for your faults and your mistakes and move on.
7205 STEREOTYPES	Girls are good at languages; boys are good at math.
7206 LAO-TZU/CHINA	Have few desires.
7207 HORACE MANN/USA/ EDUCATION	Habit is a cable; we weave a thread of it each day, and at last we cannot break it.
7208 GUSTAV MAHLER/ AUSTRIA/COMPOSER	When I reach a summit, I leave it with great reluctance, unless it is to reach for another.
7209 MAE JEMISON/USA/ ASTRONAUT	Never be limited by other people's limited imaginations. If you adopt their attitudes, then the possibility won't exist because you'll have already shut it out...You can hear other people's wisdom, but you've got to re-evaluate the world for yourself.
7210 OPRAH.COM/ ADVICE	Separate emotions from possessions
7211 REAR ADMIRAL GRACE HOPPER/US NAVY	Leadership is a two-way street, loyalty up and loyalty down. Respect for one's superiors; care for one's crew.
7212 USA/NEW YORK/GEORGE WASHINGTON PLUNKITT/POLITICIAN	There's an honest graft, and I'm an example of how it works. I might sum up the whole thing by sayin': "I seen my opportunities and I took 'em."
7213 LEARNED HAND/USA/ JUDGE	In the end it is worse to suppress dissent than to run the risk of heresy.
7214 THINKER/ARTHUR SCHOPENHAUER	Compassion is the basis of morality.
7215 MARIA SHARAPOVA/ TENNIS/RUSSIA	When you start from nothing, when you come from nothing, it makes you hungry. I am proud of where I came from and I know what I want. I want to win.
7216 ANNE RICE/AUTHOR/ THE VAMPIRE LESTAT	Sometimes fear is a warning. It's like someone putting a hand on your shoulder and saying Go No Farther.
7217 R.G. INGERSOLL/USA/ LAWYER	If I owe Smith ten dollars and God forgives me, that doesn't pay Smith.

NUMBER CATEGORY/CREDIT	TOPIC
7218 HOME/BUSINESS	Making your home or business burglarproof
7219 MAXIM GORKY/ RUSSIAN NOVELIST	You must write for children in the same way as you do for adults, only better.
7220 IMAN FAISAL ABDUL RAUF/TED.COM	The sources of human problems have to do with egotism, 'I'.
7221 ALAN WATT/USA/ WRITER	A myth is an image in terms of which we try to make sense of the world.
7222 DENNIS HONG/USA/ TED.COM/AEROSPACE	A blind person driving a vehicle safely and independently was thought to be an impossible task – until now.
7223 AN INDIAN PROVERB	Be the first at the feast but the last at the fight.
7224 PHIL BORGES/ON ENDANGERED CULTURES	Every two weeks, an elder goes to the grave carrying the last spoken work of that culture. An entire philosophy, a body of knowledge about the natural world that had been empirically gleaned over centuries, goes away.
7225 CHARLES HAZLEWOOD/ ENSEMBLE/TEDTALK	[South African musicians] don't read music. They trust their ears. You can teach a bunch of South Africans a tune in about five seconds flat. Then, as if by magic, they will spontaneously improvise a load of harmony around that tune.
7226 USA/RALPH WALDO EMERSON/ESSAYIST	In every work of genius we see our own rejected thoughts.
7227 GEORGE BERNARD SHAW/PLAYWRIGHT	There are two tragedies in life. One is not to get your heart's desire. The other is to get it.
7228 W.E.B. DU BOIS/USA/ REFORMER	The cost of liberty is less than the price of repression, even though the cost be blood.
7229 PERSONAL/JOY	What never fails to put a smile on your face
7230 TOM DYSTRA/AUSTRALIA ABORIGINAL	We cultivated our land, but in a way different from the white man. We endeavored to live with the land; they seemed to live off it.
7231 JAWAHARLAL NEHRU/ INDIA/PM	The future belongs to science and those who make friends with science.
7232 POWERFUL FORCE	Force majeure: an event or effect that cannot be reasonably anticipated
7233 SAUL BELLOW/ AMERICAN NOVELIST	Goodness is achieved not in a vacuum, but in the company of other men...
7234 PLAUTUS/ROMAN PLAYWRIGHT	No host can be hospitable enough to prevent a friend who has descended on him from becoming tiresome after three days.
7235 TINA SEELIG/USA/ ENTREPRENEUR	Ideas are like_____ because_____ therefore_____
7236 MARILYN MONROE/USA/ ACTRESS	I don't mind making jokes, but I don't want to look like one.
7237 PETER DRUCKER/USA/ MANAGEMENT/WRITER	Never mind your happiness; do your duty.
7238 AGATHA CHRISTIE/UK/ WRITER	Every murderer is probably somebody's old friend.
7239 DENG XIAOPING/CHINA	Seek truth from facts.
7240 OSCAR WILDE/IRISH WRITER/POET	We teach people how to remember, we never teach them how to grow.

NUMBER CATEGORY/CREDIT	TOPIC
7241 VACLAV HAVEL/CZECH STATESMAN/POET	Hope is definitely not the same thing as optimism. It is not the conviction that something will turn out well, but the certainty that something makes sense, regardless of how it turns out.
7242 CICERO/ROMAN PHILOSOPHER	There are some duties we owe even to those who have wronged us. There is, after all, a limit to retribution and punishment.
7243 JOAN CRAWFORD/USA/ACTRESS	I think the most important thing a woman can have – next to talent, of course – is her hairdresser.
7244 MUSINGS/DAILY YOMIURI/JAPAN	A tax increase would probably top the list of unpopular things for politicians. Even if they understand that someone must decide on a tax hike sometime, they do not want sometime to be "now" and do not want themselves to be "someone."
7245 WILLIAM SHAKESPEARE/UK/WRITER	Though this be madness, yet there is method in 't.
7246 JONATHAN SACKS/ENGLISH RABBI/THE DIGNITY OF DIFFERENCE	Just as the natural environment depends on biodiversity, so the human environment depends on cultural diversity, because no one civilization encompasses all the spiritual, ethical and artistic expressions of mankind.
7247 USA/ANNIE MURPHY PAUL/TIME MAGAZINE	More than 2,000 years ago, the philosopher Socrates wandered around Athens asking questions, an approach to finding truth that thinkers have venerated ever since.
7248 GILBERT HIGHET/USA/SCOTTISH WRITER	The relation between parents and children is essentially based on teaching.
7249 USA/DR. ABRAHAM VERGHESE/TEDTALK	I joke, but I only half joke, that if you come to one of our hospitals missing a limb, no one will believe you till they get a CAT scan, MRI or orthopedic consult.
7250 IVAN TURGENEV/RUSSIAN NOVELIST	Circumstances define us; they force us onto one road or another, and then they punish us for it.
7251 US/W.E. DEMING/JAPAN/QUALITY CONSULTANT	Quality is everyone's responsibility.
7252 HORACE MANN/USA	A house without books is like a room without windows.
7253 PERSONAL	Something you would not wish on your worst enemy.
7254 RICK WARREN/USA/EVANGELICAL PASTOR	Forgiveness must be immediate whether or not a person asks for it. Trust must be rebuilt over time. Trust requires a track record.
7255 AL SHARPTON/USA/CIVIL RIGHTS	I've seen enough things to know that if you just keep on going, if you turn the corner, the sun will be shining.
7256 JOHANNES BRAHMS/GERMAN/COMPOSER	If there is anyone here whom I have not insulted, I beg his pardon.
7257 DAPHNE ZUNIGA/AMERICAN ACTRESS	When you face your fears, you are free of them. There's nothing in the world I need to hide from again.
7258 LOUIS ARMSTONG/AMERICAN MUSICIAN	There is no such thing as 'on the way out' as long as you are still doing something interesting and good, you're in the business because you're breathing.
7259 GERMAN/FRIEDRICH NIETZSCHE/THINKER	That which does not kill us makes us stronger.
7260 EARL WARREN/USA/SUPREME COURT	I always turn to the sports pages first, which records people's accomplishments. The front page has nothing but man's failures.

NUMBER CATEGORY/CREDIT	TOPIC
7261 ALICE WALKER/THE COLOR PURPLE/USA	I think it pisses God off if you walk by the color purple in a field somewhere and don't notice it.
7262 USA/LAW/DOUBLE JEOPARDY	Nor shall any person be subject for the same offence to be twice put in jeopardy of life or limb....
7263 BLAISE PASCAL/ FRENCH/PHILOSOPHER	I lay it down as a fact that if all men knew what others say of them, there would not be four friends in the world.
7264 DEBATE/SECURITY	Wire-tapping has no place in a civilized society.
7265 ARAB PROVERB	When you shoot an arrow of truth, dip its point in honey.
7266 WRITER/WILLIAM SHAKESPEARE	To be or not to be: that is the question / Whether 'tis nobler in the mind to suffer the slings and arrows of outrageous fortune / Or to take arms against a sea of troubles, And by opposing them end then?
7267 ELIZABETH KUBLER-ROSS/PSYCHIATRIST	The opinion which other people have of you is their problem, not yours.
7268 ANDREA WREN/ GUARDIAN/BUILD A PROFITABLE BLOG	Guest-posting – writing good quality, original posts for high profile sites a in the hope that it would catch the attention of new readers and audiences.
7269 GORE VIDAL/AUTHOR	Never have children, only grandchildren.
7270 RENE DUBOS/BIOLOGIST	In most human affairs, the idea is to think globally and act locally.
7271 LOUIS L'AMOUR/ USA/WRITER	A mistake constantly made by those who should know better is to judge people of the past by our standards rather than their own. The only way men or women can be judged is against the canvas of their own time.
7272 ANTON CHEKHOV/ RUSSIAN WRITER	How unbearable at times are people who are happy, people for whom everything works out.
7273 TERRORISM	Airport security
7274 JIM HAYNES/SCOTTISH/ INVITING THE WORLD	If I had my way, I would introduce everyone in the whole world to each other.
7275 LAUREN ZALAZNICK/ TELEVISION/TEDTALK	The average American watches TV for almost 5 hours a day.
7276 HOWARD COSSELL/USA/ SPORTS/ANALYST	Sports is human life in microcosm.
7277 WOMEN/DRIVING	Ban on women driving in some countries
7278 THOMAS J. WATSON/ IBM CEO/USA/BUSINESS	Whenever an individual or a business decides that success has been attained, progress stops.
7279 SOJOURNER TRUTH/ USA/ACTIVIST	If my cup won't hold but a pint, and yours holds a quart, wouldn't you be mean not to let me have my little half measure full?
7280 MORTIMER ADLER/ USA/PHILOSOPHER	In the case of good books, the point is not to see how many of them you can get through, but how many can get through to you.
7281 CLARENCE DARROW/ AMERICAN LAWYER	Whenever I hear people discussing birth control I always remember that I was the fifth.
7282 BOB MARLEY/ MUSICIAN	You can fool some people some times but you can't fool all the people all the time.
7283 PUBLILIUS SYRUS	No one should be judge in his own case.
7284 BUNMEI TSUCHIYA/ JAPANESE POET	To the young people who impatiently wait for the coming of each year, I suggest they take a cycle of about 10 years as their scale of history.

NUMBER CATEGORY/CREDIT	TOPIC
7285 MISHA GLENNY/ TEDTALK/HACKERS	There are two types of companies in the world: those that know they've been hacked, and those that don't.
7286 CHARLES DICKENS/ UK/NOVELIST	Here's the rule for bargains: "Do other men, for they would do you." That's the true business precept.
7287 POWER/SOCIETY/ BUSINESS	Oligopoly: a market situation in which each of a few producers affects but does not control the market
7288 OSCAR WILDE/IRISH	A man who does not think for himself does not think at all.
7289 JOAN CRAWFORD/ USA/ACTRESS	If you have an ounce of common sense and one good friend you don't need an analyst.
7290 RICK WARREN/USA/ EVANGELICAL PASTOR	Our culture has accepted two huge lies. The first is that if you disagree with someone's lifestyle, you must fear or hate them. The second is that to love someone means you agree with everything they believe or do. Both are nonsense. You don't have to compromise convictions to be compassionate.
7291 RUSSIA/ALEKSANDR SOLZHENITSYN/WRITER	Live with steady solidarity over life - don't be afraid of misfortune, and do not yearn after happiness; it is after all, all the same; the bitter doesn't last forever, and the sweet never fills the cup to overflowing.
7292 JAMES THURBER/USA AUTHOR/CARTOONIST	A word to the wise is not sufficient if it doesn't make sense.
7293 MAHATMA GANDHI/ INDIAN LEADER	A man is but the product of his thoughts. What he thinks, he becomes.
7294 GABRIEL GARCÍA MÁRQUEZ/NOVELIST	Life is not what one lived, but what One remembers and how One remembers it in order to recount it.
7295 ALVIN TOFFLER/USA/ FUTURIST/ AUTHOR	The challenge of the 21st century will not be those who cannot read and write but those who cannot learn, unlearn, and relearn.
7296 CONFUCIUS/CHINA	The cautious seldom err.
7297 CLAUDE LEVI-STRAUSS/ FRENCH/SCIENTIST	The world began without man, and it will complete itself without him.
7298 JOSEPH STIGLITZ/ ECONOMIST/USA/ NOBEL LAUREATE	In debate, one randomly was assigned to one side or the other. This had at least one virtue – it made one see that there was more than one side to these complex issues.
7299 LEARNED HAND/ USA/JUDGE	Life is made up of constant calls to action, and we seldom have time for more than hastily contrived answers.
7300 SIR ARTHUR CONAN DOYLE/USA/WRITER	...there comes a time when for every addition of knowledge you forget something that you knew before. It is of the highest importance, therefore, not to have useless facts elbowing out the useful ones.
7301 ANIMAL RIGHTS	People for the Ethical Treatment of Animals (PETA)
7302 GERMAN/ARTHUR SCHOPENHAUER	Every nation ridicules other nations, and all are right.
7303 MARGARET MEAD/ ANTHROPOLOGIST	Many societies have educated their male children on the simple device of teaching them not to be women.
7304 ALAN WATTS/WRITER/ USA	...only doubtful truths need defense.
7305 RANDY PAUSCH/ PROFESSOR/COMPUTERS	We cannot change the cards we are dealt, just how we play the hand.

NUMBER CATEGORY/CREDIT	TOPIC
7306 FRIEDRICH NIETZSCHE/ GERMAN THINKER	When one has not had a good father, one must create one.
7307 USA/ROBERT G. INGERSOLL/LAWYER	Ignorance is the soil in which belief in miracles grows.
7308 RUSSIA/ALEKSANDR SOLZHENITSYN/WRITER	You can resolve to live your life with integrity. Let your credo be this: Let the lie come into the world, let it even triumph. But not through me.
7309 BILL GATES/USA/ ENTREPRENEUR	The world won't care about your self-esteem. The world will expect you to accomplish before you feel good about yourself.
7310 ZIG ZIGLAR/USA	Failure is a detour, not a dead-end street.
7311 CHINESE SAYING	You can only go halfway into the darkest forest; then you are coming out the other side.
7312 LES BROWN/USA	No one rises to low expectations.
7313 G.K. CHESTERTON/ ENGLISH WRITER	Fairy tales are more than true; not because they tell us that dragons exist, but because they tell us that dragons can be beaten.
7314 TINA SEELIG/USA/ ENTREPRENEUR	Essentially, we aren't taught to embrace problems. We're taught that problems are to be avoided, or something to complain about.
7315 ST. AUGUSTINE/ LATIN PHILOSOPHER/ THEOLOGIAN	What does love look like? It has the hands to help others. It has the feet to hasten to the poor and needy. It has eyes to see misery and want. It has the ears to hear the sights and sorrows of men. That is what love looks like.
7316 DELICACY/NUTRITION	Eating insects
7317 RUDYARD KIPLING/UK	God could not be everywhere, and therefore he made mothers.
7318 ANAIS NIN/USA/AUTHOR	And the day came when the risk to remain tight in a bud was more painful than the risk it took to blossom.
7319 AMBROSE BIERCE/USA/ JOURNALIST	Corporation; An ingenious device for obtaining individual profit without individual responsibility.
7320 CLAUDE BERNARD/ FRENCH/SCIENTIST	Art is I; science is we.
7321 CHIEF DAN GEORGE/ FIRST NATIONS/CANADA	O Great Spirit whose voice I hear in the winds...Make me strong not to be superior to my brother, but to be able to fight my greatest enemy: "Myself."
7322 RUPERT MURDOCH/ MEDIA MOGUL	I would like to be remembered if I am remembered at all, as being a catalyst for change in the world, change for good.
7323 USA/DR. MARTIN LUTHER KING JR./ CIVIL RIGHTS LEADER	If a man is called to be a street sweeper, he should sweep streets even as Michelangelo painted, or Beethoven composed music, or Shakespeare wrote poetry.
7324 RUSSIA/ALEKSANDR SOLZHENITSYN/WRITER	The sole substitute for an experience we have not ourselves lived thorugh is art and literature.
7325 CHINUA ACHEBE/ AFRICAN WRITER	While we do our good works let us not forget that the real solution lies in a world in which charity will have become unnecessary.
7326 MARILYN MANSON/USA/ MUSICIAN	Music is the strongest form of magic.
7327 ANITA DESAI/INDIAN/ NOVELIST	Do you know anyone who would – secretly, sincerely, in his innermost self – really prefer to return to childhood?
7328 CLARENCE DARROW/ AMERICAN LAWYER	We are all killers at heart...I have never taken anybody's life, but I have often read obituary notices with considerable satisfaction.

NUMBER CATEGORY/CREDIT	TOPIC
7329 OCCASIONS/EVENTS	Dress code
7330 SHUJI TERAYAMA/ AA KOYA/JAPAN	All intellectuals are like blades on a Toshiba electric fan. They rotate but do not move forward.
7331 ALICE WALKER/USA/ WRITER	No person is your friend who demands your silence, or denies your right to grow.
7332 BRIGITTE BARDOT/ FRENCH ACTRESS	A photograph can be an instant of life captured for eternity that will never cease looking back at you.
7333 MUSINGS/JAPAN/ DAILY YOMIURI/LUSHI CHUNQIU/MR. LU'S SPRING & AUTUMN ANNALS	Someone dropped a sword into a river from a boat. So, the person notched the side of the boat to mark where to look for the sword later. When the boat reached the shore after a while, the man dived into the water and searched for the sword, using the notch on the boat's side as a guide.
7334 JOAN CRAWFORD/ USA/ACTRESS	Love is a fire. But whether it is going to warm your hearth or burn down your house, you can never tell.
7335 JEAN ROSTAND/ FRENCH/SCIENTIST	Take heed of critics even when they are not fair; resist them even when they are.
7336 WRITER/ WILLIAM SHAKESPEARE	The evil that men do lives after them; The good is oft interred with their bones.
7337 MUSINGS/DAILY YOMIURI/JAPAN	"Minnabotchi": "everybody is alone even though they are surrounded by friends."
7338 AGATHA CHRISTIE/ UK/CRIME WRITER	An archaelogist is the best husband a woman can have. The older she gets the more interested he is in her.
7339 LOUIS L'AMOUR/USA/ WRITER	Start writing, no matter what. The water does not flow until the faucet is turned on.
7340 BLAISE PASCAL/MATH/ FRENCH	The heart has its reasons which reason knows nothing of.
7341 SANJIT "BUNKER" ROY/TEDTALK	What's the best way of communicating in the world today? TV? No. Telegraph? No. Telephone? No. Tell-a-woman!
7342 ERNEST HEMINGWAY/ USA/WRITER/NOBELIST	Courage is grace under pressure.
7343 HARUKI MURAKAMI/ JAPAN/WRITER	The most important thing we learn at school is the fact that the most important things can't be learned at school.
7344 COMPLAINTS	Common complaints about the workplace
7345 FRANCIS DARWIN/ UK/BOTANIST	In science credit goes to the man who convinces the world, not to the man to whom the idea first occurs.
7346 GEORGE SANTAYANA/ USA/PHILOSOPHER	Skepticism...should not be relinquished too readily.
7347 CONFUCIUS/CHINESE PHILOSOPHER	To see what is right, and not to do it is want of courage or of principle.
7348 CONNIE PODESTA/ SUCCESS MAGAZINE	We all know that life would be a whole lot easier if we didn't have to deal with those few (or many) difficult people we just can't seem to avoid.
7349 MARGARET ATWOOD/ CANADIAN NOVELIST	Ignoring isn't the same as ignorance, you have to work at it.
7350 USA/POET/DR. OLIVER WENDELL HOLMES SR.	To obtain a man's opinion of you, make him mad.

NUMBER CATEGORY/CREDIT	TOPIC
7351 SARAH MILLER/USA/ NYTIMES/WRITER	Yoga can cause injuries.
7352 JULIANA MACHADO FERREIRA/RARE ANIMAL TRAFFICKING IN BRAZIL	It is estimated that all kinds of illegal wildlife trade in Brazil withdraw from nature almost 38 million animals every year, a business worth almost $2 billion.
7353 OLIVER WENDELL HOLMES/USA/ AUTHOR/ PHYSICIAN	Don't flatter yourself that friendship authorizes you to say disagreeable things to your intimates. The nearer you come into relation with a person, the more necessary do tact and courtesy become.
7354 CICERO/ROMAN PHILOSOPHER	The wise are instructed by reason; ordinary minds by experience; the stupid, by necessity; and brutes by instinct.
7355 TOM CLANCY/USA/ NOVELIST	Never ask what sort of computer a guy drives. If he's a Mac user, he'll tell you. If not, why embarrass him?
7356 JAMES ALLEN/UK/ WRITER/SELF-HELP	A man's mind may be likened to a garden, which may be intelligently cultivated or allowed to run wild; but whether cultivated or neglected, it must, and will, *bring forth*. If no useful seeds are *put* into it, then an abundance of useless weed seeds will *fall therein*, and will continue to produce their kind.
7357 PUBLILIUS SYRUS	As men, we are all equal in the presence of death.
7358 JOHN STEINBECK/ AMERICAN WRITER	Boys are beyond the range of anybody's sure understanding, at least when they are between the ages of 18 months and 90 years.
7359 BRIGITTE BARDOT/ FRENCH/ACTRESS	Fame...brought me so much unhappiness.
7360 ORVILLE WRIGHT/ USA/INVENTOR	If we all worked on the assumption that what is accepted as true is really true, there would be little hope of advance.
7361 JEAN ROSTAND/ SCIENTIST/FRENCH	Science has made us gods even before we are worthy of being men.
7362 HENRY TAUBE/ CANADIAN SCIENTIST	This joy of discovery is real, and it is one of our rewards. So too is the approval of our work by our peers.
7363 THOMAS CARLYLE/ SCOTTISH ESSAYIST	That there should one Man die ignorant who had capacity for Knowledge, this I call tragedy.
7364 HORATIO NELSON/ BRITISH OFFICER	If a man consults whether he is to fight, when he has the power in his own hands, it is certain that his opinion is against fighting.
7365 USA/HENRY DAVID THOREAU/WRITER	When some of my friends have asked me anxiously about their boys, whether they should let them hunt, I have answered yes – remembering that it was one of the best parts of my education – make them hunters.
7366 GUILLERMO CABRERA INFANTE/CUBAN AUTHOR/ ESSAYIST	I know that may writers have had to write under censorship and yet produced good novels; for instance, Cervantes wrote Don Quixote under Catholic censorship.
7367 TALI SHAROT/THE OPTIMISM BIAS TEDTALK	We're optimistic about ourselves, we're optimistic about our kids, we're optimistic about our families, but we're not so optimistic about the guy sitting next to us.
7368 WILLIAM OSLER/ CANADIAN SCIENTIST	The good physician treats the disease; the great physician treats the patient who has the disease.
7369 TINA SEELIG/USA/ PROFESSOR/BUSINESS	Uncertainty is the essence of life.

NUMBER CATEGORY/CREDIT	TOPIC
7370 RAY DAVIES/UK/ ROCK SINGER/LOLA	Girls will be boys and boys will be girls It's a mixed up muddled up shook up world.
7371 USA/CHIEF NORM STAMPER/POLICE	I believe that violence in the home is a precursor to all forms of violence.
7372 OPRAH WINFREY/ USA/BILLIONAIRE	If it doesn't feel right, don't do it. That's the lesson. That lesson alone, will save you a lot of grief.
7373 DEBATE	Honesty is not always the best policy.
7374 ARABIC PROVERB	Your tongue is like a horse – if you take care of it, it takes are of you; if you treat it badly, it treats you badly.
7375 KATHRYN SCHULZ/ TEDTALK/AUTHOR	Regret doesn't remind us that we did badly. It reminds us that we know we can do better.
7376 USA/THURGOOD MARSHALL/JUDGE	If the First Amendment means anything, it means the state has no business telling a man, sitting alone in his house, what books he may read or what films he may watch.
7377 RYOKAN/JAPAN	Too lazy to be ambitious, I let the world take care of itself. Ten days' worth of rice in my bag; a bundle of twigs by the fireplace. Why chatter about delusion and enlightenment? Listening to the night rain on my roof, I sit comfortably, with both legs stretched out.
7378 IVAN TURGENEV/RUSSIA	I agree with no one's opinion. I have some of my own.
7379 GORE VIDAL/USA/ AUTHOR	I sometimes think it is because they are so bad at expressing themselves verbally that writers take to pen and paper in the first place.
7380 BRUCE FEILER/USA/ TEDTALK/WRITER	Take a walk with a turtle. Behold the world in a pause.
7381 PROVERB	It takes all sorts to make a world.
7382 PLATO/GREEK PHILOSOPHER	We can easily forgive a child who is afraid of the dark; the real tragedy of life is when men are afraid of the light.
7383 OPRAH WINFREY/ USA/MEDIA MOGUL	If you neglect to recharge a battery, it dies. And if you run full speed ahead without stopping for water, you lose momentum to finish the race.
7384 ALBERT EINSTEIN/ NOBELIST/SCIENTIST	Everything should be made as simple as possible, but not simpler.
7385 THOMAS MANN/ GERMAN WRITER	A writer is someone for whom writing is more difficult than it is for other people.
7386 USA/HENRY DAVID THOREAU/WRITER	What is the use of a house if you haven't got a tolerable planet to put it on?
7387 JOEY ADAMS/USA	With friends like that, who needs enemies?
7388 NY TIMES/ LEONARD MLODINOW	The need for control can inspire great achievements, such as dams, medicines, and chocolate soufflés.
7389 MUSTAFA KEMAL ATATURK/TURKEY	Justice is the infrastructure of proprietorship.
7390 USA/RALPH WALDO EMERSON/WRITER	Make yourself necessary to somebody. Do not make life hard to any.
7391 ABDUL KALAM/ INDIA/PRESIDENT	No religion has mandated killing others as a requirement for its sustenance or promotion.
7392 DOLLY PARTON/USA/ MUSICIAN	We cannot direct the wind, but we can adjust the sails.

NUMBER CATEGORY/CREDIT	TOPIC
7393 USA/OLIVER WENDELL HOLMES/AUTHOR	Knowledge and timber shouldn't be much used till they are seasoned.
7394 LOUIS L'AMOUR/ AMERICAN WRITER	The way I see it, every time a man gets up in the morning he starts his life over. Sure, the bills are there to pay, and the job is there to do, but you don't have to stay in a pattern. You can always start over, saddle a fresh horse and take another trail.
7395 KAHLIL GIBRAN/ LEBANESE POET	Keep me away from the wisdom which does not cry, the philosophy which does not laugh and the greatness which does not bow before children.
7396 ALEXIS CARREL/ FRENCH/SCIENTIST	Man cannot remake himself without suffering, for he is both the marble and the sculptor.
7397 DAVID HOCHNEY/UK/ PAINTER	If we are to change our world view, images have to change.
7398 BRIGITTE BARDOT/ FRENCH/ACTOR	I absolutely loathe luxury. It is the one thing I cannot stand.
7399 WRITER/WILLIAM SHAKESPEARE	There is a tide in the affairs of men, Which taken at the flood, leads on to fortune; Omitted, all the voyage of their life Is bound in shallows and in miseries.
7400 CHRISTOPHER MCDOUGALL/ARE WE BORN TO RUN?/ TEDTALK	There is a growing subculture of barefoot runners, people who got rid of their shoes. And what they have found uniformly is you get rid of the shoes, you get rid of the stress, you get rid of the injuries and the ailments.
7401 BEN KACYRA/TEDTALK/ DIGITAL PRESERVATIONIST	Imagine us as a human race not knowing where we came from.
7402 PUBLILIUS SYRUS	No one knows what he can do till he tries.
7403 CHIMAMANDA NGOZI ADICHIE/NIGERIA/ WRITER/TEDTALK	The single story creates stereotypes, and the problem with stereotypes is not that they are untrue, but that they are incomplete. They make one story become the only story.
7404 JOSHUA FOER/USA/ TEDTALK/MEMORY	If you want to live a memorable life, you have to be the kind of person who remembers to remember.
7405 RONALD REAGAN/ 40TH PRESIDENT/USA	Going to college offered me the chance to play football for four more years.
7406 GEORGE SANTAYANA/ SPANISH-AMERICAN PHILOSOPHER/POET	Many possessions, if they do not make a man better, are at least expected to make his children happier; and this pathetic hope is behind many exertions.
7407 DR. PASI SAHLBERG/ NY TIMES/USA	It's more difficult getting into teacher education than law or medicine.
7408 PUBLILIUS SYRUS/	Let a fool hold his tongue and he will pass for a sage.
7409 HARRY BASSETT/ USA/BUSINESS	To prosper soundly in business, you must satisfy not only your customers, but you must lay yourself out to satisfy also the men who make your product and the men who sell it.
7410 KENTETSU TAKAMORI/ JAPAN/WRITER	Many Buddhist temple priests regard their parishioners as possessions and fear their departure as a diminishing of assets.
7411 GEORGE SANTAYANA/ POET/WRITER	History is a pack of lies about events that never happened told by people who weren't there.
7412 DIFFERENCES	Comparing apples and oranges

NUMBER CATEGORY/CREDIT	TOPIC
7413 USA/ROBERT GREEN INGERSOLL/LAWYER	In nature there are neither rewards nor punishments; there are consequences.
7414 LES BROWN/USA/ MOTIVATION	Perfection does not exist – you can always do better and you can always grow.
7415 CONSTITUTION OF THE UNITED STATES	In all criminal prosecutions, the accused shall enjoy the right to a speedy and public trial, by an impartial jury...
7416 ROGER ANGELL/USA/ THE DIGNITY OF MAN/THIS I BELIEVE	I have doubts because I am still a young man, and sureness in the young is unwise and unbecoming.
7417 GILBERT HIGHET/ SCOTTISH WRITER	Many people have played themselves to death. Many people have eaten and drunk themselves to death. Nobody ever thought himself to death.
7418 ELIZABETH KUBLER-ROSS/PSYCHIATRIST	There is within each one of us a potential for goodness beyond our imagining; for giving which seeks no reward; for listening without judgment; for loving unconditionally.
7419 IVAN TURGENEV/ RUSSIAN NOVELIST	The word tomorrow was invented for indecisive people and for children.
7420 DONALD RICHIE/JAPAN/ WRITER	Japan never considers time together as time wasted. Rather, it is time invested.
7421 OPRAH WINFREY/ USA/BILLIONAIRE	If you're hurting, you need to help somebody else ease their hurt. If you're in pain, help somebody else's pain.
7422 WRITER/WILLIAM SHAKESPEARE	If all the year were playing holidays, To sport would be as tedious as to work.
7423 ALICE WALKER/USA/ WRITER	The most common way people give up their power is by thinking they don't have any.
7424 HOME/CHORES	Ways children can help at home.
7425 LATIN EXPRESSION	The loss that is not known is not a loss.
7426 DEBATE	That the elderly be able to board public transportation free of charge.
7427 EDWIN LAND/USA/ INVENTOR/BUSINESS	Politeness is the poison of collaboration.
7428 JULIEN BRYAN/USA/ THIS I BELIEVE	Wherever I went, I soon discovered that when you break bread with people and share their troubles and joys, the barriers of language, of politics, and of religion soon vanish.
7429 ROBERT HUGHES/ AUSTRALIA/ART	A determined soul will do more with a rusty monkey wrench than a loafer will accomplish with all the tools in a machine shop.
7430 THICH NHAT HANH/ VIETNAM/BUDDHISM	When you plant lettuce, if it does not grow well, you don't blame the lettuce. You look for reasons it is not doing well. It may need fertilizer, or more water, or less sun. You never blame the lettuce. Yet if we have problems with our friends or family, we blame the other person.
7431 NELSON MANDELA/ S. AFRICA/LEADER	Know your enemy -- and learn about his favorite sport.
7432 DEBATE	Alcohol is not the problem. The problem is abuse of alcohol.
7433 DARREN HARDY/ SUCCESS MAGAZINE	There are some people you might need to break away from completely.
7434 WATER/NECESSITY	Water is life.
7435 MOTHER TERESA/NUN	If you can't feed a hundred people, then feed just one.

NUMBER CATEGORY/CREDIT	TOPIC
7436 MICHELLE OBAMA/ US/FIRST LADY	Even when times are tough, in the end, you are as happy as your least happy child.
7437 BRIAN MULRONEY/ CANADIAN PM	You have to spend your political capital on great causes for your country.
7438 LOUIS L'AMOUR/ AMERICAN WRITER	I have read my books by many lights, hoarding their beauty, their wit or wisdom against the dark days when I would have no book, nor a place to read. I have known hunger of the belling kind many times over, but I have known a worse hunger: the need to know and to learn.
7439 OLIVER WENDELL HOLMES/USA/ AUTHOR/PHYSICIAN	I find the great in this world is not so much where we stand, as in what direction we are moving;: To reach the port of heaven, we must sail, sometimes with the wind and sometimes against it, but we must sail and not drift, nor lie at anchor.
7440 BERTRAND RUSSELL/ UK/PHILOSOPHER	In all affairs it's a healthy thing now and then to hang a question mark on the things you have long taken for granted.
7441 NAOMI CAMPBELL/ BRITISH MODEL	Anger is a manifestation of a deeper issue...and that, for me, is based on insecurity, self-esteem and loneliness.
7442 JOHANN WOLFGANG VON GOETHE/WRITER	Anecdotes and maxims are rich treasures to the man of the world, for he knows how to introduce the former at fit place in conversation.
7443 JAMES ALLEN/UK/ AUTHOR/SELF-HELP	Of all the beautiful truths pertaining to the soul which have been brought to light in this age, none is more gladdening of divine promise and confidence than this -- that man is the master of thought, the molder of character, and maker and shaper of condition, environment, and destiny.
7444 FRANK SINATRA/USA/ SINGER	The best revenge is massive success.
7445 KEVIN BREEL/TED/ CONFESSIONS OF A DEPRESSED COMIC/USA	The world I believe in is where embracing your light doesn't mean ignoring your dark. The world I believe in is one where we are measured by our ability to overcome adversities, not avoid them.
7446 CARL SAGAN/USA/ SCIENTIST	Science is not only compatible with spirituality; it is a profound source of spirituality.
7447 WILLIAM JAMES/USA/ PHILOSOPHER	We don't laugh because we're happy – we're happy because we laugh.
7448 USA/HENRY DAVID THOREAU/WRITER	The mass of men lead lives of quiet desperation.
7449 JOHN C. POLANYI/ CANADIAN SCIENTIST	Some dreamers demand that scientists only discover things that can be used for good.
7450 LAO TZU/CHINESE SAGE	Knowledge is a treasure but practice is the key to it.
7451 USA/MALCOLM GLADWELL/WRITER	In fact, researchers have settled on what they believe is the magic number for true expertise: ten thousand hours.
7452 BJORN LOMBORG/ GLOBAL PRIORITIES	We've had the U.N. for almost 60 years, yet we've never actually made a fundamental list of all the big things that we can do in the world, and said, "Which of them should we do first?"
7453 BRIGITTE BARDOT/ FRENCH/ACTRESS	I am against marriage, and I don't give a fig for society.
7454 ANTHONY COLDBLOOM/ USA/BUSINESS	I hate reading about other people's success. It makes me feel more of a failure.

NUMBER CATEGORY/CREDIT	TOPIC
7455 DEBATE	Money is the key to a happy marriage.
7456 BULLYING	Pushing someone's buttons
7457 JAMES ALLEN/AUTHOR/ AS A MAN THINKETH	A noble and Godlike character is not a thing of favor or chance, but is the natural result of continued effort in right thinking, the effect of long-cherished association with Godlike thoughts. An ignoble and bestial character, by the same process, is the result of the continued harboring of groveling thoughts.
7458 CHARLES DICKENS/UK/ WRITER	Accidents will occur in the best-regulated families.
7459 NICKNAMES/ PRIVACY	Use of pseudonyms online
7460 VACLAV HAVEL/ CZECH LEADER	The salvation of this human world lies nowhere else than in the human heart, in the human power to reflect, in human meekness and human responsibility.
7461 JOHN STEINBECK/USA/ WRITER	Don't get it right, just get it written.
7462 BRIGITTE BARDOT/ FRENCH ACTRESS	I have no private life at all. I am a hunted woman. I can't take a step without being questioned and surrounded.
7463 IVAN TURGENEV/ RUSSIAN NOVELIST	Most people can't understand how others can blow their noses differently than they do.
7464 HECTOR BERLIOZ/ FRENCH COMPOSER	Time is a great teacher, but unfortunately it kills all its students.
7465 JIM HAYNES/ SCOTTISH/INVITING THE WORLD TO DINNER	People are most important in my life. Many travelers go to see things like the Tower of London, the Statue of Liberty, the Eiffel Tower and so on. I travel to see friends, even – or especially –those I've never met.
7466 LAO-TZU/THINKER	Reduce selfishness.
7467 LEE IACOCCA/ CHRYSLER/CEO	In a completely rational society, the best of us would be teachers and the rest of us would have to settle for something else.
7468 ERNEST HEMINGWAY/US	Fear of death increases in exact proportion to increase in wealth.
7469 KIERKEGAARD/THINKER	Our life always expresses the result of our dominant thoughts.
7470 GERMAN/THINKER/ A. SCHOPENHAUER	To find out your real opinion of someone, judge the impression you have when you first see a letter from them.
7471 ZIG ZIGLAR/USA/ MOTIVATIONAL SPEAKER	Expect the best. Prepare for the worst. Capitalize on what comes.
7472 ANDREW CARNEGIE/ INDUSTRIALIST	Immense power is acquired by assuring yourself in your secret reveries that you were born to control affairs.
7473 FRED SWANIKER/ AFRICAN LEADERSHIP ACADEMY	I firmly believe that a leadership experience that a young person gets in their teens particularly, gives them the foundation to do something much bigger later on in their lives.
7474 LATIN EXPRESSION	All inquire whether a man is rich, no one whether he is good.
7475 HONDA MASANOBU/ JAPAN/ADVISER TO SHOGUN IEYASU	The peasant is the foundation of the state and must be governed with care. He must be allowed neither too much nor too little, but just enough rice to live on and keep for seed in the following year. The remainder must be taken from him in tax.
7476 RICHARD WOLFF/USA/ ECONOMIST	It takes a whole society to make technological breakthrough.

NUMBER CATEGORY/CREDIT	TOPIC
7477 ANN LANDERS/USA/ COLUMNIST	No person ever drowned in his own sweat.
7478 GORE VIDAL/USA/ AUTHOR	Any American who is prepared to run for president should automatically by definition be disqualified from ever doing so.
7479 GEORGE BERNARD SHAW/PLAYWRIGHT	The reasonable man adapts himself to the world; the unreasonable one persists in trying to adapt the world to himself.
7480 ALICE WALKER/USA	When the ax came into the forest the trees said the handle is one of us.
7481 VACLAV HAVEL/ CZECH PRESDIENT	There are times when we must sink to the bottom of our misery to understand truth, just as we must descend to the bottom of the well to see the stars in broad daylight.
7482 IYANLA VANZANT/USA/ TV SUCCESS COACH	When you need to be loved, you take love wherever you can find it.
7483 MOTHER TERESA/ CATHOLIC NUN	The biggest disease today is not leprosy or tuberculosis, but rather the feeling of being unwanted.
7484 VIKTOR FRANKL	To suffer unnecessarily is masochistic rather than heroic.
7485 GORE VIDAL/USA/ WRITER	The four most beautiful words in our common language: I told you so.
7486 WRITER/WILLIAM SHAKESPEARE	In peace there's nothing so becomes a man as modest stillness and humility; But when the blast of war blows in our ears, Then imitate the action of the tiger: Stiffen the sinews, summon up the blood.
7487 HECTOR BOLITHO/ UK/COMPETITION IS A SIN/THIS I BELIEVE	Instead of working today, I walked a little, and I read a little. I planted some Geranium cuttings in sand for next year. True, I put off a task I should have done, until tomorrow. But I feel calmer within myself for this idleness, and I believe that I'm right in trying to weave a new pattern in which contemplation is the chief color, and action is only a thread running through.
7488 GROUCHO MARX/USA/ COMEDIAN	Military intelligence is a contradiction in terms.
7489 SAUL BELLOW/USA / WRITER	A fool can throw a stone in a pond that 100 wise men cannot get out.
7490 AYN RAND/WRITER/ PHILOSOPHER	It is never too late to give up our prejudices.
7491 SANDRA BUCKLEY/ BROKEN SILENCE/ JAPAN	In any East Asian culture, you will find that women have a very tangible power within the household. This is often rejected by non-Asian feminists who argue that it is not real power, but...Japanese women look at the low status atttributed to the domestic labor of housewives in North America and feel that this amounts to a denigration of a fundamental social role -- whether it is performeed by a man or woman.
7492 GEORGE SANTAYANA/ POET/WRITER	Tyrants are seldom free; the cares and the instruments of their tyranny enslave them.
7493 USA/DWIGHT D. EISENHOWER/PRES.	A people that values its privilege above its principles soon loses both.
7494 ABDUL KALAM/INDIA/ PRESIDENT	Those who cannot work with their hearts achieve but a hollow, half-hearted success that breeds bitterness all around.
7495 PAUL J. MEYER/USA/ SUCCESS MAGAZINE	More damage is done by worrying than by what is being worried about.

NUMBER CATEGORY/CREDIT	TOPIC
7496 GEORGE SANTAYANA/ POET/WRITER	Friends need not agree in everything or go always together or have no comparable other friendships of the same intimacy. On the contrary, in friendship union is more about ideal things: and in that sense it is more ideal and less subject to trouble than marriage is.
7497 MOTHER TERESA/NUN	If you judge people, you have no time to love them.
7498 JONATHAN SWIFT/IRISH	Every dog must have his day.
7499 ANGELA Y. DAVIS/ USA/ACTIVIST/AN AUTOBIOGRAPHY	Jails and prisons are designed to break human beings, to convert the population into specimens in a zoo – obedient to our keepers, but dangerous to each other.
7500 P.W. SINGER/ON MILITARY ROBOTS AND THE FUTURE OF WAR	What one Predator drone pilot described of his experience fighting in the Iraq war while never leaving Nevada. 'You're going to war for 12 hours, shooting weapons at targets, directing kills on enemy combatants. Then you get in the car and you drive home, and within 20 minutes you're sitting at the dinner table talking to your kids about their homework.'
7501 KAHLIL GIBRAN/ON TEACHING	The astronomer may speak to you of his understanding of space, but he cannot give you his understanding.
7502 SANTOSH KALWAR/ NEPALESE WRITER	If I can see pain in your eyes then share with me your tears. If I can see joy in your eyes then share with me your smile.
7503 CONSTITUTION/ USA/8th AMENDMENT	Excessive bail shall not be required, nor excessive fines imposed, nor cruel and unusual punishments inflicted.
7504 STEVEN SPIELBERG/ USA/MOVIE DIRECTOR	I don't dream at night. I dream all day; I dream for a living.
7505 ELIZABETH KUBLER-ROSS/PSYCHIATRIST	There are no mistakes, no coincidences. All events are blessings given to us to learn from.
7506 THE TALMUD	Make your books your companions.
7507 SHERRY TURKLE/ TEDTALK/USA	We expect more from technology and less from each other.
7508 JANE GOODALL/ HUMANS & ANIMALS LIVE TOGETHER/ TED.COM	Chimpanzees, more than any other living creature, have helped us to understand that there is no sharp line between humans and the rest of the animal kingdom. It's a very blurry line, and it's getting more blurry all the time.
7509 GABRIEL GARCÍA MÁRQUEZ/COLOMBIA	One can be in love with several people at the same time, feel the sorrow with each, and not betray any of them.
7510 MAO TSE TUNG/ CHINESE LEADER	Communism is not love. Communism is a hammer which we use to crush the enemy.
7511 GERMAN/ARTHUR SCHOPENHAUER	To buy books would be a good thing if we also could buy the time to read them.
7512 CONFUCIUS/CHINESE PHILOSOPHER/ TR.WING-TSIT CHAN	If we are not yet able to serve man, how can we serve spiritual beings?...If we do not yet know about life how can we know about death?
7513 BOB MARLEY/SINGER	Some people feel the rain. Others just get wet.
7514 HERODOTUS/HISTORIAN	Do you see how the god always hurls his bolts at the greatest houses and the tallest trees. For he is wont to thwart whatever is greater than the rest.
7515 CANADA/PROFESSOR KIM RICHARD NOSSAL	Pinchpenny diplomacy

NUMBER CATEGORY/CREDIT	TOPIC
7516 LES BROWN/USA/ MOTIVATION	Too many of us are not living our dreams because we are living our fears.
7517 GOETHE/POET/GERMAN	Divide and rule, a sound motto. Unite and lead, a better one.
7518 M. ECKHART/THINKER	He who would be serene and pure needs but one thing, detachment.
7519 MATTHEW ARNOLD/UK/ POET	Truth sits on the lips of dying men.
7520 EARL WARREN/USA/ JUDGE	Ben Franklin may have discovered electricity – but it is the man who invented the meter who made the money.
7521 STEVEN SPIELBERG/ USA/MOVIE DIRECTOR	We pay a dollar for a bookmark? Why not use the dollar for a bookmark?
7522 WILLIAM SHAKESPEARE/ UK/PLAYWRIGHT	Although the last, not least.
7523 STEVEN SPIELBERG/ USA/MOVIE DIRECTOR	Only a generation of readers will spawn a generation of writers.
7524 MATT CURTIS/TEDTALK/ GLOBAL PARTNERSHIP	Thirty days is just about the right amount of time to add a new habit or subtract a habit – like watching the news – from your life.
7525 RULES FOR LIFE	You will NOT make $60,000 a year right out of high school. You won't be a vice-president with a car phone until you earn both.
7526 US/DANIEL LIEBESKIND/ TED.COM	Architecture is not based on concrete and steel and the elements of the soil. It's based on wonder.
7527 C. HEROLD/TED.COM	Both my nine- and seven-year olds have a stockbroker already.
7528 LONGEVITY	A story with legs
7529 WARREN BUFFETT/USA	Risk comes from not knowing what you're doing.
7530 OSCAR WILDE/IRISH	My own business always bores me to death; I prefer other people's.
7531 TINA SEELIG/AUTHOR/ STANFORD/USA	Walking away from a deal should always be considered a viable option.
7532 RITA DOVE/USA/POET	If you can't be free, be a mystery.
7533 ANTHONY HOPKINS/ ACTOR/UK	I practice each acting role 500 times before the performance.
7534 INDIAN PROVERB	Be careful of dogs that do not bark.
7535 HENRY FIELDING/UK	Love and scandal are the best sweeteners of tea.
7536 DOLLY PARTON/USA	Don't get so busy making a living that you forget to make a life.
7537 LORD ACTON/UK	Great men are almost always bad men.
7538 SENECA/ROMAN	It is the sign of a weak mind to be unable to bear wealth.
7539 BARRY COMMONER/US/ PROFESSOR/BIOLOGIST	The first law of ecology: Everything is connected to everything else.
7540 BILLIE JEAN KING/ USA/TENNIS PLAYER	Tennis is a perfect combination of violent action, taking place in an atmosphre of total tranquility.
7541 MIYAMOTO MUSASHI	Be detached from desire your whole life long.
7542 CLOTHING/MONEY	Buying new clothes versus buying pre-worn clothes
7543 GERMAN/FRIEDRICH NIETZSCHE	When a hundred men stand together, each of them loses his mind and gets another one.
7544 HERODOTUS/HISTORIAN	Illness strikes men when they are exposed to change.

NUMBER CATEGORY/CREDIT	TOPIC
7545 NIETZSCHE/GERMAN	Some are made modest by great praise, others insolent.
7546 WILL ROGERS/ AMERICAN COMEDIAN	Things run in our country run in spite of government, not by aid of it.
7547 NIALL FERGUSON/ THE 6 KILLER APPS OF PROSPERITY	It's our generation that is witnessing the end of Western predominance. The average American used to be more than 20 times richer than the average Chinese. Now it's just five times, and soon it will be 2.5 times.
7548 ALICE WALKER/USA/ WRITER	Activism is my rent for living on the planet.
7549 ISAAC MIZRAHI/ FASHION/FASHION/ CREATIVITY/TEDTALK	There are so many images out there, so many clothes out there, and the only ones that look interesting to me are the ones that look slightly mistaken.
7550 GORE VIDAL/USA/ AUTHOR	"Write what you know" will always be excellent advice for those who ought not to write at all. Write what you think, what you imagine, what you suspect.
7551 VLADIMIR NABOKOV/ RUSSIAN NOVELIST	A work of art has no importance whatever to society. It is only important to the individual.
7552 USA/DR. ALEXANDER FORBES/THIS BELIEVE	Religion is not a weakness. It is a vital element in human nature.
7553 KIM CLIJSTERS/ TENNIS/BELGIUM	You don't have to hate your opponents to beat them.
7554 JOHN W. DAVIS/ AMERICAN LAWYER AND POLITICIAN	True, we lawyers build no bridges. We raise no towers. We construct no engines. We paint no pictures...There is little of all that we do which the eye of man can see. But we smooth out difficulties, we relieve stress; we correct mistakes, we take up other men's burdens and by our efforts we make possible the peaceful life of men in a peaceful state.
7555 JOHANN WOLFGANG von GOETHE/DRAMATIST/	Enjoy when you can, and endure when you must.
7556 TOM CLANCY/USA/ NOVELIST	No matter what you or anyone else does, there will be someone who says that there's something bad about it.
7557 TONI MORRISON/ USA/NOVELIST	Everywhere, everywhere, children are the scorned people of the earth.
7558 UK/IVY COMPTON- BURNETT/NOVELIST	There is more difference within the sexes than between them.
7559 ART LAFFER/USA/ ECONOMIST	You can't love jobs and hate job creators.
7560 RAFAEL NADAL/TENNIS PLAYER/SPAIN	Losing is not my enemy...fear of losing is my enemy.
7561 INTERNATIONAL	Free trade
7562 DANISH/SOREN KIERKEGAARD	Patience is necessary, and one cannot reap immediately where one has sown.
7563 MIYAMOTO MUSASHI/ JAPANESE WARRIOR	Perceive that which cannot be seen with the eye.
7564 FOLK WISDOM	Nice guys finish last.
7565 BASHO MATSUO/ JAPANESE POET	Real poetry, is to lead a beautiful life. To live poetry is better than to write it.

NUMBER CATEGORY/CREDIT	TOPIC
7566 AL CAPONE/USA/ GANGSTER	You can go a long way with a smile. You can go a lot farther with a smile and a gun.
7567 JAMES ALLEN/UK/ AUTHOR/SELF-HELP	Act is the blossom of thought, and joy and suffering are its fruits, thus does a man garner in the sweet and bitter fruitage of his own husbandry.
7568 ANNA JULIA COOPER/ USA/EDUCATOR	The cause of freedom is not the cause of a race or a sect, a party or a class – it is the cause of human kind the very birthright of humanity.
7569 HENRY LOUIS GATES/ USA/EDUCATOR	No human culture is inaccessible to someone who makes the effort to understand, to learn, to inhabit another world.
7570 WILLIAM SHAKESPEARE	Out of nothing, nothing comes.
7571 STEPHEN PALUMBI/ TEDTALK	If the ocean ain't happy, ain't nobody happy.
7572 DR. ALEXANDER THIS I BELIEVE	I deplore the hostile conflicts between rival churches calling themselves Christian. The need for worship is expressed in many ways. The creeds and rituals that suit one type of mind, do not satisfy others.
7573 KAHLIL GIBRAN/ON FRIENDSHIP	When you part from your friend, you grieve not; For that which you love most in him may be clear in his absence, as the mountain to the climber is clearer from the plain.
7574 G.K. CHESTERTON/ UK/WRITER	Just going to church doesn't make you a Christian any more than standing in your garage makes you a car.
7575 MARCUS TULLIUS CICERO/PHILOSOPHER	Servitude is the worst of all evils, to be resisted not only by war, but even by death.
7576 ALLEN W. DULLES/USA/ THE CRAFT OF INTELLIGENCE	When the fate of a nation and the lives of its soldiers are at stake, gentlemen do read each other's mail – if they can get their hands on it.
7577 HOSEA BALLOU/USA/ CLERGY	Real happiness is cheap enough, yet how dearly we pay for its counterfeit.
7578 WILLIAM SHAKESPEARE/ UK/PLAYWRIGHT	An honest tale speeds best, being plainly told.
7579 NED KELLY/ AUSTRALIAN BUSHRANGER	If my lips teach the public that men are made mad by bad treatment, and if the police are taught that they may exasperate to madness men they persecute and ill treat, my life will not be entirely thrown away.
7580 AN INDIAN PROVERB	A book is like a garden in the pocket.
7581 STEVEN SPIELBERG/ USA/MOVIE DIRECTOR	Technology can be our best friend, and technology can also be the biggest party pooper of our lives. It interrupts our own story, interrupts our ability to have a thought or a daydream, to imagine something wonderful because we're too busy bridging the walk from the cafeteria back to the office on the cell phone.
7582 AYN RAND/WRITER/ THINKER	It only stands to reason that where there's sacrifice, there's someone collecting the sacrificial offerings.
7583 LT. GEN. D. M. MUELLER/AUSTRALIA	As a leader you must celebrate life, you must celebrate success and paradoxically, you must celebrate heroic failures.
7584 LAO-TZU/CHINA/ SAGE	Because of frugality, one is courageous.
7585 LOUIS ARMSTRONG/ USA/JAZZ MUSICIAN	Musicians don't retire; they stop when there's no more music in them.

NUMBER CATEGORY/CREDIT	TOPIC
7586 SENECA/RHETORICIAN	A hated government does not long survive.
7587 LI KA SHING/HONG KONG MILLIONAIRE	To be a successful manager, attitude and ability are equally important ingredients. A leader inspires others to greatness. A boss dominates his subordinates and makes them feel small.
7588 PLEASURE	Saving the best for last
7589 ITALY/COUNT GALEAZZO CIANO/POLITICIAN	Victory has a hundred fathers, but defeat is an orphan.
7590 ANIL GUPTA/TED.COM/ PROFESSOR/INDIA	You cannot have two principles of justice, one for yourself and one for others.
7591 STEVEN SPIELBERG/ USA/MOVIE DIRECTOR	My first reaction, every time I delve into an episode of history that I don't know very much about, is anger that my teachers never taught me about it.
7592 NAOMI CAMPBELL/UK/ MODEL	I make a lot of money and I'm worth every cent.
7593 JOHANN WOLFGANG VON GOETHE/GERMAN	If children grew up according to early indications, we should have nothing but geniuses.
7594 CONSTITUTION OF THE USA/ 13th AMENDMENT	Neither slavery nor involuntary servitude, except as a punishment for crime whereof the party shall have been duly convicted, shall exist within the United States, or any place subject to their jurisdiction.
7595 MARRIAGE/ CONFLICT	Conflict-filled marriages
7596 MATTHEW ARNOLD/UK/ POET	The freethinking of one age is the common sense of the next.
7597 TOM CLANCY/USA/ NOVELIST	People live longer today than they ever have. They live happier lives, have more knowledge, more information. All this is the result of communications technology. How is any of that bad?
7598 GABRIEL GARCÍA MÁRQUEZ/COLOMBIA	A man knows when he is growing old because he begins to look like his father.
7599 CHILDREN/READING	The practice of reading to children
7600 HECTOR BOLITHO/ UK/THIS I BELIEVE	I believe...that man's greatest enemy is fear – not fear in battle but in the moral and ethical issues of day to day life.
7601 SAYING	Don't buy the cow if she is giving away the milk for free.
7602 LEADERSHIP	The difference between the president of a nation and the CEO of a company.
7603 NATALIE GOLDBERG/ AMERICAN WRITER	After you have finished a piece of work, the work is then none of your business. Go on and do something else.
7604 SUN TZU/CHINESE GENERAL/AUTHOR	Victorious warriors win first and then go to war, while defeated warriors go to war first and then seek to win.
7605 SENECA/DRAMATIST	Enjoy present pleasures in such a way as not to injure future ones.
7606 USA/RALPH WALDO EMERSON/ESSAYIST	A friend is one before whom I may think aloud.
7607 MARGARET MEAD/ ANTHROPOLOGIST	I must admit that I personally measure success in terms of the contributions an individual makes to her or his fellow human beings.
7608 AVIS CAR RENTAL	We're number two. We try harder.
7609 MATTHEW ARNOLD/UK/ POET	To have the sense of creative activity is the greatest happiness and the great proof of being alive.

NUMBER CATEGORY/CREDIT	TOPIC
7610 ALEXANDRE DUMAS/FR.	Business? It's quite simple. It's other peoples' money.
7611 JOHANN WOLFGANG VON GOETHE/ GERMAN DRAMATIST	One ought, every day at least, to hear a little song, read a good poem, see a fine picture, and if it were possible, to speak a few reasonable words.
7612 HOBART BROWN/ USA/SCULPTOR	Money does not bring happiness. People with ten million dollars are no happier than people with nine million dollars.
7613 MEISTER ECKHART/ PHILOSOPHER	The price of inaction is far greater than the cost of making a mistake.
7614 THOMAS CARLYLE/ SCOT/HISTORIAN	I've got a great ambition to die of exhaustion rather than boredom.
7615 MEISTER ECKHART/ GERMAN	Truly, it is in darkness that one finds the light, so when we are in sorrow, then this light is nearest of all to us.
7616 BRIAN MULRONEY/ CANADIAN PM	You can't be chasing 15 rabbits. Otherwise, the public mind cannot follow you.
7617 HALLA TOMASDOTTIR/ TED.COM	I'm fed up with this tyranny of either/or choices in life – 'either it's men, or it's women.' We need to start embracing the beauty of balance.
7618 VACLAV HAVEL/CZECH/ PLAYWRIGHT	The tragedy of modern man is not that he knows less and less about the meaning of his own life, but that it bothers him less and less.
7619 MOTHER TERESA/NUN	It's not how much we give but how much love we put into the giving.
7620 MARIO PUZO/THE GODFATHER	My father taught me many things here – he taught me in this room. He taught me – keep your friends close by and your enemies closer.
7621 VACLAV HAVEL/ CZECH PLAYWRIGHT	Isn't it the moment of most profound doubt that gives birth to new certainties?
7622 SHERLOCK HOLMES/ SILVER BLAZE/DOYLE	The dog that didn't bark...
7623 LEE IACOCCA/ CHRYSLER/CEO	If you want to make good use of your time, you've got to know what's most important and then give it all you've got.
7624 CHINESE PHILOSOPHER	Recompense injury with justice, and recompense kindness with kindness.
7625 AYN RAND/WRITER	Wealth is the product of man's capacity to think.
7626 MARCUS AURELIUS ANTONINIUS	Never esteem anything as of advantage to thee that shall make thee break thy word or lose thy self-respect.
7627 GABRIEL GARCÍA MÁRQUEZ/NOVELIST	A lie is more comfortable than doubt, more useful than love, more lasting than truth.
7628 ANNE RICE/AUTHOR/ THE VAMPIRE LESTAT	Revenge is the concern of those who are at some point or other beaten.
7629 ARTHUR ASHE/USA/ TENNIS PLAYER	Success is a journey, not a destination. The doing is often more important than the outcome.
7630 RUDYARD KIPLING/UK/ WRITER	A man cannot have too much red wine, too many books, or too much ammunition.
7631 MICHAEL DIRDA/USA COLUMNIST/WAPO	...the humanities encourage the development of our own humanity. They are our instruments of self-exploration.
7632 DENG XIAOPING/CHINA	Poverty is not socialism. To be rich is glorious.
7633 THE TALMUD	The end result of wisdom is...good deeds.

NUMBER CATEGORY/CREDIT	TOPIC
7634 C. S. LEWIS/UK/ WRITER	The only people who achieve much are those who want knowledge so badly that they seek it while the conditions are still unfavorable. Favorable conditions never come.
7635 GEORGE BERNARD SHAW/PLAYWRIGHT	A life spent making mistakes is not only more honorable, but more useful than a life spent doing nothing.
7636 KAHLIL GIBRAN/POET	Knowledge of the self is the mother of all knowledge.
7637 TED TURNER/USA/ BUSINESSMAN	I've had the experience of being on top and riding the roller coaster down again, nearly to the bottom. You know, if you economize and don't buy new airplanes or long-range jets, or that sort of thing, you can get by on a billion or two.
7638 QUEEN ELIZABETH II/UK	Grief is the price we pay for love.
7639 VLADIMIR NABOKOV/ RUSSIAN NOVELIST	I cannot conceive how anybody in his right mind should go to a psychoanalyst.
7640 NOVELIST/LOUIS DE BERNIERES	Did you know that childhood is the only time in our lives when insanity is not only permitted to us, but expected?
7641 PATENTS/LAW/MONEY	Patent trolls - individuals or companies that acquire patents not for the purpose of making products but for the purpose of targeting companies that use their patents for financial compensation
7642 ZIG ZIGLAR/USA/	Every choice you make has an end result.
7643 BLAISE PASCAL/ FRENCH THINKER	Men never do evil so completely and cheerfully as when they do it from religious conviction.
7644 ST. AUGUSTINE/LATIN	A thing is not necessarily true because a man dies for it.
7645 SAM COOKE/USA/SONG	Don't know much about history. / Don't know much biology.
7646 GEORGE BERNARD SHAW/IRISH WRITER	A lifetime of happiness! No man alive could bear it; it would be hell on earth.
7647 ANN LANDERS/USA	No person who can read is ever successful at cleaning out an attic.
7648 EDWIN LAND/USA	Marketing is what you do when your product is no good.
7649 G. G. MÁRQUEZ/WRITER	Wisdom comes to us when it can no longer do any good.
7650 LEE IACOCCA/CEO/USA	I've always found that the speed of the boss is the speed of the team.
7651 NIETZSCHE/THINKER	In truth, there was only one Christian, and he died on the cross.
7652 PEACE/SAFETY	International ban on landmines
7653 MARGARET ATWOOD/ CANADIAN NOVELIST	A word after a word after a word is power.
7654 CHAUNCEY M. DEPEW/ AMERICAN LAWYER	I get my exercise serving as a pallbearer to my friends who take exercise.
7655 GEORGE SANTAYANA/US	The wisest mind has something yet to learn.
7656 CHARLES DICKENS/ ENGLISH NOVELIST	Reflect on your present blessings, of which every man has many; not on your past misfortunes, of which all men have some.
7657 MARIA MONTESSORI/ ITALIAN EDUCATOR	We teachers can only help the work going on, as servants wait upon a master.
7658 C. ACHEBE/WRITER	If you don't like someone's story, write your own.
7659 GEORGE SANTAYANA/ POET/WRITER	I like to walk about among the beautiful things that adorn the world; but private wealth I should decline, or any sort of personal possessions, because they would take away my liberty.

NUMBER CATEGORY/CREDIT	TOPIC
7660 CHARLES DICKENS/UK/ WRITER	A man must take the fat with the lean.
7661 LI KA SHING/HONG KONG MILLIONAIRE	Though a universal formula for success is difficult to come by, caution signs for failure are posted everywhere. Establishing a structure that serves to minimize failure will prove to be a shortcut to success.
7662 FRANCOIS DE LA ROCHEFOUCAULD	When we are unable to find tranquility within ourselves, it is useless to seek it elsewhere.
7663 JULIETTE BINOCHE/ FRENCH ACTRESS	I think acting is about forgetting yourself in order to give the best of yourself. It's passing through you more than you're creating it. You're not the flower, but the vase which holds the flower.
7664 CICERO/ORATOR	The good of the people is the supreme law.
7665 NAOMI CAMPBELL/ BRITISH MODEL	I've been doing my job well for 17 years. People must see something in me. Otherwise, I'd be over and out.
7666 ALICE WALKER/USA/ WRITER	Men make war to get attention. All killing is an expression of self-hate.
7667 CATHERINE LIM/ SINGAPORE/WRITER	So men make few passes at a girl who wears glasses? Well, they make even fewer passes at a girl who surpasses.
7668 LIFE/INSIGHT	Epiphany
7669 JAMES THURBER/USA	It is better to have loafed and lost, than never to have loafed at all.
7670 GILBERT HIGHET/SCOT/ PROFESSOR/WRITER	A good teacher is a determined person.
7671 SUNITHA KRISHNAN/ TEDTALK	In [India] and across the globe, hundreds and thousands of children, as young as three, four, are sold into sexual slavery.
7672 GEORGE ORWELL/UK	At fifty everyone has the face he deserves.
7673 CHARLES KETTERING/ USA/INVENTOR	No one would have crossed the ocean if he could have gotten off the ship in the storm.
7674 TINA SEELIG/WRITER/ PROFESSOR/USA	A successful career is not a straight line but a wave with ups and downs.
7675 J.K. ROWLING/UK/ WRITER	Talent and intelligence never yet inoculated anyone against the caprice of the fates.
7676 TYLER PERRY/USA/ MOVIE PRODUCER	You can't make yourself happy by causing other people's misery.
7677 USA/GUN ADVOCATES	Guns don't kill people, people kill people.
7678 DANTE ALIGHIERI/ ITALY/WRITER	My course is set for an uncharted sea.
7679 LATIN EXPRESSION	The eagle does not stoop to catch flies.
7680 USA/KAREEM ABDUL JABBAR/LIFE'S WORK	A good work ethic trumps lazy talent every time.
7681 MARGARET MEAD/USA/ CULTURAL ANTHROPOLOGIST	Nobody has ever before asked the nuclear family to live all by itself in a box the way we do. With no relatives, no support, we've put it in an impossible situation.
7682 DON TAPSCOTT/ CANADA/BUSINESS	The arc of history is a positive one and it's toward openness.

NUMBER CATEGORY/CREDIT	TOPIC
7683 JULIA BACHA/TED.COM/ BRAZIL/DOCUMENTARY	Nothing scares the army more than nonviolent opposition.
7684 DANTE ALIGHIERI/ ITALY/WRITER	The hottest places in hell are reserved for those who, in times of great moral crisis, maintain their neutrality.
7685 CALVIN COOLIDGE/ USA/PRESIDENT	I won't pass the buck.
7686 ST. BONAVENTURE/ WRITER/ITALIAN	To know much and taste nothing -- of what use is that?
7687 TYRA BANKS/USA/ MODEL	I haven't seen the Eiffel Tower, Notre Dame, the Louvre. I haven't seen anything. I don't really care.
7688 LES BROWN/USA/ MOTIVATIONAL SPEAKER	Life has no limitations, except the one you make.
7689 AMIRI BARAKA/USA/ POET	A man is either free or he is not. There cannot be any apprenticeship for freedom.
7690 USA/THURGOOD MARSHALL/JUDGE/ SUPREME COURT	None of us got where we are solely by pulling ourselves up by our bootstraps. We got here because somebody – a parent, a teacher, an Ivy League crony or a few nuns – bent down and helped us pick up our boots.
7691 ANNA JULIA COOPER/ USA/EDUCATOR	Agnosticism has nothing to impart. Its sermons are the exhortations of one who convinces you he stands on nothing and urges you to stand there too.
7692 LEO DUROCHER/USA/ BASEBALL PLAYER	I never questioned the integrity of an umpire. Their eyesight, yes.
7693 MEISTER ECKHART/ PHILOSOPHER	What we plant in the soil of contemplation, we shall reap in the harvest of action.
7694 ANNA JULIA COOPER/ USA/EDUCATOR	Bullies are always cowards at heart and may be credited with a pretty safe instinct for scenting their prey.
7695 MAE JEMISON/USA/ ASTRONAUT	Science is very important to me, but I also stress that you have to be well-rounded.
7696 MORTIMER ADLER/USA/ WRITER/EDITOR	Love without conversation is impossible.
7697 DOROTHY PARKER/ USA/HUMORIST/POET	The best way to keep children home is to make the home atmosphere pleasant – and let the air out of the tires.
7698 USA/HENRY DAVID THOREAU/WRITER	The man whose horse trots a mile in a minute does not carry the most important messages.
7699 JONATHAN SWIFT/ IRISH WRITER	I never knew a man come to greatness or eminence who lay abed late in the morning.
7700 FINNISH PROVERB	Only dead fish follow the stream.
7701 DANISH/SOREN KIERKEGAARD/ PHILOSOPHER	To dare is to lose one's footing momentarily. Not to dare is to lose oneself.
7702 ALAN GREENSPAN/ CHAIRMAN/FEDERAL RESERVE/USA	The true measure of a career is to be able to be content, even proud, that you succeeded through your own endeavors without leaving a trail of casualties in your wake.
7703 FRANCOIS-RENE DE CHATEAUBRIAND/ FRENCH/WRITER	In living literature no person is a competent judge but of works written in his own language.

NUMBER CATEGORY/CREDIT	TOPIC
7704 SAYING	Happiness is someone to love, something to do, and something to hope for.
7705 KAVITA RAMDAS/ WOMEN/INDIA/ SOCIAL ENTREPRENEURSHIP	Feminism...is not a struggle against a distinct oppressor -- it's not the ruling class or the occupiers or the colonizers -- it's against a deeply held set of beliefs and assumptions that we women, far too often, hold ourselves.
7706 GOETHE/DRAMATIST	Whatever you can do or dream, begin it.
7707 GEORGE BERNARD SHAW/PLAYWRIGHT	Democracy is a device that ensures we shall be governed no better than we deserve.
7708 FRANCOIS-RENE DE CHATEAUBRIAND/ FRENCH/WRITER	As soon as a true thought has entered our mind, it gives a light which makes us see a crowd of other objects which we have never perceived before.
7709 LOUIS L'AMOUR/USA/ WRITER	A mind, like a home, is furnished by its owner, so if one's life is cold and bare he can blame none but himself. You have a chance to select from pretty elegant furnishings.
7710 ALAIN DE BOTTON/A KINDER, GENTLER PHILOSOPHY OF SUCCESS	The problem is if you really believe in a society where those who merit to get to the top, get to the top, you'll also, by implication...believe in a society where those who deserve to get to the bottom also get to the bottom and stay there.
7711 GORE VIDAL/USA/ WRITER	A narcissist is someone better looking than you are.
7712 MILES DAVIS/USA/ JAZZ MUSICIAN/IHT	A legend is an old man with a cane known for what he used to do. I'm still doing it.
7713 OPINION	It is absolutely never all right to lie to your parents.
7714 GEORGE ORWELL/UK/ WRITER	Big Brother is watching you.
7715 VLADIMIR NABOKOV/ RUSSIAN NOVELIST	It is a short walk from the hallelujah to the hoot.
7716 ISADORA DUNCAN/ USA/DANCER/MY LIFE	Any intelligent woman who reads the marriage contract and then goes into it, deserves all the consequences.
7717 TEACHERS/RIGHTS	Teachers' unions
7718 KIRBY FERGUSON/ EMBRACE THE REMIX/TED.COM	We are not self-made. We are dependent on one another. Admitting this to ourselves isn't an embrace of mediocrity...it's a liberation from our misconceptions.
7719 LEE IACOCCA/CEO/USA/ BUSINESS	I hire people brighter than me and then I get out of their way.
7720 JAWAHARLAL NEHRU/INDIA/PM	The forces in a capitalist society, if left unchecked, tend to make the rich richer and the poor poorer.
7721 OPRAH WINFREY/ USA/MEDIA MOGUL	I believe the choice to be excellent begins with aligning your thoughts and words with the intention to require more from yourself.
7722 LATIN EXPRESSION	The camel that begs for horns loses its ears as well.
7723 MIYAMOTO MUSASHI/ JAPAN/WARRIOR	It is difficult to understand the universe if you only study one planet.
7724 CLARENCE DARROW/ USA/LAWYER	I do not consider it an insult, but rather a compliment to be called an agnostic. I do not pretend to know where many ignorant men are sure; that is all that agnosticism means.

NUMBER CATEGORY/CREDIT	TOPIC
7725 GEORGE BERNARD SHAW/IRISH WRITER	England and America are two countries separated by a common language.
7726 LOUIS L'AMOUR/ USA/WRITER	Reading without thinking is nothing, for a book is less important for what it says than for what it makes you think.
7727 LAO TSU/CHINA/SAGE	Those who know do not tell; those who tell do not know.
7728 SUN TZU/CHINA	A leader leads by example not by force.
7729 KAHLIL GIBRAN/ON FRIENDSHIP	And let your best be for your friend. If he must know the ebb of your tide, let him know its flood also.
7730 FRANCOIS-RENE DE CHATEAUBRIAND/ FRENCH/WRITER	Every institution goes through three stages -- utility, privilege, and abuse.
7731 REBECCA WEST/UK/ WRITER	There is, of course, no reason for the existence of the male sex except that sometimes one needs help with moving the piano.
7732 MALCOLM X/USA/ MINISTER/ACTIVIST	People don't realize a man's whole life can be changed by one book.
7733 LI KA SHING/HONG KONG MILLIONAIRE	Successful managers should also have a keen eye for talent. They not only select people who are smarter than themselves, but also avoid picking corporate superstars whose reputation precedes them.
7734 JAMES JOYCE/POET	A man of genius makes no mistakes. His errors are volitional and are the portals of discovery.
7735 FRANCOIS-RENE DE CHATEAUBRIAND/ FRENCH/WRITER	An original writer is one who imitates nobody, but one whom nobody can imitate.
7736 CALVIN COOLIDGE/ USA/PRESIDENT	Nothing in the world can take the place of persistence. Talent will not; nothing is more common than unsuccessful men with talent. Genius will not; unrewarded genius is almost a proverb. Education will not; the world is full of educated derelicts. Persistence and determination are omnipotent.
7737 GEORGE BERNARD SHAW/IRISH WRITER	Few people think more than two or three times a year: I have made an international reputation for myself by thinking once or twice a week.
7738 CONFLICT/WISDOM	Voice of reason
7739 JUDITH JONES/USA	Ninety percent of editing is diplomacy.
7740 OLIVER WENDELL HOLMES JR./USA/ JUDGE	A word is not a crystal, transparent and unchanged; it is the skin of a living thought and may vary greatly in color and content according to the circumstances and time in which it is used.
7741 PUBLILIUS SYRUS/ LATIN WRITER	The greatest of empires, is the empire over one's self.
7742 OSCAR WILDE/POET/ IRISH	Whenever people agree with me I always feel I must be wrong.
7743 HENRY LAWSON/ AUSTRALIAN POET	I've never seen anyone rehabilitated by punishment.
7744 LAWRENCE P. JACKS/ UK/RELIGION/MINISTER	Better that the nation grow poor for a cause we can honor, than grow rich for an end that is unknown.
7745 JOHN CHARLES POLANYI/SCIENTIST	Science never gives up searching for truth, since it never claims to have achieved it.

NUMBER CATEGORY/CREDIT	TOPIC
7746 GILBERT HIGHET/ SCOTTISH WRITER	A teacher must believe in the value and interest of his subject as a doctor believes in health.
7747 CHILDREN BEHAVIOR	Children and bad behavior in public
7748 IYANLA VANZANT/USA	Promise without a goal and a plan is like a barren cow.
7749 KAHLIL GIBRAN/POET	Life without liberty is like a body without spirit.
7750 DALE CARNEGIE/USA	You never achieve success unless you like what you are doing.
7751 CHUCK PALAHNIUK/USA	If I can't be beautiful, I want to be invisible.
7752 LAWRENCE P. JACKS/ UK/RELIGION/MINISTER	A master in the art of living draws no sharp distinction between his work and his play; his labor and his leisure; his mind and his body; his education and his recreation. He hardly knows which is which. He simply pursues his vision of excellence through whatever he is doing, and leaves others to determine whether he is working or playing.
7753 DAILY YOMIURI/JAPAN/ PRINCE TOMOHITO	I like people above anything else.
7754 PUBLILIUS SYRUS	No man is happy who does not think himself so.
7755 GEORGE BERNARD SHAW/PLAYWRIGHT	Hegel was right when he said that we learn from history that man can never learn anything from history.
7756 BENJAMIN FRANKLIN/ USA/STATESMAN	If a man empties his purse into his head, no one can take it away from him. An investment in knowledge always pays the best interest.
7757 CHARLES DICKENS/UK	Trifles make the sum of life.
7758 USA/DR. MARTIN LUTHER KING JR.	Our scientific power has outrun our spiritual power. We have guided missiles and misguided men.
7759 ABDUL KALAM/INDIA/ PRESIDENT	Be more dedicated to making solid achievements than in running after swift but synthetic happiness.
7760 LORD ALFRED DOUGLAS HOMOSEXUALITY	I am the Love that dare not speak its name.
7761 ANAIS NIN/USA/ WRITER	Dreams are necessary to life.
7762 DRIVING/TRAVEL	Driving in a foreign country
7763 CHARLES DARWIN/ UK/NATURALIST/THE DESCENT OF MAN	False facts are highly injurious to the progress of science, for they often long endure; but false views, if supported by some evidence, do little harm, as everyone takes a salutary pleasure in proving their falseness; and when this is done, one path towards error is closed and the road to truth is often at the same time opened.
7764 EDUCATION/COST	Education is an investment
7765 THOMAS J. WATSON/IBM	Good design is good business.
7766 OSCAR WILDE/IRISH WRITER/POET	Selfishness is not living as one wishes to live, it is asking others to live as one wishes to live.
7767 LOUIS D. BRANDEIS/ AMERICAN JUDGE	Most of the things worth doing in the world had been declared impossible before they were done.
7768 DR. MARTIN LUTHER KING JR./USA/	One who condones evil is just as guilty as the one who perpetrates it.
7769 KARL MARX/GERMAN/ PHILOSOPHER	From each according to his abilities, to each according to his needs.

NUMBER CATEGORY/CREDIT	TOPIC
7770 DAG HAMMARSKJOLD/ UN/SWEDEN/LEADER	Never measure the height of a mountain, until you have reached the top. Then you will see how low it was.
7771 TA-NEHISI COATES/ USA/WRITER	I did not know then that this is what life is -- just when you master the geometry of one world, it slips away, and suddenly again, you're swarmed by strange shapes and impossible angles.
7772 HERBERT L. PACKER/ USA/LEGAL SCHOLAR	We can have as much or as little crime as we please, depending on what we choose to count as criminal.
7773 GEORGE ORWELL/ UK/AUTHOR	During times of universal deceit, telling the truth becomes a revolutionary act.
7774 THE TALMUD	If one man says to thee, "Thou art a donkey" pay no heed. If two speak thus, purchase a saddle."
7775 BRIAN MULRONEY/ CANADA PM/POLITICS	In politics, Madame, you need two things: friends, but above all, an enemy.
7776 RICHARD WRIGHT/ USA/AUTHOR	Whenever my environment had failed to support or nourish me, I had clutched at books...
7777 LAWRENCE P. JACKS/ UK/RELIGION/MINISTER	We want philosophers, among other reasons, because the world is full of false philosophy.
7778 WORKPLACE	Ideal co-workers
7779 NORMAN COUSINS/ UK/AUTHOR	A book is like a piece of rope; it takes on meaning only in connection with the things it holds together.
7780 JENNA MCCARTHY/ TED.COM/MARRIAGE	Beyond the profound federal perks, married people make more money; we're healthier, physically and emotionally; we produce happier, more stable and more successful kids....we even live longer.
7781 USA/HENRY DAVID THOREAU/WRITER	I went to the woods because I wished to live deliberately, to front only the essential facts of life, and see if I could not learn what it had to teach, and not, when I came to die, discover that I had not lived.
7782 ALICE WALKER/USA	What the mind doesn't understand, it worships or fears.
7783 USA/RALPH WALDO EMERSON/ESSAYIST	Happiness is a perfume you cannot pour on others without getting a few drops on yourself.
7784 CHURCH/LEADERSHIP	Ordination of women
7785 HANS SELYE/ CANADIAN SCIENTIST	Adopting the right attitude can convert a negative stress into a positive one.
7786 ADVICE/FRIENDSHIP	Some places you recommend for meeting new, interesting people.
7787 MIYAMOTO MUSASHI	Do not, under any circumstances, depend on a partial feeling.
7788 RICHARD WRIGHT/ USA/AUTHOR	All literature is protest.
7789 CHINESE SAYING	Without rice, even the most clever housewife cannot cook.
7790 SAFETY/AIRCRAFT	Aircraft accidents
7791 OSCAR WILDE/IRISH WRITER/POET	If you want to tell people the truth, make them laugh, otherwise they'll kill you.
7792 RICHARD WRIGHT/ USA/AUTHOR	The world of most men is given to them by their culture.
7793 AGATHA CHRISTIE/ ENGLISH WRITER	Good advice is always certain to be ignored, but that's no reason not to give it.

NUMBER CATEGORY/CREDIT	TOPIC
7794 MEDICINE/TECHNOLOGY	Microsurgery
7795 EDITH WHARTON/ AMERICAN WRITER	Life is always either a tightrope or a feather bed. Give me the tightrope.
7796 GEORGE BERNARD SHAW/PLAYWRIGHT	I often quote myself. It adds spice to my conversation.
7797 RANDY KOMISAR/USA/ BUSINESS	Being an entrepreneur means seeing the world as opportunity rich.
7798 SUCCESS MAGAZINE	Act your wage
7799 CICERO/ROMAN ORATOR	The man who backbites an absent friend...that man is black at heart: mark and avoid him.
7800 ISABELLE ADJANI/FR.	I think that we all carry the divine within us.
7801 AMERICAN SAYING	A little dirt never hurt anyone.
7802 TYRA BANKS/US/MODEL	I'm competitive with myself. I always try to push past my own borders.
7803 LI KA SHING/HONG KONG MILLIONAIRE	The art of good management lies in the capacity to accept change, and the ability to meld new and traditional thinking.
7804 GEORGE ORWELL/USA	Four legs good, two legs bad.
7805 LI KA SHING/HONG KONG MILLIONAIRE	As a leader one should spend more time than others planning for the future.
7806 REV. JAMES FORBES/ COMPASSION AT THE DINNER TABLE	A Good Samaritan is not simply one whose heart is touched in an immediate act of care and charity, but one who provides a system of sustained care.
7807 RANDY PAUSCH/ USA/PROFESSOR	Showing gratitude is one of the simplest yet powerful things humans can do for each other.
7808 DR. MARTIN LUTHER KING JR./USA/ CIVIL RIGHTS LEADER	The ultimate measure of a man is not where he stands in moments of comfort and convenience, but where he stands at times of challenge and controversy.
7809 SUCCESS MAGAZINE	Pay yourself first.
7810 CHINUA ACHEBE/ AFRICAN WRITER	It is the storyteller who makes us what we are, who creates history. The storyteller creates the memory that the survivors must have – otherwise their surviving would have no meaning.
7811 REBECCA WEST/UK/ WRITER	It's always one's virtues and not one's vices that precipitate one into disaster.
7812 AUGUSTE COMPTE/FR.	Conspiracy of silence
7813 GREG BAUM/AUSTRALIA	Winning needs no explanation, losing has no alibi.
7814 UK/PM/WINSTON CHURCHILL	Criticism may not be agreeable, but it is necessary. It fulfills the same function as pain in the human body. It calls attention to an unhealthy state of things.
7815 GERMAN/FRIEDRICH NIETZSCHE/THINKER	The individual has always had to struggle to keep from being overwhelmed by the tribe. If you try it, you will be lonely often, and sometimes frightened. No price is too high to pay for the privilege of owning yourself.
7816 MARIO CUOMO/USA/ NY/GOVERNOR	Every time I've done something that doesn't feel right, it's ended up not being right.
7817 PRESIDENT DWIGHT D. EISENHOWER/USA	In preparing for battle I have always found that plans are useless, but planning is indispensable.

NUMBER CATEGORY/CREDIT	TOPIC
7818 DUPONT/SLOGAN	Better living through chemistry
7819 GOETHE/POET/GERMAN	When ideas fail, words come in very handy.
7820 WEALTH/POVERTY	Haves and have-nots
7821 LAWRENCE DURRELL/ ENGLISH/WRITER	There are only three things to be done with a woman. You can love her, suffer for her, or turn her into literature.
7822 TOM CLANCY/USA	Show me an elitist, and I'll show you a loser.
7823 SEBASTIAN FAULKS/ AUTHOR/BIRDSONGS	The function of music is to liberate in the soul those feelings which normally we keep locked up in the heart.
7824 CRIME	Rehabilitation of criminals
7825 NORMAN COUSINS/ USA/AUTHOR	A library is the delivery room for the birth of ideas, a place where history comes to life.
7826 LOUIS L'AMOUR/USA/ WRITER	Knowledge was not meant to be locked behind doors. It breathes best in the open air where all men can inhale its essence.
7827 RICHARD WRIGHT/USA/ WRITER	Wherever I found religion in my life I found strife, the attempt of one individual or group to rule another in the name of God. The naked will to power seemed always to walk in the wake of a hymn.
7828 SEBASTIAN FAULKS/ AUTHOR/ENGLEBY	This is how most people live: alive, but not conscious; conscious but not aware; aware, but intermittently.
7829 WARREN G. BENNIS/ USA/PSYCHOLOGIST	Taking charge of your own learning is a part of taking charge of your life, which is the sine qua non in becoming an integrated person.
7830 ADVICE	Everyone must try bungee jumping at least once.
7831 GERMAN/FRIEDRICH NIETZSCHE/THINKER	Insanity in individuals is something rare –but in groups, parties, nations, and epochs, it is the rule.
7832 LAW/JUSTICE	Plea bargaining
7833 MARY DALY/FEMINIST	Work is a substitute "religious" experience for many workaholics.
7834 AUSTRALIA/SAYING	Dogs must not steal from dogs.
7835 STEVE JOBS/USA/ ENTREPRENEUR	You have to trust in something, your gut, destiny, life, karma, whatever.
7836 REBECCA WEST/UK/ WRITER	I myself have never been able to find out precisely what feminism is: I only know that people call me a feminist whenever I express sentiments that differentiate me from a doormat.
7837 ANDREW CARNEGIE/ USA/BUSINESSMAN	There is not such a cradle of democracy upon the earth as the Free Public Library, this republic of letters, where neither rank, office, nor wealth receives the slightest consideration.
7838 DAPHNE ZUNIGA/ USA/ACTRESS	People go to movies or listen to music because they want to be inspired.
7839 LEARNED HAND/ USA/JUDGE	No doubt one may quote history to support any cause, as the devil quotes scripture.
7840 CHARACTER/ERROR	Honest mistake
7841 DANISH/SOREN KIERKEGAARD	The tyrant dies and his rule is over, the martyr dies and his rule begins.
7842 GEOFFREY CANADA/ EDUCATION/NY TIMES	Longer school days can lead to fewer crimes committed by young people and a decline in teen pregnancy.
7843 SENECA/DRAMATIST	Difficulties strengthen the mind, as labor does the body.

NUMBER CATEGORY/CREDIT	TOPIC
7844 PHOBIA	Scotophobia: fear of the dark
7845 CHRONICLE/USA/MOOCS	...there's a growing sense that monologues by professors are of limited effectiveness for many of today's students.
7846 MIKE BIDDLE/WE CAN RECYCLE PLASTIC	The United Nations estimates that there's about 85 billion pounds a year of electronics waste that gets discarded around the world each and every year.
7847 GORE VIDAL/USA/ AUTHOR/ESSAYIST	I wanted to be a politician and a movie star. But I was born a writer. If you're born that, you can't change it. You're going to do it whether you want to or not.
7848 BOOKER WASHINGTON/ USA/EDUCATOR	If you want to lift yourself up, lift up someone else.
7849 DEBATE	It is always wrong to marry someone that your parents do not approve of.
7850 CICERO/ORATOR/ STATESMAN	Let the punishment match the offense.
7851 ZIG ZIGLAR/USA	A lot of people quit looking for work as soon as they find a job.
7852 LI KA SHING/HONG KONG MILLIONAIRE	I do not get overly optimistic when the market is good nor overly pessimistic when the market is down.
7853 NORMAN COUSINS/ USA/AUTHOR	Death is not the greatest loss in life. The greatest loss is what dies inside us while we live.
7854 GEORGE BERNARD SHAW/WRITER	If all economists were laid end to end, they would not reach a conclusion.
7855 ANDREW DWORKIN/ USA/FEMINIST	The power of money is a distinctly male power. Money speaks, but it speaks with a male voice.
7856 BERTRAND RUSSELL/UK	War does not determine who is right – only who is left.
7857 DOROTHY PARKER/USA	The cure for boredom is curiosity. There is no cure for curiosity.
7858 LATIN EXPRESSION	The traveller with empty pockets, will sing in front of the robber.
7859 KEVIN BREEL/TEDTALK USA/COMEDIAN	Unfortunately we live in a world where when you break your arm, everyone runs over to sign your cast. But if you tell people you're depressed, everyone runs the other way.
7860 THINKER/ARTHUR SCHOPENHAUER	The two enemies of human happiness are pain and boredom.
7861 TEMPLE GRANDIN/USA/ PROFESSOR/DESIGNER	If I did not have my work, I would not have any life.
7862 SUN TZU/CHINA	The more you read and learn, the less your adversary will know.
7863 CHINUA ACHEBE/ AFRICAN WRITER	Nobody can teach me who I am. You can describe parts of me, but who I am – and what I need – is something I have to find out myself.
7864 CONFUCIUS/CHINESE PHILOSOPHER	A ruler who governs his state by virtue is like the north polar star, which remains in its place while all the other stars revolve around it.
7865 TEMPLE GRANDIN/ PROFESSOR/ ASPERGER'S ACTIVIST	Who do you think made the first stone spears? The Asperger guy. If you were to get rid of all the autism genetics, there would be no more Silicon Valley.
7866 ST AUGUSTINE/ LATIN PHILOSOPHER/ THEOLOGIAN	Men go abroad to wonder at the heights of mountains, at the huge waves of the sea, at the long courses of the rivers, at the vast compass of the ocean, at the circular motions of the stars, and they pass by themselves without wondering.

NUMBER CATEGORY/CREDIT	TOPIC
7867 SUN TZU/CHINA/ AUTHOR	If words of command are not clear and distinct, if orders are not thoroughly understood, the general is to blame.
7868 ANGELA MERKEL/ GERMAN CHANCELLOR	Spying among friends is never acceptable.
7869 VACLAV HAVEL/CZECH	Lying can never save us from another lie.
7870 ISABELLE ADJANI/ FRENCH ACTRESS	In love, one should simplify, choose persons worthy of their promises, and leave them if they don't keep them.
7871 VIKTOR FRANKL/ AUSTRIA/AUTHOR	The attempt to develop a sense of humor and to see things in a humorous light is some kind of a trick learned while mastering the art of living.
7872 DR. M.L. KING JR./USA	Wisdom born of experience should tell us that war is obsolete.
7873 AN INDIAN PROVERB	An old patient knows more than a new doctor.
7874 NIETZSCHE/THINKER	He who has a why to live can bear almost any how.
7875 USA/ELIZABETH KUBLER-ROSS/SWISS/ PSYCHIATRIST	It is very important that you only do what you love to do. You may be poor, you may go hungry, you may lose your car, you may have to move into a shabby place to live, but you will totally live.
7876 KAHLIL GIBRAN/ LEBANESE POET	Love possesses not nor will it be possessed, for love is sufficient unto love.
7877 LATIN EXPRESSION	Virtue is the safest helmet.
7878 ERASMUS/HUMANIST	A nail is driven out by another nail. Habit is overcome by habit.
7879 W.O. DOUGLAS/USA	The right to be let alone is indeed the beginning of all freedoms.
7880 REBECCA WEST/UK/ WRITER	My work expresses an infatuation with human beings. I don't believe that to understand is necessarily to pardon, but I feel that to understand makes one forget that one cannot pardon.
7881 J.M. BARRIE/PETER PAN	Life is a long lesson in humility.
7882 ELIA KAZAN/USA	You have no idea how fragile an actor's self-worth is.
7883 FELIX FRANKFURTER/US	It is simply not true that war never settles anything.
7884 W. PITT/UK/PM	Where law ends, tyranny begins.
7885 HEALTH	Food poisoning
7886 PUBLILIUS SYRUS/ LATIN WRITER	If you refuse where you have always granted you invite to theft.
7887 GERMAN/FRIEDRICH NIETZSCHE	The advantage of a bad memory is that one enjoys several times the same good things for the first time
7888 USA/HUFFPOST/A.M. MARTY STROUDMILL	Prosecutors should want justice, not convictions.
7889 CHINESE SAYING	A weasel comes to say Happy New Year to the chickens!
7890 JACK WELCH/USA/ BUSINESS	Face reality as it is, not as it was or as you wish it to be.
7891 REBECCA WEST/UK/ WRITER/FRIENDSHIP	There was a definite process by which one made people into friends, and it involved talking to them and listening to them for hours at a time.
7892 BERTRAND RUSSELL/ BRITISH AUTHOR	The fact that an opinion has been widely held is no evidence whatever that it is not utterly absurd.
7893 USA/HENRY DAVID THOREAU/WRITER	Under a government which imprisons unjustly, the true place for a just man is also a prison.

NUMBER CATEGORY/CREDIT	TOPIC
7894 GEORGE ORWELL/UK	Good writing is like a windowpane.
7895 PLAGIARISM/ ROB JENKINS/CHRONICLE	Either you can be a teacher or you can be the plagiarism police. I choose to be a teacher.
7896 TINA SEELIG/USA	Father's advice: success is sweet but transient.
7897 MOTHER TERESA/NUN	Life is a promise; fulfill it.
7898 JUSTICE/LAW/ MERRIAMWEBSTER	Restitution: a making good of or giving an equivalent for some injury
7899 MALCOLM GLADWELL	Emotion is contagious.
7900 DEREK BOK/USA/ LAWYER	I suspect that no community will become humane and caring by restricting what its members can say.
7901 REBECCA WEST/UK/ WRITER	Before a war, military science seems a real science, like astronomy; but after a war it seems more like astrology.
7902 PUBLILIUS SYRUS	Never find your delight in another's misfortune.
7903 WILLIAM BENNETT/USA/ WRITER/MORALIST	Happiness is like a cat. If you try to coax it or call it, it will avoid you. It will never come. But if you pay no attention to it and go about your business, you'll find it rubbing up against your legs and jumping into your lap.
7904 NADINE GORDIMER/ S. AFRICA/WRITER	The facts are always less than what really happened.
7905 G..B. SHAWPLAYWRIGHT	Imagination is the beginning of creation.
7906 ALICE WALKER	In nature, nothing is perfect. Trees can be contorted, bent in weird ways and they're still beautiful.
7907 EMIGRATION	Why would anyone emigrate from your home country?
7908 LATIN EXPRESSION	You must pluck out the hairs of a horse's tail one by one.
7909 CALVIN COOLIDGE/ USA/PRESIDENT	The slogan "Press on" has solved and always will solve the problems of the human race.
7910 THE TALMUD	Fish die when they are out of water, and people die without law and order.
7911 WARREN BUFFETT/ USA/INVESTOR	Of the billionaires I have known, money just brings out the basic traits in them. If they were jerks before they had money, they are simply jerks with a billion dollars.
7912 NORMAN MAILER/ USA/WRITER	There is no greater impotence in all the world like knowing you are right and that the wave of the world is wrong.
7913 PRO-GUN/USA	When guns are outlawed, only outlaws will have guns.
7914 ALEXANDER POPE/UK	A little learning is a dangerous thing.
7915 ITALY/NICCOLO MACHIAVELLI/ DIPLOMAT	Men never do good unless necessity drives them to it; but when they are free to choose and can do just as they please, confusion and disorder become rampant.
7916 SECURITY	Anti-theft devices for automobiles
7917 EMPEROR HAILE SELASSIE/HEAD OF STATE/ ETHIOPIA	We must stop confusing religion and spirituality. Religion is a set of rules, regulations and rituals created by humans, which was supposed to help people grow spiritually. Due to human imperfection religion has become corrupt, political, divisive and a tool for power struggle.
7918 NIETZSCHE/THINKER	Shared joys make a friend, not shared sufferings.
7919 JACK KEROUAC/USA/ WRITER	Houses are full of things that gather dust.

NUMBER CATEGORY/CREDIT	TOPIC
7920 PRIVACY/CRIME	Identity theft
7921 SAMUEL JOHNSON/ UK/WRITER	I am a great friend of public amusements, they keep people from vice.
7922 ANNA QUINDLEN/ USA/AUTHOR	Books are the plane, and the train, and the road. They are the destination, and the journey. They are home.
7923 FIVE PILLARS OF ISLAM	1) One God/Mohammed is HIS messenger 2) Prayer 3) Charitable giving 4) Fasting 5) Hajj: pilgrimage to Mecca
7924 FRANCOIS DE LA ROCHEFOUCAULD/ WRITER/MORALIST	We should manage our fortunes as we do our health – enjoy it when good, be patient when it is bad, and never apply violent remedies except in an extreme necessity
7925 ANN LANDERS/USA/ ADVICE COLUMNIST	Television has proved that people will look at anything rather than each other.
7926 FRENCH/ANNE BIGOT CORNUEL/SOCIETY	No man is a hero to his valet.
7927 EDUCATION	Adult illiteracy
7928 CHARLES DICKENS/ UK/NOVELIST	It is a melancholy truth that even great men have their poor relations.
7929 RANDY PAUSCH/ USA/THE LAST LECTURE	The key question to keep asking is, 'Are you spending your time on the right things?' Because time is all you have.
7930 ALDOUS HUXLEY/ UK/NOVELIST	A bad book is as much of a labor to write as a good one, it comes as sincerely from the author's soul.
7931 LATIN EXPRESSION	In writing readily, it does not follow that you write well, but in writing well, you must be able to write readily.
7932 FUN/CHALLENGE	Skydiving is the ultimate sport.
7933 LATIN EXPRESSION	Those who cross the sea change their clime but not their character.
7934 GABRIEL GARCÍA MÁRQUEZ/NOVELIST	All human beings have three lives: public, private, and secret.
7935 SERENA WILLIAMS/ USA/TENNIS PLAYER	I'm a perfectionist. I'm pretty much insatiable. I feel there's so many things I can improve on.
7936 PETER DRUCKER/USA/ MANAGEMENT	Executives owe it to the organization and to their fellow workers not to tolerate nonperforming individuals in important jobs.
7937 REPUBLICANS/USA	Get the Government Off Our Backs.
7938 WILLIAM JAMES/USA/ PHILOSOPHER	We are all ready to be savage in some cause. The difference between a good man and a bad one is the choice of the cause.
7939 WARREN BUFFETT/USA	A public-opinion poll is no substitute for thought.
7940 SAMUEL JOHNSON/ ENGLISH AUTHOR	It is better to suffer wrong than to do it, and happier to be sometimes cheated than not to trust.
7941 DOAN'S KIDNEY PILLS/ USA/ADVERTISING	Every picture tells a story.
7942 LI KA SHING/HONG KONG/ENTREPRENEUR	Self-reflection is Heaven's gift to man, a shield with which to defend his destiny.

NUMBER CATEGORY/CREDIT	TOPIC
7943 CICERO/ORATOR	The sinews of war, unlimited money.
7944 LI KA SHING/HONG KONG MILLIONAIRE	A good reputation for yourself and your company is an invaluable asset not reflected in the balance sheets.
7945 LATIN EXPRESSION	He who profits by the villainy, has perpetrated it.
7946 LES BROWN/USA/MOTIVATION	You don't have to be great to get started, but you have to get started to be great.
7947 MARIO CUOMO/USA/POLITICIAN	A smart lawyer can keep a killer out of jail, a smart accountant can keep a thief from paying taxes, a smart reporter could ruin your reputation -- unfairly.
7948 MARTHA PLIMPTON/USA/MODEL	A lot of people in this country right now are living with multiple generations under one roof, struggling to make ends meet.
7949 ZIG ZIGLAR/SPEAKER	Building a better you is the first step to building a better America.
7950 MARTIN JACQUES: UNDERSTANDING THE RISE OF CHINA/TED.COM	For 200 years, the West has been so dominant in the world that it's not really needed to understand other cultures, other civilizations. Because, at the end of the day, it could, if necessary by force, get its own way.
7951 TEDTALK/REBECCA MACKINNON/AUTHOR	The only legitimate purpose of government is to serve citizens, and.. the only legitimate purpose of technology is to improve our lives, not to manipulate or enslave us.
7952 DR. MARTIN LUTHER KING JR./USA	Freedom is never voluntarily given by the oppressor; it must be demanded by the oppressed.
7953 KAHLIL GIBRAN/ON FRIENDSHIP	For what is your friend that you should seek him with hours to kill? Seek him always with hours to live.
7954 SHEENA IYENGAR/USA/PROFESSOR	The key to getting the most from choice is to be choosy about choosing.
7955 ERNEST HEMINGWAY/AUTHOR/NOBELIST	I drink to make other people more interesting.
7956 JACQUELINE NOVOGRATZ/TEDTALK	We can send people to the Moon; we can see if there's life on Mars – why can't we get $5 [mosquito] nets to 500 million people?
7957 GEORGE SANTAYANA/PHILOSOPHER/POET	Knowledge is recognition for something absent; it is a salutation, not an embrace.
7958 AMELIA EARHARDT/USA/AVIATION	Being alone is scary, but not as scary as feeling alone in a relationship.
7959 JOHN GRISHAM/USA/WRITER	Anyone can cook a trout. The real art is in hooking the damned thing.
7960 SIDNEY SHELDON/WRITER/USA	To be successful you need friends and to be very successful you need enemies.
7961 ADVERTISING	Billboards
7962 THOMAS J. WATSON/IBM	The way to succeed is to double your error rate.
7963 GEORGE SANTAYANA/AMERICAN WRITER	Advertising is the modern substitute for argument; its function is to make the worse appear the better.
7964 WHOLE EARTH CATALOG	Stay hungry, stay foolish.
7965 W.E.B. DU BOIS/USA/REFORMER	Herein lies the tragedy of the age, not that men are poor -- all men know something of poverty, not that men are wicked -- who is good? Not that men are ignorant -- what is truth? Nay, but that men know so little of men.

NUMBER CATEGORY/CREDIT	TOPIC
7966 ICHIRO SUZUKI/JAPAN/ BASEBALL/USA	To bat my best, the pitcher also has to be at his best.
7967 WRITER/MARGARET MITCHELL	Until you've lost your reputation, you never realize what a burden it was or what freedom really is.
7968 CARL JUNG/SWISS PSYCHOLOGIST	An understanding heart is everything in a teacher, and cannot be esteemed highly enough.
7969 CHINUA ACHEBE/ NIGERIA/WRITER	Charity...is the opium of the privileged.
7970 FRAN LEBOWITZ/USA/ WRITER	Ask your child what he wants for dinner only if he's buying.
7971 JOSHUA SILVER/ TED.COM	There are some countries in sub-Saharan Africa where there's one optometrist for eight million of the population.
7972 ALDOUS HUXLEY/ ENGLISH NOVELIST	A child-like man is not a man whose development has been arrested; on the contrary, he is a man who has given himself a chance of continuing to develop long after most adults have muffled themselves in the cocoon of middle-aged habit and convention.
7973 REBECCA WEST/UK/ WRITER	You must always believe that life is as extraordinary as music says it is.
7974 MARTHA PLIMPTON/ USA/MODEL	As an actress for most of my life, I am profoundly familiar with poverty.
7975 KEN FOLLETT/USA/ NOVELIST	I like to create imaginary characters and events around a real historical situation. I want readers to feel; Ok, this probably didn't happen, but it might have.
7976 CLARENCE S. DAY/ AMERICAN WRITER	The world of books is the most remarkable creation of man. Nothing else that he builds ever lasts. Monuments fall; nations perish; civilizations grow old and die out; and, after an era of darkness, new races build others. But in the world of books are volumes that have seen this happen again and again, and yet live on, still young, still as fresh as the day they were written, still telling men's hearts of the hearts of men centuries dead.
7977 MUSINGS/DAILY YOMIURIJAPAN/POET DAIGAKU HORIGUCHI	When poet Yaso Saijo died, his rival Daigaku Horiguchi wrote a tribute that reads, "At the age of 20 / Finding a good rival in you / The whip I applied to myself was painful."
7978 LI KA SHING/HONG KONG MILLIONAIRE	It doesn't' matter how strong or capable you are; if you don't have a big heart, you will not succeed.
7979 WILLIAM FAULKNER/ USA/NOVELIST	Always dream and shoot higher than you know you can do. Do not bother just to be better than your contemporaries or predecessors. Try to be better than yourself.
7980 EARL WARREN/USA/ JUDGE/SUPREME COURT	In civilized life, law floats in a sea of ethics.
7981 SENECA/DRAMATIST	It is rash to condemn where you are ignorant.
7982 HORATIO NELSON/ BRITISH OFFICER/	When the enemy is committed to a mistake we must not interrupt him too soon.
7983 MARGARET MEAD/ USA/SCIENTIST	One of the oldest human needs is having someone to wonder where you are when you don't come home at night.
7984 LI KA SHING/HONG KONG/BILLIONAIRE	I dream of greatness, but can I rein in my passion?

NUMBER CATEGORY/CREDIT	TOPIC
7985 LEADER/QATAR/WOMEN SHEIKHA AL MAYASSA/	People have said, 'Let's build bridges,' and frankly, I want to do more than that. I would like to break the walls of ignorance between East and West.
7986 MARTHA PLIMPTON/ USA/MODEL/AWARDS	Being nominated is the win. For me, being nominated is winning. It's just unbelievable.
7987 SARA LAWRENCE-LIGHTFOOT/USA/ SOCIOLOGIST	I also believe that the boundaries of school need to be made more porous and permeable, that we need to reduce the generational segregation that defines life and learning in our society.
7988 MOTHER TERESA/ CATHOLIC NUN	Love is a fruit in season at all times, and within the reach of every hand.
7989 CARL JUNG/SWISS PSYCHOLOGIST	Every form of addiction is bad, no matter whether the narcotic be alcohol, morphine, or idealism.
7990 CHIMAMANDA NGOZI ADICHIE/WRITER	Feminism should be an inclusive party. Feminism should be a party full of different feminisms.
7991 RALPH WALDO EMERSON/USA	The bitterest tragic element in life to be derived from an intellectual source is the belief in a brute Fate or Destiny.
7992 ORGAN DONATION	Organ donation should be compulsory in a society that cares.
7993 ROALD DAHL/UK/ NOVELIST	Nowadays you can go anywhere in the world in a few hours, and nothing is fabulous any more.
7994 DEREK BOK/USA/ LAWYER	There is far too much law for those who can afford it and far too little for those who cannot.
7995 OLIVER WENDELL HOLMES SR./USA	Your right to swing your arms ends just where the other person's nose begins.
7996 CHIMAMANDA NGOZI ADICHIE/WRITER/ NIGERIA	I don't speak to provoke. I speak because I think our time on earth is short and each moment that we are not our truest selves, each moment we pretend to be what we are not, each moment we say what we do not mean because we imagine that is what somebody wants us to say, we are wasting our time on earth.
7997 USA/HENRY DAVID THOREAU/AUTHOR	What the banker sighs for, the meanest clown may have, - leisure and a quiet mind.
7998 GEORGE BERNARD SHAW/IRISH WRITER	Life does not cease to be funny when people die any more than it ceases to be serious when people laugh.
7999 NADINE GORDIMER/ S. AFRICA/WRITER	Power is something I am convinced there is no innocence this side of the womb.
8000 WILLIAM BENNET/USA/ WRITER/MORALIST	There are no menial jobs, only menial attitudes.
8001 CHINUA ACHEBE/ NIGERIA/WRITER	...stories are not always innocent...they can be used to put you in the wrong crowd...
8002 USA/HENRY DAVID THOREAU/WRITER	If a man does not keep pace with his companions, perhaps it is because he hears a different drummer. Let him step to the music which he hears, however measured or far away.
8003 DAN QUAYLE/USA/ VICE-PRESIDENT	Bearing babies irresponsibly is simply wrong. Failing to support children one has fathered is wrong.
8004 GEORGE SANTAYANA/ AMERICAN WRITER	Almost every wise saying has an opposite one, no less wise, to balance it.

NUMBER CATEGORY/CREDIT	TOPIC
8005 CHILDREN/FAMILY	Forcing children to eat certain kinds of food
8006 DISORDER	Adult baby syndrome
8007 BOOKER WASHINGTON/ USA/WRITER	I shall allow no man to belittle my soul by making me hate him.
8008 USA/IYANLA VANZANT	You can never love anyone to your own detriment.
8009 DIPLOMAT/RICHARD HOLBROOKE/USA	If women in the developing world do not have equal rights, they will not have equal health.
8010 MARTHA PLIMPTON/ USA/MODEL	I hate those people who say, "I don't own a television." I own one and I watch it whenever I can.
8011 ALICE WALKER/USA	In search of my mother's garden, I found my own.
8012 GENGHIS KHAN/ MONGOL/LEADER	If you're afraid - don't do it. If you're doing it, don't be afraid.
8013 SIR THOMAS MORE/UK/ PHILOSOPHER/WRITER	An absolutely new idea is one of the rarest things known to man.
8014 ELIZABETH KUBLER-ROSS/SWISS/USA/ PSYCHIATRIST	It is only when we truly know and understand that we have a limited time on earth – and that we have no way of knowing when our time is up – that we will begin to live each day to the fullest, as if it was the only one we had.
8015 KAHLIL GIBRAN/ LEBANESE POET	Many a doctrine is like a window pane. We see truth through it but it divides us from truth.
8016 WILLIAM OSLER/ CANADA/MEDICINE	The person who takes medicine must recover twice, once from the disease and once from the medicine.
8017 ALDOUS HUXLEY/ UK/NOVELIST	A fanatic is a man who consciously overcompensates a secret doubt.
8018 RELIGION/WILLIAM J.H.BOETCKER/LEADER	Most men believe that it would benefit them if they could get a little from those who have more. How much more would it benefit them if they would learn a little from those who know more.
8019 LES BROWN/USA	Other people's opinion of you does not have to become your reality.
8020 JONATHAN SWIFT/ IRISH WRITER	The best doctors in the world are Doctor Diet, Doctor Quiet, and Doctor Merryman.
8021 PLUTARCH/GREEK HISTORIAN/ESSAYIST	The mind is not a vessel that needs filling, but wood that needs igniting.
8022 AUSTRALIA/PROVERB ABORIGINES	Those who lose dreaming are lost.
8023 HERODOTUS/ ANCIENT GREEK HISTORIAN	If someone were to put a proposition before men bidding them choose, after examination, the best customs in the world, each nation would certainly select its own.
8024 JAMES CLAVELL/USA	Some men are born content to be second best.
8025 PUBLILIUS SYRUS/ LATIN WRITER	Prosperity makes friends, adversity tries them.
8026 RON GUTMAN/USA/ TEDTALK/BUSINESS	When you smile you don't only appear to be more likable and courteous, you appear to be more competent.
8027 JONATHAN SWIFT/IRISH	Every man desires to live long, but no man wishes to be old.
8028 RICHARD ST. JOHN/ TEDTALK	The interesting thing is: if you do it for love, the money comes anyway.

NUMBER CATEGORY/CREDIT	TOPIC
8029 SRI CHIMNOY/ INDIAN GURU	Do not try to entrap others with your haughty knowledge. To your wide surprise, they will entrap you with their lengthy ignorance.
8030 SAMUEL JOHNSON/UK	A man may be so much of everything that he is nothing of anything.
8031 NICOLAS CAGE/USA/ ACTOR	To be a good actor you have to be something like a criminal, to be willing to break the rules to strive for something new.
8032 MADELEINE L'ENGLE/ USA/WRITER	When we were children, we used to think that when we were grown-up we would no longer be vulnerable. But to grow up is to accept vulnerability… To be alive is to be vulnerable.
8033 SUN TZU/CHINA/ AUTHOR/THE ART OF WAR	Speed is the essence of war. Take advantage of the enemy's unpreparedness; travel by unexpected routes and strike him where he has taken no precautions.
8034 ALAN DERSHOWITZ/ USA/LAW/PROFESSOR	All sides in a trial want to hide at least some of the truth.
8035 PUBLILIUS SYRUS	Money alone sets all the world in motion.
8036 BOB DYLAN/USA	You don't need a weather man / To know which way the wind blows.
8037 FRAN LEBOWITZ/USA/ AUTHOR	Great people talk about ideas, average people talk about things, and small people talk about wine.
8038 AN INDIAN PROVERB	Always be well dressed, even when begging.
8039 GERMAN/LUDWIG WITTGENSTEIN/ PHILOSOPHER	The limits of my language means the limits of my world.
8040 KAHLIL GIBRAN/ON TALKING	And there are those who talk, and without knowledge or forethought reveal a truth which they themselves do not understand.
8041 DALE CARNEGIE/USA/ WRITER/LECTURER	You can close more business in two months by becoming interested in other people than you can in two years by trying to get people interested in you.
8042 GUY KAWASAKI/USA/ WRITER/FINANCE	It is better to make meaning than to make money.
8043 ALDOUS HUXLEY/UK/ NOVELIST	All gods are homemade, and it is we who pull their strings, and so, give them the power to pull ours.
8044 SUN TZU/CHINA/ AUTHOR	In the practical art of war, the best thing of all is to take the enemy's country whole and intact; to shatter and destroy it is not so good.
8045 BILL COSBY/USA/ COMEDIAN	I don't know the key to success, but the key to failure is trying to please everybody.
8046 BOB MARLEY/JAMAICA/ MUSICIAN	Love the life you live. Live the life you love.
8047 USA/FREDERICK DOUGLASS	No man can put a chain about the ankle of his fellow man without at last finding the other end fasted about his own neck.
8048 GEOFFREY BLAINEY/ AUSTRALIA	Nationalism is both a vital medicine and a dangerous drug.
8049 DR. MARTIN LUTHER KING JR.	Our lives begin to end the day we become silent about things that matter.
8050 ELVIS PRESLEY/USA/ MUSICIAN	The image is one thing and the human being is another. It's very hard to live up to an image, put it that way.

NUMBER CATEGORY/CREDIT	TOPIC
8051 RESEARCH	Being a guinea pig
8052 NATSUME SOSEKI/ JAPAN/WRITER	I believe that words uttered in passion contain a greater living truth than those words which express thoughts rationally conceived.
8053 SARAH MILLER/ NY TIMES	Because yoga is "good for us" we seem to have this fantasy that the practice of it will not create anything negative.
8054 GEORGE BERNARD SHAW/WRITER	Martyrdom is the only way in which a man can become famous without ability.
8055 CICERO/ROMAN ORATOR	Not to know what has been transacted in former times is to be always a child.
8056 KENTETSU TAKAMORI/ JAPAN/WRITER	The wave is the signature of every experience of life. By understanding the nature of waves and their characteristics, and applying that understanding to our lives, we can navigate life with a little more grace.
8057 MALCOLM GLADWELL/ WRITER/USA/CANADA	My earliest memories of my father are of seeing him work at his desk and realizing that he was happy... I did not see it then, but that was one of the most precious gifts a father can give his child.
8058 CASEY KASEM/USA/ RADIO HOST	Anytime in radio that you can reach somebody on an emotional level, you're really connecting.
8059 COUNTEE CULLEN/USA/ POET	I have no will to weep or sing, No least desire to pray or curse; The loss of love is a terrible thing; They lie who say that death is worse.
8060 THINKER/LUDWIG WITTGENSTEIN	Philosophers are often like little children, who first scribble random lines on a piece of paper with their pencils, and now ask an adult, 'What is that?'
8061 JOHN K. GALBRAITH/ ECONOMIST	If all else fails, immortality can always be assured by spectacular error.
8062 ALAN GREENSPAN/ ECONOMIST/USA	I have found no greater satisfaction than achieving success through honest dealing and strict adherence to the view that, for you to gain, those you deal with should gain as well.
8063 NICOLAS CAGE/ACTOR/ USA	I think what makes people fascinating is conflict, it's drama, it's the human condition. Nobody wants to watch perfection.
8064 RICHARD M. RORTY/ USA/PHILOSOPHER	There is nothing deep down inside us except what we have put there ourselves.
8065 GLORIA PITZER/WRITER	About the only thing that comes to us without effort is old age.
8066 OCTAVIA BUTLER/ USA/WRITER	Drowning people sometimes die fighting their rescuers.
8067 WILLIAM J. BRENNAN JR./AMERICAN JUDGE	No longer is the female destined solely for the home and the rearing of the family and only the male for the marketplace and the world of ideas.
8068 DEBATE/ CHARITY	There is nothing wrong with giving money to panhandlers.
8069 CONFUCIUS/THINKER/ TR.WING-TSIT CHAN	Is one not a superior man if he does not feel hurt even though he does not feel recognized?
8070 ARTHUR CALDWELL/ AUSTRALIA	It is better to be defeated on principle than to win on lies.
8071 RICHARD M. RORTY/ USA/PHILOSOPHER	Always strive to excel, but only on weekends.
8072 DOLLY PARTON/USA	If you want the rainbow, you have to put up with the rain.
8073 THOMAS EDISON/USA/ INVENTOR	We often miss opportunity because it's dressed in overalls and looks like work.

NUMBER CATEGORY/CREDIT	TOPIC
8074 C.S. LEWIS/IRISH NOVELIST	Education without values, as useful as it is, seems rather to make man a more clever devil.
8075 RICHARD M. RORTY/ USA/PHILOSOPHER	My sense of the holy is bound up with the hope that some day my remote descendants will live in a global civilization in which love is pretty much the only law.
8076 GEORGE ORWELL/ UK/AUTHOR	Language ought to be the joint creation of poets and manual workers.
8077 BERTRAND RUSSELL/ UK/HISTORIAN	The whole problem with the world is that fools and fanatics are always so certain of themselves, but wiser men so full of doubts.
8078 RICHARD M. RORTY/ USA/PHILOSOPHER	Philosophers get attention only when they appear to be doing something sinister -- corrupting the youth, undermining the foundations of civilization, sneering at all we hold dear.
8079 MOTHER TERESA/ CATHOLIC NUN	People who really want help may attack you if you help them. Help them anyway.
8080 ZHUANGZI/THINKER/ CHINA	Happiness is the absence of striving for happiness.
8081 ANWAR SADAT/ EGYPTIAN PRESIDENT	Peace is much more precious than a piece of land...let there be no more wars.
8082 MARIO PUZO/THE GODFATHER	Friendship is everything. Friendship is more than talent. It is more than the government. It is almost the equal of family.
8083 GORE VIDAL/USA/ WRITER	A good deed never goes unpunished.
8084 WILLIAM FAULKNER/ USA/NOVELIST	You cannot swim for new horizons until you have courage to lose sight of the shore.
8085 USA/ACTOR/DENZEL WASHINGTON	I say luck is when an opportunity comes along and you're prepared for it.
8086 BERNARD HARRIS/USA/ ASTRONAUT	...don't build your life around the expectations of others.
8087 JOEL OSTEEN/USA/ PREACHER	People of excellence go the extra mile to do what's right.
8088 GERMAN/ARTHUR SCHOPENHAUER	The longer a man's fame is likely to last, the longer it will be in coming.
8089 CHARLES DARWIN/ UK/LETTER TO J.D. HOOKER/1870	I cannot look at the universe as the result of blind chance, yet I can see no evidence of beneficent design or indeed of design of any kind, in the details.
8090 TEMPLE GRANDIN/ USA/AUTISM ADVOCATE	I know a number of autistic adults that are doing extremely well on Prozac.
8091 JOHN CHARLES POLANYI/SCIENTIST	Science exists, moreover, only as a journey toward truth. Stifle dissent and you end that journey.
8092 DANIEL GOLEMAN/ON COMPASSION/ TEDTALK	The Harvard Business Review recently had an article called, 'The Human Moment,' about how to make real contact with a person at work:...the fundamental thing you have to do is turn off your BlackBerry, close your laptop, end your daydream and pay full attention to the person.
8093 J.M. BARRIE/ AUTHOR/PETER PAN	You can have anything in life if you will sacrifice everything else for it.

NUMBER CATEGORY/CREDIT	TOPIC
8094 SIDNEY HOOK/USA/ PHILOSOPHER/ PRAGMATISM SCHOOL	Those who say that life is worth living at any cost have already written an epitaph of infamy, for there is no cause and no person that they will not betray to stay alive.
8095 JEAN KERR/USA/ WRITER	If you can keep your head about you when all about you are losing theirs, it's just possible you haven't grasped the situation.
8096 MORTIMER ADLER/ USA/PHILOSOPHER	To agree without understanding is inane. To disagree without understanding is impudent.
8097 BERNARD HARRIS/USA/ ASTRONAUT	I believe that you shouldn't let failure define you, but instead you should let failure refine you.
8098 GEORGE S. CLASON/ USA/AUTHOR	Learning was of two kinds: the one being the things we learned and knew, and the other being the training that taught us how to find out what we did not know.
8099 STRESS/OVERWORK/ MERRIAMWEBSTER	Burnout : exhaustion of physical or emotional strength or motivation usually as a result of prolonged stress or frustration.
8100 JOHN K. GALBRAITH/ ECONOMIST	In any great organization it is far, far safer to be wrong with the majority than to be right alone.
8101 LOUIS PASTEUR/ FRENCH CHEMIST	Where observation is concerned, chance favors only the prepared mind.
8102 YO YO MA/USA/ MUSICIAN	When you learn something from people or from a culture, you accept it as a gift, and it is your lifelong commitment to preserve that gift and to build on that gift.
8103 PSYCHOLOGY TODAY/ TALL PEOPLE	Height matters. Tall people get larger salaries, higher status and more respect. Furthermore, the advantage seems to be life-long.
8104 SINGLE LIFE	People who choose to remain single for life.
8105 DALE CARNEGIE/USA/ LECTURER	We all have possibilities we don't know about. We can do things we don't even dream we can do.
8106 PUBLILIUS SYRUS	It is no profit to have learned well, if you neglect to do well.
8107 J. F. KENNEDY/USA/ 35TH PRESIDENT	If a free society cannot help the many who are poor, it cannot save the few who are rich.
8108 WAYNE GRETZKY/USA/ CANADA/HOCKEY	A good hockey player plays where the puck is. A great hockey player plays where the puck is going to be.
8109 WRITER/FRANCOIS DE LA ROCHE-FOUCAULD	It is great cleverness to know how to conceal one's cleverness.
8110 RUPERT MURDOCH/ MEDIA MOGUL	Advances in the technology of telecommunications have proved an unambiguous threat to totalitarian regimes everywhere.
8111 AUSTRALIAN PROVERB	The bigger the hat, the smaller the property.
8112 CLARENCE DARROW/US	Just think of the tragedy of teaching children not to doubt.
8113 MICHAEL PORTER/ HARVARD/USA	Innovation is the central issue in economic prosperity.
8114 TUPAC SHAKUR/HIP HOP/USA	My mama always used to tell me: 'If you can't find something' to live for, you best find somethin' to die for.'
8115 BOB MARLEY/JAMAICA / MUSICIAN	Every man got a right to decide his own destiny.
8116 LATIN PROVERB	As long as I breathe, I hope.

NUMBER CATEGORY/CREDIT	TOPIC
8117 WILLIAM FAULKNER/ USA/NOVELIST	A gentleman accepts the responsibility of his actions and bears the burden of their consequences.
8118 PETER DRUCKER/ CONSULTANT/USA	We now accept the fact that learning is a lifelong process of keeping abreast of change.
8119 TONY BLAIR/UK/PM	Conflict is not inevitable, but disarmament is.
8120 PROFESSOR EDDIE OBENG/UK/PENTACLE	Events Evaporate but Patterns Persist.
8121 CARMINE GALLO/USA/ COLUMNIST	Sell dreams, not products.
8122 SAMUEL JOHNSON/ UK/POET/ESSAYIST	There are, in every age, new errors to be rectified and new prejudices to be opposed.
8123 RICHARD M. NIXON/ USA/PRESIDENT	The greatest honor history can bestow is the title of peacemaker.
8124 FRENCH/SIMONE DE BEAUVOIR/NOVELIST	One is not born, but rather becomes a woman.
8125 RANDY PAUSCH/USA/ THE LAST LECTURE	Experience is what you get when you didn't get what you wanted. And experience is often the most valuable thing you have to offer.
8126 OPRAH.COM	Stick with what works.
8127 CHARLES DICKENS/ UK/NOVELIST	Electric communication will never be a substitute for the face of someone who with their soul encourages another person to be brave and true.
8128 NORMAN COUSINS/USA/ EDITOR/WRITER/PROF.	He who keeps his cool best wins.
8129 KATHERINE HEPBURN/ ACTRESS	If you obey all the rules you miss all the fun.
8130 LORD ACTON/UK/ HISTORIAN	Liberty is not a means to a higher political end. It is itself the highest political end.
8131 HANS SELYE/CANADA	As much as we thirst for approval we dread condemnation.
8132 SOCIAL MEDIA	Virtual identity suicide: quitting the use of social media for fear of privacy violations or Internet addiction
8133 KEVIN BREEL/ TEDTALK/COMEDIAN	Real depression isn't being sad when something in your life goes wrong. Real depression is being sad when everything in your life is going right.
8134 BERTRAND RUSSELL/ BRITISH AUTHOR	There are two motives for reading a book; one, that you enjoy it; the other, that you can boast about it.
8135 SIR FRANCIS BACON/ UK/PHILOSOPHER	In taking revenge, a man is but even with his enemy; but in passing it over, he is superior.
8136 CLARENCE DARROW/US	There is no such thing as justice – in or out of court.
8137 ANTON CHEKHOV/ RUSSIAN WRITER	A good upbringing means not that you won't spill sauce on the tablecloth, but that you won't notice it when someone else does.
8138 ISAAC ASIMOV/USA/ SCIENCE/WRITER	People who think they know everything are a great annoyance to those of us who do.
8139 LOUIS ARMSTRONG/USA	If you have to ask (what jazz is), then you'll never know.
8140 MILITARY	Women in the military
8141 RALPH ELLISON/USA/ WRITER	There are few things in the world as dangerous as sleepwalkers.

NUMBER CATEGORY/CREDIT	TOPIC
8142 THE TALMUD	To break an oral agreement which is not legally binding is morally wrong.
8143 JEAN KERR/USA/ WRITER	The real menace about dealing with a five-year-old is that in no time at all you begin to sound like a five-year-old.
8144 GEORGE BERNARD SHAW/IRISH WRITER	The people who get on in this world are the people who get up and look for the circumstances they want, and, if they can't find them, make them.
8145 BERTOLT BRECHT/ GERMAN DRAMATIST	Intelligence is not to make no mistakes, but to see quickly how to make them good.
8146 KAHLIL GIBRAN/ LEBANESE POET	Out of suffering has emerged the strongest souls; the most massive characters are seared with scars.
8147 USA/MARCUS BUCKINGHAM	Great leaders rally people to a better future.
8148 RICHARD BRANSON/UK/ BUSINESS	If happiness is the goal -- and it should be -- then adventure should be a top priority.
8149 PHILIPP BLOM/NY TIMES/CULTURAL HISTORIAN	Why do we amass stuff we don't need?...Collected objects are like holy relics: conduits to another world.
8150 JOSE SARAMAGO/ PORTUGAL/JOURNALIST	You know the name you were given; you do not know the name that you have.
8151 PUBLILIUS SYRUS	Whatever you can lose, you should reckon of no account.
8152 PROBLEMS	Vicious circle
8153 THE SIMPSONS/USA/ TV SHOW/HUMOR	You tried your best and you failed miserably. The lesson is: Nver try
8154 EMILY DICKINSON/ USA/POET	Success is counted sweetest / By those who ne'eer succeed. To comprehend a nectar / Requires sorest need.
8155 OSCAR WILDE/IRISH WRITER	One's real life is often the life that one does not lead.
8156 MIYAMOTO MUSASHI/ JAPANESE WARRIOR	Do not seek pleasure for its own sake.
8157 GERMAN/THINKER/ A. SCHOPENHAUER	The greatest of follies is to sacrifice health for any other kind of happiness.
8158 USA/MARY MCLEOD BETHUNE/EDUCATOR	Cease to be a drudge, seek to be an artist.
8159 GEORGE BERNARD SHAW/PLAYWRIGHT	It is the mark of a truly intelligent person to be moved by statistics.
8160 SIR WILLIAM TEMPLE/ LOGICIAN	The only way for a rich man to be healthy is by exercise and abstinence, to live as if he were poor.
8161 OPRAH WINFREY/USA MEDIA OWNER	Every day brings a chance to start over.
8162 THE SIMPSONS/USA/ TV SHOW/HUMOR	If you pray to the wrong god, you might just make the right one madder and madder.
8163 WILLIAM PITT THE YOUNGER/UK/PM	Necessity is the plea for every infringement of human freedom. It is the argument of tyrants. It is the creed of slaves.
8164 THE SIMPSONS/USA/ TV SHOW/HUMOR	Weaseling out of things is important to learn...it's what separates us from the animals...except the weasel.

NUMBER CATEGORY/CREDIT	TOPIC
8165 CHINA/GIRLS/BOYS	Sex ratio imbalance
8166 EXPRESSION/WAR	Fog of war
8167 TERENCE/AFRICAN SLAVE/ROME	When we are well, we all have good advice for those who are ill.
8168 SOPHOCLES/THINKER	No one loves the messenger who brings bad news.
8169 NORMAN COUSINS/ AMERICAN AUTHOR	History is a vast early warning system.
8170 UK/SAMUEL JOHNSON/WRITER	A man will turn over half a library to make one book.
8171 J.H.PAYNE/USA/ ACTOR/PLAYWRIGHT	Home, Sweet Home / Be it ever so humble, there's no place like home.
8172 GEORGE BERNARD SHAW/PLAYWRIGHT	The worst sin toward our fellow creatures is not to hate them, but to be indifferent to them.
8173 WINSTON CHURCHILL	Attitude is a little thing that makes a big difference.
8174 USA/WILLIAM JULIUS WILSON/PROFESSOR	But the person who scored well on an SAT will not necessarily be the best doctor or the best lawyer or the best businessman. These tests do not measure character, leadership, creativity, perseverance.
8175 VACLAV HAVEL/ CZECH STATESMAN	Work for something because it is good, not just because it stands a chance to succeed.
8176 FRÉDÉRIC FRANÇOIS CHOPIN/COMPOSER	Simplicity is the highest goal, achievable when you have overcome all difficulties.
8177 LAKOTA PROVERB	When a man moves away from nature his heart becomes hard.
8178 UK/W. SOMERSET MAUGHAM/NOVELIST	People ask for criticism, but they only want praise.
8179 WENDELL WILKIE/ USA/LAWYER	It is from weakness that people reach for dictators and concentrated government power. Only the strong can be free. And only the productive can be strong.
8180 F. NIGHTINGALE/UK	How very little can be done under the spirit of fear.
8181 GEORGE ORWELL/UK	Power is not a means, it is an end.
8182 MORTIMER ADLER/ USA/ PHILOSOPHER	..a good book can teach you about the world and about yourself. You learn more than how to read better; you also learn more about life. You become wiser.
8183 AMBROSE BIERCE/ USA/AUTHOR	Calamities are of two kinds: misfortunes to ourselves, and good fortune to others.
8184 USA/SLOGAN/GOP	A Chicken in Every Pot. A Car in Every Garage.
8185 HILLARY CLINTON/ USA/POLITICAL LEADER	Why extremists always focus on women remains a mystery to me. But they all seem to. It doesn't matter what country they're in or what religion they claim. They want to control women. They want to control how we dress, they want to control how we act, they even want to control decisions we make about our own health and bodies.
8186 MAO TSE TUNG/CHINA	Let a hundred flowers bloom.
8187 THE SIMPSONS/USA/ TV SHOW/HUMOR	Books are useless! I only ever read one book, To Kill a Mockingbird, and it gave me absolutely no insight on how to kill mockingbirds!
8188 PUBLILIUS SYRUS	Better to be ignorant of a matter than half know it.

NUMBER CATEGORY/CREDIT	TOPIC
8189 AMBROSE BIERCE/USA	Bore: A person who talks when you wish him to listen.
8190 TONY PORTER/A CALL TO MEN/TEDTALK	If it would destroy [a 12-year-old boy] to be called a girl, what are we then teaching him about girls?
8191 JOHN IRVING/USA/ WRITER	My life is a reading list.
8192 HELEN FISHER/WHY WE LOVE + CHEAT/ TEDTALK	There's all kinds of reasons that you fall in love with one person rather than another: Timing is important. Proximity is important. Mystery is important.
8193 MOTHER TERESA/NUN	We are all pencils in the hand of God.
8194 USA/WILLIAM J. BRENNAN/JUDGE	We do not consecrate the flag by punishing its desecration, for by doing so, we dilute the freedom this cherished emblem represents.
8195 PYOTR TCHAIKOVSKY/ RUSSIAN COMPOSER	I sit down to the piano regularly at nine-o-clock in the morning and Mesdames les Muses have learned to be on time for that rendezvous.
8196 NTOZAKE SHANGE/ USA/PLAYWRIGHT	Through my tears, / I found god in myself...I loved her fiercely.
8197 THUCYDIDES/GREEK HISTORIAN	A nation that makes a great distinction between its scholars and its warriors will have its laws made by cowards and its wars fought by fools.
8198 NICOLAS CAGE/USA/ ACTOR	I know what it's like to meet someone you admire and have them be a complete jerk.
8199 HECTOR BERLIOZ/ FRENCH COMPOSER	Every composer knows the anguish and despair occasioned by forgetting ideas which one had no time to write down.
8200 SIDNEY HOOK/USA/ PHILOSOPHER	Tolerance always has limits – it cannot tolerate what is itself actively intolerant.
8201 PIANIST/BEETHOVEN	Music is...a higher revelation than all Wisdom and Philosophy.
8202 ALBERT EINSTEIN/ SCIENTIST/NOBELIST	The greatest invention of mankind is compound interest.
8203 JONATHAN SWIFT/ IRISH WRITER	Complaint is the largest tribute heaven receives, and the sincerest part of our devotion.
8204 STEVE JOBS/IMPACT/ BUSINESS/CREATIVITY	We're here to put a dent in the universe
8205 G. G. MÁRQUEZ/WRITER	Freedom is often the first casualty of war.
8206 USA/JAMES BRYANT CONANT	There is only one proved method of assisting the advancement of pure science – that of picking men of genius, backing them heavily, and leaving them to direct themselves.
8207 FINLAND/LAW	Speeding tickets are calculated based on the offender's income.
8208 USA/BOOKER T. WASHINGTON	No greater injury can be done to any youth than to let him feel that because he belongs to this or that race he will be advanced in life regardless of his own merits or efforts.
8209 ALEXANDER POPE/UK	To err is human; to forgive, divine.
8210 CONFUCIUS/CHINA/ TR.WING-TSIT CHAN	A superior man in dealing with the world is not for anything or against anything. He follows righteousness as the standard.
8211 BODY/METAPHOR	The immune system
8212 USA/BOOKER T. WASHINGTON	The individual who can do something that the world wants done will, in the end, make his way regardless of his race.

NUMBER CATEGORY/CREDIT	TOPIC
8213 GEORGE SANTAYANA/US	In Greece wise men speak and fools decide.
8214 RALPH ELLISON/USA/ WRITER/INVISIBLE MAN	What and how much had I lost by trying to do only what was expected of me instead of what I myself had wished to do?
8215 LIONEL TRILLING/ USA/AUTHOR	What marks the artist is his power to shape the material of pain we all have.
8216 NORMAN COUSINS/USA	Hope is independent of the apparatus of logic
8217 ALICE WALKER/USA	A burnt finger remembers the fire.
8218 OCTAVIA BUTLER/USA/ WRITER	
8219 MARK TWAIN/USA/ NOVELIST	Be careful when reading health books; you may die of a misprint.
8220 ADVICE	Don't do the crime if you can't do the time.
8221 WILLIAM TECUMSEH SHERMAN/USA	I think I understand what military fame is; to be killed on the field of battle and have your name misspelled in the newspaper.
8222 CERVANTES/POET	He who sings scares away his woes.
8223 CHARLOTTE BRONTE/ ENGLISH NOVELIST	Happiness quite unshared can scarcely be called happiness; it has no taste.
8224 JEAN-PAUL SARTRE/FR.	If you're lonely when you're alone, then you're in bad company.
8225 PIANIST/LUDWIG VAN BEETHOVEN	Music should strike fire from the heart of man, and bring tears from the eyes of woman.
8226 MORTIMER ADLER/ USA/PHILOSOPHER	Is it too much to expect from the schools that they train their students not only to interpret but to criticize; that is, to discriminate what is sound from error and falsehood, to suspect judgment if they are not convinced, or to judge with reason if they agree or disagree?
8227 CONFUCIUS/CHINA/ PHILOSOPHER	If a man takes no thought about what is distant, he will find sorrow near at hand.
8228 OPRAH WINFREY/ USA/MEDIA/OWNER	The key to realizing a dream is to focus not on success but significance – and then even the small steps and little victories along your path will take on greater meaning.
8229 J.D. SALINGER/USA/ WRITER	It's funny. All you have to do is say something nobody understands and they'll do practically anything you want them to.
8230 USA/NORMAN E. ROSENTHAL	Hardship toughens us, deepens our understanding of life and of ourselves and, in the end, leaves us with hard-earned wisdom.
8231 FRIEDRICH NIETZSCHE/ GERMANY/THINKER	Idleness is the parent of psychology.
8232 CONFUCIUS/CHINA	Before you embark on a journey of revenge, dig two graves.
8233 ELIA KAZAN/USA/ WRITER	What's called a difficult decision is a difficult decision because either way you go, there are penalties.
8234 CLARENCE DARROW/ AMERICAN LAWYER	I do not believe that people are in jail because they deserve to be. They are in jail because they cannot avoid it on account of circumstances which are entirely beyond their control and for which they are in no way responsible.
8235 KARL MARX/GERMAN	Landlords, like all other men, love to reap where they never sowed.
8236 SAYING	Age before beauty.

NUMBER CATEGORY/CREDIT	TOPIC
8237 YEVGENY ZAMYATIN/ SOVIET UNION/WRITER	There are books of the same chemical composition as dynamite. The only difference is that a piece of dynamite explodes once, whereas a book explodes a thousand times.
8238 WILLIAM TECUMSEH SHERMAN/USA	In our Country, one class of men makes war and leaves another to fight it out.
8239 FRÉDÉRIC FRANÇOIS CHOPIN/PIANIST	Every difficulty slurred over will be a ghost to disturb your repose later on.
8240 SAMUEL JOHNSON/UK	The first years of man must make provision for the last.
8241 JEAN KERR/USA/ WRITER	A poor person who is unhappy is in a better position than a rich person who is unhappy. Because the poor person has hope. He thinks money will help.
8242 DANIEL J. BOORSTIN/ LIBRARIAN/USA	The greatest obstacle to discovery is not ignorance – it is the illusion of knowledge.
8243 MICHAEL GATES GILL/ AUTHOR/USA	...trusting your own heart is your greatest – and only – path to happiness.
8244 UK/SAMUEL JOHNSON/WRITER	A wise man will make haste to forgive, because he knows the true value of time, and will not suffer it to pass away in unnecessary pain.
8245 PAVAN SUKHDEV/PUT A VALUE ON NATURE!/TED.COM	A billion people depend on fish for their main source of animal protein. At the rate at which we are losing fish, it is a human problem of enormous dimensions, a health problem of a kind we haven't seen before.
8246 WARREN BUFFETT/ USA/INVESTOR	It's better to hang out with people better than you. Pick out associates whose behavior is better than yours and you'll drift in that direction.
8247 ABDUL KALAM/INDIA	Do we not realize that self-respect comes with self-reliance?
8248 PLATO/GREEK PHILOSOPHER	Wise men talk because they have something to say; fools, because they have to say something.
8249 BUSINESS/JACK WELCH/USA/LEADER	Globalization has changed us into a company that searches the world, not just to sell or to source, but to find intellectual capital – the world's best talents and greatest ideas.
8250 NATALIE GOLDBERG/US	Every moment is enormous and it is all we have.
8251 TERRY PRATCHETT/UK/ WRITER	The intelligence of that creature known as the crowd is the square root of the number of people in it.
8252 PETER DRUCKER/ MANAGEMENT CONSULTANT/	Few companies that installed computers to reduce the employment of clerks have realized their expectations...they now need more, and more expensive clerks even though they call them 'operators' or 'programmers.'
8253 ITALY/NICCOLO MACHIAVELLI	The first method for estimating the intelligence of a ruler is to look at the men he has around him.
8254 MARY PETTIBONE POOLE/USA/WRITER	He who laughs, lasts!
8255 CHINUA ACHEBE/ AFRICAN WRITER	When suffering knocks at your door and you say there is no seat for him, he tells you not to worry because he has brought his own stool.
8256 USA/OLD SOUTHERN SAYING	The only way to get 30 minutes' uninterrupted rest in a hospital is to ring for a nurse.
8257 CHINUA ACHEBE/ AFRICAN WRITER/	One of the truest tests of integrity is its blunt refusal to be compromised.
8258 SOCIETY/HEALTH	Art therapy

NUMBER CATEGORY/CREDIT	TOPIC
8259 SENECA/PHILOSOPHER	He who would do great things should not attempt them all alone.
8260 GEORGE BERNARD SHAW/PLAYWRIGHT	A government that robs Peter to pay Paul can always depend on the support of Paul.
8261 PYOTR ILYICH TCHAIKOVSKY/ RUSSIAN COMPOSER	Music is indeed the most beautiful of all Heaven's gifts to humanity wandering in the darkness. Alone it calms, enlightens, and stills our souls. It is not the straw to which the drowning man clings; but a true friend, refuge, and comforter, for whose sake life is worth living.
8262 DALE CARNEGIE/ USA/WRITER	There is only one way…to get anybody to do anything. And that is by making the other person want to do it.
8263 WRITER/MALCOLM GLADWELL/BLINK/ USA/CANADA/WRITER	There can be as much value in the blink of an eye as in months of rational analysis.
8264 RABBI SHMULEY BOTEACH/USA	…teens who do not have regular family dinners are three and a half times more likely to abuse drugs.
8265 UK/W. SOMERSET MAUGHAM/NOVELIST	Follow your inclinations with due regard to the policeman round the corner.
8266 DANIEL J. BOORSTIN/ LIBRARIAN/USA	A wonderful thing about a book, in contrast to a computer screen, is that you can take it to bed with you.
8267 FRÉDÉRIC CHOPIN/ POLISH COMPOSER	I wish I could throw off the thoughts which poison my happiness. And yet I take a kind of pleasure in indulging them.
8268 SIDNEY HOOK/USA/ PHILOSOPHER	Wisdom is a kind of knowledge. It is knowledge of the nature, career, and consequences of human values.
8269 ELIE WIESEL/USA/ NOVELIST	Friendship marks a life even more deeply than love. Love risks degenerating into obsession; friendship is never anything but sharing.
8270 WOMEN/JEAN KERR/ IRISH-AMERICAN/ AUTHOR	One of the most difficult things to contend with in a hospital is the assumption on the part of the staff that because you have lost your gall bladder you have also lost your mind.
8271 JAWAHARLAL NEHRU/INDIA/PM	Life is like a game of cards. The hand that is dealt you is determinism; the way you play it is free will.
8272 GABRIEL GARCÍA MÁRQUEZ/COLOMBIA	Always remember that the most important thing in a good marriage is not happiness, but stability.
8273 ANDREW CARNEGIE/ USA/BUSINESSS	Concentrate your energies, your thoughts and your capital. The wise man puts all his eggs in one basket and watches the basket.
8274 MICHAEL PORTER/ HARVARD/USA	The essence of strategy is that you must set limits on what you're trying to accomplish.
8275 ANN LANDERS/ USA/ ADVICE COLUMNIST/ CHICAGO SUN TIMES	One out of four people in this country is mentally unbalanced. Think of your three closest friends; if they seem OK, then you're the one.
8276 RELIGION/MARRIAGE	Marrying someone of a different religion
8277 JOHN IRVING/USA/ WRITER	Half my life is an act of revision.
8278 HENRY B. ADAMS/USA/ HISTORIAN	All experience is an arch – to build upon.
8279 OLIVER WENDELL HOLMES/USA	Alas for those that never sing, but die with all their music in them

NUMBER CATEGORY/CREDIT	TOPIC
8280 PIANIST/BEETHOVEN	To play without passion is inexcusable.
8281 JEAN KERR/WRITER/USA/AUTHOR	Even though a number of people have tried, no one has ever found a way to drink for a living.
8282 WILLIAM FAULKNER/AMERICAN NOVELIST	The artist doesn't have time to listen to the critics. The ones who want to be writers read the reviews, the ones who want to write don't have the time to read reviews.
8283 WILLIAM FAULKNER/US/NOVELIST	Don't be a writer. Be writing.
8284 OPRAH WINFRENY/USA/MEDIA OWNER	Trust your instincts. Intuition doesn't lie.
8285 CHARLES DICKENS/UK	There is a wisdom of the Head, and...a wisdom of the Heart.
8286 CAMILLE PAGLIA/USA	When anything goes, it's women who lose.
8287 CICERO/ROMAN ORATOR	Laws are silent in time of war.
8288 PROTAGORAS/THINKER	Man is the measure of all things.
8289 GABBY DOUGLAS/USA/GYMNAST	The hard days are the best because that's where champions are made so if you can push through, you can push through anything!
8290 GEORGE BERNARD SHAW/WRITER	Patriotism is your conviction that this country is superior to all other countries because you were born in it.
8291 GEORGE ORWELL/BRITISH AUTHOR	One can love a child, perhaps, more deeply than one can love another adult, but it is rash to assume that the child feels any love in return.
8292 JOHN IRVING/USA/WRITER	Good habits are worth being fanatical about.
8293 PUBLILIUS SYRUS	Many receive advice, few profit by it.
8294 ALDOUS HUXLEY/UK/NOVELIST	Beauty is worse than wine, it intoxicates both the holder and beholder.
8295 J.D. SALINGER/USA/WRITER	I'm the most terrific liar you ever saw in your life. It's awful. If I'm on my way to the store to buy a magazine, even, and somebody asks me where I'm going. I'm liable to say I'm going to the opera. It's terrible.
8296 CHINUA ACHEBE/AFRICAN WRITER	An old woman is always uneasy when dry bones are mentioned in a proverb.
8297 GEORGE BALLANCHINE/RUSSIA/USA/BALLET	I don't want people who want to dance. I want people who have to dance.
8298 EZRA POUND/USA/POET	Genius is the capacity to see ten things where the ordinary man sees one...
8299 BERTRAND RUSSELL/UK	Too little liberty brings stagnation and too much brings chaos.
8300 JOHN IRVING/USA/WRITER	It's not right to hurt or deceive someone who's already been hurt and deceived.
8301 ISAAC ASIMOV/USA/WRITER/SCHOLAR	There are no happy endings in history, only crisis points that pass..
8302 CLARENCE DARROW/AMERICAN LAWYER	I am a friend of the workingman, and I would rather be his friend, than be one.
8303 OPRAH WINFRENY/USA/MEDIA OWNER	If you make a choice that goes against what everyone else thinks, the world will not fall apart.
8304 CREATE A STORY	A disturbing conversation

NUMBER CATEGORY/CREDIT	TOPIC
8305 FRENCH/NAPOLEON	Circumstances – what are circumstances? I make circumstances.
8306 FRIEDRICH NIETZSCHE/ THINKER/GERMANY	He that humbleth himself wishes to be exalted.
8307 NURSE/UK/FLORENCE NIGHTINGALE	An angel is not someone who scatters beautiful flowers but one who fights for people who are suffering.
8308 MOSHE DAYAN/ ISRAEL/POLITICIAN	If you want to make peace, you don't talk to your friends. You talk to your enemies.
8309 CINDY CRAWFORD/ USA/MODEL/ BUSINESSWOMAN	I like to work. The self-esteem and satisfaction that I get from working makes me a better person, which makes me a better mom. I feel lucky because I have the luxury of working only one or two days a week.
8310 CICERO/THINKER	A friend is, as it were, a second self.
8311 KAHLIL GIBRAN/ LEBANESE POET	Most people who ask for advice from others have already resolved to act as it pleases them.
8312 JOHN IRVING/USA/ WRITER	There's nothing I need or want to know from the writers I admire that isn't in their books. It's better to read a good writer than meet one.
8313 CHARLES DICKENS/UK	A day wasted on others is not wasted on one's self.
8314 ALAN DERSHOWITZ/ USA/LAWYER/ PROFESSOR	The prosecution wants to make sure the process by which the evidence was obtained is not truthfully presented, because, as often as not, that process will raise questions.
8315 CARL JUNG/SWISS PSYCHOLOGIST	Nothing has a stronger influence psychologically on their environment and especially on their children than the unlived life of the parent.
8316 SAMUEL JOHNSON/UK/	A man of genius has been seldom ruined but by himself.
8317 DOLLY PARTON/ AMERICAN SINGER	I'm not offended by all the dumb blonde jokes because I know I'm not dumb – and I'm not blonde either.
8318 LAURENCE J. PETER/ CANADA/EDUCATOR	An economist is an expert who will know tomorrow why the things he predicted yesterday didn't happen.
8319 JULIEN BRYAN/ FILMMAKER/FRIEND- SHIP/THIS I BELIEVE	I have come to hold a deep respect for all of man's great religions. And I have come to believe that despite their differences, all men can worship side by side.
8320 PLATO/THE REPUBLIC	The direction in which education starts a man will determine his future life.
8321 ALEXANDER POPE/UK POET	Who shall decide, when doctors disagree?
8322 RULES FOR LIFE	If you think your teacher is tough, wait till you get a boss.
8323 LES BROWN/USA/ MOTIVATIONAL SPEAKER	"BUT" is a dream killer.
8324 USA/MARY MCLEOD BETHUNE/ACTIVIST	Invest in the human soul. Who knows, it might be a diamond in the rough.
8325 LAO-TZU/THINKER	Seek not happiness too greedily.
8326 CHARLIE PARKER/ USA/JAZZ/MUSICIAN	You've got to learn your instrument. Then, you practice, practice, practice. And then, when you finally get up there on the bandstand, forget it and just wail.
8327 SENECA/DRAMATIST	He who spares the wicked injures the good.
8328 DEBATE	That students should wear school uniforms.

NUMBER CATEGORY/CREDIT	TOPIC
8329 TAX FREEDOM DAY/ WIKIPEDIA	Tax Freedom Day : Tax Freedom Day is the first day of the year in which a nation as a whole has theoretically earned enough income to fund its annual tax burden...In the United States, Tax Freedom Day for 2010 is April 3, for a total average effective tax rate of 26.9 percent of the nation's income.
8330 FRAN LEBOWITZ/USA/ AUTHOR	I must take issue with the term a 'mere child,' for it has been my invariable experience that the company of a mere child is infinitely preferable to that of a mere adult.
8331 SAMUEL BUTLER/UK/ WRITER	I reckon being ill as one of the great pleasures or life, provided one is not too ill and is not obliged to work till one is better.
8332 HENRY LOUIS GATES/ USA/EDUCATOR	The first step toward tolerance is respect and the first step toward respect is knowledge.
8333 GEORGE BERNARD SHAW/WRITER	The man who writes about himself and his own time is the only man who writes about all people and all time.
8334 BOOKER WASHINGTON/ USA/EDUCATOR	Always remember that credit is capital.
8335 ANDREW STANTON/USA/ SCREENWRITER	The greatest story commandment is: Make me care.
8336 MARY BAKER EDDY/ USA/RELIGION	Health is not a condition of matter, but of Mind; nor can the material senses bear reliable testimony on the subject of health.
8337 GREG STONE/TEDTALK/ OCEANOGRAPHER/USA	Sea levels are rising, and Kiribati, along with 42 other nations in the world, will be under water 50 to 100 years. Some of the islands have already gone under water.
8338 GEORGE BALLANCHINE/ RUSSIA/USA/BALLET	Someone once said that dancers work just as hard as policemen, always alert, always tense. But I don't agree with that because policemen don't have to be beautiful at the same time.
8339 LEE IACOCCA/CEO/ LEADERSHIP	I have always found that if I move with seventy-five percent or more of the facts that I usually never regret it. It's the guys who wait to have everything perfect that drive you crazy.
8340 RICHARD PRATT/ AUSTRALIAN BILLIONAIRE	Encourage your people to be committed to a project rather than just involved in it. You know the difference between involvement and commitment, didn't you? In a meal of bacon and eggs, the chicken is involved, the pig is committed.
8341 OSCAR WILDE/IRISH WRITER/POET	Man is least himself when he talks in his own person. Give him a mask, and he will tell you the truth.
8342 TYLER PERRY/USA/ MOVIE PRODUCER	Are you living or just existing?
8343 KEMAL ATATURK/ TURKISH SOLDIER	A nation which makes the final sacrifice for life and freedom does not get beaten.
8344 SUN TZU/AUTHOR/ CHINA	He who knows when he can fight and when he cannot will be victorious.
8345 MIYAMOTO MUSASHI/ JAPAN/WARRIOR	The ultimate aim of martial arts is not having to use them.
8346 ROGER ANGELL/USA/ THIS I BELIEVE	I am a great believer in skepticism. I think that a man should grasp a belief warily and carry it gingerly.

NUMBER CATEGORY/CREDIT	TOPIC
8347 CARL JUNG/SWISS PSYCHOLOGIST	The healthy man does not torture others – generally it is the tortured who turn into torturers.
8348 STEPHEN BREYER/ USA/JUDGE	It doesn't help to fight crime to put people in prison who are innocent.
8349 DAVID HANSON/ ROBOTS THAT "SHOW EMOTION"/ TEDTALK	Machines are becoming devastatingly capable of things like killing. Those machines have no place for empathy. There's billions of dollars being spent on that. Character robotics could plant the seed for robots that actually have empathy.
8350 ERMA BOMBECK/USA/ HUMOR COLUMNIST	Never go to a doctor whose office plants have died.
8351 FREE ADVICE/T-SHIRT MESSAGE	Face your problems, don't Facebook them.
8352 ANWAR SADAT/ EGYPTIAN PRESIDENT	There can be hope only for a society which acts as one big family, not as many separate ones.
8353 VIKTOR FRANKL/ AUSTRIA/AUTHOR	If there is meaning in life at all, then there must be meaning in suffering.
8354 HOPI PROVERB	In age, talk; in childhood, tears.
8355 JEAN COCTEAU/ FRENCH POET	We must believe in luck. For how else can we explain the success of those we don't like?
8356 RANDY PAUSCH/USA/ THE LAST LECTURE	The brick walls are there for a reason. The brick walls are not there to keep us out. The brick walls are there to give us a chance to show how badly we want something. Because the brick walls are there to stop the people who don't want it badly enough. They're there to stop the other people.
8357 JAMES JOYCE/POET/ IRISH/NOVELSIT	I will not serve that in which I no longer believe, whether it calls itself my home, my fatherland, or my church.
8358 AYN RAND/RUSSIAN-USA/WRITER	The question isn't who is going to let me; it's who is going to stop me.
8359 THELONIUS MONK/USA	Talking about music is like dancing about architecture.
8360 CONFUCIUS/THINKER/ TR.WING-TSIT CHAN	A man who reviews the old so at to find out the new is qualified to teach others.
8361 SAMUEL JOHNSON/ ENGLISH AUTHOR	Don't think of retiring from the world until the world will be sorry that you retire.
8362 SUN TZU/CHINA	What is essential in war is victory, not prolonged operations.
8363 KOREAN PROVERB	You will hate a beautiful song if you sing it often.
8364 CHINUA ACHEBE/ NIGERIAN/WRITER	We cannot trample upon the humanity of others without devaluing our own. The Igbo, always practical, put it concretely in their proverb *Onye ji onye n'ani ji onwe ya*: "He who will hold another down in the mud must stay in the mud to keep him down."
8365 JENNY JOSEPH/USA	When I am an old woman…I shall go out in my slippers in the rain and pick the flowers in other people's gardens and learn to spit.
8366 EVELYN BEATRICE HALL/UK/WRITER	I disapprove of what you say, but I will defend to the death your right to say it. (Attributed to Voltaire)
8367 MARIO PUZO/THE GODFATHER/USA	A friend should always underestimate your virtues and an enemy overestimate your faults.

NUMBER CATEGORY/CREDIT	TOPIC
8368 WILLIAM FAULKNER/ USA/NOVELIST	How often have I lain beneath rain on a strange roof, thinking of home.
8369 JOHN LENNON /UK	Everyone loves you when you're six foot in the ground.
8370 SIDNEY HOOK/USA	Fear of death has been the greatest ally of tyranny past and present.
8371 CORETTA SCOTT KING/USA/ACTIVIST	Struggle is a never ending process. Freedom is never really won. You earn it and win it in every generation.
8372 GERMAN/LUDWIG VAN BEETHOVEN	I shall seize fate by the throat; it will never bend me completely to its will.
8373 DONALD SADOWAY/ THE MISSING LINK TO RENEWABLE ENERGY/TED.COM	If we're going to get this country out of its current energy situation, we can't just conserve our way out. We can't just drill our way out. We can't bomb our way out. We're going to do it the old-fashioned, American way. We're going to invent our way out, working together.
8374 GERMAN/PIANIST/ BEETHOVEN	Nothing is more intolerable than to have to admit to yourself your own errors.
8375 MORTIMER ADLER/ USA/AUTHOR	The truly great books are the few books that are over everybody's head all of the time.
8376 SIDNEY HOOK/USA/ PHILOSOPHER	Before impugning an opponent's motives, even when they legitimately may be impugned, answer his arguments.
8377 FEDERICO FELLINI/ ITALY/MOVIE DIRECTOR	Life is a combination of magic and pasta.
8378 FEDERICO FELLINI/ ITALY/MOVIE DIRECTOR	All art is autobiographical; the pearl is the oyster's autobiography.
8379 BOB MARLEY/ MUSICIAN/REGGAE	Don't gain the world and lose your soul; wisdom is better than silver or gold.
8380 OPRAH WINFREY/USA MEDIA OWNER	Being a mother is the hardest job on earth. Women everywhere must declare it so.
8381 EDDIE WEINGART/USA	Mass shootings are becoming as American as apple pie.
8382 WILLIAM FAULKNER/ USA/WRITER/HUMOR	A mule wil labor ten years willingly and patiently for you, for the privilege of kicking you once.
8383 ALEXANDER POPE/ ENGLISH POET	T'is education forms the common mind, Just as the twig is bent, the tree's inclined.
8384 BASHO MATSUO/ JAPANESE POET	Sitting quietly, doing nothing. Spring comes, and the grass grows, by itself.
8385 USA/FREDERICK DOUGLASS/LEADER	Power concedes nothing without a demand. It never did and it never will.
8386 JOSEPH CAMPBELL/ AMERICAN AUTHOR	The goal of life is to make your heartbeat match the beat of the universe, to match your nature with Nature.
8387 OPRAH WINFREY/USA MEDIA OWNER	Love doesn't hurt. It feels really good.
8388 JOHN CAMPBELL/ USA/AUTHOR	A hero is someone who has given his or her life to something bigger than oneself.
8389 ALEXANDER THE GREAT/LEADER	I am not afraid of an army of lions led by a sheep; I am afraid of an army of sheep led by a lion.
8390 CONFUCIUS/CHINA	When anger arises, think of the consequences.

NUMBER CATEGORY/CREDIT	TOPIC
8391 KEN FOLLETT/USA/ NOVELIST	In my books, women often solve the problem. Even if the woman is not the hero, she's a strong character. She does change the plot. She'll often rescue the male character from some situation.
8392 CINDY CRAWFORD/USA/ MODEL	It's important for moms to have alone time.
8393 JOHN IRVING/USA/ WRITER	There's nothing so confusing as finding out that you don't know someone you thought you knew.
8394 CHARLES DICKENS/UK	A loving heart is the truest wisdom.
8395 GERMAN/ARTHUR SCHOPENHAUER/ PHILOSOPHER	The greatest achievements of the human mind are generally received with distrust.
8396 USA/RICHARD LEIGH/ SUSANNA CLARK/ SONGWRITERS	You've got to sing like you don't need the money; Love like you'll never get hurt; You've got to dance like nobody's watchin'; It's gotta come from the heart if you want to work.
8397 GEORGE ORWELL/ UK/AUTHOR	Each generation imagines itself to be more intelligent than the one that went before it, and wiser than the one that comes after it.
8398 RABBI HILLEL/ JEWISH LEADER	Do not say, "When I have leisure, I will study," because you may never have leisure.
8399 CARL JUN/SWISS PSYCHOLOGIST	Where love rules, there is no will to power; and where power predominates, love is lacking. The one is the shadow of the other.
8400 DAN BARBER/HOW I FELL IN LOVE WITH A FISH	For the past 50 years, we've been fishing the seas like we clear-cut forests. It's hard to overstate the destruction. Ninety percent of large fish, the ones we love – the tunas, the halibuts, the salmons, the swordfish – they've collapsed.
8401 US/POET/RALPH WALDO EMERSON/ESSAYIST	In the highest civilization, the book is still the highest delight. He who has once known its satisfactions is provided with a resource against calamity.
8402 ROBERT GATES/USA/ WAPO	The true measure of leadership is how you react when the wind leaves your sails, when the tide turns against you.
8403 G. G. MÁRQUEZ/WRITER	An early rising man is a good spouse but a bad husband.
8404 USA/FREDERICK DOUGLASS/ACTIVIST	...he is a lover of his country who rebukes and does not excuses its sins.
8405 POLITICAL SLOGAN/ VIETNAM WAR	America: Love it or leave it.
8406 MORTIMER ADLER/ USA/ PHILOSOPHER/ HOW TO READ A BOOK	Television, radio, and all the sources of amusement and information that surround us in our daily lives are also artificial props. They can give us the impression that our minds are active, because we are required to react to stimuli from the outside. But the power of those external stimuli to keep us going is limited. They are like drugs. We grow used to them and we continuously need more and more of them.
8407 SOREN KIERKEGAARD/ PHILOSOPHER	Life is not a problem to be solved, but a reality to be experienced.
8408 YEVGENY ZAMYATIN/ SOVIET UNION/WRITER	If we have no heretics we must invent them, for heresy is essential to health and growth.
8409 ERNEST SHACKLETON/ POLAR EXPLORER/USA	A man must shape himself to a new mark directly the old one goes to ground.

NUMBER CATEGORY/CREDIT	TOPIC
8410 MUSINGS/DAILY YOMIURI/JAPAN/ ADVICE/WHAT IS POLITICAN? MEMOIRS OF NOBORU TAKESHITA	Former Prime Minister Noboru Takeshita once learned from a bank president a skill that bank branch managers must master.: "As a bank branch manager, you have to carefully listen to customers who wish to receive loans from us. You must make them feel good and leave the bank satisfied. If they first realize that their loan application has been rejected upon opening the door at home, I'd say you've become qualified [as a bank branch manager.]"
8411 JUDGE/WILLIAM J. BRENNAN/USA	Religious conflict can be the bloodiest and cruelest conflicts that turn people into fanatics.
8412 G.B. SHAW/WRITER	Youth is a wonderful thing. What a crime to waste it on children.
8413 UK/W. SOMERSET MAUGHAM/WRITER	At a dinner party, one should eat wisely but not too well, and talk well but not too wisely.
8414 WILLIAM MAIR/ AUTHOR/SPEAKING	He who would speak well in public must be careful to speak well in private.
8415 DOOMSDAY/LEARNERS-DICTIONARY.COM	Apocalypse : a great disaster : a sudden and very bad event that causes much fear, loss, or destruction
8416 CHILDREN/FUN	Summer camps
8417 DANIEL WEBSTER/USA/ SENATOR/ORATOR	Falsehoods not only disagree with truths, but usually quarrel among themselves.
8418 ELDERLY/PARENTING	Elderly people having children.
8419 USA/BOOKER T. WASHINGTON	Few things can help an individual more than to place responsibility on him, and to let him know that you trust him.
8420 COMPLAINTS	Whining
8421 MARCUS TULLIUS CICERO/ORATOR	No one can speak well, unless he thoroughly understands his subject.
8422 LAO-TZU/CHINA/ THINKER	Embrace simplicity.
8423 LEE IACOCCA/USA	Every business and every product has risks. You can't get around it.
8424 MIYAMOTO MUSASHI	Accept everything just the way it is.
8425 JAMES BRYANT CONANT/ CHEMIST/HARVARD	He who enters a university walks on hallowed ground.
8426 THE TALMUD	Who is a hero? He who conquers his urges.
8427 STEVE JOBS/APPLE/ BUSINESS/USA	iPod – 1000 songs in your pocket
8428 ABDUL KALAM/ INDIA/ PRESIDENT	To succeed in your mission, you must have single-minded devotion to your goal.
8429 R.L. STEVENSON/SCOT/ WRITER	Everybody lives by selling something.
8430 CHARLES LAMB/UK	Credulity is the man's weakness, but the child's strength.
8431 G.K. CHESTERTON/ ENGLISH WRITER	There are two ways to get enough. One is to continue to accumulate more and more. The other is to desire less.
8432 RABINDRANATH TAGORE/INDIAN POET	He who is too busy doing good finds no time to be good.
8433 BLACKFOOT PROVERB	Those who lie down with dogs, get up with fleas.

NUMBER CATEGORY/CREDIT	TOPIC
8434 FEDERICO FELLINI/ ITALY/MOVIE DIRECTOR	I don't believe in total freedom for the artist. Left on his own, free to do anything he likes, the artist ends up doing nothing at all.
8435 USA/PROF/HEIDI GRANT HALVORSON	Believing in your ability to succeed is enormously helpful for creating and sustaining your motivation.
8436 DALE CARNEGIE/USA	When fate hands you a lemon, make lemonade.
8437 TONY BLAIR/PM/UK	I would have loved to have been in a band, but sadly I just wasn't good enough.
8438 USA/DAVID FOSTER WALLACE/NOVELIST	Real leaders are those who "help us overcome the limitations of our own individual laziness and selfishness and weakness and fear and get us to do better, harder things than we can get ourselves to do on our own.
8439 GERMAN/FRIEDRICH NIETZSCHE	Fear is the mother of morality.
8440 VACLAV HAVEL/ CZECH STATESMAN	The attempt to devote oneself to literature alone is a most deceptive thing, and often, paradoxically, it is literature that suffers for it.
8441 GEORGE BERNARD SHAW/PLAYWRIGHT	You see things; and you say, "Why?" But I dream of things that never were; and I say, "Why not?"
8442 CHARLES DICKENS/ UK/NOVELIST	Take nothing on its looks; take everyone on evidence. There's no better rule.
8443 WARREN G. BENNIS/ USA/PSYCHOLOGIST	The factory of the future will have only two employees, a man and a dog. The man will be there to feed the dog. The dog will be there to keep the man from touching the equipment.
8444 ROBERT FROST/US/POET	I can sum up life in three words: it goes on.
8445 VIVEK WADHWA/USA/ ENTREPRENEUR/INDIA	Genius children do not need to go to university.
8446 CHINUA ACHEBE/ AFRICAN WRITER	It's true that a child belongs to its father. But when a father beats his child, it seeks sympathy in its mother's hut.
8447 WRITER/GABRIEL GARCÍA MÁRQUEZ/	Fiction was invented the day Jonas arrived home and told his wife that he was three days late because he had been swallowed by a whale.
8448 HORATIO NELSON/UK	Desperate affairs require desperate measures.
8449 GERMAN/NIETZSCHE	In every real man a child is hidden that wants to play.
8450 ROBERT MCCRUM/UK/ THE GUARDIAN	The "overnight" success" is usually anything but.
8451 USA/RALPH WALDO EMERSON/ESSAYIST	Every great and commanding moment in the annals of the world is the triumph of some enthusiasm.
8452 JULES VERNE/ FRENCH/AUTHOR	As long as a man's heart beats, as long as a man's flesh quivers, I do not allow that a being gifted with thought and will can allow himself to despair.
8453 OSCAR WILDE/IRISH WRITER/POET	The only way to get rid of a temptation is to yield to it. Resist it, and your soul grows sick with longing for the things it has forbidden to itself.
8454 CYNTHIA JASPER/USA/ PROFESSOR/CONSUMER SCIENCE	When people interpret your way of dressing...people interpret that as something you control...You can't control how tall you're going to be or your hair and eyes, but you can control what you put on your body, and your clothing is interpreted as representing who you are.
8455 RICHARD STEELE/ BRITISH DRAMATIST	Whenever you commend, add a compelling reason for doing so; it is this which distinguishes the approbation of a man of sense from the flattery of sycophants and the admiration of fools.

NUMBER CATEGORY/CREDIT	TOPIC
8456 KATE SANBORN/ ACADEMIC/USA	Genius is 1 percent inspiration and 99 per cent perspiration. (Attributed to Inventor Thomas Edison)
8457 CAMILLE PAGLIA/ USA/WRITER/CRITIC	Beauty is our weapon against nature; by it we make objects, give them limit, symmetry, proportion.
8458 CHEYENNE PROVERB	If a man is as wise as a serpent, he can afford to be as harmless as a dove.
8459 NORMAN COUSINS/ AMERICAN AUTHOR	It makes little difference how many university courses or degrees a person may own. If he cannot use words to move an idea from one point to another, his education is incomplete.
8460 JOHN K. GALBRAITH/ ECONOMIST/USA	In the choice between changing one's mind and proving there's no need to do so, most people get busy on the proof.
8461 DEBATE	There is nothing wrong with lying to help a friend out of a jam.
8462 YO YO MA/USA/ MUSICIAN	I've been traveling all over the world for 25 years, performing, talking to people, studying their cultures and musical instruments, and I always come away with more questions in my head than can be answered.
8463 WRITER/FRANCOIS DE LA ROCHE-FOUCAULD	Before we set our hearts too much upon anything, let us examine how happy those are who already possess it.
8464 GEORGE BERNARD SHAW/WRITER	All great truths begin as blasphemies.
8465 MALCOLM GLADWELL/ CANADA/USA/WRITER	Hard work is a prison sentence only if it does not have meaning.
8466 ALAN LAKEIN/USA/ WRITER/CONSULTANT	Meetings are one of the greatest time-wasters ever invented.
8467 GEORGE ORWELL/UK/ WRITER	Serious sport is war minus the shooting.
8468 THUCYDIDES/ATHENS/ HISTORIAN	Self-control is the chief element in self-respect and self-respect is the chief element in courage.
8469 DANIEL WEBSTER/USA/ SENATOR	There are men in all ages who mean to govern well, but they mean to govern. They promise to be good masters, but they mean to be masters.
8470 WRITER/FRANCOIS DE LA ROCHE-FOUCAULD	We confess our little faults to persuade people that we have no large ones.
8471 LEE IACOCCA/USA/ CEO/ LEADERSHIP	Any supervisor worth his salt would rather deal with people who attempt too much than with those who try too little.
8472 BENNY GOODMAN/ USA/COMEDIAN	To this day, I don't like people walking on stage not looking good. You have to look good. If you feel special about yourself then you're going to play special.
8473 GABRIEL GARCIA MARQUES/COLOMBIA	'You can't eat hope,' the woman said. 'You can't eat it, but it sustains you,' the colonel replied.
8474 AGRICULTURE	Hydroponics
8475 NORMAN COUSINS/USA/ EDITOR	Life is an adventure in forgiveness.
8476 WRITER/ROBERT L. STEVENSON/SCOTTISH	For my part, I travel not to go anywhere, but to go. I travel for travel's sake. The great affair is to move.
8477 BRAM STOKER/ AUTHOR/DRACULA	How blessed are some people, whose lives have no fears, no dreads; to whom sleep is a blessing that comes nightly, and brings nothing but sweet dreams.

NUMBER CATEGORY/CREDIT	TOPIC
8478 CHILDREN/PARENTS	Living in another person's shadow
8479 KAHLIL GIBRAN/ON GOOD AND EVIL	You are good when you walk to your goal firmly and with bold steps. Yet you are not evil when you go thither limping.
8480 DALE CARNEGIE/USA/ WRITER/LECTURER	Those convinced against their will are of the same opinion still.
8481 NIETZSCHE/GERMAN	Art is the proper task of life.
8482 KAHLIL GIBRAN/POET	Perplexity is the beginning of knowledge.
8483 HBR/HEIDI GRANT HALVORSON/USA	Grit is a willingness to commit to long-term goals, and to persist in the face of difficulty.
8484 RULES FOR LIFE	Flipping burgers is not beneath your dignity. Your grandparents had a different word for burger-flipping – they called it opportunity.
8485 BOBBY McFERRIN/USA	Don't worry; be happy
8486 BOOKER WASHINGTON/ USA/EDUCATOR	Dignify and glorify common labor. It is at the bottom of life that we must begin, not at the top.
8487 MUHAMMAD ALI/USA/ BOXER	A man who views the world the same as fifty as he did at twenty has wasted thirty years of his life.
8488 FRIENDS/RIVALS	Frenemies
8489 MARK TWAIN/USA/ AUTHOR & HUMORIST	A man who carries a cat by the tail learns something he can learn in no other way.
8490 N.V. PEALE/US/AUTHOR	The Power of Positive Thinking
8491 THOMAS CARLYLE/SCOT	Popular opinion is the greatest lie in the world.
8492 PLATO/GREEK AUTHOR	You can discover more about a person in an hour of play than in a year of conversation.
8493 OLIVER WENDELL HOLMES JR./USA	A mind that is stretched by a new experience can never go back to its old dimensions.
8494 ANDREW CARNEGIE/USA	Do your duty and a little more and the future will take care of itself.
8495 THOMAS J. WATSON/ IBM CEO/USA	Every time we've moved ahead in IBM, it was because someone was willing to take a chance, put his head on the block, and try something new.
8496 ALCOHOLISM/MOTHERS	Fetal alcohol syndrome
8497 MUHAMMAD ALI/USA/ BOXER	I hated every minute of training, but I said, 'Don't quit. Suffer now and live the rest of your life as a champion.'
8498 IMMANUEL KANT/ PHILOSOPHER/GERMAN	Every answer propagates more questions.
8499 MARGARET MEAD/ USA/ANTHROPOLOGIST	We are now at a point where we must educate our children in what no one knew yesterday, and prepare our schools for what no one knows yet.
8500 USA/RALPH WALDO EMERSON/ESSAYIST	Finish each day and be done with it. You have done what you could.
8501 DOLLY PARTON/USA/ SINGER	The magic is inside you. There ain't no crystal ball.
8502 LOUIS D. BRANDEIS/ AMERICAN JUDGE	If we desire respect for the law, we must first make the law respectable.
8503 JOHN IRVING/USA/ WRITER	Of all the things you choose in life, you don't get to choose what your nightmares are. You don't pick them; they pick you.
8504 ADHD/CHILDREN	Attention Deficit Hyperactice Disorder

NUMBER CATEGORY/CREDIT	TOPIC
8505 WALLACE WATTLES/ WRITER/SUCCESS	Your present work may not be the work you want to do; but unless you can do your present work perfectly you are not ready for the work you want to do.
8506 PUBLILIUS SYRUS	It takes a long time to bring excellence to maturity.
8507 GEORGE BERNARD SHAW/PLAYWRIGHT	Silence is the most perfect expression of scorn.
8508 GEORGE ORWELL/UK/ WRITER	We have got to fight against privilege. And if the rich squeal audibly, so much the better.
8509 ARTHUR C. CLARKE/ UK/SF WRITER	When a distinguished but elderly scientist says something is possible, he is almost certainly right. When he states that something is impossible, he is very probably wrong.
8510 GALILEO GALILEI/ ITALY/PHYSICIST	If I were again beginning my studies, I would follow the advice of Plato and start with mathematics.
8511 WILL DURANT/USA/ HISTORIAN/WRITER	A statesman cannot afford to be a moralist.
8512 CICERO/ROMAN ORATOR	Never go to excess, but let moderation be your guide.
8513 FRIENDS/SOCIETY	Social proof
8514 MOTHER TERESA/ CATHOLIC NUN	What you spend years building may be destroyed overnight. Build anyway.
8515 GEORGE ORWELL/UK	The quickest way of ending a war is to lose it.
8516 HYPNOTISM	Hypnotism
8517 USA/CHRISTOPHER DARDEN/LAWYER	I no longer teach law. But when I did I advised my students that they should never accept a case if it meant that by doing so you couldn't sleep at night.
8518 JONATHAN SWIFT/IRISH	No wise man ever wished to be younger.
8519 MICHAEL JORDAN/USA/ BASKETBALL/BUSINESS	I've missed more than 9000 shots in my career. I've lost almost 300 games. Twenty-six times, I've been trusted to take the game winning shot and missed. I've failed over and over and over again in my life. And that is why I succeed.
8520 USA/BOOKER T. WASHINGTON	It means a great deal, I think, to start on a foundation which one has made for oneself.
8521 FELIX FRANKFURTER/ USA/JUDGE	Litigation is the pursuit of practical ends, not a game of chess.
8522 DEBATE/HELEN JUPITER/RESEARCH	Abstaining from alcohol significantly shortens life.
8523 BOB MARLEY/ MUSICIAN/REGGAE	The greatness of a man is not in how much wealth he acquires, but in his integrity and his ability to affect those around him positively.
8524 BILL GATES/WARREN BUFFETT/USA	The Giving Pledge (A promise by wealthy people to give at least half of their wealth away)
8525 COUNTEE CULLEN/USA/ POET	For we must be one thing or the other, an asset or a liability, the sinew in your wing to help you soar, or the chain that binds you to the earth.
8526 LEO BUSCAGLIA/USA/ WRITER	The person who risks nothing, does nothing, has nothing, is nothing, and becomes nothing. He may avoid suffering and sorrow, but he simply can't learn and feel and change and grow and love and live.

NUMBER CATEGORY/CREDIT	TOPIC
8527 CHIMAMANDA NGOZI ADICHIE/WRITER/NIGERIA	...privilege blinds because it is in the nature of privilege to blind.
8528 IYANLA VANZANT/AUTHOR/USA	Your willingness to look at your darkness is what empowers you to change.
8529 USA/ELBERT GREEN/HUBBARD/WRITER	I believe in my own divinity – and yours.
8530 GERMAN/FRIEDRICH NIETZSCHE	All truly great thoughts are conceived by walking.
8531 HERODOTUS/GREEK HISTORIAN	The most hateful human misfortune is for a wise man to have no influence.
8532 LOUIS NIZER/USA/LAWYER/READER'S DIGEST	Yes, there's such a thing as luck in trial law but it only comes at 3 o'clock in the morning...You'll still find me in the library looking for luck at 3 o'clock in the morning.
8533 MUHAMMAD ALI/USA/BOXER	Don't count the days. Make the days count.
8534 LOUIS PASTEUR/FRENCH CHEMIST	When I approach a child he inspires in me two sentiments: tenderness for what he is and respect for what he may become.
8535 ROBERT MCCRUM/UK	The majority of bestsellers are ghosted.
8536 MARIO PUZO/THE GODFATHER/USA	Revenge is a dish that tastes best when served cold.
8537 LOREN EISELEY/USA	If there is magic in this planet, it is contained in water.
8538 BRIAN PENTON/AUSTRALIA/JOURNALIST	The difference between a stupid man and a wise one is the stupid man's inability to calculate the consequences of the action. The same goes for government.
8539 CONFUCIUS/CHINA/SAGE	Ching, Duke of Ch'i, had a thousand teams of horses; but the people, on his death day, found nought in him to praise.
8540 MICHAEL PORTER/HARVARD/PROFESSOR	If all you're trying to do is essentially the same things as your rivals, then it's unlikely that you'll be very successful.
8541 FAMILY/FUN/LOVE	Dreams of a white Christmas.
8542 STEVE JOBS/APPLE INC./USA/BUSINESS	Be a yardstick of quality. Some people aren't used to an environment where excellence is expected.
8543 HERODOTUS/ANCIENT GREEK HISTORIAN	If a man insisted always on being serious, and never allowed himself a bit of fun and relaxation, he would go mad or become unstable without knowing it.
8544 APPLE INC./USA	Think different.
8545 ISADORA DUNCAN/AMERICAN DANCER	So long as little children are allowed to suffer, there is no true love in this world.
8546 RUMI/PERSIAN POET	Everyone has been made for some particular work, and the desire for that work has been put in every heart.
8547 BENJAMIN DISRAELI/UK/PRIME MINISTER	If you wish to be great, you must give men new ideas, you must teach them new words, you must modify their manners, you must change their laws, you must root out prejudices, subvert convictions.
8548 MARCEL PROUST/FRENCH NOVELIST	Remembrance of things past is not necessarily the remembrance of things as they were.

NUMBER CATEGORY/CREDIT	TOPIC
8549 USA/KENNETH BLANCHARD/BUSINESS	The key to successful leadership is influence, not authority.
8550 WILLIAM FAULKNER/ USA/NOVELIST	It's a shame that the only thing a man can do for eight hours a day is work. He can't eat for eight hours; he can't drink for eight hours…The only thing a man can do for eight hours is work.
8551 USA/ELIZABETH EDWARDS/LAWYER	I've often said that the most important thing you can give your children is wings. Because, you're not gonna always be able to bring food to the nest … sometimes…they're gonna have to be able to fly by themselves.
8552 UK/W. SOMERSET MAUGHAM/NOVELIST	It's a funny thing about life; if you refuse to accept anything but the best, you very often get it.
8553 ALICE WALKER/USA	Hard times require furious dancing.
8554 FRENCH/NAPOLEON	Impossible is a word to be found only in the dictionary of fools.
8555 ELIZABETH KUBLER-ROSS/PSYCHIATRIST	There is no need to go to India or anywhere else to find peace. You will find that deep place of silence right in your room, your garden or even your bathtub.
8556 SIGMUND FREUD/ AUSTRIA/ PSYCHOLOGIST	The great question that has never been answered, and which I have not yet been able to answer, despite my thirty years of research into the feminine soul, is "What does a woman want?
8557 RONALD REAGAN/ 40TH PRESIDENT/USA	If you're explaining, then you're losing.
8558 WINSTON CHURCHILL	An appeaser is one who feeds a crocodile, hoping it will eat him last.
8559 ARTHUR CLARKE/ UK/WRITER	The only way to discover the limits of the possible is to go beyond them to the impossible.
8560 CHARLES DICKENS/ ENGLISH NOVELIST	Great men are seldom over-scrupulous in the arrangement of their attire.
8561 CLARA BARTON/USA/ TEACHER/NURSE	The door that nobody else will go in at, seems always to swing open widely for me.
8562 ELIE WIESEL/USA/ PROFESSOR/WRITER	I do not recall a Jewish home without a book on the table.
8563 USA/RALPH WALDO EMERSON/ESSAYIST	Be not the slave of your own past.
8564 ITALY/MACCHIAVELLI	History is written by the victors.
8565 CONFUCIUS/CHINA	Everything has its beauty but not everyone sees it.
8566 DIANE BRADY/MODEL/ USA/BLOOMBERG	**Tyra Banks:** "For me, finance is intimidating. When the chalkboard starts to look like Einstein's chalkboard, I'm like, "whoa!""
8567 CHARLES DE GAULE/ FRENCH PRESIDENT	How can anyone govern a nation that has two hundred and forty-six different kinds of cheese?
8568 AN INDIAN PROVERB	A guilty conscience is an enemy in hiding.
8569 WILLIAM JENNINGS BRYAN/LAWYER/USA	If we have to give up either religion or education, we should give up education.
8570 bell hooks/USA/ WRITER/ PROFESSOR	One of the most subversive institutions in the United States is the public library.
8571 AYN RAND/WRITER/ PHILOSOPHER	All life is purposeful struggle, and your only choice is the choice of a goal.
8572 ESSO GASOLINE	Put a tiger in your tank.

NUMBER CATEGORY/CREDIT	TOPIC
8573 UK/NURSE/FLORENCE NIGHTINGALE	I attribute my success to this – I never gave or took any excuse.
8574 PUBLILIUS SYRUS	Even a single hair casts its shadow.
8575 AN INDIAN PROVERB	A thief is a thief; it matters not he steals a diamond or a cucumber.
8576 UK/W. SOMERSET MAUGHAM/NOVELIST	A mother only does her children harm if she makes them the only concern of her life.
8577 THE TALMUD	When a scholar goes to seek out a bride he should take along an ignoramus as an expert.
8578 JOSEPH HELLER/USA	Every writer I know has trouble writing.
8579 FRENCH/SIMONE DE BEAUVOIR/NOVELIST	Few tasks are more like the torture of Sisyphus than housework, with its endless repetition…The housewife wears herself out marking time; she makes nothing, simply perpetuates the present.
8580 SUN TZU/CHINA/THE ART OF WAR	To a surrounded enemy, you must leave a way of escape.
8581 EMILY DICKINSON/USA	Because I could not stop for Death – He kindly stopped for me---
8582 VOLTAIRE/FRENCH PHILOSOPHER	What can be more absurd than choosing to carry a burden that one really wants to throw to the ground?
8583 MUSINGS/DAILY YOMIURI/JAPAN	"Suki nokoshi" -- …refers to putting off eating your favorite food so you can relish it slowly later.
8584 THINKER/GEORG WILHELM HEGEL	Education is the art of making man ethical.
8585 SENECA/DRAMATIST	It is pleasant at times to play the madman.
8586 ITALY/ MACCHIAVELI/ DIPLOMAT/WRITER	It is not titles that honor men, but men that honor titles.
8587 FUN/ANIMAL CRUELTY	Dog (greyhound) racing: dogs race on a track by chasing a lure
8588 CLARA BARTON/USA/ NURSE	Everybody's business is nobody's business, and nobody's business is my business.
8589 INTOLERANCE/ JUSTICE	Moral vigilantes: people who take it upon themselves to police what is right or wrong in the public sphere
8590 CONFUCIUS/CHINA/ SAGE	There are three friends that do good…The friends that do good are a straight friend, a sincere friend, and a friend who has heard much.
8591 VIRGINIA WOOLF/UK	For most of history, Anonymous was a woman.
8592 CHILDREN/SLEEP	Best bedtime for children
8593 HAPPY DAYS/ TELEVISION/ FONZ	Jumping the shark – the point after which something that was popular begins to decline in popularity or relevance
8594 JIM ROHN/USA/	You've got to have more than one skill.
8595 FRANCIS BACON/ UK/WRITER	Reading maketh a full man, conference a ready man, and writing an exact man.
8596 PAT FORDE/GAMES' SADDEST SIGHT	This is the hard reality of the Olympics and sports in general. For everyone it lifts up in victory, it dashes others to defeat.
8597 INSOMNIA	Use of sleeping pills
8598 JOSEPH HELLER/ WRITER/CATCH-22	Some men are born mediocre, some men achieve mediocrity, and some men have mediocrity thrust upon them.

NUMBER CATEGORY/CREDIT	TOPIC
8599 GEORG BERNARD SHAW/ WRITER/IRISH	He who has never hoped can never despair.
8600 HILLARY CLINTON/ USA/POLITICIAN	Every president, if you watch what they look like when they come into office, you can se their hair turn white because it's such a hard job.
8601 MARCEL PROUST/ FRENCH NOVELIST	Let us leave pretty women to men with no imagination.
8602 MARCEL PROUST/ FRENCH NOVELIST	Desire makes everything blossom; possession makes everything wither and fade.
8603 BENJAMIN CARDOZO/ AMERICAN JUDGE	Justice is not to be taken by storm. She is to be wooed by slow advances.
8604 USA/GEN. WILLIAM WESTMORELAND	The military don't start wars. Politicians start wars.
8605 JAMES FREEMAN CLARKE/USA	A politician thinks of the next election, a statesman of the next generation.
8606 MARIO CUOMO/USA	You campaign in poetry; you govern in prose.
8607 WINSTON CHURCHILL/ UK/PRIME MINISTER	The future is unknowable but the past gives us hope.
8608 PATTI SMITH/USA/ MUSICIAN	Pollution travels across borders, but we don't want to be joined by chemicals or tainted water...We want to be joined by positive communication and clean water.
8609 NELSON MANDELA/ PRESIDENT/S. AFRICA	As I walked out the door toward my freedom I knew that if I did not leave all the anger, hatred and bitterness behind, that I would still be in prison.
8610 ALBERT EINSTEIN/ PHYSICIST/NOBELIST	Only a life lived for others is a life worthwhile.
8611 STEPHEN HAWKING/ BRITISH SCIENTIST	I have noticed even people who claim everything is predestined, and that we can do nothing to change it, look before they cross the road.
8612 SCOTT TUROW/USA/ WRITER	The law, for all its failings, has a noble goal - to make the little bit of life that people can actually control more just.
8613 MARK TWAIN/USA/ WRITER/HUMORIST	College is a place where a professor's lecture notes go straight to the students' lecture notes, without passing through the brains of either.
8614 CONFUCIUS/CHINA	Have no friends not equal to yourself.
8615 JONATHAN SWIFT/ WRITER/ANGLO-IRISH	Vision is the art of seeing things invisible.
8616 YANNIC NOAH/ FRENCH/TENNIS	I have always considered tennis as a combat in an arena between two gladiators who have their racquets and their courage as their weapons.
8617 UNIVERSE	The wonder of the universe
8618 JOHN ADAMS/USA/ 2ND PRESIDENT	As much as I converse with sages and heroes, they have very little of my love and admiration, I long for the rural and domestic scene, for the warbling of birds and the prattling of my children.
8619 SAM GOLDWYN/USA/ MOVIE PRODUCER	If you want to send a message, use Western Union.
8620 KAHLIL GIBRAN/ON CRIME/PUNISHMENT	And if it is a despot you would dethrone, see first that his throne erected within you is destroyed.
8621 ALEX HALEY/WRITER/ USA	Find the good and praise it.

NUMBER CATEGORY/CREDIT	TOPIC
8622 USA/ALEX HAMILTON/ POLITICIAN	He who stands for nothing will fall for anything.
8623 MAHATMA GANDHI/ INDIAN LEADER/NON-VIOLENCE	Your beliefs become your thoughts, Your thoughts become your words, Your words become your actions, Your actions become your habits, Your habits become your values, Your values become your destiny
8624 STEPHEN HAWKING/ BRITISH SCIENTIST/ AUTHOR	There is a fundamental difference between religion, which is based on authority, and science, which is based on observation and reason. Science will win because it works.
8625 UK/WRITER/WILLIAM SHAKESPEARE/	I dare do all that may become a man; Who dares do more, is none.
8626 ANITA RODDICK/ BUSINESS	If you think you're too small to have an impact, try going to bed with a mosquito in the room.
8627 STEVE MARABOLI/ AUTHOR	The universe doesn't give you what you ask for with your thoughts - it gives you what you demand with your actions.
8628 SAUL BELLOW/USA/ NOVELIST	You can spend the entire second half of your life recovering from the mistakes of the first half.
8629 MACBETH/WILLIAM SHAKESPEARE	Look like the innocent flower, But be the serpent under it.
8630 STEPHEN HAWKING/UK	Intelligence is the ability to adapt to change.
8631 JAMES FREEMAN CLARKE/USA	We are either progressing or retrograding all the while. There is no such thing as remaining stationary in life.
8632 MARCEL PROUST/ FRENCH NOVELIST	There is no one, no matter how wise he is, who has not in his youth said things or done things that are so unpleasant to recall in later life that he would expunge them entirely from his memory if that were possible.
8633 BRIAN TRACY/USA/ WRITER/COACH	The highest goal you can have for yourself is to become a leader, to become an outstanding man or woman who is looked up to, admired and respected by the people around you.
8634 ANDREW CARNEGIE/USA	There is little success where there's little laughter.
8635 MARCEL PROUST/ FRENCH NOVELIST	It is often hard to bear the tears that we ourselves have caused.
8636 USA/TALLULAH BANKHEAD/ACTRESS	It's the good girls who keep diaries; the bad girls never have the time.
8637 ITALY/NICCOLO MACHIAVELLI/ DIPLOMAT	A prudent man should always follow in the path trodden by great men and imitate those who are most excellent, so that if he does not attain their greatness, at any rate he will get some tinge of it.
8638 BENJAMIN DISRAELI/ BRITISH STATESMAN	As a general rule the most successful man in life is the man who has the best information.
8639 THE TALMUD	He that gives should never remember, he that receives should never forget.
8640 PERSONALITY	Blood type
8641 WILLIAM FAULKNER/ USA/NOVELIST	Never be afraid to raise your voice for honesty and truth and compassion against injustice and lying and greed. If people all over the world...would do this, it would change the earth.

NUMBER CATEGORY/CREDIT	TOPIC
8642 ROBERT GATES/USA/ WAPO	If history – and religion – teach us anything, it is that there will always be evil in the world.
8643 FRAN LEBOWITZ/ USA/AUTHOR	I never took hallucinogenic drugs because I never wanted my consciousness expanded one unnecessary iota.
8644 MARCEL PROUST/ FRENCH NOVELIST	One cannot change, that is to say become a different person, while continuing to acquiesce to the feelings of the person one has ceased to be.
8645 PUBLILIUS SYRUS	It is only the ignorant who despise education.
8646 CINDY CRAWFORD/USA	Nobody in my family ever thought that I'd be a model.
8647 SPENCER WELLS/ TED.COM	DNA ties us all together; we share ancestry with barracuda and bacteria and mushrooms, if you go far enough back.
8648 YO YO MA/USA/ MUSICIAN	I think it's just as important to play new instruments as to play new pieces. The old ones are getting scarcer and the new ones more and more wonderful.
8649 NATIVE INDIAN SAYING	Even a small mouse has anger.
8650 CHRISTOPHER NORTH/ LITERARY CRITIC	Laws were made to be broken.
8651 G.B. SHAW/WRITER	He who can, does. He who cannot, teaches.
8652 JOYCE CAROL OATES/ US/NOVELIST	The third man in the ring makes boxing possible.
8653 EMILY DICKINSON/ USA/POET	There is no Frigate like a Book To take us Lands away
8654 UK/PM/WINSTON CHURCHILL	Although personally I am quite content with existing explosives, I feel we must not stand in the path of improvement.
8655 LOUIS L'AMOUR/ AMERICAN NOVELIST	I do not think much of ages. People are people. What does it matter how old or young they are? It is a category, and I do not like categories. It is a sort of pigeonhole or a label.
8656 AN INDIAN PROVERB	A book is a good friend when it lays bare the mistakes of the past.
8657 LAURENCE J. PETER/ CANADA/WRITER	An intelligence test sometimes shows a man how smart he would have been not to have taken it.
8658 CHINUA ACHEBE/ AFRICAN WRITER	When we gather together in the moonlit village ground it is not because of the moon. Every man can see it in his own compound. We come together because it is good for kinsmen to do so.
8659 WILLIAM COWPER/ UK/POET/THE TASK	Variety's the very spice of life, That gives it all its flavor.
8660 WILLIAM JAMES/ USA/PHILOSOPHER	Whenever you're in conflict with someone, there is one factor that can make the difference between damaging your relationship and deepening it. That factor is attitude.
8661 RAISA GORBACHEV/ FIRST LADY/RUSSIA	The maltreatment of the natural world and its impoverishment leads to the impoverishment of the human society. To save the natural world today means to save what is human in humanity.
8662 ISADORA DUNCAN/ AMERICAN DANCER	The finest inheritance you can give to a child is to allow it to make its own way, completely on its own feet.
8663 AMELIA EARHART/ USA /AVIATION	Women must try to do things as men have tried. When they fail, their failure must be but a challenge to others.

NUMBER CATEGORY/CREDIT	TOPIC
8664 DAILY YOMIURI/JAPAN/ HYAKUNIN ISSHU/ONE HUNDRED POETS...	Held back by a rock / The rapid flow / Is split up / But the waters Will eventually rejoin.
8665 A.A. MILNE/ENGLISH AUTHOR	Rivers know this: there is no hurry. We shall get there someday.
8666 WILL DURANT/USA/ HISTORIAN/WRITER	Every vice was once a virtue, and may become respectable again, just as hatred becomes respectable in wartime.
8667 UK/W. SOMERSET MAUGHAM/NOVELIST	American women expect to find in their husbands a perfection that English women only hope to find in their butlers.
8668 GALILEO GALILEI/ ITALIAN PHYSICIST	I think that in the discussion of natural problems we ought to begin not with the Scriptures, but with experiments, and demonstrations.
8669 LOU HOLTZ/USA/COACH	I can't believe that God put us on this earth to be ordinary.
8670 MORTIMER ADLER/ USA/WRITER	The person who says he knows what he thinks but cannot express it usually does not know what he thinks.
8671 CLASS MATTERS/ NY TIMES/USA/2005	In working-class life, people tell you things directly, they're not subtle.
8672 JOHN K. GALBRAITH/ ECONOMIST/USA	Meetings are indispensable when you don't want to do anything.
8673 ESSYIST/RALPH WALDO EMERSON/USA	No great man ever complains of want of opportunity.
8674 PLATO/GREEK AUTHOR	You are young, my son, and, as the years go by, time will change and even reverse many of your present opinions. Refrain therefore awhile from setting yourself up as a judge of the highest matters.
8675 DIANNA BOOHER/ AUTHOR/USA	People do pay attention to those with power to reward or punish them. But they enjoy being around those who are humble, willing to serve, and give them the proverbial time of day.
8676 GLENN LLOPIS/USA	Risk is always the gap between opportunity and success.
8677 PLATO/THE REPUBLIC	The people have always some champion whom they set over them and nurse into greatness...This and no other is the root from which a tyrant springs; when he first appears he is a protector.
8678 LETTER OF ADVICE TO QUEEN VICTORIA/LIN ZIXU LIN TSE-SHI/1839/ BRITISH OPIUM TRADE	...in the new regulations, in regard to those barbarians who bring opium to China, the penalty is fixed at decapitation or strangulation. This is what is called getting rid of a harmful thing on behalf of mankind.
8679 MARY BAKER EDDY/ CHRIISTIAN SCIENCE	I would no more quarrel with a man because of his religion than I would because of his art.
8680 AMELIA EARHART/ USA/AVIATION	A single act of kindness throws out roots in all directions, and the roots spring up and make new trees.
8681 JONATHAN SWIFT/ IRISH WRITER	Good manners is the art of making those people easy with whom we converse. Whoever makes the fewest people uneasy is the best bred in the room.
8682 KAHLIL GIBRAN/ LEBANESE POET	Coming generations will learn equality from poverty, and love from woes.
8683 STEVE JOBS/ APPLE FOUNDER	Didn't see it then, but it turned out that getting fired from Apple was the best thing that could have ever happened to me.

NUMBER CATEGORY/CREDIT	TOPIC
8684 SUN TZU/CHINA/ AUTHOR	And wherefore those skilled in war bring the enemy to the field of battle and are not brought there by him.
8685 THUCYDIDES/WRITER	The secret of happiness is freedom, and the secret of freedom is courage.
8686 FAMILY/ABUSE	Spousal abuse / domestic violence
8687 DR. SUSAN NEWMAN/ SOCIAL PSYCHOLOGIST	American parents are known for putting their children first. As a result, children overall feel and know they're special.
8688 DALE CARNEGIE/ USA/AUTHOR	There are always three speeches, for every one you actually gave. The one you practiced, the one you gave, and the one you wish you gave.
8689 SELF- REFLECTION	What are you most proud of in your life?
8690 RYO ISHIKAWA/JAPAN/ PROFESSIONAL GOLFER	As my social status in Japan is getting higher, I believe that it one of the responsibilities, to provide for those people who are in need.
8691 KAHLIL GIBRAN/POET	Say not, 'I have found the truth,' but rather, 'I have found a truth.'
8692 ALBERT JAY NOCK/ USA/AUTHOR/EDITOR	As sheer casual reading matter, I still find the English dictionary the most interesting book in our language.
8693 WRITER/FLORENCE NIGHTINGALE/UK	I think one's feelings waste themselves in words; they ought all to be distilled into actions which bring results.
8694 USA/ELBERT GREEN/ HUBBARD/WRITER	I believe that the universe is planned for good.
8695 ARTHUR C.CLARKE/UK	How inappropriate to call this planet Earth when it is clearly Ocean.
8696 TA-SUNKO-WITKO/USA/ CRAZY HORSE/SIOUX	One does not sell the earth upon which the people walk.
8697 HO CHI MINH/VIETNAM/ LEADER	Write in such a way that you can be readily understood by both the young and the old, by men as well as women, even by children.
8698 OSCAR WILDE/POET	When the gods wish to punish us, they answer our prayers.
8699 PHILLIP ADAMS/ JOURNALIST	The most intense hatreds are not between political parties but within them.
8700 COMMON SAYING	What you fear, you create.
8701 MORTIMER ADLER/ USA/PHILOSOPHER	Aristotle uses a mother's love for her child as the prime example of love or friendship.
8702 MARCEL PROUST/ FRENCH NOVELIST	We must never be afraid to go too far, for truth lies beyond.
8703 G.B. SHAW/PLAYWRIGHT	Beware of false knowledge; it is more dangerous than ignorance.
8704 BOB MARLEY/REGGAE	The good times of today are the sad thoughts of tomorrow.
8705 MUHAMMAD ALI/USA/ BOXER	Champions are made from something they have deep inside them -- a desire, a dream, a vision.
8706 WILL ROGERS/USA	I don't make jokes. I just watch the government and report the facts.
8707 PROVERB	Beggars can't be choosers.
8708 HERODOTUS/HISTORY	Force has no place where there is need of skill.
8709 HOMELESSNESS	Vehicular homeless
8710 R.L. STEVENSON/SCOT	Everybody, soon or late, sits down to a banquet of consequences
8711 ECONOMY/1929- 1931	The Great Depression
8712 ALEX HALEY/USA/ WRITER	Anytime you see a turtle up on top of a fence post, you know he had some help.

NUMBER CATEGORY/CREDIT	TOPIC
8713 UK/PM/WINSTON CHURCHILL	There is only one thing worse than fighting with allies and that is fighting without them.
8714 JOHN WOODEN/USA/ BASKETBALL COACH	Make each day your masterpiece.
8715 KINGSLEY AMIS/UK/ NOVELIST	Laziness has become the chief characteristic of journalism, displacing incompetence.
8716 RALPH NADER/USA	A society that has more justice is a society that needs less charity.
8717 WILLIAM PENN/UK	Our law says it well, "To delay justice, is injustice."
8718 FRAN LEBOWITZ/ AMERICAN AUTHOR	If you are a dog and your owner suggests that you wear a sweater, suggest that he wear a tail.
8719 PETER DRUCKER/ MANAGEMENT	Unless commitment is made, there are only promises and hopes...but no plans.
8720 PUBLILIUS SYRUS	Be your money's master, not its slave.
8721 ALBERT EINSTEIN/ PHYSICIST	I am by heritage a Jew, by citizenship a Swiss, and by makeup a human being, and only a human being, without any special attachment to any state or national entity whatsoever.
8722 MARCEL PROUST/ FRENCH NOVELIST	Illness is the doctor to whom we pay most heed; to kindness, to knowledge, we make promise only; pain we obey.
8723 GEORGE BERNARD SHAW/WRITER	Take care to get what you like or you will be forced to like what you get.
8724 GERMAN/FRIEDRICH NIETZSCHE/THINKER	A pair of powerful spectacles has sometimes sufficed to cure a person in love.
8725 HUMANITY/SURVIVAL	Food security
8726 PRESIDENT DWIGHT D. EISENHOWER/USA	In war there is no substitute for victory.
8727 DR. SUSAN NEWMAN/ SOCIAL PSYCHOLOGIST	Anytime you hit or spank a child, you are teaching them that's acceptable behavior.
8728 LOUIS L'AMOUR/USA/ NOVELIST	You stick your finger in the water and you pull it out, and that is how much of a hole you leave when you're gone.
8729 GOALS/EFFORT	An uphill battle
8730 PAMELA DRUCKERMAN/ AUTHOR/PARENTING	Authority is one of the most impressive parts of French parenting. Their kids actually listen to them.
8731 FRESHMAN 15/ WEIGHT GAIN	Freshman 15: college weight gain that often afflicts new university students.
8732 MARGARET MEAD/ USA/ANTHROPOLOGIST	A small group of thoughtful people could change the world. Indeed, it's the only thing that ever has.
8733 JOAN OF ARC/FRENCH/ FIGHTER	I was admonished to adopt feminine clothes; I refused and still refuse. As for other avocations of women, there are plenty of other women to perform them.
8734 TINA SEELIG/USA/ ENTREPRENEUR	According to Nielsen Bookscan, of the approximately 1.2 million different books in print in 2004, only 25,000, or 2 percent, sold more than 5,000 copies...
8735 PUBLILIUS SYRUS	Do not turn back when you are just at the goal.
8736 SOPHOCLES/THINKER	I cannot recommend a rigid spirit.

NUMBER CATEGORY/CREDIT	TOPIC
8737 DANIEL WEBSTER/USA/ SENATOR	If all my possessions were taken from me with one exception, I would choose to keep the power of communication, for by it I would soon regain all the rest.
8738 YO YO MA/ AMERICAN MUSICIAN	I learn something not because I have to, but because I really want to. That's the same view I have for performing. I'm performing because I really want to, not because I have to bring bread back home.
8739 PAUL DICKSON/USA/ WRITER	Rowe's Rule: the odds are five to six that the light at the end of the tunnel is the headlight of an oncoming train.
8740 CINDY CRAWFORD/USA	I believe you can have it all, just not at the same time.
8741 RABBI HILLEL/ JEWISH LEADER	What is hateful to you, do not do to another. That is the whole law. The rest is commentary.
8742 DAILY YOMIURI/JAPAN/ ADVICE/HIDEO ISHII	A newspaper article is like *sumigara* (cinder). Like cinders in a stove, newspaper will be thrown away tomorrow...But they'll have kept people's hearts warm all day and all night.
8743 HENRY LOUIS GATES/ USA/EDUCATOR	Learning to sing one's own songs, to trust the particular cadences of one's own voice, is also the goal of any writer.
8744 GEORGE ORWELL/ BRITISH AUTHOR	To survive it is often necessary to fight and to fight you have to dirty yourself.
8745 MARK TWAIN/USA	A person who won't read has no advantage over one who can't.
8746 MARCEL PROUST/ FRENCH NOVELIST	A change in the weather is sufficient to recreate the world and ourselves.
8747 INTERNET/HOAXES	The spread of misinformation online
8748 HOPI PROVERB	One finger cannot lift a pebble.
8749 W. SOMERSET MAUGHAM/UK/ DRAMATIST	An author spends months writing a book, and maybe puts his heart's blood into it, and then it lies about unread till the reader has nothing else in the world to do.
8750 VOLTAIRE/FRENCH WRITER/ CANDIDE	...when man was put into the garden of Eden, he was put there with the idea that he should work the land; and this proves that man was not born to be idle.
8751 MARK PAGEL/TEDTALK/ LANGUAGE/	It might be inevitable that we have to confront the idea that our destiny is to be one world with one language.
8752 HANS SELYE/CANADA/ MEDICAL DOCTOR	If you want to live a long life, focus on making contributions.
8753 JULIA BACHA/TEDTALK/ NONVIOLENCE	Violent resistance and nonviolent resistance share one very important thing in common: They are both a form of theater seeking an audience to their cause.
8754 HATE GROUPS	Neo-Nazis
8755 DAPHNE ZUNIGA/ AMERICAN ACTRESS	The planet does nothing but support us, and we are constantly committing crimes against nature.
8756 ALBERT EINSTEIN/ PHYSICIST	I do not know how the Third World War will be fought, but I can tell you what they will use in the Fourth – rocks!
8757 R.W. EMERSON/USA	T'is the good reader that makes the good book.
8758 USA/ANAIS NIN/ AUTHOR	When we blindly adopt a religion, a political system, a literary dogma, we become automatons. We cease to grow.
8759 MARRIAGE/DEBATE	Hateful mothers-in-law: myth or reality?

NUMBER CATEGORY/CREDIT	TOPIC
8760 SIDNEY POITIER/USA	A person doesn't have to change who he is to become better.
8761 ERIC SCHMIDT/GOOGLE	The one thing you can do with bad people is shame them.
8762 ERNEST HEMINGWAY	Write drunk; edit sober.
8763 FRAN LEBOWITZ/ AMERICAN AUTHOR	Remember that as a teenager you are at the last stage of your life when you will be happy to hear that the phone is for you.
8764 DEBATE	Stealing from your friends and family is worse than stealing from strangers.
8765 FREDERICK S. PERLS/ PSYCHIATRIST/ GESTALT THERAPY	I do my thing, and you do your thing. I am not in this world to live up to your expectations. And you are not in this world to live up to mine. You are you and I am I, And if by chance we find each other, it's beautiful; If not, it can't be helped.
8766 P.W. SINGER/TED.COM/ US/POLITICAL SCIENTIST	Robots are emotionless, so they don't get upset if their buddy is killed, they don't commit crimes of rage and revenge.
8767 DIANNA BOOHER/USA/ AUTHOR	Your image can be tarnished irreparably when you use humor inappropriately.
8768 MUHAMMAD ALI/USA/ BOXER	Only a man who knows what it is like to be defeated can reach down to the bottom of his soul and come up with the extra ounce of power it takes to win when the match is even.
8769 LEE KUAN YEW/PM/ PM/SINGAPORE	Wrong ideas have to be challenged before they influence public opinion and make for problems.
8770 THE TALMUD	A person will be called to account on Judgment Day for every permissible thing he might have enjoyed but did not.
8771 GEORGE HERBERT/UK	One father is more than a hundred schoolmasters.
8772 MUHAMMAD ALI/USA/ BOXER	Often it isn't the mountains ahead that wear you out. It's the little pebble in your shoe.
8773 AMELIA EARHART/ USA/AVIATION	The most difficult thing is the decision to act, the rest is merely tenacity. The fears are paper tigers. You can do anything you decide to do
8774 WAYNE DYER/USA/ WRITER/MOTIVATION	It's never crowded along the extra mile.
8775 JOAN OF ARC/FRENCH/ LEADER	Children say that people are sometimes hung for telling the truth.
8776 DANISH/SOREN KIERKEGAARD/ PHILOSOPHER	During the first period of a man's life the greatest danger is not to take the risk. When once the risk has really been taken, then the greatest danger is to risk too much.
8777 FOOD	Genetic engineering
8778 ANTON CHEKHOV/ RUSSIAN WRITER	Advertising is the very essence of democracy.
8779 LAURA CARSTENSEN/ TEDTALK	When we recognize that we don't have all the time in the world, we see our priorities most clearly.
8780 SAMUEL JOHNSON/UK	A fishing rod is a stick with a hook at one end and a fool at the other.
8781 MARGARET ATWOOD/ CANADIAN NOVELIST	War is what happens when language fails.
8782 SIDNEY POITIER/USA	I've learned that I must find positive outlets for anger or it will destroy me.
8783 SOLON/ROMAN JUDGE	Reprove thy friend privately; commend him publicly.

NUMBER CATEGORY/CREDIT	TOPIC
8784 SOCIETY/AGE	Ageist society
8785 DALE CARNEGIE/USA/ WRITER/LECTURER	Remember that a person's name is, to that person, the sweetest and most important sound in any language.
8786 G.B. SHAW/WRITER	Assassination is the extreme form of censorship.
8787 REV. DR. IYANLA VANZANT/AUTHOR	Everything that happens to you is a reflection of what you believe about yourself.
8788 RABBI SHMULEY BOTEACH/USA	Girls who have regular family dinners with their parents are one-third less likely to develop unhealthy eating habits like anorexia or abuse diet pills.
8789 LOU HOLTZ/USA/ COACH	I never learn anything talking. I only learn things when I ask questions.
8790 JULIA WARD HOWE/ USA/MUSICIAN/ LYRICIST	I think nothing is religion which puts one individual absolutely above others, and surely nothing is religion which puts one sex above another.
8791 WILL DURANT/USA/ HISTORIAN	In my youth I stressed freedom, and in my old age I stress order. I have made the great discovery that liberty is a product of order.
8792 WRITER/FRANCOIS DE LA ROCHEFOUCAULD	We always like those who admire us; we do not always like those whom we admire.
8793 GORDON GECKO/USA/ WALLSTREET – MOVIE	Greed is good.
8794 ASHER HASAN/ MESSAGE OF PEACE FROM PAKISTAN	A rising tide lifts all boats. The rising tide of India's spectacular economic growth has lifted over 400 million Indians into a buoyant middle class; but there are still over 650 million Indians, Pakistanis, Sri Lankans, Bangladeshis, Nepalese, who remain washed up on the shores of poverty.
8795 SAMUEL JOHNSON/UK/ WRITER	Actions are visible, though motives are secret.
8796 ANTON CHEKHOV/ RUSSIA/WRITER	Any idiot can face a crisis – it's day-to-day living that wears you out.
8797 WILLIAM FAULKNER/ USA/WRITER	The past is never dead. It's not even past.
8798 BETTY FRIEDAN/USA/ FEMINIST/WRITER	Aging is not 'lost youth' but a new stage of opportunity and strength.
8799 SUN TZU/CHINA/ AUTHOR/THE ART OF WAR	Be extremely subtle, even to the point of formlessness. Be extremely mysterious, even to the point of soundlessness. Thereby you can be the director of the opponent's fate.
8800 USA/BOOKER T. WASHINGTON/ EDUCATOR	No man, who continues to add something to the material, intellectual and moral well-being of the place in which he lives, is left long without proper reward.
8801 WRITER/ARCHIBALD MacLEISH/USA	A real writer learns from earlier writers the way a boy learns from an apple orchard -- by stealing what he has a taste for, and can carry off.
8802 MARCEL PROUS/ FRENCH NOVELIST	Mystery is not about traveling to new places but about looking with new eyes.
8803 FIGHTING/IDIOM	Giving as good as one gets
8804 USA/RICHARD WILKINSON/WRITER	If Americans want to live the American dream, they should go to Denmark.

NUMBER CATEGORY/CREDIT	TOPIC
8805 MARCEL PROUST/ FRENCH NOVELIST	We do not include the pleasures we enjoy in sleep in the inventory of the pleasures we have experienced in the course of our existence.
8806 BENJAMIN CARDOZO/ USA/JUDGE	Membership in the bar is a privilege burdened with conditions.
8807 HOLIDAYS/FAMILY	Celebrating holidays with family members
8808 MUHAMMAD ALI/USA/ BOXER/SCHOOL	If they can make penicillin out of mouldy bread, then they can sure make something out of you.
8809 MARTIN SELIGMAN/US/ TED.COM	[Psychology] should be just as concerned with building strength as with repairing damage.
8810 DESMOND TUTU/ CLERGY/SOUTH AFRICA	When the missionaries came to Africa, they had the Bible and we had the land. They said, "Let us pray." We closed our eyes. When we opened them we had the Bible and they had the land.
8811 DANIEL J. BOORSTIN/ LIBRARIAN/CONGRESS	No agnostic ever burned anyone at the stake or tortured a pagan, a heretic, or an unbeliever.
8812 MARIO PUZO/THE GODFATHER/USA	Never hate your enemies. It affects your judgment.
8813 WILLIAM FAULKNER/ USA/NOVELIST	The man who removes a mountain begins by carrying away small stones.
8814 ELIZABETH KUBLER-ROSS/PSYCHIATRIST	I believe that we are solely responsible for our choices, and we have to accept the consequences of every deed, word, and thought throughout our lifetime.
8815 DANIEL J. BOORSTIN/US	Education is learning what you didn't even know you didn't know.
8816 DANIEL J. BOORSTIN/ LIBRARIAN/WRITER	We expect our two-week vacations to be romantic, exotic, cheap, and effortless.
8817 MARCEL PROUST/ FRENCH NOVELIST	The best vaccine against anger is to watch others in its throes.
8818 AMELIA EARHART/ USA/AVIATION	Never do things others can do and will do, if there are things others cannot do or will not do.
8819 ZELDA FITZGERALD/ USA/WRITER/POET	Nobody has ever measured, not even poets, how much the heart can hold.
8820 DEBATE	Sometimes, it is all right to break the law
8821 ADVICE	Never confuse politeness with respect.
8822 J.K. ROWLING/UK/ WRITER	There is an expiry date on blaming your parents for steering you in the wrong direction. The moment you are old enough to take the wheel, the responsibility lies with you.
8823 ROHINTON MISTRY/A FINE BALANCE/INDIA/ CANADIAN WRITER	He who spits *paan* on the ceiling will only blind himself. (*paan (type of food chewed like a sweet, involving betel leaf wrapped around betel nut and spices)
8824 YOGA	Yoga for kids
8825 JOSEPH CAMPBELL/ USA/AUTHOR	I think the person who takes a job in order to live – that is to say, for the money – has turned himself into a slave.
8826 WRITER/F. SCOTT FITZGERALD/USA	Forgotten is forgiven.
8827 CHARLES LAMB/UK/	He is no lawyer who cannot take two sides.

NUMBER CATEGORY/CREDIT	TOPIC
8828 WILLIAM FAULKNER/ USA/NOVELIST	A writer needs three things, experience, observation, and imagination, any two of which, at times any one of which, can supply the lack of the others.
8829 CHEYENNE PROVERB	Beware of the man who does not talk, and the dog that does not bark.
8830 SOCIETY	Anti-semitism
8831 GALILEO GALILEI/ ITALIAN PHYSICIST	I have never met a man so ignorant that I couldn't learn something from him.
8832 NTOZAKE SHANGE/POET	Where there is woman there is magic.
8833 YO YO MA/US/MUSICIAN	Good things happen when you meet strangers.
8834 HOLIDAY/FUN	Preferred holiday activities
8835 ALBERT EINSTEIN/ PHYSICIST/TIMES/ LONDON	Today in Germany I am called a German man of science, and in England I am represented as a Swiss Jew. If I come to be regarded as a bête noire, the descriptions will be reversed, and I shall become a Swiss Jew for the Germans and a German man of science for the English.
8836 GRANDMA MOSES/ AMERICAN ARTIST	I look back on my life like a good day's work; it was done and I am satisfied with it.
8837 USA/HENRY DAVID THOREAU/WRITER	Be not simply good; be good for something.
8838 MUHAMMAD ALI/USA/ BOXER	Rivers, ponds, lakes, and streams -- they all have different names, but they all contain water. Just as religions do -- they all contain truths,
8839 RICHARD BACH/USA/ NOVELIST	Allow the world to live as it chooses, and allow yourself to live as you choose.
8840 DEBATE	Every classroom must have Internet access.
8841 LOU HOLTZ/USA/ COACH	I think everyone should experience defeat at least once during their career. You learn a lot from it.
8842 SIDNEY POITIER/USA/ ACTOR	Of all my father's teachings, the most enduring was the one about the true measure of a man. That true measure was how well he provided for his children, and it stuck with me as if it were etched in my brain.
8843 USA/DWIGHT D. EISENHOWER/ 39TH PRESIDENT	I would rather try to persuade a man to go along, because once I have persuaded him he will stick. If I scare him, he will stay just as long as he is scared, and then he is gone.
8844 MARCEL PROUST/ FRENCH NOVELIST	The creation of the world did not occur at the beginning of time; it occurs every day.
8845 DESMOND TUTU/SOUTH AFRICA/CLERGY	We may be surprised at the people we find in heaven. God has a soft spot for sinners. His standards are quite low.
8846 WILLIAM J. BRENNAN JR./AMERICAN JUDGE	There are no menial jobs., only menial attitudes.
8847 MARGARET MEAD/ USA/ANTHROPOLOGIST	A city is a place where there is no need to wait for next week to get the answer to a question, to taste the food of any country, to find new voices to listen to and familiar ones to listen to again.
8848 IDIOM	Having a thick skin
8849 USA/ABRAHAM LINCOLN/PRESIDENT	It has been my experience that folks who have no vices have very few virtues.
8850 JULES VERNE/ FRENCH/WRITER	Science is eminently perfectible...each theory has constantly to give way to a fresh one.
8851 SENECA/DRAMATIST	Unjust dominion cannot be eternal.

NUMBER CATEGORY/CREDIT	TOPIC
8852 SUSAN SONTAG/USA/WRITER	Today everything exists to end in a photograph.
8853 GERMAN/KARL VON CLAUSEWITZ/LEADER	War is the realm of uncertainty; three-quarters of the factors on which action is based are wrapped in a fog of greater or lesser uncertainty.
8854 MARCUS TULLIUS CICERO/ORATOR	Natural ability without education has more often attained to glory and virtue than education without natural ability.
8855 USA/CHARLIE "BIRD" PARKER/SAXOPHONIST	If you don't live it, it won't come out of your horn.
8856 JULIA WARD HOWE/USA/MUSICIAN	When I see the elaborate study and ingenuity displayed by women in the pursuit of trifles, I feel no doubt of their capacity for the most herculean undertakings.
8857 EDUCATION	Scholarships
8858 ANATOLE FRANCE/FRENCH NOVELIST	It is only the poor who pay cash, and that not from virtue, but because they are refused credit.
8859 SUSAN SONTAG/USA/WRITER	A writer, I think, is someone who pays attention to the world.
8860 BOOKER WASHINGTON	Character is power.
8861 SUSAN SONTAG/USA/WRITER	Attention is vitality. It connects you with others. Stay eager.
8862 SUSAN SONTAG/USA/WRITER	We are told we must choose -- the old and the new. In fact, we must choose both. What is a life if not a series of negotiations between the old and the new?
8863 WILLIAM JENNINGS BRYAN/USA/LAWYER	All the ills from which America suffers can be traced to the teaching of evolution.
8864 KEN SARO-WIWA/NIGERIA/WRITER	The writer cannot be a mere storyteller; he cannot be a mere teacher; he cannot merely X-ray society's weaknesses, its ills, its perils. He or she must be actively involved in shaping its present and its future.
8865 UK/PM/WINSTON CHURCHILL	Continual effort – not strength or intelligence – is the key to unlocking our potential.
8866 DR. ALFRED ADLER/AUSTRIA/PSYCHIATRIST	It is easier to fight for one's principles than to live up to them.
8867 USA/HENRY DAVID THOREAU/WRITER	A man is rich in proportion to the number of things he can afford to let alone.
8868 SUSAN SONTAG/USA/WRITER	To paraphrase several sages: Nobody can think and hit someone at the same time.
8869 LIFE EXPERIENCE	What I do know for sure.
8870 G.K. CHESTERTON/UK/WRITER	The Christian ideal has not been tried and found wanting; it has been found difficult and left untried.
8871 GALILEO GALILEI/SCIENTIST/ITALY	The sun, with all those planets revolving around it and dependent on it, can still ripen a bunch of grapes as if it had nothing else in the universe to do.
8872 VIRGINIA WOOLF/BRITISH AUTHOR	Each has his past shut in him like the leaves of a book known to him by his heart, and his friends can only read the title.
8873 RAISING MONEY	Online fund-raising / Crowdfunding
8874 EMILY BRONTE/UK	Honest people don't hide their deeds.

NUMBER CATEGORY/CREDIT	TOPIC
8875 RIGHTS/DISABILITY	Universal access for people with physical challenges
8876 THUCYDIDES/HISTORIAN	You should punish in the same manner those who commit crimes with those who accuse falsely.
8877 MARIO PUZO/FRANCIS FORD COPPOLA/THE GODFATHER	You cannot say 'no' to the people you love, not often. That's the secret. And then when you do, it has to sound like a 'yes'. Or you have to make them say 'no.' You have to take time and trouble.
8878 WARREN G. BENNIS/USA	The manager accepts the status quo; the leader challenges it.
8879 SENECA/ROMAN DRAMATIST	You can tell the character of every man when you see how he receives praise.
8880 RICHARD BACH/USA	Argue for your limitations, and sure enough they're yours.
8881 MARGUERITE DURAS/FR.	In love there are no vacations.
8882 PEARL BUCK/USA/NOVELIST	I don't wait for moods. You accomplish nothing if you do that. Your mind must know it has got to get down to work.
8883 LOVE/ADMIRATION	The one person you are willing to "take a bullet for."
8884 JESSYE NORMAN/USA/OPERA SINGER	Pigeon holes are only comfortable for pigeons.
8885 USA/NATHANIEL HAWTHORNE/WRITER	The world owes all its onward impulses to men ill at ease. The happy man inevitably confines himself within ancient limits.
8886 USA/RUTH BADER GINSBURG/JUDGE	Dissents speak to a future age.
8887 PUBLILIUS SYRUS	It is not every question that deserves an answer.
8888 GEORGE SANTAYANA/PHILOSOPHER/POET	It is always pleasant to be urged to do something on the ground that one can do it well.
8889 PUBLILIUS SYRUS	It is more tolerable to be refused than deceived.
8890 CORAZON AQUINO/PHILIPPINES/WOMAN	Politics must not remain a bastion of male dominance, for there is much that women can bring into politics that would make our world a kinder, gentler, place for humanity to thrive in.
8891 CHIMAMANDA NGOZI ADICHIE/NIGERIA/WRITER	I recently spoke at a university where a student told me it was such a shame that Nigerian men were physical abusers like the father character in my novel. I told him that I had recently read a novel called American Psycho, and that it was such a shame that young Americans were serial murderers.
8892 MORTIMER ADLER/USA/PHILOSOPHER	Ask others about themselves, at the same time, be on guard not to talk too much about yourself.
8893 FELIX FRANKFURTER/USA/JUDGE	Old age and sickness bring out the essential characteristics of a man.
8894 OSCAR WILDE/IRISH WRITER/POET	Most people are other people. Their thoughts are someone else's opinions, their lives a mimicry, their passions a quotation.
8895 KONRAD ADENAUER/GERMAN CHANCELLOR	History is the sum total of all the things that could have been avoided.
8896 ITALY/ST. FRANCIS OF ASSISI/CATHOLIC	The deeds you do may be the only sermon some persons will hear today.
8897 USA/NATHANIEL HAWTHORNE/WRITER	Words -- so innocent and powerless, as they are standing in a dictionary, how potent for good and evil they become in the hands of one who knows how to combine them.

NUMBER CATEGORY/CREDIT	TOPIC
8898 LOU HOLTZ/USA/ COACH	If you burn your neighbor's house down, it doesn't make your house look any better.
8899 MILITARY	Boot camp
8900 SUSAN SONTAG/USA/ WRITER	The only interesting ideas are heresies.
8901 SOCRATES	Envy is the ulcer of the soul.
8902 RALPH NADER/USA/ LAWYER	John D. Rockefeller wanted to dominate oil, but Microsoft wants it all, you name it; cable, media, banking, car dealerships.
8903 TAMAR LEWIN/NYTIMES	A lot of college teaching is not very good, and everybody knows it.
8904 RICHARD DAWKINS/ BIOLOGIST/AUTHOR	Religion is about turning untested belief into unshakable truth through the power of institutions and the passage of time.
8905 KEN ROBINSON/UK/ TED.COM	We are educating people out of their creative capacities.
8906 WILL DURANT/UK/ HISTORIAN	Inquiry is fatal to certainty.
8907 DENIS DIDEROT/ FRENCH THINKER	One can fool some men, or fool all men in some places and times but one cannot fool all men in all places and ages.
8908 ESSAYIST/RALPH WALDO EMERSON/USA	To be great is to be misunderstood.
8909 FITNESS/HOME	Fitness equipment in the home
8910 ROBERT MCCRUM/UK	Literature is theft.
8911 PETER DRUCKER/ MANAGEMENT	No institution can possibly survive if it needs geniuses or supermen to manage it. It must be organized in such a way as to be able to get along under a leadership composed of average human beings.
8912 ABDUL KALAM/ INDIA/PRESIDENT	God, our Creator, has stored within our minds and personalities, great potential strength and ability. Prayer helps us tap and develop these powers.
8913 HERODOTUS/ANCIENT GREEK HISTORIAN	He is the best man who, when making his plans, fears and reflects on everything that can happen to him, but in the moment of action is bold.
8914 JOHN DOS PASSOS/ USA/NOVELIST	With people who are young and aren't scared you can do lots.
8915 CLARENCE DARROW/ AMERICAN LAWYER	History repeats itself, and that's one of the things that's wrong with history.
8916 PRESIDENT DWIGHT D. EISENHOWER/USA	When you are in any contest you should work as if there were – to the very last minute – a chance to lose it.
8917 BERTRAND RUSSELL/ UK/PHILOSOPHER	It is the preoccupation with possessions, more than anything else that prevents us from living freely and nobly.
8918 ROHINTON MISTRY/ INDIA/CANADA/WRITER	After all, our lives are but a sequence of accidents – a clanking chain of chance events.
8919 WRITER/ARCHIBALD MacLEISH/USA	There is only one thing more painful than learning from experience, and that is not learning from experience.
8920 HISTORY/GEOGRAPHY	Hunter-gatherer tribes
8921 ALICIA KEYS/USA/ MUSICIAN	Hand me the world on a silver platter, and what good would it be?

NUMBER CATEGORY/CREDIT	TOPIC
8922 ST. FRANCIS OF ASSISI/ CATHOLIC FRIAR	Start by doing what is necessary, then what is possible, and suddenly you are doing the impossible.
8923 USA/NATHANIEL HAWTHORNE/WRITER	...people always grow more foolish, unles they take care to grow wiser and wiser.
8924 USA/NATHANIEL HAWTHORNE/WRITER	The wrong-doing of one generation lives into the successive ones.
8925 TED PERRY/USA/WRITER	The earth does not belong to man; man belongs to the earth.
8926 SOCRATES/THINKER	If a man is proud of his wealth, he should not be praised until it is known how he employs it.
8927 EMILY BRONTE/UK/ NOVELIST	If I could I would always work in silence and obscurity, and let my efforts be known by their results.
8928 JAY McINERNEY/USA/ WRITER/FOOD CRITIC	I like the fact that I'm living in the world rather than in a university.
8929 OVID/ROMAN POET	Chance is always powerful. Let your hook be always cast; in the pool where you least expect it, there will be a fish.
8930 GERMAN/G.W.F. HEGEL/ PHILOSOPHER	Genuine tragedies in the world are not conflicts between right and wrong. They are conflicts between two rights.
8931 GALILEO GALILEI/ ITALIAN PHYSICIST	All truths are easy to understand once they are discovered; the point is to discover them.
8932 CHINESE PROVERB	He who cannot in his own house entertain a guest, when abroad will find few to entertain him.
8933 DAVID SUZUKI/CANADA/ SCIENTIST	We're in a giant car heading towards a brick wall and everyone's arguing over where they're going to sit.
8934 SENECA/ROMAN DRAMATIST	It is a great thing to know the season for speech and the season for silence.
8935 HEALTH	Laughter is the best medicine
8936 GERMAN/ARTHUR SCHOPENHAUER	The doctor sees all the weakness of mankind; the lawyer all the wickedness, the theologian all the stupidity.
8937 ELIA KAZAN/USA/ WRITER/ACTOR	The first thing you should do with an actor is not sign a contract with him. Take him to dinner. And take him for a walk afterwards.
8938 HARUKI MURAKAMI/ JAPAN/WRITER	If you only read the books that everyone else is reading, you can only think what everyone else is thinking.
8939 ALBERT EINSTEIN/ PHYSICIST	The unleashed power of the atom has changed everything except our modes of thinking and we thus drift toward unparalleled catastrophe.
8940 PSYCHOLOGY	Bystander effect (as the number of bystanders rises, the probability of an individual helping a person in trouble decreases)
8941 JONATHAN SWIFT/ IRISH WRITER	A man should never be ashamed to own that he has been in the wrong, which is but saying...that he is wiser today than yesterday.
8942 WRITER/ROBERT LOUIS STEVENSON	Compromise is the best and cheapest lawyer.
8943 H.L. MENCKEN/USA	Every decent man is ashamed of the government he lives under.
8944 BILL GATES/USA/ ENTREPRENEUR	Your most unhappy customers are your greatest source of learning.
8945 JEAN SIBELIUS/FINNISH COMPOSER	Pay no attention to what the critics say. A statue has never been erected in honor of a critic.

NUMBER CATEGORY/CREDIT	TOPIC
8946 NATIVE AMERICAN SAYING	It is less of a problem to be poor, than to be dishonest.
8947 E.L. DOCTOROW/USA/ AUTHOR	Planning to write is not writing. Outlining, researching, talking to people about what you're doing, none of that is writing. Writing is writing.
8948 KAHLIL GIBRAN/ LEBANESE POET	Your living is determined not so much by what life brings to you as by the attitude you bring to life; not so much by what happens to you as by the way your mind looks at what happens.
8949 HEGEL/PHILOSOPHER	Nothing great has ever been accomplished without passion.
8950 RABBI HILLEL/ JEWISH LEADER	If I am not for myself, then who will be for me? And if I am only for myself, then what am I? And if not now, when?
8951 STEPHEN KING/USA/ AUTHOR	Only enemies speak the truth; friends and lovers lie endlessly, caught in the web of duty.
8952 USA/BOOKER T. WASHINGTON	Associate yourself with people of good quality, for it is better to be alone than in bad company.
8953 NATURE/PROTECTION	Nature reserve
8954 AN INDIAN PROVERB	A man without money in his pocket is like a bow without arrows.
8955 GEORGE ORWELL/UK/ WRITER	War is evil, but it is often the lesser evil.
8956 DR. DANIEL G. AMEN/ PHYSICIAN/USA	To feel successful, you must be able to be honest about the things that are really important to you.
8957 RALPH NADER/ AMERICAN LAWYER	People are stunned to hear that one company has data files on 185 million Americans.
8958 MAURICE SENDAK/USA/ WRITER	Art has always been my salvation.
8959 SAMUEL JOHNSON/ UK/LEXICOGRAPHER	All travel has its advantages. If the passenger visits better countries, he may learn to improve his own. And if fortune carries him to worse, he may learn to enjoy it.
8960 NATIONAL ENQUIRER/ MAGAZINE/SLOGAN/USA	Enquiring minds want to know.
8961 NOBEL/USA/RICHARD P. FEYNMAN/PHYSICIST	I learned very early the difference between knowing the name of something and knowing something.
8962 AYN RAND/WRITER/ PHILOSOPHER	The man who lets a leader prescribe his course is a wreck being towed to the scrap heap.
8963 BERTRAND RUSSELL/ BRITISH AUTHOR	Of all forms of caution, caution in love is perhaps the most fatal to true happiness.
8964 WILLIAM JAMES/USA/ PHILOSOPHER	When you have to make a choice and don't make it, that in itself a choice.
8965 LAURA BUSH/1st LADY/USA	The power of a book lies in its power to turn a solitary act into a shared vision. As long as we have books, we are not alone.
8966 ABDUL KALAM/ INDIA/PRESIDENT	If a country is to be corruption free and become a nation of beautiful minds, I strongly feel there are three key societal members who can make a difference. They are the father, the mother and the teacher
8967 JEAN SIBELIUS/MUSIC/ FINNISH COMPOSER	Music begins where the possibilities of language end.

NUMBER CATEGORY/CREDIT	TOPIC
8968 IYANLA VANZANT/ AUTHOR/LIFE COACH	The only way to get what you really want is to let go of what you don't want.
8969 TENNESSEE WILLIAMS/ USA/WRITER	If I got rid of my demons, I'd lose my angels.
8970 SHERRY TURKLE/USA/ PROFESSOR/TED.COM	If we're not able to be alone, we're going to be more lonely. And if we don't teach our children to be alone, they're only going to know how to be lonely.
8971 TENNESSEE WILLIAMS/ USA/WRITER	There comes a time when you look into the mirror and you realize that what you see is all that you will ever be. And then you accept it. Or you kill yourself. Or you stop looking in mirrors.
8972 MARLENE DIETRICH/ GERMAN ACTRESS	How do you know that love is gone? If you said that you would be there at seven, you get there by nine and he or she has not called the police yet – it's gone.
8973 WILLIAM FAULKNER/ USA/NOVELIST/ ADVICE FOR WOULD-BE WRITERS	Read, read, read. Read everything – trash, classics, good and bad, and see how they do it. Just like a carpenter who works as an apprentice and studies the master. Read! You'll absorb it. Then write. If it's good, you'll find out. If it's not, throw it out of the window.
8974 NAVAJO PROVERB	You can't wake a person who is pretending to be asleep.
8975 THE TALMUD	Hire yourself out to do work, that you think is beneath you, rather than become dependent on others.
8976 STEPHEN KING/USA	The devil's voice is sweet to hear.
8977 FRANCOIS DE LA ROCHEFOUCAULD	To establish oneself in the world, one has to do all one can to appear established.
8978 KAHLIL GIBRAN/ LEBANESE POET	Your daily life is your temple and your religion. When you enter into it take with you your all.
8979 TENNESSEE WILLIAMS/ USA/WRITER	There's a time for departure even when there's no certain place to go.
8980 GALILEO GALILEI/ ITALIAN PHYSICIST	The Bible shows the way to go to heaven, not the way the heavens go.
8981 ALAN GREENSPAN/ ECONOMIST	I was a good amateur but only an average professional. I soon realized that there was a limit to how far I could rise in the music business, so I left the band and enrolled at New York University.
8982 WINSTON CHURCHILL/ UK/PRIME MINISTER	The price of greatness is responsibility.
8983 ELIE WIESEL/USA/ NOVELIST	I have not lost faith in God. I have moments of anger and protest. Sometimes I've been closer to him for that reason.
8984 PHYSICIST/JAMES CLERK MAXWELL/SCOT	It is of geat advantage to the student of any subject to read the original memoirs on that subject…
8985 TYLER PERRY/USA	You can't build your life around hurts from the past.
8986 KAREN VON BLIXEN/ ISAK DINESEN/AUTHOR	All sorrows can be borne if you put them into a story or tell a story about them.
8987 F. SCOTT FITZGERALD/ USA/WRITER	Never confuse a single defeat with a final defeat.
8988 AFRICAN PROVERB	He who is carried on another's back does not appreciate how far off the town is.
8989 TENNESSEE WILLIAMS/ USA/WRITER	When so many are lonely as seem to be lonely, it would be inexcusably selfish to be lonely alone.

NUMBER CATEGORY/CREDIT	TOPIC
8990 GEIL BROWNING/USA/ WRITER/INC. MAGAZINE	Being a confident talker and a persuasive speaker can get you attention in meetings, get you the sale, and even get you elected. No one gets kudos for sitting quietly.
8991 SOCRATES	Regard your good name as the richest jewel you can possibly be possessed of.
8992 USA/WILLIAM DEAN HOWELLS/WRITER	Some people stay longer in an hour than others do in a month.
8993 KELLY CUTRONE/USA/ ENTREPRENEUR	If you don't have a well-thought out dream, you can start by figuring out where you want to go.
8994 RICHARD BACH/USA/ NOVELIST	Bad things are not the worst things that can happen to us. Nothing is the worst thing that can happen to us!
8995 RICHARD DAWKINS/ BIOLOGIST	Let us try to teach generosity and altruism, because we are born selfish.
8996 EMILY BRONTE/UK/ NOVELIST	The tyrant grinds down his slaves and they don't turn against him, they crush those beneath them.
8997 MALCOLM X/USA/ ACTIVIST	Education is our passport to the future, for tomorrow belongs to the people who prepare for it today.
8998 J.K. GALBRAITH/USA	More die in the United States of too much food than of too little.
8999 TENNESSEE WILLIAMS/ USA/WRITER	All cruel people describe themselves as paragons of frankness.
9000 GEORGE ORWELL/UK	War is peace. Freedom is slavery. Ignorance is strength.
9001 OVID/ROMAN POET	If you would marry suitably, marry your equal.
9002 RASTAFARIANS	Dreadlocks
9003 HENRY JAMES/USA/ WRITER	Three things in human life are important: the first is to be kind; the second is to be kind; and the third is to be kind.
9004 US ARMY/SLOGAN	Be all you can be.
9005 LAURENCE J. PETER/ WRITER/USA	Every man serves a useful purpose: A miser, for example, makes a wonderful ancestor.
9006 USA/LAWRENCE SUMMERS/USA/ ACADEMIC	There are children who are working in textile businesses in Asia who would be prostitutes on the streets if they did not have these jobs.
9007 TENNESSEE WILLIAMS/ USA/WRITER	You can be young without money, but you can't be old without it.
9008 ECONOMICS/JOSEPH SCHUMPETER/ AUSTRIAN-AMERICAN	Creative destruction
9009 ROHINTON MISTRY/ CANADA/WRITER	You have to maintain a fine balance between hope and despair. In the end it's all a question of balance.
9010 CHOICE/VIEWPOINTS	Competing realities
9011 MARKETING	Multi-level marketing
9012 WILLIAM JENNINGS BRYAN/USA/LAWYER	If the Bible had said that Jonah swallowed the whale, I would believe it.
9013 LAWRENCE HILL/ CANADA/WRITER	I had learned that there were times when fighting was impossible, when the best thing to do was to wait and to learn.

NUMBER CATEGORY/CREDIT	TOPIC
9014 PUBLILIUS SYRUS	It is better to learn late than never.
9015 PIANIST/LUDWIG VAN BEETHOVEN/GERMAN	There are and always will be thousands of princes, but there is only one Beethoven!
9016 LOU HOLTZ/USA/COACH	It's not the load that breaks you down, it's the way you carry it.
9017 THE TALMUD	For the unlearned, old age is winter; for the learned it is the season of harvest.
9018 BILL CLINTON/USA	I tried marijuana once. I did not inhale.
9019 WILL DURANT/USA	Knowledge is the eye of desire and can become the pilot of the soul.
9020 STEPHEN KING/USA	The trust of the innocent is the liar's most useful tool.
9021 RICHARD BACH/USA NOVELIST	Don't be dismayed by good-byes. A farewell is necessary before you can meet again. And meeting again, after moments or lifetimes, is certain for those who are friends.
9022 WILLIAM J. CLINTON/ PRESIDENT/USA	In today's knowledge-based economy, what you earn depends on what you learn. Jobs in the information technology sector, for example, pay 85 percent more than the private sector average.
9023 GRANDMA MOSES/USA	Painting's not important. The important thing is keeping busy.
9024 MARK ROTHKO/USA	There is no such thing as a good painting about nothing.
9025 GAY/LESBIAN/ CHRISTIANITY	Praying the gay away
9026 USA/ELIZABETH CADY STANTON/WOMEN	The Bible and the Church have been the greatest stumbling blocks in the way of women's emancipation.
9027 J. HECTOR ST. JOHN CREVECOEUR/ ESSAYIST	Lawyers are plants that ill grow in any soil that is cultivated by the hands of others; and when once they have taken root they will extinguish every other vegetable that grows around them.
9028 HENRY JAMES/USA/UK/ WRITER	I don't want everyone to like me; I should think less of myself if some people did.
9029 DOLORES IBARRURI/ SPANISH LEADER	It is better to die on your feet than to live on your knees.
9030 HENRY JAMES/USA/ WRITER	Never say you know the last word about any human heart.
9031 MASLOW/HIERARCHY OF NEEDS	Maslow's Hierarchy of Needs: Physiological, Safety, Love & Belonging, Esteem, Self-actualization
9032 SOCIETY/WOMEN	Women's progress
9033 TOBIAS WOLFF/ AMERICAN WRITER	Fearlessness in those without power is maddening to those who have it.
9034 SOPHOCLES/ GREEK TRAGEDIAN	Truly, to tell lies is not honorable; but when the truth entails tremendous ruin, To speak dishonorably is pardonable.
9035 bell hooksAMERICAN WRITER/PROFESSOR	I entered the classroom with the conviction that it was crucial for me and every other student to be an active participant, not a passive consumer... Learning is a place where paradise can be created.
9036 LANGSTON HUGHES/ USA/WRITER	What happens to a dream deferred? Does it dry up like a raisin in the sun? Or fester like a sore -- And then run?
9037 WINSTON CHURCHILL/ UK/PRIME MINISTER	Success consists of going from failure to failure without loss of enthusiasm.

NUMBER CATEGORY/CREDIT	TOPIC
9038 PATRICK deWITT/ CANADA/WRITER	I will never be a leader of men...and neither do I want to be led...I want to lead only myself.
9039 SOCRATES	Remember that there is nothing stable in human affairs: therefore avoid undue elevation in prosperity, or undue depression in adversity.
9040 MARCUS TULLIUS CICERO/ROMAN ORATOR	Liberty is rendered even more precious by the recollection of servitude.
9041 CHIEF JOSEPH/USA	I am tired of talk that comes to nothing.
9042 SENECA/DRAMATIST	The best ideas are common property.
9043 EDITOR/ARIANNA HUFFINGTON/USA	I think while all mothers deal with feelings of guilt, working mothers are plagued by guilt on steroids.
9044 LEE KUAN YEW/PRIME MINISTER/SINGAPORE	I started off believing all men were equal. I now know that's the most unlikely thing ever to have been.
9045 LANGSTON HUGHES/ USA/WRITER	Hold fast to dreams. For if dreams die, Life is a broken-winged bird that cannot fly.
9046 GALILEO GALILEI/ ITALIAN PHYSICIST	I do not feel obliged to believe that the same God who has endowed us with sense, reason, and intellect has intended us to forgo their use.
9047 OVID/ROMAN POET	Take rest; a field that has rested gives a bountiful crop.
9048 THE TALMUD	He that is gentle to the brutal will end up being brutal to the gentle.
9049 SUN TZU/CHINA/ THE ART OF WAR	The good fighters of old first put themselves beyond the possibility of defeat, and then waited for an opportunity of defeating the enemy.
9050 JOHN WOODEN/USA BASKETBALL COACH	We are many, but are we much?
9051 LEWIS CARROLL/UK/ WRITER/LOGICIAN	Sometimes I've believed as many as six impossible things before breakfast.
9052 DOLLY PARTON/USA/ SINGER	I always just thought if you see somebody without a smile, give 'em yours.
9053 BILL COSBY/USA/ COMEDY	My grandfather said when you become senile you won't know it.
9054 ELIA KAZAN/USA/ WRITER	I value peace when it is not bought at the price of fundamental decencies.
9055 BASHO MATSUO/ JAPANESE POET	Do not seek to follow in the footsteps of the wise; seek what they sought.
9056 PETER DRUCKER/USA/ MANAGEMENT	Follow effective action with quiet reflection. From the quiet reflection will come even more effective action.
9057 MARGARET MEAD/ USA/ANTHROPOLOGIST	Always remember that you are absolutely unique. Just like everyone else.
9058 VERA NAZARIAN/USA/ ARMENIA/RUSSIA	The world is shaped by two things -- stories told and the memories they leave behind.
9059 HENRY JAMES/USA/ WRITER	Try to be one of those on whom nothing is lost.
9060 AMI McKAY/CANADA/ THE BIRTH HOUSE	No matter what you do, someone always knew you would.
9061 GRANT HILL/USA/ BASKETBALL	Yelling doesn't get your point across; it only makes it louder.

NUMBER CATEGORY/CREDIT	TOPIC
9062 JACKSON POLLOCK/ AMERICAN ARTIST	I have no fear of making changes, destroying the image, etc., because the painting has a life of its own.
9063 KAHLIL GIBRAN/ LEBANESE POET	To understand the heart and mind of a person, look not that he has already achieved, but at what he aspires to.
9064 BRIAN COX/WHAT WENT WRONG AT THE LHC/TED.COM	The Large Hadron Collider is the largest scientific experiment ever attempted – 27 kilometers in circumference. Its job is to re-create the conditions that were present less than a billionth of a second after the universe began, up to 600 million times a second. It's nothing if not ambitious.
9065 VINCENT VAN GOGH/ DUTCH ARTIST	The fishermen know that the sea is dangerous and the storm terrible, but they have never found these dangers sufficient reason for remaining ashore.
9066 LEONARDO DA VINCI/ ITALY/ARTIST	Anyone who conducts an argument by appealing to authority is not using his intelligence; he is just using his memory.
9067 WILLIAM J. CLINTON/ USA/PRESIDENT	Never pick a fight with people who buy ink by the barrel.
9068 LAURENCE J. PETER/ CANADA/AUTHOR	The Peter Principle: In a hierarchy every employee tends to rise to his level of incompetence.
9069 DALE CARNEGIE/USA/ WRITER/LECTURER	The successful man will profit from his mistakes and try again in a different way.
9070 LOU HOLTZ/USA/COACH	No one has ever drowned in sweat.
9071 BARUCH SPINOZA/ DUTCH PHILOSOPHER	Freedom is absolutely necessary for progress in science and the liberal arts.
9072 STEVE JOBS/USA/ APPLE COMPUTERS	I was worth...over a million dollars when I was twenty-three and over ten million dollars when I was twenty-four, and over a hundred million dollar when I was twenty-five and it wasn't that important because I never did it for the money.
9073 PLATO/GREEK THINKER	Be kind, for everyone you meet is fighting a hard battle.
9074 WRITER/GABRIEL GARCÍA MÁRQUEZ	He who awaits much can expect little.
9075 JACKIE ROBINSON/ USA/BASEBALL PLAYER	A life is not important except in the impact it has on other lives.
9076 RACISM/LAW	Hate crimes
9077 ANAHAD O'CONNOR/ SURGEONS /NY TIMES	Every year in the United States, 4,000 cases of "retained surgical items" are left inside patients.
9078 MAXWELL MALTZ/USA	Self image sets the boundaries of individual accomplishment.
9079 JACKSON POLLOCK/ AMERICAN ARTIST	New needs need new techniques. And the modern artists have found new ways and new means of making their statements...the modern painter cannot express this age, the airplane, the atom bomb, the radio, in the old forms of the Renaissance or of any other past culture.
9080 NATALIE GOLDBERG/ AMERICAN WRITER	We heard about people who go back to their roots. That is good, but don't get stuck in the root. There is the branch, the leaf, the flower – all reaching towards the immense sky.
9081 HENRY JAMES/USA/ WRITER	Money's a horrid thing to follow,, but a charming thing to me.
9082 PRODUCTS/SAFETY	Importance of product labeling

NUMBER CATEGORY/CREDIT	TOPIC
9083 FLORENCE SCOVEL SHINN/USA/ARTIST	The game of life is a game of boomerangs. Our thoughts, deeds and words return to us sooner or later with astounding accuracy.
9084 THUCYDIDES/HISTORY	He who graduates the harshest school, succeeds.
9085 ALEXANDER THE GREAT/MACEDONIA	Remember upon the conduct of each depends the fate of all.
9086 OVID/ROMAN POET	Nothing is stronger than habit.
9087 ALBERT EINSTEIN/ PHYSICIST/LETTER TO CHAIM WEIZMAN/1929/ ISRAEL	Should we be unable to find a way to honest co-operation and honest pacts with the Arabs, then we shall have learned nothing from our 2,000 years of suffering and will deserve our fate.
9088 FLORENCE SCOVEL SHINN/USA/ARTIST	There is a supply for every demand.
9089 SOCRATES/THINKER	Remember what is unbecoming to do is also unbecoming to speak of.
9090 BARUCH SPINOZA/ DUTCH PHILOSOPHER	I call him free who is led solely by reason.
9091 RANDY O. FROST/NY TIMES	A passion for collecting is a healthy outlet and an activity that keeps people connected to the world around them.
9092 KAHLIL GIBRAN/ LEBANESE POET	Your children are not your children. They are the sons and daughters of Life's longing for itself. They came through you but not from you and though they are with you yet they belong not to you.
9093 RABBI HILLEL/LEADER	He who refuses to learn deserves extinction.
9094 JUDGMENT/WASTE	How to spend time when caught in a traffic jam
9095 HENRY JAMES/USA/ WRITER	If you are going to be pushed, you had better jump.
9096 IAN KIERNAN/CLEAN UP AUSTRALIA DAY	Ordinary people need to lead and not sit there and think that governments are going to spoon-feed them.
9097 USA/BOOKER T. WASHINGTON	There are two ways of exerting one's strength: one is pushing down, the other is pulling up.
9098 SLOGAN/LISTERINE	Even your closest friends won't tell you.
9099 HENRY JAMES/USA/ WRITER	You can do a great many things if you are rich which would be severely criticized if you were poor.
9100 ARISTOPHANES/ GREEK/PLAYWRIGHT	Quickly, bring me a beaker of wine, so that I may wet my mind and say something clever.
9101 FRIENDSHIP	How you handle misunderstanding with a friend
9102 ARISTOPHANES	A man can learn wisdom even from a foe.
9103 AYN RAND/WRITER/ PHILOSOPHER	Civilization is the process of setting man free from men.
9104 LAO-TZU/CHINESE PHILOSPHER	To know that you do not know is the best. To pretend to know when you do not know is a disease.
9105 WILL DURANT/USA	Woe to him who teaches men faster than they can learn.
9106 OSCAR WILDE/IRISH WRITER/POET	The reason we all like to think so well of others is that we are all afraid for ourselves. The basis of optimism is sheer terror.
9107 MORTIMER ADLER/USA/ WRITER	Friendship is a very taxing and arduous form of leisure activity.

NUMBER CATEGORY/CREDIT	TOPIC
9108 JOHN RAWLS/USA/ PHILOSOPHER	The bad man desires arbitrary power.
9109 MARGUERITE DURAS/ FRENCH NOVELIST	The best way to fill time is to waste it.
9110 DEEPAK CHOPRA/USA/ INDIA/WRITER	Every time you are tempted to react in the same old way, ask if you want to be a prisoner of the past or a pioneer of the future.
9111 WORK/IMPORTANCE	Speed versus accuracy
9112 FREDERICK DOUGLASS/ USA/WRITER/ACTIVIST	A little learning, indeed, may be a dangerous thing, but the want of learning is a calamity to any people.
9113 WRITER/FRANCOIS DE LA ROCHEFOUCAULD	Preserving health by too severe a rule is a worrisome malady.
9114 KAHLIL GIBRAN/ON GIVING	You often say, "I would give, but only to the deserving." The trees in your orchard say not so, nor the flocks in your pasture.
9115 ABRAHAM LINCOLN/USA/ 16TH PRESIDENT	In the end, it's not the years in your life that count. It's the life in your years.
9116 ROBERT SMITHSON/USA	Artists themselves are not confined, but their output is.
9117 WILL DURANT/USA/ HISTORIAN	Man became free when he recognized that he was subject to law.
9118 JILL TARTER/JOIN THE SETI SEARCH	Ultimately, we actually all belong to only one tribe, to Earthlings.
9119 HORATIO NELSON/ UK/LEADER	Duty is the great business of a sea officer; all private considerations must give way to it, however painful it may be.
9120 THOMAS A. EDISON/ INVENTOR/USA	Our greatest weakness lies in giving up. The most certain way to succeed is always to try just one more time.
9121 ANDREW CARNEGIE/ USA/INDUSTRIALIST	The man who acquires the ability to take full possession of his own mind may take possession of anything else to which he is justly entitled.
9122 DREUX RICHARD/ METROPOLIS MAGAZINE	Kaz Taira (Hair Salon Owner): "Fashion shouldn't be an arms race."
9123 THOMAS MERTON/USA	Man was made for the highest activity, which is, in fact, his rest.
9124 DEEPAK CHOPRA/USA/ INDIA/WRITER	To acquire true self power you have to feel beneath no one, be immune to criticism and be fearless.
9125 KYUNG-SOOK SHIN/ SOUTH KOREA/WRITER	Either a mother and daughter know each other very well or they are strangers.
9126 J.K. ROWLING/ BRITISH WRITER	You will never truly know yourself or the strength of your relationships until both have been tested by adversity.
9127 LITERACY VOLUNTEERS OF AMERICA	Volunteering is reaching your hand out into the darkness to pull another's hand back into the light, only to realize that it's your own.
9128 DEMOSTHENES/GREEK/ ORATOR	As a vessel is known by its sound whether it be cracked or not, so men are proved by their speeches whether they be wise or foolish.
9129 DALE CARNEGIE/ USA/WRITER	Take a chance! All life is a chance. The man who goes furthest is generally the one who is willing to do and dare.
9130 WILLIAM HAZLITT/ ENGLISH CRITIC	Even in the common affairs of life, in love, friendship, and marriage, how little security have we when we trust our happiness in the hands of others!
9131 WOMEN	Continuing to work after marriage

NUMBER CATEGORY/CREDIT	TOPIC
9132 REAR ADM. GRACE HOPPER/US NAVY	It is often easier to ask for forgiveness than to ask for permission.
9133 ROBERT FULGHUM/USA/ WRITER	If you break your neck, if you have nothing to eat, if your house is on fire, then you've got a problem. Everything else is an inconvenience. Life is inconvenient. Life is lumpy. A lump in the oatmeal, a lump in the throat, and a lump in the breast are not the same kind of lump.
9134 ERIC SCHMIDT/GOOGLE/ USA/BUSINESS	Texting is not a substitute for human contact.
9135 GALILEO GALILEI/ ITALIAN PHYSICIST	In questions of science, the authority of a thousand is not worth the humble reasoning of a single individual.
9136 CHIEF JOSEPH/USA/ NATIVE AMERICAN	An Indian respects a brave man, but he despises a coward.
9137 CHINESE SAYING	You can't prevent a bird from flying over your head, but you can prevent it from building a nest in your hair.
9138 PABLO PICASSO/ SPANISH PAINTER/ LIFE WITH PICASSO	God is really only another artist. He invented the giraffe, the elephant, and the cat. He has no real style. He just goes on trying other things.
9139 MUSINGS/DAILY YOMIURI/JAPAN	Even though they do not do particularly bad things, spiders are treated badly due to their appearance. They may lament, "We are creatures with no connection to beauty."
9140 ROBERT DIGGS/USA/ HIP HOP ARTIST	Song title: C.R.E.A.M. Cash Rules Everything Around Me
9141 STEPHEN CARTER/ USA/LAWYER	When you shoot someone who is fleeing, it's not self-defense. It's an execution.
9142 USA/JACQUELINE NOVOGRATZ/TED.COM	Your job is not to be perfect. Your job is only to be human.
9143 NORMAN MAILER/ USA/WRITER	Any war that requires the suspension of reason as a necessity for support is a bad war.
9144 ABIGAIL ADAMS/USA/ 1ST LADY	These are the times in which a genius would wish to live. It is not in the still calm of life...that great characters are formed...Great necessities call out great virtues.
9145 GEORG W F HEGEL/ GERMAN/ PHILOSOPHER	We do not need to be shoemakers to know if our shoes fit, and just as little have we any need to be professionals to acquire knowledge of matters of universal interest.
9146 R. ADMIRAL GRACE HOPPER/USA	One accurate measurement is worth a thousand expert opinions.
9147 MAYA ANGELOU/USA/ WRITER	You may encounter many defeats, but you must not be defeated. It may even be necessary to encounter the defeats so you can know yourself.
9148 COLE PORTER/USA/ COMPOSER/MUSIC	My sole inspiration is a telephone call from a director.
9149 KAHLIL GIBRAN/ON CRIME AND PUNISHMENT	And you who would understand justice, how shall you unless you look upon all deeds in the fullness of light? Only then shall you know that the erect and the fallen are but one man standing in twilight between the night of his pigmy-self and the day of his god-self.
9150 SENECA/DRAMATIST	It is quality rather than quantity that matters.

NUMBER CATEGORY/CREDIT	TOPIC
9151 CHIMAMANDA NGOZI ADICHIE/THE DANGER OF A SINGLE STORY/TEDTALK	Stories matter. Many stories matter. Stories have been used to dispossess and to malign, but stories can also be used to empower and to humanize. Stories can break the dignity of a people, but stories can also repair that broken dignity.
9152 SALMA HAYEK/ MEXICAN ACTRESS	Every woman who thinks she is the only victim of violence has to know that there are many more.
9153 SOCRATES/THINKER	Think not those faithful who praise all thy words and actions; but those who kindly reprove thy faults.
9154 CHINESE PROVERB	Waiting for a rabbit to hit a tree and be killed in order to catch it.
9155 VINCENT VAN GOGH/ DUTCH ARTIST	If you hear a voice within you say 'you cannot paint,' then by all means pain, and that voice will be silenced.
9156 UK/PM/WINSTON CHURCHILL	All the great things are simple and many can be expressed in a single word: freedom, justice, honor, duty, mercy, hope.
9157 DIFFERENCE	Being different in the world of business is a great thing.
9158 bell hooks/USA/ WRITER/ PROFESSOR	If we want a beloved community, we must stand for justice, have recognition for difference without attaching difference to privilege.
9159 ADBUSTERS/USA	"Buy Nothing Day"
9160 JOHN K GALBRAITH/USA	Nothing is admirable in politics as a short memory.
9161 FAMILY/BUDGET	Buying things in bulk
9162 DEEPAK CHOPRA/USA/ INDIA/WRITER	Don't try to steer the river.
9163 MAO TSE TUNG/ CHINESE LEADER	A revolution is not a dinner party, or writing an essay, or painting a picture, or doing embroidery.
9164 CONFUCIUS/CHINA/ PHILOSOPHER	They must often change who would be constant in happiness or wisdom.
9165 MIYAMOTO MUSASHI/ JAPANESE WARRIOR	Today is victory over yourself of yesterday; tomorrow is your victory over lesser men.
9166 JAY McINERNEY/USA/ WRITER	Your heartbreak is just another version of the same old story.
9167 HANS SELYE/CANADA	It's not stress that kills us; it is our reaction to it.
9168 EDWARD ABBEY/USA/ ESSAYIST	You can't study the darkness by flooding it with light.
9169 POET/RALPH WALDO EMERSON/USA/	Sometimes a scream is better than a thesis.
9170 MUHAMMAD ALI/USA/ BOXER	It's the repetition of affirmation that leads to belief. And once that belief becomes a deep conviction, things begin to happen.
9171 LOUIS D. BRANDEIS/ USA/JUDGE	In the frank expression of conflicting opinions lies the greatest promise of wisdom in governmental action.
9172 BENNY GOODMAN/ USA/COMEDIAN	Too many young musicians today want to win polls before they learn their instruments.
9173 ANNIE DILLARD/USA	The life of sensation is the life of greed; It requires more and more.
9174 SADE/UK/MUSICIAN	I only talk when there's something to be said.
9175 CHINUA ACHEBE/ NIGERIAN WRITER	Writers don't give prescriptions. They give headaches!

NUMBER CATEGORY/CREDIT	TOPIC
9176 TRENDS/ GLOBALIZATION	Memes : an idea, behavior, style, or usage that spreads from person to person within a culture
9177 WILLIAM DEMILLE/ USA/FILM DIRECTOR	I have always admired the ability to bite off more than one can chew and then chew it.
9178 THE TALMUD	Into the well which supplies thee with water, cast no stones.
9179 EDWARD ABBEY/USA/ ESSAYIST	Freedom begins between the ears.
9180 USA/DANICA PATRICK FORMULA 1 RACER	What makes you different makes you great.
9181 KELLY CUTRONE/ USA/ENTREPRENER	In today's disposable culture, we throw away people like we do razors, always assuming there's someone better out there to hang out with.
9182 NATIONALISM	Pledging allegiance to a nation.
9183 USA/R.W. EMERSON	Whoso would be a man must be a nonconformist.
9184 MICHELANGELO/ITALY/ ARTIST	If people knew how hard I worked to get my mastery, it wouldn't seem so wonderful at all.
9185 RICHARD BACH/USA/ NOVELIST	Here is a test to find whether your mission on Earth is finished; If you're alive, it isn't.
9186 RICHARD DAWKINS/ AUTHOR/BIOLOGIST	It has become almost a cliché to remark that nobody boasts of ignorance of literature, but it is socially acceptable to boast ignorance of science and proudly claim incompetence in mathematics.
9187 KAHLIL GIBRAN/ LEBANESE POET	You pray in your distress and in your need; would that you might also pray in the fullness of your joy and in your days of abundance.
9188 OVID/ROMAN POET	We can learn even from our enemies.
9189 LAO-TZU/CHINA/ PHILOSOPHER	He who loves the world as his body may be entrusted with the empire.
9190 ELIE WIESEL/USA/ PROFESSOR/NOVELIST	I write to understand as much as to be understood.
9191 LEONARDO DA VINCI/ ITALY/ARTIST	There are three classes of people: those who see, those who see when they are shown, those who do not see.
9192 CHINUA ACHEBE/ AFRICAN WRITER	A man who pays respect to the great paves the way for his own greatness.
9193 NATALIE GOLDBERG/ USA/WRITER	Sometimes people say to me, "I want to write, but I have five kids, a full-time job, a wife who beats me, a tremendous debt to my parents," and so on. I say to them, "There is no excuse. If you want to write, write. This is your life…You will not live forever."
9194 MARK TWAIN/USA/ AUTHOR & HUMORIST	A round man cannot be expected to fit in a square hold right away. He must have time to modify his shape.
9195 LEONARDO DA VINCI/ ITALY/ARTIST	He who wishes to be rich in a day will be hanged in a year.
9196 BRIAN TRACY/USA/ AUTHOR/SUCCESS COACH	The greatest gift that you can give to others is the gift of unconditional love and acceptance.
9197 WRITER/MICHAEL BASSEY JOHNSON/ NIGERIA	I don't fancy colors of the face; I'm always attracted to colors of the mind.

NUMBER CATEGORY/CREDIT	TOPIC
9198 RABBI SHMULEY BOTEACH/USA	When you don't get the love you need, attention becomes a desperate, though ultimately, unfulfilling substitute.
9199 LEE KUAN YEW/PM/ SINGAPORE	I ignore polling as a method of government. I think that shows a certain weakness of mind.
9200 PETER VAN UHM/WHY I CHOSE A GUN/TED.COM	Until the day comes when we can do away with the gun, I hope we all agree that peace and stability do not come free of charge.
9201 DR. ALEXANDER FORBES/THIS I BELIEVE	Dogmatic insistence that one form of worship is right and all others wrong is as alien to the spirit of freedom, to which our Western world is dedicated, as the tyranny of the dictator.
9202 SOCRATES/ PHILOSOPHER	Thou shouldst eat to live; not live to eat.
9203 USA/JACQUELINE NOVOGRATZ/TED.COM	At the end of the day, dignity is more important to the human spirit than wealth.
9204 TINA SEELIG/USA/ ENTREPRENEUR	I've become increasingly aware that the world is divided into people who wait for others to give them permission to do the things they want to do and people who grant themselves permission.
9205 KEN ROBINSON/ SCHOOLS KILL CREATIVITY	Every education system on Earth has the same hierarchy of subjects: at the top are mathematics and languages, then the humanities, and the bottom are the arts.
9206 GERMAN/KARL VON CLAUSEWITZ/SOLDIER	War is the continuation of politics by other means.
9207 TAXATION/RICH/ POOR/DICTIONARY. CAMBRIDGE.ORG	Robin Hood Tax : a suggested set of taxes on banks and financial transactions (= the buying and selling of shares, bonds, etc.) that would provide money to protect public services and the environment, help the poor, etc.
9208 O.A. BATTISTA/ CANADIAN CHEMIST	One of the hardest things to teach a child is that the truth is more important than the consequences.
9209 SAMUEL BECKETT/ IRISH PLAYWRIGHT	Do we mean love, when we say love?
9210 EDWARD ABBEY/USA/ ESSAYIST	I am not an atheist but an earthiest. Be true to the earth.
9211 CHINESE PROVERB	You say you have Lost your horse but who knows but that it will Return to you with a whole herd some day.
9212 MICHELANGELO/ITALY/ ARTIST	The greater danger for most of us lies not in setting our aim too high and falling short, but in setting our aim too low, and achieving our mark.
9213 THOMAS J. WATSON/ IBM CEO	If you stand up and be counted, from time to time you may get yourself knocked down.
9214 BOB MARLEY/ MUSICIAN	Live for yourself and you will live in vain; Live for others, and you will live again.
9215 SAMUEL BECKETT/ IRISH PLAYWRIGHT	I regret nothing; all I regret is having been born.
9216 KEMAL ATATURK/ TURKISH SOLDIER	A nation devoid of art and artists cannot have a full existence.
9217 ESI ADUGYAN/CANADA/ WRITER	Ain't no glory made from being dependable.

NUMBER CATEGORY/CREDIT	TOPIC
9218 GIORGIO VASCARI/ ITALY/ARTIST	Men of genius sometimes accomplish most when they work the least, for they are thinking out inventions and forming in their minds the perfect idea that they subsequently express with their hands.
9219 WATTY PIPER/USA	I think I can. I think I can. I think I can.
9220 MAYA ANGELOU/USA/ WRITER/PROFESSOR	Achievement brings its own anticlimax.
9221 PYTHAGORAS/MATH	Do not talk a little on many subjects, but much on a few.
9222 DAVID STEINDL-RAST/ WRITER/MONK	The root of joy is gratefulness...It is not joy that makes us grateful; it is gratitude that makes us joyful.
9223 JAPAN/DAILY YOMIURI/ KYOICHI HANYA	A man should not be afraid of contracting a disease....He should be afraid of having no means to cure it.
9224 EDGER DIJKSTRA/ COMPUTER SCIENTIST	The question of whether Machines Can Think...is about as relevant as the question of whether Submarines Can Swim.
9225 IRINA DUNN/FEMINIST/ AUSTRALIAN WRITER	A woman needs a man like a fish needs a bicycle.
9226 PYTHAGORAS/GREEK/ MATHEMATICIAN	Friends are as companions on a journey, who ought to aid each other to persevere in the road to a happier life.
9227 EDWARD ABBEY/USA/ ESSAYIST	The idea of wilderness needs no defense; it only needs defenders.
9228 EDWARD ABBEY/USA/ ESSAYIST	When a man's best friend is his dog, the dog has a problem.
9229 JIM ROHN/US/WRITER/ BUSINESS/MOTIVATION	Take advantage of every opportunity to practice your communication skills so that when important occasions arise, you will have the gift, the style, the sharpness, the clarity, and the emotions to affect other people.
9230 SAMUEL GOLDWYN/ USA/MOVIE PRODUCER	A hospital is no place to be sick.
9231 J.M. BARRIE/ AUTHOR/PETER PAN	Nothing is really work unless you would rather be doing something else.
9232 QUENTIN CRISP/UK/ THE NAKED CIVIL SERVANT	The young always have the same problem – how to rebel and conform at the same time. They have now solved this by defying their parents and copying one another.
9233 WORLD WAR II/USA/ SAYING	Loose lips sink ships.
9234 EDWARD ABBEY/USA/ ESSAYIST	A drink a day keeps the shrink away.
9235 LAURENCE J. PETER/ WRITER/USA	Originality is the fine art of remembering what you hear but forgetting where you heard it.
9236 GEORGE SANTAYANA/US	A child educated only at school is an uneducated child.
9237 DR. PASI SAHLBERG/ FINLAND	The primary aim of education is to serve as an equalizing instrument for society.
9238 KAREEM ABDUL /USA JABBAR/LIFE'S WORK	Being prepared, having a good understanding of your strengths and limitations, and having a good game plan; Those are essential elements of success.
9239 MAGIC JOHNSON/USA/ NBA/BASKETBALL	Ask not what your teammates can do for you. Ask what you can do for your teammates.

NUMBER CATEGORY/CREDIT	TOPIC
9240 MARCUS FABIUS QUINTILIAN/ROMAN/ RHETORICIAN	A laugh, if purchased at the expense of propriety, costs too much.
9241 LEADERSHIP	Confusing charisma with competence.
9242 GEORGE WILLIAM CURTIS/USA/WRITER	It is not the ship so much as the skillful sailing that assures the prosperous voyage.
9243 USA/MARILYNNE ROBINSON/ESSAYIST	It is not man's working hours that is important, it is how he spends his leisure time.
9244 WARREN G. BENNIS/ USA/PSYCHOLOGIST	The manager has a short-range view; the leader has a long-range perspective.
9245 EDWARD ABBEY/USA/ ESSAYIST	When the situation is hopeless, there's nothing to worry about.
9246 JIM ROHN/US/WRITER/ BUSINESS/MOTIVATION	Some people plant in the spring and leave in the summer. If you're signed up for a season, see it through. You don't have to stay forever, but at least, stay until you see it through.
9247 KAHLIL GIBRAN/ ON WORK	And if you cannot work with love but only with distaste, it is better that you should leave your work and sit at the gate of the temple and take alms of those who work with joy.
9248 JIM ROHN/USA/ WRITER/MOTIVATION	The book you don't read won't help.
9249 WILL DURANT/USA	Moral codes adjust themselves to environmental conditions.
9250 EDWARD ABBEY/USA/ ESSAYIST	From the point of view of a tapeworm, man was created by God to serve the appetite of the tapeworm.
9251 USA/MARILYNNE ROBINSON/ESSAYIST	There is a saying that to understand is to forgive, but that is an error, so Papa used to say. You must forgive in order to understand.
9252 PYTHAGORAS/GREEK PHILOSOPHER	In this theater of man's life, it is reserved only for God and angels to be lookers-on.
9253 AYN RAND/USA/ PHILOSOPHER	Only the man who does not need it, is fit to inherit wealth, the man who would make his fortune no matter where he started.
9254 INDIA/JAWAHARLAL NEHRU/PM	The policy of being too cautious is the greatest risk of all.
9255 MARILYN MONROE/ USA/ACTRESS	I don't mind living in a man's world, as long as I can be a woman in it.
9256 JENNY JOSEPH/ WARNING - WHEN I AM AN OLD WOMAN...	When I grow old...I shall sit down on the pavement when I am tired and gobble up samples in shops and press alarm bells and run my stick along the public railings and make up for the sobriety of my youth.
9257 KENNETH CHANG//NY TIMES/USA	Researchers found that university science professors widely regard female students as less competent than male ones.
9258 ANAIS NIN/USA/WRITER	When you make a world tolerable for yourself you make a world tolerable for others.
9259 R.L. STEVENSON/ SCOTTISH WRITER	An aim in life is the only fortune worth finding.
9260 G.K. CHESTERTON/ UK/WRITER	The Bible tells us to love our neighbors, and also to love our enemies; probably because generally they are the same people.
9261 USA/ALFIE KOHN	Competition turns all of us into losers.

NUMBER CATEGORY/CREDIT	TOPIC
9262 USA/AUTHOR/ F. SCOTT FITZGERALD	First you take a drink, then the drink takes a drink, then the drink takes you.
9263 PETER DRUCKER/USA MANAGEMENT	Today knowledge has power. It controls access to opportunity and advancement.
9264 ERASMUS/THEOLOGIAN	A good portion of speaking will consist in knowing how to lie.
9265 SOCRATES	Having the fewest wants, I am nearest to the gods.
9266 CYNTHIA OZICK/USA/ NOVELIST	In saying what is obvious, never choose cunning. Yelling works better.
9267 SAMUEL BUTLER/UK	Friendship is like money, easier made than kept.
9268 bell hooks/USA/ WRITER/PROFESSOR	When we face pain in relationships our first response is often to sever bonds rather than to maintain commitment.
9269 SARAH VOWELL/USA	History is full of really good stories.
9270 THAI PROVERB	Those who dance poorly often blame the musician.
9271 KAHLIL GIBRAN/ LEBANESE POET	When we turn to one another for counsel we reduce the number of our enemies.
9272 JIM ROHN/USA/WRITER/ BUSINESS/MOTIVATION	The reason that fiction is more interesting than any other form of literature, to those who really like to study people, is that in fiction the author can really tell the truth without humiliating himself.
9273 EDWARD ABBEY/USA/ ESSAYIST	A pretty girl can do no wrong.
9274 bell hooks/USA/WRITER	To know love we have to invest time and commitment.
9275 ALEXANDER THE GREAT/MACEDONIA	I am indebted to my father for living, but to my teacher for living well.
9276 PERICLES/GREEK STATESMAN	Having knowledge but lacking the power to express it clearly is no better than never having any ideas at all.
9277 AN INDIAN PROVERB	A beautiful woman belongs to everyone; an ugly one is yours alone.
9278 USA/MIKE MYATT/ FORBES/USA	Leadership is pursuit – pursuit of excellence, of elegance, of truth, of what's next, of what if, of change, of value, of results, of relationships, of service, of knowledge, and of something bigger than themselves
9279 CHARLES A. DANA/USA	If a dog bites a man it is not news, but if a man bites a dog it is.
9280 MARGARET MEAD/USA/ ANTHROPOLOGIST	Every time we liberate a woman, we liberate a man.
9281 H. W. ARNOLD/WRITER	The worst bankrupt in the world is the man who has lost his enthusiasm.
9282 SOPHOCLES/WRITER	Wisdom outweighs any wealth.
9283 VOLTAIRE/WRITER/ FRENCH/PHILOSOPHER	The best way to be boring is to leave nothing out.
9284 VIRGINIA WOOLF/ BRITISH AUTHOR	As a woman I have no country. As a woman my country is the whole world.
9285 EDGAR WATSON HOWE/USA/AUTHOR	Families with babies and families without babies are sorry for each other.
9286 EDWARD ABBEY/USA/ ESSAYIST	All governments need enemies. How else to justify their existence?
9287 JOHN F. KENNEDY/USA/ PRESIDENT	War will exist until that distant day when the conscientious objector enjoys the same reputation and prestige that the warrior does today.

NUMBER CATEGORY/CREDIT	TOPIC
9288 NAPOLEON BONAPARTE/ USA/FRENCH LEADER	The people to fear are not those who disagree with you, but those who disagree with you but are too cowardly to let you know.
9289 SAINT AUGUSTINE	Complete abstinence is easier than perfect moderation.
9290 RICHARD CARLSON/USA	Don't sweat the small stuff...and it's all small stuff.
9291 JOAN DIDION/USA/ AUTHOR	Writers are always selling somebody out.
9292 JIM ROHN/US/WRITER/ BUSINESS/MOTIVATION	Things that I felt absolutely sure of a few years ago, I do not believe now. This thought makes me see more clearly how foolish it would be to expect all men to agree with me.
9293 SOCRATES/THINKER	I know nothing except the fact of my ignorance.
9294 PROTECTION/ SAFETY	Taking precautions
9295 DR. PHIL MCGRAW/USA/ PSYCHOLOGIST	You can't make sense out of nonsense.
9296 ANDREW CARNEGIE/ SCOTISH-AMERICAN BUSINESSMAN	The thorough man of business knows that only by years of patient, unremitting attention to affairs can he earn his reward, which is the result, not of chance, but of well-devised means for the attainment to ends.
9297 CHINESE SAYING	Your fingers can't be of the same length.
9298 E.L. DOCTOROW/ USA/WRITER	Writing is an exploration. You start from nothing and learn as you go.
9299 SARAH VOWELL/ AMERICAN AUTHOR	In death, you get upgraded into a saint no matter how much people hated you in life.
9300 ADAM GOPNIK/USA/ WRITER	The loneliness of the expatriate is of an odd and complicated kind, for it is inseparable from the feeling of being free, of having escaped.
9301 WARREN FARRELL/ USA/ AUTHOR	Every day in about half the advertisements, a man sees the constant reminder of the woman he was not worthy of.
9302 STEPHEN CARTER/USA	Teaching civility is an obligation of the family.
9303 USA/MARILYNNE ROBINSON/ESSAYIST	I think hope is the worst thing in the world. I really do. It makes a fool of you while it lasts. And then when it's gone, it's like there's nothing left of you at all...
9304 USA/MOLEFI KETE ASANTE/PROFESSOR	A wise person speaks carefully and with truth, for every word that passes between one's teeth is meant for something.
9305 SENECA/ROMAN DRAMATIST	If a man does not know to what port he is steering, no wind is favorable to him.
9306 FRIENDSHIP	It is important to maintain friendships from the past.
9307 BERTRAND RUSSELL/ UK/AUTHOR	One of the symptoms of an approaching nervous breakdown is the belief that one's work is terribly important.
9308 FELIX FRANKFURTER/ USA/SUPREME COURT	The mode by which the inevitable is reached is effort.
9309 USA/CHARLES KETTERING/INVENTOR	Inventing is a combination of brains and materials. The more brains you use, the less material you need.
9310 RUMI/PERSIAN POET	My head is bursting with the joy of the unknown.
9311 SOCRATES	There is only one good, knowledge, and one evil, ignorance.
9312 NATURE	Vanishing lakes

NUMBER CATEGORY/CREDIT	TOPIC
9313 MALCOLM X/USA/ACTIVIST	I'm for truth, no matter who tells it. I'm for justice, no matter who it is for or against.
9314 PETER DRUCKER/USA/MANAGEMENT	Knowledge has to be improved, challenged, and increased constantly, or it vanishes.
9315 HOBBY	Coin collecting
9316 KELLY CUTRONE/USA/ENTREPRENER	I happen to believe the world will change only when we change ourselves.
9317 JUVENAL/ANCIENT ROME	Who will guard the guardians and who will watch the watchers?
9318 FASCISM/LEARNERS DICTIONARY.COM	Fascism: a way of organizing a society in which a government ruled by a dictator controls the lives of the people and in which people are not allowed to disagree with the government
9319 bell hooks/WRITER	Living simply makes loving simple.
9320 PYTHAGORAS/SCIENTIST	No one is free who has not obtained the empire of himself.
9321 MEDICINE/ADVANCES/JAPAN	Use of dogs to identify early stage cancer even when patients do not know they are sick.
9322 RICHARD CARLSON/USA/WRITER	One of the most dynamic and significant changes you can make in your life is to make the commitment to drop all negative references to your past.
9323 USA/MARILYNNE ROBINSON/ESSAYIST	It is a good thing to know what it is to be poor, and a better thing if you can do it in company.
9324 SARAH VOWELL/USA/AUTHOR	Like Lincoln, I would like to believe that the ballot is stronger than the bullet. Then again, he said that before he got shot.
9325 ROGER ANGELL/USA/THE DIGNITY OF MAN/THIS I BELIEVE	I am a believer in children. I love children, it seems to me, because they have not yet learned to hide their humanity, to protect it behind words and customs, and lonely fears and suspicions.
9326 JONATHAN SWIFT/IRISH WRITER	And surely one of the best rules in conversation is, never to say a thing which any of the company can reasonably wish had been left unsaid...
9327 MICHAEL PORTER/USA/BUSINESS/PROFESSOR	Billions are wasted on ineffective philanthropy.
9328 GABRIEL GARCÍA MÁRQUEZ/NOVELIST	I don't believe in God, but I'm afraid of him.
9329 USA/FREDERICK DOUGLASS/CIVIL RIGHTS LEADER/1852	What, to the American slave, is your 4th of July? I answer; a day that reveals to him, more than all other days in the year, the gross injustice and cruelty to which he is the constant victim. To him, your celebration is a sham.
9330 HENRI POINCARE/FRENCH/ MATH	To doubt everything or to believe everything are two equally convenient solutions: both dispense with the necessity of reflection.
9331 LOUIS D. BRANDEIS/USA/JUDGE	I abhor averages. I like the individual case. A man may have six meals a day and one the next, making an average of three meals per day but that is not a good way to live.
9332 DUKE ELLINGTON/USA/MUSICIAN	Fate is being kind to me. Fate doesn't want me to be too famous too young.
9333 LYNN TOLER/USA/JUDGE	There are no 'buts' in the expression of love.

NUMBER CATEGORY/CREDIT	TOPIC
9334 LYNN TOLER/USA/ JUDGE	I never ever award pain and suffering in here because I think pain and suffering is a part of life.
9335 KARL MARX/GERMAN/ PHILOSOPHER	Medicine heals doubts as well as diseases.
9336 LYNN TOLER/JUDGE	You marry the guy you date, not the one he promises to become.
9337 PHYLLIS DILLER/USA/ COMEDIAN	Cleaning your house while your kids are still growing is like shoveling the walk before it stops snowing.
9338 WALT DISNEY/USA/ ANIMATOR	I only hope that we never lose sight of one thing – that it was all started by a mouse.
9339 SENECA/ROMAN DRAMATIST	It is not the man who has too little, but the man who craves more, that is poor.
9340 CICERO/ROMAN ORATOR	Let your desires be ruled by reason.
9341 SRI CHIMNOY/ INDIAN GURU	An unaspiring person believes according to what he achieves. An aspiring person achieves according to what he believes.
9342 MORTGAGE/LOANS	Pre-payment penalty
9343 WRITER/FRANCOIS DE LA ROCHEFOUCAULD	It is merely for an excuse that we say things are impossible.
9344 bell hooks/AMERICAN WRITER/PROFESSOR	For me, forgiveness and compassion are always linked; how do we hold people accountable for wrongdoing and yet at the same time remain in touch with their humanity enough to believe in their capacity to be transformed?
9345 USA/DR. ROBERT A. BURTON/AUTHOR	Pathological altruism – generosity taken to extremes can end up causing harm
9346 RALPH WALDO EMERSON/USA	When you strike at a king, you must kill him.
9347 CLAUDIAN/EPIC POET/ ALEXANDRIAN	Clemency alone makes us closer to the gods.
9348 BOETHIUS/GREEK	No man is rich who shakes and groans, convinced that he needs more.
9349 JIM HAYNES/UK	No one can ever really understand anyone else, but you can love them or at least accept them.
9350 USA/HENRY DAVID THOREAU/WRITER	We have more and more ways to communicate and yet less and less to say to each other.
9351 USA/DR. MARTIN LUTHER KING JR.	It may be true that the law cannot make a man love me, but it can stop him from lynching me, and I think that's pretty important.
9352 TYLER PERRY/USA/ MOVIE PRODUCER	You will always find jealous people. They're the ones promoting you.
9353 WILLIAM OSLER/ CANADIAN SCIENTIST	The philosophies of one age have become the absurdities of the next, and the foolishness of yesterday has become the wisdom of tomorrow.
9354 WARREN BUFFETT/ AMERICAN INVESTOR	I always knew I was going to be rich. I don't think I ever doubted it for a minute.
9355 JOHN ADAMS/USA/ PRESIDENT	A government of laws, and not of men.
9356 G.K. CHESTERTON/UK/ WRITER	There are no uninteresting things, only uninterested people.

NUMBER CATEGORY/CREDIT	TOPIC
9357 JIM ROHN/USA/WRITER/ BUSINESS/MOTIVATION	To solve any probem, here are three questions to ask yourself: First, what could I do? Second, what could I read? And third, Who could I ask?
9358 NATURE	Insect-eating plants
9359 SUN TZU/CHINESE GENERAL	The general who wins the battle makes as many calculations in his temple before the battle is fought. The general who loses makes but few calculations beforehand.
9360 WILL DURANT/USA/ HISTORIAN/WRITER	Our knowledge is a receding mirage in an expanding desert of ignorance.
9361 WALTER PIRSIG/USA/ WRITER/TEACHER	When people are fanatically devoted to political or religious faiths or any other kinds of dogmas or goals, it's always because these dogmas or goals are in doubt.
9362 UK/PM/WINSTON CHURCHILL	A prisoner of war is a man who tries to kill you and fails, and then asks you not to kill him.
9363 G.K. CHESTERTON/ UK/WRITER	Dogma does not mean the absence of thought, but the end of thought.
9364 KAHLIL GIBRAN/ LEBANESE POET	You give but little when you give of your possessions. It is when you give of yourself that you truly give.
9365 SOCRATES	I am not an Athenian or a Greek, but a citizen of the world.
9366 JERRY SPRINGER/USA	You don't love women if you treat them like dirt.
9367 E.B. WHITE/USA	Genius is more often found in a cracked pot than in a whole one.
9368 FLEXIBILITY/CHANGE	Teleworking
9369 GUILLERMO DEL TORO/ MEXICO/FILM MAKER	Awareness of insanity does not make one any less insane. Awareness of drowning does not make one any less of a drowning person -- it only adds to the burden of panic.
9370 USA/RUTH BADER GINSBURG/JUDGE	My mother told me to be a lady. And for her, that meant be your own person, be independent.
9371 USA/JEFFREY SACHS/ ECONOMIST	Roosevelt talked not only about Freedom from Fear, but also Freedom from Want.
9372 JONATHAN SWIFT/ IRISH WRITER	Nothing is so great an instance of ill manners as flattery. If you flatter all the company, you please none; if you flatter only one or two, you affront the rest.
9373 DOLLY PARTON/USA	Storms make trees take deeper roots.
9374 DAPHNE ZUNIGA/USA	To play a bag woman is brave for any woman.
9375 EDUCATION/ASIA	Cram schools (after school study centers)
9376 DALE CARNEGIE	Count your blessings, not your troubles.
9377 DUKE ELLINGTON/USA	Gray skies are just clouds passing over.
9378 JAMES ALLEN/UK/ AUTHOR	A man sooner or later discovers that he is the master-gardener of his soul, the director of his life.
9379 CULTURE	Cross cultural understanding
9380 OLIVER WENDELL HOLMES JR./USA	A man is usually more careful of his money than of his principles.
9381 GUILLERMO DEL TORO/ MEXICO/FILM MAKER	...video games are the comic books of our time...It's a medium that gains no respect among the intelligentsia.
9382 PUBLILIUS SYRUS	Every day should be passed as if it were to be our last.

NUMBER CATEGORY/CREDIT	TOPIC
9383 USA/ABRAHAM LINCOLN/PRESIDENT	If you would win a man to your cause, first convince him that you are his sincere friend.
9384 JIM ROHN/USA/ BUSINESS/MOTIVATION	Work harder on yourself than you do on your job.
9385 OSCAR WILDE/IRISH WRITER/POET	Anybody can sympathize with the sufferings of a friend, but it requires a very fine nature to sympathize with a friend's success.
9386 PUBLILIUS SYRUS	It is a bad plan that admits of no modification.
9387 D. H. LAWRENCE/UK/ WRITER	A woman unsatisfied must have luxuries. But a woman who loves a man would sleep on a board.
9388 USA/MARILYNNE ROBINSON/ESSAYIST	I think the attempt to defend belief can unsettle it, in fact, because there is always an inadequacy in argument about ultimate things.
9389 RESEARCH/SOCIETY	Difference between correlation and causation
9390 GEIL BROWNING/USA/ BUSINESS	Be aware that other people are not mind readers.
9391 DEBATE/ COMPUTERS	Tablet computers are the future of the Internet.
9392 RALPH ELLISON/USA	Education is all a matter of building bridges.
9393 RUMI/PERSIAN POET	If in thirst you drink water from a cup, you see God in it.
9394 SOCRATES	The unexamined life is not worth living.
9395 WADE DAVIS/DREAMS FROM ENDANGERED CULTURES/TED.COM	Genocide, the physical extinction of people, is universally condemned, but ethnocide, the destruction of people's way of life, is not only not condemned, it's universally celebrated as part of development strategy.
9396 GUILLERMO DEL TORO/ MEXICO/FILM MAKER	Science has made many advances in my lifetime, but the instrument has yet to be invented that can see clearly into the marriage of a man and a woman.
9397 bell hooks/USA/ WRITER/PROFESSOR	I will not have my life narrowed down. I will not bow down to somebody else's whim or to someone else's ignorance.
9398 GUILLERMO DEL TORO/ MEXICO/FILM MAKER	The doctor's code is, 'First - do no harm.' The politician's code is, 'First -- go on television.'
9399 JONATHAN SWIFT/ IRISH WRITER	Laws are like cobwebs, which may catch small flies, but let wasps and hornets through.
9400 ABBA EBAN/ISRAEL/ DIPLOMAT/LEADER	History teaches us that men and nations behave wisely once they have exhausted all other alternatives.
9401 DERRICK BELL/USA/ HARVARD/LAW	Self-esteem is like a difficult-to-cultivate flower. It requires frequent nurturing that occurs when you keep your word and follow through on your promises.
9402 JIM ROHN/USA/ MOTIVATION	You don't get paid for the hour. You get paid for the value you bring to the hour.
9403 JANE ADDAMS/USA/ SOCIAL WORKER	The cure for the ills of Democracy is more Democracy.
9404 CONNIE PODESTA/USA/ MOTIVATION/SPEAKER	We reward difficult people by giving in to their needs.
9405 ENTERTAINMENT	Buskers
9406 WILLIAM JENNINGS BRYAN/USA/LAWYER	Eloquent speech is not from lip to ear, but rather from heart to heart.

NUMBER CATEGORY/CREDIT	TOPIC
9407 GUILLERMO DEL TORO/ MEXICO/FILM MAKER	The butterfly does not look back upon its caterpillar self, either fondly or wistfully; it simply flies on.
9408 MAGIC JOHNSON/USA/ NBA/BASKETBALL	My father is my idol, so I always did everything like him. He used to work two jobs and still come home happy every night. He didn't let anyone smoke in the house. Those are the rules I adopted too.
9409 GEORGE ORWELL/ UK/AUTHOR	Every war when it comes, or before it comes, is represented not as a war but as an act of self-defense against a homicidal maniac.
9410 IMMIGRANTS/ DEBATE	Immigrants must be forced to adopt the customs of their adopted country.
9411 VIRGINIA WOOLF/ USA/AUTHOR	A woman must have money and a room of her own if she is to write fiction.
9412 SAINT AUGUSTINE/ THEOLOGIAN	Do you wish to rise? Begin by descending. You plan a tower that will pierce the clouds? Lay first the foundation of humility.
9413 RABBI SHMULEY BOTEACH/USA	2/2/2 theme: two hours of family dinner, with the family inviting two friends as guests, and with two subjects suggested for all to discuss.
9414 MUSINGS/DISASTER/ DAILY YOMIURI/JAPAN	Even if one city were to be devastated by a disaster, other cities should be able to take up the functions of the affected one.
9415 ALAN WATTS/USA/ WRITER	Hurrying and delaying are alike ways of trying to resist the present.
9416 CONNIE CHUNG/USA/ BROADCASTER	I was just going at this career -- boom, boom, boom! Then all of a sudden, at 38, Oh, my God -- I forgot to get married!
9417 PYTHAGORAS/GREEK MATHEMATICIAN	Rest satisfied with doing well, and leave others to talk of you as they will.
9418 ROBERT BROWNING/ UK/POET	Ah, but a man's reach should exceed his grasp, Or what's a heaven for?
9419 RICHARD CARLSON/ USA/WRITER	Reading is a gift. It's something you can do almost anytime and anywhere. It can be a tremendous way to learn, relax and even escape.
9420 KELLY CUTRONE/USA/ FASHION PUBLICIST	Dreams won't always take you on a straight path to destiny.
9421 FRANCIS BACON/UK/ PHILOSOPHER	Much bending breaks the bow, much unbending the mind.
9422 USA/ZORA NEALE HURSTON/WRITER	Those that don't got it, can't show it. Those that got it, can't hide it.
9423 CLARENCE DARROW/ USA/LAWYER	I do not believe there is any sort of distinction between the real moral conditions of the people in and out of jail. One is just as good as the other.
9424 MIYAMOTO MUSASHI/ JAPAN/WARRIOR	You can only fight the way you practice.
9425 ELIA KAZAN/USA	Every fighter has one fight that makes or breaks him.
9426 THOMAS J. WATSON/ IBM CEO/USA	A man flattened by an opponent can get up again. A man flattened by conformity stays down for good.
9427 GEORGE SANTAYANA/ USA/WRITER	A man's feet should be planted in his country, but his eyes should survey the world.
9428 SOPHOCLES/ GREEK PLAYWRIGHT	Show me the man who keeps his house in order and he's fit for public authority.

NUMBER CATEGORY/CREDIT	TOPIC
9429 DEBI THOMAS/USA/ SURGEON/SKATER	I tell people I'm too stupid to know what's impossible. I have ridiculously large dreams and half the time they come true.
9430 SARAH VOWELL/USA	Relics are treasured as something close to the divine.
9431 HORATIO NELSON/UK/ MILITARY LEADER	I cannot command winds and weather.
9432 GROUCHO MARX/USA	When you're in jail, a good friend will be trying to bail you out. A best friend wil be in the cell next to you saying, 'Damn, that was fun.'
9433 RUMI/PERSIAN POET	If an ant seeks the rank of Solomon, / Don't smile contemptuously upon its quest / Everything you possess of skill, and wealth and handicraft, / Wasn't it first merely a thought and quest?
9434 PYTHAGORAS/ PHYSICIST/GREEK	Strength of mind rests in sobriety; for this keeps your reason unclouded by passion.
9435 ITALY/ST. FRANCIS OF ASSISI/CATHOLIC FRIAR	O Divine Master, grant that I may not so much seek to be consoled as to console, to be understood as to understand, to be loved, as to love.
9436 DALE CARNEGIE/USA/ WRITER/LECTURER	The person who seeks all their applause from outside has their happiness in another's keeping.
9437 KAHLIL GIBRAN/ LEBANESE POET	You are the bows from which your children as living arrows are sent forth.
9438 MAGGIE KUHN/USA/ ACTIVIST	When you least expect it, someone may actually listen to what you have to say.
9439 W.H. AUDEN/POET/ ANGLO-AMERICAN	Between friends, differences in taste or opinion are irritating in direct proportion to their triviality.
9440 WILLIAM FAULKNER/ USA/NOVELIST	I have found that the greatest help in meeting any problem with decency and self-respect and whatever courage is demanded, is to know where you yourself stand.
9441 HENRY JAMES/USA/ WRITER	A man who pretends to understand women is bad manners. For him to really understand them is bad morals.
9442 LEE KUAN YEW/PM/ SINGAPORE	If you can't force or are unwilling to force your people to follow you, with or without threats, you are not a leader.
9443 RALPH ELLISON/USA/ WRITER	Hibernation is a covert preparation for a more overt action.
9444 BENJAMIN DISRAELI/UK	To be a great lawyer, I must give up my chance of being a great man.
9445 PUBLILIUS SYRUS	It is folly to punish your neighbor by fire when you live next door.
9446 SAMUEL BECKETT/IRISH	I can't go on. I'll go on.
9447 NATALIE GOLDBERG/ USA/WRITER/	To encounter a fine book and have time to read it is a wonderful thing.
9448 R. MISTRY/CANADA	Walk, first, through the fire, then philosophize.
9449 AMBROSE BIERCE/ USA/AUTHOR/	Absurdity: A statement or belief manifestly inconsistent with one's own opinion.
9450 GERMAN/ARTHUR SCHOPENHAUER	Talent hits a target no one else can hit; Genius hits a target no one else can see.
9451 ROBERT MENZIES/ AUSTRALIAN PM	A man may be a tough, concentrated, successful money-maker and never contribute to his country anything more than a horrible example.
9452 JULES VERNE/ AUTHOR/FRENCH	The chance which now seems lost may present itself at the last moment.

NUMBER CATEGORY/CREDIT	TOPIC
9453 MAGIC JOHNSON/USA/ NBA/BASKETBALL	When you are honest and open with young people, they let you in.
9454 IKKYU/JAPAN/ZEN MONK	Many paths lead from the foot of the mountain, but at the peak we all gaze at the single bright moon.
9455 ECCLESIASTES 7:16/ ADVICE/BIBLE	Do not be extremely righteous and do not be overly wise. Why should you destroy yourself?
9456 WILL DURANT/USA	The family is the nucleus of civilization.
9457 CHARLES DICKENS/UK	If there were no bad people, there would be no good lawyers.
9458 JAROD KINTZ/WRITER/ USA	Who leads the world in consumption? America! Who has more lawyers per capita? America! Who has the highest incarceration rate? America! What is the greatest country on earth? America!
9459 CHINESE SAYING	The struggle between "for" and "against" is the mind's worst disease.
9460 MERYL STARR/NY TIMES	Collections are wonder. They bring us joy and great memories.
9461 THUCYDIDES/ HISTORIAN	The bravest are surely those who have the clearest vision of what is before them, glory and danger alike, and yet notwithstanding, go out to meet it.
9462 UK/PM/WINSTON CHURCHILL	A pessimist sees the difficulty in every opportunity; an optimist sees the opportunity in every difficulty.
9463 CHARLIE ROSE/USA/ TV INTERVIEWER	Sometimes, it's more important not to try to prove something but to learn something.
9464 KOFI ANNAN/GHANA/ UNITED NATIONS	People of different religions and cultures live side by side in almost every part of the world, and most of us have overlapping identities which unite us with very different groups. We can love what we are, without hating what -- and who -- we are not. We can thrive in our own tradition, even as we learn from others, and come to respect their teachings.
9465 E.B. WHITE/US/WRITER	Luck is not something you can mention in the presence of self-made men.
9466 FRANCOIS DE LA ROCHE-FOUCAULD	He who lives without folly isn't so wise as he thinks.
9467 PERSONAL TALENT	What do you consider to be your personal gifts?
9468 CHILDREN	Interfering when other people's children behave badly in public
9469 SUN TZU/ CHINESE GENERAL	When torrential water tosses boulders, it is because of its momentum. When the strike of a hawk breaks the body of its prey, it is because of timing.
9470 A.A. MILNE/UK/AUTHOR	How lucky I am to have something that makes saying goodbye so hard.
9471 BELLA ABZUG/USA/ POLITICIAN	Women have been trained to speak softly and carry a lipstick. Those days are over.
9472 DUKE ELLINGTON/USA	My attitude is never to be satisfied, never enough, never.
9473 GEORGE ORWELL/ UK/AUTHOR	As with the Christian religion, the worst advertisement for Socialism is its adherents.
9474 ARTHUR ASHE/USA/ TENNIS PLAYER	If I were to say, "God, why me?" about the bad things, then I should have said, "God, why me?" about the good things that happened in my life.
9475 HENRY J. KAISER/ USA/INDUSTRIALIST	You can't sit on the lid of progresss. If you do, you will be blown to pieces.
9476 MAGIC JOHNSON/USA/ BUSINESS/BASKETBALL	If you're a competitive person, that stays with you. You don't stop. You always look over your shoulder.

NUMBER CATEGORY/CREDIT	TOPIC
9477 SENECA/DRAMATIST	He who boasts of his ancestry is praising the deed of another.
9478 RALPH ELLISON/USA/ AUTHOR	I am not ashamed of my grandparents for having been slaves. I am only ashamed of myself for having at one time been ashamed.
9479 CARL SAGAN/USA/ SCIENTIST	Who are we? We find that we live on an insignificant planet of a humdrum star lost in a galaxy tucked away in some forgotten corner of a universe in which there far more galaxies than people.
9480 YOSHIDA KENKO/ ESSAYS IN IDLENESS/ JAPAN	If you must take care that your opinions do not differ in the least from those of the person with whom you are talking, you might just as well be alone.
9481 SOPHOCLES/GREEK TRAGEDIAN	Ignorant men don't know what good they hold in their hands until they've flung it away.
9482 ALBERT EINSTEIN/ PHYSICIST	As a human being, one has been endowed with just enough intelligence to be able to see clearly how utterly inadequate that intelligence is when confronted with what exists.
9483 YOSHIDA KENKO/ ESSAYS IN IDLENESS/ JAPAN	In everything, no matter what it may be, uniformity is undesirable. Leaving something incomplete makes it interesting, and gives one the feeling that there is room for growth.
9484 bell hooks/USA/ WRITER/PROFESSOR	Love is a combination of care, commitment, knowledge, responsibility, respect and trust.
9485 PERICLES/GREEK STATESMAN	Just because you are not interested in politics does not mean that politics will not take an interest in you.
9486 BUSINESS/SHELL CORPORATIONS	Shell (shelf) corporations – Businesses incorporated but not active and available for sale to those who need to form a company quickly.
9487 PYTHAGORAS/GREEK MATHEMATICIAN	The oldest, shortest words – "yes" and "no" – are those which require the most thought.
9488 DALE CARNEGIE/USA/ WRITER/LECTURER	You can make more friends in two months by becoming interested in other people than you can in two years by trying to get other people interested in you.
9489 GENGHIS KHAN/ MICHAEL PRAWDIN	Conquering the world on horseback is easy; it is dismounting and governing that is hard.
9490 BENJAMIN DISRAELI/UK	We cannot learn men from books.
9491 DALE CARNEGIE/USA/ WRITER	Success is getting what you want; happiness is wanting what you get.
9492 ELIE WIESEL/USA/ NOVELIST	Mankind must remember that peace is not God's gift to his creatures; peace is our gift to each other.
9493 THOMAS CARLYLE/ SCOTTISH AUTHOR	Our main business is not to see what lies dimly at a distance but to do what lies clearly at hand.
9494 YOSHIDA KENKO/ ESSAYS IN IDLENESS/ JAPAN	Are we to look at cherry blossoms only in full bloom, at the moon only when it is cloudless?...Branches about to blossom or gardens strewn with faded flowers are worthier of our admiration.
9495 D. H. LAWRENCE/UK/ WRITER	I like trying things and discovering how I hate them.
9496 ERIKA ANDERSEN/ FORBES/USA	People only become true and effective leaders when those around them accept their leadership.
9497 YOSHIDA KENKO/JAPAN	The most precious thing in life is its uncertainty.

NUMBER CATEGORY/CREDIT	TOPIC
9498 ABRAHAM MASLOW/ USA/PSYCHOLOGIST	The story of the human race is the story of men and women selling themselves short.
9499 GERRY SPENCE/USA	When it comes to plain talk, lawyers are the worst.
9500 INDIAN PROVERB	A house without children is a graveyard.
9501 bell hooks/PROF/USA	Feminism is for everybody.
9502 FRANK LLOYD WRIGHT/ USA/ARCHITECT	An architect's most useful tools are an eraser at the drafting board and a wrecking ball at the site.
9503 SHONDA RHIMES/USA/ MOVIE PRODUCER/TV	Whenever you see me somewhere succeeding in one area of my life, that almost certainly means I am failing in another area of my life.
9504 MUSTAFA AKYOL/ TEDTALK	I think forcing people to uncover their head is as tyrannical as forcing them to cover it.
9505 ZUANGZI/CHINA	Great wisdom is generous; petty wisdom is contentious.
9506 FERDINAND MAGELLAN/ EXPLORER	The church says the earth is flat, but I know that it is round, for I have seen the shadow on the moon, and I have more faith in a shadow than in the church.
9507 STEPHEN KING/USA/ HORROR WRITER	People think that I must be a very strange person. This is not correct. I have the heart of a small boy. It is in a glass jar on my desk.
9508 TINA SEELIG/USA/ ENTREPRENEURSHIP	The majority of people who claim great success have made it happen on their own.
9509 ABORIGINAL PROVERB	Keep your eyes on the sun and you will not see the shadows.
9510 ARTHUR C. CLARKE/ UK/SCIFI WRITER	Any sufficiently advanced technology is indistinguishable from magic.
9511 HEALTH/MEDICINE	Acupuncture
9512 ABRAHAM LINCOLN/ 16th PRESIDENT/USA	Better to remain silent and be thought a fool than to speak out and remove all doubt.
9513 ADOLF HITLER/NAZI	Success is the sole earthly judge of right and wrong.
9514 CHINUA ACHEBE/ AFRICAN WRITER/	Let me say that I do think decency and civilization would insist that the writer take sides with the powerless.
9515 LOUIS D. BRANDEIS/ USA/JUDGE	Men long for an afterlife in which there apparently is nothing to do but delight in heaven's wonders.
9516 OLIVER WENDELL HOLMES JR./USA	A child's education should begin at least one hundred years before he is born.
9517 JAMES ALLEN/UK	People seek guidance of him who is master of himself.
9518 ANDREW CARNEGIE/ SCOTTISH-AMERICAN	Surplus wealth is a sacred trust which its possessor is bound to administer in his lifetime for the good of the community.
9519 MARGARET MEAD/USA	We won't have a society if we destroy the environment.
9520 ANNE HEYWOOD/USA/ THIS I BELIEVE	I know that the unhappy periods of our lives offer us concrete and useful plus-values, chief among them a heightened understanding and compassion for others.
9521 R.W. EMERSON/USA	The years teach much which the days never know.
9522 E.B. WHITE/USA/ WRITER	I arise in the morning torn between a desire to improve the world and a desire to enjoy the world. This makes it hard to plan the day.
9523 CLARENCE DARROW/US/ LAWYER	The trouble with law is lawyers.

NUMBER CATEGORY/CREDIT	TOPIC
9524 CICERO/ORATOR	It is a true saying that "One falsehood leads easily to another."
9525 AMA ATA AIDOO/ WRITER/GHANA	People are worms, and even the God who created them is immensely bored with their antics.
9526 WILLIAM JENNINGS BRYAN/USA/LAWYER	Burn down your cities and leave our farms, and your cities will spring up again is if by magic; but destroy our farms and the grass will grow in he streets of every city in the country.
9527 DEBATE/RELIGION	There are different paths to the divine.
9528 HABITS/WILL POWER	Breaking bad habits
9529 KELLY CUTRONE/USA/ ENTREPRENER	When you're the most happening person at the party, 'tis time to leave.
9530 RALPH ELLISON/USA/ AUTHOR	Life is to be lived, not controlled; and humanity is won by continuing to play in the face of certain defeat.
9531 RABBI SHMULEY BOTEACH/USA	Someone without value cannot confer value on you.
9532 WILL DURANT/USA/ HISTORIAN/WRITER	The trouble with most people is that they think with their hopes or fears or wishes rather than with their minds.
9533 AMA ATA AIDOO/ WRITER/GHANA	It's a sad moment, really, when parents first become a bit frightened of their children.
9534 SOPHOCLES	Much speech is one thing, well-timed speech is another.
9535 EDUCATION/COST	Increasing cost of education
9536 F. SCOTT FITZGERALD/ USA/WRITER	A great social success is a pretty girl who plays her cards as carefully as if she were plain.
9537 CLARENCE DARROW/ USA/LAWYER	Even if you do learn to speak correct English, whom are you going to speak it to?
9538 AYI KWEI ARMAH/ GHANA/WRITER	Disgust with injustice may sharpen the desire for justice.
9539 HARDSHIP/SURVIVAL	Resilience
9540 FEDERAL EXPRESS	When it absolutely, positively has to be there overnight.
9541 MORTIMER ADLER/USA	Freedom is the emancipation from the arbitrary rule or other men.
9542 TOBIAS WOLFF/USA	We are made to persist; that's how we find out who we are.
9543 ARTHUR ASHE/USA	The ideal attitude is to be physically loose and mentally tight.
9544 BERTRAND RUSSELL/ BRITISH AUTHOR	To fear love is to fear life, and those who fear life are already three parts dead.
9545 MICHAEL ONDAATJE/ CANADA/WRITER	I have spent weeks in the desert, forgetting to look at the moon, he says, as a married man may spend days never looking into the face of his wife. These are not sins of omission but signs of preoccupation.
9546 DIANNA BOOHER/USA/ COMMUNICATIONS	Dress for the part you want to play.
9547 NGUGI WA THIONG'O/ KENYA/WRITER	If poverty was to be sold three cents today, I can't buy it.
9548 WILLIAM HAZLITT/ UK/CRITIC	An honest man speaks the truth, though it may give offence; a vain man, in order that it may.
9549 JURGEN HABERMAS/ GERMAN/THINKER	Each murder is one too many.

NUMBER CATEGORY/CREDIT	TOPIC
9550 THOMAS PICKETTY/ ECONOMIST/USA/ FRANCE	For millions of people, "wealth" amounts to little more than a few weeks' wages in a checking account or low-interest savings account, a car, and a few pieces of furniture.
9551 CHILDREN/ OBESITY	Increase in childhood obesity
9552 ESSAYIST/RALPH WALDO EMERSON/USA	What you do speaks so loud that I cannot hear what you say.
9553 MALCOLM FORBES/USA/ EDITOR/BUSINESS	Once in a civil service job, one needs only to live to rise. It's near impossible to be fired for incompetence, indifference, woeful attendance, insubordination, or even being caught red-handed in the cookie jar.
9554 BEAUTY/SKILL	Interior decorating
9555 DANIEL DEFOE/UK	All men would be tyrants if they could.
9556 SCIENTIST/NICHOLAS COPERNICUS/POLISH	For I am not so enamored of my own opinions that I disregard what others may think of them.
9557 KEN ROBINSON/UK/USA/ TEDTALK/EDUCATOR	I believe this passionately; that we don't grow into creativity, we grow out of it. Or rather, we get educated out of it.
9558 OSCAR WILDE/IRISH WRITER/POET	It is through disobedience and rebellion that progress has been made.
9559 bell hooks/USA/ WRITER/ PROFESSOR	When we drop fear, we can draw nearer to people, we can draw nearer to the earth, we can draw nearer to all the heavenly creatures that surround us.
9560 HANS ROSLING/M.D./ TEDTALK/STATISTICS	My experience from 20 years of Africa is that the seemingly impossible is possible.
9561 RICHARD CARLSON/ USA/WRITER	Effective listening is more than simply avoiding the bad habit of interrupting others while they are speaking or finishing their sentences.
9562 THE TALMUD	He who promises runs in debt.
9563 LAO-TZU/CHINESE PHILOSPHER	Because of not daring to be ahead of the world, one becomes the leader of the world.
9564 TONY KUSHNER/ PLAYWRIGHT	Every student needs someone who says, simply, "You mean something. You count."
9565 USA/DWIGHT D. EISENHOWER/ 39TH PRESIDENT	Though force can protect in emergency, only justice, fairness, consideration and co-operation can finally lead men to the dawn of eternal peace.
9566 SCIENCE	Cloning of animals
9567 CHARLIE PARKER/USA	Don't play the saxophone. Let it play you.
9568 SECURITY	Data protection in the Internet age
9569 G.K. CHESTERTON/UK	The way to love anything is to realize it may be lost.
9570 MARK TWAIN/USA/ NOVELIST	A person with a new idea is a crank until the idea succeeds.
9571 STEVE JOBS/APPLE FOUNDER/USA	Sometimes life is going to hit you in the head with a brick. Don't lose faith.
9572 JULIUS CAESAR/ROME/ LEADER	It is easier to find men who will volunteer to die, than to find those who are willing to endure pain with patience.
9573 JEREMY BENTHAM/ UK/PHILOSOPHER	Lawyers are the only persons in whom ignorance of the law is not punished.

NUMBER CATEGORY/CREDIT	TOPIC
9574 FELA KUTI/NIGERIA/ MUSICIAN	To be spiritual is not by praying and going to church. Spiritualism is the understanding of the universe so that it can be a better place.
9575 ALAN WATTS/USA/ WRITER	Paradoxical as it may seem, the purposeful life has no content, no point. It hurries on and on and misses everything. Not hurrying, the purposeless life misses nothing, for it is only when there is no goal and no rush that the human senses are fully open to receive the world.
9576 JOAN DIDION/USA/ WRITER	Life changes in the instant. The ordinary instant.
9577 KEN ROBINSON/ SCHOOLS KILL CREATIVITY/TED.COM	You were probably steered benignly away from things at school when you were a kid – things you liked – on the grounds that you would never get a job doing that: 'Don't do music, you're not going to be a musician,. Don't do art., you won't be an artist.' Benign advice – now profoundly mistaken.
9578 RUMI/PERSIAN POET	Gamble everything for love if you are a true human being.
9579 GEORGE ORWELL/ UK/AUTHOR	Who controls the past controls the future. Who controls the present controls the past.
9580 RUMI/PERSIAN POET	Do not grieve. Anything you lose comes round in another form.
9581 ALAN WATTS/USA/ WRITER	People become concerned with being more humble than other people.
9582 ADOLF HITLER/NAZI LEADER	By the skilful and sustained use of propaganda, we can make a people see even heaven as hell or an extremely wretched life as paradise.
9583 RUMI/PERSIAN POET	Good and bad are mixed. If you don't have both, you don't belong with us.
9584 PETER DRUCKER/ MANAGEMENT/WRITER	Time is the scarcest resource and unless it is managed nothing else can be managed.
9585 JOHN K GALBRAITH/ ECONOMIST	Politics is the art of choosing between the disastrous and the unpalatable.
9586 AL CAPONE/USA/ GANGSTER	Once in the racket you're always in it.
9587 USA/ABRAHAM LINCOLN/PRESIDENT	A friend is one who has the same enemies as you have.
9588 ANDREW CARNEGIE/USA	The first man gets the oyster, the second man gets the shell.
9589 CONFUCIUS/THINKER	Ignorance is the night of the mind, but a night without moon and star.
9590 KOFI ANNAN/GHANA/ UNITED NATIONS	Landmines are among the most barbaric weapons of war, because they continue to kill and maim innocent people long after the war itself has ended.
9591 TECHNOLOGY	Biometric signatures
9592 THOMAS PICKETTY/ ECONOMIST/FRANCE	Democracy will never be supplanted by a republic of experts -- and that is a very good thing.
9593 G.K. CHESTERTON/ UK/WRITER	The true soldier fights not because he hates what is in front of him, but because he loves what is behind him.
9594 JULES VERNE/AUTHOR	The earth does not need new continents, but new men.
9595 FRANS DE WAAL/DUTCH PRIMATOLOGIST/ TEDTALK	Humanity is actually much more cooperative and empathetic than [it's] given credit for.
9596 AUGUSTUS CAESAR/ LEADER/ROME	Hasten slowly.

NUMBER CATEGORY/CREDIT	TOPIC
9597 RICHARD DAWKINS/ BIOLOGIST/AUTHOR	I am against religion because it teaches us to be satisfied with not understanding the world.
9598 KOFI ANNAN/UN/ GHANA	To live is to choose. But to choose well, you must know who you are and what you stand for, where you want to go and why you want to get there.
9599 GANDHI/INDIA/LEADER	No culture can live if it attempts to be exclusive.
9600 UK/SOMERSET MAUGHAM/WRITER	Sometimes the greatest journey is the distance between two people.
9601 LILLIAN HELLMAN/ USA/PLAYWRIGH	Cocaine isn't habit-forming. I should know – I've been using it for years.
9602 PUBLILIUS SYRUS	He doubly benefits the needy who gives quickly.
9603 WILMA ASKINAS/USA	A friend is one who sees through you and still enjoys the view.
9604 SRI LANKA/CHANDRIKA B. KUMARATUNGA	Peace is a battle.
9605 ANNE FRANK/JEWISH AUTHOR/ HOLOCAUST	Women should be respected as well! Generally speaking, men are held in great esteem in all parts of the world, so why shouldn't women have their share?
9606 WILL DURANT/USA/ HISTORIAN/WRITER	To speak ill of others is a dishonest way of praising ourselves. Nothing is often a good thing to say, and always a clever thing to say.
9607 RALPH ELLISON/USA/	When I discover who I am, I'll be free.
9608 RUMI/PERSIAN POET	Whoever gives reverence receives reverence.
9609 KAHLIL GIBRAN/ON CLOTHES	Your clothes conceal much of your beauty, yet they hide not the unbeautiful. And though you seek in garments the freedom of privacy you may find in them a harness and a chain.
9610 GEORGE SANTAYANA/ WRITER	Intolerance is a form of egotism, and to condemn egotism intolerantly is to share it.
9611 CRIMINAL JUSTICE/2001/ ECONOMIST	In France parading suspects in public is banned.
9612 USA/ELEANOR ROOSEVELT/1ST LADY	To handle yourself, use your head; to handle others, use your heart.
9613 WARREN FARRELL/ USA/WRITER	Throughout my life I have always been amazed that people couldn't listen to other people, that they couldn't hear their best intent, that there seemed to be an enormous need to demonize.
9614 SAMUEL JOHNSON/ UK/AUTHOR/	Curiosity is one of the permanent and certain characteristics of a vigorous mind.
9615 DEBATE	Computers connect people to happiness.
9616 GEORGE ORWELL/ UK/AUTHOR	All the war-propaganda, all the screaming and lies and hatred, comes invariably from people who are not fighting.
9617 F. S. FITZGERALD/USA	Family quarrels are bitter things.
9618 ROBERT FROST/USA/ POET	The jury consists of twelve persons chosen to decide who has the better lawyer.
9619 KOFI ANNAN/UN/ GHANA	Literacy is a bridge from misery to hope.
9620 ELDRIDGE CLEAVER/US/ CIVIL RIGHTS ACTIVIST	You're either part of the solution or you're part of the problem.

NUMBER CATEGORY/CREDIT	TOPIC
9621 DALAI LAMA XIV/ TIBET/LEADER	This is my simple religion. There is no need for temples; no need for complicated philosophy. Our own brain, our own heart is our temple; the philosophy is kindness.
9622 SOPHOCLES	One word frees us of all the weight and pain of life. That word is love.
9623 JEFFREY EUGENIDES/ USA/WRITER	Biology gives you a brain. Life turns it into a mind.
9624 PATRICK AWUAH/ ASHESI UNIV. FOUNDER/ GHANA/TEDTALK	While I was at Microsoft, the annual revenues grew larger than the GDP of the Republic of Ghana.
9625 THUCYDIDES/ HISTORIAN	In a democracy, someone who fails to get elected to office can always console himself with the thought that there was something not quite fair about it.
9626 MICHIO KAKU/USA/ PHYSICIST/ HYPERSPACE	Some people seek meaning in life through personal gain, through personal relationships, or through personal experience. However, it seems to me that being blessed with the intellect to divine the ultimate secrets of nature gives meaning enough to life.
9627 WILLIAM JENNINGS BRYAN/USA/LAWYER	Destiny is no matter of chance. It is a mater of choice. It is not a thing to be waited for; it is a thing to be achieved.
9628 DAVID BROOKS/USA/ WRITER/BOBOS IN PARADISE	To get the most attention, the essay should be wrong. Logical essays are read and understood. But an illogical or wrong essay will prompt dozens of other writers to rise and respond, thus giving the author mounds of publicity.
9629 E.B. WHITE/USA/WRITER	One of the most time-consuming things is to have an enemy.
9630 TONY KUSHNER/USA/ PLAYWRIGHT	The smallest indivisible human unit is two people, not one; one is a fiction. From such nets of souls societies, the social world, human life springs.
9631 UNIVERSITIES	Academic freedom
9632 TONY KUSHNER/USA	Here's another piece of advice: only date people who have read a different set of books than you have read. It will save you lots of time in the library.
9633 ARTIST/JEAN-MICHEL BASQUIAT/USA	Fire will attract more attention than any other cry for help.
9634 GARY NUTTING/NY TIMES/PHILOSOPHER	Does it matter whether God exists?
9635 CHARLES DICKENS/UK	No one is useless in this world who lightens the burdens of another.
9636 REMBRANDT/PAINTER/ DUTCH	Choose only one master -- Nature.
9637 ALAN WATTS/USA/ WRITER	Eskimos have five words for different kinds of snow because they live with it and it is important to them. But the Aztec langauge has but one word for snow, rain, and hail.
9638 FRENCH/GEORGES CLEMENCEAU/PM	My home policy: I wage war; my foreign policy; I wage war. All the time I wage war.
9639 SOPHOCLES	Numberless are the world's wonders, but none more wonderful than man.
9640 EMPLOYEES' CREDO	If you want it bad, you'll get it...bad!
9641 INDIAN PROVERB	A harvest of peace germinates from seeds of contentment.
9642 OSCAR WILDE/IRISH POET	Wisdom comes with winters.

NUMBER CATEGORY/CREDIT	TOPIC
9643 SOPHOCLES/WRITER	What you cannot enforce, do not command.
9644 NATALIE ANGIER/USA/NY TIMES/WRITER	Empathetic nurses burn out and leave the profession more quickly than do their peers who remain aloof.
9645 SCIENTIST/NICHOLAS COPERNICUS/POLISH	Mathematics is written for mathematicians.
9646 bell hooks/AMERICAN WRITER/ PROFESSOR	I am passionate about everything in my life – first and foremost, passionate about ideas.
9647 ABORIGINAL PROVERB	The more you know, the less you need.
9648 SOREN KIERKEGAARD/PHILOSOPHER	Be that self which one truly is.
9649 MARCO TEMPEST/MAGIC/TEDTALK	The Chinese general Sun Tzu said that all war was based on deception. Oscar Wilde said the same thing of romance.
9650 KAHLIL GIBRAN/ON CRIME AND PUNISHMENT	And as a single leaf turns not yellow but with the silent knowledge of the whole tree, so the wrongdoer cannot do wrong without the hidden will of you all.
9651 KOFI ANNAN/GHANA/UNITED NATIONS	Fierce national competition over water resources has prompted fears that water issues contain the seeds of violent conflict.
9652 SOPHOCLES/WRITER	No man loves life like him that's growing old.
9653 RICHARD CARLSON/USA/WRITER/DON'T SWEAT THE SMALL STUFF	The need to be right stems from an unhealthy relationship to your own thoughts. Do you believe your thoughts are representative of reality and need to be defended, or do you realize that realities are seen through different eyes?
9654 CICERO/ORATOR	It is a great thing to know our vices.
9655 TUPAC SHAKUR/HIP HOP/USA/ARTISTE	It seems like every time you come up something happens to bring you back down.
9656 USA/RICHARD P. FEYNMAN/WINNER	I believe that a scientist looking at nonscientific problems is just as dumb as the next guy.
9657 THOMAS MANN/WRITER	Tolerance becomes a crime when applied to evil.
9658 JOHN C. MAXWELL/USA/CONSULTANT	Leadership is not about titles, positions or flowcharts. It is about one life influencing another.
9659 A. G. WELLS/UK/WRITER	All men, however highly educated, retain some superstitious inklings.
9660 SENECA/ROMAN DRAMATIST	Without an adversary, prowess shrivels. We see how great and efficient it really is only when it shows by endurance what it is capable of.
9661 USA/DWIGHT D. EISENHOWER/PRESIDENT	Don't join the book burners. Don't think you're going to conceal faults by concealing evidence that they ever existed. Don't be afraid to go in your library and read every book.
9662 ROBERT FROST/US POET	A successful lawsuit is the one worn by a policeman.
9663 BENJAMIN DISRAELI/BRITISH STATESMAN	Grief is the agony of an instant, the indulgence of grief the blunder of a life.
9664 FRANK LLOYD WRIGHT/USA/ARCHITECT	A man is a fool if he drank before he reaches the age of fifty, and a fool if he doesn't afterward.
9665 RICHARD CARLSON/USA/WRITER/DON'T SWEAT THE SMALL STUFF	The old adage, "If it sounds too good to be true, it probably is" isn't always correct. In fact, the suspicion, cynicisms, and doubt that are inherent in this belief can and does keep people from taking advantage of excellent opportunities.

NUMBER CATEGORY/CREDIT	TOPIC
9666 ANDREA DWORKIN/USA	Feminism is hated beause women are hated.
9667 WRITER/FRANCOIS DE LA ROCHEFOUCAULD	Gratitude is merely the secret hope of further favors.
9668 GEORGE ORWELL/UK	Whoever is winning at the moment will always seem to be invincible.
9669 ABRAHAM LINCOLN/ USA/16TH PRESIDENT	Discourage litigation. Persuade your neighbors to compromise whenever you can.
9670 ALAN WATTS/WRITER	Belief clings, but faith lets go.
9671 THE TALMUD	The parent who does not teach the child a useful trade is teaching him or her to steal.
9672 RABBI SHMULEY BOTEACH/USA	Everyone who seeks the spotlight, whether in sports, television or politics, does so to compensate for some feeling of inadequacy.
9673 RICHARD CARLSON/ USA/WRITER	Ironically, when you surrender your need to hog the glory, the attention you used to need from other people is replaced by a quiet inner confidence that is derived from letting others have it.
9674 LILLIAN HELLMAN/USA/ DRAMATIST	I like people who refuse to speak until they are ready to speak.
9675 WILL DURANT/ USA/HISTORIAN	Truth always originates in a minority of one, and every custom begins as a broken precedent.
9676 JIMMY CLIFF/SINGER	I'd rather be a free man in my grave, than living as a puppet or a slave.
9677 JAMES ALLEN/UK/ AUTHOR	A man has to learn that he cannot command things, but that he can command himself; that he cannot coerce the wills of others, but that he can mold and master his own will.
9678 REMBRANDT/PAINTER/ DUTCH	Life etches itself onto our faces as we grow older, showing our violence, excesses or kindnesses.
9679 THOMAS J. WATSON/ IBM CEO	Nothing so conclusively proves a man's ability to lead others as what he does from day to day to lead himself.
9680 JENNY JOSEPH/ WARNING	When I am an old woman, I shall wear purple with a red hat that doesn't go, and doesn't suit me.
9681 ABRAHAN LINCOLN/ USA/PRESIDENT	I regard no man as poor who has a godly mother.
9682 BENJAMIN DISRAELI/ BRITISH STATESMAN	Cleanliness and order are not matters of instinct; they are matters of education, and like most great things, you must cultivate a taste for them.
9683 HENRY D. THOREAU/ USA/WRITER	It is not desirable to cultivate a respect for law, so much as a respect for right.
9684 ST. FRANCIS OF ASSISI/CATHOLIC FRIAR	For it is in giving that we receive. It is in pardoning that we are pardoned.
9685 JOHN SCOPES/USA/ SCIENCE TEACHER	The best time to scotch the snake is when it starts to wiggle.
9686 PICO IYER/WRITER/ WHARTON/USA	...the more time-saving gadgets we have in our lives, the less time we have.
9687 TYRA BANKS/MODEL/ OPEN LETTER/THE DAILY BEAST	I would love for models to be protected by a guild. Even when I was a teen model, I didn't think it was fair that I had to enter the acting world to get insurance.
9688 ALBERT EINSTEIN/ SCIENTIST/NOBELIST	Science without religion is lame, religion without science is blind.

NUMBER CATEGORY/CREDIT	TOPIC
9689 SOPHOCLES/WRITER	To him who is in fear everything rustles.
9690 H. G. WELLS/UK/WRITER	Will is stronger than fact; it can mold and overcome fact.
9691 OSCAR WILDE/IRISH WRITER/POET	There are many things that we would throw away if we were not afraid that others might pick them up.
9692 DANISH/SOREN KIERKEGAARD	Boredom is the root of all evil...
9693 JULES VERNE/WRITER	Science...is made up of mistakes, but they are mistakes which it is useful to make, because they lead little by little to the truth.
9694 ALAN WATTS/WRITER	I owe my solitude to other people.
9695 AN INDIAN PROVERB	A house without a woman is the devil's own residence.
9696 H. G. WELLS/WRITER/UK	Every time I see an adult on a bicycle, I no longer despair for the future of the human race.
9697 ARTHUR ASHE/USA	Racism is not an excuse to not do the best you can.
9698 USA/WILLIAM O. DOUGLAS/JUDGE/USA	The right to revolt has sources deep in our history.
9699 AYN RAND/WRITER	Money is the barometer of a society's virtue.
9700 THE CREATIVITY CRISIS/ NEWSWEEK/JULY 2010	A recent IBM poll of 1,500 CEOs identified creativity as the No. 1 'leadership competency' of the future.
9701 R.W. EMERSON/WRITER	All I have seen teaches me to trust the creator for all I have not seen.
9702 STEFFI GRAF/TENNIS	I never look back. I look forward.
9703 MARILYN MANSON/ AMERICAN MUSICIAN	A lot of people don't want to make their own decisions. They're too scared. It's much easier to be told what to do.
9704 SUN TZU/CHINESE GENERAL/AUTHOR/ THE ART OF WAR	The general who advances without coveting fame and retreats without fearing disgrace, whose only thought is to protect his country and do good service for his sovereign, is the jewel of the kingdom.
9705 CHARLES LAMB/UK/ WRITER	It is good to love the unknown.
9706 WILLIAM HAZLITT/UK	A wise traveler never despises his own country.
9707 JASON FRIED/WHY WORK DOESN'T HAPPEN AT WORK/ TED.COM	[Facebook and Twitter] aren't the real problems in the office. The real problems are what I like to call the M & M's, the Managers and the Meetings.
9708 BLAISE PASCAL/FRENCH	Law, without force, is impotent.
9709 JIM ROHN/USA/ BUSINESS/MOTIVATION	Miss a meal if you have to, but don't miss a book.
9710 JIM ROHN/USA	Excuses are the nails used to build a house of failure.
9711 COMMON SAYING	The early bird may catch the worm, but the second mouse gets the cheese.
9712 bell hooks/USA/ WRITER/ PROFESSOR	Often men who have been emotionally neglected and abused as children by dominating mothers bond with assertive women, only to have their childhood feelings of being engulfed surface.
9713 JACQUES BARZUN/USA/ EDITOR/WRITER	Teaching is not a lost art, but the regard for it is a lost tradition.
9714 DAVID SHIELDS/USA	Anything processed by memory is fiction.
9715 bell hooks/USA/ WRITER/PROFESSOR	...no woman writer can write "too much." No woman has ever written enough.

NUMBER CATEGORY/CREDIT	TOPIC
9716 WILLIAM JENNINGS BRYAN/USA/LAWYER	Do not compute the totality of your poultry population until all the manifestations of incubation have been entirely completed.
9717 JOAN DIDION/USA/ WRITER	Character – the willingness to accept responsibility for one's own life – is the source from which self-respect springs.
9718 KELLY CUTRONE/ USA/ENTREPRENER	Things will change...sometimes the hardest lessons to learn are the ones your soul needs most.
9719 ALAN WATTS/WRITER	One learns a great deal sometimes from being sick.
9720 ALBERT EINSTEIN/ LETTER TO CORNEL LANCZOS/1942	It is hard to sneak a look at God's cards. But that he would choose to play dice with the world...is something I cannot believe for a single moment.
9721 bell hooks/USA/ WRITER/ PROFESSOR	Visionary feminism is a wise and loving politics. It is rooted in the love of male and female being, refusing to privilege one over the other.
9722 SOPHOCLES	How dreadful it is when the right judge judges wrong!
9723 LEE IACOCCA/ CHRYSLER/CEO/ LEADERSHIP	One of the things the government can't do is run anything. The only things our government runs are the post office and the railroads, and both of them are bankrupt.
9724 ALBERT ELLIS/USA/ PSYCHOLOGIST	By not caring too much about what people think, I'm able to think for myself and propagate ideas which are very unpopular. And I succeed.
9725 MARRIAGE/WEDDING	Wedding ceremonies in your home country
9726 WILLIAM OSLER/ CANADIAN SCIENTIST	The greater the ignorance the greater the dogmatism.
9727 PETER DRUCKER/ PROFESSOR/USA	There is nothing so useless as doing efficiently that which should not be done at all.
9728 DR. WAYNE DYER/USA/ WRITER/MOTIVATION	What comes out of you when you are squeezed is what is inside you.
9729 TINA SEELIG/USA/	Failure: the secret sauce of Silicon Valley
9730 JIM ROHN/USA	Either you run the day or the day runs you.
9731 STACEY KRAMER/ TED.COM	The next time you're faced with something that's unexpected, unwanted and uncertain, consider that it just may be a gift.
9732 DAVID OGILVY/ ADVERTISING INDUSTRY LEADER	Advertising is a business of words, but advertising agencies are infested with men and women who cannot write. They cannot write advertisements and they cannot write plans. They are helpless as deaf mutes on the stage of the Metropolitan Opera.
9733 USA/ABRAHAM LINCOLN/16th PRESIDENT	Force is all-conquering, but its victories are short-lived.
9734 TAN LE/MY IMMIGRATION STORY/TEDTALK	It is okay to be an outsider, a recent arrival, new on the scene – and not just okay, but something to be thankful for...Because being an insider can so easily mean collapsing the horizons, can so easily mean accepting the presumptions of your province.
9735 KAHLIL GIBRAN/ON CRIME & PUNISHMENT	And how shall you punish those whose remorse is already greater than their misdeeds?
9736 DALE CARNEGIE/ USA/WRITER	When dealing with people, let us remember we are not dealing with creatures of logic. We are dealing with creatures of emotion.
9737 ANNIE DILLARD/USA/ WRITER	You can't test courage cautiously.

NUMBER CATEGORY/CREDIT	TOPIC
9738 BRENÉ BROWN/USA/ TEDTALK/PROFESSOR	The two most powerful words when we're in struggle: me too.
9739 COMMON SAYING	If three people tell you that you are drunk, you better lie down.
9740 BENJAMIN DISRAELI/ BRITISH STATESMAN	Circumstances are beyond human control, but our conduct is in our own power.
9741 CHINESE SAYING	You won't help shoots grow by pulling them up higher.
9742 KATHRYN SCHULZ/ TEDTALK/JOURNALIST	If you Google 'regret and tattoo,' you will get 11.5 million hits.
9743 BENJAMIN DISRAELI/ UK/PRIME MINISTER	In England when a new character appears in our inner circles, the first question always is, "Who is he?" In France it is, "What is he?" In England "How much a year?" In France, "What has he done?"
9744 JOHN CHARLES POLANYI/CANADA	If we treasure our own experience and regard it as real, we must also treasure other people's experiences.
9745 WARREN BUFFETT/ BILLIONAIRE/USA	I don't look to jump over 7-foot bars. I look around for 1-foot bars that I can step over.
9746 KAHLIL GIBRAN/ LEBANESE POET	And forget not that the earth delights to feel your bare feet and the winds long to play with your hair.
9747 PETER DRUCKER/USA	What gets measured gets done.
9748 ASHLEIGH BRILLIAN/ UK/AUTHOR	Sometimes the most urgent and vital thing you can possibly do is take a complete rest.
9749 WILLIAM HAZLITT/UK	A hair in the head is worth two in the brush.
9750 MIYAMOTO MUSASHI	If you wish to control others you must first control yourself.
9751 CONFUCIUS/CHINA	Is it not delightful to have friends coming from afar?
9752 NGUGI WA THIONG'O/ WIZARD OF THE CROW	Your own actions are a better mirror of your life than the actions of all your enemies put together.
9753 NELSON MANDELA/ S. AFRICA/PRESIDENT	Education is the most powerful weapon which you can use to change the world.
9754 PIETRO ARETINO/ ITALY/POET	I keep my friends as misers to their treasure, because, of all things granted us by wisdom, none is greater or better than friendship.
9755 F. SCOTT FITZGERALD/ USA/AUTHOR	After all, life hasn't much to offer except youth, and I suppose for older people, the love of youth in others.
9756 TYRA BANKS/MODEL/ OPEN LETTER/USA	To moms everywhere, we need to educate our girls not to fall prey to *thinspirational* images of beauty.
9757 PUBLILIUS SYRUS	For a good cause, wrongdoing is virtuous.
9758 MARC PACHTER/THE ART OF THE INTERVIEW/TEDTALK	Everybody in their lives is really waiting for people to ask them questions, so that they can be truthful about who they are and how they became what they are.
9759 PHILIP ZIMBARDO/ THE DEMISE OF GUYS?/ TEDTALK	Boys are 30 percent more likely than girls to drop out of school. In Canada five boys drop out for every three girls. Girls outperform boys now at every level, from elementary school to graduate school.
9760 PAUL GAUGUIN/ FRENCH/PAINTER	I shut my eyes in order to see.
9761 bell hooks/USA/WRITER	Love is an action, never simply a feeling.

NUMBER CATEGORY/CREDIT	TOPIC
9762 DAVID BROOKS/USA/ WRITER/THE SOCIAL ANIMAL	The point of being a teacher is to do more than impart facts, it's to shape the way students perceive the world, to help a student absorb the rules of a discipline. The teachers who do that get remembered.
9763 USA/JOHN QUINCY ADAMS/2nd PRESIDENT	Public business, my son, must always be done by somebody. It will be done by somebody or another. If wise men decline it, others will not; if honest men refuse it, others will not.
9764 MERYL STARR/USA/ NY TIMES/	Clutter immobilizes you.
9765 FRANTZ FANNON/ CARIBBEAN/ PSYCHIATRIST	Sometimes people hold a core belief that is very strong. When they are presented with evidence that works against that belief, the new evidence cannot be accepted. It would create a feeling that is extremely uncomfortable, called cognitive dissonance. And because it is so important to protect the core belief, they will rationalize, ignore and even deny anything that doesn't fit in with the core belief.
9766 PLATO/AUTHOR/ PHILOSOPHER	Never discourage anyone who continually makes progress, no matter how slow.
9767 PUBLILIUS SYRUS	In a heated argument we are apt to lose sight of the truth.
9768 TINA SEELIG/USA/ ENTREPRENEUR	The sweet spot is where your passions overlap with your skills and the market.
9769 RANDY PAUSCH/USA/ COMPUTER SCIENTIST	I'd compare college tuition to paying for a personal trainer at an athletic club. We professors play the roles of trainers, giving people access to the equipment (books, labs, our expertise) and after that, it is our job to be demanding.
9770 AMERICAN EXPRESS	Don't leave home without it.
9771 HELEN FISHER/WHY WE LOVE + CHEAT/ TEDTALK	People live for love. They kill for love. They die for love. They have songs, poems, novels, sculptures, paintings, myths, legends. It's one of the most powerful brain systems on Earth for both great joy and great sorrow.
9772 BOB HOPE/USA/ COMEDIAN	A bank is a place that will lend you money if you can prove that you don't need it.
9773 RACHEL CARSON/USA/ SCIENTIST/WRITER	But man is a part of nature, and his war against nature is inevitably a war against himself.
9774 JOSEPH CAMPBELL/USA/ WRITER	Opportunities to find deeper powers within ourselves come when life seems most challenging.
9775 FRANK WARREN/USA/ SECRETS/TED.COM	Secrets can remind us of the countless human dramas, of frailty and heroism playing out silently in the lives of people all around us.
9776 JAMES WATSON/USA	A predisposition does not a predetermination make.
9777 MICHIO KAKU/USA/ PHYSICIST/ HYPERSPACE	By 2100, our destiny is to become like the gods we once worshipped and feared. But our tools will not be magic wands and potions but the science of computers, nanotechnology, artificial intelligence, biotechnology, and most all...quantum theory.
9778 BOB PROCTOR/USA	The only competition you will ever face is with your own ignorance.
9779 CHARLES M. BLOW/USA/ COLUMNIST	One doesn't have to operate with great malice to do great harm. The absence of empathy and understanding are sufficient. In fact, a man convinced of his virtue even in the midst of his vice is the worst kind of man.

NUMBER CATEGORY/CREDIT	TOPIC
9780 ROBERTH HUGHES/ AUSTRALIA/AUTHOR	The greater the artist, the greater the doubt. Perfect confidence is granted to the less talented as a consolation prize.
9781 bell hooks/USA/ WRITER/PROFESSOR	Contrary to what we may have been taught to think, unnecessary and unchosen suffering wounds us but need not scar us for life. It does mark us. What we allow the mark of our suffering to become is in our own hands.
9782 RACHEL CARSON/USA/ SCIENTIST/AUTHOR	There is something infinitely healing in the repeated refrains of nature -- the assurance that dawn comes after night, and spring after winter.
9783 COUNTEE CULLEN/USA/ POET	For we must be one thing or the other, an asset or a liability, the sinew in your wing to help you soar, or the chain to bind you to earth.
9784 ALAIN DE BOTTON/ SUCCESS/ TED.COM	A snob is anybody who takes a small part of you and uses that to come to a complete vision of who you are.
9785 MICHIO KAKU/USA/ PHYSICIST	Physicists are made of atoms. A physicist is an attempt by an atom to understand itself.
9786 INDIA/JAWAHARLAL NEHRU/PM	Evil unchecked grows, evil tolerated poisons the whole system.
9787 SAMUEL BECKETT/ IRISH PLAYWRIGHT	I have my faults but changing my tune is not one of them.
9788 ACTOR/USA/DENZEL WASHINGTON	I made a commitment to completely cut out drinking and anything that might hamper me from getting my mind and body together. And the floodgates of goodness have opened for me – spiritually and financially.
9789 ROBERT JARVIK/USA/ SCIENTIST	Leaders are visionaries with a poorly developed sense of fear, and no concept of the odds against them. They make the impossible happen.
9790 FRAUD/CHARITY	Charity scams
9791 PUBLILIUS SYRUS	Admonish thy friends in secret, praise them openly.
9792 JON KRAKAUER/THE NEW YORKER/USA	Even when some parts of a plant are known to be edible, other parts of the same species may contain dangerous concentrations of toxic compounds.
9793 AUTHOR/F. SCOTT FITZGERALD/USA	An author ought to write for the youth of his own generation, the critics of the next, and the schoolmaster of ever afterwards.
9794 DR. IMANI PERRY/USA/ PROFESSOR	For me, the book holds immense aesthetic appeal. I like the smell of the paper, the varying fonts, the sound of a new spine cracking, the weight in my palm. Give me a cup of tea, a good book, and a cotton blanket on a rainy day and I'm blissful.
9795 SE SMITH/GUARDIAN/UK	For people with physical disabilities, buying clothes can be an exercise in frustration.
9796 ROBERT HUGHES/ART	The new job of art is to sit on the wall and get more expensive.
9797 USA/GEN. WILLIAM WESTMORELAND	I don't take criticism lying down.
9798 HO CHI MINH/VIETNAM/ LEADER	To reap a return in ten years, plant trees. To reap a return in 100, cultivate the people.
9799 MARK BEZOS/TED.COM/ BUSINESS	Not every day is going to offer us a chance to save somebody's life, but every day offers us an opportunity to affect one.
9800 TAL GOLESWORTHY/ TEDTALK/HEART	When you have a group of people who've had a different professional training, a different professional experience, they not only have a different knowledge base, but they have a different perspective on everything.

NUMBER CATEGORY/CREDIT	TOPIC
9801 THOMAS JEFFERSON/ USA/LEADER	Determine never to be idle...It is wonderful how much may be done if we are always doing.
9802 CHARLES M. BLOW/USA	The only way to vanquish cowardice is to brandish courage.
9803 HERB COHEN/USA/ NEGOTIATOR	Most of us, in our civilized society, rely too heavily on reasoning capacity to make things happen. We've been raised to believe that logic will prevail. Logic, in and of itself, will rarely influence people.
9804 KATIE COURIC/USA/ BROADCASTER	A boat is always safe in the harbor, but that's not what boats are built for.
9805 CHIEF SEATTLE/USA	We did not spin the web of life. We are all strands in it. And whatever we do to the web, we do to ourselves.
9806 WILLIAM URY/USA/ BUSHMEN/AFRICA	Sharing resources as a way of preventing disputes is widely taught and practiced.
9807 HOWARD HUGHES/USA/ NEGOTIATION	Play off everyone against each other so that you have more avenues of action open to you.
9808 WILLIAM URY/USA/ NEGOTIATION	At the heart of most disputes are emotions: frustration, fear, anger, and distrust.
9809 SWAMI DAYANANDA SARASWATI/TED.COM	One cannot contribute unless one feels secure, one feels big, one feels: 'I have enough.'
9810 HOMER/THE ILIAD	Hateful to me as the gates of Hades is that man who hides one thing in his heart and speaks another.
9811 KATHY SIERRA/USA	People aren't passionate about things they suck at.
9812 STEVEN JOBS/USA/ART BUSINESS	It's rare that you see an artist in his 30s or 40s able to really contribute something amazing.
9813 HOMER/THE ILIAD	There is strength in the union even of very sorry men.
9814 THOMAS JEFFERSON/US	Question with boldness even the existence of a God; because, if there be one, he must more approve of the homage of reason than that of blindfolded fear.
9815 STEVE JOBS/USA/ APPLE/BUSINESSWEEK	I'm as proud of what we don't do as I am of what we do.
9816 STEVEN JOBS/USA/ART BUSINESS	I'm convinced that about half of what separates the successful entrepreneurs from the non-successful ones is pure perseverance.
9817 HOMER/THE ILIAD	Young men's minds are always changeable, but when an old man is concerned in a matter, he looks both before and after.
9818 THOMAS JEFFERSON/ USA/LEADER	Do not bite at the bait of pleasure till you know there is no hook beneath it.
9819 HO CHI MINH/VIETNAM/ LEADER	After the rain, good weather. In the wink of an eye, the universe throws off its muddy clothes.
9820 THOMAS JEFFERSON/ USA/LEADER	The man who reads nothing at all is better educated than the man who reads nothing but newspapers.
9821 DR. IMANI PERRY/USA/ PROFESSOR	I have often found myself wishing that instead of encouraging every woman to feel she is beautiful...that we could find a way to make it such that beauty is not at the center of self-esteem.
9822 PAMELA MEYER/HOW TO SPOT A LIAR/TED	Lying is an attempt to bridge a gap, to connect our wishes and our fantasies, about who we wish we were, how we could be, with what we're really like.

NUMBER CATEGORY/CREDIT	TOPIC
9823 JOSEPH HELLER/ WRITER/CATCH-22	The enemy is anybody who's going to get you killed, no matter which side he is on.
9824 THERESA BROWN/NY TIMES/USA	A lot of what we do in medicine, and especially in modern hospital care, adheres to this same formulation. We hurt people because it's the only way we know to make them better.
9825 STEVE JOBS/USA/ LEADER/BUSINESS	Design is not just what it looks like and feels like. Design is how it works.
9826 NEW SCHOOL/USA	Graphic designers are ambassadors of meaning.
9827 LUCILLE BALL/USA/ ACTOR	I think knowing what you cannot do is more important than knowing what you can.
9828 HERBIE HANCOCK/USA/ MUSICIAN	I have to be careful not to let the world dazzle me so much that I forget that I'm a husband and a father.
9829 WILLIAM URY/USA/ NEGOTIATION	Power is the ability to satisfy one's interests with or without the cooperation of others.
9830 CHARLES M. BLOW/USA/ COLUMNIST	A lie is like a cat: you need to stop it before it gets out the door or it's really hard to catch.
9831 PHILIP PULLMAN/USA/ WRITER	After nourishment, shelter and companionship, stories are the thing we need most in the world.
9832 L. RON HUBBARD/USA/ WRITER/SCIENTOLOGY	Probably the most neglected friend you have is you. And yet every man, before he can be a true friend to the world, must first become a friend to himself.
9833 DAVID BROOKS/USA/ WRITER/THE SOCIAL ANIMAL	I had thought that the magic of the information age was that it allowed us to know more, but then I realized the magic of the information age is that it allows us to know less.
9834 MICHELLE KWAN/USA/ FIGURE SKATER	There's a lot of emotions that always come out after a skate of a lifetime. I always start crying because there is so much buildup to that competition.
9835 JOSEPH HELLER/ WRITER/CATCH-22	It doesn't make a damned bit of difference who wins the war to someone who's dead.
9836 THOMAS JEFFERSON/ USA/LEADER	Every citizen should be a soldier. This was the case with the Greeks and Romans, and must be that of every free state.
9837 ERICH FROMM/ GERMAN/PSYCHOLOGY	If I am what I have and I lose what I have, who then am I?
9838 HOMER/THE ODYSSEY	A small rock holds back a great wave.
9839 HERBIE HANCOCK/USA/ MUSICIAN	Creativity and artistic endeavors have a mission that goes far beyond just making music for the sake of music.
9840 PHILIP PULLMAN/USA/ THE AMBER SPYGLASS	I stopped believing there was a power of good and a power of evil that were outside us. And I came to believe that good and evil are names for what people do, not for what they are.
9841 A.A. MILNE/ENGLISH AUTHOR	Good judgment comes from experience, and experience -- well, that comes from poor judgment.
9842 DAPHNE DU MAURIER/ WRITER/REBECCA	I am glad it cannot happen twice, the fever of first love. For it is a fever, and a burden, too, whatever the poets may say.
9843 KENNETH GRAHAME/ UK/WRITER	After all, the best part of a holiday is perhaps not so much to be resting yourself, as to see all the other fellows busy working.

NUMBER CATEGORY/CREDIT	TOPIC
9844 JOSEPH HELLER/ WRITER/CATCH-22	It doesn't matter whether they mean it or not. That's why they make little kids pledge allegiance even before they know what 'pledge' and 'allegiance' mean.
9845 CHARLES M. BLOW/USA/ COLUMNIST/NY TIMES	It has been my experience that the "hardest" people in the world are actually the most fragile and the most soft-spoken are the strongest.
9846 HERBIE HANCOCK/USA	It is people's hearts that move the age.
9847 A.A. MILNE/ENGLISH AUTHOR	One advantage of being disorderly is that one is constantly making exciting discoveries.
9848 H. G. WELLS/UK/WRITER	No passion in the world is equal to the passion to alter someone else's draft.
9849 STEVE JOBS/USA/ BUSINESS/APPLE COMPUTERS INC.	Here's to the crazy ones, the misfits, the rebels, the troublemakers, the round pegs in the square holes...the ones who see things differently -- they're not fond of rules...they push the human race forward, and while some may see them as the crazy ones, we see genius, because the ones who are crazy enough to think that they can change the world, are the ones who do.
9850 PUBLILIUS SYRUS	I have often regretted my speech, never my silence.
9851 SAMUEL GOLDWYN/ MOVIE PRODUCER/USA	An oral contract isn't worth the paper it's written on.
9852 NOVELIST/LOUIS DE BERNIERES	Love itself is what is left over when being in love has burned away, and this is both an art and a fortunate accident.
9853 HO CHI MINH/VIETNAM/ LEADER	Remember that the storm is a good opportunity for the pine and the cypress to show their strength and their stability.
9854 HOMER/POET/ODYSSEY	It is tedious to tell again tales already plainly told.
9855 ALFRED HITCHCOCK/ MOVIE PRODUCER/USA	There is no terror in the bang, only in the anticipation of it.
9856 RANDY PAUSCH/PROF/ THE LAST LECTURE/USA	Getting people to welcome feedback was the hardest thing I ever had to do as an educator.
9857 A.A. MILNE/POOH'S... INSTRUCTION BOOK	When carrying a jar of honey to give to a friend for his birthday, don't stop and eat it along the way.
9858 KENNETH GRAHAME/ UK/WRITER	Children are the only people who accept a mood of wonderment, who are ready to welcome a perfect miracle at any hour of the day or night.
9859 JOSEPH HELLER/ WRITER/CATCH-22	Destiny is a good thing to accept when it's going your way. When it isn't, don't call it destiny; call it injustice, treachery, or simple bad luck.
9860 JOSEPH HELLER/USa	For war, there is always enough. It's peace that's expensive.
9861 A.A. MILNE/ENGLISH AUTHOR	Promise me you'll always remember: You're braver than you believe, stronger than you seem, and smarter than you think.
9862 JOSEPH HELLER/SOME-THING HAPPENED/USA	I know at last what I want to be when I grow up. When I grow up I want to be a little boy.
9863 LOUIS DE BERNIERE/UK	History is the propaganda of the victors.
9864 LEO TOLSTOY/WRITER/ RUSSIA	All happy families are alike; each unhappy family is unhappy in its own way.
9865 KEN FOLLETT/WRITER/ USA	Hunger is the best seasoning.

NUMBER CATEGORY/CREDIT	TOPIC
9866 CHARLES M. BLOW/USA/COLUMNIST	We don't vote for people because they are the exact embodiment of our values, but because they are likely to be the most responsive to them.
9867 KEN FOLLETT/WRITER/USA	...excessive pride is a familiar sin, but a man may just as easily frustrate the will of God through excessive humility.
9868 GERALDINE BROOKS/USA/MARCH	For to know a man's library is, in some measure, to know his mind.
9869 JEFFREY EUGENIDES/USA/NOVELIST/THE MARRIAGE PLOT	Depression is like a bruise that never goes away. A bruise in your mind. You just got to be careful not to touch it where it hurts. It's always there, though.
9870 KEN FOLLETT/WRITER/USA	Marriage is a promise. You can't keep a promise only when it suits you. You have to keep it against your inclination. That's what it means.
9871 LOUIS DE BERNIERE/UK	No man is a man until he has been a soldier.
9872 KEN FOLLETT/WRITER	Being a monk was the strangest and most perverted way of life imaginable...They deliberately shunned anything good -- girls, sports, feasting and family life.
9873 LYDIA MILLET/WRITER	You don't see a fish in a chair often.
9874 RICHARD POWERS/USA/NOVELIST	Evil is the refusal to see one's self in others.
9875 NASSIM NICHOLAS TALEB/WRITER	Half of the people lie with their lips; the other half with their tears.
9876 ROBERT FROST/USA/POET	A poem begins with a lump in the throat, a sense of wrong, a homesickness, a lovesickness.
9877 HOMER/THE ODYSSEY	The wine urges me on, the bewitching wine, which sets even a wise man to singing and to laughing gently and rouses him up to dance and brings forth words which were better unspoken.
9878 PHILIP PULLMAN/USA/THE AMBER SPYGLASS	All the history of human life has been a struggle between wisdom and stupidity.
9879 THOMAS JEFFERSON/USA/LEADER	We in America do not have government by the majority. We have government by the majority who participate.
9880 KENNETH GRAHAME/WIND IN THE WILLOWS	Packing the basket was not quite such pleasant work as unpacking the basket. It never is.
9881 JOSEPH HELLER/WRITER/CATCH-22	I'm not running away from my responsibilities. I'm running to them. There's nothing negative about running away to save my life.
9882 LEO TOLSTOY/WRITER	If you look for perfection, you'll never be content.
9883 KEN FOLLETT/WRITER/USA	A man hates the person he has wronged, paradoxically. I think it's because the victim is a perpetual reminder that he behaved shamefully.
9884 RICHARD POWERS/USA/NOVELIST	Maybe happiness is like a virus. Maybe it's one of those bugs that sits for a long time, so we don't even know that we are infected.
9885 LIFE/SOCIETY	Conversations with strangers
9886 LEO TOLSTOY/WRITER	It is amazing how complete is the delusion that beauty is goodness.
9887 KEN FOLLETT/WRITER/WORLD WITHOUT END	We who are born poor have to use cunning to get what we want. Scruples are for the privileged.
9888 CORMAC McCARTHY/ALL THE PRETTY HORSES	Scars have the strange power to remind us that our past is real.

NUMBER CATEGORY/CREDIT	TOPIC
9889 E.L. DOCTOROW/USA/WRITER	There is music in words, and it can be heard, you know, by thinking.
9890 RICHARD BRANSON/UK/BUSINESS	Don't think about fun as a reward; think of it as a responsibility.
9891 VERNA MYERS/USA/DIVERSITY/TEDTALK	Biases are the stories we make up about people before we know who they actually are. But how are we going to know who they are when we've been told to avoid and be afraid of them?
9892 EDDIE ADAMS/USA/PHOTOGRAPHER	If it makes you laugh, if it makes you cry, if it rips out your heart, that's a good picture.
9893 THOMAS JEFFERSON/USA/PRESIDENT	When the government fears the people, there is liberty. When the people fear the government, there is tyranny.
9894 NASSIM NICHOLAS TALEB/AUTHOR/USA	The three most harmful addictions are heroin, carbohydrates, and a monthly salary.
9895 PHILIP PULLMAN/USA/THE AMBER SPYGLASS	When you choose one way out of many, all the ways you don't take are snuffed out like candles, as if they'd never existed.
9896 JEFFREY EUGENIDES/USA/NOVELIST	There were some books that reached through the noise of life to grab you by the collar and speak only of the truest things.
9897 KATHERINE BOO/USA/INVESTIGATIVE JOURNALIST	Though every community is different, my personal rule is pretty much the same: It's O.K. to feel like an idiot going in as long as you don't sound like an idiot coming out.
9898 JEFFREY EUGENIDES/USA/NOVELIST	Children learn to speak Male or Female the way they learn to speak English or French.
9899 RAY BRADBURY/USA	You don't have to burn books to destroy a culture. Just get people to stop reading them.
9900 AMY HARMON/THE LAW OF MOSES	Everyone always talks about being color blind. And I get that. I do. But instead of being color blind, we should celebrate color, in all its shades.
9901 RAY BRADBURY/USA/WRITER	If we listened to our intellect we'd never have a love affair. We'd never have a friendship. We'd never go in business because we'd be cynical.
9902 AMY HARMON/USA	Sometimes a beautiful face is false advertising.
9903 A.A. MILNE/UK/WRITER	The things that make me different are the things that make me.
9904 LEO TOLSTOY/WRITER	Respect was invented to cover the empty place where love should be.
9905 JANE GOODALL/UK/PRIMATOLOGIST	Change happens by listening and then starting a dialogue with the people who are doing something you don't believe is right.
9906 CHANG-RAE LEE/USA/KOREA/WRITER/	Imagination might not be limitless. It's still tethered to the universe of what we know.
9907 JANE GOODALL/UK/PRIMATOLOGIST	What you do makes a difference, and you have to decide what kind of difference you want to make.
9908 GERALDINE BROOKS/USA/MARCH	If there is one class of person I have never quite trusted, it is a man who knows no doubt.
9909 JEFFREY EUGENIDES/USA/NOVELIST	Capitalism has resulted in material well-being but spiritual bankruptcy.
9910 HOMER BIGART/USA	Jobs are physically easier, but the worker now takes home worries instead of an aching back.

NUMBER CATEGORY/CREDIT	TOPIC
9911 NASSIM NICHOLAS TALEB/WRITER/PHILOSOPHER	Missing a train is only painful if you run after it! Likewise, not matching the idea of success others expect from you is only painful if that's what you are seeking.
9912 ANNE LAMOTT/USA/WRITER	Don't look at your feet to see if you're doing it right. Just dance.
9913 THOMAS JEFFERSON/USA/3RD PRESIDENT	Delay is preferable to error.
9914 THOMAS JEFFERSON/US/PRESIDENT	Health is worth more than learning.
9915 JEFFREY EUGENIDES/USA/NOVELIST	Great discoveries, whether of silk or gravity, are always windfalls. They happen to people loafing under trees.
9916 LANI GUINIERE/USA/LAW PROFESSOR/NY TIMES/TAMAR LEWIN	Studies show that groups made up of the highest-performing individuals are not as good at solving complex multidimensional problems - like designing environmental policies, cracking codes or creating social welfare systems -- as groups with a mix of skills, backgrounds and ways of thinking, even if the individuals in the group are not all high performers.
9917 AMY HARMON/USA/JOURNALIST	Everybody is a main character to someone.
9918 J. HOPE FRANKLIN/USA/HISTORIAN	If the house is to be set in order, one cannot begin with the present: he must begin with the past.
9919 GERALDINE BROOKS/US	..poverty requires aptitude.
9920 EDWIN LOUIS COLE/US/CHRISTIAN MINISTER	A man's talent can take him where his character cannot sustain him.
9921 ALAN WATTS/USA/WRITER	The clash between science and religion has not shown that religion is false and science is true. It has shown that all systems of definition are relative to various purposes, and that none of them actually 'grasp' reality.
9922 JEFFREY EUGENIDES/US	Winter is the season of alcoholism and despair.
9923 JEFFREY EUGENIDES/USA/NOVELIST	The monster always approaches from the direction you did not expect.
9924 RAY BRADBURY/USA	Learning to let go should be learned before learning to get. Life should be touched, not strangled.
9925 DAVID HALBERSTAM/US	Sometimes the best virtue learned on the battlefield is modesty.
9926 JEFFREY EUGENIDES/USA/NOVELIST	Pregnancy humbles husbands. After an initial rush of male pride they quickly recognise the minor role that nature had assigned them in the drama of reproduction.
9927 RAY BRADBURY/USA/MARTIAN CHRONICLES	It's good to renew one's wonder, said the philosopher. Space travel has again made children of us all.
9928 JULIUS IRVING/NBA/USA	Being a professional is doing the things you love to do, on the days you don't feel like doing them.
9929 LEO TOLSTOY/WRITER/RUSSIA	Nothing is so necessary for a young man as the company of intelligent women.
9930 RAY BRADBURY/USA	We are all rich and ignore the buried fact of accumulated wisdom.
9931 ANNE LAMOTT/USA	Having a baby is like suddenly getting the world's worst roommate.
9932 PHILIP PULLMAN/USA/WRITER	Children are not less intelligent than adults; what they are is less informed.

NUMBER CATEGORY/CREDIT	TOPIC
9933 ELLEN GOODMAN/USA/ JOURNALIST	There's a trick to the 'graceful exit.' It begins with the vision to recognize when a job, a life stage, or a relationship is over -- and let it go.
9934 WALTER LIPPMAN/USA/ JOURNALIST	It requires wisdom to understand wisdom: the music is nothing if the audience is deaf.
9935 ANNE LAMOTT/USA/ BIRD BY BIRD/WRITER	One thing I know for sure about raising children is that every single day a kid needs discipline...But also every single day a kid needs a break.
9936 ELLEN GOODMAN/USA/ JOURNALIST	When you live alone, you can be sure that the person who squeezed the toothpaste tube in the middle wasn't committing a hostile act.
9937 ALICE MUNRO/CANADA/ NOBEL PRIZE	Never underestimate the meanness in people's souls. Even when they're being kind...especially when they're being kind.
9938 THICH NHAT HANH/ MINDFULNESS	If you're washing dishes then wash dishes, and don't be planning on what you're going to do after the dishes are done.
9939 JUSTICE WILLIAM J. BRENNAN JR./USA/ SUPREME COURT	Use of a mentally ill person's involuntary confession is antithetical to the notion of fundamental fairness embodied in the due process clause.
9940 THOMAS JEFFERSON/ USA	Advertisements...contain the only truths to be relied on in a newspaper.
9941 ERIK ERIKSON/USA/ PSYCHOLOGIST/GERMAN	The richest and fullest lives attempt to achieve an inner balance between three realms: work, love, and play.
9942 MURIEL SPARK/WRITER/ USA	- "How do you know when you're in love?" she said. - "The traffic improves and the cost of living seems low. "
9943 PETER MCWILLIAMS/ AUTHOR	Be willing to be uncomfortable. Be comfortable being uncomfortable. It may get tough, but it's a small price to pay for living a dream.
9944 DAVID STEINDL-RAST/ WRITER/MONK	You think that this is just another day in your life...It's not just another day. It's the one day that is given to you -- today.
9945 JIM ROHN/US/BUSINESS	How long should you try? Until.
9946 RAY BRADBURY/USA	I believe in libraries because most students don't have any money. When I graduated from high school, it was during the Depression and we had no money. I couldn't go to college, so I went to the library three days a week for 10 years.
9947 ANNE LAMOTT/USA/ BIRD BY BIRD/WRITER	Perfectionism is the voice of the oppressor, the enemy of the people.
9948 CORMAC McCARTHY/ USA/WRITER	My daddy used to tell me not to chew on something that was eating you.
9949 PAUL CEZANNE/ARTIST/ FRENCH	It's so fine and so terrible to stand in front of a blank canvas.
9950 ELI BROAD/USA/ PHILANTHROPIST	Civilizations are not remembered by their business people, their bankers or lawyers. They're remembered by the arts.
9951 EDVARD MUNCH/ART	At different moments you see with different eyes. You see differently in the morning than you do in the evening. In addition, how you see is also dependent on your emotional state.
9952 RAY DALIO/QUANT/USA/ BUSINESS	Nature gave us pain as a messaging device to tell us that we are approaching, or that we have exceeded, our limits in some way.
9953 STEPHEN LEACOCK/ HUMORIST/CANADA	It may be that those who do most, dream most.

NUMBER CATEGORY/CREDIT	TOPIC
9954 PHILIP PULLMAN/USA/ THE AMBER SPYGLASS	You don't win races by wishing, you win them by running faster than everyone else does.
9955 EDMUND BURKE/IRISH/ STATESMAN	The only thing necessary for the triumph of evil is for good men to do nothing.
9956 PAUL CEZANNE/ARTIST/ FRENCH	Painting from nature is not copying the object, it is realizing one's sensations.
9957 HERMAN MELVILLE/US	Ignorance is the parent of fear.
9958 GERALDINE BROOKS/ USA/MARCH	The great thing about being always among people of noble manners was the inevitable elevation of one's own.
9959 JIM ROHN/USA/WRITER	Finding is reserved for those that search.
9960 NASSIM NICHOLAS TALEB/WRITER	If you want to annoy a poet, explain his poetry.
9961 GLENN GOULD/CANADA/ MUSICIAN	If an artist wants to use his mind for creative work, cutting oneself off from society is a necessary thing.
9962 NASSIM NICHOLAS TALEB/WRITER	People focus on role models; it is more effective to find antimodels -- people you don't want to resemble when you grow up.
9963 GUY FIERI/USA/CHEF/ USA	No matter how tough the meat may be, it's going to be tender if you slice it thin enough.
9964 PHILIP PULLMAN/USA/ THE SUBTLE KNIFE	Every little increase in human freedom has been fought over ferociously between those who want us to know more and be wiser and stronger, and those who want us to obey and be humble and submit.
9965 CALVIN COOLIDGE/USA	Don't expect to build up the weak by pulling down the strong.
9966 CORMAC McCARTHY/USA	The freedom of birds is an insult to me.
9967 DAVID STEINDL-RAST/ WRITER/MONK	Open your heart to the incredible gifts that civilization gives to us. You flip a switch and there is electric light. You turn a faucet and there is warm water, and cold water, and drinkable water...
9968 DAVID COPPERFIELD/US MAGICIAN/NY TIMES	People in the hate business need an "us" and a "them." Without an enemy they can't function.
9969 HERMAN MELVILLE/USA	Better sleep with a sober cannibal than a drunk Christian.
9970 MUNIR VIRANI/TED.COM WHY I LOVE VULTURES	Vultures are our natural garbage collectors. They clean up carcasses right to the bone.
9971 ELI BROAD/USA/ PHILANTHROPIST	You can have great teachers, but if you don't have a good principal, you won't have a good school.
9972 EDMUND BURKE/IRISH/ WRITER	It is a general popular error to imagine the loudest complainers for the public to be the most anxious for its welfare.
9973 USA/MARK CUBAN/ BILLIONAIRE	I don't think I would encourage executives that work for me to blog. There can be only one public vision for any organization.
9974 CALVIN COOLIDGE/USA	We cannot do everything at once, but we can do something at once.
9975 THOMAS JEFFERSON/ USA	If our house be on fire, without inquiring whether it was fired from within or without, we must try to extinguish it.
9976 EDMUND BURKE/IRISH	Rudeness is the weak man's imitation of strength.
9977 WILLIAM ZINSSER/USA	Writing is thinking on paper.
9978 CALVIN COOLIDGE/ USA/PRESIDENT	Prosperity is only an instrument to be used, not a deity to be worshipped.

NUMBER CATEGORY/CREDIT	TOPIC
9979 EDITH SITWELL/POET/ UK/CRITIC	I am patient with stupidity but now with those who are proud of it.
9980 ANNE LAMOTT/USA	It's good to do uncomfortable things. It's weight training for life.
9981 L. RON HUBBARD/USA/ WRITER/SCIENTOLOGY	If you want to make a little money, write a book. If you want to make a lot of money, create a religion.
9982 MAHATMA GANDHI/ INDIA/LEADER	I had no shoes, until I met a man who had no feet.
9983 JUSTIN P. McBRAYE/USA NY TIMES/PHILOSOPHY	Things can be true even though no one can prove it.
9984 HAFIZ/PERSIAN POET	The words you speak become the house you live in.
9985 PAULO FREIRE/BRAZIL/ EDUCATOR	No one can be authentically human while he prevents others from being so.
9986 KARL POPPER/THINKER/ AUSTRIAN/UK	Those who promised us paradise on earth never produced anything but a hell.
9987 THOMAS JEFFERSON/ USA	An honest man can feel no pleasure in the exercise of power over his fellow citizens.
9988 NASSIM NICHOLAS TALEB/WRITER	Meditation is a way to be narcissistic without hurting anyone
9989 PHILIP PULLMAN/USA/ THE AMBER SPYGLASS	Thou Shalt Not is soon forgotten, but Once Upon a Time is forever.
9990 CORMAC McCARTHY/ USA	People don't pay attention. And then one day there's an accounting. And after that, nothing is the same.
9991 BECCI MANSON/PHOTOS TED.COM	[Photos are] our memory-keepers and our histories, the last thing we would grab [in a crisis], and the first thing you'd go back to look for.
9992 EL ANATSUI/SCULPTOR/ GHANA	An artist in India is the same as an artist in Africa, Ghana, Japan, or America. We all want to be known as artists, not a Japanese artist, American artist, or Ghanaian artist.
9993 NASSIM NICHOLAS TALEB/WRITER	To bankrupt a fool, give him information.
9994 MIKE TYSON/BOXER/US	Everyone has a plan until he gets punched in the face.
9995 ELI BROAD/USA/ PHILANTHROPIST	Every artist is unreasonable, because he or she is doing something that hasn't been done before.
9996 ANNE LAMOTT/USA/ WRITER	The road to enlightenment is long and difficult, and you should try not to forget snacks and magazines.
9997 THOMAS PAINE/USA/ PHILOSOPHER	I prefer peace, but if trouble must come, let it come in my time, so that my children can live in peace.
9998 GUSTAVO DUDAMEL/US/ VENEZUELA/MUSIC	Exclusion is the problem of our society. When you give a child an instrument, you are including them immediately.
9999 ANDREW CARNEGIE/ USA/PHILANTHROPIST	He who dies in wealth dies in shame.
10K +1 RAY BRADBURY/USA	There's no use going to school unless your final destination is the library.

NOTES

NOTES

NOTES

Everett Ofori holds an MBA from Heriot-Watt University (Scotland, UK). He teaches Public Speaking, Management, and English for Specific Purposes (Business Writing, Medical Writing, Meeting Facilitation, etc.). Everett has helped hundreds of high school and university students around the world to improve their writing and grades. He has worked extensively with business executives (including those at the C-level) but is equally at home with helping young people hone their writing skills or become more effective in expressing themselves verbally.

Everett has worked with clients/students from the following organizations and more:	
• Accenture	• Actelion
• Asahi Kasei Medical	• Asahi Soft Drink Research, Moriya
• Barclays	• Becton Dickinson
• Disney	• ExxonMobil
• Fujitsu	• Goldman Sachs
• Hitachi Design	• IIJ (Internet Initiative Japan)
• Johnson & Johnson (Janssen)	• McKinsey Japan
• Mitsubishi (Shoji)	• Moody's
• National Institute of Land and Infrastructure Management, Tsukuba, Japan (NILIM)	• Orix
• PriceWaterhouseCoopers (PWC)	• Recruit
• Sckizenkai Nursing School, Soga, Kanagawa	• Sumitomo
• Summit Agro International	• Suntory
• Tokyo International Business College, Asakusabashi, Tokyo	• Yokohama Child Welfare College (Hoiku Fukushi), Higashi Totsuka, Kanagawa

Note to Users:

If you have used this book and you are happy with it, please write a review on the Amazon and/or Barnes and Noble website, or on a book review site of your choice.

If you have any comments regarding this book please contact Everett Ofori, at one of the following:

Email: everettofori@gmail.com

Mailing address:
Everett Ofori
Takarazuka University of Art and Design
Tokyo Campus Bldg 1F, 123 (MBE)
7-11-1 Nishi Shinjuku
Shinjuku ku, Tokyo Japan 160-0023

www.ingramcontent.com/pod-product-compliance
Lightning Source LLC
Chambersburg PA
CBHW081103080526
44587CB00021B/3427